Evolution of Hindu Nationalism -
Icons of HMS, RSS and BJS

OrangeBooks Publication

1st Floor, Rajhans Arcade, Mall Road, Kohka, Bhilai, Chhattisgarh 490020

Website:**www.orangebooks.in**

© **Copyright, 2024, Author**

All rights reserved. No part of this book may be reproduced, stored in a retrieval system, or transmitted, in any form by any means, electronic, mechanical, magnetic, optical, chemical, manual, photocopying, recording or otherwise, without the prior written consent of its writer.

First Edition, 2024
ISBN: 978-93-5621-770-6

EVOLUTION OF HINDU NATIONALISM
ICONS OF HMS, RSS & BJS

SANKARA NARAYANAN T

OrangeBooks Publication
www.orangebooks.in

Dedicated to all Swayamsevaks and karyakarthas who work tirelessly for the cause of param vaibhavam - Pinnacle of glory.

Preface

Various authors have published their work on Hindu nationalist organisations namely Hindu Mahasabha, RSS and Bharatiya Jana Sangh and the icons in pre independence era of India, However malicious propaganda by left ecosystem on Icons of Hindu nationalism prompted me to write this book for which I analysed many biographies of various national leaders and books related to Hindu nationalism to complete this work, Indian National congress of pre independence era was umbrella organisation for all ideologies for a common cause that is to attain independence. There were leaders who led other organisations and political parties also even as they remained leaders of Indian national congress.

This book is an attempt to unravel the relationship between the organisations and its leaders. This book provides detailed account on the life and works of Hindu Nationalist icons of Hindu Mahasabha, RSS and BJS with excerpts from their select speeches on various occasions.

Since 1900s, there seems to have been resurgence of socio cultural 'religious movements across the country, these movements have been enormously influential in shaping public policies. The Emergence of Hindu Cultural nationalism as a movement in the country, has its roots and its past core concepts are provided by Hindu Nationalist of modern India.

The BJS has its roots in the RSS and in other dharmic, cultural and nationalist movements before it. So, to understand, we have to go to the roots, the formations, the ideas, the leaders and the ideological frameworks of the BJS, the RSS and the other movements before them, right back to the Arya Samaj & Hindu Mahasabha.

This study is a 're-reading' of the writings of these personalities in order to trace the intellectual history of the present-day Hindu Cultural nationalism.

To my understanding, the BJP of today is the latest political manifestation of the years of nationalist movements that India has seen. As the Congress ruled the government for decades after Independence and the left ruled the academia, the story of the nationalist movement—from the Arya Samaj to the Hindu Mahasabha to the Rashtriya Swayamsevak Sangh (RSS) to the Bharatiya Jana Sangh (the BJS) to the Bharatiya Janata Party (BJP)—never got narrated in its entirety and purity.

I thank the readers and appeal to pass on suggestions and to refer authentic material if any which can help me improvise this volume in further editions.

- Sankara Narayanan T

Table of Contents

Evolution of ideology	1
Akhil Bharat Hindu Mahasabha	**27**
❖ Lala Lajpat Rai	50
❖ Madan Mohan Malaviya	82
❖ C Vijayaraghavachariar	102
❖ Balakrishna Shivaram Moonje	110
❖ Narasimha Chintaman Kelkar	121
❖ Bhai Parmanand	127
❖ Swami Shraddhanand	140
❖ Ganesh Damodar Savarkar	151
❖ Vinayak Damodar Savarkar	166
Rashtriya Swayamsevak Sangh	**222**
❖ Dr. Keshav Baliram Hedgewar	278
❖ Madhav Sadashiv Golwalkar	321
Bharatiya Jana Sangh	**370**
❖ Syama Prasad Mukherjee	400
❖ Deendayal Upadhyaya	439
Bibliography	**482**

Evolution of ideology

Bharat Varsha, from the Himalayas to Kanyakumari, is and has been a living organism through the ages – geographically, culturally and historically. Bharat is an ancient nation and Bharatiya nationalism, therefore, must naturally be based on undivided allegiance to Bharat as a whole and her great and ancient culture, which distinguishes her from other lands.

Since ancient times, the word "Hindu" has been used to describe the native traditions and people of India without defining it. It was only in the late 18th century that the word "Hindu" came to be used extensively with religious connotations, while still being used as a synecdoche describing the indigenous traditions. Hindu nationalist ideologies and political languages were highly diverse, both linguistically and socially. Since Hinduism does not represent an identifiable religious group, terms such as 'Hindu nationalism', and 'Hindu', are considered in the case of religious and nationalist discourse. The Hindu community was recognized as a homogeneous group, so some Congress leaders were able to imbue a symbolism with "Hindu" meaning within a secular nationalist stance.

The diversity of Indian cultural groups and moderate positions of Hindu nationalism have sometimes made it regarded as cultural nationalism than a religious one.

Shivaji, with his quests, is noted to have founded a firm footing for Hindu nationalism with the foundation of Maratha Empire. Shivaji was also an inspiration for Hindu nationalist activists such as Bal Gangadhar Tilak.

The Hindu Samaj (Bharatvarsha Hindu Samaj) is the oldest Hindu organization in India (formed in 1849 at Kolkata) to define Hindutva (Hindu way of life), remove corruption and moral degeneration in Hinduism, and achieve complete independence for Hindus culminating in a

Hindu nation. Lala Lajpat Rai, a Hindu nationalist, was inspired by Navin Chandra Rai, who chaired the special Congress session held in Lahore in 1921.[1]

Who is a Hindu?

The Hindu Samaj defines that every person who believes in the Supreme Being (or Supreme Power), who alone is to be worshipped, as a Hindu, irrespective of whichever denominational religion they follow.

Akhand Hindustan

The indivisibility of the land, extending from the Himalayas down to the Southern and Eastern Seas, is an article of faith with Hindus.

Hindu Nationalism

Hindu nationalism is a product of a challenge internal to democracy. Post-1857, it became clear that India was going to adopt, albeit gradually, some form of democratic governance. For the first time, the Muslim elite in India found itself without political power. This set-in motion a complex politics regarding the political identity in India. In a democracy, the framework of a majority and a minority acquires political significance. But at a very basic level, once the concept of minority and majority was accepted as the basic conceptual framing, the definition of a 'religious minority' made sense only against the idea of a 'majority' who might have posed a potential political threat to the minority; the two concepts co-created each other.

The Hindu nationalism is no different from other nationalisms that are legitimized all over the world. Most nations often appeal to potent principles of cultural unity. The basis of India's unity is not simply an allegiance to constitutionalism; it requires recognition of our common identity as Hindus. The second is to signal that Hindu nationalism is not reactionary; it is a way of reassuring modernist Hindus that the project of producing cultural unity does not imply regression to a religious or a theocratic state. In fact, a Hindu Rashtra can have as modern a state as it needs. The third is to reclaim the story of India's identity and to posit the existence of a Hindu nation back into the deep recesses of India's history, one that transcends the flow of time, changes in political regimes, and the existence of social divisions.

What it requires of citizens, especially minorities, is not just an allegiance to the terms of the social contract as set out in constitutional principles or to the institutions and processes of the state. It requires everyone to acknowledge the symbols of Hindu unity, such as the sacredness of territory, the importance of Hindu symbols, and the overall glory of Hindu civilization. But it also provides fertile ground for creating a moving target of threats to this cultural unity, defining their identity on their own terms.

Hindus are a distinct ideological group comprising a large percentage of the human population. They possess a distinctive way of looking at life, a well-defined cultural background, and a very strong historical tradition that are easily distinguished from everyone else. The "National Home" of this race was forcibly captured by foreign invaders and even their present alleged freedom is no more real to the Hindus than the independence of America was to the Red Indians.

Modern age and the Hindu Renaissance in the 19th century:

In the nineteenth century, there were many Hindu reform movements. The Upanishads and Vedas were interpreted differently as a result of these movements, which also stressed social reforms. The marked feature of these movements was that they countered the notion of the superiority of Western culture during the colonial era. This led to the upsurge of patriotic ideas that formed the cultural and an ideological basis for the independence movement in Colonial India.

Brahmo Samaj

The Brahmo Samaj was started by a Bengali scholar, Ram Mohan Roy, in 1828. Ram Mohan Roy endeavored to create, from the ancient Upanishadic texts, a vision of rationalist 'modern' India. Socially, he criticized the ongoing superstitions and believed in a monotheistic Vedic religion. His major emphasis was on social reform. He fought against caste discrimination and advocated equal rights for women. Although the Brahmo samaj found a favourable response from the British government and Westernized Indians, it was largely isolated from the larger Hindu society due to its intellectual Vedantic and Unitarian views. However its efforts to systematize Hindu spirituality based on rational and logical interpretation of the ancient Indian texts would be carried forward by other movements in Bengal and across India.[2]

Ram Mohan Roy's impact on modern Indian history included his revival of the pure and ethical principles of the Vedanta school of philosophy as found in the Upanishads. He preached the unity of God, made early translations of Vedic scriptures into English, co-founded the Calcutta Unitarian Society and founded the Brahma Samaj. The Brahmo Samaj played a major role in reforming and modernizing the Indian society. He successfully campaigned against sati, the practice of burning widows. He sought to integrate Western culture with the best features of his own country's traditions. He established a number of schools to popularize a modern system of education in India. He promoted a rational, ethical, non-authoritarian, this-worldly, and social-reform Hinduism. His writings also sparked interest among British and American Unitarians.[3]

Sri Aurobindo

Sri Aurobindo was a nationalist and one of the first to embrace the idea of complete political independence for India. He was inspired by the writings of Swami Vivekananda and the novels of Bankim Chandra Chattopadhyay. He based his claim for freedom for India on the inherent right to freedom, not on any charge of misgovernment or oppression". He believed that the primary requisite for national progress and reform is the free habit of free and healthy national thought and action, which is impossible in a state of servitude. He was part of the Anushilan Samiti, a revolutionary group working towards the goal of Indian independence. In his brief political career spanning only four years, he led a delegation from Bengal to the Indian National Congress session of 1907 and contributed to the revolutionary newspaper Bande Mataram.

In his famous Uttarpara Speech, he outlined the essence and the goal of India's nationalist movement thus:"I say no longer that nationalism is a creed, a religion, a faith; I say that it is the Sanatan Dharma which for us is nationalism. This Hindu nation was born with the Sanatan Dharma, with it, it moves and with it, it grows. When the Sanatan Dharma declines, then the nation declines, and if the Sanatan Dharma were capable of perishing, with the Sanatan Dharma it would perish."

In the same speech, he also provided a comprehensive perspective of Hinduism, which is at variance with the geocentric view developed by later-day Hindu nationalist ideologues such as Veer Savarkar and Deendayal Upadhyay:

"But what is the Hindu religion? What is this religion which we call Sanatan, eternal? It is the Hindu religion only because the Hindu nation has kept it, because in this Peninsula it grew up in the seclusion of the sea and the Himalayas, because in this sacred and ancient land it was given as a charge to the Aryan race to preserve through the ages.

But it is not circumscribed by the confines of a single country; it does not belong peculiarly and forever to a bounded part of the world. That which we call the Hindu religion is really the eternal religion, because it is the universal religion which embraces all others. If a religion is not universal, it cannot be eternal. A narrow religion, a sectarian religion, an exclusive religion can live only for a limited time and a limited purpose. This is the one religion that can triumph over materialism by including and anticipating the discoveries of science and the speculations of philosophy."

In 1910, he withdrew from political life and spent the rest of his life engaged in spiritual exercises and writing. However, his works continued to inspire revolutionaries and struggles for independence, including the famous Chittagong Uprising. Both Swami Vivekananda and Sri Aurobindo are credited with laying the foundation for a vision of freedom and glory for India rooted in the spirituality and heritage of Hinduism.[4]

Hindu reformist Ishwar Chandra Vidyasagar was highly educated and influenced by Oriental thoughts and ideas. When Ramakrishna met Vidyasagar, he praised him as the ocean of wisdom. Vidyasagar championed the upliftment of the status of women in India, particularly in his native Bengal. Unlike some other reformers who sought to set up alternative societies or systems, he sought to transform society from within. He was the most prominent campaigner for Hindu widow remarriage, petitioning the Legislative Council despite severe opposition, including a counter petition (by Radhakanta Deb and the Dharma Sabha) which had nearly four times as many signatures. Even though widow remarriage was considered a flagrant breach of Hindu customs and was staunchly opposed, Lord Dalhousie personally finalized the bill and the Hindu Widows' Remarriage Act of 1856 was passed. Against child marriage, efforts of Vidyasagar led to Age of Consent Act of 1891. He was a keen advocate of education for women and rightly viewed education as the primary way for women to emancipate themselves from the social oppression they faced at the time. He went door to door, asking family heads to allow their daughters to be enrolled in schools. Across Bengal, he opened 35 women's schools and succeeded in enrolling 1,300 students, Vidyasagar spent the last 18 years of his life living among Santhal tribals in present day Jharkhand, where he started what is possibly India's first school for Santhal girls.[5]

Swami Vivekananda

Swami Vivekananda on the Platform of the Parliament of the World's Religions.

Another 19th century Hindu reformer was Swami Vivekananda. As a student, Vivekananda was educated in contemporary Western thought. He joined the Brahmo Samaj briefly before meeting Ramakrishna, a priest in the temple of the goddess Kali in Calcutta, who would become his guru. Under the influence of Orientalism, Perennialism and Universalism, Vivekananda re- interpreted Advaita Vedanta, presenting it as the essence of Hindu spirituality and the development of human's religiosity. This project began with Ram Mohan Roy of Brahmo Samaj, who propagated a strict monotheism. This reinterpretation produced neo-Vedanta, in which Advaita Vedanta was combined with disciplines such as yoga and the concept of social service to attain perfection, drawing from the ascetic traditions in what Vivekananda called "practical Vedanta". The practical side essentially included participation in social reform.

He made Hindu spirituality, intellectually accessible to the Westernized audience. His famous speech at the Parliament of the World's Religions in Chicago on 11 September 1893, was followed by a huge reception of his thought in the West and made him a well-known figure in the West and subsequently in India too. His influence can still be recognized in popular western spirituality, such as nondualism, the New Age and the veneration of Ramana Maharshi. Swami Vivekananda stirred the hearts and minds of Indians with enthusiasm for strength and fearlessness, ready for service and self-sacrifice for nation.

Vivekananda played a major role in the growing Indian nationalist sentiments in the late 19th and the 20th century, encouraging many Indians with his success and appeal in the West. His example helped to build pride in India's cultural and religious heritage and supported the Indian independence movement. Vivekananda participated in several of these movements, calling for Indian independence from British rule. Swami Vivekananda believed that India is the blessed punyabhumi, the "land of virtue": "...the land where humanity has attained its highest towards generosity, towards purity, towards calmness, above all, the land of introspection and of spirituality - it is India.

According to Vivekananda, a country's future depends on its people, stating that "man-making is my mission." Religion plays a central role in this man-making, as he stated "to preach unto mankind their divinity, and how to make it manifest in every movement of life." He believed that coordinated willpower would lead to independence, even with forty million Britons ruling three hundred million people in India. According to Vivekananda, those forty million Britons put their wills together, resulting in infinite power, and that was the reason for their success. Vivekananda prescribed that to make a great future India, the whole secret lies in organization, accumulation of power, co-ordination of wills.

The land of India holds special sacred significance for Vivekananda, and he refers to India as a punyabhumi. He uses the term, however, in a more descriptive manner to describe India as a land of spirituality and as the place of origin for several of the world's religions. it is clear that Vivekananda locates the meaning of Hindu identity in an ecumenical hermeneutic consisting of shared religious doctrines.

Training of workers

"My plan is to start institutions in India, to train our young men. Men, men-these are wanted:

everything else will be ready, but strong, vigorous, believing young men, sincere to the backbone, are wanted. A hundred such and the world will become revolutionized. The will is stronger than anything else.

"Of course, this is a very big scheme, a very big plan. I do not know whether it will ever work out. But we must begin the work. But how? Take Madras, for instance. We must have a temple, for with Hindus, religion must come first. Then, you may say, all sects will quarrel about it. But we will make it a non-sectarian temple, having only "Om" as the symbol, the greatest symbol of any sect. If there is any sect here which believes that "Om" ought not to be the symbol, it has no right to call itself Hindu. All will have the right to interpret Hinduism, each one according to his own sect ideas, but we must have a common temple. Here should be taught the common grounds of our different sects, and at the same time, the different sects should have perfect liberty to come and teach their doctrines, with only one restriction, that is, not to quarrel with other sects. Secondly, in connection with this temple there should be an institution to train teachers who must go about preaching religion and giving secular education to our people; they must carry both. Then the work will extend through these bands of teachers and preachers, and gradually we shall have similar temples in other places, until we have covered the whole of India. That is my plan. It may appear gigantic, but it is much needed. You may ask, where is the money? Money is not needed. Money is nothing. For the last twelve years of my life, I did not know where the next meal would come from; but money and everything else I want must come because they are my slaves, and not I theirs. Must that is the word. Where are the men? That is the question. Young men of Madras, my hope is in you. Will you respond to the call of your nation?" [6]

A major element of Vivekananda's message was nationalist. He saw his effort very much in terms of a revitalization of the Hindu nation, which carried Hindu spirituality and could counter Western materialism. The notion of the superiority of Western culture against the culture of India was to be questioned based on Hindu spirituality. This also became a main inspiration for Hindu nationalism today. One of the most revered leaders of the Rashtriya Swayamsevak Sangh (RSS), Babasaheb Apte, often said, "Vivekananda is like the Gita for the RSS." Some historians have observed that this helped the nascent Independence movement develop a distinct national identity and kept it from being a simple derivative function of European nationalisms.

Influence of Swami Vivekananda on Hindutva ideology

Swami Vivekananda interpreted the Bhagavad-Gita along the lines of Bal Gangadhar Tilak, insisting on action or karma-yoga. Tilak wrote in the Mahratta that Swami Vivekananda is the real father of modern nationalism. He founded the Ramakrishna Mission in order to teach karma-yoga and shakti (power, energy). His karma-yoga influenced Tilak and Aurobindo. Shakti is the feminine aspect of divinity, symbolizing power and energy. Vivekananda believed that national rejuvenation would come only when Indians tapped this potential source of power. He advocated the Shakti cult, which was later taken up by Aurobindo Ghose and his brother Barindra Ghose.

The RSS has found Vivekananda's message of Hindu revivalism quite compatible with its own belief system. In fact, he has become an important symbol within the RSS and an inspiration for a Hindu lay order dedicated to strengthening Hindu identity among groups vulnerable to other creeds. M.S. Golwalkar translated Vivekananda's speeches into Marathi. Vivekananda's picture hangs on the walls of many swayamsevaks' homes and books about him serve as primers on nationalism. His message of self-esteem and national revitalization is the subject of innumerable RSS baudhik (intellectual discourses) sessions.

To commemorate the Swami Vivekananda's birth centenary in 1963, the RSS leadership decided to bring out a collection of Vivekananda's writings. Eknath Ranade was commissioned to edit the volume. After completing the book, Ranade became intrigued by the idea of further popularising the views of Vivekananda and in time decided to establish a secular lay-order to do so. Vivekananda's thoughts have also influenced the Bharatiya Jana Sangh.

Arya Samaj

Arya Samaj is considered one of the overarching Hindu renaissance movements of the late nineteenth century. Swami Dayananda, the founder of Arya Samaj, rejected idolatry, caste restrictions and untouchability, child marriage and advocated equal status and opportunities for women. Arya Samaj was the first Hindu organization to introduce proselytization in Hinduism. The organization has also worked towards the growth of civil rights movement in India since the 1800s.

Dayananda was not only a religious leader and social reformer but also a political thinker. He derived his nationalist ideas from the originality of his own understanding of Indian culture and without any direct influence of Western thought. He noted that a nation is a people that is conscious of its historical identity, cultural uniqueness, common language, common territory and claim to self-rule. Dayananda's concept of nationalism met all these requirements and he arrived at it about 1875, a decade before even the Indian National Congress was founded. Though the Arya Samaj is not a political organisation in the strict sense, it has a political philosophy of its own. It is a national movement in the Indian context because it has a definite approach in all matters affecting the lives of the people and the country - religious, social, educational, cultural and political. Among the aims of Arya Samaj, we read: "Its [Arya Samaj's] prosperity and future depend upon the reconciliation of Hinduism with that greater Indian Nationalism." [7]

Dayananda's Ideology and Hindutva

An ideology can be considered to have succeeded when new generations of people begin to speak its language. Though more than a century has passed since Dayananda's death, his religious philosophy continues to inspire a significant portion of the Hindu intelligentsia in India.

There is an ideological link between Dayananda's religious ideas and the present-day Hindutva. Dayananda was perhaps the first in modern times to politicise the Hindu religion. Through his interpretation of the Vedas, he politicised Hinduism in a subtle way and to a degree no other Indian thinker had done before him. He attempted to justify that Hindu culture was to be the natural and necessary basis of nationalism. Dayananda considered the Vedic Dharma as the exclusively and absolutely true faith and therefore superior to all others. Hence, he gave a clarion call to all Hindus to "return to the Vedas". He says: "The prosperity of a country depends upon the fulfilment of certain conditions, such as the study of the Vedas and the Vedic literature, due observance of the rules of the four Ashramas, Brahmacharya etc." He also spoke of a Golden Age in which the Aryans of the Vedic era is presented as the chosen people to whom God revealed perfect knowledge of the Veda. Dayananda also considered India as the land of the Aryans and that Indians were Aryans. We read in Satyartha Prakash: "Now, we shall examine the merits and demerits of the religion professed by the Aryas or people of the country of Aryavarta [India]. In the whole world there is no country like India. For this reason, did the Aryas come to this land and settle here in the beginning of the universe." He also used the term Aryavarta for India, Indraprashta for modern Delhi, Prayag for Allahabad and Avantika for Ujjain.[8]

Although Arya Samaj was often considered a social movement, many revolutionaries and political leaders of the Indian Independence movement, like Lala Lajpat Rai, Bhai Paramanand, Shyamji Krishnavarma, Ramprasad Bismil and Bhagat Singh, were inspired by it. Shraddhanand led the Shuddhi movement, which aimed to bring Hindus who had converted to other religions back to Hinduism. In the early 1900s, the Samaj (or organizations inspired by it, such as Jat Pat Todak Mandal) campaigned against caste discrimination. They also campaigned for widow remarriage and women's education. Bhagat Singh's grandfather followed Arya Samaj, which had a considerable influence on Bhagat Singh. In the 1930s, when the Hindu Nationalist group, the Rashtriya Swayamsevak Sangh, grew in prominence in northern India, they found support from the Arya Samaj of Punjab. The Samaj was active in Sindh at the end of the 19th and the beginning of the 20th century. The activities of the Samaj in the region included using shuddhi to integrate half-Muslim or low-caste communities into the organization. A Hindu Sindhi leader, K. R. Malkani, later became prominent in the Rashtriya Swayamsevak Sangh (RSS). According to Malkani, the Arya Samaj created a "new pride" among the Hindu Sindhis by opening gymnasia and Sanskrit pathshalas in the 1920s. Chadra Nath Basu's book Hindutva was published in 1892 by Gurudas Chatterjee. The first recorded use of the word Hindutva, at least in print, is believed to have been made in this book. In the Calcutta Review's July 1894 issue (Vol. 99), the 'vernacular literature' section carried a two-and-a-half- page review of Hindutva. The review describes the book as 'evidently a work of Hindu revival'.[9]

Bankimchandra Chattopadhyaya and the Impact of 'Hindu Nation'

The novels, as well as the journalistic, sociological and political writings and religious interpretations of Bankimchandra Chattopadhyaya (1838-94), present a complex legacy for both Hindu and secular nationalism. Bankim is considered to be the 'father' of the modern Bengali novel and perhaps the most important figure in the Bengal Renaissance from the late 1860s. His huge body of work is subject to various interpretations. In particular, a regular distinction is made between his earlier writings, committed to humanistic forms of social, religious and gender equality, and his later ones that seem to celebrate Hindu nationalist supremacism.

In the tradition of what is conceived to be secular nationalism, the themes of nationalism in Bankim's writings can be glossed over. Conversely, for Hindu nationalists, his earlier writings on gender equality and the conception of sexual freedom, and his satirical, humorous and mocking prose directed against Hindu sadhus and Bengali babus are significant. Particularly notable is his glorification of Hindu religious-territorial nationalism in his song 'Bande Mataram', a virtual anthem for the contemporary Hindutva movement. As important for both secular and religious appropriations was Bankim's view that, while Western science (and indeed the West as the home of empirical science) was valuable and important for Indian sensibilities to learn from, it was India and Hinduism that had provided advanced philosophical and religious learning that the west had barely reached, let alone moved beyond. The Kantian ideal of humanity as an end was, in principle, reachable not by Western utilitarian atheism, as some Western philosophers argued, but by a devotionalism to a humanized god - this was one of the distinctive potentials of Indian or Hindu philosophy.

Bankim can be rather effortlessly appropriated by or uncritically enfolded into apparently secular nationalist tendencies despite the thoroughgoing Hindu religious nationalist imaginary that not only permeated especially his later and most important writings but quite fundamentally structured them. 'Hindu nationalist' novels that can work against the exclusivist religious nationalism he was ostensibly promoting. The discussion below has a different aim: to highlight the Hindu nationalist themes in his work in the context of a telos of nationalist development that characterised his critical (and initially enthusiastic, but later diminishing) appropriation of Positivism.

'Ananda Math' had emerged as an exemplar of the idea of Hindu nationalism. 'Vande Mataram' ("Hail to the Motherland"), the first song to represent India as the Motherland, was published in this novel in 1882.

Bankim's later novels and writings were important for articulating an often rather didactic aesthetic of Hindu nationalism through their symbolisation first of the Bengal 'motherland' and then 'the Hindu nation' in visceral gendered and religious terms. While Bankim's novels were often occupied with apparently reforming concerns within Hinduism, especially in relation to poverty, equality and gender (Samya), in four of his novels and 'Krishnacharita', these concerns were either displaced or intertwined with powerful themes of Hindu resilience and suffering, Hindu resistance to British colonialism, and what was conceived to be Mughal tyranny in Bengal or in medieval and colonial India. The merging of religion with nationalism in his novels is striking not simply because nationalism was often conceived as a battle against British colonists, but because of his deployment of a powerful affective dimension as an integral component of what Hindu belonging to the Motherland must mean. Bankim recognized that political affect had to be made central to religious-nationalist affiliation. This sympathetic pity identified the sorrow at the historic plight of the symbolically conceived Motherland with the affect manifest in the inability of his masculine characters to exactly decide their future in the face of unanswerable aporias and limits to their national condition. This was a consistent, familial and gendered theme in Hindu-leaning nationalist discourse: a cultivation and invocation of a strictly grievous emotional wounding as an abyss that both defined the Hindu man and turned him towards perpetually futile action against his 'enemies'. This theme of love for a suffering motherland was often crudely supplemented in Hindu nationalist discourse with past glories, the present need for militant action against perceived 'enemies', and future redemption. Of salience was a powerful metonymic relation established between domestic maternal suffering and affliction, the consequent effect of the son, and the imagined historical injury to the nation.

The affective configuration of Hindu nationalism in Bankim's novels may appear to sit uneasily with Bankim's critical sociological and philosophical commitments, notably to that distinctive combination of utilitarianism, strong positivism and social evolutionism that was flourishing, at least for a period, in nineteenth-century Bengal intellectual circles. Not only was Bankim familiar with the dominant trinity of Comtean positivism, John Stuart Mill's utilitarianism and Herbert Spencer's evolutionist sociology, but he had also engaged with various other European writers.

Aspects of what appears to be rationalism make an appearance in his writings, in particular the transmutation of Kant's conception of the faculties of mind in Bankim's distinctive idea of the harmonious cultivation of the human faculties. Bankim also appeared to be familiar with the abstracted conception of God and religious existence in German idealism (as demonstrated, for example, by Schelling, Fichte and Schleiermacher) which Bankim sought to displace with a humanized neo-Puranic God (Krishna) and a conception of anushilan dharma – a neo-Kantian harmonious cultivation of the human faculties in accordance with the necessity of action in a field defined by culture. In Bankim, there was a displacement of an abstracted metaphysical-spiritual idea of religion for one in which the 'cultural cultivation' of religious affect was made central. He was also familiar with the work of some Indologists, such as William Jones and Max Muller, as well as the philosophies of Bentham, Hume, Rousseau, Locke and the Mills. However, Bankim's engagement with both Utilitarianism and Spencerianism was critical and he was to reject the atheistic and individual rights-based thrust of utilitarian liberal political philosophy in favour of a view that inserted love, duties and obligations to the national or social collective under an overarching Hindu religious conception of humanism. Of all the objects of his 'faculty of love', the love for one's nation was of the highest kind.[10]

Anushilan Samiti

Anushilan Samiti was an Indian fitness club that actually served as an underground society for anti-British revolutionaries. In the first quarter of the 20th century, it supported revolutionary violence as a means to end British rule in India. The organisation arose from a conglomeration of local youth groups and gyms (akhara) in Bengal in 1902.

The Samiti was influenced by the writings of the Bengali nationalist author Bankim Chandra Chattopadhyay. The name of the organisation, Anushilan, is derived from Bankim's works espousing hard work and spartan life. Bankim's cultural and martial nationalism, exemplified in Anandamath, along with his reinterpretation of the Bhagavat Gita, were strong influences on the strain of nationalism that inspired the early societies that later became Anushilan Samiti. A search of the Dacca Anushilan Samiti library in 1908 showed that Bankim's Bhagavat Gita was the most widely read book in the library.

The philosophies and teachings of Swami Vivekananda were later integrated into this philosophy. The "Rules of Membership" in the Dacca library strongly recommended reading his books. These books emphasized "Strong muscles and nerves of steel", which some historians consider to be strongly influenced by Hindu Shakti Philosophy. This interest in physical improvement and proto-national spirit among young Bengalis was driven by an effort to break away from the stereotype of effeminacy that the British had imposed on the Bengalis. Physical fitness was symbolic of the recovery of masculinity, and was part of a larger moral and spiritual training to cultivate control over the body, and to develop national pride and a sense of social responsibility and service. The Samiti had three pillars in their ideologies: "cultural independence", "political independence", and "economic independence". In terms of economic independence, the Samiti diverged from the Swadeshi movement, which they decried as a "trader's movement". The organisation moved away from its philosophy of violence in the 1920s due to the influence of the Indian National Congress and the Gandhian non-violent movement. However, a section of the group, notably those associated with Sachindranath Sanyal, remained active in the revolutionary movement, founding the Hindustan Republican Association in north India. A number of Congress leaders from Bengal, especially Subhash Chandra Bose, were accused by the British Government of having links with the organisation during this time.

Anushilan Samiti was organized on different lines, reflecting their divergence. The Samiti was centrally organized, with rigid discipline and a vertical hierarchy. Membership was predominantly made up of Hindus, at least initially, which was ascribed to the religious oath of initiation. Physical fitness was symbolic of the recovery of masculinity and was part of a larger moral and spiritual training to cultivate control over the body and develop national pride and a sense of social responsibility and service. The Samiti was involved in a number of noted incidents of revolutionary attacks against British interests.[11]

Indian National Congress - In first half of 20th century, factions of the Indian National Congress continued to be identified with "Hindu politics" and ideas of a Hindu nation. Initially, various congress leaders were involved in the Hindu nationalist cause. The period from 1885 to 1905 was known as the period of the moderates because they dominated the Indian National Congress. The Moderates used petitions, prayers, meetings, leaflets, pamphlets, memorandums, and delegations to present their demands to the British government.

Their only notable achievements were the expansion of the legislative council by the Indian Councils Act of 1892, which created dissatisfaction among the people. A further split occurred between Hindu and Muslim nationalists due to the militant nationalism that had long existed, set in place by the multifaceted culture and tradition. By 1905, a division opened between the moderates, who downplayed public agitation, and the new extremists, who advocated agitation and regarded the pursuit of social reform as a distraction from nationalism. The extremists tried to mobilise Hindu Indians by appealing to an explicitly Hindu political identity. In the light of the split, the Moderates restated the goal of Congress to be the attainment of self-government within the British Empire. The Indian National Congress was also split into two different groups: Moderates and Radicals. The Moderates wanted to oppose the British peacefully, while the Radicals wanted to use violent means, but the aim of both was to expel or suppress the British Empire from India. The Moderates believed in the policy of settling minor issues with the government through deliberations, but the Radicals believed in agitation, strikes, and boycotts. Nationalists led by Lokmanya Tilak agitated against the Moderates. The split between these two sections became visible at the end of Congress' Banaras Session (1905). Lokmanya Tilak and his followers held a separate conference and formed the Extremist Party. However, they decided to work as a part of the INC. The difference between moderates and extremists widened during Congress' Calcutta Session (1906) and attempts were made to select one of them as the president. The moderates opposed the resolutions on Swaraj, Swadeshi, the boycott of foreign goods, and National Education and requested to withdraw from the policy laid down in the Calcutta session. But the extremists were not ready to do so.

In the Surat Session of 1907, the Radicals or Extremists wanted Lala Lajpat Rai or Tilak as the presidential candidate, while the Moderates supported Rash Behari Ghosh. However, Lala Lajpat Rai stepped down and Rash Behari Ghosh became the President. The colonial authorities immediately clamped down on the extremists and their newspapers were suppressed. Lokmanya Tilak, their main leader, was imprisoned in Mandalay for six years.[12]

Bal Gangadhar Tilak (23 July 1856 – 1 August 1920) was the first leader of the Indian independence movement. The British colonial authorities called him "The father of the Indian unrest". He was also conferred with the title "Lokmanya", which means "accepted by the people as their leader". Gandhi called him "The Maker of Modern India".

Tilak was one of the first and strongest advocates of Swaraj ('self-rule') and a strong radical in Indian consciousness. He is known for his quote in Marathi: "Swaraj is my birthright and I shall have it!". He formed a close alliance with many Indian National Congress leaders, including Bipin Chandra Pal, Lala Lajpat Rai, Aurobindo Ghose and V. O. Chidambaram Pillai.

Impact of Bal Gangadhar Tilak's Ethics:

The manner in which a religion chooses to interpret its sacred scriptures in conflict resolution has far-reaching consequences. The ethics of Gita Rahasya took the form of militant Hinduism and political extremism. It found practical expression in a number of initiatives that promoted nationalism and politics based on religion, such as the celebration of Ganesh festivals, Shivaji festivals, gymnastic societies, extremist journalism and militant activities. These initiatives awakened Hindu consciousness among many Hindus.

Ganesh festivals

Tilak was perhaps the first Indian political leader to realised the strength of the masses. He developed many programs to bring people together, arguing that hero worship is at the root of nationality, social order and religion. Nehru remarked that Tilak was the first political leader of the new India who reached the masses and drew strength from them.

In 1895, Tilak inaugurated the Ganapati festivals. Ganesh is one of the most popular deities worshipped by Hindus. The Ganapati movement, inaugurated by Tilak, included participation from Hindus of the lower castes. Until then, Ganapati festivals had nothing of a public character. However, Tilak succeeded in transforming a simple domestic rite into a public celebration.

In 1894, Tilak with the help of the Natu brothers was responsible for making the festival a public event lasting ten days, with music and an organised procession involving boys from schools and colleges. Songs were sung in praise of Tilak and Shivaji. Boys were engaged in fencing and other physical exercises, and the Natu brothers taught them sword and single-stick exercises.

Through the Ganapati festivals, Tilak succeeded in bringing together the hitherto ignored urban and peasant lower classes, indoctrinating them with political songs and speeches, drilling young men to march about town in militant groups and imparting to Hinduism a congregational character previously unknown to it. During the processions, they shouted: "O Heroes of Hind" and "Adore your country as God."

In 1894 and 1895, Tilak held special Ganapati meetings in his own house at Poona where songs were sung that denounced moderate Hindus and the British government, and Tilak approved of these songs.

The worship of Ganesh was reinvented in Maharashtra by the great independent leader Tilak. Today, the Ganesh festival is the largest Hindu public religious performance in Maharashtra.

Tilak's use of the Ganesh festivals was an example of the use of traditional religious symbols to mobilise Hindus in the cause of Hindu nationalism.

Shivaji festivals

Tilak was also instrumental in reviving the memory of Shivaji and initiating a great national propaganda which culminated in 1895 with the celebration of Shivaji's reputed birthday at the chief centres of Brahmin activity in the Deccan. According to Tilak, the Shivaji festivals served like manure to the seeds of enthusiasm and the spirit of nationalism. He saw in this festival a peculiar value for the whole country and argued that it was the duty of everyone to ensure that this character of the festival was neither ignored or misrepresented. The Shivaji festivals were also attempts to consolidate Hindu consciousness.

Shivaji as a role model

Shivaji, the Maratha leader, provided a kind of exemplar for Tilak of his ethics of violence as higher duty, whose festivals he ardently promoted, though M K Gandhi considered Shivaji as a misguided patriot. In 1896, Tilak lamented the neglect of the sites associated with the life and death of Shivaji.

He said: "That the place of coronation and the tomb of that great man who gave the joy of independence to Maharashtra for two centuries should have been so utterly forgotten by the Marathas is indeed a misfortune." On 24 June 1906, Tilak wrote an article in his newspaper, Mahratta, entitled "Is Shivaji not a National Hero?" He called Shivaji a 'swadeshi hero' and argued that "Shivaji is the only hero to be found in Indian history". Tilak also began the modern projection of Shivaji as the leader of Maratha independence in Maharashtra. He urged children to read a portion of a historical novel entitled Ushahkal dealing with the times of Shivaji. According to him, what makes Shivaji a national hero is the spirit that guided him throughout and not his deeds as such.

Moreover, knowing about other ambivalent features of Tilak's political behaviour, one might conclude that Tilak chose the Shivaji precisely because it was ambivalent: it permitted him to appeal to the chivalrous and heroic elements of the Maratha leader's lofty character while at the same time allowing him to trade upon some of Shivaji's qualities.

The 'great chivalric hero' Shivaji arrived with concealed deadly weapons to meet Afzal Khan. At his first opportunity, Shivaji murdered Afzal Khan on the very spot where they had agreed to talk peace. What followed was the massacre of Afzal Khan's entire retinue. Now leaderless, the Mughal army dispersed and Shivaji won what Marathi patriots have celebrated as a great victory.

Shivaji is not just an inspirational historical figure but a symbol of resistance against oppression and a cultural renaissance of sorts. Indian nationalist historians saw him as the founder of the Maratha, and thereby Indian, nation. The Hindutva interpretation of Shivaji is essentially derived from this position. Shivaji employed people of all castes and religions in his administration and armed forces.

Shivaji's greatest legacy was laying the foundation for the Maratha Empire, which played a significant role in undermining the military and economic strength and prestige of the Mughal

Empire. At its peak, the Maratha empire stretched from modern-day Maharashtra in the south to the Sutlej River in the north, and to Orissa in the east, replacing the Mughals as dominant power. The Marathas remained the pre-eminent power in India until their defeat by the British in the Second and Third Anglo- Maratha wars.

Shivaji's legacy varied by observer and time, but nearly two centuries after his death, he began to take on increased importance with the emergence of the Indian independence movement. Many Indian nationalists, like Tilak and Savarkar, elevated him as a proto-nationalist and hero of the Hindus.

Gymnastic Societies

Tilak maintained that unless Hindus learned to employ force, they must expect to be impotent witness of the gradual downfall of their ancient institutions. Therefore, he proceeded to organise Gymnastic Societies in which physical training and the use of more or less primitive weapons were taught to develop the martial instincts of the rising generation.

The Natu brothers were recognized leaders of Hindu orthodoxy. They carried Tilak's propaganda to schools and colleges, proclaiming that unless they learned to employ force, the Hindus must expect to be impotent witnesses to the gradual downfall of all their ancient institutions.

His Gymnastic Societies sometimes resorted themselves to forming juvenile bands to swell the coffers of swaraj against the British. Young Hindus were taught to use arms and induced to believe it to be their duty to employ them against the enemy.

Extremist Journalism: Tilak started two newspapers, Kesari and Mahratta. He wrote articles to encourage militant nationalism and used his newspapers to incite the Hindus to assert their rights. He vilified the British. From June through August of 1902, Kesari ran a highly provocative series of nine editorials entitled 'Guerrilla Warfare'. Sometimes, Kesari contained articles on the methods of the Russian revolutionaries and the cult of the bomb in Bengal. He openly advocated Russian methods of retaliation. Writing in Kesari on 16 July 1907, he exhorted Indians to follow the Russian methods of political agitation. Tilak also wrote some articles proposing to the government to make gymnastics a compulsory subject in schools.

In the Kesari of 28 May 1907, he exhorted Indian leaders to emulate the example of Russian democrats in their methods of political agitation. He also spoke of how the Russians managed to evade press censorship. On 27 July 1907, Tilak wrote in Kesari: "We find in Mr. Savarkar's book a true echo of the thoughts of Mazzini, his secret and the open attempts to bring about the unification of Italy." "We find in Mazzini's writings a clear enumeration of the noble principles of democratic politics."

When Tilak began Kesari and Mahratta, he stated that the aim of the two newspapers would be to provide a fearless account of the existing conditions in the country, to review Indian books and to give correct estimates of political affairs in Britain. However, his columns went beyond this scope and promoted extremism and militancy. They became vehicles for his radical political views and ethics of violence.

Esteem for Swami Vivekananda

Tilak and Swami Vivekananda had great mutual respect and esteem for each other. They met accidentally while travelling by train in 1892, and Tilak had Vivekananda as a guest in his house. A person who was present there (Basukaka) heard that it was agreed between Vivekananda and Tilak that Tilak would work towards nationalism in the "political" arena, while Vivekananda would work for nationalism in the "religious" arena. When Vivekananda died at a young age, Tilak expressed great sorrow and paid tributes to him in the Kesari. Tilak said about Vivekananda:

"No Hindu, who has the interests of Hinduism at heart, could help feeling grieved over Vivekananda's samadhi. Vivekananda, in short, had taken the work of keeping the banner of Advaita philosophy forever flying among all the nations of the world and made them realize the true greatness of Hindu religion and of the Hindu people. He had hoped that he would crown his achievement with the fulfilment of this task by virtue of his learning, eloquence, enthusiasm and sincerity, just as he had laid a secure foundation for it; but with Swami's samadhi, these hopes have gone. Thousands of years ago, another saint, Shankaracharya, showed to the world the glory of Advaita philosophy, and Vivekananda continued this great tradition."

Tilak was the founder of the militant revolutionary school in the national movement. He seemed to have had connections with the secret societies in Nasik, Bengal and elsewhere. He felt strong enough to capture the Congress organisation in 1907, though it was not successful. The fight between the moderates and the extremists, carried on in the political arena, led to a split in the Indian National Congress. The extremists founded a party of their own. However, Tilak said that the extremists of today will be the moderates of tomorrow, just as the moderates of today were extremists yesterday. In 1907, at Surat, Tilak and his revolutionary group, including Aurobindo Ghose, were expelled from the Congress for their radicalisation of Indian politics. The rift was only healed in 1914 when Tilak finalised a pact with the Muslim League for a joint front against the British.

It has been argued that in the murder of Walter Charles Rand and Charles Egerton Ayerst at Nasik, the assassins were only giving effect to Tilak's teachings. During the anti-cow killing agitation of 1893, which caused disturbances throughout the country and much loss of life and property, he showed himself as an open advocate of violence and the cult of physical force. Sometimes he advocated insurrection and argued that the Boer system of warfare, which had been successful against the British, should be emulated. In 1908, Tilak was tried for sedition because of an attempt on the life of Kingsford, a British judge at Muzaffarpur. Though the intention was to murder Kingsford, the assassins missed the target, and two ladies were killed. Tilak in his writings, supported the bomb throwers. This bomb outrage offered the government a golden chance to arrest Tilak. Tilak was sentenced for six years in prison.

Tilak was convicted for inciting disaffection against the British in his writings in Marathi, but he claimed that the English renderings were defective. The trial ended in his incarceration, and he was sent to Mandalay (Myanmar), where he composed his influential commentary on the Gita, the Gitarahasya.

Tilak and Hindu Nationalism

Bala Gangadhar Tilak needs special discussion for the following reasons: first, he not only attempted to draw the outline of a Hindu nation, but he also actively and effectively mobilized the Hindus to crystallize Hindu identity; secondly Dr. K. B. Hedgewar and his political guru Dr. B. S. Moonje were ardent followers of Tilak. The ideology of the RSS undoubtedly took its cue from Tilak.

In his writings-The Orion and The Arctic Home in the Vedas-Tilak attempted to prove that his Aryan ancestors had actually planted the seed of civilization. Though Tilak's thesis did not have a strong scholarly foundation, his conclusion certainly generated a sense of psychological superiority among the Hindus. "In a land where antiquity was generally equated with superiority, few contributions to the inflation of the national ego were of greater significance."

Tilak had developed his thinking in terms of a Hindu nation: "The common factor in Indian society is the feeling of Hindutva (Hinduness)". When he talked of Indian society, he meant Hindu society. He considered the Hindus of different regions as one, all of them believing in a Hindu dharma. He observed, "There may be different doctrines in the Hindu dharma, but certain principles can be found in common, and because of this alone a sort of feeling that we belong to one religion has remained among people speaking different languages in such a vast country". This feeling of oneness among the Hindus was further strengthened by different institutions of the Hindu religion, like temples and places of pilgrimage, he analysed.

Tilak believed that religion was a vital element in nationality and argued that India was a self-contained nation during Vedic times. He observed, "A Hindu of this place is as much as a Hindu as one from Madras or Bombay . . . the inner sentiments which move you are the same. The study of Gita, Ramayana and Mahabharata produce the same ideas throughout the country. Are not these common allegiances to the Vedas, Gita and Ramayana our common heritage?" Tilak believed that the divergent sects of India could converge to form a "mighty Hindu nation" if they would only follow the original principles of the Hindu tradition as set forth in such texts as the Ramayana and the Bhagavadgita. This convergence should be the goal of all Hindus. The writings of the RSS very much reflect these ideas.

Promotion of Hindu nationalism

Tilak was the first to connect Hindu symbolism with the freedom struggle and he interpreted the Gita in terms of political activism. It was during the British rule that Hindu nationalism took birth. "The father of Indian unrest' was in many respects one of the figures who nurtured it. Tilak was a Hindu nationalist to the core who made - no distinction between religion and politics. According to Tilak, religion is an element of nationality. He buttressed the claims of Hindu chauvinism through his scholarship. He said: "The common factor in Indian society is the feeling of Hindutva (Hinduness)" The Hindu religion provides to the Indian society a moral as well as social tie. During the Vedic times India was a self-contained country and a great nation united by a common culture. That unity disappeared and it brought upon the nation great degradation. But it is the duty of the leaders of India to revive that union.

Tilak stood for the establishment of a Hindu Rashtra in India. It is argued that Tilak had a part in the so-called 'Nepal plot'. The idea presumably was to convince the king of Nepal to invade India, sparking in turn an uprising within the country in his support, since if the independent king of the only independent Hindu kingdom conquered India there would be one sovereign Hindu nation.

Emulation of a great past is axiomatic to any cultural renaissance. Tilak argued that truths that are being discovered by the West were known to the rishis of India. Modern science is gradually justifying and vindicating the ancient wisdom of India. He says: "Are not these common allegiances to the Vedas, the Gita and the Ramayana our common heritage? If we lay stress on it forgetting all the minor differences that exist between different sects, then by the grace of providence we shall be able to consolidate all the different sects into a mighty Hindu nation. This ought to be the ambition of every Hindu."

Religio-Political Views

Tilak sought to unite the Indian population for mass political action throughout his life. For this to happen, he believed there needed to be a comprehensive justification for anti-British, pro-Hindu activism. To this end, he sought justification in the supposed original principles of the Ramayana and the Bhagavad Gita. He named this call to activism karma-yoga, or the yoga of action. In his interpretation, the Bhagavad Gita reveals this principle in the conversation between Krishna and Arjuna when Krishna exhorts Arjuna to fight his enemies (which, in this case, included many members of his family) because it is his duty. In Tilak's opinion, the Bhagavad Gita provided a strong justification for activism. However, this conflicted with the mainstream exegesis of the text at the time, which was dominated by renunciate views and the idea of acts purely for God. These views were represented by the two mainstream interpretations of the time, those of Ramanuja and Adi Shankara.

To find support for this philosophy, Tilak wrote his own interpretations of the relevant passages of the Gita and backed his views using Jnanadeva's commentary on the Gita, Ramanuja's critical commentary and his own translation of the Gita. His main battle was against the renunciate views of the time, which conflicted with worldly activism. To fight this, he went to great lengths to reinterpret words such as karma, dharma and yoga, as well as the concept of renunciation itself. Because he founded his rationalization on Hindu religious symbols and lines of thought, his approach resonated deeply with many Hindus.

The Gita Rahasya is essentially a work of nationalist literature rather than of philosophy. Through it, Tilak made a stirring call to his countrymen to take action in order to claim their birthright, which is swaraj (self-rule). He argued that in this process, it is legitimate to indulge in violence, in imitation of Arjuna and Shivaji. It is the motive rather than the action itself that matters. In other words, the end justifies the means.

Claim of the superiority of Hinduism

Tilak advocated the superiority of Hinduism over all other religions. In his address in Benares in 1906, he said: "There is no other religion on the face of the earth except the Hindu religion wherein we find such a hopeful promise, a promise that God comes to us as many times as necessary. After Mohammed, no Prophet is promised, and Jesus Christ came once forever. No religion holds such a promise full of hope. A time will come when our religious thoughts and our rights will be vindicated."

According to Tilak, all the different sects of Hinduism are in fact branches of the Vedic religion. He claimed that the term Sanatana dharma ('eternal religion') shows that Hinduism is very old - as old as history of the human race itself. Vedic religion was the religion of the Aryans from a very early time. Hindu religion as a whole is made up of different parts co-related to each other as many sons and daughters of one great religion.

Tilak claimed that all religions, except Hinduism, are partial truths. He said: "They [non-Hindu religions] are partial truth while our Hindu religion is based on the whole, the Sanatana truth. "He added: "Hindu religion is very comprehensive - as comprehensive as its literature itself; we have a wonderful literature. Wisdom, as is concentrated in the Gita and epitomized in about 700 verses, that wisdom, I am confident, cannot be defeated or overcome by any philosophy, be it Western or any other."

In many of his speeches, Tilak asked for greater coordination of all the sections of Hinduism under the banner of Bharata Dharma Mahamandala ('All India Religious Association'). He also emphasised the value of numbers. He said: "Numerical strength also is a great strength. Can the religion which counts its followers by crores die? Never, unless the crores of our fellow-followers are suddenly swept away, our religion will not die. All that is required for our glorious triumph and success is that we should unite all the different sects on a common platform and let the stream of Hindu religion flow through one channel."

Tilak also proudly maintained that Hinduism is the most tolerant religion in the world. According to him, it tolerates all religions. He asked: "If there be any religion in the world which advocates toleration of other religious beliefs and instructs one to stick to one's own religion, it is the religion of the Hindus alone." He added: "Shri Krishna does not say that the followers of other religions would be doomed to eternal hell. I challenge anybody to point out to me a similar text from the scriptures of other religions. It cannot be found in any other religion." [13]

Bipin Chandra Pal

Bipin Chandra Pal has the distinction of being one of "the mightiest prophets of nationalism" in India. He was the "Pal" of the famous triumvirate of Lal-Bal-Pal. A journalist by profession, he is credited with the launch of the journal "New India" and the daily "Bande Mataram", which was also edited by Aurobindo Ghose. While Pal has been overshadowed to some extent by Lal and Bal in contemporary times, his writings are critical for contextualizing some of the issues that are formative to the idea of India and continue to be discussed and debated even today.

Bipin Chandra Pal was a proponent of aggressive nationalism and was associated with revolutionary groups. He gave a clarion call for attaining "Purna Swaraj", advocated the boycott of foreign goods and the adoption of 'swadeshi'. Pal was acutely aware that India was not an island unto herself and was keenly interested in international affairs. He authored several pieces with a sense of foreboding for India in the background of the geopolitical changes happening in China and other parts of the world.

Bipin Chandra Pal is often referred to as the 'Father of Revolutionary Thoughts' in India because of his staunch advocacy for radical changes in the political and social fabric of the country. Like many freedom fighters of his time, Bipin Chandra Pal was focused on educating the masses, eradicating social ills, and working towards the economic upliftment of the common Indian citizen. He not only opposed the caste system but also worked towards what can be termed 'women empowerment' in his context.

This piece summarizes two essays titled – 'Hinduism and Indian Nationalism' and 'Hinduism Nationalism: What it Stands For' authored by the great freedom fighter – Shri Bipin Chandra Pal and not only provide brilliant insights into certain aspects of our nation building but also offer food for thought in contemporary times.

Gleanings from Bipin Chandra Pal's Essays

In 'Hinduism and Indian Nationalism', Bipin Chandra Pal laid down the tenets of a new brand of nationalism. He explained that the new spirit of nationalism is 'intensely realistic' and 'not imitative' in character. While it has the transformation of ancient symbols and philosophy at its core to establish a connection with the masses, it is not only limited to a revival of religious ideas but also focusses on social reformation. Pal elevated the idea of 'Swaraj' to a goal that is not just political in nature but also has associated spiritual and religious underpinnings.

There is a new idea of nationalism that is now pervading the minds of political leaders spearheading the revival of nationalistic fervor. These leaders are men and women who have managed to synthesize their rationalist perspectives, which were primarily born from their Euro-centric education, with the meanings and inspirations of the 'ancient symbols and sacraments of their people'. They have revived their faith 'in national institutions and scriptures' and their 'religious spirit, at once so real and so conservative' is 'rehabilitating the old beliefs and trying to adjust them to the demands of the modern life and thought.'

The leaders are cognizant of the fact that 'statesmanship is not concerned with the rationality, but simply with the reality, of popular faiths. For it is this reality, the earnestness and sincerity with which particular faiths are held, that lends vitality and strength to historic movements.' They know that 'Hinduism is not dead, but still living; the religion of the Hindu is not idolatry, not even idolatry; the old gods are no mere myths.' It is in light of these partly philosophical and partly political truths that they are creating new symbols or a new form of idolatry 'representing the apotheosis of the geographical habitat of the race.'

A few examples quoted by the author deserve special mention. The interpretation and transformation of the popular Hindu goddess Jagaddhatri (जगद्धात्री) as symbolic of the different stages of nationalism and Shree Krishna as a nation-builder and the divine exemplar for Hindus in all times to come are symbols that have invigorated the masses. The author states, 'This wonderful transfiguration of the old gods and goddesses is carrying the message of new nationalism to the women and the masses of the country.'

Daily mundane rituals, like purification of the physical body with mantras that invoke the sacred rivers of India's geography, have acquired intensely spiritual connotations and have also become symbolic of the geographic unity of the land and its people.

'Gangeca, yamunecaiva, Godavari, Sarasvati,

Narmada, Sindhu, Kaveri, jalesmin sannidhim kuru.'

May the Ganges, the Jumna, the Sarasvati, the Narmada, the Indus, and the Kaveri, enter into this water.

The new Nationalist Movement is not limited to religious revival but has led to a great social revival in the country. 'There has been at work a slow and silent process of the liberalization of old social ideas. The old bigotry that anathematized the least deviation from the rules of caste or the authority of custom is openly giving way to a spirit of new tolerance. The imperious necessities of national struggle and national life are slowly breaking down, except in purely ceremonial affairs, the old restrictions of caste.'

Neo-Vedantism and/or Neo-Hinduism are at work and are 'seeking to realize the old spiritual ideals of the race, not through monkish negations or medieval abstractions, but by the idealization and the spiritualization of the concrete contents and actual relations of life.' They demand, 'consequently, a social, an economic, and a political reconstruction, such as will be helpful to the highest spiritual life of every individual member of the community.'

While 'the spiritual note of the present Nationalist Movement in India is entirely derived from this revived Vedantic thought', the limited influence of European thoughts and ideals is admitted. The author states that the new social revival should not be read superficially as a 'conflict between the progressive and conservative elements of Indian society', but as 'a conflict between aggressive European and progressive Indian culture.'

Pacifism and non-violence are not a given to achieve desired ends. The 'real spirit of Indian Nationalism' is essentially religious and 'its end is the realisation of God-life in and through the activities of social and political life. That end is absolutely assured, but whether it will be reached by peaceful means or not will be determined by the capacity or incapacity of British statesmanship to work out the problem that faces it in India.'

'Swaraj', the proclaimed ideal of the Indian people, is more than a political term and conveys much more than 'self-government', which is assumed to be a given. The term borrowed from ancient Vedantic philosophy is essentially a positive concept which, for political purposes, implies 'not merely the absence of bondage', like freedom, but also includes in its purview 'the settlement of all disputes due to conflict of interests, either national or international'. The concept involves not merely national freedom, but universal federation also, without which nations can never be established in perfect harmony with one another.'

The word not only 'signifies the highest spiritual end' but also 'represents the highest political ideal'.

In the second essay titled 'Hinduism Nationalism: What it Stands For', Bipin Chandra Pal collectively referred to the points mentioned above as 'Hindu Nationalism'. However, he boldly and broadly asserted that this brand of nationalism is characterised by an essentially universal and synthesizing spirit. It is focused on inclusion and not exclusion.

Hindu nationalism has the term 'Narayana' as its cornerstone. Each human being is an indivisible part of 'Narayana' and hence the ultimate aim of Hindu nationalism is to rise above all distinctions of colour, creed, country or caste; to believe in 'vasudhaiva kutumbakam' and to strive for national and universal well-being. Hindu nationalism is thus universal in nature and encompasses all nations of the world.

'Our holy men have known and revered every human individual, whatever his colour, creed, country or caste, as Narayana himself. Every human, the lowest socially as well as the highest, is uniformly saluted by the holiest of our holy men all over India as Narayana. The collective life of the various tribes, races, and nations of the world is equally regarded by the highest Hindu thought as diverse vehicles and manifestations of Narayana. This Narayana or Humanity, is the Whole; the different nations of the world are parts of that Whole. Narayana or Humanity, is the Body; the different tribalities, racialities and nationalities are limbs of that Body. The whole is implied in the parts, the organism in the organs. Narayana or Universal Humanity, is therefore logically implicit in every tribe, race, and nation. And the end and aim of the evolution of all these various social units must, therefore, be to make explicit this hidden life of Narayana in their own life and activities.'

'Hindu Nationalism implies neither selfish conflicts with, nor arrogant isolation from, other nations of the world.' 'Hindu Nationalism stands, therefore, not only for the furtherance of the cause of true freedom in India, which includes the fullest scope and opportunity for the utmost possible development and perfection of the special genius, culture and civilization of our people. With the view to be able to bear our share of the work of universal humanity and to make our special contribution to the culture and character of the race—but also for the continuance of the British connection with us for the immense possibilities of that federal internationalism which may be most easily secured for our nation through this connection.'

Hindu nationalism recognises that there is a cultural basis to national differences, beyond just territorial demarcations. It recognises that 'the whole structure of the civilization of our rulers is based, as Lecky says, 'upon the belief that it is a good thing to cultivate intellectual and material capacities even at the cost of certain moral evils which we are able accurately to foresee.' It challenges the preference for material and intellectual ends over moral and spiritual ends.'

Hindu nationalism accepts that India is but a part of the whole and is characterised by a passion for unity that 'underlies all forms and classes of diversities and differences.'

'Even as advocates of Hindu culture and Hindu civilization, we cannot, consistent with the teachings of Hinduism itself, refuse to admit that our culture and civilization represent only a part of universal human culture and civilization. At their best, they have so far rendered only a few notes of that universal humanity which includes all the different races and cultures of the world.'

'For we hold that God has left no country or people without witnesses unto his spirit or proofs of his providence; and that the universal is present behind the particular everywhere. Universal Humanity is the regulative idea in all historic evolutions. Particular culture-histories are therefore only parts of the history of universal culture and have consequently a close kinship with one another. Their unity is necessary and basal. Their divergences, however wide and vital, are due either to differences of race-consciousness—which is the element of permanence in racial evolution—or to physical environments or historic associations or differences in the stages of evolution in which these severally stand.' [14]

Mohandas Karamchand Gandhi [1869-1948] gained unprecedented authority over the Indian National Congress through a complex process that brought him into conflict with the Hindu Mahasabha and its elite politics in the 1920s and 1930s.Although he attended the inaugural meeting of the Hindu Mahasabha in Haridwar in 1915, the Mahasabha's old style of politics had collapsed since Gandhi's emergence as the leader of the Congress's mass campaigns in India following the Khilafat- Non-cooperation movement in 1919-1921. The Congress was transformed into a mass organisation and strove to attract a wider cross-section of the population to its fold, diverting much of the support that the Mahasabha had received from the Hindu classes. Gandhi's leadership presented a radical challenge to the Mahasabha's definition of nationalism and vision of the Indian nation by emphasizing an 'inclusive' Indian nation based on the coexistence of diverse creeds and religions. Gandhi advanced an alternative to Hindutva, articulating the Hindu tradition of religious pluralism, which envisioned religious diversity as a plurality of 'expressions of truth'. His ideals of ahimsa [non- violence] and Hindu-Muslim unity constituted the basis of a struggle for India's freedom, conflicting with the Mahasabha's discourse of a majoritarian 'Hindu nation' based on military power. Gandhi's dominance of national-level politics, having proclaimed the 'secular' to be sacred, blunted the Mahasabha's leadership. The Mahasabha, which led a drive to make India a 'Hindu' state, resisted Gandhian nationalist struggles most virulently in the country. Gandhi's dialogue and conflict with the Mahasabha over the methods of the freedom struggle and the nature of the future nation-state that was to emerge in India in the early twentieth century were significant.

Gandhi's religion

Gandhi tried to grapple with the enigma of Hinduism, which had represented his strongest bond and a great influence on his life. His understanding of Hinduism was largely based on reading and reflection, yet it remained shallow and abstract, offering an insight into one of the most distinctive doctrines of Vedanta - the doctrine of religious pluralism, or sarva dharma samabhava [equality of religions]. Gandhi read Vivekananda's Rajayoga, M.N. Dwivedi's two commentaries on the Yoga Sutras, and the Bhagavad Gita - the principal scripture that deeply influenced him on the principle of aparigraha [non-possession] and renunciation.

He described Hindus as that branch of Aryans who had migrated to the trans-Indus region of India. "A thousand years ago," he explained, "the army of Ghazni invaded India in order to spread Islam. Hindu idols were broken, and the invasions carried as far as Somnath. Thus, we have seen how there have been three assaults on Hinduism, coming from Islam and then Christianity, but on the whole it came out of them unscathed." Gandhi identified Hinduism with the Sanatana dharma, the 'eternal' or 'universal religion' which underlay all religions, comprising the Vedic tradition based on the 'equality of religions. He defined Hinduism as the most tolerant of all religions known to him, in which non- violence found the highest expression and application. 'Its freedom from dogma,' he explained, "gives the votary the largest scope for self-expression. Not being an exclusive religion, it enables the followers of that faith not merely to respect all the other religions, but to admire and assimilate whatever may be good in the other faiths."

Hinduism, according to Gandhi, 'is as broad as the Universe and takes in its fold all that is good in this world', and 'whatever of substance contained in any other religion is always to be found in it'. To Gandhi, Hinduism signified pluralism and non- violence, representing the best impulses of its classical texts, besides being 'inclusive', 'tolerant' and productive of 'diversity'. It became the model for spiritual humanism that drew upon the best of all religions, looking beyond the narrow limits of ethnicity and nationality.

Gandhi claimed that he was a sanatani [orthodox] Hindu, a Vaishnavite Hindu grounded in the ancient and traditional beliefs and values of Hinduism. 'I am a Hindu,' he confessed, 'not merely because I was born in the Hindu fold, but I am one by conviction and choice.... As I know it [Hinduism] and interpret it, it gives me all the solace I need both here and hereafter.' He declared: 'I have been born a Hindu and I shall die a Hindu, a Sanatani Hindu. If there is salvation for me, it must be as a Hindu.' He had little interest in the outer forms of Hinduism, its rituals, or pilgrimages. Placing reason above scripture as authoritative and relying on an 'inner voice' - the 'still, small voice that must always be the final arbiter'- Gandhi represented a tradition of modernity and reform within Hinduism. [15]

Gandhi and Rama Rajya

Though Gandhi never called himself a "Hindu nationalist"; he believed in and propagated concepts like Dharma and introduced the concept of " Rama Rajya " (Rule of Lord Rāma) as part of his social and political philosophy. Gandhi said "By political independence, I do not mean an imitation of the British House of commons, the soviet rule of Russia or the Fascist rule of Italy or the Nazi rule of Germany. They have systems suited to their genius. We must have ours suited to ours. What that can be is more than I can tell. I have described it as Rama Rajya i.e., sovereignty of the people based on pure moral authority."

Gandhi emphasised that "Rama Rajya" to him meant peace and justice, adding that "the ancient ideal of Rama Rajya is undoubtedly one of true democracy in which the meanest citizen could be sure of swift justice without an elaborate and costly procedure". He also emphasised that it meant respect for all religions: "My Hinduism teaches me to respect all religions. In this lies the secret of Rama Rajya".

While Gandhi had clarified that "by Ram Rajya I do not mean Hindu Raj. I mean by Ram Rajya, Divine Raj, the kingdom of God," his concept of "Rama Rajya" became a major concept in Hindu nationalism. [16]

Subhas Chandra Bose

Subhas Chandra Bose was one of the most prominent leaders and highly respected independence fighters from Bengal in the Indian independence movement.

Apart from Gandhi, revolutionary leader Netaji Subhas Chandra Bose referred to Vedanta and the Bhagavad Gita as sources of inspiration for the struggle for Indian independence. Swami Vivekananda's teachings on universalism, his nationalist thoughts and his emphasis on social service and reform had all inspired Subhas Chandra Bose from his very young days. The fresh interpretation of India's ancient scriptures appealed immensely to Subhas. Hindu spirituality formed an essential part of his political and social thought throughout his adult life, although there was no sense of bigotry or orthodoxy in it. Subhas, who called himself a socialist, believed that socialism in India owed its origins to Swami Vivekananda. In a sense, that would mark the posthumous homecoming for a nationalist who believed that Rashtra bhakti is a synthesis of religion and nationalism, of the spiritual and the political.

In the early decades of this century, when others were looking up to Mohandas Karamchand Gandhi for inspiration, Bose was looking elsewhere for guidance. His search for a religious philosophy that would spur political activism led him to explore the teachings of Swami Vivekananda and the writings of Aurobindo Ghosh. The latter made a lasting impression on his mind, providing his political activism with a religious side.

The profound Impact that Aurobindo Ghosh had on Subhas Chandra Bose is reflected in his autobiography: "In my undergraduate days, Aurobindo Ghosh was easily the most popular leader in Bengal... a mixture of spirituality and politics had given him a halo of mysticism and made his personality more fascinating to those who were religiously inclined... We felt convinced that spiritual enlightenment was necessary for effective national service..."

It is, therefore, not surprising that he should have also been influenced by Bankim Chandra Chatterjee's construction of nationalism. Like Aurobindo Ghosh, Bankim Chandra Chatterjee and Bal Gangadhar Tilak, the Indian nation for him extended beyond the geographical to the devotional plane. During his college days, he discovered the wretchedness of not India but "impoverished Mother India."

Curiously, his view of the other India, the one which appears so distant from the fashionable drawing rooms and glittering malls of our cities, is not different from those who believe that a divide separates 'us' and 'them'. For, "the picture of real India", which Subhas Chandra Bose described as "the India of the villages where poverty stalks the land, men die like flies, and illiteracy is the prevailing order", is also the India which many believe should receive priority over that India which revels in rejecting anything that carries the label 'Made in India', including Hindu spirituality and religious philosophy.

In his book, Brothers Against the Raj, Leonard A Gordon writes about Bose's quest for a religious philosophy to serve as the core of nationalism and sustain his political activism: "Inner religious explorations continued to be a part of his adult life. This set him apart from the slowly growing number of atheistic socialists and communists who dotted the Indian landscape." It was this "religious exploration" that set Subhas Chandra Bose apart from Jawaharlal Nehru, for whom "this was a vain quest". Although Bose scrupulously avoided publishing his faith or his quest, he remained firm in his belief that "Hinduism was an essential part of his Indianness", his Bharatiyata. In other words, he subscribed to cultural nationalism or, call it if you must by its other name, Hindutva.

But he had grown up in the first two decades of the twentieth century in Bengal, where, owing to the influence of Bankim Chandra Chatterjee and Swami Vivekananda, there was a fusion of religion and nationalism. As a result, nationalist feeling had a pronounced Hindu complexion and Hinduism had a pronounced political character.

This "fusion of religion and nationalism" and Hinduism with a "pronounced political character" came into play in 1925 when, during his incarceration at Mandalay prison, Subhas Chandra Bose, along with other Bengali prisoners, organised Durga Puja on the jail premises and demanded that the expenses be borne by the authorities. When the latter refused, Bose converted his spiritual quest into a political campaign by launching a hunger strike. This practice of political Hinduism had an electrifying impact on public opinion and soon the Swarajists lent their voice to the popular demand for the release of all political prisoners who had not been charged with specific crimes.

Those who deride nationalism, more so cultural nationalism, as narrow, selfish and aggressive, a hindrance to the promotion of internationalism, would do well to go through Bose's speech at Poona after being elected president of the Maharashtra Provincial Conference. "Indian nationalism," Subhas Chandra Bose asserted, "is inspired by the highest ideals of the human race, Satyam, Shivam, Sundaram. Nationalism in India has… roused the creative faculties which for centuries had been lying dormant in our people…" [17]

"Inner religious explorations continued to be a part of his adult life. This set him apart from the slowly growing number of atheistic socialists and communists who dotted the Indian landscape." Hinduism was an essential part of his Indianness. His strategy against the British colonial government also included the use of Hindu symbols and festivals. In 1925, while in Mandalay jail, he went on a hunger strike when Durga puja was not supported by prison authorities. The revolutionary leader Netaji Subhas Chandra Bose always referred to Vedanta and the Bhagavad-Gita as sources of inspiration for the struggle against the British. Swami Vivekananda's teachings on universalism, his nationalist thoughts and his emphasis on social service and reform had all inspired Subhas Chandra Bose from his very young days. The fresh interpretation of the India's ancient scriptures appealed immensely to Subhas. Hindu spirituality formed the essential part of his political and social thought through his adult life, although there was no sense of bigotry or orthodoxy in it. Subhas, who called himself a socialist, believed that socialism in India owed its origins to Swami Vivekananda.

Subhas, from an early age, possessed a deep devotion to Dharma and meditated for hours as a perfect son of the freedom movement. Asceticism once appeared to him as the best path because of his dedication to Hindu Dharma. The literature of Swami Vivekananda provided solace to him after a lot of failed attempts and disappointments; he regarded Swami as his Guru. A Bengali book titled Taruner Swapna, a story about a young boy's dream of worshipping Mother Land, reflects Subhas' true vision of worshiping Mother Land. In a similar manner, Rishi Bankimchandra, Swami Vivekananda, and Sri Aurobindo also envisioned Motherland as sacred.

Subhas was considered by his comrades as the ideal convergence of Bhakti (devotion) and Shakti (Strength) even. It is quite amazing to note that even in his tiring times, whether it was the formation of the Bengal Volunteers during the 1928 Kolkata session of the Indian National Congress, his election as the president of Indian National Congress or his expulsion from the same party, he would read the Shrimad Bhagavad Gita and other Hindu religious books daily. Numerous citations can be quoted to prove this. Netaji was significantly influenced by V.D. Savarkar, the renowned theoretician and leader of All India Hindu Mahasabha, who suggested a change in the track of his actions. As per Savarkar, Bose was wasting time agitating for the removal of the Holwell Monument in then Calcutta, and he suggested waging the war of national liberation from outside India. This suggestion indeed changed Bose's life completely.

Exponents of alleged secularism in India can be silenced by the fact that Netaji had high regard for Savarkar and recognized his role. In his speech on Azad Hind Radio (June 25, 1944), he acknowledged Savarkar's wisdom with these words: "When, due to misguided political whims and lack of vision, almost all the leaders of the Congress party have been decrying all the soldiers in the Indian Army as mercenaries, it is heartening to know that Veer Savarkar is fearlessly exhorting the youths of India to enlist in the armed forces. These enlisted youths themselves provide us with trained men and soldiers for our Indian National Army."

Testaments also prove that even when the Indian National Army (Azad Hind Fauj) was engaged in a life-and-death struggle, Netaji used to read the Shrimad Bhagavad Gita and Sri Sri Chandi and perform puja daily. [18]

Akhil Bharat Hindu Mahasabha

History of Hindu Maha Sabha
Hindu Sahaik Sabhas

A broad unity on the basis of an emerging Hindu consciousness had gained momentum in the Punjab since the 1900s, where the Arya Samaj shaped the 'first blueprint' of Hindu nationalism. The formation of the All-India Muslim League in December 1906 triggered a competing 'Hindu unity' narrative, strengthening the notion that 'Hindu interests' needed representation in colonial politics. A series of Hindu Sahaik Sabhas were established through the initiatives of local Arya Samajs in the cities of the Punjab. Ram Bhaj Datta, an Arya Samajist of the College faction, founded a Hindu Sahaik Sabha in Lahore in 1906 in protest against the government's 'pro-Muslim bias', calling for the development of a 'Hindu politics'. A Hindu Sabha was formed in Lahore on 4th August 1906 by prominent Arya Samaj and Hindu Sanatanist leaders: Lala Lajpat Rai, Shadi Lal, Harkrishna Lal, Raja Narendra Nath, Ram Saran Das, Ruchi Ram Sahini, Ram Bhaj Datta, and Lala Hans Raj. Its main objective was to improve the 'moral, intellectual and material conditions' of Hindus. A provincial Hindu Sabha was formed in Lahore in 1907 to safeguard the interests of Hindus, showing a vigorous action on issues concerning Hindus. The Hindu Sabhas retained religious and social objectives, focusing on 'Hindu unity' and 'renewal'. They did not have a crystallised ideology, but fulfilled religious and social roles by promoting 'self-help and mutual co-operation' in the Hindu community, even though they swore loyalty to the British. Sections of the educated Hindu elite embraced the Sabhas, for the Congress had not addressed their dilemmas and anxieties in the years before the First World War.

Through June 1909, a string of letters, titled 'Hindu: A Dying Race', written by Lt Col. U.N. Mukerji, an Indian Medical Service officer, appeared in Bengalee, a Kolkata-based English-language newspaper owned and edited by veteran Congress leader Surendranath Banerjea. Historians identified these letters, later compiled into a pamphlet and also published as a book, as the founding basis of the notion that Hindus were in danger and they needed to wake up and act.

One prominent influence behind the birth of the Hindu Sabha movement in the Punjab was Rai Bahadur Lal Chand [1852-1912], a prominent Arya Samajist and a judge in Lahore. Lal Chand wrote in 1909 a series of 15 articles in Punjabee of Lahore, the newspaper founded by Lajpat Rai, under the title 'Self Abnegation in Politics', which was published as Self-Abnegation in Politics in 1938. Lal Chand's thesis represented Hindutva discourse on the 'political rights' of Hindus and their 'plight' in colonial India. He attacked the attitude of Hindus towards politics as one of 'self-denial' which allowed the claims of Muslims to take the 'precedence', separate electorates being an 'apotheosis of surrender' by Hindus. Hindus, he explained, were weak and divided in view of British 'hostility' and 'opposition' by Muslims; 'Hindu nationality' and 'Hindu sentiments' were being obliterated, 'if not pushed out of existence'. Lal Chand put the blame for the loss of 'Hindu self-assertion on the Congress, an organisation that 'makes the Hindu forget that he is a Hindu and tends to swamp this communal individuality into an Indian ideal, making him break with all his past traditions and past glory'. The Congress's ideal of a composite nationhood, he argued, was 'erroneous' and had become unrealistic under the declared 'hostile attitude' of Muslims. Any concessions by Hindus to 'Muslim separatism' would end in a failure. Hindu unity and political action alone would, he asserted, save the community and bring about a 'reconciliation' with Muslims. 'My own belief," he declared, 'is that if we succeed in establishing a strong, independent Hindu organisation, the Muslims would, in course of time, join us in making a common demand for redress of common grievances'. Lal Chand favoured a 'Hindu politics' as an alternative to the Congress's national politics, proposing the substitution of Hindu Sabhas for Congress committees and of the Hindu press for the Congress press as a basis for the protection of 'Hindu interests'. "The point I wish to urge,' he went on, 'is that patriotism ought to be communal and not merely geographical." The idea is to love everything owned by the community. It may be religion, it may be a tract of country, or it may be a phase of civilization. Lal Chand's work laid the foundation for a 'Hindu politics', setting a pattern for the strengthening of the Hindu Sabha movement as a powerful symbol of Hindu unity and cohesiveness in the Punjab. [19]

Origins of the Hindu Mahasabha emerged in connection with the disputes after the partition of Bengal in 1905 in British India. Under the then viceroy Lord Curzon, the division of the province of Bengal was in two new provinces of East Bengal and Assam, as well as Bengal. The new province of Bengal had a Hindu majority, the province of East Bengal and Assam was mostly Muslim. The division was justified by the British for administrative reasons.

A broad unity on the basis of an emerging Hindu Consciousness had gained momentum in the Punjab since 1900s. The formation of the All-India Muslim League in 1906 and the British India government's creation of separate Muslim electorate under the Morley-Minto reforms was a catalyst for Hindu leaders coming together to create pan India organisation to protect the rights of the Hindu community members.

All these statements can be made by any leader of the Maha Sabha in any Conference. These statements indicate the basic principles of the formation of the Maha Sabha. In December 1900, at a meeting of leading Hindus held at Allahabad, it was decided that an all-India Hindu Maha Sabha should be formed.

In 1909, Lal Chand and U.N. Mukerji established the Punjab Hindu Sabha ("Punjab Hindu Assembly").

The Sabha stated that it was not a sectarian organisation, but an "all-embracing movement" that aimed to safeguard the interests of "the entire Hindu community". During 21–22 October, 1909, it organised the Punjab Provincial Hindu Conference, which criticized the Indian National Congress for failing to defend Hindu interests and called for promotion of Hindu-centred politics. Nearly 800 delegates from different parts of the province attended the two days sitting. Pandit Madan mohan Malviya participated in the session and gave inaugural speech. It was stated that sabha was 'not sectarian, but an all-embracing movement' with an aim to safeguard the 'interests of the entire Hindu community'.

Full report of this Conference was published in book form (200 pages) and copies are still preserved in Hindu Maha Sabha records. Lala Lajpat Rai who took a prominent part in the Hindu Maha Sabha movement afterwards attended the conference and made a long speech on the first resolution on "Desirability of feeling of Hindu Nationality and Hindu Unity.". The Sabha organised five more annual provincial conferences in Punjab,

The first Hindu Sabha was established in the Punjab in the year 1907 with the following objects:-

1) "To Promote brotherly feelings amongst the various sections of the Hindu community

2) To help destitute and disabled Hindus

3) To act as trustees of such properties as may be entrusted to the Sabha for charitable, religious, educational and other purposes

4) To improve the moral, intellectual and material condition of Hindus

5) Generally protect, promote and represent the interests of the Hindu community

6) To help the establishment of similar Sabhas in other important towns.

Note: (1) The Sabha will not side with any particular system of religious thought and action and will observe perfect toleration towards all the different religious views. Note: (2) The Sabha will have no connection with any political body. As such, the Sabha is not a sectarian nor a denominational, but an all-embracing movement. While meaning no offence to any other movement, whether Hindu or non-Hindus, it aims to be ardent and watchful in safeguarding the interests of the entire Hindu community in all respects."

It will be seen that the present aim and objects of the Hindu Maha Sabha have been evolved gradually from these primary objects. Several phrases in the first draft of objects are still preserved and continued in the aim and objects of the present Hindu Maha Sabha. Every primary member of the Hindu Maha Sabha has to subscribe in writing to this aim and the objects. The present form is as follows: -

To organise and consolidate all sections of the Hindu society into one organic whole; to protect and promote Hindu interests whenever and wherever necessary; To remove untouchability and generally to ameliorate and improve the condition of the so-called depressed classes amongst the Hindus; To revive and promote the glorious ideals of Hindu woman-hood; to promote cow-protection; To improve the physique of the Hindus and promote martial spirit amongst them by establishing military schools and organising volunteer corps; To reclaim all those who have left the Hindu-fold; To found orphanages and rescue homes for orphans and homeless women; Generally to take steps for promoting religious, educational, social, economic and political interests and rights of the Hindus. To promote good feelings between the Hindus and non-Hindu communities in Hindustan, and to act in a friendly way with them with a view to evolve a united and self-governing Bharatiya Nation based on equality of civic rights and duties irrespective of caste and creed.

The development of the broad work for Hindu unity that started in the early 20th century in Punjab was a precursor for the formation of the All-India Hindu Sabha. Over the next few years, several such Hindu Sabhas were established outside Punjab, including United Provinces, Bihar, Bengal, Central Provinces and Berar, and Bombay Presidency.

A formal move to establish an umbrella All-India Hindu Sabha was made at the Allahabad session of Congress in 1910. A committee headed by Lala Baij Nath was set up to draw up a constitution, but it did not make much progress. Another conference of Hindu leaders in Allahabad also took the initial step to establish an All-India Hindu Sabha in 1910, but this organisation did not become operational due to factional strife. On 8th December 1913, the Punjab Hindu Sabha passed a resolution to create an All-India Hindu Sabha at its Ambala session. The Conference proposed holding a general conference of Hindu leaders from all over India at the 1915 Kumbh Mela in Haridwar. The objects and rules were drafted, and office-bearers were elected. The first Akhil Bharatiya Hindu Maha Sabha Conference was held in 1915 at Haridwar.

Preparatory sessions of the All-India Hindu Sabha were held at Haridwar (13 February 1915), Lucknow (17 February 1915) and Delhi (27 February 1915). In April 1915, Sarvadeshak (All India) Hindu Sabha was formed as an umbrella organisation of regional Hindu Sabhas, at the Kumbh Mela in Haridwar. M.K.Gandhi and Swami Shraddhanand were also present at the conference and were supportive of the formation of All India Hindu Sabha. The Sabha laid emphasis on Hindu solidarity and the need for social reform. [20]

Amongst the Mahasabha's early leaders were the prominent nationalist, educationalist and four times Indian National Congress president Pandit Madan Mohan Malaviya, who founded the Benaras Hindu University; the Punjabi populist Lala Lajpat Rai and Lajpat Rai's mentor, Navin Chandra Rai of the Hindu Samaj, chaired the special Congress session of 1921 held at Lahore, which gave the call for non-cooperation. Under Malaviya, the Mahasabha campaigned for Hindu political unity, for the education and economic development of Hindus as well as for the conversion of Muslims to Hinduism.

At its sixth session in April 1921, the Sarvadeshak Hindu Sabha formally changed its name to Akhil Bharat Hindu Mahasabha on the model of the Indian National Congress. Presided over by Manindra Chandra Nandi, it amended its constitution to remove the clause about loyalty to the

British and added a clause committing the organisation to a "united and self-governing" Indian nation.

Till 1928, Pandit Madan Mohan Malaviya and Lala Lajpat Rai led the Hindu Maha Sabha Movement. The Sessions of the Hindu Maha Sabha were mostly held since 1922 along with the Congress Sessions. The Jubbulpur Session in 1928 under the presidentship of Shri. N. C. Kelkar marked the turning point of the organisation evolving independent of Congress.

The Eminent personalities who founded this Organisation and who presided over the All India Sessions held are: Pandit Madan Mohan Malaviya, Lal Lajpat Rai, Swami Sharadhanand, Shankaracharya Dr Kurtkoti, N.C.Kelkar, Raja Narendranath, Ramanand Chatterjee, C.Vijayaraghavacharya, Dr B. S. Moonje, Bhai Parmanand, Bhikustootama, Vinayak Damodar Savarkar, Dr Shyama Prasad Mukherjee, Dr N.B.Khare, N.C.Chaterjee, Prof V.G.Deshpande, N.N.Banerjee.

In pre independence era, Dr.Rajendra Prasad, Babu Jagjivan Ram, Jairamdas Daulatram, S.K.Patil, M.R.Jaykar, Dr. Choitram Gidwani, SriKrishna Sinha, Meherchand Khanna and several other Congress Leaders were actively associated with Hindu Mahasabha and were office bearers. In 1925, Shri Vitthalbhai Patel and Motilal Nehru had attended the session at Calcutta (Kolkatta). In the 1925 election to Provincial Legislatures, nationalists supported by Hindu Mahasabha were elected in Sindh, Bengal, Punjab, C.P (Central Province)& U.P (Uttar Pradesh) including personalities like Lal Lajpat Rai in Punjab, Dr B.S.Moonje in C.P and Shri G.D.Birla in U.P. In 1944, at Bilaspur Session of All India Hindu Mahasabha under the Presidentship of Dr. Shyama Parsed Mukherjee, a model Constitution of India was adopted similar to the present Constitution so far as the salient features are concerned.[21]

Formative Years:

Hindu sabha was established in Delhi in 1918. Delhi is one of the smallest provincial units of India, but as capital of India its position is unique and significant. So, the Provincial Delhi Hindu sabha's activities are generally reflected mostly through the activities of the All India Hindu Mahasabha, whose head office is located in New Delhi. The Delhi Provincial Hindu Sabha was established in 1918 during the 5th Session of the Hindu Mahasabha, which met under presidentship of Raja Rampal singh of Oudh and was invited to Delhi. But the Provincial Hindu Sabha came into prominence in 1925, when Lala Lajpat Rai, during the tenure of his presidentship, transferred the Head office of Hindu Mahasabha from Varanasi to Delhi.

Provincial Hindu Sabha in United Provinces (Present Uttar Pradesh) was established in 1919 from 1919 to the year 1934. The provincial Hindu Sabha continued to work but not very actively. During these years, 48 branches of the provincial Hindu Sabha representing almost all districts of these provinces have been organised. It is through these branches that the central sabha keeps itself informed of all events likely to affect the rights and interests of the Hindus. Local organisations have been doing useful work in protecting the life and property of those who stand in need of the same. A number of prominent workers were associated with the main organisation of the All India Hindu Mahasabha. During these years, among those who has been supporting the Provincial Hindu Sabha were R.B.Vikramjit Singh, Rani Phul Kumari Sahiba of Sherkot, Jwala Prasad Srivasatva and Raja Bahadur Vishwanath Singh Sahib of Tiloi.

Provincial Hindu Sabha was established in Bihar in 1922. A special session of the Hindu Mahasabha was held at Gaya with Pandit Madan Mohan Malviya as President and Babu Rajendra prasad as Reception Committee. It was highly successful. Pandit Malviya prepared fully for next Annual Session at Varanasi. In the meantime, the Shuddhi movement, with Swami Shraddhanand as it head, was in full swing and was popular Hindu Mahasabha session at Benares, for which Swami Shraddhanand under took a Country wide tour.

Thus, the work of the Bihar Provincial Hindu Sabha began systematically in the province. A district conference was held at Motihari along with the provincial political conference and was a great success. The first Bihar Provincial Hindu conference was held at Darbhanga under the Presidentship of Jagat Guru Swami Bharti Krishnan Tirtha. The session was a complete success. After the Session, Swami Bharti Krishan and Jagat Narain Lal made a prolonged tour throughout the province.

A band of whole-time workers, for almost every district was appointed in the province and almost 50 Sabhas were established across the province. The next session of the Bihar provincial Hindu Conference was held at Muzaffarpur under the Presidentship of Lala Lajpat Rai in 1925, amid scene of unparalleled enthusiasm. The Third Session was held at Chapra in 1926 under the Presidentship of Madan Mohan Malviya, amid a large and distinguished gathering. The Fourth Session of the Bihar Provincial Hindu Conference was held at Bhagalpur in 1927 under Bhai Paramanand and Fifth Session of the Bihar Provincial Hindu Conference was held at Purnea under the Presidentship of Dr.B.S.Moonje in 1929.

The removal of untouchability conferences and Shuddhi Conferences were also held along with these conferences. Several Hindu Orphanages were established at Patna,Bhagalpur,Gaya,Kathiar and other places in the wake of Hindu Maha Sabha Movement.

The Shuddhi and untouchable departments of the Bihar Provincial Hindu Sabha were working actively for several years in various parts of Bihar. SriKrishna Sinha led the Dalit entry into the Baidyanath Dham temple (Vaidyanath Temple, Deoghar), which reflected his commitment towards the upliftment and social empowerment of the Dalits. Babu Rajendra Prasad and SriKrishna Sinha were involved with this movements till the period when parted ways with Mahasabha on account of the conflict between the Hindu Sabha and Congress in assembly elections.

The work for the protection of the aboriginal Hindu tribes was carried in different parts of Chhota Nagpur and Ranchi till the Shraddhanand mission was established here on the behalf of the All-India Shraddhanand mission. During the natural calamities in Bihar, Bihar Hindu Sabha relief committee rendered great service, saving Human life at Patna, Muzarfur and Darbhanga.

The Central Provinces Hindu Sabha was started at Nagpur for the first time in November 1923. Then, for the first time, the C.P and Berar Provincial Hindu conference was held at Nagpur in 1927, with Sir Sankaran Nair presiding. This session was a grand success. Ananth Vidyarthi Griha was started by Sir GovindRao Holkar. Right from Brahmins to Harijans, more than 250 were enjoying the shelter of the Griha. The institution constructed a building of its own for hostel and school purposes.

In 1924, on the 10th January, a branch of the Hindu Mahasabha was opened at Poona. Sixty branches were started across all over Maharashtra. To give impetus to the work already begun by the Poona branch, a tour programme of Dr. B.S. Moonje was arranged in 1927. The dignified personality and thundering declarations of Dr. B.S Moonje made the whole atmosphere in Maharashtra vibrating with Hindutva. People were roused from their Slumbers. Dr. Moonje visited in his tours—Poona, Satara, Nasik, Solapur and other principal cities and toured over the southern Maratha states.

In 1933, Bhai Parmanand and Dr. Moonje with R.G. Bhide in 1935 went on lecturing tours and carried the message of the Mahasabha to every corner of Maharashtra. The session of All India Hindu Mahasabha was held under Presidentship of Madan Mohan Malviya in Poona in 1935, which was unique and grand success. The session helped to remove perverse ideas of some sceptics about the aims and ideals of Hindu Mahasabha. Though the branch of the Hindu Mahasabha was opened at Poona in 1924, Maharashtra was practically doing work for Sabha since 1920. The 1st Maharashtra Hindu Dharma conference was held in Nasik in 1920 under the Presidentship of his Holiness Shankarcharya Kurkoti.

Maharashtra has done appreciable work in the field of Shuddhi. In the first year, 100 converts has been brought to Hindu fold. Its Shuddhi work in Goa was above expectation. About 6000 Gavadas were reconverted 'en masse'. The Dharma Samrakshana Sabha was performing feats in this work.

The propaganda and movements among the Bhils in Satpuda hills are taught to lead pure and simple life. They were completely addicted to drinks, but through the systematic propaganda by Rajaram Maharaj, head of the Sangh, they are almost cured of the evil, as the whole community has become self-conscious and assertive.

The Sonya Maruti Satyagraha in Poona, started under the auspices of the Hindu Sabha, was unique from many points of view. The most important and notable aspect of that Satyagraha was that it was for the first time in the living memory of Hindus that Hindus, as Hindus, launched a movement of Satyagraha in defence of their religious rights—the rights of worship and rights to play music. The Hindus, without any distinction of caste or creed, rallied around and offered satyagraha, Thousands of Hindus of all ranks participated in the movement. The Maharashtra Hindu Sabha, with the support of the Varnashram Swarajya Sangh, systematically carried the movement. The satyagraha movement spelled advantageous in the work of sanghathan.

The condition of Hindus in the Hyderabad state worsened to the limit. The people in the state were deprived of the elementary rights of citizenship, Liberty of speech, association, meeting etc., was denied to them. Mahasabha decided to start the movement of satyagraha against tyranny of Nizam. The Hindutva Nishta Satyagraha Mandal was established in Poona under the Presidentship of G V Ketkar. It was arranged to send volunteers by batches to the territories of the Nizam of Hyderabad to offer satyagraha. The Hindus were prepared to conduct the fight till their demands are satisfactorily fulfilled. Maharashtra, with greater affinity to Hyderabad Hindus, was supportive of the struggle.

Untouchability was prevalent in Ratnagiri. Mahasabha made untouchability a thing of past. Shree Patit Pavan Mandir, meant for all Hindus, was constructed as an initiative with the help of Shriman Bhagoji Seth. Every Hindu, of whatever gradation of the Hindu society, came to the temple, forgetting all the differences of castes under Hindu Bhagwa Dwaja and performed puja, bhajan, darshan and vedapathan jointly. When people enter the mandir, all Hindus transcend all caste differences. Every year, the celebration of Ganesh Chaturthi and Visarjan is a very prominent feature in Maharastra. Public celebration of Ganesh Chaturthi was initiated by Bala Gangadhar Tilak to spur Nationalism though spiritual means. Utsava happened for 10 days. Every Hindu, without Caste distinction, took part in the celebration. Keertan, Geetapath, carrying idols and dining was done without any caste distinction.

Berar Provincial Hindu Sabha came into existence in 1924. It extended it hands in to various actions, which strengthened the Hindu Sanghathan movement. With this object, the Hindu Sabha made efforts to conversion to other religion and by inducing the orthodox section of upper class under took reconversion work against strong opposition. In order to eradicate untouchability, the Provincial Hindu Sabha wrote to all district councils to open all public wells and school to all Hindus irrespective of the caste. Through the efforts of the Hindu Sabha, many temples were open to worship irrespective of the caste. A number of lecture tours were arranged throughout the province to preach on the evils of untouchability. Another sphere of the activity of Provincial Hindu Sabha was opening of orphanages and Vidhwas ashrams and Vidhwa Viwah Samstha. The Berar Provincial Hindu Sabha invited Akhil Bharatiya Hindu Mahasabha and its session was held at Akola in 1929 under the Presidentship of Madan Mohan Malviya. A joint session of CP and Berar in 1937 at Akola under the presidentship of V.D. Savarkar and a resolution was passed aiming at 'complete independence' as ultimate goal of the Hindu Aspirations.

The Bengal Provincial Hindu Sabha members had preachers touring every district propagating the message of the Hindu Sabha. The Bengal Provincial Hindu Sabha has a clearly defined constructive programme, which aims at welding the different castes and communities by pursuing programmes on untouchability, dowry system, child marriage, protection of women, widow remarriage, upliftment of backward classes, organisation of Sarvajan Pujas for the benefit of all Hindus of all castes, establishment of akharas for the physical regeneration of youth. These programmes were popular among the backward classes, and the Sabha had a solid backing of the backward classes.

The Hindu Maha Sabha movement was initiated in Bengal by Tushar Kanti Ghosh of Amrita Bazar Patrika in the year 1924. In 1925, All Indian Hindu Mahasabha session was held in Calcutta under the presidentship of Lala Lajpat Rai and the first session of Bengal Hindu Provincial conference was held at Sirajganj which was presided by Babu Sasadhar Roy, Advocate of Calcutta high court and was attended by Swami Shraddhananda. Subsequent Meetings of Provincial Hindu Sabha was held at Calcutta, Mymensingh, Dacca, Burdwan and Maldah.

The Sindh Provincial Hindu Sabha was founded in 1926. When a Provincial Hindu Conference was organised under the presidentship of Lala Lajpat Rai, Jai Ram Daulatram was prominent Hindu Sabha leader. In October 1937, a Hindu Conference was held at Karachi under the presidentship of Bhai Paramanand, where representatives from all parts of Sindh participated. Several resolutions were passed such as resolution against passing of discriminatory bills and appointment of important cadres in Sindh on communal basis. The other resolutions were on Sanghathan of Hindus and Shuddhi.

The Rajasthan Provincial Hindu Sabha was founded 1927. Rajasthan Provincial Sabha has been taking keen interest in the upliftment of the depressed classes and in Shuddhi and Sangadhan. In 1933, 15th Session of All India Hindu Maha Sabha was held in Ajmer, under the presidentship of Bhai Parmanand.

Some work for the interest of Hindus in general was done in Nowgong by few people in the town. But the death of Swami Shraddhananda has been an eye opener to many Hindus in Assam. Till this event, the Hindus in Assam failed to realise the working of the non-Hindus organisations in Assam, which vitally affected the interests of the Hindus. The idea of struggle to protect and promote the common interests of the Hindus arose from that time.

In 1928, the Provincial Hindu Conference of Assam was held in the town of Nowgong under the presidency of Dr. B.S. Moonje. All influential Hindus, irrespective of caste and creed gathered to hear the message of Dr. B.S. Moonje. Besides, some schools and temples were established by Assam Hindu Sabha for backward tribes and tea garden labourers. During Floods, committee was formed know as 'Hindu Sabha Relief Committee' for the purpose of relief during natural calamities. The committee distributed Clothes and ration for the needy. Tarun Ram Phukan was a prominent member of Hindu Mahasabha. Phookan played an important part in forming the Assam Branch of the Indian National Congress in 1921. He was elected its first President. When the Non-Cooperation Movement was started, Phookan took a leading part in it and he toured various parts of Assam carrying the message of Non-Cooperation Movement. He was sentenced to one year's rigorous imprisonment in 1921.

He undertook several programmes for the upliftment of the under-privileged sections of society. He established a Leper Asylum in Guwahati. He was a great orator and also a prominent writer. He served as the President of the Assam Sahitya Sabha. He also served as President of the Assam Chhatra Sammelan in 1928.

All India Congress Committee session was hosted by the APCC in 1926, at Pandu, Guwahati, which was presided over by S. Srinivasa Iyengar and national leaders like Motilal Nehru, Sardar Vallabhbhai Patel, Dr. Rajendra Prasad, Madan Mohan Malaviya, Muhammad Ali, Shaukat Ali, Sarojini Naidu, S. Satyamurti, Abul Kalam Azad and others attended the session. Provincial Hindu Sabha session was also held parallelly.

Hindu Sabha in Kolhapur worked extensively on removal of untouchability and Shuddhi movement.[22]

Shuddhi:

Sangadhan gathered force in view of the threat of conversions from Hindu society, with Shuddhi being revived as a ritual of decisive importance for reclaiming Hindu converts from Islam and Christianity. The Hindu Mahasabha became explicit in its ideological support for Shuddhi, strengthening its drive to combat conversions in India. At its Banaras Session in 1923, Swami Shraddhanand, Party Vice President, moved two resolutions, linking Shuddhi to the need for the development of the Sangathan movement. The first resolution dealt specifically with the Malkana Rajputs of the western UP and second one more generally with Shuddhi as a process of conversion from other religion. The Mahasabha adopted the first resolution, stating that the 'Malkanas' should be taken back into the Hindu Fold in the caste to which they originally belonged. On the second resolution, it declared at its special session on 4th February 1924, 'Any non-Hindu was welcomed to enter the fold of Hinduism though he could not be taken into any caste'. Shuddhi was to be conducted by the All India Shuddhi Sabha actively supported by the Mahasabha. The Mahasabha amended its constitution at its Nasik Session in February 1924, incorporating Shuddhi among its 'Aim and objects'.

M.M Malviya who had forged the Mahasabha's alliance with the Arya Samaj, linked shuddhi to sangathan's efforts to reverse the perceived decline of Hindu numbers. Malviya explained, Hindu society was 'Physically, socially and morally feeble'. "There was a lower birth rate among Hindus", he argued, "what would be our condition in future with a much-reduced Hindu population if we allow this rate of conversion from Hinduism and do not allow reconversion into Hinduism?" The Mahasabha accepted as lawful the reconversion and reintegration of Hindu apostates from Islam and Christianity into Hinduism, tradionally a non proselytising religion, through shuddhi, which represented a campaign to preserve the social and political strength of the Hindu community in India. [23]

Integration of untouchables:

Sangathan carried a strong element of social critique, expressing a positive and constructive search for nation-building through the correction of 'internal failings' and 'corruption' in India. It demanded a 'unified' Hindu community, a necessity that moved the Hindu Mahasabha into the position of a radical caste reform. By far, the most ambitious project launched by the Mahasabha in the 1920s was the attempt to forge a greater Hindu political community by uniting the disparate castes and tribes of the 'Hindu family' into a single 'homogeneous' entity. The Mahasabha aimed to create a monolithic 'Hindu identity', under- playing diverse caste identities in its discourse of sangathan. However, the crucial dilemma was the incorporation of Antyajas [untouchables and tribals] - a category of outcastes outside the varna [caste] hierarchy. They constituted the Panchama [fifth 'estate'], posing a threat to the hierarchically conceived varnashrama dharma [caste order] - the 'nobility and purity' of the upper castes. The Mahasabha underlined the need for solidarity among the different castes of Hindus and amended its constitution at its Hardwar session in April 1921, formally adding the 'lower castes' to its definition of a 'Hindu'. By the late 1920s, it had advocated programmes for untouchable uplift and the removal of caste barriers, as social inequalities and poverty largely resulted in the conversion of the lower castes to Islam and Christianity." There were many emotional appeals Sangathan ideology in support of untouchable uplift in this period. The Leader strongly pleaded for the uplift of the untouchables, appealing for a 'vyavastha [decree] from sanatanist [orthodox Hindu] pandits of recognised eminence' in favour of the removal of untouchability. The upper-caste Hindus were urged to 'immediately bring lower castes within Hindu fold'; otherwise, the latter were becoming Muslims. The 'decline' of the Hindu numbers was blamed on the 'carelessness of the Hindu jati [race]' and its 'abhorrence' of the lower castes. The popular emphasis was on untouchable integration, as a 'cohesive' Hindu community had become central to Hindu 'solidarity and strength' in the country.

The protection of Hindu rights and interests in the struggle for power under the colonial reforms had, in part, strengthened the drive for untouchable integration in India. The numerical strength of religious communities played a decisive role in determining the allocation of seats in India's legislatures. The 1919 Montagu-Chelmsford reforms brought into a sharp focus the issue of the relative numbers of various religious groups, recognising the principle of representation on the basis of communities and classes in the legislatures. M.R. Jayakar explained: "Now that the Montagu-Chelmsford Report has put a value on each individual. If a single Hindu be taken out of his religious faith owing to we resent that causes which have nothing to do with religious change of mind conversion." 'Democracy,' B.S. Moonje argued, 'means a government which is based on the counting of heads. In India ... the Muslim heads and the Christian heads are yearly increasing in numbers and are hopefully aspiring to swallow up the majority community of the Hindus or to reduce it to a minority community. The untouchables numbering over 60 million proved critical to possible Hindu gains, if integrated into Hindu society, in terms of the greater share of provincial power in India'. The heavy interlinkage between community representation based on religious/caste affiliations and the colonial reforms had substantially shaped sangathan narrative on untouchable integration, aiming to enlarge and strengthen Hindu political gains.

The Hindu Mahasabha put the abolition of untouchability at the heart of sangathan as part of the reform of Hindu society in the 1920s and 1930s. At its Banaras session in August 1923, Swami Shraddhanand called in a resolution for practical measures as a 'prelude to the assimilation of the untouchables into the great body of the Aryan fraternity'. "The question of uprooting the curse of untouchability, he explained, 'was the "sine qua non" of Nationality in India". The task of Hindu sangathan could not become a reality if serious steps were not taken towards the abolition of 'caste barriers' and a full integration of the untouchables. The Mahasabha voted in favour of Shraddhananda's resolution, calling for the access of the untouchables to roads, schools, wells, and temples in India.

The programme of untouchable integration remained at the centre of the Hindu Mahasabha's sangathan narrative, more so in its efforts to make Hindus socially and politically strong in India. At the Mahasabha's session in Nasik in February 1924, Dr Kurtkoti explained: 'If in these hard times Hindus do not take seriously in hand this holy work of "conversion" and prevent their brethren from embracing alien faiths through mistaken views, I say here as I stand that within ten decades you shall find no Hindu on the surface of this earth. "The best way to prevent conversions, he pointed out, was to remove 'social disabilities' on the 'depressed classes' - the untouchables." At a special session held in Belgaum in December 1924, the Mahasabha had declared that its chief focus would be on the removal of untouchability, with M.M. Malaviya explaining that Hindus should oppose caste disabilities out of a 'sense of duty to their brethren Untouchables'. The Mahasabha's Belgaum session amended its constitution, incorporating a broader definition of 'Hinduism' that recognised all those professing a faith indigenous to India as 'Hindu': Buddhists, Jains, and Sikhs were deemed as integral to Hinduism. At the Mahasabha's session in 1926, Dr Choithram Gidwani of Sind launched an appeal for the removal of the 'blot of untouchability', as Islamic and Christian missionaries had exploited the 'weaknesses' of the Hindu social system. At the Jabalpur session on 8 April 1928, the party reaffirmed its opposition to caste disabilities, passing a resolution on the removal of untouchability.

N.C. Kelkar, in his presidential address, insisted that India must remove untouchability in order to justify its claim to swaraj [freedom]. At the Akola session in Maharashtra in August 1931, the Mahasabha invited the aboriginals to take on caste Hindu names and register their caste as 'kshatriya' [warrior caste] in the census. By the early 1930s, the Mahasabha's approach had signified a new dynamism, reinforcing a reformist resolve to end untouchability and build one 'Hindu nation' or 'jati' in India. [24]

Akharas:

In the 1920s and 1930s, Hindu nationalism became explicitly linked to physical training practised through akharas [wrestling gymnasiums], which had body building in order to create 'strong and heroic' men in India. Physical fitness, an essential element of masculinity, was promoted by stick and sword exercises together with wrestling. In the UP, Hindu organisations and mercantile notables had made financial donations for the establishment of akharas as a form of expression of 'Hindu power'. The akharas proliferated in Banaras, Gorakhpur, and Lucknow as the centres of physical culture, wrestling, sword and club wielding, and lathi [staff] fighting. An estimated 13 Hindu akharas staged displays of arms and drills with 300 participants in the towns of the UP in late 1923. About '150 Hindus in nine akharas learnt swordsmanship and wrestling in Allahabad in one week' in 1923. Over 5,000 were involved in the display of swordsmanship in Allahabad in 1924. The akharas placed primacy on celibacy - a practice which aimed to develop and maintain power [brahmacharya] and enhance 'masculine strength'. They became the basic units of mobilisation for a collective action by Hindu volunteer corps Bhimsen Dal, the Abhimanyu Dal, and the Mahabir Dal - which had emerged in the towns of the UP, particularly Banaras and Kanpur. Popular self-assertion by the lower castes in the akharas and their active participation in festivals imparted a 'martial image' to Hinduism. The akharas were often in conflict with the state and suspected by the British as 'dangerous societies', which hatched 'plots' and had as their object the 'corruption of youth and spread of revolutionary ideas'. Crucially, the akharas were implicitly viewed as the centres of 'revitalisation' and 'salvation' for Hindu society, emphasising physical culture as a means of promoting the values of citizenship and self-development for a strong Indian nation.

The Hindu Mahasabha adopted the akharas as the centres of building Hindu 'strength and power', defining the aspects of physical culture in the framework of sangathan narrative. It drew its drive for akhara promotion from the Indian National Congress, which had pioneered prabhat pheris [drills in groups held each morning] - the earliest form of nationalist mobilisation in order to strengthen the Indian nation physically and spiritually in the freedom struggle. At the centre of the Mahasabha's discourse lay the programme of wrestling and gymnastics, which were practised in the akharas with an emphasis on the glorification of India's military and religious heroes and 'selfless service' to the nation. The organisation of the akharas and physical fitness troupes was among the most popular activities undertaken by the local Hindu Sabhas in the UP. The formation of akharas and armed volunteer armies was defended as a vital means of building India's 'national strength'. M.M. Malaviya proposed a programme to establish akharas and local volunteer corps in order to protect Hindus. At the Mahasabha's Banaras session in 1923, he urged the building of a small Hanuman temple and an akhara in every village and Mohalla [urban quarter] of India. He viewed wrestling as a means of 'national reform', insisting that Hindus should 'establish akharas, listen to the Mahabharat and the Ramayan and learn to become fighters' in India's struggle for freedom. The Mahasabha proposed to establish an All-India Central Athletic Association, which would 'organise competitions and plan measures for improving the health of the youth of the country'. It resolved that samaj sewak dals [community service corps] were to be formed on the model of akharas in every village and town for the 'social service of the Hindu community and its protection' when necessary. Lajpat Rai made the formation of akharas an integral part of the sangathan project as Mahasabha president in 1925. In the UP, the Hindu Sabhas propagated Hindu unity and consolidation, urging physical fitness and military training in the cause of India's freedom. The UP Hindu Sabha had established the Lajpat physical training camp in Ghazipur; and the Agra Hindu Sabha planned to form physical training centres under the guidance of Harihar Rao Deshpande in different parts of the province in the early 1920s. In 1928 N.C. Kelkar proposed that Hanuman be regarded as the presiding deity of Hindus, and that the Mahasabha encourage the formation of local sports clubs and gymnasiums in order to revive the strength of Hindus in the country. Evidently, the new constitution adopted by the Mahasabha at its Ahmedabad session in December 1937 had pledged to 'improve the physique of Hindus and promote martial spirit' by establishing military schools and volunteer corps in India. The Mahasabha emphasised military valour and training as an integral part of sangathan, urging Hindus to whip up military enthusiasm for the promotion of Hindu strength and power in India. Hence, the Provincial Hindu Sabhas were formed in the Punjab, Sind, Delhi, Bihar, Rajputana, Bengal, Assam, Bombay and Madras Presidency. By the end of 1926, the party established 362 Hindu Sabhas all over India. Of the 362 Hindu Sabhas, the UP comprised 160 Sabhas, the Punjab 65, Bihar 65, Bombay presidency 22, Central Provinces 16, Bengal 11, Madras Presidency 11, Burma 3, Rajputana 3, Assam, Sind, Kenya, South Africa and Mesopotamia one each.[25]

Relationship between Congress and the Hindu Maha Sabha:

Pandit Madan Mohan Malviya, Bhai Parmanand, Dr Moonje, VD Savarkar, Swami Shraddhananda and Lala Lajpat Rai were involved in a much-focused manner in the plans regarding the future of the Hindu community. Their views on the question of nationalism were by and large in congruence with each other. The Congress was trying to articulate a composite nationalism. It was wary of being labelled as an entity that was 'Hindu in character' and in order to charter a middle path, the Congress leadership always tried to cloak Muslim communalism, fanaticism and its provocative behaviour vis- à-vis Hindus. Unfortunately, the Congress had no qualms about treating Muslim separatists with reverence and awe but maintained its distance from the Hindu Mahasabha. Till the day of Partition, its doors were open to the Muslim League for 'dialogue', but the Hindu Mahasabha was treated as a political pariah.

One has to admit that the then Hindu nationalists played no small role in portraying Hindutva and the Hindu nation in a narrow sense and thereby reducing its potency. They took recourse to meetings, conferences, propaganda and political programmes and thereby limiting Hindutva to the educated intellectuals and middleclass Hindu families. Their appeal centred around one facet: the Congress policy of appeasement of Muslims and the separatist character of the Muslim League. As a result, the social base of contemporary Hindu organizations remained limited. They paid scant attention to the fundamental issues that plagued the Hindu society like untouchability, hierarchical divisions among different castes and acute individualism. Social harmony, in their view, was dependent on a change of heart among Hindus themselves. Moreover, much of the prevalent Hindu leadership was from the elite class, and its penchant for positions of power meant that it failed to influence the common Hindu, despite the innumerable failures of the Congress. Therefore, Hindutva in that particular phase of our history came to be largely defined as a 'majoritarian' political concept. The Mahasabha, during early 1930s was not a full-fledged political party. It was treated as a socio-cultural organization that acted as a pressure group within the Congress. This is evident in the fact that there were common leaders in both the organizations — particularly people like Lala Lajpat Rai, Madan Mohan Malaviya, Gauri Shankar Mishra, Sampurnanand, etc. The local branches were almost indistinguishable in North Indian towns, particularly in the UP. During this period, Varadarajulu Naidu joined the Hindu Mahasabha and presided over its Madras Presidency unit for five years. he was all-India vice president of the Hindu Mahasabha. Varadarajulu Naidu actively participated in the temple-entry movements in Madras Presidency . Both organizations lent cadres and organizational space to each other. It was an external factor and subsidiary to the congress's Struggle for India's independence, exercising little influence on the conduct of the nationalist movement.

In Early twentieth century, the Mahasabha distinction from the congress had been quite vague, as both organizations were not seen to antagonistic to each other at the social base in the localities. The boundaries between a secular imagination of the nation and more a sectarian vision of it as constituted by religious communities were blurred and overlapping.

In the UP, the congress and the local Hindu Sabhas were 'interlocked' assumedly benefitting from the relationship, until the end of the 1930s. The early Mahasabha was not a political party in its own right and decisively tied to its links with the congress and often described as a 'pressure group' within the latter, it was controlled by Madan Mohan Malviya, the leader of the Hindu wing of the congress.

Several congress leaders—prominently Gokarannath Mishra, Narayan Gurtu, Hridaynath Kunzuru, Gauri Shankar Mishra, J P Srivastava, Krishna Gurtu Narain, Shivprasad Gupta, Dharmadeo Shastri, Sriprakash, Jyothishankar Dikshit and Iswar Saran had been involved in the Mahasabha movement in the UP. In August 1923, Mahasabha Benares session was attended by Prominent Congressmen – Rajendra Prasad, Purushottam Das Tandon, Bhagwan Das, Ghanshyam Das Birla. In 1924, Malaviya presided over the Mahasabha's session held at the congress venue in Belgaum, which was attended by M K Gandhi and Motilal Nehru. Yogi Digvijaynath who was associated with Congress in 1920s, and participated in the non-cooperation movement in 1922. Yogi Digvijaynath joined the Hindu Mahasabha rose to become the head of the party in the United Provinces. His status as the Mahant of the Gorakhpur Math as well as his political acumen helped him to take the organisation forward in Hindi heartland. Sections of the Mahasabha leaders had held a dual membership, working for the protection of Hindu interests within Congress and the solidarities of the community conflated the interests of the "Hindu community" with those of the 'Indian nation'. The prestige associated with the congress, the growing sentiment of national unity and the secure sources of financing were powerful attractions, which made local Hindu Sabhas and their front-rank leaders retain their association with congress. Linkage between Congress and Hindu institutions were more widespread. Dr. Jawaharlal Rohtagi, G.G.Jog, Balkrishna Sharma, Ram Swarup, Narayan Prasad Arora and Lala Ram Ratan Gupta and middle ranking congress figures retained affiliation with Mahasabha in 1930s.

K M Ashraf, a congress socialist protested that influential Mahasabhaites were allowed to occupy responsible positions in Congress organisation and permitted to join the congress committees.

Paradoxically Moonje suggested that all the Mahasabhaites should join the congress as a prophylactic action. The inability of the UP Congress to overcome the Mahasabha Cadres pointed to the presence of a "Hindu Idiom" among the Party ranks and congress radicalism coexisted with the elements of 'Hindu Politics'. Congress leaders retained fewer formal associations with the Mahasabha, believing that the congress worked as the main political organization, whereas the Hindu, the Hindu Sabhas dealt with the socio and cultural issues of Indian Society. The Hindu Mahasabha had retained a strong association with the Hindu 'Right Wing' of the Congress. Sampurnanand maintained close Hindu Sabha connections and was involved in the organisation of Hindu Sabha meeting to mobilise support for Gandhi's Harijan campaign in October 1932.

Muslim leaders like Shaukat Ali rued that the Congress had been "taken over by the Mahasabha". However, the growing adoption of the "secular" rhetoric by the Congress and its increasing espousal of "territorial nationalism" started distancing the two from each other.[26]

Tej Bahadur Tapru a member of the Hindu Sabha committee in UP. Narmada Prasad Singh, general secretary of the Hindu Sabha in Agra in 1920s was a well-known congressman, a member of the UP congress committee and leader of Malviya group in the Allahabad congress. In many instances, the Hindu Sabhas and the congress right wing had shared resources and personnel in the towns, their active organisational overlap continued well in to the late 1930s.

At the National level, the Hindu Mahasabha had evolved itself as an 'alternative platform' for Congressmen to express an ideology of nationalism in a 'Hindu Idiom'. A substantial section of the congress old guard had shifted to the Mahasabha in the UP, Central Provinces and Maharashtra in 1930s. Lala Lajpat Rai had remained vanguard of the sangathan politics, working together with M.M Malviya at the helm of the Mahasabha until his death in Lahore in 1928.

Swami Shraddhanand, a prominent sanghathan leader had been associated with the Congress before joining the Mahasabha in the 1920s. K B Hedgewar, who became Mahasabha general secretary before founding the RSS in 1925, had first been in Congress and elected to the Central Provinces Congress Committees as its joint secretary. He was part of Resolution Committee in 1920. Tangutri Prakasam of Andhra and Jairamdas Daulat Daulatram, a Congress Leader from Maharashtra had been involved in the Mahasabha activities and programmes in the 1920s and 30s

The Congressmen who had been Tilak's associate largely took control of Mahasabha organisation in North India in 1920s and 30s. The most prominent of the Tilakites were, B.S. Moonje, the leading figure in Central Provinces, Madhav Srihari Aney, an influential congress politician from the Berar, Narsimha Chintaman Kelkar, the congress legislator in Poona, and Mukund Ramrao Jayakar, the Congress -Swarajist party leader from Bombay. They were inspired by the political activism of Bala Gangadhar Tilak, including his 1905 Clarion call to Self-rule (Swaraj is my birth right and I will have it) and his belief in the compatibility of social reform with nationalist agitations. The Middle ranking Tilakites, Lakshman B Bhopatkar, Chandragupta Vedalankar, Ganpat Rai and Indra Prakash had once been congressmen before becoming the Mahasabha Hardliners. Evidently, several prominent congressmen became important leaders in the Mahasabha Organization in the 1920s.

Dr. G V Ketkar was the grandson of Lokmanya Bal Gangadhar Tilak. He was convicted in the bout of the Civil Disobedience movement and was sentenced to 9 months imprisonment on 22nd April 1930. In 1935, he was the President of the Maharashtra Provincial Congress Committee -

MPCC. He headed many different local organizations. He was a part of the Hindu Mahasabha. He was the Editor of Kesari, Maratha, and Tarun Bharat and contributed to various other newspapers. His interpretation of Salt Satyagraha in his journalism intensified his interest in the movement. Ketkar, then joined the famous 'Dandi March'. During these years, he got involved with the leadership of the Maharashtra Provincial Congress Committee -MPCC, but also, on his close association with the revolutionary leader V D Savarkar and the 'Hindu Mahasabha'. [27]

Laxman Bhopatkar was an exercise scientist and was also the founder of Maharashtra Mandal Shikshan Sanstha. He was involved with Congress before joining Hindu Mahasabha. During the Indian freedom struggle, Bhopatkar hoisted the national flag on the Solapur Municipal Council on April 6, 1930. He also participated in the Hyderabad Satyagraha of 1937. He was sentenced to prison for that. [28]

As a committed freedom fighter and Congressman, Jagat Narain Lal was imprisoned during the Non-Cooperation, Civil Disobedience and the Quit India Movements and spent close to a decade in jail. As the assistant secretary of the Provincial Congress Committee, he played a major role in the success of the Gaya Congress in 1922 after his release from Buxer jail. He was sentenced to prison for a second time in 1929 under the charges of sedition for having become, as he writes, 'the bête noir to the Government and the police chief of the province, thanks to my bitter and scathing criticism of their bungling which had resulted in communal antagonism and riots.' After he was released from Hazaribagh Central jail in 1929, he lent his support to and spearheaded the Salt Satyagraha as the President of the Patna District Congress Committee.

Jagat Narain Lal under the influence of Madan Mohan Malviya and B.S. Moonje, also acquired dual membership of the Hindu Mahasabha & Congress. His association with the All India Hindu Mahasabha strengthened and he became its General Secretary at its Calcutta session in 1926. Beginning early 1930s, his enchantment with the Hindu Mahasabha began to wane. On his release from Hazaribagh Central Jail in 1932, he joined the Servants of Hindu Society. He wrote: '[When] Bhai Paramanand was elected president of the Hindu Mahasabha, he openly advocated a pro-government and anti-Congress policy, in defiance of all earlier traditions. The rift between us grew wider and wider until…'I felt I could no longer associated with him.' In protest, and to register his disenchantment, Jagat Narain Lal finally stopped taking his allowance from the Mahasabha. His disenchantment with the Hindu Mahasabha was complete by the time the first provincial assembly elections took place in 1937 when he fought the elections on a Congress ticket defeated the Mahasabha candidate who stood against him. [29]

The rift over the communal question became even wider with the Nehru Report of 1928. The Mahasabha forced the Congress to not give into such extortionate demands, and thus the Nehru Report only accepted separate electorates and reservation of seats for Muslims in minority provinces. The Congress, however, quickly distanced itself from the Report and started fresh discussions on the communal question, which angered the Mahasabha further. Nothing came out of the Round Table Conferences. While Malaviya and Lajpat Rai were conciliatory towards the Congress, subsequent presidents like BS Moonje or Bhai Parmanand were not. The growing opposition of the Mahasabha to Congress policies finally led to a resolution being adopted in the Haripura Session of the Congress in 1938, which categorically excluded members of the Congress from becoming members of either the Hindu Mahasabha or the Muslim League.

Dr B.S. Moonje had represented Hindu Mahasabha in the Round Table Conference. Such is the Political Graph of the Hindu Mahasabha. In 1944, at Bilaspur Session of All India Hindu Mahasabha under the Presidentship of Dr. Shyama Prasad Mukherjee, a model Constitution of India was adopted similar to the present Constitution so far as the salient features are concerned.

Sheth Jugal Kishore Birla was scion of the Birla family. He was a noted industrialist, philanthropist and vocal supporter of Hindu philosophy.

Jugal Kishore Birla devoted much time and money to charity, building numerous temples, the Kolkata Medical College, Marwadi Balika Vidyalaya in Kolkata for girls, and numerous other such institutions. A devout Hindu, Jugal Kishore Birla was also the moving force behind the building of many of the early Birla Mandirs across India, including the first in Delhi, and those in Kolkata and Bhopal. Supporting Gaushalas (cow shelters) and pinjrapols (animal and bird feeding mangers) was another cause dear to his heart. He also donated money to various Hindu causes and organisations, including Hindu Mahasabha and Rashtriya Swayamsevak Sangh. At the same time, supporting finances of Mahatma Gandhi and Indian National Congress and India's freedom movement were looked after together by Ghanshyam das Birla and others.

He along with his brother Ghanshyam Das donated funds to start girls' school under their private trust, a school named Marwari Balika Vidyalaya, which has grown into the noted Shri Shikshayatan School and Shri Shikshayatan College.

He spent much of his personal wealth in building Hindu temples known as Birla Temples and Dharamshalas across major metropolitan towns of India and promotion of schools and universities and hospitals and adopting many villages in times of famine and natural disasters.

In his old age, he took the leading role to fulfill the unfinished dream of Madan Mohan Malaviya of building Krishna Janmabhoomi Kesava Deo Temple, for which he is fondly remembered by believers of Hindu religion. In his old age he also donated initial funds for building of Vivekananda Rock Memorial and also arranged for further funds for the project from his brothers, the construction of which, however, began several years after his death. [30]

N.B. Khare was member of Indian National Congress from 1916 to 1938. He was the president of the Central Provinces Provincial Congress Committee, Harijan Sewak Sangh, Nagpur and a member of the All-India Congress Committee for several years. Khare was elected as a member of the Second Legislative Council of the Central Provinces from 1923 to 1926 and again to the Third Legislative Council from 1927 to 1930. Khare resigned from the Legislative Council in pursuance of the mandate by the Lahore Congress and was imprisoned for participating in Civil Disobedience Movement. From 1935 to 1937, he was a member of the Legislative Assembly, where he initiated the Arya Marriage Validation Bill which was later put on the Statute Book. During the Quit India Movement in 1942, mobs in Ashti and Chimur killed some policemen. Thirty people were tried and sentenced to hang. Khare formed the Capital Punishment Relief Society to help the prisoners of Ashti and Chimur. He later joined Hindu Mahasabha on 15th August 1949 and served as its President for few years

In the 1940s, the Muslim League stepped up its demand for a separate Muslim state of Pakistan. The League's great popularity amongst Muslims forced the Congress leaders to hold talks with the League President, Muhammad Ali Jinnah. Even though Savarkar recognised Hindus and

Muslims to be separate nations, he condemned Gandhi's eagerness to hold talks with Jinnah and regain Muslim support for the Congress as appeasement. After communal violence claimed the lives of thousands in 1946, Savarkar claimed that Gandhi's adherence to non-violence had left Hindus vulnerable to armed attacks by militant Muslims. When the Congress agreed to divide India in June 1947 after months of talks of power-sharing between the Congress and the League, the Mahasabha condemned the Congress and Gandhi for dividing India.

The Mahasabha leaders had till then participated in the 'Indian' politics, carried on by the Congress. But it must be noted that even there they formed a group in favour of parliamentary and constitutional activities and against Non-cooperation policy and Gandhism in general. The first breaking away with the Congress began with the disapproval by Mahasabha leaders and followers of the "appeasement" policy of the Congress with regard to the political constitution of the country. The difference became more prominent when Congress adopted the attitude of neutrality towards the Communal Award. The same difference was visible, when with regard to the policy in legislatures the Mahasabha felt the necessity of setting up candidates on the Mahasabha ticket as opposed to the Congress. After the actual experience of the working of the Congress ministries in several provinces and especially in U.P., the breaking away from the Congress in the Parliamentary programme became complete.

With the relinquishment of the ministries by the Congress, its adoption of anti-militarisation policy and Satyagraha for the principle of non-violence, the political divergence between the Hindu Mahasabha and the Congress has become almost complete.

The creed of the Hindu Maha Sabha is "Complete political Independence" for Hindustan. But since the beginning of this war the Hindu Mahasabha is demanding Dominion Status as a step towards the goal to be taken at the end of the war.

All India Hindu Mahasabha was founded in 1915 to bring together the diverse local Hindu movements which had roots in North Indian public life, reaching back as far as the previous century. It was remodelled much on the lines of the Congress in the early 1920s by its founders including UP's Pandit Madan Mohan Malaviya. With branches in most parts of India, it put emphasis on social and religious work among Hindus and untouchables, on protection of cows and in the spread of Hindi. The organisation remained more interested in protecting Hindu interests, particularly at times when the Congress tactics seemed to endanger them.

Since the mid-1920s, the Hindu Mahasabha's operations in Bengal remained mostly concentrated around the removal of untouchability. The leaders of the Hindu Mahasabha, with the support of local Congressmen undertook campaigns in favour of the social uplift of the untouchable communities. The Mahasabha's involvement with the lower castes gained much prominence in the early 1930s, especially in the aftermath of Macdonald's Communal Award. The Hindu Mahasabha invited aboriginals to adopt caste Hindu names and register their caste as Kshatriya during the census enumeration. In Malda district, Mahasabha activists tried to persuade the aboriginal labourers and sharecroppers to stop work in the fields of Muslim jotedars. They encouraged aboriginals to make a common cause with local Hindu politicians on the one hand and break their connections with the Muslim employers on the other. They thought that such efforts would enable them to thwart the efforts of the leftists to win over the sharecroppers in the northern districts. In the late 1930s, the Mahasabha also lent support to several new Hindu organisations to carry out campaigns in favour of unification of Hindu society. In several districts, Mahasabha activists-maintained links with the lower caste leadership. However, this sort of campaign to bring the lower castes into the Hindu community resulted in communal clashes between the lower castes and the Muslims which often took the form of communal riots. Instances of rioting and arson involving the Muslims and the lower caste Hindus were reported from Burdwan, Khulna, Jessore, Dhaka, and Noakhali districts.

The Session voted against separation of Sind with an overwhelming majority against the advice of the revered Pandit Madan Mohan Malaviya, who urged that the Mahasabha should not take the "odium" upon itself of making a settlement impossible by its flat denial but "to wait for the report of the sub-committee appointed by the Madras Congress." [31]

In 1944, the All India Hindu Mahasabha adopted the Constitution of the Hindustan Free State (CHFS) as a possible draft constitution. The party's ideological line—only those who considered the land between the Sindhu and the Sindhu Sagar both their pitrubhumi (fatherland-where one's ancestors came from) and punyabhumi (holy land) could form the common brotherhood of Hindus. By definition, this included Sikhs, Jains, Buddhists and atheists and excluded Muslims, Christians, Jews. And despite some internal reservations, Savarkar himself had Zoroastrians as well.

But this exclusionary dogma was kept aside when drafting the Constitution. Written by four men, DV Gokhale, Laxman Bhopatkar, KV Kelkar and MR Dharmadhere, with a foreword by N.C. Kelkar, this is the only known example of an avowedly Hindu party setting forth its own constitutional ideas in concrete form.

The ideas in this Constitution were directly inspired by Savarkar's speech at the Mahasabha session in Calcutta in 1939, where he outlined his views on the future constitution of India.

The contents of the CHFS, a fleshed-out version of that speech, might come as a surprise to many.

We, the people of Hindustan

The CHFS consisted of 111 articles and was much shorter than the eventual Constitution of India. Like the Constitution, it derived its legitimacy from the people and claimed to speak in their name. Unlike our Constitution, however, this draft placed much greater faith in principles of direct democracy. The framers of the CHFS believed that democracy in India had evolved to such a stage that people were entitled to "a direct voice in respect of their social and economic well-being and political destiny." It thus made provisions for:

- Initiative – This was an innovative proposal by which citizens of the country could directly initiate legislation or constitutional amendments. A minimum number of voters would have to propose legislation, which would then be voted on by the whole adult population through a referendum.

- Referendum – Any initiative for legislation or any other significant law could be put to vote in a yes/no referendum before the entire adult population. This could happen when a minimum number of voters or a minimum number of representatives initiated the process.

- Recall – Arguably the most significant proposal, the right to recall, gave voters a right to depose their elected representatives before the completion of their term. One-tenth of the voters in a constituency would have to propose such a motion and it could lead to a representative being fired if a majority voted in its favor.

To the framers of the Indian Constitution, these ideas were too radical. India had to be gently guided towards democracy and not thrust into it, as these proposals were attempting. Like much else in our present Constitution, the framers wisely decided to take things slowly and ignore these proposals.

Neither India nor Bharat

The framers of the CHFS dwelt only briefly on the name for the country. "India" for them was "a meaningless term" and there was "absolutely no warrant in the past history of this country for styling it as India (sic)". The present alternative "Bharat" was not discussed at all, despite copious references to the term in Sanskrit as well as several Indian languages. For Savarkar, Bharatavarsha, despite originating in the Vishnu Purana, was a suppression of "our cradle name "Sindhus or Hindus". As a result, "Hindustan" was chosen in the Constitution without any dissenting voices.

Attached to the Indic term "Hindustan" was a distinctly un-Indic suffix "Free State" to give the country its full name—Hindustan Free State. In fact, the phrase was taken from Ireland, where the Irish Free State had successfully managed to free itself from colonial rule. The framers saw no contradiction in an indigenous name with a borrowed suffix. This was a recurring theme of the entire drafting process of the CHFS. As a matter of rhetoric, the CHFS was presented as the product of native Indian thought. But on matters of substance, they liberally borrowed from constitutions around the world.

Equally, they adopted the standard Anglo-American constitutional model of a government based on separation of powers with the legislature, executive and the judiciary checking and balancing each other. More indigenous ideas of panchayats and local councils, with a focus on moral rights and wrongs rather than checks and balances, were scarcely discussed. An independent Hindustan would.

A secular State, no State religion

Perhaps the most surprising aspect of this constitutional framework was a ringing endorsement of India's secular nature. Article 7(xv) of the CHFS provided that the Hindustan Free State would have no State religion. The possibility of a constitutional Hindu Rashtra was firmly shut. Article 7(xi) gave every citizen the freedom to practice and profess their own religion and protect their own culture and language. There was no constitutional mandate to homogenize the nation. Equally, Articles 6 and 7(i) and (ii) guaranteed equal citizenship to all citizens with equal civic rights. No law could treat Hindus and Muslims differently.

There were clear political compulsions underlying these provisions. The Hindu Mahasabha had come into the political mainstream by forming a coalition government in Bengal during the Second World War. But after exiting that government, the Mahasabha became a fringe player in national politics. The Muslim League was on the rise and the RSS was fast emerging as the principal organiser of the Hindu community. The Congress was of course the centre of nationalist efforts. To remain relevant, the Hindu Mahasabha chose to be balanced and reasonable. The CHFS reflects that choice. While history can never serve as an assurance for the future, it can certainly be a guide. With the fortunes of parties that belong to the Sangh Parivar now firmly in the ascendant, they would do well to look to their predecessors and the spirit that animated their constitutional thought while drafting the CHFS. That spirit was one of inclusion over ideology. Hindustan would be a country that every person irrespective of religious denomination could call home. The Constitution would reflect that broad-mindedness without being hemmed in by the narrow currents of parochialism or polarisation. Opponents of the Sangh Parivar too ought to take note of the CHFS. Calls to draft a new constitution cannot automatically be conflated with creating a Hindu Rashtra. As Babasaheb Ambedkar himself said, quoting Thomas Jefferson, "every generation should be free to debate its own constitutional ideas. India today should be no exception." [32]

Interestingly, the 1940s also witnessed a political discord between the Congress and the Mahasabha. The Bengal Congress by selecting caste Hindu candidates could win over the majority of the Hindu Nationalist and Sabha voters. Congress leaders tried to prove that they could represent Hindu interests better than the Hindu Mahasabha. The great Calcutta riot, following the Muslim League's Direct Action Day on 16th August 1946, and Naokhali became turning point. Shyama Prasad Mukherjee, along with N C Chatterjee toured Bengal. 10 relief organisations and medical missions performed relief work in Noakhali as a part of Mahasabha relief activity. Syama Prasad Mookerjee, Nirmal Chandra Chatterjee and Pandit Narendranath Das, along with other workers, flew to Comilla and entered the affected area with military escorts. Ashutosh Lahiry, the General Secretary of Hindu Mahasabha, immediately left for Chandpur. A plane was requisitioned and dispatched to the affected area loaded with rice, chira, bread, milk, biscuits, barley and medicines. Other consignments of relief supplies were dispatched by train. The affected people who took refuge in Kolkata were given protection in about 60 centres in the city and suburbs. Syama Prasad Mookerjee appointed P. K. Mitter & Co., a Kolkata-based accountancy firm, to control the collection, disbursement and audit of funds contributed by the public.

Nirmal Chandra Chatterjee, the acting President of the Bengal Provincial Hindu Mahasabha; Debendranath Mukherjee, the general secretary; and Nagendranath Bose, the Assistant Secretary, proceeded to the affected areas of Noakhali and Tipperah. Chatterjee consulted Larkin, the Relief Commissioner, and considered zonal settlement to be the best method for providing relief and safety, keeping in mind the future resettlement of the victims in their respective villages. Accordingly, relief centres were opened at Bamni under the Raipur police station, Dalalbazar under the Lakshmipur police station and Paikpara under the Faridganj police station. M. L. Biswas, the Secretary of the Bengal Provincial Hindu Mahasabha; P. Bardhan, the Medical Secretary; and J. N. Banerjee, the Treasurer, were sent to the other affected areas to set up relief centres. Each of the relief centres was provided with a mobile medical unit under medical officers. Sanat Kumar Roy Chowdhury, the vice-president of the Bengal Provincial Hindu Mahasabha, inaugurated a well-equipped 25-bed hospital at Lakshmipur in the memory of Rajendralal Raychaudhuri. Dr. Subhodh Mitra was placed in charge of the hospital. Nirmal

Chandra Chatterjee visited Noakhali for a third time and inaugurated a students' home at Bajapati named 'Shyamaprasad Chhatrabas'. Shyama Prasad Mukherjee, in this situation, emerged as the sole spokesman of the Hindu Mahasabha in Bengal. As communal politics took over the scene, the Hindu Mahasabha became more interested in setting up Hindu volunteer corps for the defence of Hindu life and property. The Mahasabha even supported the idea of supplying firearms and ammunitions to Hindu organisations. The Mahasabha also arranged military training to Hindu youths by ex-servicemen. By 1946, the Hindu Mahasabha was successful in mobilising a substantial section of Bengali Hindus of Calcutta in support of its politics of Hindu nationalism. Many scholars believe that Hindu Mahasabha was responsible for the partition of Bengal in 1947. After it became apparent that the division of India on the basis of the two-nation theory would almost certainly result in the partition of Bengal along religious lines, the Bengal provincial Muslim League leader Huseyn Shaheed Suhrawardy came up with a new plan to create an independent Bengal state, which would join neither Pakistan nor India and remain unpartitioned. Suhrawardy realised that if Bengal was partitioned, it would be economically disastrous for East Bengal as all coal mines, all but two jute mills and other industrial plants would certainly go to the western part since they were in overwhelmingly-Hindu areas. Most importantly, Calcutta, the largest city in India and an industrial and commercial hub and the largest port, would also go to the western part. For the Congress, only a handful of leaders agreed to the plan, such as the influential Bengal provincial Congress leader Sarat Chandra Bose, the elder brother of Netaji and Kiran Shankar Roy. However, most other leaders and Congress leaders, including Jawaharlal Nehru and Vallabhbhai Patel, rejected the plan. The nationalist Hindu Mahasabha, under the leadership of Shyama Prasad Mukherjee, vehemently opposed it and considered it nothing but a ploy by Suhrawardy to stop the partition of the state so that its industrial west, including the city of Kolkata, would remain under League control. It also claimed that even if the plan was for a sovereign Bengal state, it would be a virtual Pakistan. Following the partition of Bengal, between the Hindu-majority West Bengal and the Muslim-majority East Bengal, there was an influx of Bengali Hindu/Bengali Muslim refugees from both sides.

On January 6, 1948, in a speech in Lucknow, Sardar Patel invited the Hindu Mahasabha to amalgamate with the Congress. He held out the same invitation to members of the RSS, criticising Nehru obliquely: "In the Congress, those who are in power feel that by virtue of authority they will be able to crush the Mahasabha and the RSS. You cannot crush an organisation by using the danda [stick]. The danda is meant for thieves and dacoits. They are patriots who love their country. Only their trend of thought is different. They are to be won over by Congressmen with love."

On January 30, 1948, Nathuram Godse shot Mahatma Gandhi three times and killed him in Delhi. Godse was identified as member of the Hindu Mahasabha and former member of RSS. Along with them, police arrested Savarkar. While the trial resulted in convictions and judgments against the others, Savarkar was released due to lack of evidence. Many leaders, including Dr Babasaheb Ambedkar were convinced that Savarkar's arrest was nothing but a political vendetta. The Kapur Commission said, Godse and his accomplices' decision to kill Gandhi was determined by the circumstances of Partition and the death of Hindus in the course of the communal violence of 1947.

The involvement of the Mahasabha in Gandhi's murder led to a severe backlash, pushing it to get further marginalised. Though active as an organisation, the Congress Government lost no opportunity in not only arresting the perpetrators but branding the Mahasabha and the RSS itself as guilty. RSS offices were attacked throughout the country and many of the cadre were even killed. Narayan Savarkar, the younger brother of V.D. Savarkar was lynched to death. Around 4000 Marathi Brahmins were killed by Congressmen just because the community was more prominent in the Mahasabha-RSS groups. This chain of events culminated in a ban placed upon on the RSS. Even though the ban was lifted after a year and the Hindu Mahasabha still continued as a party (with leaders like Mukherjee still in the Government), it had dented the whole organization.[33]

The assassination of Mahatma Gandhi by Godse-one of its staunch supporters, dealt a severe blow to its prestige. It was under eclipse till its leaders were excoriated of this heinous charge of Gandhi's assassination by the Tribunal which took up Gandhi murder case.

It suspended its political activities temporarily but re-entered the political arena after All India Council of Hindu Mahasabha renounced the policy and programme in December, 1948. Ultimately, Mukherjee himself felt that the organization was not doing enough to represent non-Hindus and left the organization to form his own party. He also advised the organization to stay politically inactive in the aftermath of Gandhi's murder, which contributed to its further decline. Later, Mukherjee formed the Bharatiya Jana Sangh with the help of the RSS. As a result, the Mahasabha became a defunct body. Even when it contested the first parliamentary elections and won some seats, the party could not win even one per cent of votes, it gradually lost space to the more energetic and resourceful Jana Sangh. The results of the General Elections reflect that Hindu Mahasabha failed to appeal to the sentiments of the people.

The Mahasabha officially continues to exist even today. It is only known to appear in the press through ludicrous acts and utterances. However, despite the degeneration of this organization in the early 50's, it had to its credit a lot of achievements which helped serve Hinduism and the Hindu community. The example of this organization should continue to inspire organizations and forces working for the cause of Hindu renaissance and nationalism.

Lala Lajpat Rai

Lajpat Rai (28 January 1865 - 17 November 1928), generally known as Lala Lajpat Rai (the term 'Lala' is a honorific). He was popularly known as Punjab Kesari, and also as 'Punjab da Sher' which literally means the 'Lion of Punjab'.

Freedom fighters were responsible for achieving the political unity of India from Kashmir to Kanyakumari, from Sindh to Kamarup - an ideal which neither Asoka nor Samudragupta could conceive, which neither the Moghuls nor Marathas could achieve and which the British, during the century and a half of their rule, could not constitutionally enforce. They are undaunted and even their failures were glorious. Lala Lajpat Rai personified the indomitable spirit of rebellion. Along with Bal Gangadhar Tilak and Bipin Chandra Pal, he converted his simple and somnolent countrymen into brave freedom fighters in thousands, having derived inspiration from Mazzini, Garibaldi, and Swami Dayananda Saraswati.

He was born on January 27, 1865, in a poor Bania family of the Punjab. His father was an Urdu teacher. His mother was a lady of fortitude. As a student, he was intelligent and industrious, and he qualified himself as a lawyer in 1885. Commencing his practice at Hissar, he soon became the leader. Since Punjab was annexed by the British only in 1849, national life was fragmented there. But, Arya Samaj had beneficent impact on them, since its founder, Dayananda Saraswati, first gave currency to the ideal of Swaraj.

Lalaji joined hands with Hansraj and Guru Jnani Dutt to propagate and popularise Arya Samaj. Dayananda Anglo-Vedic College with Lalaji as Secretary was founded in Lahore. He also became the Secretary of Hissar Municipality. He attended the third session of the Congress held at Allahabad in 1888 with George Yule presiding. He shifted to Lahore, the capital of Punjab, in 1892, and soon occupied the position of a front-rank lawyer. Fascinated by social work, he founded an orphanage. He formed a relief committee to cope with the famine of 1897. He rushed to the help of victims of the earthquake in 1905.

The participation of Lajpat Rai in the Congress session in Bombay in 1904 marked his promotion to the rank of a national leader; the Swadeshi Movement of 1905 then reinforced the adherence of the Arya Samajists to the Congress. In 1907, at the time of the Surat split, Lajpat Rai, the leader of the Congress in Punjab, preferred to attempt a mediation between the 'Moderates' and the 'Extremists'. But the exclusion of the 'Extremists' by the 'Moderates' incited the Arya Samajists, who had openly aligned themselves with Tilak during the 1906 Congress, to consider themselves as being outside the Congress.

At the provincial level, also, the Arya Samajists had chosen to act alone; in 1907, finding that the Congress was unwilling to take up the cause of the urban Hindus, they directed their attacks against the British and cited the defence of their Hindu nationality as well as their economic interest as the basis for their action.

He also accompanied Gopala Krishna Gokhale to England to acquaint the English with the Indian aspirations. Incidentally, he toured countries of Europe and the USA and made a keen study of international affairs.

On his return to India, he joined the Swadeshi movement, an off shoot of anti-Partition (of Bengal) agitation in reply to Curzon's moves. He was a protagonist of national education. His speeches and writings made a deep impression, particularly on the youth. His name was sponsored for the Presidentship of the Surat Session by extremists in 1907, which ended in a fiasco. Government of India took a serious view of his political activities, detained him under Bengal Regulation of 1818 and whisked him away to Mandalay Fort in Burma. But far from proceeding out of corporatist motivations alone, the ideology of the new Hindu Sabha is founded to be a kind of extension the Arya Samajist nationalism. Proof of this lies in the fact that Lajpat Rai, at the Punjab Provincial Hindu Conference of October 1909, after having insisted on the necessity of constituting a 'Hindu Congress' in order, notably, to make a protest against these confidential circulars of the government which aim at giving preferential treatment to the other communities at the expense of the Hindus'. It laid stress on the status of nationhood integral to the Hindus by invoking the same characteristics of ethnic nationalism (history, culture, ...) as the founders twenty years earlier of the Arya Samajist nationalism:

It may be that the Hindus by themselves, cannot form a nation in the modern sense of the term, but that is only a play on words. Modern nations are political units…. That is, the sense in which the expression is used in connection with the body called the 'Indian National Congress'. But, that is not the only sense in which it is or can be used. In fact, the German word 'Nation' did not necessarily signify a political nation or a State. In that language, it connoted what is generally conveyed by the English expression that 'people', implying a community in possessing a certain civilisation and culture. Using it in sense, there can be no doubt that Hindus are a 'nation' in themselves, because they represent a civilisation all their own. In the present struggle between Indian communities, I will be a Hindu first and an Indian afterwards, but outside India or even in India against non-Indians, I am and shall ever be an Indian first and a Hindu afterwards.

This declaration, which was tantamount to a statement certifying the birth of Hindu nationalism-as a sub-assembly of Indian nationalism, testifies all the more to the relationship of continuity existing between this ideology and that of the Arya Samajists of the 'College faction, its promoters, since it drew its inspiration explicitly from an article written by Lajpat Rai in the Hindustan Review (Allahabad), officially in 1899, at a time when the Arya Samajists had not yet proclaimed themselves as being Hindus. The Hindu Sabha, over and above the nationalist ideology of the Arya Samajists, also adopted the sociological model of the nation developed by the Arya Samaj, as suggested by Lal Chand while transferring it simply on the political plane:

Weak and disunited, we are divided into various sects. But the remedy ties in bringing the sections on a common political platform where they should realise that they are merely branches of the same stock and community. He was founder of the Punjab National Bank.

On his return from deportation, he became a hero to the classes and masses alike. Constructive aspect of public life commanded his attention. He created a fund to assist public workers in acquiring knowledge of national and international affairs and, for that purpose, he established People's Society with the English Weekly "The People", as its organ. He was also one of the sponsors of "The Hindustan Times." Presiding over the first session of the Indian Trade Union Congress at Bombay in 1920, he diverted public attention to the labour problems. He pleaded for the public trial of Sir Michael O'Dwyer, who was responsible for the Jallianwallah Bagh atrocities. Though he presided over the special session of the Congress at Calcutta, which was attended by a number of liberal, leaders, in the same year, Gandhiji's technique of Satyagraha did not appeal to him, and he opposed the boycott of schools and Courts. The special session of the Indian National Congress was held at Calcutta in the first week of September 1920. Lala Lajpat Rai occupied the presidential chair on account of his consistent patriotic service to the cause of India's struggle for freedom. Some crucial decisions were to be made at this Congress, because it was meeting after a few months of the Congress session held at Amritsar in December 1919 under the presidentship of Pandit Motilal Nehru.

In his presidential address, Lajpat Rai surveyed the political situation in India in a comprehensive way. At the outset, he made it clear to delegates assembled in the pandal that the days of passing resolutions, making prayers and sending memorials were over. He reminded the nation that it was passing through a revolutionary period. The changes made by the Raj in our economic, political and educational system were severely criticised by him. 'We are thus face to face with a great struggle between the forces of democratic change, English and Indian, and reactionary militarism. In order to go through the struggle successfully, we will require all the manliness and strength, all the wisdom and tact, and all the determination and struggle we are capable of putting forth'. [34]

He further explained the major national problems including Punjab disorders, Jallianwala Bagh tragedy, martial law in the Punjab and the great resentment by the people of the region and elsewhere, the question of Khilafat and its implications, reform rules and regulations passed by the Act of 1919, the programme of the non-cooperation—a call given to the nation by Gandhi, and the despotism depicted by the Raj in our country.

He displayed dignity and decorum in conducting the proceedings. He condemned shouting down moderates and checked a speaker from denouncing Jews. At the same time, he supported the Khilafat agitation.

In the elections to the Central Assembly, he drifted away from the Congress and joined hands with Madan mohan Malaviya, Dr. Moonje, N.C. Kelkar and M.R. Jayakar, and formed the Nationalist Party. When Miss Mayo brought out her notorious book "Mother India", aptly described by Mahatma Gandhi as a drain inspector's report, Lalaji gave a fitting reply through his well-documented work entitled 'Unhappy India'. Besides, he wrote stirring biographies of Lord Krishna, Chatrapati Shivaji, Swami Dayananda Saraswati, Mazzini and Garibald. Besides being a Director of the Punjab National Bank, he founded textile mills in collaboration with Lala Harikishen Lal, known as Napoleon of Indian finance, and facilitated industrialisation of the country.

From Arya Samaj to Congress to Hindu Mahasabha

Amidst these developments before and after the First World War, Lala Lajpat Rai's symbolic trajectory from the Brahmo Samaj to the Arya Samaj, then variously into and out of Congress, his alignment with the 'Extremist' section of Congress and some revolutionary nationalist activities, and then his emergence as a key figure in both the pre-Savarkarite Hindu Mahasabha and the Hindu Sangathan movement is both evocative and characteristic of the shape of Hindu nationalism in this period.

Lajpat Rai was important in the development of the Anglo Vedic College and was to head the 'College' faction of the Arya Samaj after its split. He had first come across Arya Samajists at the Government College at Lahore after 1881. He had previously been under the guidance of Pandit Shiv Narain Agnihotri, a Brahmo Samaj leader, who was also initially associated with Dayananda and had subsequently fallen out with him, eventually starting his own Dev Samaj. Lajpat Rai joined the Arya Samaj in 1882 and rapidly became an influential figure. He became a legal representative in Jagraon and Rothak, and finally a lawyer, working first in Hissar, south Punjab and then in Lahore in the early 1890s. It was during this period, starting from 1893, that Lajpat Rai became practically involved in Congress activities. His interests in educational and industrial development (the latter becoming explicitly socialist in the following decades, particularly after his meetings with British socialists such as Hyndman) led to him becoming a member of the Indian National Congress Committee in 1901. While during his political career, Lajpat Rai was heavily involved in a wide range of social reform, industrial, anti-colonial and political activities, and in 1907 was deported to Mandalay Prison with Ajit Singh for revolutionary and seditionist activities. This chapter will primarily focus on those of his activities that related to specifically political Hindu concerns.

Prior to his serious involvement in Congress, Lajpat Rai had published a series of Open Letters to Sir Syed Ahmed Khan between October and December 1888. In 1887, Syed Ahmad Khan had both criticized Congress proposals for representative councils as 'seditious' and had declared that the interests of Muslims and Hindus were not identical as far as political representation in the councils was concerned, claiming that proposals for representation would mean Hindu majority domination over Muslims. If this was an example of what was frequently viewed in Hindu nationalist discourse as the early stirrings of Muslim separatism and Muslim collaboration with the British colonial government, its trajectory was by no means set.

Lajpat Rai's critique of Syed Ahmad Khan used the latter's earlier patriotic declarations against himself, particular those that argued for a common nationhood based on geography and irrespective of religious, 'racial' or linguistic differences. However, while Lajpat Rai criticized Ahmad Khan for suggesting that the interests of Muslims and Hindus were different, he did not powerfully state in those letters that the interests of Hindus and Muslims were the same or defined by a common nationhood. It was this formative lacuna or asymmetry that constituted an important characteristic of early Hindu nationalism, and allowed the latter to slide between Congress nationalism and an instinctive Hindu supremacism until it faced a different ideological challenge after the 1920s. Elaborating on the Hindu contours existing in pre-1920s, Indian nationalism is not a difficult task and is illustrated by a variety of currents in the national movement, both moderate and revolutionary. Some of these areas are at least partially illustrated by Lajpat Rai's own views about Hindu nationalism elaborated from the late 1890s onwards.[35]

Lajpat Rai and Hindu Nationalism

In 1899, Lajpat Rai published an article for the Indian National Congress in the Hindustan Review in which he declared that 'Hindus are a nation in themselves, because they represent a civilization all their own'. This was not a new idea even then. However, for Lajpat Rai, this idea was directly influenced by a conception of Hindu nationalism in the aftermath of the 'purification' of Hinduism by the Arya Samaj. In 1902, Lajpat Rai entered a debate occurring in the pages of Hindustan Review and Kayastha Samachar between an anonymous "Hindu Nationalist' and Pandit Madhao Ram about the basis for creating a 'Hindu Nationalism'. Indeed, discussion about the idea of 'Hindu Nationalism' spread from the pages of Hindustan Review and Kayastha Samachar and into the Times of India between 1900-1902.

Lajpat Rai agreed with the main prescriptions of 'Hindu Nationalist', arguing that these echoed his earlier writings. It was his areas of disagreement with the 'Hindu Nationalist' that are important here. The 'Hindu Nationalist' had asserted that the concept of nationalism was a modern, European idea that could be appropriated by Hindus in their project of coming to nationhood. Lajpat Rai disagreed both with the view that the origins of the national idea were to be found in Europe and with the view that Hindus had historically possessed no sense of nationality.

He is also seen as having sown the seeds of Hindu nationalism in the first decade of the twentieth century. Exploring Lajpat Rai's thought between the 1880s and 1915, this article traces how felt imperatives of Hindu nation-building impelled him to regularly re-define Hinduism. These first prompted Rai to articulate a 'thin' Hinduism, defined less in terms of an insistence on a complex set of beliefs and more in broad, simple terms. In Lajpat Rai's thought, the production of the Religions Hindu nation amidst the diversity of Hinduism led him to first de-emphasise doctrinal complexity and purity, and belief more generally, and then emphasise a culturalized Hinduism—'Hindu culture'— over Hindu religion. This reveals the distinctive effects that Hindu nationalism had on the conceptualization of Hinduism in the thought of a prominent Arya Samajist and Hindu politician– thinker. Rai's thought both reflected and shaped broader intellectual trends and represented a significant strand of Hindu thinking about Hindu identity and Hinduism. An examination of Rai's ideas reveals the latent and even unselfconscious political manoeuvres sometimes embodied in conceptualizations of what is ostensibly Hindu religion. Scholars have noted that nationalism drove articulations of a homogenised Hinduism around which Hindus could rally. Rai's thought shows that this sometimes entailed re-defining Hinduism in terms of fewer, simple beliefs rather than many, elaborate beliefs and in ways that de-emphasised belief and observance altogether. It further shows that nationalism could drive a prioritisation of Hindu culture (conceived in broadly non-religious terms) over Hindu religion. In being predicated on a conceptualisation of Hinduism that de-emphasised belief and a prioritization of 'Hindu culture' over Hinduism. Rai's Hindu nationalism converged with Savarkar's. This is an important revelation considering dominant historiographical interpretations of Rai's Hindu nationalism as an ideological antecedent of Savarkarite Hindutva. By the 1890s, the felt urgency of regenerating a Hindu nation impelled Lajpat Rai to not only de-emphasise elaborate religious beliefs and thin down Hinduism but also side-line Hinduism in favour of the language, literature, and history—or the profane 'culture'—of Hindus. This represented a move from an emphasis on belief towards the explicit recasting of Hindu identity in primarily de-sacralised 'cultural' terms, the latter constituting the culturalization of Hinduism. Hindu nationalism, therefore, prompted Lajpat Rai not just to 'thin down' Hinduism but soon turn instead to Hindu 'culture'. To be sure, Hindu religion appeared in Rai's Hindu history. Lajpat Rai relinquished his earlier Arya Samaj influenced definition of Hinduism as Vedic monotheism. Accepting the Samaj as one of Hinduism's many sects, and moving towards a broad-based definition of Hinduism, Rai now embraced Hinduism's multiple post-Vedic texts. He also omitted emphasis on God and belief to define Hinduism as social and national spirit. In short, in the very early years of the new century, imperatives of Hindu nation-building despite Hinduism's tremendous internal diversity motivated Rai to side line the Samaj and the question of belief altogether as he defined Hinduism. Put differently, Rai seemed to sense that a particular Arya Samajist based definition of Hinduism would alienate the majority of non-Arya Samajist Hindus, given the diversity of Hindu beliefs. To crystallise a Hindu nation that included diverse followers of Hinduism, Rai espoused a definition of Hinduism that de-emphasised not just specific Arya tenets but religious belief more generally. Hindu nationalism impelled Rai to argue that the multiple Hindu texts revered by Hindus preached a 'Hinduism' that equalled a social and national spirit. By following this true 'Hinduism', Hindus with different beliefs could realise the Hindu nation. In his article titled 'Hinduism and Common Nationality' (1907), Rai contested arguments that because Hinduism 'does not represent one set of beliefs', nothing substantial bound 'one Hindu to another in ties of national brotherhood', and Hinduism was more a 'congeries of different religions . . . holding diverse and not unoften diametrically opposite views on matters of faith and doctrine' and constituted neither a 'religion' nor a 'religious nationality' in 1909. Lajpat Rai participated in the Punjab Hindu Sabha, following the grant of separate electorates and weighted representation to Muslims. His drive to build his most capacious Hindu nation now resulted in not a radical re-formulation of Hinduism—entailing the emptying of its convictional content—but Hinduism itself being firmly superseded by 'Hindu culture'. Rai now believed that grounding the Hindu nation in Hinduism would exclude 'our friends of the Brahmo Samaj, Jains and some Sikhs' who did not 'subscribe to the scriptural authority of the Vedas'. To include such groups, he now explicitly argued that it was sufficient for them to 'studiously retain, and laboriously maintain, the distinguishing features of Hindu culture in their thought and life'. 'Community of religion', he said, was not necessary for the formation of a 'nation', the 'essence' of which lay in its 'culture' . This was different from Chatterjee's stance that Rai had echoed before. Chatterjee and, similar to him, Rai had argued that the substance or essence of Hindu religion was culture. Rai was now arguing that the essence of the Hindu nation was not religion but culture. Efforts to build a broad-based Hindu nation—including Brahmos, Sikhs, Jains, and Buddhists—had Rai displace even the Vedas in favour of Hindu culture as he defined Hindu nationhood. Hindu nation-building now caused Rai to displace even this surface level marker of 'Hinduism hitherto' retained to bind the diverse followers of Hinduism into a Hindu nation. Culturalized Hinduism, phenomena imagined as decoupled from belief and observance, and conceived as 'Hindu culture', was made the centre of Hindu nationhood to realize Rai's most capaciously defined Hindu nation. The de-emphasis on the finer points of belief and the emphasis on 'Hindu culture' as a means of crafting a capacious 'Hindu nation'—which included Sikhs, Jains and Buddhists but excluded Muslims and Christians—would be similarly evident in the definitions of Hinduism and Hindu nationalism Savarkar articulated in 1923. In Essentials of Hindutva, Savarkar emphasised that while 'Hinduism' was a 'sectarian term' signifying 'spiritual or religious dogma', 'Hindutva' or Hindu-ness was broader than Hinduism, 'not primarily' or 'mainly' concerned with 'any particular theocratic or religious dogma'. Religious belief, he averred, is substantially unimportant for Hindutva or Hindu national belonging. While residence in and love for India constituted the first 'essential' of Hindutva and possession of Hindu blood the second, these remained insufficient essentials for Hindu national belonging. The third 'essential'—reverence for 'Hindu culture' or Sanskriti—was crucial. This 'Hindu culture' was represented in the literature, art, architecture, history, mythology, law, festivals, rites, rituals, customs, ceremonies, and sacraments of Hindus, Lajpat Rai saw his Hindu nation as compatible with a larger 'Indian nation: 'By aiming at unity and solidarity amongst the Hindus, we do not contemplate a blow at Indian unity . . . I believe that the political salvation of India must come out of the combination and union of all communities into one national whole . . . that decidedly is the goal' . Rai conceived the Hindu nation in a pre-nationalist sense to signify a cultural community. Even if politically charged, this nation was not imagined in a modern nationalist sense to signify a political community that deserved a self-ruling state over a particular territory. When Rai used the term nation in this modern nationalist sense, he imagined an 'Indian' nation, including Hindus and non Hindus. Although Rai did not define the cultural identity of this common Indian nation, his not asserting a superior claim of Hinduism and Hindu culture over India, and not demanding assimilation, revealed a basic respect for India's diversity.

In several key passages of his response, Lajpat Rai expressed a series of gestatory ideas, many of which were to find their way virtually unchanged in Savarkar's definitive Hindutva. Lajpat Rai dismissed the argument that the term 'Hindu' was a Persian term of abuse invented by 'Mohammedan invaders'. He argued that it had a much more ancient history, and only became a pejorative term under Muslim rule because it signified the fall of the 'Hindu nation'. However (as Savarkar was also to reiterate) it was used in ancient times as a name that others - such as the Persians used to describe the inhabitants of India. This formative idea that the name 'Hindu' was a patronymic that had been conferred by a constitutive outside, rather than as emergent from within Vedic or other religious texts, is both highly significant and proved repeatedly troublesome for later Hindu nationalists who could find no such name in the archaic texts of 'Hinduism' itself.

However, while ancient Hindu literature did not use the word 'Hindu' as a self-description, but instead the term Arya, for Lajpat Rai even these ancient texts contained the sentiment of nationality, expressed most strongly in Aryan battles against their enemies, the dasyus, chandalas and mlechhas. Against the view of 'Hindu Nationalist' that nationalism was a modern invention, Lajpat Rai explicitly situated the birth of 'Hindu nationality' in the Aryan Vedic period. This heritage, he argued, 'must be the fulcrum of the lever with which we are to rise as a nation'. He argued that the history of India had still to be written from 'a Hindu point of view', a task which would demonstrate Hinduism's ancient nationalism.

We the English educated Hindus of the present day, who claimed to have imbibed the new spirit of nationality and patriotism from the West would really do well to study a few chapters of the Vedic literature with care and thought.

In opposing the view that nationalism was invented in nineteenth-century Europe, Lajpat Rai used precisely the method and epistemology of the latter to discern what he believed to be an earlier idea of nationalism in the Vedas. The idea that the foundations of modern nationalism were to be found in archaic primordialism was a key component in the eighteenth- and nineteenth-century European invention of nationalism.

For Lajpat Rai, 'Hindu ritualism', and not the absence of the spirit of nationality, was the bane of the Hindus. This antagonistic separation of Hindu nationality from caste Hindu religious tradition was an archetypal Arya Samaj formulation that was to find its way into the 'post-religious' nationalism of the Rashtriya Swayamsevak Sangh, but was also to become of source of tension within Hindu nationalism, both before and after independence. Lajpat Rai also situated the historical expression of Hindu nationality in the 'efforts of the Mahrattas and the Rajputs to throw off the foreign yoke and found a Hindu empire'. This transcendental conception of a temporal link between an ancient and a medieval 'Hindu nation' is significant and was stated most militantly by Savarkar.

After having stated that nationality did not imply a complete union in all the details of religious, social, economic and sectarian life, Lajpat Rai asserted a comprehensive definition of nationality:

Run on a few basal principles in religion, on the community of a sacred language, and on the community of interests, the Hindus ought to foster the growth of a national sentiment which should be sufficiently strong to enable them to work for the common good in the different ways and according to the lights vouchsafed to each. Let us keep one ideal before us. Let our ideal be sufficiently high to cover all, sufficiently broad and extensive to include all, who take pride in a common name, a common ancestry, a common history, a common religion, a common language and a common future. We will not advance the cause of nationality by one inch if we decide to preserve an attitude of silent quietude and non-disturbing peace in all matters, religious and social. Such an attitude can only mean stagnation and gradual extinction. Struggle, hard struggle is the law of progress. Yes struggle we must, both inter se as well [as with] others.

With one possible exception, the idea of a common 'race', perhaps indicated above by 'ancestry', this formulation of nation is virtually equivalent to that of Savarkar and vividly elides the distinction between a 'Hindu' and an 'Indian' nationalism.

As important was the thoroughgoing influence of Spencerian evolutionist political sociology, indicated above in the 'hard struggle' that was the 'law of progress'. This frequently defined the field of intellectual production for many colonial and anti-colonial currents. The consequences of this epistemology were brought out most clearly by Lajpat Rai in an article published in 1907:

A question has often haunted us, asleep or awake, as to why is it that notwithstanding the presence among us of great, vigorous and elevating truths, and of the very highest conception of morality, we [Hindus] have been a subject race, held down for so many centuries by sets of people who were neither physically nor spiritually nor even intellectually so superior to us as a fortiori to demand our subjection.

This powerful formulation that encapsulated both 'Hindu weakness' and 'Hindu strength' has been foundational to successive waves of post-independence Hindu nationalism. The translation of the question, articulated in the colonial period, of why British colonialism had occurred into an entirely different imaginary of why Hindus had 'repeatedly failed to repel foreign invaders' over some ten to thirteen centuries is striking and considerable ideological and political content follows from posing the logic of a transcendental 'Hindu history' in this way. It was precisely this question that preoccupied Dr. K.B. Hedgewar, from which he derived the Rashtriya Swayamsevak Sangh as the answer. In a densely fascinating way, a logic was started that severely minimized British colonialism within a much longer 'historical' frame of Hindu resistance to what were conceived as all 'foreign invaders'.

This logic culminated in Savarkar's Hindutva who is a Hindu (1923), and Swami Shraddhanand's Hindu Sangathan-Saviour of a dying race (1926), both written in the midst of one of the most violent and troubled periods of anti-colonial agitation during the first manifestation of a genuinely mass anti-colonial movement, but which can be read with barely any indication within them that British colonialism was even present. (A similar theme preoccupied later Hindutva ideologues: the British colonial period was effectively dismissed or conceived as relatively benign, even civilizing and moral in character in comparison with the early or high medieval periods of Mughal rule, which were seen as periods of ruthless oppression and genocide of Hindus.)

The framing of colonial subjugation in such terms had distinctive intellectual conditions of possibility. As Lajpat Rai said:

We do not require a Herbert Spencer to tell us that the social efficiency of a social organism as such, depends upon the sense of social responsibility amongst the members of such an organism. The greater and the intense the sense of responsibility amongst the individual members, regarding the safety and welfare of the whole, the greater and the stronger the efficiency of the organism.

Lajpat Rai's political speeches frequently employed Spencerian themes of organisms, social flexibility, adaptability and adaptation, efficiency and inefficiency, survival and extinction. In particular, Spencer's critical combination of ideas of the collective survival of the fittest with individual liberty from domination was to have significant resonance in colonial India. Spencerianism allowed for the development of a specifically naturalistic, 'physiological' and 'biological' theory of imperialism and anti-colonialism.

Lajpat Rai claimed that Hinduism did contain an organic sense of responsibility and survival, since it had continued to 'reign supreme' even after 'twelve centuries of Islamic propaganda backed by all the forces of political ascendancy and moral superiority which is the anchor sheet of a virgin religion and a conquering creed', and after a further '400 years of active evangelical work done in the name of Christ'. The fact that Hinduism existed at all was testimony to its strength and power. This was a key teleological and functionalist component of evolutionary sociology: the elementary fact of the contemporary existence of a social phenomenon was evinced as proof both of its inherent functional fitness and an indication of its telos. In essence, this was a naturalistic theory of imperialism, a transmutation of Spencer by those fighting colonialism. The use of Spencerian themes would inevitably lead to a focus on Hindu biological and physiological 'fitness', reproductive 'efficiency' and the necessity of strengthening the fertility of Hindu women.

One consequence of conceiving both nationalism and colonialism in naturalistic and 'physiological' terms was the requirement to explain a strong and powerful Hinduism able to resist other 'conquering' religions and the 'historical weakness' of Hindus unable to repel 'foreign invasions'. Both themes, central to Lajpat Rai's political epistemology, were to travel through Savarkar's formulation of Hindu identity and then into the 'man-moulding' activities of the RSS. Lajpat Rai articulated the strength and resilience of Hindus through their simple existence in the face of repeated 'foreign invasions'.

What then was the cause of the 'weakness' of Hindus and Hinduism, demonstrated most clearly for Lajpat Rai by the elementary fact of British colonial domination? He argued that this was primarily because of individual selfishness, greed and calculation that prevented organismic consciousness of the greater society and nation. The political remedy for Lajpat Rai was to inculcate a 'sense of social responsibility which requires each and every member of the organism to place the interests of the community or the nation over and above those of his own'. A political sociology of the collectively, drawing on influences such as Spencer, were mobilized to provide an organic view of the over integrative capacities of Hinduism, the latter indeed dovetailing neatly into extant colonial discourses about Hinduism's amalgamating properties.

In his conceptions of nationalism, Lajpat Rai discussed Hindu nationality in a 'commonsense' and naturalized way as an integrative function that elided its difference from Indian nationality. This is an historical and theoretical issue of considerable importance during a period when distinct and sophisticated political languages of secularism were not available. After the 1920s, the distinction between Hindu nationalism and anti-communal (but not necessarily 'secular') Indian nationalism was to be politically forged, but a naturalized British discourse of group communalism and group rights substituted for a deeper elaboration of the meaning of secularism as constituting a substantive field distinct from a principled 'anti-colonial anti-communalism'.

Hence, Lajpat Rai both appeared to accept and frequently stated that Hindus and Muslims had something like a common national destiny, and severely castigated Syed Ahmad Khan for suggesting otherwise, and yet articulated Indian nationality as a Hindu nationalism. The faithful and imaginative holding of both these positions continued to be reproduced in Hindutva literature after the 1920s and is still central for what are viewed as the 'moderate' tendencies in the contemporary Hindutva movement. Lajpat Rai cultivated associations with both Gandhi and Jinnah, with 'moderates' and 'radicals' in Congress, and with organizations that explicitly called for 'Hindu Raj' and Hindu self-organization against Muslims. This was a convergence between an Indian nationalist who happened to have been raised within and affiliated to a Hindu religious tradition, and a Hindu supremacist for whom Hinduism was nationalism.

Lajpat Rai's view of a Hindu nation represented a general intellectual current manifested around the turn of the century in colonial India. The distinctive aspect of this was the view that Hindus were historically a nation, and that they were a nation solely because of the associated view that Hinduism was an ancient civilization. There were various examples, often associated with Arya

Samajist currents, which articulated a similar equivalence between the alleged historical existence of a Hindu nationality in India that was claimed to be primordial precisely because of another, different claim that there existed a primordial civilization that was in all its important aspects 'Hindu'. The term 'civilization' was neither neutral nor unrelated to a longer intellectual project that disputed, while emulating, British claims about the civilizing mission while vehemently criticizing, and offering historical explanations for what were perceived as the uncivilized, barbaric or degenerate aspects of Hinduism. This intellectual equivalence between imagined nationalism and imagined civilization was extremely important and the civilizational method was indeed definitive. The early Hindu nationalist organizations indeed had a civilizing mission that promised another ostensibly 'indigenous' path into modernity for those wayward populations that were deemed to require 'upliftment' into Hinduism, a mission that continues to this day.[36]

The Bombay Provincial Hindu Sabha had been organised by Raja Narayanlal Pitti, Pt. Mukunda Malaviya and others and they had come down to attend the Belgaum Special Session of the Hindu Sabha which was also organised by them. The next regular session of the Hindu Mahasabha was held at Calcutta in the month of April. L. Lajpat Rai, who had taken up the movement with the courage and earnestness characteristic of him, was the President-elect and great enthusiasm was being felt for the Conference. L. Lajpat Rai left for Calcutta after presiding over the second Behar Provincial Hindu Conference at Muzaffarpur, where thousands of people had gathered. Great enthusiasm had been created owing to the advent of Bhai Parmanandji along with Lalaji. Sir P. C. Ray was the Chairman of the Reception Committee of the Calcutta Session. The Conference was a roaring success.

Immediately after the Calcutta Session, Lalaji reached Assam, toured the province and entrusted the work of Hindu Sangathan to Mr. T. R. Phookon with a monthly grant of five hundred rupees. During the course of the year, Lalaji visited Bombay where a Provincial Hindu Conference presided over by him was held and Mr. M. R. Jayakar, the Congress veteran - leader of Bombay, was drawn into the Hindu Mahasabha as the President of its Provincial Branch at Bombay. He next visited Burma and presided over the first Burma Provincial Hindu Conference. This visit of Lalaji created a great awakening amongst the Hindus of that province. Lalaji visited Sindh and C. P. also that year. The Sindh Provincial Hindu Sabha had been firmly organised by two of the most prominent Congress Hindu leaders of the province. Dr. Choithram and Mr. Jairamdas - formerly the trusted lieutenants of Mr. Gandhi and who have since then again gone back to the Congress, took up the work earnestly with their companions and co-workers and made it a real, living and effective body in those parts.

The office of the Hindu Mahasabha was relocated to Delhi this year to suit the convenience of Lalaji and to take advantage of the presence of the representatives of the different provinces coming to attend the sittings of the Legislative Assembly during its Winter Session. The two years previous to it had seen the tangible dawn of Renaissance, and this year, with the Presidentship of Lalaji, was laid the foundation of the real work of the Renaissance, which has since then gone on steadily in a more and more organised shape.

On the occasion of the Cawnpore Congress in December, 1925, another Special Session of the Hindu Mahasabha was held, which was presided over by Shri. N. C. Kelkar who had already identified himself with the cause of the Renaissance.

Lajpat Rai, 'Cooperation' and Hindu Interests

Lajpat Rai's political trajectory and concerns after 1924, until his death in 1928, form an illustrative ideological map of the kinds of complex positions that were ostensibly central to the national movement but clearly favoured Hindu interests. Lajpat Rai appealed for purely Hindu interests and consistently argued against the 'policy of appeasement' of Muslims. He provided strong leadership for the Hindu Mahasabha (of which he was President in 1925), Hindu Sangathan and the Shuddhi movements, urging the growth of the latter against the corresponding tabligh and tanzim activities among Muslim communities. He opposed the politicization of the Hindu Mahasabha, and talk of 'Hindu Raj' or 'Muslim Raj' while bemoaning the historic weakness of Hindus, claiming that Hindu Sangathan and Indian nationalism were entirely compatible and necessary for each other. Lajpat Rai was an extremely influential member of Congress who accepted the need for Hindu-Muslim unity, that Hindus and Muslims shared a common interest, even a composite nationality. But he had already declared in 1917 that he was 'a Hindu nationalist'. While a willing supporter of non-cooperation ('Speech at 35th session of Indian National Congress, Nagpur, December 1920') who was extremely critical of Gandhi's suspension of civil disobedience, he consistently adopted a more pragmatic position towards absolute non-cooperation and absolute independence, typically arguing that these were legitimate aims, but the reality of political possibilities demanded a more compromised position, if not their absolute rejection.

His conception of the politically possible delineated his movement towards an explicitly Hindu communalist position within a few years. In discussing the 'Hindu-Muslim problem' during 1924, following his resignation from Congress, Lajpat Rai (using Spencer) bemoaned the growth of the idea of absolute freedom and absolute rights in religious matters, at the expense of duties towards the nation: All organic relations depend upon the mutual obligations of the members comprising the organism. No part of the organism has any absolute right'. While consistently viewing communalism as an invention of British statecraft, he traced its growth to the principle of separate communal organization, cooperation with the British and opposition to self-rule of Sir Syed Ahmed Khan and the Muslim leadership that followed in his wake - 'the Aligarh School of Muhammadans became characteristically anti-Hindu and pro-Government'. He portrayed Islam as an intolerant, dogmatic religion in comparison with Hinduism, which despite its caste system, was 'the most tolerant of all great religions in the world'. Gandhi was criticized for asking Hindus to concede to Muslim religious demands while never making a similar request to Muslims; similarly Gandhi's assertion that Muslims had accepted non-cooperation 'was absolutely unwarranted'. Remarkably, he said that untouchability must have arisen as a result of Hindu 'non-cooperation' with foreign. However, the 'enemies' of previous centuries were now neither foreigners nor rulers and were an integral part of the Indian nation. Despite this, he argued, Muslims leaders over the past fifty years had implanted the idea in the Muslim masses that Hindus were 'Kafirs'.

Lajpat Rai's narrative which depicted Muslim communalism as exclusive, self-seeking, anti-national, anti-Indian and in complete alliance with the British, whereas Hindu communalism was both a response to Muslim separatism and represented a 'cult of political freedom' from British imperialism, was central to his justification for the flourishing of Hindu communalist organizations from the mid-1920s. This discourse was pivotal in legitimizing Hindu nationalist strategies of cooperation with the ruling British power and of opposing both the Congress and the national movement, especially strands in the latter that were to remain committed to absolute non-cooperation, obstruction of British rule and immediate and complete independence.

Lajpat Rai argued that many Muslims had genuinely committed themselves to the non-cooperation movement, but 'in very many cases, their nationalism seemed to be secondary to their Pan-Islamism'. Muslims, he argued, were opposed to the British mainly because the British had been at war against other Muslim countries, and not because of their unconditional love for India and its freedom. 'Divided allegiance and divided love cannot produce either good nationalists or good patriots'. Moreover, it was only in India that exclusivist and Pan-Islamic Muslims could be found, whereas in every other Muslim country, the task of nation-building had predominated. Conversely:

Hindus cannot be anything but Indians. They have no other country and no other nation to look to. They cannot, therefore, be accused of any kind of Pan-Hinduism, in the sense in which the term is used in relation to Islam. Hinduism and Indianism are, in their case, synonymous terms.

Lajpat Rai's discussions of the Shuddhi and Sangathan movements were couched in similar terms. While critical of Swami Shraddhanand and the earlier Arya Samaj shuddhi activities, he defended shuddhi as 'non-political', and its adoption by the Hindu Mahasabha as 'partly political, partly communal and partly humanitarian'. The shuddhi movement, he argued, had come to stay and had to be accepted; it could not be stopped as long as non-Hindu agencies were undertaking proselytizing work. Similarly, the sangathan (Hindu Sabha) movement need not be inherently anti-Muslim, but, in comparison, tanzim activities were 'obviously anti-Hindu'.

The thrust of his analysis of communalism was criticism of Muslims and of Muslim communal representation since, he argued, this was the surest way of not achieving Swaraj. After iterating a fear among some Hindu leaders that Muslim communal representation of electorates was designed, with the assistance of foreign Muslim states, to establish Muslim rule of Hindustan, Lajpat Rai argued on the one hand for proportional communal representation in the provincial legislatures and local bodies where Muslims were in a majority; but on the other hand, opposed separate electorates, the principle of 'effective' minority representation in the provinces where Muslims were in a minority, and communal representation, government service or educational institutions.

In 1923, Lajpat Rai argued that Muslims should have four states (the Pathan province, western Punjab, the Sind and eastern Bengal), but he added, 'it should be distinctly understood that this is not a united India. It means a clear partition of India into a Muslim India and a non-Muslim India'. He used the term non-Muslim India because 'all that the Muslims are anxious for is a guarantee of their own rights. All other communities they lump into one as non-Muslims'.

His message in 1924 to both Muslims and Hindus is worth quoting at length, since it encapsulated the ideological map of a primordial, majoritarian Hinduism that grew rapidly from 1923-25. Let us live and struggle for freedom as brothers whose interests are one and indivisible... India is neither Hindu nor Muslim. It is not even both. It is one. It is India.

Leaving the Swaraj Party

Lajpat Rai's withdrawal from the Swaraj Party is equally instructive. Lajpat Rai opposed 'unreserved' non-cooperation because in his view the national movement was too weak and disunited to paralyse the administration or bring it to a standstill. Characteristically arguing that the principles of non-cooperation were correct, he nevertheless opposed the practice of uniform obstruction, because the movement had not correctly estimated the facts and conditions of national life. After resigning from the Swaraj Party in September 1926 and forming the Nationalist Party, with Madan Mohan Malaviya, Lajpat Rai argued that non-cooperation had been frustrated because of the separatism of the Muslim community. Hence, the policy of non-cooperation or obstruction by only Hindus would also fail. Conversely, the Muslims would continue to cooperate with the British to secure their own rights, the acceptance of which would reduce the Hindu community to a position of inferiority and subordination. 'What would be the position of the Hindus after 10 or 20 years hereafter if the present alliance of the Government and the Muslims continues, and the Hindus continue to allow themselves to be influenced by the mentality of [non] cooperation and boycott?'. Contrasting his nationalism, with that of the Swaraj Party, he said, his nationalism would be consistent with 'justice' to the Hindu community, and it would not abide the formation of national unity at the cost of 'Hindu rights'. While rejecting the conversion of all Muslims in India to Hinduism and establishing a Hindu Raj, and while claiming that his policy was not that of unfettered cooperation with the British, he urged instead what he called a 'balanced' and 'reasoned' approach to the issue of cooperation: 'I do not want to change masters'. Hence, the answer to Muslim communalism was Hindu communalism, cooperative with the British and in accordance with the separate sphere of exclusively Hindu interests.

Such sentiments were to gain greater force in Lajpat Rai's activities as president of the Hindu Mahasabha and in his Sangathanist activities. In his speech to the Bombay Hindu Provincial Conference in 1925 (as President of the Hindu Mahasabha) the theme of 'Hindus in danger' was very strong: 'it was incumbent on Hindus to take active steps to repel the attacks and to resist the attempts that are being made to destroy their unity and communal existence' by Muslims, the latter wishing to become 'the dominant communal entity' in India. Failure to do this would mean Muslim domination. He asserted that if organizing Hindus 'is anti-Muslim or anti-national, then I frankly confess that the Hindu Sabha movement is both'. Hindus should cultivate internal unity and unity with the Christians and Parsees. Similarly, in a reference to the upsurge of the Non-Brahman movement in Maharashtra in the early to mid-1920s, he argued that the Brahmins must 'destroy' the movement for the separate political existence of the non-Brahmins and bring into the shudra fold all 'untouchables'. Hinduism was a living organism and life implied adaptability and growth; hence, Hindus had to move every nerve' to become communally efficient and united. Of additional significance was the fact that the national movement's attempts, under uniquely difficult political circumstances, at cultivating a non-communal, non-sectarian political strategy was viewed by Lajpat Rai as a matter of inefficiency.

If these Spencerian, organicist themes are prominent (and were propounded in a similarly forceful way by Swami Shraddhanand, who was indeed explicit about the metaphoric usefulness of bodily tropes), it should not be surprising that Lajpat Rai, like Shraddhanand, focused on the biological and physiological weakness of the Hindu race, which could only be remedied by the reproductive strengthening of Hindu women:

The Hindus of today are inefficient, lacking in courage, lacking in enterprise, lacking in the zest for life, lacking in enthusiasm, lacking in solidarity, scattered units of a once great race because the condition of their women is not what may be called healthy.

The answer to this 'physical disability' was to attend to 'our girls', living in ignorance and superstition, physically poor because of the social restrictions of Hindu orthodoxy and early child marriage, while girls in other countries are at school, developing their muscles and nerves, hands and feet by suitable exercise'., He contrasted this with 'ancient times', during which Hindu women were independent, assertive, self-reliant, physically competent and as free as men, and produced brave, kind, self-confident, able-bodied and strong Hindu children.

He also accompanied Gopala Krishna Gokhale to England to acquaint the English with the Indian aspirations. Incidentally, he toured countries of Europe and the USA and made a keen study of international affairs.

In 1914, he quit law practise to dedicate himself to the Indian independence movement and travelled to Britain, and then to the United States in 1917. In October 1917, he founded the Indian Home Rule League of America in New York. He stayed in the United States from 1917 to 1920. His early freedom struggle was impacted by Arya Samaj and Hindu Mahasabha.

After joining the Indian National Congress and taking part in political agitation in Punjab, Lala Lajpat Rai was deported to Mandalay, but there was insufficient evidence to hold him for subversion. Lajpat Rai's supporters attempted to secure his election to the presidency of the party session at Surat in December 1907, but he did not succeed.

Graduates of the National College, which he founded inside the Bradlaugh Hall at Lahore as an alternative to British-style institutions, included Bhagat Singh. He was elected President of the Indian National Congress in the Calcutta Special Session of 1920. In 1921, he founded Servants of the People Society, a non-profit welfare organisation, in Lahore, which shifted its base to Delhi after partition, and has branches in many parts of India. According to him, Hindu society needs to fight its own battle with caste system, position of women and untouchability. Vedas were an important part of Hindu religion but the lower castes were not allowed to read them. Lala Lajpat Rai approved that the lower caste should be allowed to read them and recite the mantras. He believed that everyone should be allowed to read and learn from the Vedas.[37]

The First Hindu Conference

The first Punjab Provincial Hindu Conference was held in 1909 at Lahore. Nearly 800 delegates from different parts of the province attended the two days sitting 21st and 22nd October, 1909. Full report of this Conference was published in book form (200 pages) and copies are still preserved in Hindu Mahasabha records. The late Lala Lajpat Rai, who took a prominent part in the Hindu Mahasabha movement, afterwards attended the conference and made a long speech on the first resolution on "Desirability of feeling of Hindu Nationality and Hindu Unity."

In his speech, late Lajpat Rai quoted a very significant passage from his article on the Indian National Congress written ten years before (i. e, in 1899) in the Hindustan Review of Allahabad. The following extract from this article, written years ago, will explain the motives behind the genesis of the Hindu Mahasabha:

"The number of subjects upon which there is any likelihood of reasonable friction existing or coming into existence between members of different religious nationalities in India ought to be reduced to minimum, if there is any room for the same, in the agenda paper of the general assembly. Such subjects being reserved for separate treatment by the inclusive organizations of the nationalities. This will lead to a Hindu political or semi-political Congress or Conference being organised and the sooner it is done the better. As at present situated, the absence of such an organisation places the Hindus at a distinct disadvantage, and takes away from them the chances of a united action or a united expression of opinion upon matters which affect the unity, prosperity and well-being, and generally the interest of Hindus all over India. In order to leave no doubt, as to the necessity of this step, I will be more specific. In my opinion, it should be the business of a Hindu Congress or Conference to support and take as far as possible such steps which might conduct to their unity and strength as a religious nationality, as for instance, the language question, the question of character, the advisability of having common text-book, the teaching of Sanskrit language and literature all over India, the taking of steps which might lead to the protection of Hindu orphan from the hands of proselytising agencies of other denominations, and if necessary, to record a protest against those confidential circulars of Government, which aim at the favouring of other communities to the loss of Hindus".

Lala Lajpat Rai also explained how the Hindus by themselves formed a Nation. He said: "It may be that the Hindus by themselves cannot form themselves into a nation in the modern sense of the term, but that is only a play on words. Modern nations are political units. A political unit ordinarily includes all the people who live under one common political system and form a State. The word 'nation' and 'state' when thus considered are practically interchangeable phrases. That is the sense in which the expression in used in connection with the body called the "Indian National Congress". That is, no doubt, one use of the word and the one which is commonly adopted in modern political literature. But that is not the only sense in which it is or can be used. In fact, the German word 'Nation' did not necessarily signify a political nation or a State. In that language it connoted what is generally conveyed by the English expression "people" implying a community in possessing a certain civilisation and culture. Using it in that sense, there can be no doubt that Hindus are a "nation" in themselves, because they represent a type of civilisation all their own".

With regard to the attitude of the Hindu Maha Sabha towards other communities in India Lalaji said:-

"In the present struggle between Indian communities, I will be a Hindu first and an Indian afterwards, but outside India, or even in India against non-Indian, I am and shall ever be an Indian first and a Hindu afterward. That is, in short, my position in the matter.

"Holding that position, I bear no ill-will to my countrymen of other faiths. I wish them all joy and prosperity. In their efforts to ameliorate the condition of their own community and to secure a position of advantage for their co-religionists I do not find fault with them. In the existing political conditions of India they are perfectly justified in looking to the interests of their own community as long as by doing that they do not injure the Hindus by an unholy alliance with non-Indians."

The movement was comprehensive from the beginning. Lalaji said:-"The Hindu movement inaugurated by the organisers of this conference does not contemplate the exclusion of anyone who is prepared to sail under the Hindu flag and take the credit or discredit which attaches thereto."

Full text of Lala Lajpat Rai's address delivered on 5 December 1925 at the Provincial Hindu Sabha held at Bombay.[38]

In explaining the article, *I may be permitted to state that the Sabha aims at creating a spirit of unity between the different sections of the Hindu society, without any ulterior design against any other community or class of persons outside that society. Ours is a unifying and integrating function and in no way a disuniting and disintegrating one. The Hindu community is the largest and the biggest in the country that goes by one name. Outside India the word "Hindu" stands for "Indian." It may be a surprise to you to learn that even in Egypt a pre-eminently Muslim country, in the compound of the greatest Muslim University (that of Al-Azhar) in the world, Indian Muslims are called Hindus, and the quarter reserved for their residence is known as the Hindu section of their Boarding House. In America, both North and South, all Indians are called and described as Hindus. This would have been an ideal condition of things if the non-Hindu inhabitants of this country had adopted that name without giving up an iota of their respective religious faiths or departing in any way from their religious practices. The name of the country is Hindustan and all those who accept it as their home ought to be called or known as Hindus. But we know that is not so. There are large groups of humanity having their homes in this country who resent being called Hindus, and in its efforts to keep up these differences.*

This is, however, by the way. though it emphasises the necessity of the Hindus doing something to counteract this mischievous tendency and keeping together under one designation all those who take pride in Hindu culture and are not ashamed of acknowledging their Hindu origin. Active efforts are being made by Government and non-Government agencies to divide the Hindus and split them into smaller groups so as to reduce their strength, their importance, and their influence. Unfortunately, the prevailing social system of the Hindus lends support to these efforts. The existing caste distinctions are the weakest spot in the Hindu system and if the Hindu community and Hindu culture have to outlive these ridiculous and mischievous attacks, it is incumbent on the Hindus to take active steps to repel the attacks and to resist the attempts that are being made to destroy their unity and their communal existence. Religion, in all countries, does impose a certain type of communal existence and create artificial barriers to free intercourse between man and man. I have found such distinctions even in the freest country in the world. In the United States there is a thick wall that separates the Jews and the Christians. In fact, the division is not between the Jews and the Christians but between Jews and non-Jews. Nor is the distinction of the making of the Jews alone. There are Jewish hotels where non-Jews are not admitted, and there are non-Jewish hotels where Jews and black men are not admitted. The Government of the country, however, recognises no such distinctions and a time is sure to come when these distinctions will altogether disappear even from the social field. This might have been the case in India as well, if the Government had not intervened and created communal compartments for political purposes and out of political motives. Religious sentiment and religious bias is no doubt very strong in the world but so also are political and economic forces. Where the latter are converted into aids to the former there a state of things is produced which makes any eventual obliteration of communal distinction impossible. Personally I would like my country to recognise no communal distinction in the political and the economic fields. In fact, I would go farther and recognise no communal distinction even in social life. I would like to see people professing different faiths intermingle in social life absolutely freely. But under the existing conditions that is not to be. Insistence on communal distinctions by one community followed by Government recognition of its separate political existence as a necessary element of political life, reacts on peoples of other faiths and leaves them no alternative but to organise themselves communally, if they do not desire to be eventually merged in the former.

It must be recognised that separate communal existence for political purposes intensifies religious and communal differences. Under such a system the communal ego of such a community becomes intense while that of the others becomes loose, so much so that in the course of time the latter are eaten up and devoured by the former. That is the condition of things that now faces us in India. Islam has a distinctive individuality of its own not only as a religious but also as a political and social system. The best interests of the Indian body-politic require that while it may retain the former, it should let the latter go. The same may be said of the Hindus. The meeting together of the two on the same political and economic platform would in that case have led to the evolution of such a socio-political system as would retain the best features of both without destroying their religious individualities. But communal distinctions on political lines are calculated to produce exactly the contrary effect. The question then resolves itself into this. The Muslims are determined to preserve and perpetuate not only their religious but also their political system as far as it may be possible for them to do so. They are not prepared to merge their separate entity into a body-politic which might be a composite entity composed of all the religious communities that claim India as their home. They insist on communal representation all along the political line and also on organising their separate communal entity so completely as to become the dominating communal entity in India. This is bound to come about if other communities refuse to organise themselves. Their refusal or neglect to do so means acquiescence in a condition of things which must sooner or later end in. their merging in or subordination to the other community. Organization means power, influence and prestige. Those who 'neglect to organise must give way to the organised. The power of the British lies in their organising capacity. Their numbers are small but their organising capacity is great. Similarly, if the Muslims organise as Muslims and Hindus refuse or neglect to organise, the consequences are plain. The question of the desirability or otherwise of such consequences is not relevant. The fact remains that the bulk of the Hindus do not desire them, and for good reasons. I will say nothing about the Christians and the Parsees. Under the circumstances it becomes absolutely essential for the Hindus to organise themselves in order to avert those consequences. If organising for that purpose is anti-Muslim or anti-national, then I frankly confess that the Hindu Sabha movement is both. But I don't admit that such an organization is either anti-Muslim or anti-national. The desire for separate political existence and the move to secure that end has come from the Muslims. The Hindus are whole-heartedly opposed to that policy and are prepared to merge their separate communal entity into a common Indian nation. But they form the majority and the Muslims are afraid of not receiving justice at their hands without the necessary guarantees for the protection and safeguarding of their communal or minority interests. These they believe can only be secured by communal electorates and by communal representation even in the services and on the local bodies. But this plea can only hold good if it be conceded that Hindus and

Muslims have separate political and economic interests. So far as religious freedom is concerned one can appreciate the fear but it may be safeguarded by the constitution. But so far as secular interests are considered, why should anyone claim any such rights as a Muslim or as a Hindu if the idea be to evolve a common nationhood? The whole idea of the existence of such separate interests is a negation of nationhood and it must be frankly confessed that those who desire a perpetuation of religious-communal distinctions in the secular line must be considered to be opposed to nationalism. New York is the biggest Jewish city in the world and even there the Jews are in a minority as against the Christians, yet they have never put forward a claim for communal representation. The same may be said of the coloured people of the U.S.A. who socially form an entirely separate community with whom the white have hardly any social relations at all. The population of the United States is a polyglot population consisting of the British, the Germans, the Italians, the French, the Russians. the Spanish, the Arabs, etc. It is a standing complaint of American publicists that these groups keep up their separate communal existence for several generations, but no one has ever asked for communal representation. In fact, of all great countries the idea is singular to India. Its acceptance is entirely due to the desire of the foreign rulers to perpetuate our differences and thus make impossible the evolution of a common nationality. The plea that it is a temporary phase and will cease after some time is untenable on the face of it, as experience has now abundantly proved that the principle is one which tends to perpetuate itself when put into practice even for a short time. I have already remarked that it is a principle of such a kind that if you concede it in favour of one community you cannot deny it in the case of others. I hope I have made it sufficiently clear that circumstances have made it absolutely essential for the Hindus to organise themselves so as to reduce the amount of mischief which the separate organisation of one community politically, religiously, and socially, in spite of the non-organisation of other communities is bound to produce.

Communal organization has thus been thrust upon us. At the same time, it is our bounden duty to be perpetually vigilant so as to avoid its degeneration into a communal war. One way of doing it is to create a new bond of alliance between communities that are opposed to communal representation in the political field. As a Hindu I consider it my duty to take all measures that will effectively prevent a Hindu's conversion to any other religion, be it Islam or Christianity; subject to that qualification, I see no reason why there should not be the freest social interaction between the different religious communities, so as to remove, or at least reduce effectively, the acerbities which are a necessary consequence of political communal representation. Inter-dining and inter-marriage between different religious communities is interdicted by Hindu customs. It is not always allowed even between different castes and sub-castes. It is thus out of the question to expect Hindus to inter-dine and inter-marry with Muslims and Christians. Inter-marriage between Hindus and Muslims is not recognised even by Islamic Law, as at present understood and interpreted by Maulvies. According to the latter the moment a married Hindu, man or woman, is converted to Islam. the marriage tie is dissolved, but that is not so if he or she becomes a Christian. Thus, while a marriage ties between a Christian and a Hindu is legally possible, it is not possible between a Hindu and a Muslim. In the former case the parties to the marriage can retain their respective faiths, but in the latter both must become either Muslims or Hindus. I am mentioning this in order to show that in this respect there is a greater possibility of a freer social interaction between the Hindus and the Christians than between the former and the Muslims. The Indian Christians have declared against communal representation (some have recently pronounced in favour of it) in the political field though they are also organising their community for non-political purposes. Here the Hindus and the Christians are on common ground and nearer to each other than Hindus and Muslims. More or less the same may be said of the Parsees. The two cultures (Hindu and Parsee) have much more in common than any other two cultures in the world. Several of their religious customs and ceremonies seem to be closely allied to each other, such as Homa and Yajnopavit. Be that as it may, I would beg of the Hindus, Christians and Parsees to keep together as far as may be possible, so as to fight out the disease of communal representation in the political field successfully. This perhaps is more easily said than done, in face of the numerous divisions in the Hindu society itself. The infection is spreading and in the West and the South there is a regular war between the Brahmans and the Non-Brahmans. The Non-Brahmans have formed themselves into a separate community. But this is an arrangement which lacks the elements of permanence. If the Hindus were to organise themselves on a broad basis, the distinction between Brahmans and Non-Brahmans is bound to disappear. Hinduism is sufficiently broad-based to include and tolerate all differences of faith, culture, custom, and caste within its fold. In Upper India, the Hindus are not divided into Brahmans and Non-Brahmans. The bureaucracy tried to create that division but their efforts have not been successful. They are now trying to create a division between Jats and Non-Jats, but there again if the Hindu community behaves wisely and tactfully, the division will be averted. A fresh division is now being attempted between the Caste-Hindus and the untouchables, but that is an all-India question, and I will come to it presently. My point is that an organisation of the Hindus, as such, is necessary to counteract the evil effects of communal representation in the political field which is insisted upon by our Muslim countrymen; secondly, that the Hindus must cultivate more friendly relations with the Christians and the Parsees; and thirdly, that they should do everything possible to avert political divisions among the different sections of their community. I will now take up this last question.

Hindus are divided into castes and sub-castes. Hindu Shastras recognise no such distinction as between Brahmans and Non-Brahmans. In North India we know of no such distinction. In the South and the West, the distinction has come into existence because of the original Varna system not having been enforced here. In the North there is very little difference between the Brahmans and the other Dwijas. All the Dwijas whether Brahmans or Non-Brahmans, are entitled to wear the Yajnopavita, perform Yajnas, and study the Vedas. All of them are entitled to the Gayatri. The functions of the priesthood are no doubt confined to the Brahmans. In the South and the West, however, Yajnopavita and Gayatri and the Vedas are denied to all Non-Brahmans. We have sufficient evidence in Hindu Shastras and Hindu history that in ancient times the caste distinctions were not so 'rigid as they are today. Intercourse between castes was fairly common. A Brahman was sometimes degraded to the position of a Shudra and a Shudra had opportunities to rise to Brahman hood. Anyway, there is no authority for Yajnopavita and Gayatri being denied to those who are entitled to the position of Dwijas under the Shastras. There is also abundant authority for the proposition that those who became Antyajas by ceasing to wear Yajnopavita and preform Yajnas, were re-admitted to these rights by the performance of the necessary prayashchit. Under the circumstances, it is easy for the Hindus of the South and the West to fall back on the ancient custom and admit at least those Non-Brahmans who are Dwijas by occupation as laid down in the Dharma Shastras and other ancient books on Hindu Law and ritual, to the rights of Yajnopavita and Yajnas. The Brahmans of the South and the West can thus destroy the movement for the separate political existence of the Non-Brahmans by broadening the basis of their Brahmanism and admitting into its fold all those Non-Brahmans who are not doing the work of the Shudras. Brahmanism will thus become synonymous with Hinduism. I am certain the movement for separation is exploited by a few educated men. The Non-Brahman shopkeeper, cultivator, craftsman, etc., have no interest in it. If the Brahmans of the South were to concede to them the rights of Dwijas which are theirs under the Hindu Shastras, their separatist tendencies will disappear. It is in the best interests of Hinduism as well as nationalism that this should happen and I beg to implore the Brahmans of the Western and Southern Presidencies to lose no time in coming to an understanding with the Non-Brahmans. I am not afraid of the latter, even if they continue to receive the favoured treatment they are now getting from the Government, because I am certain that ultimately, they cannot go adrift from the Hindu Samaj, but the sooner the division is healed up the better.

Now I come to the Shudras and the untouchables. The case of the untouchables is clear enough so far as untouchability is concerned. On no account and for no consideration can untouchability be allowed to disfigure the fair face of Hinduism. Once untouchability is removed, the present-day untouchables become one with the Shudras. We have abundant authority for the proposition, as already remarked, that caste in ancient times was not so rigid and so permanent as it is now. Shudras were allowed by proved fitness to rise to higher castes and people in the latter were degraded to the position of Shudras by reason of misconduct. The present-day caste system is not an ancient system. All sensible and intelligent Hindus are agreed that the prevailing system of numerous castes and sub-castes cannot be defended. It requires substantial changes. Time and circumstances are against it. However wrathful the Varna-Ashram may be against the reforms, they are destroying the existing caste system inch by inch by their own conduct. Theirs is a dying cause, for the simple reason that the time forces are against it. Let us first take the Varna system. It is clear that the present numerous divisions have no justification in the ancient Hindu Shastras which divided society into four Varnas. The present system must then be a development of later days, and is thus open to change according to the needs of the time. The advocates of Varna-Ashramas themselves do not fully observe either the rules of ancient Varnas or the customary restrictions of the present Varnas. The customary practices are opposed both in spirit and in letter to the ancient system, but the actual conduct of the orthodox today is opposed even to the sanctioned customary practices of 100 years ago. There are many among the so-called orthodox who have no objection to the use of European medicine, or sacred waters, or pipe-water, or articles of food manufactured in Europe and America. Some of them dine at the Government House or in the company of the Europeans and also preside at Sanatan Dharma Sammelans (conferences). They go to Europe and do not perform any prayashchit (expiation ceremony) on their return. This is particularly true of the ruling Princes. How can they then advocate the maintenance of the caste system in its present shape? Their own conduct belies their professions of faith.

Let us next take the Ashramas. Here again, their conduct and practice is entirely opposed to the spirit and the letter of the Ashrama-Dharma. The rules as to Ashrama-Dharma do not contemplate early marriage, at least among the Dwijas. The present-day Hindus have cut the root of the Ashrama-Dharma by the institution of child-marriage. How many of them retire to the forests or become Sanyasis as required by the Ashrama-Dharma? For people who marry their children at the age of twelve or under, who do not teach the latter even rudiments of Sanskrit, who send them to schools managed by non-Hindus, who stick to Grihastha life after sixty, nay some of whom even re-marry at that age, to call themselves defenders and champions of the Varna-Asharam-Dharma is mere mockery worthy of the Pharisees. The best thing for us is to deliberately change our social Code, and for that there is ample authority and provision in the ancient scriptures. Samaj Dharma is always regulated by Desh and Kal (i.e. place and time). The Hindus have, from time to time, changed it, according to their altered needs and circumstances; and this has given them stability and permanence. Life implies adaptability and growth. Hinduism is a living organism, has always been so. Its social Code, has been changing, is changing, and will continue to change according to the needs of Desh and Kal. The opposition of the orthodox is good so for as it militates against too rapid a change and too outlandish a transformation, but it is harmful and injurious when it threatens to thwart all progress and militates against the regeneration of life according to the needs of the time.

The greatest need of the community is to take the best care it can of the mothers of the community. To a Hindu, a woman is Lakshmi, Saraswati and Shakti, combined. That means that she is the foundation of all that is beautiful and desirable and leads to power. And very deservedly too. The mothers of the race are its makers and unless their condition is healthy, the race cannot be expected to be anything better. When we say healthy, we include in it all that makes life enjoyable, progressive and potent.

The efficiency and prosperity of a social or political unit must eventually be a reflex of the efficiency and prosperity of its women. The Hindus of today are inefficient, lacking in courage, lacking in enterprise, lacking in the zest for life, lacking in enthusiasm, lacking in solidarity, scattered units of a once great race because the condition of their women is not what may be called healthy. The great feature of present-day Hindu life is passivity. "Let it be so," sums up all their psychology, individual and social. Active effort to change the conditions of life, to change the current of their tendencies, to be masters of their fate, to grapple with difficulties that hamper their progress and solidarity, is wanting. They have got into the habit of taking things lying down. They have imbibed this tendency and this psychology and this habit from their mothers. It seems as if it was in their blood. There is no question that all this bas to be changed if the Hindus are to become efficient, enterprising and courageous. The best, the easiest and the most effective way is to attend to our girls. Our women labour under many handicaps. It is not only ignorance and superstition that corrode their intelligence, but even physically they are a poor race. Their physical disabilities are generally due to the social restrictions from which they suffer. They become mothers at an age, at which girls in other countries are at school, developing their muscles and nerves, hands and feet by suitable physical exercises. The first delivery is the death of a good number of them, and disables many more. They become a kind of invalids for the rest of their lives. Those who breed, breed too many, and thus lead miserable, wretched lives from which all zest and enthusiasm disappears. As a rule, they are careless about their food. Their chief concern is to feed their men well. For themselves they can live and subsist on anything. The Hindus are an awfully careless people in the matter of their food. The rich eat too much and the poor too little. The middle class does not exist. In middle class and poor families, the women are all day long engaged in cooking food. Both men and women are supremely ignorant about the food value of the things they eat and drink. As for regularity of meals, no one understands the value thereof. Women get very little open air and almost no exercise. How on earth is the race then to improve and become efficient? A large number of our women develop consumption and die at an early age. Such of them as are mothers, infect their children also. Segregation of cases affected by tuberculosis is almost impossible. Mothers won't leave the children alone. They must have them by their side.

The hardships from which our women suffer, react most injuriously on the condition of men too. We put up with all kinds of tyranny and impudence from others, because we are in the habit of making others put up with such things at our hands. Our women are extremely shy and dependent. Modesty is a great virtue, but not so helplessness and dependence. I want the Hindu woman to retain her modesty, her selflessness, her devotion to duty towards her children and her man, but at the same time I want her to learn a bit of self-assertiveness. People who lack in that quality can never be free. They are always looking to others for protection. It is not praiseworthy to be offensive and aggressive, but it does not pay to be always on the defensive. There are occasions in life when one has to take the offensive if one wants to save one's life and liberty. Offensiveness in such a condition is really another name for self-preservation. The ancient history of the Hindus proves that in ancient times, Hindu women were more independent, more assertive, more self-reliant and physically more competent than they are now. They were as free as men, and their children were brave, kind, self-confident and able bodied. If the Hindus want to get out of the slump in which they find themselves at present, they must attend to and improve their women.

A craze has set in for University diplomas and degrees. These examinations are a great curse. Yet the best among our educated people are mad after examinations. I place no limitations on women's right to knowledge and scholarship but diplomas and degrees do not necessarily produce these results. Woman is the goddess of home, but she is also the presiding genius of social life. To educate her is pre-eminently desirable but that kind of doubtful education that is a passport for diplomas and degrees is not only not necessary for her, but is even undesirable. The present system of education is a great drain even on boys' health. Much more must it be so in the case of girls. But our people are crazy after degrees. The first two words of the English alphabet have a charm for them which they can't disregard. Oh! how fallen and how helpless we are! We cannot even give suitable education to our girls because we cannot start and maintain good and well-equipped institutions of our own for their education. If we could establish and maintain national Vidya Pithas for our girls, we would bestow a real boon on the nation. I will beg of my countrymen to save their girls, to give them suitable opportunities for developing healthy bodies, and psychologically fit minds. Our girls and women must be freed from all superstitions which breed carelessness in life, indifference to food, distaste for struggle, lack of energy, the habit of taking things lying down and a psychology of dependence and fear. Let me not be misunderstood. There is nothing so hateful as a quarrelsome, unnecessarily assertive, impudent, ill-mannered woman but even if that were the only road which the Hindu woman must traverse in order to be an efficient, courageous, independent and physically fit mother, I would prefer it to the existing state of things. In concluding this part of my address, I will say to my countrymen. "Your women are your makers, save them and educate them."

Friends, I think I have already taken too much of your time. I will briefly put in a categorical form; the chief points I have sought to press on your attention in this address:

1. *The need of and justification for the Hindu Sanghathan.*
2. *Opening the life of Dwijas to the Non-Brahmans.*
3. *The immediate removal of untouchability and the uplift of the Sudras.*
4. *Immediate improvement in the conditions of Hindu women and provision for their education.*
5. *Taking necessary steps to prevent the division of the Hindu community into different political compartments.*

Presidential addresses by Lala Lajpat Rai at Hindu Mahasabha annual meetings, The Indian Quarterly Register, vol. 1, January-June 1925, pp. 377-85. as Reported (1925) 38

Lala Lajpat Rai in the course of his Presidential Address said: "The Hindus have no political aims of their own separate from those of their countrymen of other faiths. There was a time when good many of the Hindu leaders wanted the Hindus to abstain from all political activity and to engage only in religious exercises. That class has now almost disappeared. But another class has come to the front who hold out that Hindu leaders have injured the Hindu community by taking to too much anti-government political activities and by raising the standard of Swaraj, and that it is time that we should make up with the Government and give up all anti-government activities. I am afraid I cannot agree with them. I am not at all sorry for the part the Hindu leaders have so far played in the development of the movement of freedom. The future historian of India will I hope, give them credit for their activities in this direction. It must be understood that no living nation can avoid politics. Politics is the very breath of associated life and political activities of a healthy kind are absolutely necessary for social progress and national prosperity. In this respect the following quotation from the MahaBharata ought to be very carefully borne in mind by such Hindu leaders as preach to us political inactivity:

When Politics become lifeless, the triple Veda sinks, all the Dharmas (i.e., the basis of civilization) (howsoever) developed, completely decay.

When traditional State-Ethics are departed from, all the divisions of individual life are shattered, In Politics are realised all the forms of renunciation, in Politics are united all Sacraments, in Politics are combined all knowledge; in Politics are centred all the Worlds'. Mahabharata Shantiparva-63-28-29.

Political activities are of two kinds anti-government and pro-government. It will be foolish to oppose Government for the sake of opposition. It will be equally foolish to support Government with the object of individual or communal gain. The Hindus have so far followed a National policy and, I think, they must stick to that. They will be stultifying themselves if they replace their nationalism by communism. Yet we cannot ignore the fact that there are some communities in India who want to take undue advantage of our nationalism and are pushing forward their communalism to such an extent as is injurious to the interests of the whole nation and certainly disastrous to those of the Hindu community. Such communalism we are bound to oppose as, in our judgment, it can only lead to permanent slavery, permanent disunity and a state of perpetual dependence.

Hindus do not Want a Hindu Raj: "There is some apprehension in the mind of a certain section of our Muslim countrymen that the Hindus are working for a Hindu Raj. It is to be deplored that some Hindus, too, should have taken to that line of argument in retaliation to the Mohammedan cry for Muslim Raj. We know that all Mohammedans do not want a Muslim Raj, and we also know as a fact that the bulk of the Hindus do not want a Hindu Raj. What the latter are striving after is a National Government founded on justice to all communities, all classes and all interests. In my judgment, the cry of a Hindu Raj or a Muslim Raj is purely mischievous and ought to be discouraged.

'Some time ago I had the occasion to read in one of the Muslim papers an article on Muslim Raj. The writer dismissed the idea of establishing Muslim Raj by the help of foreign Mohammedan states, such as Kabul and Turkey. And he also dismissed the idea of establishing a Muslim Raj by deceiving the Hindus into a unity for turning out the British and then establishing a Muslim Raj. But he actually advocated the policy of co-operation with the Government which might in the course of time lead that Government to hand over their power to the Muslims as the best organised and the most powerful body of men fit to rule. It seems to me that the writer has done great injustice to the Mohammedans by this line of argument as his conclusion seems to be more in the interests of Anglo-India than of the Muslim community. I am confident that this conclusion is not shared by the whole Mohammedan community, though unfortunately the utterances and actions of some of the foremost Muslim leaders do lend colour to it. Anyway, I am clear in my mind that neither a Hindu Raj nor a Muslim Raja is in the realm of possibility. The correct thing for us to do is to strive for a democratic Raj in which the Hindus, Muslims and the other communities of India may participate as Indians and not as followers of any particular religion.

So far as Politics are concerned, the Hindu Mahasabha has no special political functions except to define the position of the community in relation to other communities. The Hindus as a community are opposed to communal representation as such in any shape or form. The preponderance of opinion seems to be that the Lucknow Pact was a mistake but it is wrong to represent, as has been done by Mr. M.A. Jinnah recently at Aligarh, that the Hindus are altogether opposed to revision or reconsideration of the Lucknow Pact. In conversations at Delhi, the position of the Hindu representatives was that they would accept any uniform principle of representation applicable to the whole of India subject to one consideration that the electorates in all cases should be mixed and that the principle of communal representation shall not be extended beyond the legislature. In face of this to say that the Hindus as such are opposed to any compromise is not true. I do not consider that an understanding between the Hindus and the Mohammedans is impossible, but it must be clearly understood that the Hindus will not submit to any coercion whatsoever in arriving at some settlement. No amount of riots and disturbances will make them enter into any agreement which they do not consider fair and just.

The Problem of North-West Frontier-The Fear of Invasion: It is said that the Hindus are very much obsessed by a fear of the Indian Mohammedans making a common cause with the Mohammedan Powers beyond the North West Frontier to establish Mohammedan dominions in India. In this connection we have been assured by some Mohammedan leaders that the apprehension is absolutely unfounded, and is in fact a reflection on their patriotism. They are as much interested in the independence of India of any foreign control, be it a Mohammedan or a non-Mohammedan, as the Hindus. I have no doubt that this assurance is perfectly bonafide and *sincere as far as it goes. But there is no guarantee that the Mohammedans of the North West Frontier Province, the Punjab and Sindh, are likely to take the same view if any such situation arises. If anything, the indications are to the contrary. We have several evidences of the mentality of the Frontier Mohammedans in this respect. Some Mohammedans have already suggested that all the territories which lie between Peshawar and Agra should be handed over to the Mohammedans in which they might establish Mohammedan Government as a member of the Mohammedan League of Nations. At the last session of the Muslim League held at Bombay, M. Mohammad Ali actually suggested that the Mohammedans of the Frontier Province should have the right of self-determination to chose between an affiliation with India or with Kabul.*

'*Now I have reasons to believe that this opinion is shared by a large number of Mohammedans in the Frontier Province and the Punjab and Sindh. In the light of this evidence, the Hindu apprehension cannot be dismissed as entirely unfounded. The question of the Frontier very important to the whole of India and it specially concerns the safety and security of the Hindu community. It is not right to say that the territories beyond Indus were taken possession of by the British Government from the Mahomedans. Just like Alsace-Lorraine, the territories between the Indus and Peshawar have continuously been changing hands in the historical period and have been a bone of contention between the Government of India and other Governments situated beyond Peshawar. Speaking historically, they have been for a larger part of the historical period a portion of the Indian territories than otherwise. There was a time when all the territories between Indus and the eastern boundary of Persia proper formed part of the Indian province of the Iranian Empire.*

Then came the Empire of the Hindu Morians which included all these territories as a part of the Indian Empire. On the rise of Islam, the Moslem Generals of the Khalifa conquered these territories from the Hindus and the several sovereigns of the Ghazni families fought pitched battles with the Hindus on the North West Frontier side to Peshawar. Since then the territories comprising the North West Frontier Province have often been changing hands. They have several times been in the possession of Afghans, at others, formed part of the Indian Empire. The Sikhs held possession of these territories as a part of their Empire, and the British Government took possession of these provinces from the Sikhs. So far as Hindus are concerned, the question is one of pure Frontier defence and should be judged purely on its merits as such. The Hindus do not desire any domination over the Mohammedan population. What they want is the safeguarding of their interests and that of India generally.

I have nothing more to say about politics. Real politics must be left to political associations like the Congress and the Liberal League. The Hindus must not on any account give up the Congress. That would be prejudicial to the best interests of the country, and the Hindu Sabhas should make no encroachment on the province of the Congress, except so far as purely communal questions are concerned.

Sangathan: The Hindu community is being furiously attacked on all sides on account of the Sangathan movement. I can see no justification in these attacks. Every religious community is trying to unify itself and organise itself in different ways. It is true that the Hindus have so far neglected that work, but if they have learnt the lesson from the example of other communities and are doing the right thing towards their own community, no one has a right to find fault with them on that ground. Looking at the history of Hindu Sangathan movement, it is not a new movement at all though it has taken a more tangible shape now and for obvious reasons. It is the duty of the Hindus to organise themselves and bring about unity of action in their relations with other communities and the Government. The Hindu Mahasabha stands for this unity of action and I appeal to all the different sections of the Hindu community to lay aside their difference and unite under the flag of the Hindu Mahasabha. We must recognize the common dangers, both internal and external. The external dangers I have already referred to. The internal dangers are still more formidable. We are too much dis-united on account of the divisions and sub-divisions of the community into so many creeds and castes. Now I have no intention of finding fault with any creed or caste. But we must recognise the necessity of all-round fusion for the purpose of meeting common dangers and performing common duties. The community must realise the absolute necessity of internal consolidation for the purpose of getting sufficiently strong to live its own life and not lag behind other communities in progress and in numbers. We cannot afford to lose very many of our people. The old game of throwing out people on very small pretences must be given up and occasions must be sought to bring people back into our fold without injuring anybody's scruples. Depressed Classes: I will take the Depressed Classes first. The Depressed Classes, it is said, number about six or seven crores, but these numbers are unreliable. The figures have been swelled either intentionally or unintentionally. There are many classes included under this heading who are not untouchables anyway. Again there are some classes who are untouchables in one province and not so in another. If we were to take the figures of those who are untouchables in all provinces, the number will dwindle down to a very small figure. Now I beg of the Hindu community to remove the untouchability of all because it is wrong to consider any human being as untouchable, particularly when he belongs to one's own religion; in any case there ought to be no untouchability in relation to those classes who are not uniformly untouchables throughout India. There is a great deal of controversy between the orthodox people and those who favour the entire removal of untouchability about the extent to which untouchability should be removed. Personally, I am in favour of untouchability being removed altogether. Personally, I will go much farther than the minimum laid down by the Hindu Mahasabha at its Special Session held at Allahabad. But with the object of conciliating my orthodox brothers, I will not urge upon the Mahasabha to go farther. I think it should be left to the Provincial Sabhas to consult Hindu opinion in their Provinces with regard to the actual steps they would sanction for the removal of untouchability and the uplift of the Depressed Classes. This should satisfy the orthodox opinion because they can do what they think best in their spheres of influence with regard to this matter. But there is a great danger in our continual neglect of these classes. There are other people out to absorb them who have greater secular influence and larger resources to take them into their own folds. For the Hindus at this stage to neglect the Depressed Classes will be simply suicidal and I will beg of them to take a broader view of the question than they may be inclined to do on the ground of their religious scruples. One glory of Hinduism consists in its adaptability to the circumstances of the times, and but for this the Hindus would have been nowhere by this time. They would have been absorbed by other communities and would have disappeared. The crying need of the time is to adapt ourselves to the exigencies of the present. We can at least all join together in providing education and economic facilities for the uplift of the Depressed Classes. In this respect all credit is due to those Hindu philanthropists who with great sacrifice and labour are working in this cause.

Lala Lajpat Rai on Dalits and Conversions

There can be no denying the fact that the rigidity of the Hindu caste system is the bane of Hindu society. It is a great barrier in the way of the social and national progress of Hindus. It confronts them at every step and slackens the speed with which, otherwise, the nation would climb up to the heights of national solidarity. The condition of the 'low' castes, sometimes described as 'untouchables', at other times as the 'depressed classes' is nothing short of disgraceful. It is a disgrace to our humanity, our sense of justice, and our feeling of social affinity. It is useless to hope for any solidarity so long as the depressed classes continue to be so low in the social scale as they are. The intellectual and moral status of the community as a whole cannot be appreciably raised without the co-operation of all the classes forming the community. So then, as there are classes amongst us who are untouchable by the so-called superior classes, because of their having been born of certain parents, the moral and intellectual elevation of the community as a whole can only proceed by slow, very slow, degrees. The condition of the depressed classes is a standing blot on our social organization, and we must remove that blot if we are really desirous of securing the efficiency of our social organism. All parts of the whole must be raised, not necessarily to the same level but to a level from which they can, by their individual efforts, talents and achievements, rise to the highest possible position, within the reach of members of the social organism.

The present arrangement is a cruel and unjust arrangement. Besides, it is both economically and politically unsound. A community which allows so much valuable human material to rot in a state of utter depression and helplessness, cannot be said to be economically wise. As to the political danger involved by the continuance of these classes in their present condition, one need only look at the arguments advanced by our friends of the Muslim League in support of their contention for a larger representation on the Legislative Councils than they are entitled to by virtue of their numerical strength. Quite ignoring the fact that they are as much affected by these classes as the Hindus, they make it a point to say that in counting the Hindus for the purposes of representation the untouchables enumerated with them should be excluded. Whatever may be the value of this argument for the purpose for which it is used, there can be no doubt that the existence of these classes in their present deplorable condition is a menace to the power and influence of the Hindu community. The line of argument adopted by our Muslim friends and by some missionary critics of the Reforms Scheme, ought to open the eyes of the Hindus to the absolute necessity and urgency of raising the social status of their fellow-religionists, called and known as the members of the depressed classes. Thus from every point of view, whether that of humanity, justice or fair play, or that of self-interest, it is the bounden duty of the so-called high-caste Hindus to give a helping hand to their brothers of the 'low castes' and raise them socially as well as intellectually. We are living in a democratic age. The tendencies of democracy are towards the levelling down of all inequalities.

That there are forces working amongst us which will sooner or later demolish all artificial barriers due to accidents of birth between man and man, is patent to all far-sighted people. Under any circumstances, then, the day of the depressed classes is bound to come. If so, would it not be wise to take time by the forelock, and to take in hand, in all willingness, what other forces, which are not in our control, must perforce bring about? I say this not because I have the least doubt about the shocking injustice involved in the existing arrangements, but because it is perfectly legitimate to point out the moral of our neglecting to do what is right and by the weight of that moral to ask people to avoid the evil consequences of letting the forces of nature to have their own revenge. Morality requires that we should take to the work of elevating the depressed classes out of a sheer sense of justice and humanity regardless of any outside considerations. But to appeal in the name of expediency, when the latter strengthens the demands of morality and humanity, involves no breach of principle, and we may very well point out that the communal interest of the Hindus also lies that way. There are agencies at work which are doing their best to remove these Hindus from the pale of Hinduism, which, bereft of these classes, might live, but only as an exhausted frame. The classes themselves are anxious to remain Hindus even though the latter may not promise them the fullest social privileges which they may be in a position to obtain by change of religion. The only thing for Hinduism to do is to meet them halfway at once and remove at least the principal grounds of their depression. The least that we can do without delay is to make the untouchables touchable and take away the sting out of their names. Hindu who is not prepared to do even this is an enemy to the community, however unconscious he may be of the great injury he is causing it thereby. I confess, we, the educated Hindus, are not doing our duty in the matter honestly and manfully. Most of our time and energies are employed in agitating for trivial political rights, the good of which can at best be remote, to the neglect of questions upon the right solution of which depends our immediate safety as a nation. I am only repeating what I have already said times out of number, that the work of nation-building must be begun from below. The nation that has to be built up lives in huts and not in palaces. Legislative Councils principally composed of the latter are not likely to be the best instruments of building the nation from below. I say this without in any way disparaging the agitation to obtain more legislative powers. But I cannot help saying that to me there seems to be a lack of proportion in the importance that is being attached to a scheme which for the present at least altogether ignores the masses as well as the lower middle classes.

II

In educated circles there seems to be fairly practical unanimity as to the inherent injustice and monstrosity of the existing system; nay, even further, there seems to be an agreement as to the desirability of taking steps to elevate the moral, material and social condition of the caste system. What stands in the way of progress in this direction, however, is the prejudice of the illiterate and the apathy of the educated classes. The former are wanting in that broad outlook on human affairs without which the consciousness of a sense of corporate social responsibility is slow to awaken, the latter lack in that backbone without which it is impossible to bring about changes which look radical but the absence of which blocks the avenues that lead to national consciousness and national solidarity.

For the latter purpose what is required is fairness and humanity at least, if not perfect equality in the relations of the different units that compose the social organism.

At the present moment the greatest strength of the Hindus consists in their number. It is true that intellectually and educationally, in trade and commerce, in brain and body, in mind and muscle, in the arts of peace and war, they are second to none. But in their numerical strength lies that power which is not shared by any other community in this country. This numerical strength, however, may easily be converted into the chief source of their weakness if not properly organised for national purposes. At first sight the Hindus look a heterogeneous mass of untidy humanity without any ties to bind them to one another. Their lack of homogeneity is their curse. To an outsider they seem to agree in nothing. Caste and inter-caste jealousies block the way to progress. The energies which should be spent in bringing about solidarity are being spent in rearing up individuality in the different social units which make up the community. The Brahman, the Khatri, the Banya, the Kayastha, the Rajput, the Jat; among Brahmans the Gaur, the Sandhya, the Nagar, the Kanaujia; &c &c. are all dominated by separatist tendencies. Their collective ambition moves in the circumscribed circle of their own little group, which gives a sectional or rather only a sub-sectional colour to their patriotism or nationalism, but what is even worse is their attitude towards the lower classes and the latter's attempt to retaliate. The former's denial of equal or any opportunities of worship to the latter in their temples or shrines is a standing disgrace to the good name of Hinduism. The so much boasted of tolerance of the Hindus disappears the moment that tolerance is demanded by the classes lower in the social scale. The high-caste Hindus of the present day, men who have received their education under Western ideals, are often heard to speak with pride of the spirit of toleration possessed and shown by Hinduism towards other religions and other communities, but a critic may very well say that this toleration is the offspring of fear or greed. You dare not be uncivil or unkind to Mohammedans or Christians because they can make matters unpleasant for you, but you are insolent towards your own people, whom you think you can defy without any fear of retaliation. The consequences are plain and can be seen even running. The Hindus are going down in numbers. Your insolence towards the lower classes of Hindus is being repaid by the latter running [sic] their back on you. Mohammedanism and Christianity are extending their arms to embrace them and indications are not wanting of the readiness of the lower classes of Hindus to accept the hospitality of non-Hindu religions and social systems. Why, the reason is obvious. As a Hindu you won't touch him; you would not let him sit on the same carpet with you, you would not offer him water in your cups, you would not accept water or food touched by him; you would not let him enter your temples, in fact you would not treat him like a human being. The moment, however, he becomes a Mohammedan or a Christian, without even giving up his ancestral occupation you are all smiles to him, you welcome him to your home; and have no objection at times to offer him drink and food in utensils etc. It is a deep-rooted sentiment that has so far prevented the depressed classes of Hindus from deserting Hinduism en-masse [sic]. Sentiments are, however, melting away before the matter-of-fact civilization of the West. The time does not seem to be very distant when sentiment will cease to control the desire of the depressed classes to better their social position, if it cannot be had otherwise than by a change of faith. There are circumstances and causes in the environments of these classes which are working with effect to bring about that consummation and if the Hindus want to avoid that catastrophe, it is time that they subordinated there caste-pride to the exigencies of the situation and took time by the forelock..

These quotations should leave no doubt in the mind of any Hindu as to the urgency and importance of the question of improving the lot of the depressed classes and of raising their social status. I am of opinion that the matter should be taken in hand in each province by influential provincial committees composed of men of provincial reputation.

Depressed classes missions for smaller area should be organised under the guidance and control of these committees and the work pushed through with earnestness and zeal. The sympathies of young men should be enlisted, from whom eventually some may be inclined to make it their life-work. The subject has an important bearing on famine relief and the development of home industries, from which point of view I intend to discuss it in another article.

Hindu Sabha a Unifying Force

Lala Lajpat Rai addressed a crowded audience at Madras conference on the lines of Hindu reorganisation. He said that while not deprecating communal organisation for social and religious reform, it was his view that political communal organisations must of necessity produce an atmosphere antagonistic to the growth of national feeling. However, after reading the proceedings of the last session of the Muslim League and the Khilafat Conference, he was convinced that the time had come for Hindus also to organise themselves on communal lines. He regarded the Hindu Sabha as unifying force among the Hindus as its platform is open to all Hindus irrespective of caste and creed and also to Buddhists, Jains and Sikhs. He did not want the Hindu Sabha to supplant the National Congress or lower its prestige or influence, and for this purpose it was necessary that the Sabha should not deal with political questions, but should confine itself to matters communal. He saw no reason why staunch Hindu Congressmen should not take the same interest in the Sabha as Mahomed Ali and Shaukat Ali and other leaders took in Muslim league. The main work of the Hindu Sabha, he said, should be to strengthen and organise the Hindu community in every respect, and he also indicated the various ways in which the Sabha could work for the welfare of the community, such as organising relief for sufferers from communal disturbances, taking steps to improve the physical condition of Hindus, uplifting of the depressed classes and the untouchables, etc.

He pleaded for the public trial of Sir Michael O'Dwyer, who was responsible for the Jallianwallah Bagh atrocities. Through he presided over the special session of the Congress at Calcutta, which was attended by a number of liberal, leaders, in the same year, Gandhiji's technique of Satyagraha did not appeal to him and he opposed the boycott of schools and Courts. He displayed dignity and decorum in conducting the proceedings. He condemned shouting down moderates and checked a speaker from denouncing Jews. At the same time, he supported the Khilafat agitation.

In the elections to the Central Assembly, he drifted away from the Congress and joined hands with Malaviya, Dr.Moonje, Kelkar and Jayakar and formed the Nationalist Party. When Miss Mayo brought out her notorious book "Mother India" aptly described by Mahatma Gandhi as a drain inspector's report, Lalaji gave a sitting reply through his well-documented work entitled 'Unhappy India'. Besides, he wrote stirring biographies of Lord Krishna, Chatrapati Shivaji, Swami Dayananda Saraswati, Mazzini and Garibald. Besides being a Director of the Punjab National Bank, he founded textile mills in collaboration with Lala Harikishen Lal, known as Napoleon of Indian finance, and facilitated industrialisation of the country.

Lajpat Rai was a heavyweight veteran leader of the Indian Nationalist Movement, Indian independence movement led by the Indian National Congress, Hindu reform movements and Arya Samaj, who inspired young men of his generation and kindled latent spirit of patriotism in their hearts with journalistic writings and lead-by-example activism. Young men in the independence movement, such as Chandrasekhar Azad and Bhagat Singh, were inspired by Lajpat Rai.

In 1928, the United Kingdom set up the Simon Commission, headed by Sir John Simon to report on the political situation in India. The commission was boycotted by Indian political parties because it did not include any Indian members, and it was met with country-wide protests. When the Commission visited Lahore on 30 October 1928, Lajpat Rai led a non-violent march in protest against it and gave the slogan "Simon Go Back!". The protesters chanted the slogan and carried black flags.

The police superintendent in Lahore, James A. Scott, ordered the police to lathi charge the protesters and personally assaulted Rai. Despite being severely injured, Rai subsequently addressed the crowd and said "I declare that the blows struck at me today will be the last nails in the coffin of British rule in India".

Rai did not fully recover from his injuries and died on 17 November 1928. Doctors thought that James Scott's blows had hastened his death. However, when the matter was raised in the British Parliament, the British government denied any role in Rai's death. Bhagat Singh, an HSRA revolutionary who was a witness to the event, swore to avenge the death of Rai, who was a significant leader of the Indian independence movement. He joined other revolutionaries, Shivaram Rajguru, Sukhdev Thapar and Chandra Shekhar Azad, in a plot to kill Scott to send a message to the British government. However, in a case of mistaken identity, Singh was signalled to shoot on the appearance of John P. Saunders, an assistant superintendent of the Lahore Police. He was shot by Rajguru and Singh while leaving the District Police Headquarters in Lahore on 17 December 1928. Chanan Singh, a head constable who was chasing them, was fatally injured by Azad's covering fire.

This case did not stop Singh and his fellow-members of the Hindustan Socialist Republican Association from claiming that retribution had been exacted.[39]

Young revolutionaries Bhagat Singh, Rajguru and Sukhdev, attempted to wreak vengeance on Saunders, they were implicated in Lahore Conspiracy Case and sent to gallows. He was selfless to the core. When a purse of over a lakh of rupees was presented to him as a mark of appreciation for his public life, he created a public trust with that amount. He won laurels as a religious and social reformer, patriot, spell-binding orator, finished writer and distinguished journalist, working on many fronts with crusading zeal and became a tribune of his people fighting British imperialism to the last breath of his life. His life is the history of India during an epoch-making period of evolution of our national renaissance. He lived and died like a hero.

Madan Mohan Malaviya

In any age, only few are privileged to make history; of those, some conceive great and noble things for the benefit of their fellow beings, and some are given the good fortune to see their noble conceptions adequately realised by their efforts during their lifetime itself. Pandit Madan Mohan Malaviya was one of those who fulfilled their mission during their lifetime.

Madan Mohan Malaviya (25 December 1861—12 November 1946) was an Indian scholar, educational reformer and politician notable for his role in the Indian independence movement. He was president of the Indian National Congress four times and the founder of Akhil Bharat Hindu Mahasabha. He was addressed as Pandit, a title of respect, and also as Mahamana (Great Soul).

He was born at Prayag (Allahabad) on December 25, 1861, in a family of Sanskrit scholars noted for piety and devotion. Since his forefathers came from Malwa, members of this clan came to be known as Malaviyas. After graduation, he worked as a teacher for some time. On taking the Law Degree, his career was one of striking success at the Bar. His life was remarkable in a variety of ways.

When public life was a hobby and a sort of relaxation to upper classes, he took it seriously and became a whole time and whole-hearted devotee, sacrificing lucrative practice at the Bar. Such a turn in his life was neither an accident not a plunge. He took to public life as a duck takes to water. When he spoke at the second session of the Congress in 1886 at Calcutta, Dadabhai Naoroji, who presided over the Session, complimented him thus: "Mother India is herself resonant in the voice of this young man." [40]

Malaviya started his political career in 1886 with an address to the Indian National Congress session in Calcutta. Malaviya would go on to become one of the most powerful political leaders of his time, being elected Congress president on four occasions.

In December 1886, Malaviya attended the second Indian National Congress session in Calcutta under the chairmanship of Dadabhai Naoroji, where he spoke on the issue of representation in Councils. His address not only impressed Dadabhai, but also Raja Rampal Singh, ruler of Kalakankar estate near Allahabad, who had founded a Hindi weekly, Hindustan, but was still looking for a suitable editor to turn it into a daily. In July 1887, Malaviya resigned from the school and joined as editor of the nationalist weekly. He remained for two and a half years, and left for Allahabad to study for his L.L.B. In Allahabad, he was offered the co-editorship of The Indian Opinion, an English daily. After finishing his law degree, he started practicing law at Allahabad District Court in 1891 and moved to Allahabad High Court by December 1893. Bharat Dharma Mahamandala was a prominent Hindu organization founded by Pandit Din Dayalu Sharma in Hardwar in 1887, Scholars from all over the country were present during its formation ,Madan Mohan Malviya was also part of this group.Its objective was to bring together all leaders of the orthodox Hindu community and to work together for the preservation of Sanatan Dharma.The offshoots of the Mahamandala were the Sanatan Dharma Sabhas(1895), founded for the defense of Hinduism from critics both within the community and outside it. In the early years of the 20th century, Pandit Madan Mohan Malaviya was very closely associated with the Mahamandala and the Sanatan Dharma movements.

Malaviya became the President of the Indian National Congress in 1909, a position he held also in 1918 and 1932. He was a moderate leader and opposed separate electorates for Muslims under the Lucknow Pact of 1916. The "Mahamana" title was conferred on him by Mahatma Gandhi. An unflinching supporter and leader of the anti-British struggle, he participated in the anti-Rowlatt Satyagraha, mobilised parties and groups for the Simon-boycott and the Civil Disobedience movement. He worked closely with Gandhi during the Second Round Table Conference. He was also instrumental in bringing about the Poona Pact and was a signatory to it. However, he was opposed to the principle of separate electorate and to the integration of Khilafat question with the Non-Cooperation movement. He disagreed with the idea of boycott of educational institutions, disliked the Swarajist policy of entering the legislatures and then creating obstructions, and stood up against the Communal Award as also the Congress's attitude of indecisiveness on it. Gandhi and Malaviya remained life-long associates fondly addressing each other as brothers. Gandhi even considered Malaviya as his conscience keeper, referring to him as Dharmatma [righteous soul]. Both were outstanding social and political leaders, and their life and discourse defied the conventional logic (or rather definition) of modernity. Both charted, in one way or the other, independent paths in their life. Malaviya, though being a leader of the Congress and the Hindu Mahasabha, would tow an independent line if he was not convinced of the party-line on important questions affecting the progress of the nation.

Malaviya renounced his practice of law in 1911 to fulfil his resolve to serve the causes of education and social service. Despite this vow, on one occasion, when 177 freedom fighters were convicted to be hanged in the Chauri-chaura case, he appeared before the court and won the acquittal of 156 freedom fighters. He followed the tradition of Sannyasa throughout his life, adhering to his avowed commitment to live on the support of society. Malaviya strove to promote modern education among Indians and co-founded the Banaras Hindu University (BHU) at Varanasi in 1916.

He was a member of the Imperial Legislative Council from 1912 until 1919, when it was converted to the Central Legislative Assembly, of which he remained a member until 1926. Malaviya was an important figure in the Non-cooperation movement. He was opposed to the politics of appeasement and the participation of Congress in the Khilafat movement.

In 1928, he joined Lala Lajpat Rai, Jawaharlal Nehru, and many others in protesting against the Simon Commission, which had been set up by the British to consider India's future. Just as the "Buy British" campaign was sweeping England, he issued a manifesto on 30 May 1932 urging concentration on the "Buy Indian" movement in India. Malaviya was a delegate at the Second Round Table Conference in 1931.

During the Salt March, he was arrested on 25 April 1932 along with 450 other Congress volunteers in Delhi, only a few days after he was appointed as the President of Congress, following the arrest of Sarojini Naidu. In 1933, at Calcutta, Malaviya was again appointed as the President of the Congress. Before Independence, Malaviya was the only leader of the Indian National Congress to be appointed as its president for four terms.

On 24 September 1932, an agreement known as Poona Pact was signed between Dr. B R Ambedkar (on behalf of the depressed classes among Hindus) and Mahatma Gandhi (on behalf of the other Hindus). The agreement guaranteed reserved seats for the depressed classes in the Provisional legislatures within the general electorate, and not by creating a separate electorate. Due to the pact, the depressed class received 148 seats in the legislature, instead of the 71 as allocated in the Communal Award proposal of the British Prime Minister Ramsay MacDonald. After the pact, the Communal Award was modified to include the terms as per the pacts. The text uses the term "Depressed Classes" to denote Untouchables among Hindus who were later called Scheduled Castes and Scheduled Tribes under India Act 1935, and in the Indian Constitution of 1950.

In protest against the Communal Award, to provide separate electorates for minorities, Malaviya and Madhav Shrihari Aney left the Congress and started the Congress Nationalist Party. The party contested the 1934 elections to the central legislature and won 12 seats.

As a publicist, he was a striking success. Having edited "HINDUSTAN" in Hindi, he founded "THE LEADER," an English Daily, at Allahabad, which quickly became a power to be reckoned with in upper India under the able editorship of C. Y. Chintamani. He preferred to go out instead of easing out the Editor when differences arose. Later on, he shouldered the burden of guiding the "HINDUSTAN TIMES' at Delhi as Chairman of the Board of Directors.

Besides his services to Allahabad as city father and to Uttar Pradesh as its representative in the Provincial Council, he was all along an all-India figure. He never became a back-number. He presided over two annual sessions of the Congress before the advent of Gandhiji, besides being elected as President of two banned Sessions at Calcutta and Delhi. He braved the rigours of jail life and crossed the seas to plead for Indian freedom at the Second Round Table Conference. He was always respected by the people and powers-that-be.

As a parliamentarian, he rose to his full stature in the old Imperial Legislative Council and the Central Assembly. By virtue of his social charm, unruffled dignity and urbane eloquence, he was a model and a marvel of his contemporaries. His speeches on Sedition Bill, Press Laws and Imperial Preference became historic. He was impeccably dressed in white robes with a turban.

Education claimed his attention from the beginning. He realised his life's dream of founding the Banaras Hindu University when Annie Besant handed over to him the Central Hindu College founded by her. He soon made it a nationalist institution in 1916, with Sir Sunder Lal as Vice-Chancellor. Sir P.S. Sivaswami Iyer succeeded him. Alfred King, an Englishman, was appointed as Principal of the Engineering College. The professoriate was drawn from every part of the country. He assumed charge as founder Vice-Chancellor. It became catholic in character and composition. He passed on his mantle as Vice Chancellor to the eminent educationist, Dr.S. Radhakrishnan, even while being alive. Thus, he had always the best interest of the institution at heart. He was indeed the finest flower of Hindu culture, radiating fragrance far and wide, and was aptly called 'Dharmatma.'

The University is a fitting monument for his lifelong work. Religion and patriotism are the two pillars, on which the arch of the Hindu University rests. The Arya Samajists have their Mandir and Sikhs their Gurdwara and a mosque within its precincts. The University was the recipient of substantial benefactions from the Nawab of Rampur, Nawab of Chatrai, and Aga Khan. He blended ancient tradition with modern temper and was well-versed in our classics and epics. He was a puritan in private life.He did not lag behind the social reformers. His efforts for the uplift of Harijans were steady and sustained, and they were given special facilities and personal attention at the University. He evinced active interest in secular movements like scouting and founded the Hindustan Scouts Association, when he detected that the scout movement in India was becoming subservient to foreign rulers. He did not tolerate self-respect being trifled with.

During the national struggle, the Government of India stopped its annual grant to the University. The Maharajahs and business magnates also hesitated to extend the usual help. But the Maharanis passed on their valuable jewellery to Panditji to tide over the crisis. The self-sacrificing professoriate voluntarily cut their salaries. Such was the loyalty he commanded from one and all. Students regarded him as a father figure. Their respect for him bordered on reverence.

He was more than an elder statesman. He did not hesitate to found the Hindu Mahasabha when he was convinced that the vital interests of Hindus were being sacrificed in the guise of nationalism of placate communalism of the minorities. He also advocated reconversion to Hinduism of those who were earlier lured into Christianity and Islam. At the same time, he always strove for communal unity and respected all faiths.

In spite of ill-health, advancing years and incidental infirmities, he was always youth in spirit and served as an invaluable link between the younger and older generations. He was stout but sympathetic, unbending but open to conviction and, above all, just and even generous to his opponents. With the solitary and inevitable exception of Gandhiji, there is none in our history comparable to him for the range of public service or for an equal record of selfless dedication. He is justly regarded as one of the foremost makers of modern India.

Pandit Madan Mohan Malaviya was one of those who fulfilled their mission during their lifetime. Malaviya played an important part in the removal of untouchability and in giving direction to the Harijan movement. The Harijan Sevak Sangh was founded at a meeting in 1933 at which Pandit Malaviya presided.

Malaviya asserted – if you admit internal purity of human soul, you or your religion can never get impure or defiled in any way by touch or association with any man.

To solve the problem of untouchability, Malaviya followed a Hindu method, of giving Mantradīkshā to untouchables. He said, "Mantras would be a certain means of their upliftment socially, politically and spiritually." He worked for the eradication of caste barriers in temples and other social barriers. Malaviya contributed significantly to ensuring the entry of the so-called untouchables into any Hindu temple. In March 1936, Hindu Dalit (Harijan) leader, P. N. Rajbhoj, along with a group of 200 Dalit people demanded entry at the Kalaram Temple on a Rath Yatra day. Malaviya in the presence of priests of Kalaram Temple, gave diksha to the assembled people and facilitated their entry into the temple. They then also participated in the Rath Yatra of Kalaram Temple. On the issue of removal of untouchability, fighting the indentured labour system, promoting cow protection, popularising Hindi, upholding Swadeshi, showing faith in Sanatanism and imbibing simplicity in personal lives, Gandhi and Malaviya were on the same page. While Gandhi was focussed on politics as a leader of the Congress and engaged in social and constructive works through his unique ways, Malaviya would, apart from leading the Congress, also work in the Hindu Mahasabha, Sanatanist organisations such as the Bharat Dharma Mahamandal and the Sanatan Dharma Mahasabha, and advocate Hindu sangathan [organisational unity].

In any age, only few are privileged to make history; of those, some conceive great and noble things for the benefit of their fellow beings and some are given the good fortune to see their noble conceptions adequately realised by their efforts during their lifetime itself.[41]

Malaviya and Hindu Mahasabha:

Malaviya was one of the founder of Hindu Mahasabha. Malviya was President of Hindu Mahasabha thrice. The thrust of his speech was that the unity and amity among different communities could only be based on justice and fair play. It was therefore, the responsibility not only of the Hindus but also of others communities to work for that unity in India. An attempt in this direction was made in the famous Congress-League Pact of 1916, otherwise known as the Lucknow Pact. Malaviya was entirely opposed to the communal aspects of the pact but kept quiet largely because of the support extended to the measure by Tilak. However, the Hindu Mahasabha was dismayed by the stand taken by the Congress in 1916. It argued that if Tilak could make such concessions, others might go even further in this direction in future. Opposition to the Lucknow Pact was particularly strong in Punjab. The Punjab Hindu Sabha raised a hue and cry against the provisions of the pact in several meetings all over the province. However, keeping in view the all-India interest of forging communal harmony between the Hindus and Muslims, they did not demand the rejection of the measure. Even so, the provincial Hindu leaders expressed their disappointment at the soft stand taken by Malaviya and other senior leaders at the Lucknow Congress session.

The 1918 session of the Hindu Mahasabha later made a symbolic protest against the pact. When Gandhi decided to extend the support of the Congress to the Khilafat movement, Malaviya was in complete agreement with his move. One of the highlights of the Khilafat agitation was that the pioneer of the Hindu Mahasabha, Swami Shraddhanand, spoke at Jama Masjid to the Muslims of Delhi in favour of the Khilafat cause.

In its first phase, up to 1922, the Hindu Mahasabha was at best, an inter-provincial organization linking Hindu movements in UP and Punjab. As its conferences were held in conjunction with the annual Congress sessions, it attracted casual support from other provinces. Predominantly urban in character, it was concentrated in the larger trading cities of northern India. A small groups of professionals, mainly lawyers and the banking and landholding families, controlled the Mahasabha. The Hindu Mahasabha and the Congress had much in common as the same men who had been pioneers in the Congress also influenced the Mahasabha's activities.

Impact of Non Cooperation movement and other events:

The most alarming development after the sudden suspension of the non-cooperation movement was the increasing communal distrust, resulting in numerous Hindu-Muslim riots in different parts of the country. The Hindu-Muslim unity of the years of the non-cooperation movement was now a 'mere memory'; 'trust had given way to distrust' and 'there was a new bitterness in politics'. This was a sad anti-climax to the spirit of fraternization so assiduously built by Gandhi.

By bringing in the ulama (a body of Muslim scholars) and by overtly using a religious symbol, the Khilafat movement evoked religious emotions among the Muslim masses. Violent tendencies appeared in the Khilafat movement as the masses lost self-discipline and the leaders failed to control them. The worst case was the Moplah uprising in Malabar in August 1921, where the Moplah peasants, emboldened by the Khilafat spirit, rose against the Hindu landlords and the government. For months, the press in northern India was obsessed with detailed accounts of the forced conversions of Hindus in Malabar and with the means of reclaiming their lost brothers.

The question of forcible conversions was too sensitive, an issue for those involved and the nationalist leaders sought to minimize the divisive effects of the Moplah rebellion on the Hindus. In spite of their efforts, the reports of the atrocities and forcible conversions, whether exaggerated or not, stirred fears of violence among the Hindus. Thus the alliance between the Khilafat movement and the Congress proved artificial and short-lived. Furthermore, the alliance was responsible for the injection of an overdose of religion into politics. When the bubble of unity was burst-first by the Moplah atrocities in Malabar and then by the suspension of the non-cooperation movement by Gandhi, the two communities drifted apart and fell back to their old positions and whipped up old prejudices and fears with renewed vehemence. The result was that the Muslim League and the Hindu Mahasabha, whose activities were dormant during the days of non-cooperation, became more active with communalist politics.

The year 1922 was a turning point in the history of the Mahasabha, largely due to events which dramatized a Muslim threat to the Hindu community. In September 1922, there was a riot in Multan. At this time, Malaviya was in Punjab, investigating the Akali Sikh troubles of Guru Ka Bagh. Along with Rajendra Prasad and Hakim Ajmal Khan, Malaviya visited Multan as a member of the subcommittee appointed by the Congress. He addressed largely attended public meetings in Amritsar and Lahore and heard details of heart-rending incidents about the riots. He criticized Hindus for their failure to organize their own defence and proposed the formation of citizen guard units regardless of religious affiliations. He impressed upon the Hindus, the need for unity, with a view to resisting attacks on their lives and property.

The unfortunate result of the Moplah revolt in combination with the Multan riots was the increasing communal distrust between the two communities that led Malaviya to advise the Hindus to organize and defend themselves. Events that took place in 1922 and 1923 led to the revival of the Hindu Mahasabha into a full-fledged organisation.

Gaya Session of the Hindu Mahasabha:

The Hindu Mahasabha held its important annual conference at the Congress session grounds in Gaya in the last week of December 1922 with Rajendra Prasad as the chairman of the Reception Committee and Malaviya as its President. Malaviya set the tone of the session by terming the level of degeneration of the Hindu community, the worst of any in India, as evidenced by the low birth rate, high death rate, lower longevity, and cowardice in the face of attack. He blamed the Hindu weakness for the poor state of Hindu-Muslim relations. Malaviya maintained that the Hindu 'dharma' required that its followers be non-aggressive and show respect for all religious. It also required that they should give their lives, if necessary, in order to defend themselves when under attack. He proposed the formation of Hindu Sabhas in every village to promote Hindu unity and regeneration, which in turn would eventually contribute to the improvement of inter-communal relations. The resolutions adopted in the Mahasabha session echoed Malaviya's speech and evidenced a more militant stance. One of these called upon the Hindu religious leaders of Malabar to 'unhesitatingly re-embrace all the converts and restore them to their former caste and social status'. Another resolution called for an improved and extended network of Hindu organizations 'for the fulfilment of the first essential condition of attaining Swaraj viz. Hindu-Muslim unity as well as the self-preservation and religious safety of the Hindu community'.

In the first half of 1923, Hindu leaders were looking to the past and the future in the course of reassessing their strategies and goals. A general attitude becoming influential among Hindus that was cutting across political and religious lines was expressed in a newspaper editorial in the following words:

Banaras session of Hindu Mahasabha:

Contrary to earlier practice, the Hindu Mahasabha session held in Banaras in August 1923 did not coincide with the annual Congress session. In order to stimulate attendance, Malaviya published an appeal in which he referred to the 'lamentable condition of the Hindus', the 'inability of the community to defend itself', and held out the hope that 'the meeting at Benaras would consider the remedial measures as well as a series of important social and religious issues'. An estimated 1,500 delegates attended the Mahasabha session at Banaras and there were 4,000 visitors in attendance, including representatives of the Jain, Buddhist, Parsi, and Sikh communities. A Sanskrit motto over the gateway of the pandal warned that by killing religion, you are yourself killed and by protecting it, you are yourself protected. That may have indicated the spirit of the session, but giving shape to it in the deliberations, resolutions, and activities of the meeting proved to be a challenging task. Malaviya played a crucial role in moderating the views of diverse Hindu interests.

Defining the task before the conference, the chairman of the Reception Committee, Raja Moti Chand, pointed out that the Mahasabha's 'aim was to unite the different sects of Hindus in a bond of love'. A prominent participant, C.Y. Chintamani, desired that 'the result of the success of this movement would be not an increase in the differences between Hindus and Mahomedans but greater unification'.

In his long address, Malaviya began with the review of the history of the Hindus from ancient times to the Muslim conquest and British rule, and noted that in the latter period, the community had begun to suffer from many evils in its society. He stressed that strength and consolidation were the keys to repair the damage done to Hinduism, and proposed a number of restoratives including celibacy, minimum age for marriage, female education, and dowry expenses. Rejecting the charge that in seeking to reconstruct the society, Hindus had any sinister motives or designs against the Muslims, he declared, 'I solemnly affirm before God that I never mean to hurt Muslims or desire supremacy of Hindus over Muslims. If that be my sentiment God may give me the greatest punishment.' Nor was he prepared to agree that there was any valid reason for apprehensions regarding the fate and future of Hindu-Muslim unity in case the Hindu Mahasabha succeeded in its endeavours to breathe a new life and spirit into Hindu society. Malaviya repeatedly blamed a handful of bad elements for the Hindu-Muslim riots and called upon the Hindus to reorganize themselves against such elements in different parts of the country. He emphasized the need of harmonious communal relations between the two communities in the beginning as well as the concluding part of his presidential address.

He warned his supporters against insulting or showing any disrespect to other religions in the following words: 'Hindu-Muslim unity is an essential condition for the attainment of Swaraj. Therefore, look with reverence at places of worship of other religions' mosques and churches, speak with respect with followers of other religions, and give no cause of complaint in these respects.

The controversial issues before the conference were shuddhi (a process of purifying' certain Muslims and admitting them into the Hindu fold) and untouchability. As an arbiter behind the scenes, Malaviya attempted to assist the Sanatanists and the Arya Samajists to come to an agreement. A resolution proposed by Swami Shraddhanand that acknowledged the need for making arrangements to allow untouchables to draw water, enter schools and temples, and sit in public places. The resolution was adopted largely due to Malaviya's efforts. The shuddhi question was subjected to a similar compromise.

The Banaras session of the Mahasabha attracted attention all over India and various leading newspapers offered editorial comments. The Daily Express welcomed Malaviya's 'moving appeal', the Hindu wrote that the 'solemn presidential address' and the 'declaration of the Sabha of inter-communal unity ... leaves no room for apprehension in the matter'. The Amrita Bazar Patrika noted that there was 'great earnestness and enthusiasm' all along the session. The Indian Social Reformer was happy that the 'first blow has been struck' by Malaviya against Hindu orthodoxy. The Justice was of the view that 'it has to be gratefully acknowledged that Malaviya gave a right lead'. These leading newspapers of the country desired that the Hindu Mahasabha fight against the prevailing social evils of the Hindu society. However, the Urdu press expressed hostility to Malaviya's efforts from the very beginning. The Medina wrote that his effort was to 'annihilate Islam from India'.

Malaviya actively led the Mahasabha for five years from 1922 to 1927, attended its sessions, and was actively involved with its affairs. As one of its top-most leaders, Malaviya influenced the Mahasabha's decisions during these years. Therefore, it would be appropriate to probe his association with the Mahasabha during this period as well as his disenchantment from it thereafter. Since the membership of the Congress and the Mahasabha were not mutually exclusive, they often held their annual sessions together, with the result that a considerable number of Congressmen came under the influence of the Mahasabha. At the session, he urged the building of a small Hanuman temple and an akhara in every village and mohalla [urban quarter] of India.

The Hindu Mahasabha revival of 1923 was the product of developments of events in Punjab and UP and was closely linked with the re-awakening of religious enthusiasm in reaction to Khilafat revivalism. Its emphasis upon religious issues, shuddhi, and reclamation of untouchables was a response to the quickening pace of social reform within Hindu society. The Mahasabha worked to unite a variety of movements and carried out various activities through the Arya Samaj, the Sanatan Dharma Sabha, the Hindu societies, and various caste associations. The Mahasabha was still a loose organization, essentially a platform for the Hindu unity movement in northern India. A prominent Hindi nationalist weekly, Pratap, editorially commented that the Mahasabha was the 'natural result' of the understanding of those Hindus who thought that 'it was necessary for the Hindus to organize themselves against the attacks of Muslims'. The paper conceded that such an organization would necessarily be 'reactive' and 'confrontationist' in nature. [42]

Important resolution passed in Benares session in 1923 are:

Volunteer Corps: The Mahasabha Desires the formation of Hindu Volunteer corps at every village and town for the social service of the Hindu community and its protection when necessary and declares it to be the duty of the members of these corps to preserve peace and order in the locality in cooperation with followers of other religions.

Use of Swadeshi: The Hindu Mahasabha enjoins upon all Hindus in the interest of economic and religious welfare of country of using indigenous cloths and products.

Reclamation of Malkanas: The Mahasabha declare it to be perfectly legitimate and proper to retake such Malkana Hindus into the fold of Hinduism as have all along observed Hindu customs whether they are Rajput, Brahmans, Vaishyas, Jats, Gujjars or depressed classes or member of any other castes. [43]

Belgaum Session:

The next session of the Mahasabha was held at Belgaum in December 1924 at the same time and place as the annual session of the Congress, which was presided over by Gandhi. It was attended by several leading Congress leaders including Gandhi, Motilal Nehru, Lajpat Rai, C.R. Das, Satyamurti, Swami Shraddhanand. Malaviya dominated the proceedings and was delighted at the favourable response received from several provinces. Immediately after the Belgaum session, Malaviya gave the following account of the progress of the Mahasabha.

There has been a very great change in favour of the Hindu Mahasabha movement since we talked of it at Gaya. The last session at Belgaum was a great success. Nearly all the prominent Hindu leaders have come round to the opinion that along with the Congress movement, there must be the Hindu Mahasabha movement, and that it should not confine itself to questions of socio-religious character but should deal with political questions also as far us they affect the Hindus.

The Belgaum session of the Mahasabha marked an increased concern about the communal electorates in the anticipated constitutional reforms. A committee was appointed under the chairmanship of Lala Lajpat Rai 'to ascertain and formulate Hindu opinion on the subject of Hindu-Muslim problem'. The other members of the committee were C.Y. Chintamani, Rajendra Prasad, B.S. Moonje, Narendra Nath, and Hans Raj. Malaviya explained the need for such an enquiry in the following words:

The main question is whether representation in the Legislatures should be based upon the proportion of Hindus and Musalmans in the population or whether it should be on non-communal general qualifications and also whether the principle should be extended to local boards and the services.

When the Congress organized an All Parties Conference in Delhi in January 1925 under the chairmanship of Gandhi, several political parties, groups, and interests took part in its deliberations. The Mahasabha was represented in the conference by the members of the committee appointed earlier under the chairmanship of Lala Lajpat Rai. The conference failed to arrive at any definite conclusions as several leaders were more interested in an 'unseemly selfish scramble for power and office' and 'Muslim representatives' appetite had grown by what it had fed on. Malaviya urged Muslims to lay their cards on the table and explain what they wanted so that the Mahasabha could consult the Hindu community and arrive at conclusions. The prevailing mood of suspicion between the Hindu and Muslim representatives led to the failure of this conference.

The regular session of the Mahasabha was held in Calcutta in April 1925. The Hindu-Muslim tragedy of Kohat and prohibition of playing music before the mosques by Hindus at Allahabad and other places created an atmosphere of bitterness. These issues were brought before the representatives of the session by Malaviya who recorded his protest against the policies of different provincial governments. Malaviya further demanded effective relief for those who were suffering after the Kohat tragedy. The Mahasabha also adopted a resolution opposing separate communal representation on the ground that it was 'harmful and detrimental' to the creation of national solidarity.

Malaviya attempted to use the Mahasabha forum for social reforms such as the uplift of backward sections of society and improvement of the condition of women as he was fully aware of the fact that without undertaking these measures, Hindus were likely to remain backward and disunited. Foremost among Malaviya's activities were those that were against untouchability. He attached the highest importance to the problems of the people in these social groups in different Mahasabha sessions. In the Delhi session of the Mahasabha that was held in March 1926, serious differences emerged during discussions over the resolutions on various social reforms proposed by the organizers. Malaviya mediated between those who supported progressive measures and the orthodox section among the Hindus. It was with great difficulty and because of Malaviya's persuasion that the delegates agreed to the wording of the resolutions recommending social changes in the Hindu society.

The ascendancy of the Arya Samajists in the Mahasabha was the result of local conditions in UP and Punjab, and affected the new alignments that were to dominate the movement. The chief exponent of the shuddhi movement, Swami Shraddhanand, secured Malaviya's help in bringing back a large number of Malkhana Rajputs into the fold of Hinduism. When the Mahasabha adopted the shuddhi programme as its own, it led to considerable tensions between Hindus and Muslims.

Although Malaviya was fully aware of the risks involved in the adoption of the shuddhi programme by the Mahasabha, he succumbed to the demand of the Arya Samajists.

The Mahasabha and Electoral Politics:

Since 1926, the Mahasabha began to move towards becoming a more explicitly political organization. When it met in Delhi that year, Bhai Parmanand conducted an intensive campaign to convince delegates that the Mahasabha should become a political party, so that Hindus would be sure to find candidates in the third election to the provincial legislative councils later that year. There were heated discussions on this proposal as several leading figures of the Mahasabha, including Malaviya and Lala Lajpat Rai, were unwilling to allow the Mahasabha to directly participate in the forthcoming elections. Ultimately, a compromise was reached authorizing the Provincial Hindu Sabhas to take all proper steps, which included putting forward or supporting its own candidates, for the next elections. The Mahasabha itself would not nominate candidates but its provincial branches could do so or could support candidates of other parties. The compromise was a victory for Malaviya as the old core of the Mahasabha from UP and Punjab wanted the organization to work for Hindu unity through a moderate political programme.

The Mahasabha's decision to enter the political arena came at a time when the Swaraj Party had gained complete control of the Congress. Even though the Swaraj Party kept its own identity intact, it had assumed full authority to take part in the next elections on behalf of the Congress as it thought fit and proper. Under the circumstances, Motilal Nehru began to guide the Congress as well as the Swaraj Party. In March 1926, he attended the Delhi session of the Mahasabha in an attempt to bring it under the Congress fold. The elder Nehru suggested that 'the true remedy lay in Hindusabha as a body joining the Indian National Congress and thereby influencing the whole programme of work in the councils'. In this appeal Motilal Nehru pointed out:

There is no use concealing the fact that the Indian National Congress is predominantly a Hindu organization. It started and developed as such and whatever strength it received from the Musalmans from time to time is fast decreasing by the revival of independent Muslim Organizations.

During the middle of 1926, Malaviya was busy in his negotiations with the Responsivists and the Swaraj Party. He discussed various proposals with them, had his eyes set on UP and Punjab, and with this end in view, desired to arrive at an understanding with the Swarajists as well. Motilal Nehru was, however, in no mood to oblige Malaviya and had his own plans to turn the tables on him. Throughout July and August, he supported moves to capture the Bihar and UP Hindu Sabhas so as to win their support in favour of the Congress candidates for the membership of the provincial councils. Motilal outlined his plan of action in the following words:

I cannot understand Malaviyaji's game and have not heard what he intends to do in the matter of U.P. elections. The Bihar Hindu Sabha has thrown him overboard and bodily adopted the whole list of nominations made by the Congress Executive. I am told a meeting of the U.P. section of the Hindu Sabha was to be held about the end of last month but it has not taken place. I am trying to get the U.P. section to follow the example of Bihar and there is every hope of success.

Motilal Nehru intended to swamp the annual conference of the Agra Hindu Sabha in support of the anti-Malaviya faction. He deputed Sitla Sahai to execute the plan and he immediately went into action. Sahai reported to Motilal on 13 July that 'the election comes off on the 1st of August and Pandit Madan Mohan Malaviya will be present on the occasion. It is very probable that we may capture the Hindu Sabha. I am glad to inform you that the whole affair is quite confidential and the Hindu Mahasabha is unaware of our intentions.' A week later, he informed Motilal Nehru: 'We are trying our best to capture the Hindu Sabha and you will judge our effort by the result.' On the eve of the election for the post of the president of the Provincial Hindu Sabha, a confident Sitla Sahai wrote again:

The Hindu Sabha people are still unaware. Our men will remain solid. We will ask Anandi Prasad Dubey to announce his candidature for Presidentship. This is sure to create differences in the Hindu Sabha members for Raja Tirwa is the candidate of the orthodox section. We shall therefore have not much difficulty in winning the elections. Our policy is to create differences among the original members of the Hindu Sabha.

As Motilal's representative, Sitla Sahai repeatedly emphasized that he was doing everything possible to 'create division in the original Hindu Sabha'. The gameplan was to weaken Malaviya's hold over the Agra Hindu Sabha by removing his nominee from the post of President and getting Motilal Nehru's stooge elected in his place. Malaviya's camp was, however, vigilant on the election day and foiled all attempts by Motilal Nehru to get AP Dubey elected as the President of the Agra Hindu Sabha.

The Agra Provincial Hindu Sabha formed an elections board in August 1926 to 'protect Hindu interests'. A similar committee was organized by the Oudh Provincial Sabha that was to work in consultation with its counterpart in Agra. Malaviya now made a final attempt to come to terms with Motilal Nehru. When he failed to persuade the latter, Malaviya announced the formation of the Independent Congress Party in the first week of September. The leading members of the party were, in fact, the Mahasabha politicians and the executive committees of the Hindu Sabhas and the Independent Congress Party were practically identical. Although the party was the electoral front of the Mahasabha, the party candidates did not represent various strands of the movement.

Growing differences within Hindu Mahasabha:

The special session of the Hindu Mahasabha met at the Congress pandal in Madras on 29 December 1927 under the presidentship of Malaviya who made a fervent appeal to the Mahasabha leaders to adopt the following resolution:

The Hindu Mahasabha, in association with the Indian National Congress and other bodies, calls upon the people to boycott the Simon Commission at every stage, in every manner.

A section of the Mahasabha led by Bhai Parmanand and B.S. Moonje was unwilling to boycott the Simon Commission as they thought that they had an opportunity of securing advantages over Muslims or stalling concessions made to them. But their opposition proved to be of no avail. Malaviya, Lala Lajpat Rai, and M.R. Jayakar successfully prevailed upon the members present at the Mahasabha session to pass the resolution. Thus the Mahasabha finally decided to move forward with the Congress with regard to the Simon Commission.[44]

The decision of the Mahasabha was endorsed by all its branches in the country except in Punjab. Bhai Parmanand persuaded the Punjab Hindu Sabha to oppose the resolution passed by the Madras session of the Mahasabha. In accordance with his wishes, the Punjab Hindu Sabha decided to cooperate with the Simon Commission and expected to gain certain benefits from the government by taking such a step. Contrary to the decision of the All-India Hindu Mahasabha, it presented a memorandum before the Simon Commission dealing with the exclusive rights of the Hindus. This led to 'a serious split in the ranks of the Congress'. Bhai Parmanand later justified his step by arguing that 'M.M. Malaviya and Lajpat Rai were so incensed at the exclusion of Indians from the Commission that regardless of all other differences they went over to and joined forces with Motilal Nehru'.

This was indicative of the emergence of a separate bloc in the Mahasabha working openly against Malaviya. The Patna session of the Hindu Mahasabha held in April 1927, further confirmed the trend. The new president of the sabha, B.S. Moonje, openly pleaded in favour of a swaraj scheme for the country in which Hindus would be supreme and dominant. This was contrary to Malaviya's views as he had repeatedly urged against making any attempts to establish Hindu Raj in India. He was totally opposed to any plans of spelling out any such policy from the Mahasabha platform. Under these circumstances, fundamental differences began to emerge between Malaviya and the newly emerging Mahasabha leadership.

The differences between Malaviya and certain other leaders of the Mahasabha again surfaced when M.A. Jinnah demanded the separation of Sindh from the Bombay Presidency and the reservation of seats for Muslims. Since the Congress and some other parties and groups were willing to accept the separation of Sindh from the Bombay Presidency, Malaviya was also prepared to accept this demand as a step to bring about a harmonious relationship between Hindus and Muslims. He thought that a broad understanding between the Congress and other political parties and groups was in the national interest. But the newly emerging Mahasabha leadership did not appreciate Malaviya's stand and accused him of being much too deep in the Congress camp. The viceroy gave the following assessment of the situation within the Mahasabha:

Hindu Mahasabha itself is not quite a happy family at present. A good many of them appear to look upon Malaviya and Lajpat Rai as too much in the pocket of the Congress.

The viceroy was apparently referring to the growing rift within the Hindu Mahasabha that ultimately changed its course and character. Malaviya and Lajpat Rai, who were actively associated with the Congress, were deeply committed to carrying on the anti-imperialist struggle under its banner and were prepared to work with it within the broad nationalist framework of

Hindu-Muslim unity. While presiding over the special session of the Hindu Mahasabha on 29 December 1927, Malaviya reiterated his views, explained the challenges before the Mahasabha, and defined its strategy for the years to come. He called upon the delegates 'to remember that this Hindu Mahasabha was never brought into existence as a communal organization to fight against any community'. He further stressed that the prime objective before the Mahasabha should be to promote greater unity and solidarity among all sections of the Hindu community and to promote good feelings between Hindus and other communities.

Malaviya used the opportunity to impress upon the delegates that 'ever since its inception up to date not a single resolution has been passed by this Sabha which any reasonable man who has any sense of nationalism in him can take exception to'.

As a publicist, he was a striking success. Having edited "HINDUSTAN" in Hindi, he founded "THE LEADER," an English Daily, at Allahabad, which quickly became a power to be reckoned with in upper India under the able editorship of C. Y. Chintamani. He preferred to go out instead of easing out the Editor when differences arose. Later on, he shouldered the burden of guiding the "HINDUSTAN TIMES' at Delhi as Chairman of the Board of Directors. The key figure in all these developments was Madan Mohan Malaviya (1861-1946), a pandit from Allahabad, whose family was highly respected for its orthodoxy and command of the sacred texts of Hinduism. A lawyer by training, Malaviya became a member of the Congress upon its inception, and was a professional politician. He was appointed president of Congress in 1909, and in 1918, got himself first elected to the Municipal Council of Allahabad and then to the Provincial Legislative Council without interruption for decades. He constantly defended moderate positions on the British presence in India, as well as conservative views of social reform. He was the archetypal orthodox Brahmin. He started the Hindu Samaj (Hindu Society) in 1880 to defend the region's Hindu festivals, in particular the yearly Magh Mela, which he felt was under threat on account of missionaries. Soon afterwards, he launched plans for a Hindu university. This was to become the Banaras Hindu University (BHU) in 1916. The idea was to preserve Hindu tradition, including a hereditary caste system. Soon after the opening of BHU, in 1922, Malaviya was instrumental in reviving the Hindu Mahasabha within Congress.

Presidential Addresses at Hindu Mahasabha Annual Meetings Madan Mohan Malaviya: Presidential Address, as Reported (1923).

Pt Malaviya began his address with Veda path (recitation of Vedic mantras) and heartily thanked the audience for electing him president. He laid emphasis on the greatness of Hindu civilisation, the four varnas (castes) and four ashramas (stages) of Hindu society. Paying respects to Buddha, he said Lord Buddha, the thrice greatest benefactor of mankind, is worshipped by Hindus as one of the ten incarnations of God. The ten Buddhistic commandments exactly tally with Manu's rules about 'achar' and there is no difference between Hindus and Buddhists. He said that the ashrama system of Hindu society was unparalleled in its perfection, which divided life into four parts of brahmacharya, grehastha, vanaprastha and sanyasa. Ancient great men and sages, Ram and Krishna, Bhishma, Drona, Yudhistira, Arjuna, Vasishta, Gautama and others were seers of the Hindu civilisation. Tolerance and forgiveness were characteristics of the Hindu society and even in the later age, Prithvi Raj captured Mohammad Ghori and set him free. The Hindu ideal is never to hurt or be aggressive to anybody, but at the same time, Hindus wished that they should not also be hurt or attacked by others.

The Hindu religion sustained many attacks. Hindus never cared so much for rajya as for dharma. We had fallen down, and before the British advent, anarchy and chaos reigned supreme in India. Hindus and Mahomedans both had fallen down and were fighting one another.

The British came to India and ruled over India, of course with a selfish motive and interest, but some common advantages have been derived by us. People of different and farthest corners have been brought nearer and together due to railways and telegraphs, and on account of a common language and common laws, mutual relations have increased and they have ample facility for coming together. From 1885 to 1915, the Congress strove its utmost and worked hard for India's uplift, although the Mahomedans, as a community kept themselves aloof, except a few liberal-minded statesmen. In 1916, all of us joined and drew up a scheme for reform. Something was given, but it was insufficient and incomplete. Since then our condition has been worse. The greatest of Indians and the saint of the world, Mahatma Gandhi (cheers), was most unjustly imprisoned by the Government (Shame) and we have not yet been able to get him released--our weakness and helplessness cannot be greater than this, that we have not yet been able to effect his release. The heart of India is most pained at this Government attitude and explosives are collecting [sic] which may one day prove very dangerous. Besides this, our trade and commerce are destroyed. Traders and merchants are impoverished. Government is increasing taxation and our condition and status are pitiable. Formerly the Government had some fear of us, but since Mahatma Gandhi's preaching's of non-violence the Government's attitude had completely changed. We have now to consider what is our duty in the present circumstances, what relations we have to maintain towards the Government, Mahomedans, Parsis and other Indian communities.

1. Presidential addresses by M.M. Malaviya at Hindu Mahasabha annual meetings, Indian Annual Register, 1923, pp. 127-40.

Referring to relations with Mahomedans the Pandit said that it was an unhappy, a painful episode. The relations between Hindus and Mahomedans have not been as happy and cordial as they ought to be. During the Bengal Partition days, the Government were inciting Mahomedans to attack Hindus. In 1916 in Eastern Bengal, inhuman, brutal, unparalleled atrocities were perpetrated on Hindus. Hindu women were outraged by fanatic Mahomedans and many Hindu women had to take shelter in rivers and tanks to protect their honour. Then came the Great War in 1914. In 1914 in the frontier districts, particularly Muzaffarnagar, Hindu houses were regularly looted and Hindu women dishonoured, but Indian patriots preached not to heed them. By Mahatma Gandhi's advice, Hindus worked with Mahomedans and helped them in the Khilafat cause, not because the former wanted something in return, but because they were for the liberty and freedom of every nation and also because of their sympathy for fellow Muslim brothers. The speaker emphasised that he did not attribute such inhuman attacks to good and gentle Mahomedans but to rogues, vagabonds and bad elements of the Muslim society. Again in 1920, brutal and inhuman atrocities were perpetrated on Hindus by Moplahs in Malabar. Hindu houses were looted, women were outraged, male and female butchered with the greatest cruelty for refusing to embrace Islam and many were forced into Islam at the point of the sword. The speaker pathetically and movingly said that it is better to die than to be beaten and oppressed anywhere and everywhere, than to see women's modesty outraged, temples attacked and burnt and idols broken. The whole of India was severely pained and afflicted at these horrible inhumanities. Due to tolerance, we patiently bore all this and drank the bitter dose simply with anxiety and desire that no ill-feeling and differences be created between the two sister communities. The Amritsar episode is not out of memory. At Multan, temples were burnt down and women's chastity was outraged, and latter [sic] on, burnt Geeta and Granth Saheb and broken temple idols were found. Next an appeal was issued to maintain unity and peace on Bakrid day, but riots occurred at several places, although not so many as were expected. Our ladies do not consider they are as safe as 50 years ago. In Amritsar, Hindu women do not come out of houses so frequently and abruptly as they used to do formerly. Every moment, they fear of being dishonoured. Everybody knows what happened at Panipat and at Ajmer. Temples were broken and burnt, and idols were destroyed.

In such circumstances, it is our individual and social duty to increase our strength and be on terms of love and good-will with Muslims. It is most deplorable that Hindus are so fallen that a handful of foreigners can be ruling over us. Fie on the Hindus who live to see the breaking of temples and the outrage of women. Miss Ellis was kidnapped and the vibration pervaded the whole British Empire. Behind English girls and women, there is national strength which protects them wherever they go. So also with Mahomedan women. There was a time when Hindu ladies had also such national backings behind them. Unless we have such strength, we cannot continue among strong nations of the world. Whatever steps we adopt, we should see that we may not harm others and put hindrance to national unity. The main reason of the present disunity is that Hindus are comparatively weak and cannot protect their religion and women. Unity and good-will can exist only between two equally strong parties. When the irresponsible element of Muslims will realise that we can react to the policy of tit for tat they would never venture to attack us.

The Pandit continued: 'I solemnly affirm before God I never mean to hurt Muslims or have the supremacy of Hindus over Muslims. If that be the sentiment in me, God may give me the greatest punishment, but I wish that my Hindu brethren be wiped off this earth if they cannot protect their sisters, daughters and others, cannot save the honour of our religion. We are responsible for our weakness. We have forgotten our duty. We should not fight shy of being called Hindus. When Hindus are oppressed we should approach Muslim leaders to devise means to settle disputes. In case riots occur we should settle matters in consultation with leaders of both communities.'

Pandit Malaviya then emphasised on girls' education. He laid great emphasis on the importance and necessity of brahmacharya, physical strength and exercise, and urged the establishment of wrestling places (Akharas) in every quarter, every town and village. He next urged economy in social functions such as marriages, upanayan and others. He denounced dowry and urged its wholesale stoppage. Regarding untouchability, the Pandit spoke very feelingly, and tears were trickling down his cheeks when he referred to the untouchables. He said the Hindu Sabha comprises all sects of Hindus. Our untouchables follow the Hindu religion, worship Rama, Krishna and other Hindu gods, take their meal after bath, and if wealthy, even build temples (Swami Shraddhanand interrupted: But then they are not allowed to enter those temples and worship there.). With tears in his eyes, the Pandit then took out the turban from his head and said: 'Why should I not place my turban at the feet of my untouchable brother who follows the Hindu religion? Why should I not allow my untouchable brother to have darshan in temples? Full of sins as I am, what right have I to stop my untouchable brother from entering temples?'

Referring to permission to untouchables for drawing water from wells the president said that Christians and Mahomedans are asking untouchables to embrace their religion, for so long as they remain. Hindus are not allowed to draw water from wells, and if they accept their faith, they will not be so outcasted, insulted and disallowed. Pertinently remarked Pandit Malaviya: 'An untouchable comes under the hottest sun from your labour and is extremely thirsty. I ask what true Hindu is there who will so cruelly prevent these untouchables from drawing water from wells while they do not object untouchables' entry in houses when their services are required. Teach them to be clean. When they travel with us in trains, when they sit with us in schools, we do not object because this has been forced upon us by the Government.'

Re-conversion: Referring to the Shuddhi movement, Pandit Malaviya said there are forty-eight crores of Muslims in India of whom not more than fifty lakhs are those who might have come from outside. The rest were converted from Hinduism. Theirs is a proselytising religion while our religion has closed the doors for those who wish to come in our fold. Mullas have recently prepared an expansive scheme for reconversion of Hindus on a grand active scale in their private very confidential meeting and have scrupulously given no publication to this resolution and they have also collected fifty lakhs, but you will be surprised to know that it has not been scrupulously kept secret. Hindus are converted by dupes. In Gujrat, some Mussalmans with notices bearing prints of 'Om preach Kalauki incarnation is H.H. Aga Khan' say that they should join that sect. Within three years, one lakh of Hindus has been converted by Khojas. He asked: 'Is there no prayashchitta for those who unknowingly took anything touched by non-Hindus. Malkanas ought to be taken into Hinduism. He asked: What Hindu is there who has this right to say that some particular man has no right to offer prayers after coming into the Hindu fold?

The President then referred to a verse in Dharmshastra Mahaprabandha which lays down that those who had been converted to other religion either by force or willingly can be taken back to the Hindu religion if they so desire. He asked the audience to decide this question. Replying to those, who say that we should not care for our numerical strength and that those who have already been converted should not be taken into Hinduism, the Pandit said: 'When now we are so badly treated with a numerical strength of 22 crores, what would be our condition in future with a much-reduced Hindu population, if we allow this rate of conversion from Hinduism and do not allow reconversion into Hinduism?

Besides his services to Allahabad as city father and to Uttar Pradesh as its representative in the Provincial Council, he was all along an all-India figure. He never became a back-number. He presided over two annual sessions of the Congress before the advent of Gandhiji, besides being elected as President of two banned Sessions at Calcutta and Delhi. He braved the rigours of jail life and crossed the seas to plead for Indian freedom at the Second Round Table Conference. He was always respected by the people and powers-that-be.

As a parliamentarian, he rose to his full stature in the old Imperial Legislative Council and the Central Assembly. By virtue of his social charm, unruffled dignity and urbane eloquence, he was a model and a marvel of his contemporaries. His speeches on Sedition Bill, Press Laws and Imperial Preference became historic. He was impeccably dressed in white robes with a turban.

Education claimed his attention from the beginning. He realised his life's dream of founding the Banaras Hindu University when Annie Besant handed over to him the Central Hindu College founded by her. He soon made it a nationalist institution in 1916, with Sir Sunder Lal as Vice-Chancellor. Sir P.S.Sivaswami Iyer succeeded him. Alfred King, an Englishman, was appointed as Principal of the Engineering College. The professoriate was drawn from every part of the country. He assumed charge as founder Vice-Chancellor. It became catholic in character and composition. He passed on his mantle as Vice Chancellor to the eminent educationist, Dr.S.Radhakrishnan, even while being alive. Thus, he had always the best interest of the institution at heart. He was indeed the finest flower of Hindu culture, radiating fragrance far and wide, and was aptly called 'Dharmatma.'

His capacity to collect funds amounting to rupees one crore was unique. Mahatma Gandhi called him Prince among beggars.

The Poona Session

Pandit M. M. Malaviya, one of the premier pioneers of the Renaissance, who since the Jubbulpore Session (1928) had ceased to take active interest in the affairs of Hindu Mahasabha, though he continued to remain as one of its Vice-Presidents, presided over the Poona Session held on 29, 30 and 31st December 1935. In his presidential address, he eulogised the services of Dr. Moonje and Bhai Parmanand and in the end, announced that within 12 months, he would collect a sum of Rs. one crore for the Hindu Mahasabha to carry on the work according to its own programme, which he clearly and at great length explained to the huge audience.

The two most important and contested resolutions that were passed under the Presidentship of Panditji, concerned with the Removal of Untouchability and the Council entry programme of the Hindu Mahasabha. They may be quoted below verbatim:

1) "The Hindu Maha Sabha further affirms its faith that untouchability must not be regarded as a part of Hindu religion or social system."

2) "The Mahasabha recommends to the Hindus, the abolition of all distinctions in the Hindu Society based on birth or caste in the spheres of public, social and political life in which such distinctions ought to have no application and are out of place in the present age."

3) "The Mahasabha is of opinion that elections to Legislatures should be contested with a view to protecting and upholding the Hindu interest in the Legislatures and leave it to the Provincial Hindu Sabhas to take steps in that connection wherever necessary."

About two nights were spent in discussing the resolution on Untouchability. Mr. M. R. Jayakar, Pt. Malaviya and other very important personalities participated in the discussion. It was ultimately carried with an overwhelming majority.

Resolution Passed in Poona Session Under Presidentship of M.M.Malviya:

1) Constitution of the Army and other forces : HMS Protests against policy of the Government in preferring persons from a few Provinces and Specified classes only.

2) Military schools and Volunteer corps : HMS is opinion that in order to enable the Hindus to defend their interest and have proper share defence forces, HMS welcomes establishment of Central Hindu Military Education society at the instance Dr.B.S.Moonje.

3) HMS strongly protests putting unnecessary restrictions upon the movements and activities of V.D.Savarkar by Confining him to Ratnagiri for yesrs together,It notes the splendid service which Savarkar has been rendering to the cause of Hinduism and urges Govt to remove all restrictions on him. [46]

The decision regarding the Council entry was also a momentous one but when the time of election to the Provincial Legislatures came, a conflict arose between the U.P. Provincial Hindu Sabha and Pandit M. M. Malaviya. Although the ostensible cause of the difference was the recognition of a particular Provincial Hindu Sabha, there came into existence two rival parties in the United Province. This rivalry between the parties was of a few years' standing. The Hindu Mahasabha at the Poona Session decided to conduct their elections and authorised Babu Padam Raj Jain to do the needful in this connection.

At Agra, the elections took place under the supervision of Bhai Parmananda and Babu Padam Raj Jain, and the U. P. Provincial Hindu Sabha was properly recognised. Not satisfied with all these certain interested persons, approached Pandit Malaviyaji for interference which resulted in some conflict in the Working Committee of the Hindu Mahasabha, and after a number of Working Committee meetings held at Delhi and Benares, the problem was finally solved at the Lahore Session of the Hindu Mahasabha when Malaviyaji chose to withdraw.

The Lahore Session of the Hindu Mahasabha was presided over by His Holiness Jagatguru Shankaracharya, Dr. Kurtakoti. Dan Veer Seth Jugal Kishore Birla also attended the Session.

Up to the Ahmedabad Session (1937), Bhai Parmanand, for all practical purposes, was the Working President of the Mahasabha and guided its policy with all the firmness and courage in him. During this period, he made the Hindu Mahasabha a living organisation. The days of keeping the Mahasabha as a subsidiary or a corollary organisation to the Congress with half way policy was no longer to be continued and hence it was re-organised as quite independent of the Congress with its own principles, aims and objects, policy and programme.

The University is a fitting monument for his lifelong work. Religion and patriotism are the two pillars, on which the arch of the Hindu University rests. The Arya Samajists has their Mandir, and Sikhs have their Gurdwara within its precincts when a mosque was destroyed during Hindu Muslim riots at Varanasi. He got it reconstructed at his own cost. The University was the recipient of substantial benefactions from the Nawab of Rampur, Nawab of Chatrai, and Aga Khan. He blended ancient tradition with modern temper and was well-versed in our classics and epics. He was a puritan in private life.

He did not lag behind the social reformers. His efforts for the uplift of Harijans were steady and sustained, and they were given special facilities and personal attention at the University. He evinced active interest in secular movements like scouting and founded the Hindustan Scouts Association, when he detected that the scout movement in India was becoming subservient to foreign rulers. He did not tolerate self-respect being trifled with.

During the national struggle, the Government of India stopped its annual grant to the University. The Maharajahs and business magnates also hesitated to extend the usual help. But the Maharanis passed on their valuable jewellery to Panditji to tide over the crisis. The self-sacrificing professoriate voluntarily cut their salaries. Such was the loyalty he commanded from one and all. Students regarded him as a father figure. Their respect for him bordered on reverence.

He was more than an elder statesman. He did not hesitate to found the Hindu Mahasabha, when he was convinced that the vital interests of Hindus were being sacrificed in the guise of nationalism of placate communalism of the minorities. He also advocated reconversion to Hinduism of those who were earlier lured into Christianity and Islam. At the same time, he always strove for communal unity and respected all faiths.

In spite of ill-health, advancing years and incidental infirmities, he was always youth in spirit and served as an invaluable link between the younger and older generations. He was stout but sympathetic, unbending but open to conviction and, above all, just and even generous to his opponents. Atrocities perpetrated on the Hindu minority at Noakhali moved him deeply, and he succumbed to that shock on November 12, 1946. C. Y. Chintamani described him as heart from head to feet. With the solitary and inevitable exception of Gandhiji, there is none in our history comparable to him for the range of public service or for an equal record of selfless dedication. He is justly regarded as one of the foremost makers of modern India.

C Vijayaraghavachariar

F ew succeed in keeping pace with changing times. Of the few, one in a thousand remains in limelight throughout his life. Chakravarti Vijayaraghavachariar of Salem was one such fortunate man. His very surname means an emperor. He was indeed an emperor for over 60 years in our public life with few to equal and none to surpass.

He was born on June 18, 1852, in an orthodox Srivaishnava family. Till his 12th year, he studied Sanskrit and the Vedas and blossomed into a Sanskrit scholar and Sanatanist of high repute. With this classical foundation, he matriculated in 1870, standing second in the Madras Presidency. He graduated in 1875, winning a number of prizes. After working as a teacher at Madras, Mangalore and Salem, he privately qualified himself as a pleader and set up practice at Salem in 1881.

The Salem Riots and his spirit of Resistance

In 1882, a brief time after he set up practice at Salem, a Hindu-Muslim riot broke out in Salem, when some Muslims prevented a temple procession from passing through a street even though they had obtained permission from the court. Vijayaraghavachariar was implicated in Hindu-Muslim riots alleging that he personally directed the operations of rioters, resulting in demolition of a mosque. Failing to obtain bail, he had to remain in prison for some time.

He was sentenced to 10 years imprisonment along with nine other co-accused and to be sent to Andaman. He fought relentlessly in the courts, appointing Eardley Norton, a famous lawyer, to argue his case in the high court. The judge who was hearing the case was surprised to see Norton reading the letter written to him by Vijayaraghavachariar saying, the contents of the letter is sufficient to put across his arguments and sat down. The judge had never seen Norton reading out from somebody else's brief. The arguments based on the letter got him released straightaway. He was not only acquitted but he also won the encomium of the full bench of the High Court for his bold, manly and upright stand.

Angered by their loss of face, the Governor of Madras Presidency ordered Vijayaraghavachariar to be removed from the municipal council. Vijayaraghavachariar was not a person to take injustice lying down. He not only fought to get himself re-instated but also sued the Secretary of State for India for compensation for the act, and was awarded Rupees hundred. Then he moved the courts, and with his legal acumen, fought to get all his co-accused who were languishing in Andaman jail, convicted for ten years, released. The witnesses who gave false evidence were also not spared and were prosecuted. Salem riots of 1882 made Vijayaraghavachariar famous overnight. He was hailed by the press from all over the country for his spirit of fighting and called him "The Lion of South India."

Afterwards, he proceeded against the witnesses who falsely deposed against him and got them convicted. He saw that his defense witnesses, who were victimized, were duly reinstated in service. He pleaded for clemency before Lord Rippon, the then Governor-General, for those convicted along with him and rotting in Andamans and secured pardon for them. Purity was to him not an accident of adornment but an essential structure. This was indicated by dress and department. He cut a characteristic personality in any gathering and could easily be spotted out.

The Governor of Madras got him removed from the Salem Municipal Commission with vengeance without assigning any reason. He successfully fought against this disqualification and also displayed rare courage in suing the Secretary of State for India, for damages amounting to Rs. 10,000 and got a verdict in his favor for Rs. 100 as damages. "Amrita Bazar Patrika" of Calcutta, hailed him as the "Hero of Salem."

Learned in Law, adept in marshalling facts, powerful in advocacy, dignified in bearing with commanding personality, he soon built-up roaring practice and was the acknowledged leader of the bar for four decades. He cared more for principles than for briefs. When a client did not disclose the truth, he threw away the brief with fees. When a Judge was rude to a member of the bar, he made him apologize. Something of Puritan's moral earnestness and strength of character blended in him with the gravity of culture and the spirit of 'noblesse obliges.'

He became a member of the Madras Legislature in 1895. With his unrivalled knowledge of public affairs and fearless expression of views, he was head and shoulders above the rest. In 1909, he retired in favor of Malaviya for the Presidentship of the Congress for the Session at Lahore. Malaviya, in his turn, regarded him as an elder brother. Entering the Imperial Legislative Council in 1913, he proved to be an outstanding parliamentarian in the company of Gokhale and others during the Viceroyalty of Hardinge. When he was present, Government members were alert. Edwin Montague, Secretary of State for India, in his 'Indian Diary', described him as the most vigorous thinker, though some of his ideas were impracticable. His powerful pleading for clemency saved Bhai Paramananda of the Punjab from the gallows.

Formation of the Indian National Congress:

He was a statesman having an excellent relationship with many British administrators, who exhibited a sympathetic attitude towards Indians. Prominent among them was Allan Octavian Hume, who later founded Indian National Congress. Even before the congress was born in 1885,

Vijayaraghavachariar wrote to his friend Hume that a national organization like the Indian National Congress which he was proposing to create should be political in outlook and at the same time should look into the economic and social needs of the masses. He felt that only then the influence of such a body could spread wide all over the country. He was invited to the first session of Congress by Hume as a special invitee to participate in its deliberations. Thus, Vijayaraghavachariar was involved with the Indian National Congress from day one. He was considered in the organization along with the founders, Dadabhai Naoroji (1825– 1917), Pheroze Shah Mehta (1845-1915), Dinshaw Wacha (1844-1936), S. Subramania Iyer (1842–1924), and G. Subramania Iyer (1855-1916). At the age of thirty-six, in 1888, Vijayaraghavachariar drafted the Constitution of the Congress Party.

During the 1891 Nagpur session, INC passed a resolution that the British Government should give more powers to Indians in the Legislative councils. Based on this, Lord Cross's Act of Council Reform was passed in 1892. In this formative period of the congress, Vijayaraghavachariar, along with Surendranath Banerjee, Pheroze Shah Mehta, and Dadabhai Naoroji prevailed in all matters of policy decisions. Vijayaraghavachariar played a key role during this period, in making the Indian National congress an effective political organization with a focus on unity, development, and national consciousness.

Land settlement of Tenure and Land reforms:

In 1899, he was appointed as a member of the Congress Propaganda Committee. At the Calcutta Session in 1906, Vijayaraghavachariar moved a resolution relating to the Permanent Land Settlement of Land Tenures. He argued that the people owned the land in India since time immemorial, and the ruler was only paid a share of the produce. He said, "The ruler never owned everything, and a shift in thought and action was the result of colonial tendencies and reeked of European feudalism." This paved the way for Land reforms. This was one of the contentious issues for those Zamindars and Pannayars who were possessing large holding of land against the congress, and they started tilting towards the British. British used this opportunity and gave a religious and community color to it to divide and rule.

Hardliner and Tilak's Associate:

A towering, uncompromising, and fearless personality, Vijayaraghavachariar naturally went along with Balagangadhar Tilak, a hardliner, after the Great split between hardliner and moderate factions at Surat in 1907. He kept away from congress (not from social activity) for a brief period after the split. V.O. Chidambaram Pillai, Subramanya Bharathi, Va Ve Su Iyer, Subramanya Siva and Neelakanda Brahmachary were others who followed the same path.

Divide and rule policy of the British-Division of Bengal:

Minto-Morley Reforms of 1909 was made to appease the Muslims in keeping with the British policy of Divide and Rule following the mass Swadeshi Movement against the partition of Bengal. The British Government brought in a scheme for separate communal electorates for the Muslims. Congress strongly disapproved of the scheme for separate electorates.

Vijiaraghavachariar stated to this effect: "I condemn the scheme for separate communal electorates. It will cut at the root of the Nation's unity and endanger its Constitutional progress."

In 1913 he was elected to the Imperial Legislative Council with which he was associated till the year 1916. In Delhi, he worked in close cooperation with great leaders like Madan Mohan Malaviya, Surendranath Banerjea, and Gopala Krishna Gokhale.

President of Congress:

The Nagpur Session took place in 1920, and Vijayaraghavachariar was made the President of the party. It is at this session that Gandhi proposed the Non-Cooperation Movement. It was announced in the backdrop of the Rowlatt Act and the Jallianwala Bagh tragedy. The 1920 session of the Indian National Congress held in Nagpur, which was the biggest conference ever then, a total number of 14583 delegates were present. A volunteer organisation called Bharat Swayamsewak Mandal was formed to undertake the arrangements of the conference. Vijayaraghavachariar told Gandhi, Non-Cooperation movement's aim must be only to get Swarajya and nothing short. It was a time when Jinnah was against Non-cooperation. On the way back from Nagpur, a compartment was to be attached to the train towards Chennai and the authorities refused to do so, angered by the Resolution of Non-Cooperation passed at that session. Vijayaraghavachariar, along with five hundred delegates, laid themselves flat on the railway track and prevented any train from moving out, forcing the authorities to relent (Maybe that was the first Rail Roko!). Similarly, when he was traveling in a first-class compartment, the Collector of Coimbatore was also traveling in it, his baggage was thrown out onto the platform. He promptly took the baggage of the European too and threw it out (unimaginable guts in those days). It is another matter that they became good friends later. He, with his powerful oratory, argued against C. R. Das and Motilal Nehru on the question of the Council Entry Programme drawn up by them. Motilal Nehru made a sarcastic remark that since he is a practicing lawyer, he is opposing it. C.V had the last laugh when he said equally sarcastically that "he has discussed this with Gandhi and only Mahatmas can understand", not the others.[47]

Head of Unity Conference:

The year 1932 saw the 80-year-old Vijayaraghavachariar heading the Unity Conference in Prayagraj. Throughout his life, he strived for unity among Hindus, a hardliner, and moderate factions and said that, it is this freedom movement that has brought all the people from various social classes together and is the only thing that will nourish the congress as a political party.

Other social activities:

Vijayaraghavachariar advocated post-puberty marriage for women and the right of a daughter to have a share in her father's property. He advocated the much-needed change in the Hindu law at a time when any talk about it was taboo. He rendered great assistance to Swami Shraddhanand in his work connected with the Anti-Untouchability League. His multi-sided personality also found expression in his participation in the organization of the Hindu Mahasabha. He presided over the All India Hindu Mahasabha Sessions at Akola in 1931.

He earned a fortune in his profession but spent them on public cause, and in establishing institutions. The Anti-Untouchability League and the Congress Propaganda Organization in England, in its early days, received liberal financial support from him. Even in those days, he used to spend his summer in Kodaikanal and used to vigorously row boats in the lake and ride horses.

He was a great nationalist, a reformer with uncompromising qualities. His vision was our county's progress without compromising on our ancient values. Even the imperial council, headed by Viceroy Hardinge, had great admiration and respect for his advocacy for the rights of the underprivileged class, and his courage in taking up even unpopular but deserving demands. He died in 1944 at the age of ninety-two, before his dream of swaraj was obtained. He left behind a great legacy for us to emulate and follow. His life as a poor priest's son reaching the pinnacle is itself the essence of democracy for which he fought. His valuable collections were treasured in the Memorial Library and Lecture Halls, specially constructed and named after him in Salem.

On the political plane, his position was unique. He was a special invitee to the first session of the Congress held in 1885 at Bombay, and he was closely associated with A.O. Hume, its founder. He was intimate with Charles Bradulaugh and Annie Besant. In 1887, he drafted a constitution for the Congress. Steeped in Victorian liberalism, he became the harbinger of Gandhian era. In 1919, he took prominent part in discussing the technique of civil disobedience with Gandhiji.

He presided over the Congress Session at Nagpur in 1920, which marked the advent of the hegemony of Mahatma Gandhi. His address was logical, lucid, cogent and convincing. He pooh-poohed the claim of the British Parliament to be the sole Judge as to the time and manner of each instalment of constitutional reforms. Such a claim, he contended, was a negation of all principles of sovereignty in a people and of the first principles of self-determination, for whose protection England and her allies fought. He hailed the League of Nations as the hope of humanity.

He was rigidly logical and did not fully approve Gandhi's line of action. But he conducted the proceedings with great dignity and decorum by vacating the chair whenever a subject came up involving differences of opinion. He drafted a Swaraj Constitution for India. The idea of fighting the Government from within the councils did not appeal to him. At the meeting of the Subjects Committee of Congress at the Kakinada Session in 1923, he opposed Council entry. Then Motilal Nehru, sponsor of Council entry, angrily remarked at the fun of a practicing lawyer opposing him. Then, Vijayaraghavachariar retorted emotionally that he did not join the Congress after amassing wealth. He was in the Congress since his student days, and all his earnings were spent for public service. He was obliged to continue at the Bar with the permission of Gandhiji to make both ends meet and only a Mahatma could understand him. Mohamud Ali, as President, expressed his inability to intervene when two former Presidents and veterans were crossing swords. Sensing the mood of the House, Motilal withdrew his remarks and apologized. But, he approved the boycott of Simon Commission and thought poorly of the outcome of the Round Table Conference. He also assisted in drafting the Nehru Report. He was rightly regarded as a constitutional pundit by one and all. He was respected as a patriot without self or stain.

He advocated post-puberty marriages and right of Share to daughter. He championed the rights of depressed classes and carried on anti-untouchability campaign. He condemned racial discrimination and sponsored the claims of the labor. He spurned titles and resisted the lure of office.

When he felt that the rights of Hindus were sacrificed to appease Muslim communalism, he presided over the annual session of the Hindu Mahasabha held at Akola in 1931 to give a constructive lead. He presided over the Unity Conference at Allahabad in 1932 to deal with the situation created by the British Prime Minister's communal award and the Poona Pact.[48]

PRESIDENTIAL SPEECH OF C. VIJAYARAGHAVACHARIAR, AKOLA, AUGUST 1931

Passing very briefly over the origin and progress of the Sabha he discusses the Indian Problem chiefly with reference to the solution of Hindu-Muslim unity. "The problem of minorities," he says, "has assumed unique dominance in Indian politics. It is a remarkable fact that the Minority which is most numerous and which by wealth, education and above all organization is most powerful is also the most insistent for numerous special safe-guards for the protection of its rights. It needs no great research for discovering the factors (other than those which throughout the rest of the world constitute the pure Minority problem) which influence our Muslim fellow countrymen to conceive and formulate, as they have done, their special rights, real and subjective. I may be pardoned here for stating at once that our difficulty in solving this problem is due almost entirely to certain foreign and irrelevant elements that subjectively constitute this problem. The policy of conciliating the Muslims by special patronage and concessions began in this country between the seventies and eighties of the last century, almost simultaneously with the starting of Pan-Islamism by Abdul Hamid, Sultan of Turkey. And this problem has been ever since growing in volume and intensity, with the active encouragement of the Bureaucracy more than under the auspices of the Government. The result is, it has become so complex, that it is impossible now for Muhammadans themselves to arrive at a reasoned and unanimous solution. Neither the Government nor non- Muslims are able to arrive at a settlement with them. Prominent Muslims, such as Sir Mirza Ismail, the Dewan of Mysore, are clearly of opinion that no satisfactory solution would be reached in the near future. Therefore the one important question before us is, what is the remedy? Are we to postpone the constitutional reforms and the political salvation of the country until we reach a solution of this problem so as to give satisfaction to everybody in the country? It would be disastrous to adopt such an unreasonable attitude, look at it how you may. Rather the effort must be to analyse and separate the purely local question of the adjustment of claims and interests from the national one of securing power into Indian hand. To my mind a solution of the minority problem is near at hand, the only solution we can think of. And that is to invoke the assistance of the great International Institution, the League of Nations."

He answers the objections and allays the fear of those who think that the solution of the problem of minority is purely a domestic matter and that therefore the League of Nations could not interfere. "This is a mistake." He says, "No doubt it is true that neither the Hindus nor the Muslims, nor both of them together, can submit this question for arbitration to the League of Nations. But the Government of British India, or better the Government of the coming Dominions, of its own motion can and ought to do so to save the situation."

Moreover, he believes that "when the new Government of British India is thus started on its legs, the Minority problem, or the Muslim problem to put it more accurately will cease to be a problem of domestic politics. We may be sure that there will be no grievance. History shows that ancient Hindusthan was the safest place in the world to live in. The freedom and security enjoyed through the ages by the Jews of Cochin, the Syrian Christians of Malabar and the Parsees of Gujrat and Bombay illustrate this fact. Nothing would prevail upon these communities to return to Palestine or Persia. So there is absolutely no need for our Muslim brethren and sisters to fear that their special rights would not be safe in our country itself. However, if they have a grievance, there is the League of Nations ready to enquire and settle it impartially."

The learned President passed on to a consideration of the Constitutional question. He is definitely against Federalism. According to him "the sort of political mechanism invented at the Round Table Conference is Federalism only in name. Fantastic in structure and novel and startling in function, if at all it can be established, it would be dangerous for British India and ruinous for the Indian States."

He discusses the subject at length and in all important aspects of it. He is of the opinion that "the Constitution should be unitary and parliamentary and not by any means Federal in the sense proposed at the Round Table Conference. Not only it is a physical and meta-physical impossibility, in the oft-quoted words of Carlyle, but it is in the highest degree dangerous to the people of both the, India's. I might here sound a note of warning to our rulers. The well accepted international doctrine that a change in the form of. Constitutional Government of a country cannot absolve that country from all the legal obligations contracted by its unreformed ancestor, cannot in my humble view apply to a State constructed out of the political debris of British India on the one hand, and metamorphosed Indian States on the other. There should be no. Reservations and Crown subjects beyond the full reach of the new Government as regards Defense, Foreign Relations and Finance except in so far as the declarations of wars are concerned, and to which we should have the same right of voice as the Dominions. Compromises may be made by treaties between treaties between the reformed Government of British India, and Britishers and Irishmen, residents in India whether as officials or non-officials, but who are not national, provided that the terms of such compromises do not constitute them a privileged class."

"He criticised the policies of Indian national congress in as much as in calling Hindu Mahasabha as a communal body". In the end he added "The Hindu Mahasabha does not seek to have for Hindus any political economic or civic rights privileges to which they are not entitled by their numbers, educational and other qualifications character, ability, public spirit and tax paying capacity and in particular the Hindu Mahasabha does not want for Hindus any fixed share for anything which may indirectly leave an unequitable portion for others, it stands for open and fair competition, for an open door for talent irrespective of considerations of race, creed or complexion. It is one of its objects to promote good feelings between the Hindus and other communities in Hindustan and to act in a friendly way with them with a view to evolve a united and self governing Indian Nation".[49]

Resolutions passed under Vijayaraghavachariar presidency:

Resolutions on Census of India, participation of Hindu Mahasabha in Round Table conference, future reforms in Round Table conference and Unity talks were passed in Akola Session.[49]

He welcomed the Congress declaration to accept office in 1937. During World War II, he declared that India's cooperation was out of the question in the absence of immediate assurance of granting her dominion status.

He was keen on spending summer at Ootacamund, the queen of hill stations. His intellectual range covered constitutional treatises, Parliamentary reports, dramas of Shakespeare and the poetry of Milton. There was something Olympian about him and he had a truly Hellenic mind free from every type of prejudice and responsive to all good influences.

He warned that no good would come out of Cripps' proposals. He disapproved Rajaji's move to appease the Muslim League on the question of Pakistan. He had a firm faith in the destiny of India. He enjoyed the privilege of friendship with three generations of patriots represented by Dadabhai Naoroji, Mahatma Gandhi and Subhas Chandra Bose. He was never a back-number at any time. He was a mighty stream absorbing all the currents and crosscurrents of life and served as a link between successive generations.

His passing away on April 19, 1944, at the ripe old age of 92, marked the end of an epoch of sturdy nationalism and constructive statesmanship. There is a hall and library at Salem to perpetuate the memory of this stalwart, who strode over the political arena like a colossus for over 60 years.

Balakrishna Shivaram Moonje

Balakrishna S Moonje was born into a Deshastha Rigvedi Brahmin (DRB) family in 1872 at Bilaspur in Central Provinces. He completed his Medical Degree from Grant Medical College in Mumbai in 1898, and was employed in Bombay Municipal Corporation as a Medical Officer. He left his job to participate in the Boer War in South Africa through the medical wing, as the King's Commissioned Officer. After returning from South Africa, he started his medical practice at Nagpur. He invented the method of operating cataract after testing his skills on dead bodies of goats. He also presented his thesis in a Medical Association, but since it was dominated by British members, he could not receive due credit. He could not pursue the claim afterwards since he got involved in social and political activities, dedicating his entire life to India's freedom struggle, thus leaving his stable Medical Practice in early age. He was also a Sanskrit scholar, a very close associate of Sri Aurobindo in freedom struggle. He visited Pondicherry to persuade him to rejoin politics.

Dr. Moonje was a prominent freedom fighter and a strong supporter of Lokmanya Bal Gangadhar Tilak. The Congress Party's annual session was held at Surat (Gujarat) in 1907. Trouble broke out between the Moderate (Soft Faction) and the Extremist (Hardline Faction) factions of the Congress party over the selection of a new President. The Congress party split into two factions. The extremists were led by the triumvirate of Lala Lajpat Rai, Bal Gangadhar Tilak, Bipin Chandra Pal (known as LAL-BAL-PAL). Dr Moonje and his followers literally gave physical protection to Tilak when he was attacked by few people throwing chairs. From then onwards, the relationship between Tilak and Moonje became very close. Dr. Moonje toured the entire Central India and collected huge funds for Tilak on many occasions. Dr. Moonje also introduced Ganesh and Shivaji Festivals in Central India and also accompanied Tilak to Calcutta for this purpose. He was The General Secretary of Central Indian Provincial Congress for many years.[51]

Dr. Moonje, a famous eye surgeon and a prominent leader of the Central Province, decided to persuade Sri Aurobindo to return to British India and accept the leadership of the Congress. In his trip to Pondicherry, he was accompanied by Dr. Hedgewar. Those were the days when public workers led a frugal life. So Dr. Moonje traveled in a second class compartment, and his companion Dr. Hedgewar in the third class compartment. On the way to Pondicherry, at a junction, Dr. Hedgewar got into the second class compartment to meet Dr. Moonje. Before he could finish the work and return to his third class compartment, the train started moving. Hedgewar was stunned. Suddenly, a ticket examiner appeared and started verifying the tickets. On seeing the third class ticket with Hedgewar, he became angry and chided him. However, much Hedgewar explained the situation, the examiner was not prepared to believe. Moonje, who was observing the scene, intervened and in a reprimanding tone, cautioned the examiner to remember that he was paid from the passengers' fare and should refrain from uttering harsh words.

Following the death of Bal Gangadhar Tilak in 1920, Moonje dissociated from Congress. He disagreed with the policies of M. K. Gandhi. His association with Hindu Mahasabha increased and he was also political mentor of Dr. Hedgewar, who founded RSS in 1925. He was popularly called as "Dharamveer".

Sangathan emerged at the centre of a social and political crisis in north India in the early 1920s due to the outbreak of the Malabar-crisis, which revived the image of 'Hindus under a siege'. The Moplah revolt of Muslim peasants against their predominantly Hindu landlords in Malabar in August 1921 - a result of both Hindu 'landlord oppression' and the perception of Islam in danger' - triggered a self- conscious 'Hindu predicament'. The revolt, resulting in the murder of over 600 Hindus, became significant due to its association with Islamic conversions', dealing a decisive blow to the Non-cooperation movement. The Arya Samaj's Pratinidhi Sabha undertook the reclamation of between 2,500 and 3,000 Hindu converts through shuddhi [ritual purification] under the leadership of Pandit Rishi Ram, guided by the fourth-century text Devalasmriti, in Malabar. The forced conversions of Hindus had unified large segments of Hindu public opinion, revealing the evident 'oppression and disunity' of Hinduism.

B.S. Moonje, who headed the Nagpur commission on the Malabar riots, claimed that the 'chronic disunity and weakness' of Hindus. Hindus, he explained, were divided by caste [varna], which had created 'so many water-tight compartments, each having a social culture and life of its own, that there is hardly any association between them in the wider field of social activities. The Mahomedans, on the other hand, are one organic community, religiously well-organised. Muslims grew in 'numbers, strength, material welfare and solidarity', but Hindus were hastening towards 'disintegration'. Moonje argued that India had lost seven crores of Hindus to Islam and Christianity over the past 900 years through conversions; others reckoned the figure to be millions, but some argued that all the Muslims living in India were 'Hindu apostates', or the casualties of 'Islamic proselytization'. He proposed the settlement of the Marathas, Rajputs, Sikhs, etc., in Malabar, which alone, I think, can solve the Moplah terrorism over meek and helpless Hindus'. He appealed to Hindus to resist the 'aggressiveness' and match their 'virility' through a communitarian organisation and unity. The Moplah crisis signified the loss of 'Hindu strength' in view of conversions, driving the popular opinion to argue for Hindu consolidation in order to protect and extend the Hindu religion.

Meanwhile Dr. Hedgewar founded RSS on Vijayadashmi day in 1925. Dr.Moonje was present in Nagpur on the momentous day.

A shakha (branch) of Hindu teenagers and youngsters was started by Dr. Hedgewar in the ruins of Salubai Mohite's wada in Mahal area of Nagpur. This was the beginning of the Rashtriya Swayamsevak Sangh (RSS).

Moonje was the All India President of the Hindu Mahasabha from 1927 until he handed over the charge to Vinayak Damodar Savarkar in 1937. Until his death, he was active in the Mahasabha and toured all over India. Savarkar had his strong support. He also attended the Round Table Conferences (in London) twice, despite strong opposition from Congress leaders on his views.

PRESIDENTIAL SPEECH OF DR. B. S. MOONJE, PATNA, APRIL 1927.

"I shudder to think what shall happen to Bengal, say 50 years hence, if this course of rapid decline of the Hindus of Bengal is not checked. I am afraid Bengal is fairly on the way to become another Kashmere of India in this respect. I feel from what I have seen and read of the daily happenings in East Bengal particularly that Bengalees alone and unaided by Hindus outside Bengal are absolutely incapable of resisting the inroads of Islam into the preserves of Hinduism there. Let Bengal clearly understand that it may exercise some pressure on the Govt. through the cult of the Bomb and the Pistol, but it will not be able to maintain the pressure until it develops the Lathi cult and proves its capacity of putting down the mischievously aggressive mass Hooliganism."

"The Afghan, before he was allowed to be captured, was fighting for the preservation and maintenance of Hindu religion and culture with the same tenacity and fearlessness of death as he was fighting for their destruction only three or four centuries later on, after Islam was forced on him through sheer compulsion in a moment of helplessness of defeat suffered in wars with his Moslem invaders of Central Asia. But how did the Hindu India of the time react to this forcible shearing of its most powerful wings? Does History record any evidence of any pang felt in the then entirely Hindu Hindusthan, when such a big and enviable slice as Afghanistan was cut out of it? Did the Hindu Hindusthan of those days make any concerted move to avert the calamity then overtaking Afghanisthan? As for Kashmir and Malabar, history tells the same sorry tale, being repeated over there much in the same fashion as in Afghanistan."

"Yet after the Moghul Empire was subverted and the Sikhs in the Punjab and the Marathas in the rest of India had re-established the Hindu Empire, did the Hindus who were as paramount in India then as the Moslems were in their days before they had been conquered, move a finger to recoup the loss in their number sustained through Moslem aggression? Other parts of India also show marks of Moslem aggression narrating equally eloquent tales of Moslem efficiency and hunger of man power on one hand and of Hindu supineness and indifference on the other."

The indifference and the present sociology and orthodoxy of the Hindus together with proverbial mildness and docility of temper, and their indulgence in sentimentalism of various kinds of their own creations such as the excesses of Bhakti Sampradaya and of Ahimsa and non-violence have been the chief contributors to their monumental success. Their daily work of proselytization and of building up of their community brick by brick, was so long going on so unmolested and without any noise, that the hope was manufactured in them and they had come to believe as a matter of course that a time will soon come when the 7 crores of the untouchables which the Hindus regard as the refuse of their community shall have been devoured, digested, and assimilated in the Islamic society. They were thus building up castles in their mind that if they can once reach the Hindus at par by assimilation of the untouchables, their aggressiveness in which they feel supreme confidence will stand them in good stead to give such a push to the mild Hindu as to send him down headlong along the inclined plane of extinction. Thus they were dreaming of absorbing the whole of Hindu India into themselves so that the whole of Hindusthan may ultimately belong to them and be changed into Muslimsthan as the whole of Afghanisthan now belongs to the Moslems.

"Now let us further analyse the Hindu mentality. It is hopelessly perplexing. The Hindu seems to be obsessed with the desire for Swaraj. It is a very noble and manly ambition, but has he ever indulged in a little introspection and examined his own inner self with a view to satisfy himself if he is really fit for Swaraj? In the quite loneliness of his room, when he is all to himself alone, if he were to ask himself a question "if I cannot guarantee safety and immunity from molestation to my women folk and temples from those of my Moslem brethren who are only armed with Lathies, how can I aspire to wrest Swaraj from and maintain it against the cupidity of those armed with machine guns," what answer can he give? While trying to invent or discover an answer let him picture to himself in the loneliness of his room the daily occurrences of Hindu's running away for life when attacked by Moslem ruffians, leaving behind their women-folk to be dealt with by them as they may please."

"Unity based on the principle of bargaining can never be stable, particularly when it has to be purchased by making concessions. The moment they say that Swaraj cannot be attained without Hindu-Moslem Unity, that unity becomes a marketable article and all the laws of economies concerning Demand and Supply immediately come into operation on it."

"I have no value, not the least, for that Swaraj where the Hindoo declines daily both in numbers and in influence. I can only imagine that Swaraj where the Hindu in his forefathers' land of Hindustan shall be prospering and supreme, capable of radiating peace and love and brotherhood all round. How can he attain it, living as he does at the present moment, under the dual domination of the British Machine-gun and the Moslem Lathi? Shuddhi and Sangathan are the means prescribed by the Hindu Sabha Movement and both reason and commonsense dictate that success in this enterprise shall be the harbinger of stable and permanent Hindu-Moslem Unity and the Swaraj that shall be covetable."

"Just as England belongs to the English, France to the French, and Germany to the Germans, India belongs to the Hindus. If Hindus get organized, they can humble the English.... The Hindus henceforth create their own world which will prosper through Shuddhi".

"I feel that I should repeat my conviction that if the Hindus leave the Moslems severely alone for some time to come to do as they please even in association with the Government and cease talking any further of the Hindu Moslem Unity, the Moslems themselves will see the folly of their own insistence on separatist communalism and may eventually come to feel that it shall be to their real interest as also to that of India as a whole if they veer round and merge themselves in the Indian Nationalism for the common good of India, which commodes their Communal prosperity also."

Perhaps what has more than else made the Hindu Mahasabha popular is its efforts 'to preserve and increase the numerical strength of Hindus, which is one of its declared objects. Hindu Communities in Hindustan have increased vastly at the expense of Hindus. Therefore, anything done to arrest this process cannot be looked upon with favour by the followers of those non Indian faiths. Still, more unpleasant must be the reversal of the process be to them, but I do not see how one can logically and justly object to the Hindus doing what the others have been doing to Hindus for centuries, particularly as the Hindus have not gone in for the accession to the ranks of "Rice" Hindus, men tempted to come over by the prospect of marriage, persons induced to be converted by the prospect of economic advantage and of persons forced to be converted by terrorism of any kind. The Hindu Mahasabha and Hindu missions connected with it formally or informally want reconversion. Like the work of conversion and reconversion, there are some other items in the programme of Hindu Mahasabha and missions which have brought upon them the charge of communalism. Once such activity is the amelioration improvement of the condition of the so called low caste of the Hindu community and even the efforts made by Hindus to get their widows married are for obvious reasons disliked by other non Indian religions. He strongly pleads of the cause of the so called 'acchuts' and asks Hindu Mahasabha to take some action in the direction of providing educational facilities both general and vocational for them to an adequate extent. "In the end he exhorted the Hindus to be considerate towards their fellow brethren of depressed classes and to make changes in their social and religious practices and thus to consolidate their own ground internally". He said I long for the day when we shall all be known only as Hindus all in enjoyment of equal social dignity. He vehemently said that "the sooner the expression, 'Depressed classes' falls into disuse the better" and he feels for the daily decrease in number of Hindus in every province. This leads him to discuss briefly the cause of the decay of nations and people. He rightly points out that, "If in any Hindu Caste or Hindus in any area are decreasing, it should be investigated whether owing to any cause their has been suppressed and hope creased" and further say "I shall only say only this in brief that, as in the past, so at present and also in the future the Hindus will not shrink from facing all dangers and making all the sacrifices necessary for winning the freedom for all communities." [52]

The Round Table Conference

Dr. Moonje, as the Working President of the Hindu Mahasabha, was invited to the Round Table Conference. Besides him, some of the prominent Hindus were also invited in their private capacity. Among them, the names of Raja Narendra Nath, and Pandit Nanak Chand may be mentioned. All of them tried their best to present the Hindu point of view before the British statesmen and the delegates.

First Round Table Conference was held for a federal formula for the Government of India to "make it possible to give a semblance of responsible government. It was represented by Hindu Mahasabha. B. S. Moonje attended conference along with M. R. Jayakar, and Diwan Bahadur Raja Narendra Nath. Liberals represented by J. N. Basu, Tej Bahadur Sapru, C. Y. Chintamani, V. S. Srinivasa Sastri, C.P. Ramaswami Iyer, Justice Party by Arcot Ramasamy Mudaliar, and Depressed Classes by B. R. Ambedkar, Rettamalai Srinivasan. The conference started with six plenary meetings where delegates put forward their issues. Nine sub-committees were formed to deal with several different matters including federal structure, and provincial constitution. The

British agreed that representative government should be introduced on provincial level. In Second Round Table Conference, the Gandhi–Irwin Pact opened the way for Congress participation in this conference. Along with the leaders, who attended the 1st Round table, Gandhi was invited from India and attended as the official Congress representative accompanied by Sarojini Naidu and also Madan Mohan Malaviya, Ghanshyam Das Birla, S.K. Dutta and Sir Syed Ali Imam. Gandhi claimed that the Congress alone represented political India; that the Untouchables were Hindus and should not be treated as a "minority"; and that there should be no separate electorates or special safeguards for Muslims or other minorities.

He attended the Round Table Conferences (in London) twice to place the side of Hindus, despite strong opposition from Congress leaders. Incidentally, the Congress leaders, who opposed Dr Moonje for his participation in first Round Table Conference, took part in second Round Table Conference.[53]

In 1931, Moonje travelled to Italy, where he met with Prime Minister Benito Mussolini and was shown the militarization of society through a guided tour of organizations such as Balilla, the Accademia della Farnesina and other military schools and educational institutions. He visited many Military Schools in Britain, Germany, France, Spain and Italy. He met many Generals of First World War to study the military training imparted.

Moonje was deeply influenced by these organizations, in which he saw an opportunity to militarize Hindu society in order to fight against external threats. After returning from his Italy visit, he set up Bhonsala Military School in Nasik. Critics of RSS often comment that RSS was modelled on Fascist organisation Balilla. But the fact was, RSS was founded in 1925, on the lines of Bharthiya Swayamsevak Mandal and Hindustani Seva Dal and basic organisational setup was in place. RSS has expanded to Vidarbha and Central Provinces when Dr.B.S. Moonje visited Europe as a member of Round table conference and later visited Italy and met Benito Mussolini in 1931.

As a social reformer, he established many social Institutions and Organizations such as Schools, Orphanages, Gymnasiums, Rifle Clubs, Hostels for Untouchables/Dalits. All the institutions he founded are still running in good condition, some of them have completed the Diamond Jubilee. He also started a Marathi Newspaper known as Daily Maharashtra in Nagpur.

Dr. Moonje was in favor of Responsive Cooperation rather than total Non-Cooperation. Later on, Congress adopted this Policy of Responsive Cooperation, realizing its effectiveness.

He, along with Veer Savarkar, strongly advised Dr Ambedkar to convert to any religion of Indian origin (and not any Abrahamic creed), when the question of Dalit exodus from Hinduism gained fire. Initially, Ambedkar thought of joining Sikhism, but later settled for Buddhism.

In April, 1927, Dr. B. S. Moonje presided over the Patna Session of the Akhil Bharatiya Hindu Mahasabha. Some were a bit frightened at Dr. Moonje's election as the president. As he was regarded one of the strongest and most fiery advocates of the Hindu cause, it was feared he might give a bold set-back to the Congress movement. The wavering attitude of our leaders was clearly witnessed when, through this vague fear, he was prevailed upon by these prominent Hindu Sabha and Congress leaders not to read his address, which he had already written, to the audience, and satisfying them simply with a verbal speech from the pulpit. Dr. Moonje, though often yielding to environments, has always remained loyal and true to the Hindu Sabha cause, which he boldy espoused and has tenaciously stuck to it through sun and shade with a life-long service to his credit.

Before this 'Moonje-period' in the History of Hindu Sabha Movement, the Hindu leaders and Hindu public had awakened, as we have already mentioned, to the great need of self-defence and self-preservation. But, unfortunately, the Hindu leaders could not take their stand for a long time. They lost ground, obsessed of the Congress that by the sentimental ideal 'served as a film to obscure their vision from the right path.'

The Memorable Ajmer session and after :

Dr. B. S. Moonje was still in England when the memorable session of the Akhil Bharatiya Hindu Mahasabha was held at Ajmer on October 13, 14 and 15, 1933, under the presidentship of Bhai Parmanandji—a practical politician and staunchest champion of the Hindu Cause.

In his Presidential Address, he enunciated his views on the conditions through which the country was passing. At that time, many public men, like Pandit Jawaharlal Nehru and the Congress Newspapers in the country ran down his views on the ground that he preached co-operation with the Government as he advised the Hindus to capture the Legislatures. But only four months after this, these same critics began to subscribe to his views and came to look upon the Council entry as the only political work of any importance. And now what do we see? The Congress Raj is prevalent in seven provinces of Hindustan. Is it non-co-operation with the Government?

Immediately after assuming the Presidentship or the Akhil Bharatiya Hindu Mahasabha, Bhai Parmanand undertook an all-India tour. He visited important towns in all the provinces of Hindusthan, i. e. Agra and Oudh, Bihar, Bengal, Bombay Presidency, Maharashtra, the N. W. F. Province and the Punjab. In Maharashtra Province, Dr. B. S. Moonje and Sri. R. G. Bhidey also joined him. In almost all the cities, mass meetings of the Hindus were held and unanimous resolutions condemning the so-called Communal Award were passed, texts of which were communicated to the Government and to the Joint Parliamentary Committee.

While concluding the Ajmer Session, it would be well to mention certain outstanding events connected with Hindu Mahasabha's policy that was clearly marked in extending its sphere of influence and activity beyond the British India.

The Hindu Mahasabha did not rest content by sending only a cable-gram to the League of Nations, communicating its resolutions and appealing to the League for interference and for application of the League Covenant to the Communal problems in India. But it stirred itself to make serious efforts to end the long cultural isolation of the Hindus at home and of the Hindus in islands, countries and other colonies outside India. The Hindu Maha-sabha, therefore, carefully looked to the grievances of the Hindus of Goa and made various attempts to get them removed. Taking advantage of Dr. Moonje's stay in England after the evidence before the Joint Parliamentary Select Committee in London, the Goanese Indians requested him to visit Lisbon, the capital of Portugal, and to represent their grievances to the Home Govt. of the Portuguese.[54]

'Rajah-Moonje Pact' (R-MP) signed in early 1932 between Dr B.S. Moonje and M. C. Rajah. It provided a model for walking a path that would not compromise on justice nor would fall prey to the divide and rule policy created by the British.

The bitter lessons learned in the circumstances surrounding the controversy led to the pact becoming important in building unity among the then scheduled communities (SCs). In fact, R-MP served as the precursor to the much celebrated 'Ambedkar-Gandhi' Pact (A-GP).[55]

The Signatories

Mylai Chinna Thambi Pillai Rajah (17 June 1883-20 August 1943) was a Dalit politician and a social and political activist from Tamil Nadu.

Born to a poor Tamil family in Madras, he entered politics after graduating from college and became a leader of Paraiyars (a Scheduled Castes community) in the Justice Party. But, he left the party in 1923 over the treatment of Dalits and allied with Dr BR Ambedkar.

At one point, Rajah was considered to be a person equal in stature to Ambedkar. Rajah, along with Ambedkar and Rettamalai Srinivasan, represented the Dalits at the Second Round Table Conference in London.

During late 1935, Rajah chose to not support Dr Ambedkar's decision to leave Hinduism. Rajah, felt that conversion from Hinduism would weaken the determination of the Dalit and Hindu social reformers involved in fighting caste anomalies.

B S Moonje was a resilient follower of Lokmanya Tilak. He was the general secretary of Central Indian Provincial Congress for many years.

After the demise of Tilak in 1920, Moonje separated from Congress and took up the leadership of the Hindu Mahasabha until he handed over the charge to Veer Savarkar in 1937. Till his death, he was active in the Mahasabha and used to tour across India.

A prominent social reformer, Moonje, founded many social institutions including schools, gymnasiums, and hostels for Dalit children. The Bhonsala Military School in Nashik was started by him to provide military training to young Hindus irrespective of caste.

It is a historical fact today that Rajah-Moonje Pact was the first-ever agreement on reservation between the so-called Caste Hindus and the SCs. Later, M C Rajah pointed out the significance of the pact as the one between 'the only central organisation of the depressed classes' and the 'organised body of Hindus taken as a whole'.

He also hailed the 'hand of fraternity' extended by 'our co-religionists, the Caste Hindus'. The heart of the problem was the issue of joint or separate electorates for the so-called depressed classes.

Originally, Rajah stood for the Separate Electorates and Ambedkar for the Joint Electorates with Adult Suffrage and Reservation of seats. But, Ambedkar changed his state of mind to the separate electorate, putting forth separate electorates as a united demand of the then Depressed Classes due to the pressure from Rajah and Madras Presidency Organisations in 1931. However, Rajah changed his mind to Joint Electorates with reserved seats on population basis due to lower representation of the Minority Pact in 1932. So, he concluded a pact with the All India President of the Hindu Mahasabha, B. S. Moonje. This was known as the Rajah–Moonje pact. According to this pact, Moonje offered reserved seats to the Scheduled Castes in return for Rajah's support. The Rajah-Moonje Pact was a precursor for the Poona Pact.

Dr Ambedkar had returned from the round table conference and started vehemently supporting separate electorates for the scheduled communities. On the other hand, M C Rajah was in favour of joint electorates.

The then British prime minister had favoured separate electorates through the 'Communal Award' by which the separate electorates, hitherto given to the Muslims, were now extended to the SCs. Gandhi wrote a letter to the British Prime Minister that he would launch a fast unto death if separate electorates for the SCs were not withdrawn. But, Dr Ambedkar considered the communal award 'a priceless privilege' and declared that with dual vote and separate electorate the 'untouchables would have been in a position to determine if not dictate the issue of the general election'.

However, Rajah pointed out that the communal award actually took more than it gave. Thus, while the Simon Commission gave 117 seats out of 1,436 in provincial legislature for the SCs, and 237 under minorities pact (which Dr Ambedkar himself had signed), 90 seats according to the recommendations of the Indian Central Committee, the communal award gave scheduled communities just 71 seats.

Rajah further argued in favour of the joint electorates with reservation for SCs from the point of view of a healthy democracy and social empowerment:

"I do not know why the Prime Minister calls the scheme of joint electorates with reservation of seats as impracticable. It is already in force in local bodies in Madras and some other provinces and has worked very satisfactorily. I am surprised at the argument of the Prime Minister that there is no segregation because we can vote for Caste Hindus who will have to solicit our votes. But, Sir, how can we bring about a common ideal of citizenship when Depressed Class representatives are not to solicit the votes of (so-called) higher castes?"

Then he went on to argue the need for reforming the Hindu society from within and not by alienating them through separate electorates:

"We Depressed Classes, feel ourselves as true Hindus as any Caste Hindu can be and we feel that the moral conscience of the Hindus have been roused to the extent that our salvation lies in bringing about a change from within the main body of Hindu society and not segregating ourselves from them."

The British were over-concerned about the Rajah-Moonje Pact, and secretary of state for India from London asked the viceroy if he could send 'any estimates' regarding 'the extent to which the pact is likely to receive general acceptance by the interests involved.'

In Tamil Nadu, K Bashyam, a Gandhian leader, who was active in anti-untouchability campaign met Rajah and expressed his support for the Rajah-Moonje Pact. This was duly noted by British intelligence (Under Secretary's Safe File No 804). That was in 1932. The British interest was not in social justice but in the 'politically very considerable advantages in having two substantial minorities' as Lord Amery wrote to Viceroy Lord Linlithgow, a decade after the separate electorate-communal award was thwarted.

The opposition to the pact was violent and vehement. In the All India Depressed Classes Conference held at Kamptee in 1932, a prominent SC leader Raj Bhoj, who supported the R-MP, was attacked physically by the supporters of separate electorate and was admitted to the hospital. However, there was also widespread support.

In the Hindustan Times, dated 29 February 1932, the special correspondent reported that the R-MP was sent to the Prime Minister of England. On 9th March, the paper reported that 'Hindu and Sikh MLAs support'the Rajah-Moonje Pact. On 16 March 1932, a procession was taken out in support of the pact by Deorukhker, a nationalist SCs leader. On 17th March, on behalf of Shraddhanand Memorial Trust, the pact was hailed by SCs leaders.

The Tribune from Lahore, in its issue dated 25 March 1932, hailed the pact as 'the best solution' and it wrote:

"If only the other minorities in India had the same wisdom, clear-headedness and sagacity that Mr Rajah and his Association possess they would have come to exactly the same conclusion to which the latter have come. If the depressed classes are socially an integral part of the Hindu community, the Muslims and other non-Hindu Minorities are politically an equally integral part of the Indian nation..."

The Statesman, dated 30 March 1932, reported that in New Delhi, All India Shradhanand Dalit-Uddhar Sabha took out a procession in support of the pact. They raised the 'Bharat Mata ki Jai' slogan and carried banners that declared 'We are Hindus of Hindus.' When the Pune Pact was signed between Gandhi and Dr Ambedkar, Rajah gave his full support to the pact without any ego though it was mostly a replica of Rajah-Moonje Pact.

In the speech delivered at the legislative assembly on 13 September 1932, he gave his wholehearted support for Ambedkar-Gandhi Pact. In this, he was supported by Swami Sahajananda, another social reformer and a scheduled community representative.

It is interesting that in the context of present-day Indian politics, the words of Dr Ambedkar on minority rights (social minorities and not religious minorities) echo the spirit of Rajah-Moonje Pact. He saw reservations as provisions for homogenising the majority and minorities. He said:

"In this country both the minorities and the majorities have followed a wrong path. It is wrong for the majority to deny the existence of minorities. It is equally wrong for the minorities to perpetuate themselves."

Just as how Rajah placed hopes and aspirations of the SCs in the hands of the larger Hindu society, Dr Ambedkar stated that: 'the minorities in India have agreed to place their existence in the hands of the majority' and pointed out that 'the moment the majority loses the habit of discriminating against minority, the minorities can have no ground to exist...

In other words, Rajah-Moonje Pact saw the British plan to perpetuate minorities in India for their political advantage and opted joint electorates with reservations as a means to achieve social integration.

Later, Dr Ambedkar also came to the conclusion that the social minorities should merge with the majorities with the latter removing the discrimination, and that reservations are only tools towards this end. Interestingly, now the pseudo-secular forces in India have taken the place of the British, who want the perpetuation of minorities for the 'politically very considerable advantages'.

Indianisation of the military and militarization of India

He had a keen interest in "Indianisation of the military and militarization of India". He was member of the "First Defence Committee of India" under the Chairmanship of General Chetwood, and also member of Central Legislative Council (now known as the Parliament).

Taking the advantage of new recruitment opened by British Government during World War II, he conducted several Recruitment Rallies for inducting young men into the British Army, thinking that the well trained Indian Blood (at the cost of British) will revolt against British when nation needs it. Bhonsala Military School, Nasik was established by Dharamaveer Dr Balkrishna Shivramji Moonje, who was a firm believer of Indianisation of the Armed Forces during the British rule and indispensability of military training to Indian youth. He took initiative in starting Indian Military Academy at Dehradun as the first Indian Academy in 1936. After this tour, he established Central Hindu Military Education Society at Nashik in 1935 and started Bhonsala Military School in 1937 as a feeder Institute to IMA, Dehradun. The school started functioning in the Surgana Palace in Nasik city with 90 students on its roll. The Maharaja of erstwhile Gwalior state, H H Shriman Jivajirao Scindia inaugurated the main building of the school. In his inaugural speech, he said, "It is not a mere coincidence that within a short period of the opening of a first rate public school in India (he was referring to the Doon School, Dehradun), we are here today to open a first rate Military School." Such was the charisma, charm and aura of the founder, that he made the then Governor of Bombay State, Sir Roger Lumley to lay the foundation stone of the present main building of the school. Over the years, the school has established itself as a premier residential school catering for educational needs of students from all over India and also as a focal point for military education.

He was disturbed with partition and ensuing consequences. He was ill and passed away on 3rd March 1948, few months after independence. His contribution in reference to 'Simon Commission', 'Budget Provision for Defence', 'Founding of Military schools' and 'Social Reform', has been proudly acknowledged by society at large.

Narasimha Chintaman Kelkar

Narasimha Chintaman Kelkar (N. C. Kelkar), popularly known as Sahityasamrat Tatyasaheb Kelkar (24 August 1872–14 October 1947), was a lawyer from Miraj as well as a dramatist, novelist, short story writer, poet, biographer, critic, historian, writer on philosophical and political themes. He was born in Chitpavan Brahmin family. Narsimha Chintaman Kelkar was born in Miraj on 24 August 1872. He spent most of his life in Pune. Kelkar studied law, and was a prominent literary, political and social figure in the early twentieth century Maharashtra. Kelkar carved a niche for himself in the political and cultural life of Maharashtrians. In 1912 and 1918, he was respectively the Vice President and the President of Pune Municipality, and Mayor for six years of the 25 years he was its member.

N.C. Kelkar was a close associate of Lokmanya Tilak. About 15 years younger, Kelkar worked with Tilak over many initiatives. Following Tilak's death, he became one of the key leaders of the 'Tilak faction' of the Indian National Congress. Kelkar was the editor of Kesari twice during Tilak's imprisonments (1897-1899 and 1908-1914). He continued working with Kesari after Tilak's death (in 1920) and wrote the first comprehensive biography of Tilak in 1921. In 1918, he was Secretary of the Indian delegation to the United Kingdom for the Indian National Congress and the All India Home Rule League. In 1919, while in the UK, he edited the British India Congress Committee India newsletter. Later, he was the Chairman of the Joint Provincial Council of both the Congress and the Home Rule League in Solapur in 1920.

Kelkar was elected to the Central Legislative Assembly and served from 1923 to 1929. He participated in the first Round Table Conference in 1930. He was president of the Akhil Bharatiya Hindu Mahasabha twice at Jabalpur in 1928 and Delhi in 1932.

He was a literary and political figure in Maharashtra, India, and also both editor and trustee of the newspaper Kesari. He served as editor twice when Tilak was imprisoned in 1897 and 1908.

He was associated with Shikshana Prasarak Mandali Pune, an education society in Pune, established in 1904. He was also closely associated with Bal Gangadhar Tilak in the Indian independence movement. He had also served as the president of Marathi Granth Sangrahalaya, Thane.[56]

After the death of Tilak in 1920, he became one of the foremost leaders of the Tilak faction in the Congress party. He was elected to the Central Legislative Assembly, the lower house of the Imperial Legislative Council in 1923 and served until 1929. He was president of Akhil Bharatiya Hindu Mahasabha twice at Jabalpur in 1928, and Delhi at 1932. He was also known as 'Tatyasaheb' Kelkar.

N.C. Kelkar was a very prominent figure in Maharashtra in early 20th century. Unfortunately, his work is not very well known today. "Therefore, when the next annual session of the Hindu Mahasabha met at Jubbulpore under the distinguished presidentship of N. C. Kelkar, the change was complete and even Pandit. Malaviya was thrown overboard by the Hindu representatives in spite of all their reverence for him on this question. For, when the Sindh question came up before the Mahasabha, Pandit Malaviya again advised the Mahasabha not to take "odium" upon itself of making a settlement impossible by its flat denial but to wait for the report of the sub-committee appointed by the Madras Congress."

But, the Sindh representatives, headed by Dr. Choithram and Prof. Ghansham, made a touching and emphatic appeal to the gathering, asking them not to play the game of "Hide and Seek", but to reject clearly and in plain terms a demand unreasonable on the face of it and accepted as such on all hands. Pandit Malaviya formally opposed it, and was heard with the full respect due to him. Dr. Moonje first wanted the representatives to bow to Panditji's advice, but when he found that they were unwilling, he also respectfully opposed Panditji. Mr. Kelkar, though himself uncommitted also agreed with Dr. Moonje. But, very few delegates voted with Pandit Malaviya and all the rest voted for the rejection of the proposed separation of Sindh. Thus the father (of the Renaissance) saw at least, that the child had outgrown the father.

PRESIDENTIAL SPEECH OF N. C. KELKAR, JUBBULPORE, APRIL 1928

"They, the Hindus, have a stake in the country, greater than any other community in India. In the recent troubles the Indian Mohammedans could at least think of such a thing as Hijrat, though of course, they could not practice it successfully. But where in the whole wide world is there an inch of space which the poor, befriended and threatened Hindu can call his own, outside Hindusthan? Other communities have their whole bases of operations and world-wide lines of communication, and flotillas of boats and transports which can replenish them in India at need. The Hindu Society, on the other hand, has long ago burnt its boats, cut off every possible line of communication with the world with its own hands, and has cooped itself up unwisely with a ditch around itself and a foolish contrivance in which the valve shuts against itself but opens out for any hostile soldier, adventurer or camp-follower to safely come across and give the best account of the slightest capacity of mischief or harm which he may possess. The only hope, therefore, of this beleaguered community now lies in strongly fortifying itself at all points of attack, making friends with all amongst itself, taking good care of the blind, the lame and the diseased, and in enthusing the whole garrison with the hope that it can save itself even now, if it makes up its

mind, the hope being reinforced by the warning that it is doomed to destruction if it faints or falters for a moment. Hindus not only wish to attain political Swaraj in India, but they also wish to have their proper share of it, remaining Hindus. We cannot Swaraj will not be worth having if purchase it with any price less than the loss of Hinduism itself."

"The removal of conflict between the different members and organs of the Hindu Society and the establishment of good understanding between them is only a foundation upon which the real structural work of strengthening and organizing the Hindu society is to be done."

"Conferences are being held for the last three years to settle the points of differences between the Hindus and Mohammedans, in matters religious as well as political. But things went from bad to worse even after that. The attempt at the settlement of political differences has shared the same fate. The question therefore arises, what next? My reply to that is 'wait and see'. But I do not give that reply in any cynical spirit. For I really think that the compromise proposals perhaps require some rest. It is now better to see the tree of communal good-will grow from a distance than pull it up frequently by its roots, as it were, to see how it is growing. The discussions and deliberations held during the last three or four years cannot all go for nothing. The discovery of the fundamental positions where both Hindus and Mohmedans stand is in itself a great gain. Digging up of foundations is a necessary operation for undertaking a structure."

"The Hindus should, in my view, spend greater attention and energy on the consideration of the question as to how they will, so far as they can, give the best account of themselves, in the work of achieving political Swarajya."

"I can challenge any one to cite any well-known or proved instances of reconversions to Hinduism which were obtained by fraud or force, ever since the Shuddhi and Sanghathan movements were set on foot. That being so, are Hindus to be branded as communal anti-national? Is it a sin for them to wish to remain Hindus and participate in the future Swaraj as Hindus? It is well if the other communities co-operate with the Hindus in a fair spirit in the work of achieving Swarajya, But if they do not, that is well also, if not so well. The Hindu pilgrim's never failing experience is that if he starts on the journey with a determination to complete his pilgrimage though all alone, he soon begins to get fellow pilgrims on the way as he proceeds. Companionship is indeed good, but self-reliance is always better."

PRESIDENTIAL SPEECH OF N. C. KELKAR, DELHI, SEPTEMBER 1932

Shri N. C. Kelkar discussed and dealt with the Communal Award of 17th August and observed, "My very first word of comment upon the Award would be that it is not the Award of an arbitrator, but simply a decision by the British Government arrived at on its own responsibility like any other administrative decision. Individual members of the Round Table Conference or its Consultative Committee, who were weak or incautious enough to accept Government, even in the last resort, as chosen judges or arbitrators, may naturally feel estopped from contesting the Award. But the Hindu Mahasabha as an association was not called upon to send any chosen delegates to the Round Table Conference. And the Sabha may legitimately feel itself not bound or estopped by the Cabinet decree of 17th August. No doubt the Round Table Conference gave the appearance of certain representatives of the Indian people being consulted, and allowed to suggest to Government decisions, which would be binding if they embodied a common agreement among the leaders of different communities. But Government knew in their heart of hearts that no such agreement would be arrived at, and they also took pretty good care from time to time that such agreement would be made almost impossible. Openly as well as secretly they showed partiality to minorities, especially Muslims among them, and the minorities were consequently inspired or encouraged to set up a higher key to the tune of their communal demand. Government knew full well that they could make great capital out of the communal disagreement in Hindusthan, as communal leaders chosen for the purpose were bound to disagree, though invited to a R. T. Conference."

"If the Government of India," he goes on, "honestly wanted to set up an Indian Nation on its feet in this country, they might have followed the example of League of Nations. But far from doing this, they have decided the matter in such a way that communal confusion in Hindusthan would be worse confounded, owing to communal distinctions being recognised in public and political affairs as much as in private life." "The so-called Award can be impeached," according to him, "on many grounds. The provisions in it have conceded special electorates not only to Mahomedans, who demanded them, but also to Anglo-Indians, Indian Christians and even Indian women who never asked for them. They went beyond even the Simon Commission which did not recommend an assured majority in the legislatures for the majority communities in the provinces, nor special electorates for Depressed Classes or Indian Christians. They have also exceeded the demands put forward even by the official Government of the Punjab in the interest of the Muslims. For whereas an excess of two seats was suggested by them for Muslims over Hindus, a majority of nearly 10 has been conceded by the Award. If Government thought that minorities really should be given representation according to population basis, they should have done for the Hindu minorities in different provinces what they have done for Muslim minorities. But they have perpetrated injustice to the Hindu minorities alone both in Bengal and the Punjab. The Award thus cannot be justified on any common principle. But it is obviously the result of secret partiality to certain minority communities, and the desire also to cripple as far as possible the Hindu community which, in the opinion of Government, has been evincing perhaps an unpleasant or excessive political activity and national consciousness in this country. Broadly, the object of Government seems to be to make it impossible for the legislature in any province to effectively control the Executive Administration. Group would be set up against group. Patronage would do its destructive work. And the foreigner would be able to manipulate the sea-saw of political power; so that the resulting profit of the position would always fall in his own lap."

He further tries to show very clearly how injustice has been done to the Hindus in each province, either by the grant of separate electorates or excessive weightage. He, then, refers to the vow which Mahatma Gandhi took to enter up on a fast unto death as a protest against separate electorates being given to the depressed classes. He very curtly reveals that "Truth in my humble opinion is that this method of self-immolation is not valid. It is grand but not politics." As for the consequences which such a fast and its result are to bring about, he says, "For the Hindu Community generally it would be a painful humiliation. The Depressed class representatives, though they may for the moment yield to Gandhi will perpetually nurse that concession as a great grievance."[57]

Resolutions passed under N.C.Kelkar's Presidentship:

1) The Hindu Mahasabha appreciated the efforts of Dr.Hedgewar for starting strong organisation of Hindus named Rashtriya Swayamsevak Sangh in C.P and Berar, and recommends that its branches be established in all provinces so that it may be an Akhil Bharatiya organisation.

2) **Provincial council elections** -This session of the Mahasabha is of opinion that the forth coming elections to the provincial councils should be contested with a view to protecting and upholding the Hindu interest in the legislatures and leaves it to the Provincial sabhas to take necessary steps in that connection.

3) **Removal of Untouchability** – The Hindu Mahasabha reaffirms its previous resolutions for giving equal access to all Hindus irrespective of their particular caste or creed and to all public amenities and institutions such as temples, schools, wells, tanks, ghats, places of water supply, hotels, roads, parks, dharamshalas, public places of worship, Burning ghats and the like. [58]

The Hindu Mahasabha further affirms its faith that untouchability must not be regarded as a part of Hindu religion or social system. The Mahasabha recommends to Hindus the abolition of all distinctions in the Hindu Society based on Birth or caste in the spheres of public, social and political life, in which such distinctions ought to have no application and are out of place in the present age.

Kelkar played key leadership roles in many institutions across political, social and commerce areas. He was associated with virtually every major institution in Pune. He was a founding member of the Mahratta Chamber of Commerce and the Cosmos Bank. Kelkar was actively involved in the Bhandarkar Oriental Research Institute in several capacities, ever since its inception in 1917. He was a member of the Regulating Council of the Institute continuously from 1918 to 1947, and served as its Chairman from 1930 to 1942.

Three great leaders (19/20th C), can be called as 'the face of Maharashtra': Justice Ranade, Lokmanya Tilak and N.C. Kelkar. Ranade laid the foundation of many great institutions. Tilak nurtured them, and Kelkar grew and expanded them.

N C Kelkar, was a great literary mind of 20th-century Maharashtra. A lawyer, dramatist, novelist, short story writer, poet, essayist, biographer, critic, historian, philosophical and political theme writer, editor, and a nationalist politician, he was a trusted, but moderate lieutenant of Bal Gangadhar Tilak.

For almost five decades, Kelkar carved a niche for himself in the political and cultural life of Maharashtrians. In 1912 and 1918, he was respectively the Vice President and the President of Pune Municipality, and Mayor for six years of the 25 years he was its member.

In 1918, he was Secretary of the Indian delegation to the United Kingdom for the Indian National Congress and the All India Home Rule League. In 1919, while in the UK, he edited the British India Congress Committee India newsletter. Later, he was the Chairman of the Joint Provincial Council of both the Congress and the Home Rule League in Solapur in 1920.

After Tilak's death in 1920, he became one of the foremost leaders of the Tilak faction in the Congress party and joined Gandhi & Non-cooperation Movement, and was a member of the

Congress executive. Elected to the Legislative Assembly in 1923, he served it until 1929. He was president of Akhil Bharatiya Hindu Mahasabha twice at Jabalpur in 1928, and Delhi at 1932.

In 1932, Kelkar served as a member of the London Round Table Conference with the British government to discuss India's Independence. But after Gandhi withdrew his movement, Kelkar joined the Swarajya Party, formed with the aim of implementing reforms and entering the legislature to fight British politics.

Popularly known in Maharashtra as Sahitya Samrat (king of literature) Tatyasaheb Kelkar, he made Marathi readers and writers, truly fond of literature. He covered literary questions like: the relationship between humour and poetry; the cause for laughter; what a metaphor decisively meant; the nature of the interrelationship between prose and verse and how it affects the classification of poetry; the nature of dramatic verses; how literary criticism is fed by memories; what is the role of legends, etc.

His interests included history, philosophy, political science, pedagogy, sociology, court cases, philosophy and politics. His body of work numbers around 15,000. The Kelkar Literary Series, consisting of 12 volumes, released in 1938, was followed by the Kelkar Essay Series (Sahyadri Volume). He wrote plays, novels, short stories, poems, essays, travelogues, biographies, memoirs, and literary reviews. His literary works include 10 plays, eight novels, two collections of poems, two collections of short stories, biographies, and 30-40 critical treatises.

Associated with Shikshana Prasarak Mandali, Pune, established in 1904, he was the President of the Akhil Bharatiya Marathi Sahitya Sammelan held in Baroda in 1921 and it's Secretary in Pune in 1927. He was Chairman of the first session of the Baroda Literary Council (1931), and the President of the Central Indian Poetry Conference held in Ujjain in 1931.

As Trustee of Tilak's daily newspaper Kesari, established in 1881, he was the editor twice when Tilak was imprisoned in 1897 and 1908. He edited the magazine Sahyadri from 1935 to 1947.

Lokmanya Tilak Yanche Charitra, was his biography of Tilak; and Gatagoshti (1939), his autobiographical book. His notable plays were Totayache Band (1913) and Krishnarjuna Yuddha (1915). Among his critical works are Subhashit aani Vinod (1908), Marathe va Ingrej (1918), Rajyashastra (1932), Bharatiya Tattvajyan (1934), and Hasyavinodamimansa (1937).

At 65, Kelkar retired from public life for literary pursuits. He passed away on 14 October 1947, aged 75, at his home on Prabhat Road in Pune, barely two hours after composing two poems on death. A huge number of people attended N.C. Kelkar's funeral in Pune, including Maharishi Karve and Veer Savarkar.

Savarkar in his brief 'Shradhanjali' mentioned:

When Nana Phadnis died (in 1800), all of Pune was drowned in an ocean of grief. Today, it is in a similar state...

Bhai Parmanand

Parmanand was born into a prominent family of the Punjab, Mohyal Brahmins. His father, Tara Chand Mohyal, came from Kariala, Jhelum District and was an active religious missionary with the Arya Samaj movement. In October 1905, Parmanand visited South Africa and stayed with Mahatma Gandhi as a Vedic missionary. Parmanand visited Guyana in 1910 which was the centre of the Arya Samaj movement in the Caribbean. His lectures increased their following there. In 1911, he visited Lala Hardayal when he was on retreat in Martinique. Parmanand persuaded Hardayal to go to the United States to found a centre for the propagation of the ancient culture of the Aryan people. Hardayal left for America, but soon located himself in Hawaii, where he again went on retreat on Waikiki Beach. A letter from Parmanand prompted his departure for San Francisco where he became an activist in the anarchist movement.

While reading letters of Lala Lajpat Rai to him, in 1909, he had jotted an idea that 'the territory beyond Sindh could be united with North-West Frontier Province into a great Musulman Kingdom. The Hindus of the region should come away, while at the same time the Musulmans in the rest of the country should go and settle in this territory'. He was first Hindu leader to come with such idea although there has been such proposal from Syed Ahmed Khan and other Muslim leaders in the past.

Parmanand actually agreed that Muslims should be given a separate nation. But that doesn't mean he was propagating Two-Nation Theory. One has to understand that in the end, entire India accepted that Muslims should be given a separate nation but it doesn't mean that India was wishing her own division. Because of the kind violence which erupted, people agreed that it's better to give their own nation. Parmanand actually wanted a united India, for that, he along with Dayanand Saraswati went to Sir Syed Ahmad [Father of Two-Nation Theory] to hold talks about Hindu-Muslim unity, but then they understood that Syed Ahmad is not willing to accept their proposal. Hence, it seems, Parmanand shaped his view that holding talks about Hindu-Muslim unity is fruitless.

Parmanand toured several British colonies in South America before re-joining Hardayal in San Francisco. He was a founder member of the Ghadar Party. He accompanied Hardayal on a speaking tour to Portland in 1914 and wrote a book for the Ghadar Party called Tarikh-I-Hind. He returned to India as part of the Ghadar Conspiracy, claiming he was accompanied by 5,000 Ghadarites. He was part of the leadership of the revolt, and was sent to promote the revolt in Peshawar. He was arrested in connection with the First Lahore Conspiracy Case and was sentenced to death in 1915. The sentence was later commuted to one of transportation for life: he was imprisoned in the Andaman Islands until 1920 and subjected to hard labour. In protest against such harsh treatment of political prisoners, Bhai Parmanand went on hunger strike for two months. The King-Emperor, George V, released him in 1920 as the result of a general amnesty order.[59]

Bhai Parmanand: Lesser-known Hindu Mahasabha Leader's Saga of Sacrifice

At that time, Bhai Parmanand was in the Andamans jail, suffering 'transportation with forfeiture. The 'forfeiture' had deprived his family of even the cooking utensils and now his wife was supporting the family with a scanty pay, from her work as a primary school teacher in an Arya Samaj school.

Earlier, Bhai Parmanand worked as a lecturer of history and political economics. As a life-member of Arya Samaj, with a vow to teach at a fixed allowance of 75, he had declined a higher career from Punjab University, as it would have raised his salary above the limit of his vow. He had later gone to the United States to coordinate the overseas attempts by Indians to achieve Independence, where he was active in the Ghadar movement. His cousin Bhai Balmukund came in the line of Bhai Matidas, the disciple of Guru Tegh Bahadur, who was martyred by Aurangzeb. When the British hanged Bhai Balmukund to death, his wife, Ram Rakhi, married only for a year, ended her life.

Bhai Parmanand was deported to Andaman. Here he, along with other convicts, had to extract fine coconut fibre from the bundle of coconut fibre given to them. They had to grind oil in the mill tied to the yoke like draught animals. British used tandeels-black uniforms given to convicts to harass the convicts who beat up and abused them, particularly the political prisoners Rev Andrews, learning about the plight of Bhai Parmanand, wrote:

The thought has come home to me again and again... how futile, how stupid, how insensate it is to keep one of the brightest and keenest intellects in modern India, a man with such noble qualities of mind and heart, imprisoned along with the lowest criminals for the rest of his life and engaged in the useless, senseless and meaningless occupation of grinding hour after hour at the mill.

Solitary confinement, restriction of movement by having an iron-stake between the legs, handcuffs on the wrists and handcuffing behind the back, and whipping with a maximum of 30 lashes. The prisoners had to endure all these tortures. Often the prisoners became suicidal. Bhai Parmanand records:

For the future-blank despair, for the present, the severity of punishment and of hard labour; under such conditions many prisoners become indifferent to life and resolve to destroy themselves. Though there is a search every evening and the warder keeps going round the lines at night with lamp in hand, they manage to conceal a piece of rope or improvise one by tearing to pieces their shirt or breeches and hang themselves to death. Several such cases occurred during my stay there and these served to impress firmly on our minds, how near the life and death was our place of residence.

Suicidal thoughts and a complete sense of purposelessness in rotting away his entire life in the sub-human conditions in the prison started taking its toll on him.

My own mind was kept agitated by the thought, 'Why should I live longer?' A sort of special feeling of uneasiness occupied my heart. Every moment, I was debating within myself whether I should cut shot my life or continue to live.

As Bhai Parmanand toiled in prison, the First World War was coming to a close. His observations regarding the war show a very humanistic and Indic vision. He saw the war rooted in 'the very essence of European civilization, whose one ideal has been self-aggrandizement, by whatever means, at the expense of others. Unlike some other nationalists, he did not harbour the motion that had Germany won the war, India would have become liberated.

He observed with cold and remarkable objectivity thus:

As regards the English nation, although it has kept us down and trampled on our rights, I had little hope that the atrocities would be less if the Germans came. No doubt, if both powers should fight in India, there might be a chance of improving our position.

If Indian political prisoners had any hope that with the end of the War, the government would release them, they were smashed with the behaviour of the government which enacted the Rowlatt Committee. Meanwhile, the Chief Commissioner of Andamans, at that time was one Col. Douglas, who happened to be a great friend of Sir Michael O'Dwyer.

One day, he came to Bhai Parmanand and informed him that O'Dwyer still remembered him and asked if he was still alive. Meanwhile, some of the letters of Bhai Parmanand which described the sordid conditions of the Andamans, got published in the Punjab Tribune. This led to the solitary confinement of Bhai Parmanand. At this point, Bhat Parmanand started a fast unto death. After a week, the authorities started force-feeding him. The doctor, who came to see the prisoners, came with a tube for forcing the milk into the stomach through the nose. Bhai Parmanand writes:

Hands and feet were held tight, and a long rubber tube was introduced through the nose into the stomach through which the milk was passed down. The process was painful, but this is the usual thing in jail and was done by force.

The struggle went on for eight weeks. And after much persuasion by a new Superintendent who took an admiration for him, Bhai Parmanand gave up the hunger strike which nearly killed him. In 1920, he was released after five years of incarceration. Upon returning home, he found it hard to get a job and made peace with the idea that his wife would work in the school and he would look after the house. Some friends sent him to Kashmir in 1930 to regain his health. There he observed, 'Yes, great injustice had everywhere been done to Hindus in respect to their religion, but such treatment had exceeded all the limits in Kashmir'. The sight of Kashmiri Hindu women and children with the vermillion on their forehead and religious marks, made him 'unconsciously bow' his head remembering the great sacrifice made by Guru Tegh Bahadur.

Soon, he took up the work that was dearer to his heart-teaching. He wanted to create an educational system that was completely Indic. Therefore, when Gandhi started his national educational programme, 'Bhaiji' as he was called, gave his full cooperation. When he started teaching again in the college one of the students who had enrolled received his particular attention. His name was Bhagat Singh.

Bhai Parmanand had a great respect for Gandhi, but he was highly critical of the Khilafat movement which he rightly recognized as having 'fanned bigotry and fanaticism in the minds of the Muslims. Attacks on Hindus had already started taking place throughout the country: Malabar, Multan, Kohat, Calcutta etc. At Saharanpur, where he went personally for relief work, he saw the utterly helpless plight of Hindus and discovered that the local Khilafat committee leaders were the ones indulging in the riots. When eminent Hindu leaders of the Congress like Swami Shraddhanand, Pandit Madan Mohan Malviya and Lala Lajpat Rai realized the danger the Hindu society was facing and started a movement for Hindu Sanghatan, Bhai Parmanand also joined the movement The communal award system with which the British were playing havoc with social harmony and to which the Congress had largely compromised, pained the visionary in him. He stated that 'if the communal award remains the way to Swaraj would be closed for Hindus forever and that they would be subjected to double slavery.

When Congress leaders started attacking him that he was being fearful, he remarked caustically that he knew no fear even when imprisonment was dreadful, so why he should be afraid of going to jail now when even such persons as have passed all their lives in wine and women could court two or three-months' imprisonment and come to be known as fearless or brave patriots. For the Congressmen, it would not have been lost upon them as to whom he targeted this rebuke. Though a great admirer of Gandhi, he never lost sight of what he considered as the truth, in the awe of the Mahatma. He rejected the idea that it was Gandhi who made Congress and national struggle a people's movement. Given the fact that even today, this idea that Gandhi made the independence movement a mass movement prevails, the observations of Bhai Parmanand need to be quoted at length:

Very often I am told that the Congress, in spite of all its defects, has at least done one great good to India. It has brought awakening in the land. If Mahatma Gandhi and the Congress did anything it was this: they harnessed that universal sentiment to the service of their own movement.

Bhai Parmanand was also a caste abolitionist and started the Caste-Elimination movement within Arya Samaj. He also adopted a child from another community as his own son and brought him up. Like M. C. Rajah of Tamil Nadu, he also held that before Hindu-Muslim unity, first Hindu unity should be achieved. In 1932, a tragedy struck him in the form of the death of his wife who had given him constant support in all his struggles. In 1939, his youngest daughter died too.

His Sanghatan Views

Bhai Parmanand wrote Hindu Sanghatan in Hindi. The book was translated into English by Prof. Lal Chand Dhawan and was published in 1936 by the Central Hindu Yuvak Sabha of Lahore. At the very beginning of the book, Bhai Parmanand distinguishes between dogmatic religion and the Hindu spiritual traditions. He underscores freedom from dogmas as the unique positive feature of Hindu Dharma:

What is the foundation of religion? Religion lays down a few dogmas and teaches us that these and these alone are true, and everything against them is untruth. It also teaches that salvation for man lies in having faith in those dogmas alone. These two things, however, will put an end to all freedom of opinion in the world. How can an intelligent man be ever compelled to believe against his reason that there is only one God, that he possesses certain characteristics and reveals his will in different ways?

Religion presupposes the truth of a few postulates, and thus lays the foundations of narrow-mindedness and bigotry. And what if these postulates themselves happen to be wrong? The Hindu Shastras do not proceed on any such suppositions or hypotheses. They take note of the universe around us, and in trying to solve the mystery of the existence of the universe, they infer the existence of the power that controls the universe. Beyond this, they confess everything is unknowable. No one can ever that he knows him; even he who says that he does not know him is wrong. The following verse of the Gita shows how important and venerable freedom of opinion is: "All roads lead to me. He who seeks me, whatever way he may follow, shall surely find me. The author of the Gita, too, had many postulates at his disposal. He could lay down one or two of these as obligatory and kill all freedom of thought. But he preferred that freedom to everything else; for therein lay the welfare of mankind"

Then he proceeds to define who is a Hindu. While admiringly accepting the Savarkarite definition as 'the only correct and complete definition, he himself desires a much simpler definition and states that anyone who calls and considers himself a Hindu is a Hindu. A non-historian Parmanand does not delve into the truth of the Aryan race theory and he seems to have no problem in accepting the

Aryans as a race, but it does not matter much to him. He approvingly quotes a scholar saying that Hindu as a name of the country might date back to pre-Aryan times.

His analysis of the phenomenon of religion, shaping the human mindscape anticipates the modern neuro-psychological approach to the phenomenon of religion. In his view, the religion becomes the carrier of values and is a motivating force for humans to sacrifice themselves for a cause greater that individual interests. However, as religions claim ownership to competing and at times mutually exclusive 'truths, one needs to apply to reason rather than to dogma and belief. In this, he criticized even his fellow Arya Samajists as well as proselytizing religions. Again, this is an approach that one finds in almost all Hindu Sanghatanist worldviews. The passage needs to be quoted here in detailed manner, for it expresses one important aspect of Hindutva and the Hindu Sanghatan movement:

"In spite of the fact that the countless wrongs and atrocities have been perpetrated on account of the spread of religions and creeds, the world has got the same respect for them as before, and people are still prepared to sacrifice their everything for their respective religions. Man begins to love the religion or thoughts of his birth as much as his native soil and society. Belief in religious dogmas has a special advantage also. Piety and Devotion, born of faith, are not to be found in reason and argumentation. The principles in which we have faith, fix certain ideas on our minds in which a form that we believe them alone to be true and become prepared to sacrifice our all for their sake. It is a noble aspect of man's nature that he is prepared to make any and every sacrifice for the sake of what he thinks and believes to be true. But for religions, this side of human nature would have remained undeveloped. To keep alive this spirit in man is a good thing and this has been made possible by religion. But it should not be inferred from this that what the followers (of) different religions regard as true is in reality true. An idea of the mentality of such men can be gathered from this alone that in the teeth of reason and proofs, they still persist in believing the earth to be flat and are ready to break the head of any one who differs with them. Is there no true religion in the whole wide world? The fact that religion is really true, though in a sense, all religions are true; for a religion is true for him who believes in it. The common saying that 'Truth always triumphs' means nothing more than that the truth in which more men or more powerful men have faith, triumphs. In reality what is Truth? To know and to judge this, man's reason alone is the means. According as a man's intellect is his understanding of truth will be. Hence, the prayer contained in the Gaitri mantra is that our reason and intellect may be sound. In the Punjab the Arya Samaj is considered to be the most active and powerful religious body among the Hindus. Now, consider the case of the Arya Samaj. If anyone has the courage to say today that he doubts if the Vedas are revealed, plans will be made at once to turn him out of the Samaj. Such statements make for weakness of belief in doctrines; and it is feared that the weakening of belief in its doctrines will weaken Arya Samaj itself. If this is really so, then the Arya Samaj is nothing but a creed."

One can see here that Bhai Parmanand points out how the religion serves an important role in human evolution, particularly how it makes individual members of human species sacrifice their own genetic survival for the group, and the genetic survival of those belonging to the same memetic clan (which usually also may have ethnic supremacist underpinning, like Islam enhances ultimately Arabic supremacism and Maoism Han-racism). However, he points out that while the kindling of martyrdom is an important achievement of religion, the other side of it is the fanaticism which rejects reason and breeds Intolerance. With 'truth' being a construct, ultimately the appeal has to be reason. This is an important conceptual evolution in the Arya Samaj thought process which has been ignored by many Western observers of Hindutva and also 'South Asian' academic informants for the Western knowledge production. Arya Samaj, in their narratives is merely shown as a monotheist projection of Vedic religion, a kind of 'return to Vedic purity' influenced by colonial encounters. However, the clear placing of reason over dogma and even belief in Vedas by an Arya Samajist leader makes such a characterization of the Arya Samaj movement.

Though Bhai Parmanand tends to accept the dominant narrative that Buddhism abolished 'caste system, a term 'he' (or the translator) seems to confound with Varna, he considers that as a negative feature of Buddhism.

Buddhism abolished the caste system and laid emphasis merely on the duties of the individual. The consequence was that the nation lost all sense of national and patriotic duties. It must be borne in mind that the distinction of castes was based on differences of work and worth and not, as in the present times, on birth.

He further emphasizes that one of the important reasons for the fall of Hindus is because the basis of the Varna system shifted from worth to birth: As birth came into greater and greater prominence, worth and character sank into greater and greater oblivion, till at last all castes Brahmanas, Kshatriyas, Vaishya and Shudras alike fell from their ideals and lost sight of their duties altogether. In my opinion, the greatest and most harmful consequence of the importation of birth into the caste system was that as Brahmanas, Kshatriyas, etc. began to be regarded as such by birth, no one paid any heed to his duties nor was any one under the necessity of doing so. Only this slight change from worth to birth in the cave system dragged the nation from the summit of glory down into the bottomless pit of degradation.

So according to him, the Hindu nation had become old and weak and needed rejuvenation. Towards this end, Bhai Parmanand strongly advocates intercaste marriages:

The four Varnas or divisions of society date back to the very remote past. The sub-castes came into being much later, and are unnatural. These have split up our society into countless small sub-divisions, so that the coming into being of the national sentiment is out of the question. The scope for marriages has become very restricted. Castes have also restricted the mingling of blood a great deal. For instance, certain sections of society are growing more and more cowardly on account of confining their blood to their own castes. The low are becoming lower still. It is a law of nature that the more distant the bloods that mingle the better will be the offspring. There is but one remedy for decay, namely, that new blood should be infused into the community. I think, therefore, that it is necessary to permit free inter-marriages with those castes among the Hindus which have got fresh blood in them so that a new life and spirit may be born in the community.

There is a striking aspect of Hindu Sanghatan worldview here, which sees endogamy as the reason for the physical fall of the Hindus. While world over the racists and racism-motivated eugenics stood for disallowing the racial mix-up, the Hindu Sanghatanists stood for the mixing of 'blood' and lifting the prohibitions of intermarriages. The narrative that Bhai Parmanand constructs where the Varnas were originally occupation-based and not birth-based and, later, as they became birth-based, the coming up of the proliferation of sub-castes and along with that, the restrictions of marriages between the castes, has a striking similarity to the narrative developed by Dr Ambedkar. In both narratives, the restriction on marriages did not transform Varna to caste, but there were other processes. According to Bhai Parmanand, this was the gradual emphasis on birth, which became more and more central to the identification of one's Varna, while Dr Ambedkar puts the blame entirely on the process which he terms as 'Brahminism. Dr Ambedkar based his speculation on:

Varna is not hereditary either in status or occupation. On the other hand, caste implies a system in which status and occupation are hereditary and descend from father to son. The change was accomplished by stages. In the transformation of Varna into Caste, three stages are quite well marked. The first stage was the stage in which the duration of Varna i.e., of status and occupation of a person was for a prescribed period of time only. The second stage was a stage in which the status and occupation involved the Varna of a person ensured during lifetime only. The third stage was a stage in which the status and occupation of the Varna became hereditary. According to ancient tradition as embodied in the Puranas, the period for which the Varna of a person was fixed by Manu and Saptarshi was a period of four years and was called Yug. At the end of the period of four years, there occurred the Manwantar, whereby every fourth year the list was revised. Under the revision some changed their old Varna, some retained it, some lost it and some gained it. The original system seems to have in contemplation the determination of the Varna of adults. It was not based on prior training or close scrutiny of bias and aptitude. The determination of the Varna was done in a rough and tumble manner. This system seems to have gone into abeyance. A new system grew up in its place. It was known as the Gurukul system. The Gurukul was a school maintained by a Guru (teacher) also called Acharya (learned man). All children went to this Gurukul for their education. The period of education extended for twelve years. Upanayan by the Acharyas was the new method of determining Varna which came into vogue in place of methods determination by Manu and Saptarshi. The new method was undoubtedly super to the old method. The principal change made by Brahmanism was the transfer of authority from the Guru to the father in the matter of performing Upanayan. The result was that the father having the right to perform the Upanayan of his child gave his own Varna to the child and thus made it hereditary. It is by divesting the Gar of his authority to determine the Varna and vesting it in the father that Brahman ultimately converted Varna into Caste.

One can note that both in Dr Ambedkar and Bhai Parmanand's views, the narrative core is the same which is that the original Varna system was not birth-based but worth-based. Both consider the fall from Varna to caste (which Parmanand - or his translator - calls sub-caste), as a great national misfortune. Thus, in a way one can say that though Dr Ambedkar positioned himself as against the Arya Samaj or even Hindu revivalists, he agreed that during the Vedic period, the original system was not one of oppression and was not unjust. On the other hand, the point of departure between most Hindu Sanghatanists and Dr Ambedkar is of the view that the latter puts the blame on 'Brahminism and thinks of a motivated, almost a conspiratorial process, which intentionally changed the right of upanayana from the Guru to the father.

Another important element of Bhai Parmanand's worldview that comes in his Hindu Sanghatan is the process of samanvaya. Though he did not name it in the book, it comes out forcefully with respect to two issues. One is in the accommodation of so-called idol worship, and another was the cooperation between the traditionalists and the reformers' factions in the Hindu Sanghatan movement itself. As an Arya Samajist, he was required to be against idol worship. But his own experience in the Andamans Cellular Jail reduced his aversion for the worship of the Divine in forms:

The greatest doctrine of the Arya Samaj is the refutation of idol-worship. Perhaps even the Sanatanists will admit that no image of God can be ever made; but where lies the harm in making idols of Rama, Krishna, etc., and raising temples to them. I was in the Andaman jail. I have no faith (in) idol-worship. But a deep study of the Gita produced in me a special reverence and devotion for Krishna. At that time, my one grief was that I had not seen Brindavan, one of my greatest desires then was that in case I was set at liberty I must go on a sort of pilgrimage to the holy land of Brindavan. Later, when I had the good fortune to visit that place, thoughts that welled up in my mind were too deep for words. Every particle of dust there seemed to me to be worthy of worship. Who knows but Krishna might have touched that particle with his feet? This line recurred to my memory again and again. "Every particle of the dust of my mother land is like a god to me". Have we left off keeping with us pictures of great men? Admitted that they were of God, but they did reveal in their life and actions the power (of) God the greatest. If, therefore, Krishna or Rama was called an incarnation of that power, where lay the harm or sin?

The second samanvaya process that he discerned was with respect to the two factions within Hindu society which were bitterly opposed to each other with respect to social reforms. Hence, this is even more important with respect to the Hindu Sanghatan movement. He pointed out that the radical Arya Sumajists then spearheading social reforms in Hindu society, by themselves alone, would not be able to effect changes. On the contrary, the social reforms proved to be more effective when the reformers while initiating the reforms, also had the orthodoxy convinced and got them roped in as well in integrating the reforms in the society. He explained:

"The Sanatan Dharm Sabhas, which had been brought into being with the sole object of offering opposition to the Arya Samaj, opposed all these things, even though it was not part of the Sanatanists' religion or doctrines to do so. Many years have since elapsed, and that opposition and the differences between these two religious bodies have grown much less, so much so that the Sanatan Dharm Sabhas themselves are now prepared to undertake all those reforms. Although the Arya Samaj preached the necessity of these reforms, yet it did not meet with any considerable success in the absence of support from the Hindus in general. Now there can be, owing to the Sanatanists joining hands with Arya Samajists, hope of real success in this direction, provided we all co-operate heart and soul and be determined to effect those reforms. Another effect of this has been that the work of social reform is no longer confined to the Arya Samaj."

The next frequent common strand, also found in Bhai Parmanand is the oneness of humanity. This is a common theme in both Savarkar and Parmanand, in that they both saw the entire humanity as essentially one. While for Savarkar this was the ultimate reality, all distinctions man-made temporary, and would ultimately yield to the oneness of human species. For Bhai Parmanand, this was an ideal vision towards which humanity - now selfish and fragmented - should strive for:

"It is but a natural and ordinary thing for men to emerge from the individual or wild state of existence and found a family or clan. Their relationship by blood makes them friends and helpers to another and companions in weal and woe. On the other hand, mankind as a whole may be regarded as a big family and all men as brothers. But it is the gods alone who can do so. The human race will reach that stage only if and when there is a fundamental change in human nature, and man rises above all petty self-interests and imbibes some god-like characteristics. Maybe mankind is marching towards that goal, but there is no visible sign of it as yet. The stage which mankind has reached so far lies midway between these two: it is the stage of nationalism. But so far, the wish or thought of marching towards the final stage is hardly in evidence anywhere." Bhai Parmanand, *Hindu Sanghatan and Crossing the Genders*

Summing up, Bhai Parmanand wanted the Sanghatan to be one made of love - a love similar to one Radha had for Krishna. He compares the Sanghatanist to Radha and Krishna to the soul of India.

"Sabhas and Sewak Dals are all useful and necessary, but so long as the flame of love does not fire your soul, Sangathan is out of question. This is the true cement. Krishna is the soul of this nation. Have that deep and boundless love for it as Radha had for Krishna. Like a devotee of Krishna, bearing lotus flowers in his hands as offering, offer your life and soul to this Krishna of yours. This is the true worship of your Krishna; this, true devotion to Him."

This passage filled with emotions, particularly coming from a patriot who lost his own daughter who had died in the arms of her mother, because of the self-imposed poverty and the cellular jail imprisonment of the father, is also significant for another reason. Hindu Sanghatan movement has often been portrayed by the Western academics as well as their Indian academic informants, as an exclusive call to masculinity. Here is a typical such academic portrayal of Hindutva as a masculine call for making 'men' out of Hindus:

Masculine Hinduism anchored the image of strength within the Hindu nationalist discourse. While the discourse that centred on masculine Hinduism constituted a form of resistance to colonial British hierarchy, which itself was founded upon ideas of hegemonic masculinity, Indian masculine Hinduism was not a mechanical incorporation of British ideas dressed in Hindu cultural garb, nor was it monolithic. Rather the Indian construct essentially was a creative response to British disparagement of Indian men. Savarkar clearly perceived masculine Hinduism in terms of virile Aryan warriors riding onwards from a legacy of Indian (i.e., Hindu) imperialism; Vivekananda's image of masculine Hinduism - reflecting purity and stance of a warrior-monk and derived from notions of a mythic ascetic warriorhood - was delineated most eloquently in Chatterjee's Anandamath. In Vivekananda's vision of masculine Hinduism, spiritual strength sat in the foreground; Savarkar's vision emphasized martial prowess. Both viewed physical strength as an important condition for expressing images of masculinity. Madam Cama, Sister Nivedita, and Sarala Debi drew on a figure of manhood that was closer to Savarkar's Aryan soldier than Vivekananda's fighting monk.

Most missionaries portrayed Hinduism as an effeminate religion. They associated idolatry with effeminacy, and effeminacy with all possible vices, such as lying, dishonesty, perjury, and immorality. For Orientalists, by contrast, Hindu effeminacy was a mark of infancy rather than depravity. Most missionaries saw Hindu gods and goddesses as embodiments of vice, lacking in moral virtues and qualities, and therefore thought that those who worshipped them imbibed the immoral qualities of their deities. The missionary concept of Hinduism as an effeminate religion formed part of the larger colonial construction of India as an effeminate nation and as lacking any sense of order, progress, rationality, or the history that characterized Protestant Christianity and Western civilization. The implication was that India and Indian women could not be protected by effeminate men but only manly British men. Colonialists and missionaries justified their continued presence and intervention by constructing an effeminate India, which was incapable of uplifting itself.

Contrary to Dr Sugirtha Rajah saying that the missionary portrayal of the Hindu nation was effeminate as part of a colonial project, now it is clear that it is the other way round. In India today, Christian evangelism, Catholic liberation theology, Islamism and Marxism have inherited, nurtured and propagated this missionary view of Hinduism and Hindu society in academia, media and polity with not a less significant success.

The ninth Annual Session of the Hindu Mahasabha was held at Delhi on the eve of the departure of the members of the Central Legislatures to their homes. General sensation and curiosity were felt in political circles, specially in the Congress Camp, about the resolutions to be passed in that Session. For Bhai Parmanand, one of the most prominent and earnest Hindu Sabha leaders, whose name had been recommended for Presidentship by almost all the Provinces and who would have been certainly elected President had he not himself chosen to withdraw, had been carrying on intense agitation in the papers and on the platform, asking the Mahasabha to send its own nominees to the legislatures as Congress nominees did not consider themselves responsible to the Hindu public opinion and had failed to guard Hindu interests, whereas Mussalmans always guarded their own separate Muslim interests and fought for the same.

Bhai Parmanand's arguments were cogent and forceful and based on facts too. A good section of the Hindu public opinion favoured his views while another differed from them. L. Lajpat Rai, till then the Deputy Leader of the Swarajya Party, was already disgusted with the 'walk in' and 'walk out' policy of the party, but was still not prepared to allow the Hindu Mahasabha to put its hands directly in the matter. Pt. Malaviya was undecided. The dual seemed to be between Lalaji and Bhai Parmanand. Almost all the prominent Congress Hindu leaders for the first time in the history of the Hindu Mahasabha showed their deep anxiety to be present at this Session - though only to thwart the proposals of Bhaiji. So, several Hindu Congressmen came in as delegates and entered the Subject Committee for this very purpose, while most of the more prominent among them, including shri Vithalbhai Patel - the Assembly President, Pt. Motilal Nehru and others chose to bring about indirect pressure upon them by their presence, persuasion, assurance, reason and so-forth.

This Mahasabha Session had therefore gathered a peculiar interest round it. The Session was presided over by Raja Narendra Nath of Lahore, a liberal and moderate in politics, but a man full of the most youthful enthusiasm for the Hindu cause in spite of his old age.

It is in this context that one needs to view the 'make me a man' call of Vivekananda. Swami Vivekananda inverted the missionary and colonial caricature of Hindu effeminacy on its head. He accused the rootlessness caused by British education to the perceived effeminacy in Indian upper classes. And even his pure ascetic warrior-monk came from a tradition that has strong roots in the Divine Feminine.

This passage of Swami Vivekananda shows how remarkably the 'make me a man' call of Hinduness was rooted in the Divine Feminine rather than on a masculinity that downgraded or marginalized the feminine. In another letter written in 1897 to his Guru Bhai Brahmananda, Swami Vivekananda explained how seeing Shashi Babu - probably Shashipada Banerjee, founder of the Widows' Home of Baranagore - 'with his feminine retiringness stirred to work' his own courage had gone up by leaps and bounds. So, if the evangelists and colonialists, the feminine in Indian men was an evil, Vivekananda saw the ability to feel and animate the feminine in men a must for becoming pure and service-minded towards the society. When seen in this context, the passage of Bhai Parmanand represents a continuity in the Hindu Sanghatan thought process, if it can be called that. In his passage, we have a characterization where the Sanghatanist or the patriot is seen as a counterpart the feminine Radha rather than a masculine, virile warrior out to destroy the enemies or worse, spearhead an expansionist imperialism.

As the modern age, through colonialism and evangelism, encountered Hindutva, the resultant churn brought out a wide variety of magnificent thought processes. Internalizing Darwin, Freud, and Marx on the one hand, struggling for the independence of their own nation and looking into their own history, tradition and fighting incursive expansionist theologies along with colonialism, the Hindutva Sanghatan movement enriched the Indian mindscape with quite a rich diversity. The life and thoughts of Lala Har Dayal (1884-1939) demonstrate the inherent plasticity and universal nature in Hindutva which came out when it interacted with the Western modern age.[60]

In 1930, he was the chair of the Sind Provincial Hindu Conference, where he expressed concern that Muslim creation of Pakistan would divide India. He met Gandhi again in 1933 where he analysed India as being composed of three elements: Hindus, Muslims and the British. He suggested that Gandhi had tried to bring the first two together to drive out the British, but that the British had succeeded in gaining the support of the Muslims. Gandhi replied that he was an optimist, and look forward to the day when Muslims would join with Hindus. Parmanand suggested that only if Hindus organised amongst themselves would Muslims join them as nobody associates with the weak."

In 1930s, He was also elected the working President of the Hindu Mahasabha and remained at the helm of affairs consecutively for 4 years, During this period he made Mahasabha a living organization. The days of keeping the Mahasabha as a subsidiary or Corollary organization to the Congress with a half way policy were no longer to be continued and hence it was reorganized as quite a separate body from the Congress with its own principles, aims and objects, policy and programmes.

He founded a Hindu sewa ashram for training persons who would devote their lives to Hindu Sanghathan movement. For the construction of the Hindu Maha Sabha Bhawan the main credit should go to Bhai Parmanand for taking all the initiative for getting such a wonderful building constructed. He also started a new movement within the fold of samaj and founded the Jat pat torak Mandal(Society for the abolition of the caste system).His is a life of sacrifice and suffering for the cause of his country and the Hindu Community.[61]

When at last in 1947, freedom came with the vivisection of India, Bhai Parmanand saw Hindus becoming refugees in their own land over a single night. He had long ago proposed a phased regrouping of people. In hindsight, one can say that had his words been listened to, much human tragedy and suffering could have been averted. Yet, he saw an independent India before he died on 8th December 1947.

His son, Dr. Bhai Mahavir, grew up with an Arya Samaj background and Mahavir joined the RSS in 1938, in a shakha established by Raja Bhau Paturkar in Lahore. He became a pracharak in 1942, and worked in that capacity in Jalandhar for 2 years. Between 1944 and 1947 he was the Secretary of RSS in Lahore. After the partition, he settled down in Jalandhar and worked as a lecturer. He moved to Delhi in 1956, working as a lecturer in the Panjab University College established for the Panjabi refugees.[62]

Towards the end of 1950, Shyama Prasad Mukherjee gathered in Delh,i a core group of activists to form a new political party, the future Bharatiya Jana Sangh. Bhai Mahavir was among this group, along with Vasantrao Oak and Balraj Madhok, all RSS Pracharaks. The three of them founded the Panjab-Delhi branch of the Jana Sangh in Jalandhar on 27 May 1951, which later became part of the nationwide `Bharatiya' Jana Sangh, established on 21 October 1951.

Swami Shraddhanand

Swami Shraddhanand also known as Mahatma Munshi Ram Vij. He was born on 22 February 1856 in the village of Talwan in the Jalandhar District of the Punjab Province of India. He was the youngest child in the family of Lala Nanak Chand, who was a Police Inspector in the United Provinces (now Uttar Pradesh), then administered by the East India Company. His given name was Brihaspati Vij, but later he was called Munshi Ram Vij by his father, a name that stayed with him till he took sanyas in 1917, variously as Lala Munshi Ram Vij and Mahatma Munshi Ram.

Meeting Dayanand

He first met Dayanand Saraswati, when Dayanand visited Bareilly to give lectures. His father was handling arrangements and security at the events, due to the attendance of some prominent personalities and British officers. Munshiram attend the lectures at his father's request. He originally went with the intent of spoiling the arrangements, then claimed to be strongly influenced by Dayanand's courage, skill, and strong personality. After completing his studies, Munshiram started his practice as lawyer.

Schools

In 1892, Arya Samaj was split into two factions after a controversy over whether to make Vedic education the core curriculum at the DAV College Lahore. He left the organization and formed the Punjab Arya Samaj. The Arya Samaj was divided between the Gurukul Section and the DAV Section. Shraddhanand headed for Gurukuls. In 1897, when Lala Lekh Ram was assassinated, Shraddhanand succeeded him. He headed the 'Punjab Arya Pratinidhi Sabha', and started its monthly journal, Arya Musafir. In 1902, he established a Gurukul in Kangri, India, near Haridwar. This school is now recognized as Gurukul Kangri University.

In 1917, Mahatma Munshi Ram took sanyas as "Swami Shradhanand Saraswati". Shraddhanand established gurukul Indraprashtha in Aravali near Faridabad, Haryana.

Activism

In 1917, Shraddhanand left Gurukul to become an active member of the Hindu reform movements and the Indian Independence movement. He began working with the Congress, which he invited to hold its session at Amritsar in 1919. This was because of the Jalianwala Massacre, and no one in the Congress Committee agreed to have a session at Amritsar.

He also joined the nationwide protest against the Rowlatt Act. The same year, he protested in front of a posse of Gurkha soldiers at the Clock Tower in Chandni Chowk, then was allowed to proceed. In the early 1920s, he emerged as an important force in the Hindu Sangathan (consolidation) movement, which was a by product of the now revitalised Hindu Maha Sabha.

Swami Shradhanand was the only Hindu Sanyasi who addressed a huge gathering from the minarets of the main Jama Masjid New Delhi, for national solidarity and vedic dharma, starting his speech with the recitation of ved mantras.

He wrote on religious issues in both Hindi and Urdu. He published newspapers in the two languages as well. He promoted Hindi in the Devanagri script, helped the poor and promoted the education of women. By 1923, he left the social arena and plunged whole-heartedly into his earlier work of the shuddhi movement (re-conversion to Hinduism), which he turned into an important force within Hinduism. In 1922, Dr Ambedkar called Shraddhanand, "the greatest and most sincere champion of the Untouchables".

In late 1923, he became the president of Bhartiya Hindu Shuddhi Sabha, created with an aim of reconverting Muslims, specifically 'Malkana Rajputs' in the western United Province. This brought him into direct confrontation with Muslim clerics and leaders of the time. 1,63,000 Malkana Rajputs were converted back to Hindu fold due to this movement.[63]

Shraddhanand, Biopolitics and Hindu Sangathan

In 1909, Lt Colonel U. N. Mukerji of the Indian military service had published an influential pamphlet, Hindus - A dying race, based on his articles to The Bengalee. Using the results of the 1901 Colonial Census, he had argued rather simplistically that in just over 400 years, Hindus would cease to exist both because of the relative increase in the Christian population (due to missionary activity) and the increase in the Muslim population (resulting from conversions to Islam and allegedly higher birth rates). This terrifying invocation of biological Hindu extinction had a remedy: a focus on those groups of the Indian population that were otherwise considered marginal – the 'tribals' and 'untouchables' who were seen as willing if misguided fodder for missionaries. The pamphlet hugely influenced an Arya Samajist, Munshi Ram (1857-1926), who had become a sannyasi, Swami Shraddhanand, and was a key founder of the Hindu Sangathan movement that emerged from the revitalized Hindu Mahasabha of the early 1920s.

Swami Shraddhanand was previously leader of the 'Mahatma' faction during its dispute with the Dayananda Anglo-Vedic 'College' faction within the Arya Samaj that led to its first major split. He subsequently headed the Punjab Arya Samaj (becoming president of the Punjab Arya Pratinidhi Sabha) and founded his own Gurukul Kangri (school) in 1900, which was itself subject to bitter internecine disputes about curriculum and doctrinal purpose. Similarly, vicious disputes about the status and fallibility of Dayananda's teachings continued to affect both Arya Samaj factions. Shraddhanand, like the previous head of the opposing 'College' faction, Lajpat Rai, was also to be involved in Congress activities in the 1920s; to differing degrees, both were associated with Hindu Mahasabha activities from the same period.

In the period from 1905 until 1919, Shraddhanand had severely criticized anti-British political agitation, whether revolutionary or reformist. When the Arya Samaj had come under suspicion for seditious activities, particularly after the arrest and deportation of Lajpat Rai and Ajit Singh in 1907, Shraddhanand, while opposed to the arrests, portrayed the Arya Samaj as a loyal, non-political, purely religious organization having no subversive or seditious aims. He viewed politics as, in essence, an impure diversion from religious learning.

However, he had strongly agitated for a range of reforms within Hinduism, mostly within the framework of Arya Samaj ideology but with significant modifications that were to be consequential for his militant Hindu nationalism.

Shraddhanand had remained aloof from the national movement until he met Gandhi. According to one of his biographers, it was Gandhi's religious simplicity and commitment that transformed Shraddhanand towards active support for the satyagraha and non-cooperation campaigns. Shraddhanand is frequently viewed as a central figure in the 1920s anti-Rowlatt satyagraha, and often portrayed as a major and unique symbol of Hindu-Muslim unity, especially because of his preaching of national unity from the pulpit of the Jama Masjid in Delhi and his singular bravery in the face of armed colonial police. However, his active involvement in the non-cooperation movement and Congress spans just a few years from 1919 until 1922, when Congress opposed participation in his Shuddhi campaigns. Thereafter, from 1923, he devoted himself to Hindu nationalist and Hindu interests on an India-wide scale. Again, his trajectory into and out of Congress, like that of Lajpat Rai, muddies an easy understanding of the 'secular' foundations of Congress.

In 1912, Shraddhanand met U. N. Mukerji in Calcutta, who explained to him his fear of Hindu extinction. Shraddhanand claimed to have then spent the next thirteen years as a student of statistics, analysing the census reports for 1901, 1911 and 1921. These resulted in his book, Hindu Sangathan: Saviour of the dying race, written in 1924 as the 'solution' to Mukherji's Hindus - The dying race.

The great Aryan Nation is said, at the present moment, to be a dying race not because its numbers are dwindling but because it is completely disorganised. Individually, man to man, second to none on earth in intellect and physique, possessing a code of morality, unapproachable by any other race of humanity, the Hindu Nation is still helpless on account of its manifold divisions and selfishness.

Shraddhanand's influential tract was important for its reiteration of the fear of Hindu extinction, and because it proposed a solution, sangathan or the strategic organization of Hindu society, to the perceived problem of Hindu numerical decline and degeneration into the system of sub-castes. Hindu Sangathan knitted together Shraddhanand's quite dogmatic Arya Samajist philosophy into a political programme for Hindu organization while presenting a renewed framework for interpreting Indian history and the place of Hindus within it. Hindu Sangathan was written within the same few years as Savarkar's Hindutva (while it does not refer to the latter, Shraddhanand does commend Savarkar in other texts). It can be seen as a product of the consolidation of Hindu nationalist ideology in the 1920s, following Gandhi's withdrawal of the non-cooperation movement, and in the political aftermath of the Khilafat agitations.

Hindu Sangathan is a prominent example of the products of late nineteenth-century and turn-of-century 'neo-Vedic' ideology, bearing the unmistakable stamp of the Arya Samaj. For Shraddhanand, who based his historical methodology primarily colonial and Orientalist writers, ancient India had been ruled by the Aryan race for 'millions' of years and had colonized and given birth to the entire civilized world (The term 'Aryan' would have been based on the ethnological and anthropometric studies of Herbert Hope Risley and his collaborators, studies adjacent to the colonial censuses that Shraddhanand claimed to have read and that were readily available in India). Aryan colonists, he claimed, had been sent from India to both poles, to bring civilization and knowledge to both hemispheres. The Aryans, who gave the ancient name of Aryavarta 'to our motherland', possessed 'a real civilization which has not been equalled even up till now'. Similarly, the Aryan social policy was an ideal organized according to the varna vyavastha or system of four castes, which, according to Shraddhanand meant the organic and functional organization of society according to one's 'attributes and works, quality and action, character and conduct' rather than because of heredity. This displacement of individual heredity for a hierarchically defined social organism retained biological tropes while apparently claiming to dismiss hereditarianism. As with Lajpat Rai, Shraddhanand usurped and strategically reversed colonial discourse, while demonstrating a modernist preoccupation with biopolitics and population demographics.

The 'downfall of the nation', according to Shraddhanand, occurred because of the rise of pride and jealousy, as shown in the Mahabharata war between the Pandavas and Kauravas. The system of brahmacharya, in which the Brahmin-Hindu renounced the world and sought spiritual education, was replaced by heredity, blind faith, superstition and fetish worship. Sub-castes mushroomed, untouchability (the 'panchamas' or fifth 'caste') arose and with it grew the shudras and 'untouchables', a third of the population, living under 'a social and economic tyranny unparalleled in the history of the world'. If this is one reason for 'the dying of the Hindu race', Shraddhanand was also at pains to highlight at length what he viewed as the conversions by violence, force, fraud and inducements of those groups by Muslim conquerors and Christian missionaries (These long sections of Hindu Sangathan could be virtually reproduced unchanged today and would be barely distinguishable from the Vishwa Hindu Parishad).

While Shraddhanand was clear that it was the tyranny of orthodoxy that often drove some groups to Islam or Christianity, he also needed to demonstrate the resilience of 'Hinduism' in the face of the corrupt and dishonest methods of conversion allegedly used by Islamic and Christian proselytisers. In this sense, deeply resonant today, the strength of Hinduism is simply that it existed despite the fraudulent attempts to disparage it. There were precise intellectual conditions of possibility by which the Arya Samaj, an explicitly unorthodox, and initially an avowedly non-

Hindu movement, could undertake conversion campaigns legitimately while considering those undertaken by Christianity or Islam as inherently illegitimate.

Shraddhanand proposed several remedies to restore to Hindus their 'ancient status in the world'. He recommended the revivification of the practice of ashram dharma. Opposing the Hindu Sabha's lower minimum ages for the marriage of boys and girls, he urged Dayananda's prescriptions of 25 years for males and 16 years for females. Shraddhanand's reasons were twofold progeny of younger adults was biologically weaker, and hence a source of weakness for the 'Hindu race'; and that the recommended ages allowed for the education of youth, and the institution of brahmacharya, whose knowledge would filter down and strengthen the Hindu community. He also proposed that all child widows be allowed to remarry, and provided various remedies for widowhood.

Shraddhanand's partial opposition to jati, aspects of gender inequality and untouchability has to be considered within his narrative against what he perceived as the threatening demography of Islam and Christianity. His prescriptions on child marriage were directly related to his belief that early marriage and conception led to physically weak children and thus physiologically weak Hindus. His belief that young widows be allowed to remarry was precisely related to his fear that young widows could not procreate if they remained unmarried. He compared traditional Hindu prescriptions about child marriage and widowhood directly with Muslim and Christian age variations in marriage and widowhood, as well as the allegedly more prolific Muslim birth rate. Christians and Muslims, he argued, also married later and thus had biologically stronger and numerically greater progeny.

Similarly, his attacks on the Hindu Mahasabha for earlier passing a resolution against untouchability that (in the face of Sanatan Dharma opposition) nevertheless did not go so far as to allow 'untouchables' to draw water from a common well, attend any Hindu temple or wear the sacred thread, was compared directly to Muslims and Christians who could use the same water wells as caste Hindus. 'Muslim prostitutes', he argued, were allowed to dance in front of temples that 'untouchables' could not enter. In each of the caste and gender reforms he proposed, the treatment of 'untouchables' by Brahmin and other caste Hindus was explicitly contrasted with the favourable treatment enjoyed by Christians and Muslims.

One of the most consistent arguments of Shraddhanand concerned 'the untouchables', who he argued should be immediately brought into the shudra caste. 'Untouchables', including 'tribals', he argued, once belonged to one of the three higher castes of Hinduism. They had become 'socially degraded' probably because of their 'moral degradation' but once 'uplifted' and having reformed their way of life and morality, 'nothing should stand in the way of their regaining their former positions.' It is clear throughout the text of Hindu Sangathan that the mass of those outside the Hindu caste system were important precisely because of their numerical and demographic strength for Hinduism and of the fear, consistently projected by Shraddhanand that they would be lost to Islam or Christianity, and thence contribute to the extinction of the Hindu race. His argument was not that scheduled castes should as of right, and with reference only to their condition, enjoy greater freedoms and liberties. It was rather that Christians and Muslims already had such liberties, whereas those who were only important because they could potentially become incorporated as low castes within a hierarchical Hinduism and increase its numerical strength, did not. This orientation, whereby the strategy towards populations outside the caste system should be to bring them into a hierarchical system of caste was definitive of sangathan, and is a key characteristic of today's Hindutva movement.

Syncretism and Repugnance

The main practical remedy Shraddhanand proposed to prevent the decline of the Hindus was to oppose the 'evil' of conversions to Islam and Christianity. He recounted an incident in 1923 during which, while Congress was meeting with Khilafat leaders, the All India Kshatriya Mahasabha had resolved to 'take back' 450,000 Malkana Rajputs into the kshatriya caste. The Malkana Rajputs practised a form of religion that was syncretic and comprised Hindu and Islamic beliefs and practices, but they were often seen as Muslims. The first large-scale 'reconversion' campaigns Shraddhanand highlighted, as indicative of the growth of the Hindu Sangathan movement concerned not a Muslim population but a syncretic one that could not be categorized unambiguously by 'Hindu' or 'Muslim' labels. Of similar importance was Shraddhanand's concern that 'Muslim proselytizers' had targeted this same community. Shraddhanand proposed in 1923, the formation of the Bharatiya (All-India) Hindu Shuddhi Sabha to undertake India-wide conversions, initially of those termed 'neo-Muslims', but often comprising communities with syncretic religious traditions. This syncretism was interpreted by Shraddhanand as the 'casting of yearning glances towards their Hindu brethren for the past two centuries or more' by communities whose entry into Hinduism was forbidden by orthodoxy. He hence urged the 'reclamation' of these 'strayed brethren', the neo-Muslims and neo-Christian.

Two conspicuous processes, the logic of modernist demographic enumeration and the imperative of unambiguous classification, are glaringly obvious throughout Shraddhanand's text. These processes of numerical and categorical reasoning are distinctive to modernist configurations of the populace, groups and nations. As Datta has argued, groups that could not be enumerated or categorized under dominant religious classifications were problematized by Hindu communalism. Of additional importance, here is the logic of purity and danger highlighted by Mary Douglas (1991) in which the target groups for Hindu supremacism were not Muslims and Christians but those who offended and created. Revulsion for the Hindu chauvinist sensibility because they could not be nominated as Christians, Muslims, or Hindus. Instructively, a circular by E. A. Gait, census commissioner for the 1911 census, proposed syncretic 'Hindu-Muslim' categories and the classification of 'untouchables' as 'not Hindus'. This was received by Arya Samajists and Hindu leaders in the Punjab and United Provinces as the potential 'loss' of sixty million 'Hindus', and resulted in the political galvanization of Hindu 'orthodoxy' against the census categories, combined with an intensification of Arya Samaj Shuddhi activities.

The central thrust of these activities was about the disciplining and 'purification' of Indian groups and communities that were economically, politically and culturally marginal, and yet numerically large 'untouchables' and hybrid communities were important because they could be nominated as 'Hindu'. As important was the different civilizing mission, based on 'purification', 'social hygiene' and 'upliftment', whose intellectual conditions of thinkability were those of British colonialism itself: how could a minority claim political hegemony over a majority, if not by modernist processes of nominal reasoning, as subjects of the British King-Emperor, or as subjects of a Hindu nation? Finally, Shraddhanand urged the adoption of Hindi and the Devanagari script throughout India, and, as the first step towards Hindu national solidarity and unity (sangathan), building of a Hindu Rashtra (Hindu Nation) mandir (temple) in every town and major city, which would hold at least as many people as the major mosques in northern India. The Hindu Rashtra mandir would be based on the worship of the cow as mother, the goddess of knowledge, and the motherland.

Swami Shraddhananda exemplifies a peculiar Arya Samajist tradition, combining asceticism and social activism. The life of Munshi Ram - Shraddhananda's name before his initiation to spiritual life--was transformed in the 1880s after he read Satyarth Prakash and later met Guru Dutt (1864–1890), Dayananda's most religious disciple. He became a vanaprastha (voluntary exile in the forest) in 1902 and then a sannyasi in 1917, when he changed his name. Alongside these spiritual inclinations, Shraddhananda remained true to Arya Samaj ideology. He claimed that the plateau of Tibet was the first to come out of water and therefore the revelation of the Vedas was imparted to early humanity at the sacred soil. Mankind was then divided into the good or virtuous and the bad or vicious. The first were named "Aryas", and the latter "Dasyus" in the Veda itself.

Also true to the Arya Samaj worldview, Shraddhananda believed Hindus underwent a steady decline since the Vedic golden age and that foreign invasions - the Muslim ones to begin with-- but also a constant degradation of culture and society, were responsible for this state of decadence. The slow death of the Hindus was, he believed, measured in the census figures that the British had produced every ten years since 1871 (and more thoroughly since 1881) because they bore testimony to a steady erosion of the population share of the majority community. Ergo, Hindus were bound to be turned into a minority in the foreseeable future. As P.K. Datta demonstrates, this obsession with figures has been long associated with the Hindu's cultural and physical features in Hindu nationalist writings: the Hindus are here seen as weak, notably because of their division into castes, whereas social classes in England are seen as bonded by common sentiments, 'such as those provided by sports, defence requirements and church activities. Islam too had produced a sense of commonness through masjid congregations.' Discourses like Shraddhananda's gave birth to what Datta calls 'the production of Hindu communal common sense', a process through which communal stereotypes tended to form a routinized discourse, stressing the need for a Hindu nationalist reaction.

For Shraddhananda, the making of the Hindu nation implied seriously implementing the agenda of the Hindu Sangathan movement. Here, social reform was the cornerstone of the desired unity among Hindus. He showed the way himself by having his daughter married to an Arora (he was from a Khatri family himself). More importantly, Shraddhananda fought untouchability. He did this by resorting to the old Arya Samajist recipe of Shuddhi. This ritual formula, which was traditionally used by upper-caste Hindus who happened to be polluted by some hypothetically impure contact, had as we saw been reinterpreted by Dayananda and his followers to 'purify' converts to other religions who wanted to return to the Hindu fold. Shraddhananda systematized this technique in order to integrate Untouchables into mainstream Hindu society. This radical method of social change alienated the Hindu Sabhaites of Sanatanist obedience to such an extent that, eventually, Swami Shraddhananda left the Hindu Mahasabha.[64]

Extract from Hindu Sangathan: Saviour of the Dying Race [65]

The Hindu Sabha has also resolved that those non-Hindus who have faith in Hindu Samskars and Hindu Dharma should be taken within the fold of the Hindu Dharma. This means that every non-Hindu has a right to be absorbed in Hinduism if he has faith in the Hindu religion and culture, in short it means that every Christian, Muhammadan, Jew & c., can be converted to the Hindu Dharma without any hindrance according to the dictum of the Hindu Mahasabha. Thus moral sanction of the Hindu community as a whole is with the reformers in this respect. But the task is uphill. Without sufficient funds and enthusiastic workers, the work is languishing. Therefore, the first remedy is to make the Bhartiya Hindu Shuddhi Sabha a living body, to collect lakhs of rupees for pushing on work in all directions and to induce selfless men of pure intents to go about persuading Hindus to take back to their bosom their strayed brethren.

The second remedy is to revivify the ancient Ashram Dharma and to place it on a sound basis. The Hindu Sabha has laid down the minimum marriageable age at 18 years in the case of males and of 12 years in the case of girls. This reform by doles won't do. Let the minimum marriageable age be fixed at 25 for males and 16 for females and let Hindu society become strict in the enforcement of this scientific rule. Then, no widower ought to be allowed to marry a virgin. If, after the death of the first wife, the widower cannot lead a life of Brahmacharya let him marry a widow. Then, polygamy in the North and polyandry in the South should also be unequivocally condemned. And, in order to protect and educate Hindus properly separate Gurukulas for boys and girls ought to be opened in all parts of the country.

1. **Swami Shraddhananda, Hindu Sangathan: Saviour of the Dying Race (Delhi: Arjun Press, 1926), pp. 130-41.**

If a Hindu commits a sin or neglects to act according to a virtuous dictum he must expiate for it. Proper prayashchit alone can wash away the fruits of a sin in the case of individuals as well as of nations. The orthodox Hindu professes to believe in the Vedas, the Smritis as well as the Puranas. The Vedas lay down the Eternal Dharma which is true for all ages. The Veda is the original source of Dharma.

But the Smritis, which are not opposed to the teachings of the Vedas, should also be followed. These Smritis lay down the rules to be followed in times of extreme distress or calamity and such rules constitute what is called Apaddharma.

In the first place all distinctions of sub-castes must cease, and no non-caste sects among Hindus should be recognized. I realize the difficulty in remodelling the Hindu Samaj according to the ancient Varnadharma at once. But there should be no difficulty in all the sub-castes, and even non-castes consisting of the so-called untouchables, being absorbed in the four principal castes. The Brahman caste must be self-contained in the sense that no sub-division into Panchgauras, Panchdravidas, Bhumihars, Tagas &c. should be recognized. The Kshatriya caste should include Rajputs, Khatris, Jats, Gujars &c. and should be one recognized society of protectors of the nation. All the castes and sub-castes engaged in trade and agriculture should be included in the Vaishya caste. And the rest should constitute the Shudra caste and serve society. There should be free marriage relations, to begin with, within the castes and Anuloma marriages should not be interfered with. Then gradually Pratiloma marriages ought to be introduced. And lastly character and conduct should become the determining factors in fixing the Varna of a Hindu.

But interdining among all the castes should be commenced at once - not promiscuous eating out of the same cup and dish like Muhammadans, but partaking of food in separate cups and dishes, cooked and served by decent Shudras. This alone can solve the problem of untouchability and exclusiveness among the Hindus.

The Hindu Mahasabha has passed a lengthy resolution purporting to deal with the problem of untouchability, but it has resulted in confounding confusion worse. It all depends upon the local Hindus whether the so-called untouchables are to be allowed to draw water from common wells which are not prohibited to Muhammadans and Christians. And then if a devout untouchable goes to worship the image of his favourite deity in a Hindu temple the priest has the option of allowing or not allowing him to approach the place where Muhammadan prostitutes are asked to dance accompanied by Muhammadan players on [sic] music. As regards allowing admission to the children of the so-called untouchables in public Schools and Colleges, the less said the better. But the climax is reached when, after allowing all the above mentioned ambiguous privileges, the Hindu Mahasabha lays down the authoritative dogma that 'initiating the untouchables with sacred thread, teaching them the Vedas and to interdine with them is against the Shastras and custom according to Sanatan Dharma.'

Basis for Hindu Sangathan: The above fourfold remedies in my humble opinion, constitute the basis of real Hindu Sangathan: the success of all the minor resolutions passed by the Hindu Mahasabha depend upon the right application of these remedies.

It is true that protection of the cow is a powerful factor not only in giving the Hindu community a common plane for joint action but in contributing to the physical development and strength of its several members. But if the drain upon the depressed classes continues and they go on leaving their ancestral religion on account of the social tyranny of their co-religionists and the onrush of Hindu widows towards prostitution and Muhammadanism, on account of the brutal treatment of [sic] their relations, is not stopped by allowing them to remarry in their own community, the number of beef-eaters will increase and Gauraksha will remain only a dream of unpractical sentimentalists. And what would the Hindu Raksha Sangham be able to accomplish against the inroads of non-Hindu Gundas, if their own house is not in order? The best way to avoid conflict with Muhammadans is to take care of your own women and children.

The introduction of uniform Devanagar script and Hindi lingua franca throughout is absolutely necessary, because a common language brings all the individuals speaking that language nearer one another in thought and action, but unless caste and sectarian prejudices vanish there is no likelihood of a common language and literature being evolved.

The salvation of the community depends upon common action taken by the Hindu Samaj as a whole, but individual salvation is the lookout of individuals. Theoretical Dharma is connected with indvidual salvation and, therefore, there is room for Theists, Pantheists, Henotheists and even Atheists in the broad lap of the organized Hindu Samaj. But the code of practical Dharma has to do with the community as a whole and, therefore here the plea of individual Dharma should not be allowed to prevail nor should it hamper the efforts of the organized Hindu Samaj towards national salvation.

The First Step: The question naturally arises-What is the first step to be taken in our advance towards Hindu Sangathan? In my tour throughout India I have seen educated Hindus reluctant to mix with each other. It is only on rare occasions that they meet to discuss common social problems. The reason is that they have no common meeting place. Their sectarian temples have not sufficient space where even a hundred or two could sit together. In Delhi, besides the Juma and Fatehpuri mosques which can accommodate big audiences consisting of 25 to 30 thousands of Muhammadans, there are several old mosques which can serve as meeting places for thousands. But for Hindus, the only enclosed meeting place is Lakshmi Narayana's Dharamshala which can hardly accommodate some 8 hundred, with this difference that while the Muhammadan meetings are free from all noise, the hubbub of voices from travelers in the Dharamshala hardly allows the speakers to be distinctly heard.

The first step which I propose is to build one Hindu Rashtra Mandir at least in every city and important town, with a compound which could contain an audience of 25 thousands and a hall in which Katha from Bhagavad Gita, the Upanishads and the great epics of Ramayana and Mahabharat could be daily recited. The Rashtra Mandir will be in charge of the local Hindu Sabha which will manage to have Akharas for wrestling and gatka &c. plays in the same compound. While the sectarian Hindu temples are dominated by their own individual deities, the Hindu Mandir should be devoted to the worship of the three mother-spirits the Gaumata, the Saraswatimata and the Bhumimata. Let some living cows be there to represent plenty, let 'Savitri' be inscribed over the gate of the hall to remind every Hindu of his duty to expel all ignorance and let a life-like map of Mother-Bharat be constructed in a prominent place, giving all its characteristics in vivid colours so that every child of the Matru Bhumi may daily bow before the Mother and renew his pledge to restore her to the ancient pinnacle of glory from which she has fallen!

If a beginning, on lines proposed by me in all humility and love, is made with faith, I hope that all the necessary reforms will follow, as night is followed by the day, and the progeny of the ancient Aryans will once more step forward to give salvation to humanity.

Assassination

To protect Hindu society from the onslaught of Christianity and Islam's forced conversions, the Arya Samaj represented by him, started the 'Shuddhi' (purification) movement to reconvert to the Hindu fold the converts of Christianity and Islam. This led to increasing communalisation of social life during the 1920s, and later snowballed into communal political consciousness. Consequently, on 23 December 1926, he was assassinated by Abdul Rashid. Swami Shraddhanand's Shuddhi mission of reconverting Malkana Rajputs did not go down well with Gandhi. In the 1922 issue of his magazine, Young India, he is reported to have criticised Swami Shraddhanand in an article, titled 'Hindu-Muslim-Tensions: Causes and Resistance'.

Gandhi wrote: "Swami Shraddhanand has also become a character of disbelief. I know that his speeches are often provocative. Just as most Muslims think, that every non-Muslim will one day convert to Islam. Shraddhanand also believes that, every Muslim can be initiated into the Hindu fold."

As a tribute to the man who was martyred for the Hindu cause, Savarkar's brother Narayanrao decided to start a weekly titled Shraddhanand from Bombay, beginning 10 January 1927. Savarkar contributed several articles to this weekly under pen-names.

Today, the 'Swami Shraddhanand Kaksha' at the archaeological museum of the Gurukul Kangri University in Haridwar, houses a photographic journey of his life.

A statue of him was placed in front of Delhi Town Hall after independence, replacing a statue of Queen Victoria. This location in Old Delhi is termed Ghantaghar because the old clock tower stood here until the 1950s.

Ganesh Damodar Savarkar

Ganesh Damodar Savarkar was born on 13 June 1879 in the Marathi Chitpavan Brahmin to Damodar and Radhabai Savarkar in the village of Bhagur, near the city of Nashik. Soon after completion of his Marathi education at a local school ,He shifted to Nashik for higher studies in English , After completion of the studies ,Ganesh Savarakar learned Yoga Mudras(Yogic Poses),He used to spend 14-15 hours daily practising Yoga.He had knowledge of Ayurveda,Samudrikas,Sastras,Astrology , Yoga and Vedanta. Ganesh Savarkar was a follower of the Teachings of swami Vivekananda and swami Ramtirta,He used to perform religious activities for long hours was a religious man who believed in worshipping Hindu Gods, Ganesh Savarkar was a associate of Lokamanya Tilak,During his participation in Independence movement,Ganesh Savarkar used to contribute articles to well known publications such as Kesari (Pune) ,Lokamanya (Bombay), Maharastra(Nagpur), Sakaal(Bombay), Aadhesh(Nagpur) and Vande Mataram(Bombay).Ganesh Savarkar was indeed a Forgotten Hero. The cellular jail was a place which would break any freedom fighter, when India was a colony under the British Empire. The punishments ranged from solitary confinement to standing handcuff punishments. This was where both the Savarkar brothers – Ganesh and Vinayak spent nearly a decade, undergoing the worst.

This was not the first prison sentence of Ganesh Savarkar, who was known for his revolutionary activities. He had to take the responsibility of bringing up his family at a young age, thereby sacrificing his education. He pinned his hopes on his brother Tatyarao (Veer Savarkar) who went to London to complete his studies and become a Barrister. Meeting Tatyarao at the cellular jail in Andaman was a shock for Babarao, when the latter arrived there a year later.[66]

Mitramela and Abhinav Bharat

Rashtrabhaktasamooha was formed in 1899 by VD Savarkar and in 1900, it was rechristened as Mitramela. This would later pave way for the secret society called Abhinav Bharat. The primary activities were organising public celebrations of festivals, inviting other freedom fighters and intellectuals to join them. It included Lokamanya Tilak, Aurobindo, Syed Haidar Raza etc. In 1904, Abhinav Bharat began its work under that name. The inspiration came from Mazzini's Young Italy, an Italian secret society which was created to unify Italy.

Abhinav Bharat had proclaimed that India cannot progress without complete independence. They wanted Swaraj (self-rule), not a dominion status under the British Crown. Indian National Congress adopted this as a resolution only in 1929, during the Lahore session. Babarao headed both the Mitra Mela and Abhinav Bharat.

Babarao organised lectures to awaken the people. There would be charged sloganeering for freedom. In 1905, the first public bonfire of foreign clothes was organised by Ganesh in Nashik and by Vinayak in Pune. This was to protest against the partitioning of Bengal.

On a Dussehra procession, the Mitramela marched the streets with loud "Vande mataram" slogans. Babarao and some members were arrested as they thrashed a policeman who hit Babarao with a baton. They were tried, found guilty and punished with fines. This was known in Maharashtra (then the Bombay Province) as Vande Mataram trial.

Imprisonment under false charges

Babarao was arrested in Bombay for a duel with Muhammad Hussain, a sub inspector posted for controlling a crowd. He had come forward to save a Khoja gentleman in an altercation with the policeman. After he was arrested, JF Guyder, the Superintendent of Police, found a Russian revolutionary's book with him. Once he found out that he had the Tiger of Nashik in his clutches, he left no stone unturned to ensure Babarao's conviction. The first accusation was organizing an illegal gathering to free Paranjpe, which was dismissed. This was because the crowd had come to see the editor of Hind Swarajya, not Paranjpe of Kaal. Babarao had to argue on his own as he did not manage to find a lawyer. Finally, he was punished for disobeying the Sub Inspector and had to spend a month in prison, where he would meet Lokmanya Tilak for the last time.

Now, the Savarkar residence was under surveillance and Babarao had detectives following him everywhere. However, he managed to give them a slip and distribute manuals on bomb making. He was also expecting a consignment of guns from his brother, Veer Savarkar.

He was arrested from Mumbai where he had reached for a discussion, after evading the detectives who were behind him. Babarao was then taken to Nashik as an undertrial. The policemen who were watching him were figuring out the secret communication he had with his visitors. This led to a raid of his house where they recovered enough evidence to prove him guilty under Section 121.

Laghu Abhinav Bharat Mala, which was a collection of 18 Poems, was mentioned in the judgement where he was held guilty for waging war against the Empire. His trial was initially before the Nashik District Collector, Jackson who ensured Savarkar's Transportation of life. The judgement was pronounced on 8th June 1909, which happened to be Babarao's birthday as per the Hindu calendar.

Wrath of the patriots

The news of Babarao being condemned to the Andaman Cellular jail spread far and wide. This made the blood of the 'Indian revolutionaries' boil. On 1st July, Madanlal Dhingra, a patriot assassinated Curzon Wylie as a "humble revenge for hangings and deportation of patriotic Indians". Dhingra was hanged to death.

In November 1909, the Bombay High Court upheld the lower court verdict on Babarao's transportation. Anant Laxman Kanhere, a 19-year old student hatched a plot to kill Jackson, the DC of Nashik. He was the kingpin behind Babarao's sentence and the one who saved a Britisher who killed an Indian. On 21 December 1909, they killed Jackson. Kanhere, Karve, and Deshpande were executed. The Britishers conducted several raids and arrests to prevent further retaliation.

Babarao's days in Andaman Cellular Jail

Before he reached the Andaman Island in 1910, he was jailed in Nashik, Yerawada (Pune), Thane and Alipur jails. He was constantly tortured to reveal the names of other revolutionaries. Babarao's will was so strong that not even electric shocks made him reveal a single name. However, his health deteriorated.

He was tortured by a sadistic Irish jailor named Barrie, who was notorious for the cruelty he meted out. Babarao had to spend 6 months in solitary imprisonment. He was later made to do hard labour like rope making from coconuts, push the rod of the 'kolu' to extract oil. His health wouldn't permit that and he had to face tough punishment for missing the 'target'.

Some of these involved 'standing handcuffs', where he was hooked to a handcuff in standing position for hours together. Sometimes, the food would be mixed with kerosene causing abdominal cramps and diarrhoea. An article won't be enough to describe the tortures these brave men went through in the prison and on the way.

In 1911, Veer Savarkar joined his brother in Andaman. He was found guilty for various crimes, mainly the supply of guns to kill Jackson. However, they were not allowed to communicate and were separated. They organised 'Shuddhi', to bring back those Hindus who had converted to Islam. It acted as a way to prevent forced conversions by the Muslim jailors. There were informers and traitors too, among the inmates. One of them, who were known as Ainewala Babu, had plotted to accuse Babarao of a murder and later tried to poison him.

'Ditcher's Diary' in The Capital

The Capital was a periodical in which a defamatory article against the Savarkars was published. It was called 'Ditcher's Diary'. It was a propaganda piece written to complicate the release of the Savarkars and break their support. It sounded like Babarao had invited Germans to attack the Andaman.

Narayanrao dragged the Editor of the periodical to court for slander. They apologised unconditionally and withdrew the article two months later on 28th July 1909. Today, it's Congress who is playing this role of defaming Savarkar.

Narayanarao, the younger Savarkar who was in India ran from pillar to post all the while to save his brothers from the Andaman jail. He used to do it under the banner of "National Union". He had approached Gandhi who supported the demand of their release but said that he would not agree to 'the cult of violence'. Finally, on 2nd May 1921, the Savarkars were released from Andaman and repatriated. He came out of jail on a stretcher and he was in a critical stage. He knew that death awaited him, as the Civil Surgeon did not predict he would live beyond a few days. Fortunately, he managed to recover and dedicated his life to awaken the Hindus.

Gandhi Amanullah Pact

The brothers were separated after they reached mainland India. Babarao was sent to the Bijapur jail where he had to undergo torture and was near dead when Narayanrao came to meet him. With the help of 'Bombay Chronicle', he spread the word about the condition of Babarao in Bijapur prison. As a result of this, he was moved to Sabarmati jail.

There, he met Maulana Mohani, a fellow inmate who was part of the Khilafat movement. It whipped up the pan-Islamist sentiments of Indian Muslims in support of the Ottoman Empire. He learnt about the sinister Gandhi-Amanullah pact from the Maulana. According to this, Amir Amanullah of Afghanistan was 'invited' to invade India to drive the Britishers away. Apparently, this was intended to help the Hindus as well. He smelt something fishy in this and researched more.

Critical analysis of Gandhian thought

Babarao was familiar with few Gandhians whom he met in prison. He learnt about Gandhian school of thought from them. Some of the incidents he observed in jail are as follows. These are excerpts from Babarao's biography.

This is when he realised the loopholes in such a philosophy and the damage it was doing to the cause of Swarajya. Babaro disagreed with Gandhi's theory of 'Go to jail for patriotism'. He felt the ideas like spinning charkhas and filling up prisons would not win the cause. He felt that Gandhi was refusing to adapt to the industrial age, which was needed in any modern country. He felt that the ideals of Gandhi like ahimsa was acting as 'shackles' in the fight for freedom.

It would be unfair to omit the pain and suffering of Ganesh Savarkar's wife in this story. She had lost everything when Babarao was transported for life. She has lost two daughters in their infancy and was lonely. It was a shocking news for her when she realised that Babarao's entire property would be confiscated. She had to spend the rest of her life in Rambhau Datar's house as the two families were close.

Savarkar's other friends also pitched in to help her in all ways they could. Narayanrao was the other source of support but, since he was also in jail, he couldn't do much. Yesuvahini wrote about her plight to Veer Savarkar in England. His poetic reply 'Saantvan' is seen as a brilliant literary work.

Tarun Hindu Sabha

Babarao knew that the Hindus would have to be presented with a constructive alternative. He plunged into the activities of the Hindu Mahasabha. Babarao knew that for any ideology to take firm roots, it must capture the hearts and minds of the youth. To enlist the support of the youth into the Mahasabha, Babarao founded a separate "Tarun Hindu Sabha" ('Young Hindus' Conference) in 1923-24. For the next 4-5 years, Babarao traveled extensively to start branches of the Tarun Hindu Sabha. He would correspond extensively and give encouragement to youngsters to keep up the activities of the Tarun Hindu Sabha. In 4-5 years, Babarao could start 25-30 branches of the Tarun Hindu Sabha and enlist some 500 youths under its banner. The Tarun Hindu Sabha was open to any Hindu male from 16 to 40 years of age irrespective of his caste and sect. The members would celebrate festivals such as the coronation day of Chhatrapati Shivaji, Vijayadashmi and Makar Sankraman. The members would meet once a week and deliberate on issues facing the Hindus. They would prevent Hindu girls from falling prey to the machinations of Muslim youth. They would receive training in lathis and march-past. The members would start professions and businesses wherein non-Hindus had entrenched themselves. They would participate in shuddhi and abolition of caste discrimination. The members would contribute eight annas (roughly fifty paise or half an Indian rupee) on a yearly basis and thus take care of the finances. Babarao paid attention to minute details in the working of the Tarun Hindu Sabha. Several volunteers of the Tarun Hindu Sabha attended the annual Hindu Mahasabha session held in Surat in 1929. It was Babarao's first attempt to give an impetus to the Tarun Hindu Sabha. This attempt met with mixed success. In the same year in April, Babarao made a similar attempt at a conference of the Hindu Mahasabha, held in Akola. This attempt met with considerable success and the Tarun Hindu Sabha received a fillip.

The Conference in Akola was marked by successful sub-conferences of the Berar Provincial Hindu Sabha, Akhil Maharashtra Tarun Parishad, Shuddhi Parishad and Asprushyoddhaar Parishad (Conference for Upliftment of Untouchables). Babarao had stationed himself at Akola for several days before the Conference. While he would guide the workers of the different sub-conferences, his real interest lay in the 'Akhil Maharashtra Tarun Parishad'. He made strenuous efforts for its success. The Conference of the 'Akhil Maharashtra Tarun Parishad' was held on 20 April 1929 under the Chairmanship of Dr. Narayanrao Savarkar. Leaders such as Dr. Hedgewar, Dr. Moonje, Masurkar Maharaj, Loknayak MS Aney, Swami Shivanand, Panchlegaonkar Maharaj, Dr. Shivajirao Patwardhan, Brijlal Biyani attended the Conference. Dr. Savarkar delivered a brilliant speech. To channelize the enthusiasm generated by the Conference, a working committee was formed. Babarao was the moving spirit of the Conference. However, such was his self-effacing nature that he saw to it that his name did not figure anywhere among the luminaries.

Tarun Hindu Sabha, RSS and Babarao

Dr. Keshav Baliram Hedgewar, a former member of the revolutionary organization Anushilan Samiti, had completed his medical education at the National Medical College, Calcutta (now Kolkata), and returned to Nagpur in 1914. Instead of starting medical practice, he had decided to devote himself wholly to the motherland. In 1919, Dr. Hedgewar started an organization of youngsters called 'National Union'. After two years, he merged this organization into Dr.

Moonje's party. In 1920, Dr. Hedgewar worked as 'Officer Commanding' at the Nagpur session of the Indian National Congress. In 1922, Dr. Hedgewar played a major role in the 'Officers' Training Camp' that was held preparatory to starting the volunteer wing of the Indian National Congress. In 1923, as secretary of the Nagpur Hindu Sabha, Dr. Hedgewar was in the forefront of a satyagraha launched in the Ganesh Peth area of Nagpur. However, Dr. Hedgewar had started getting the feeling that all these efforts were isolated and disjointed. He resolved to start a nation-wide, well-oiled volunteer organization of the Hindus.

Towards the end of 1924, Babarao arrived in Nagpur. He was put up at the residence of Advocate Vishwanathrao Kelkar who was his distant relative and Dr. Hedgewar's close friend. Babarao used to attract youngsters wherever he went. His stay in Nagpur saw several youngsters visiting him and discussing the state of the Hindu society. Among these youngsters was Dr. Hedgewar. He used to attend these meetings with Babarao for hours together but would speak rarely. Babarao had now created a group of committed Hindu youngsters. He started a branch of the Tarun Hindu Sabha in Nagpur. When the time came for Babarao to leave Nagpur, he decided to entrust the responsibility of the Tarun Hindu Sabha to a suitable person. On discussing the matter with Kelkar, Babarao became convinced that there was no one more suitable than Dr. Hedgewar to carry forward the activities of the Tarun Hindu Sabha. It was with a sense of great satisfaction that Babarao entrusted the Tarun Hindu Sabha to Dr. Hedgewar when he left Nagpur.

Dr. Hedgewar translated his long-cherished dream into reality on Vijayadashmi day in 1925. A shakha (branch) of Hindu teenagers and youngsters was started by Dr. Hedgewar in the ruins of Salubai Mohite's wada in Mahal area of Nagpur. This was the beginning of the Rashtriya Swayamsevak Sangh (RSS). The organization received its name after it was actually founded. Babarao Savarkar was present in Nagpur on this momentous day. He was happy to know that a new organization of Hindus had started. He would engage in frequent discussions with Dr. Hedgewar regarding the RSS. Babarao felt great affection towards the RSS. From his sickbed, he would think constantly of its progress.

Dr. Hedgewar in turn had the highest respect for Babarao. He requested Babarao to prepare the RSS flag with his own hands. The Bhagwa (saffron) flag that was prepared was the age-old symbol of the Hindu nation. Dr. Hedgewar also asked Babarao to prepare the RSS pledge. Babarao had earlier prepared the pledge of the Abhinav Bharat and the Tarun Hindu Sabha. Dr. Hedgewar made some minor changes in Babarao's draft. Thus, the RSS pledge was prepared. The RSS pledge mentioned the words 'Hindu Rashtra'. This had deep significance. For the first time ever, the words 'Hindu Rashtra' were officially accepted on an organizational basis. One cannot but marvel at the vision of both Babarao and Dr. Hedgewar.

Merging of the Tarun Hindu Sabha and the Sangh

The Tarun Hindu Sabha and the Sangh had similar aims and objectives. Their methodology of functioning was also similar. The only difference was that the Sangh shakha was organized on a daily basis whereas the members of the Tarun Hindu Sabha worked on a weekly basis. Usually, two organizations that work towards the same goal develop differences and clash of egos. However, this never took place in the case of these two organizations. The principal reason for this was the deep affection and respect that both Babarao and Dr. Hedgewar felt towards each other. Dr. Hedgewar would refrain from starting shakhas in places that had a functioning Tarun Hindu Sabha branch. Babarao would reciprocate likewise. This continued till 1931.

Babarao's health continued to be indifferent. He did not have the strength to tour the country which was a requirement for expanding his organization. In Dr. Hedgewar, he was seeing a young man with exceptional organizational abilities. Babarao felt that it was unnecessary for two organizations with similar goals and methodology to function separately. He was now slowly veering towards the thought of merging his Tarun Hindu Sabha in the Sangh.

Dr. Hedgewar was in Kashi till 01 April. During this time, he nursed Babarao with all his heart. One day, Babarao told Dr. Hedgewar, "Doctor, I have dissolved my Tarun Sabha today. Please allow it to be merged in your Sangh. I shall henceforth use all my goodwill for the sake of the Sangh work. I bless the Sangh and wish it immortality and success!" Babarao promptly wrote to all the branches of the Tarun Hindu Sabha asking them to dissolve themselves and merge into the Sangh. The Tarun Hindu Sabha and the Sangh became one. The meeting of the Ganga and Yamuna rivers occurs in Kashi. The mingling of these two organizations occurred in the same sacred town. In merging his organization into the Sangh, Babarao again showed his self-effacing nature.

Touring for the Sangh

After merging his organization into the Sangh, Babarao plunged into Sangh work. In 1932, Babarao planned a tour of Maharashtra for the expansion of the Sangh work. On 17 July 1932, Babarao wrote a letter to Dr. Hedgewar inviting him to tour Western Maharashtra. Bowing to Babarao's wish, Dr. Hedgewar left Nagpur on 05th August and reached Mumbai. The two then undertook a joint tour to expand the Sangh work. They toured Pune, Satara, Karad, Sangli, Kolhapur, Ratnagiri, Thane and Kalyan and started Sangh shakhas at different places. At Babarao's instance, his younger brother, Dr. Narayanrao became Sanghachalak (local Sangh head) of Mumbai. In fact, the first Sangh shakha in Mumbai started in Dr. Narayanrao's clinic. In April 1932, Babarao wrote to Dr. Hedgewar and urged him to attend the Akhil Bharatiya Tarun Hindu Parishad that was to be held in Karachi in May. Dr. Hedgewar was always on the lookout for opportunities to meet youngsters. However, Dr. Hedgewar was busy with the Officers' Training Camp that was to be held in Nagpur at the same time. The question of the expenses involved in going to Karachi also bothered him. He apprised Babarao of his difficulties. Like Dr. Hedgewar, Babarao also had no funds to go to Karachi. The correspondence that followed not only indicates the fondness between these two stalwarts but also underscores the difficult circumstances in which they were working.

Being aware of Babarao's meagre financial resources, Bhai Parmananda offered to bear Babarao's traveling expenses. Babarao typically wrote to Dr. Hedgewar, "... We shall share the available funds between the two of us and lighten the burden." Such was the warmth between the two. On Dr. Hedgewar's suggestion that Babarao should speak to the assembled youth regarding the Sangh, Babarao modestly replied, "Though I have totally devoted myself to the Sangh, I do not as yet consider myself fully equipped to propagate the Sangh. You should come. Bhaiji has asked me regarding you and desires that you should attend." Another letter dated 20 April is in the same vein. Babarao writes to Dr. Hedgewar, …'Though I am whole-heartedly in the Sangh, I am not fully clear in my mind as to the method of putting forth its aims, definite answers to various queries, complete knowledge of its functioning... Hence, you should attend the Conference. When you answer various queries and expound fundamentally on functioning and methodology of the Sangh in my presence, I shall be able to understand these things fully...'

The plan to attend the Conference in Karachi finally took shape. On 02nd May, Dr.Hedgewar left Nagpur for Mumbai. From there, both Babarao and Dr. Hedgewar left by the night train on 03rd May. Both of them were in Karachi for six days.

Babarao brought many prominent individuals into the Sangh. For example, Bhaurao Damle at whose residence Babarao stayed in Kashi took on the responsibility of Sanghachalak of Kashi at Babarao's instance. In 1931, when the Tarun Hindu Sabha merged into the Sangh, Dr. Hedgewar spent around 15-20 days persuading Bhaurao to take up responsibility as the first Sanghachalak of Kashi. But Bhaurao would not agree. Finally, Babarao requested Bhaurao to accede to the proposal. Babarao spoke with such fervour that tears welled up in his eyes. Bhaurao could not now refuse the responsibility.

Babarao used his good offices in the Hindu Mahasabha to further the Sangh work. It was through Babarao's efforts that resolutions commending the Sangh were passed at the 14th (1932, Delhi, under presidentship of NC Kelkar), 15th (Ajmer, under presidentship of Bhai Parmanand) and 19th (Karnavati, under presidentship of Tatyarao Veer Savarkar) sessions of the Akhil Bharat Hindu Mahasabha. As a result, the fledgling Sangh drew nation-wide attention. Hindu Mahasabha workers across the country started joining the Sangh. Leaders such as Babu Padmaraj Jain became acquainted with the Sangh due to the resolutions passed in the Hindu Mahasabha sessions.

Shielding the Sangh

On one occasion, the issue of the Sangh cropped up at a meeting of the Hindu Sabha in Delhi. Babarao was chairing the meeting. Speaking at the meeting, Babu Jagat Narain remarked that the Sangh should play second fiddle to the Hindu Mahasabha. Babarao immediately opposed this sentiment. In a speech marked by tremendous insight and clarity of thought, Babarao said, "The Sangh and the Sabha are two organizations with different method of functioning. One is styled on military lines while the other is civilian in nature. As the Hindu Sabha is civilian in nature and hence subject to public opinion, its leaders will constantly change. The Hindu Sabha has to be guided by fickle public opinion. Hence one cannot give a guarantee that its leaders will always be the best. Under these circumstances, if an organization like the Sangh is run by the Sabha, its work cannot continue unhindered and will be ruined. Hence, the Sangh should exist separately and remain ekachaalakaanuvarti (run by a single leader). It should not come under the control of the Sabha." Babarao's argument failed to convince those present. However, Meher Chand Khanna, a delegate from the Frontier provinces got up and said, "Babaji's stand is one hundred percent correct." Khanna's support turned the tide and Babarao's original resolution supporting the Sangh was approved!

Babarao stood by the Sangh once again in 1939. The Bhaagyanagar (Hyderabad) Unarmed Resistance movement was in full swing. The Sangh was under fire from pro-Hindu quarters for not participating in the movement as an organization. GG Adhikari, the pro-Hindu editor of the

'Vande Mataram' weekly from Mumbai criticized the Sangh. When Babarao read Adhikari's article, he wrote a counter article defending the stand taken by the Sangh. The article entitled 'Sanghaachya aadnyechi khoti sabab' (the false excuse of the Sangh's command) was published in the issue of 'Vande Mataram' dated 21 June 1939. Babarao wrote, "Those individuals whose minds have been fired by love and pride of Hindutva through the teachings of the Sangh have never shirked from their duty towards Hindutva in times of need. They have discharged their duty diligently. The number of such individuals may be less or more than expected but there is no doubt that it is there." Babarao thus gallantly defended the Sangh.

Babarao implied that true Sangh workers participated in the Bhaagyanagar movement out of their innate pride in Hindutva without waiting for a formal command from the Sangh. Those Sangh workers who worked half-heartedly remained aloof. There was no merit in the argument that the Sangh does not command its workers to participate in a particular movement. Once Babarao's article appeared, the columns of the 'Vande Mataram' weekly fell silent in their criticism of the Sangh.

Strengthening the Sangh

Babarao did not rest content with merging his own Tarun Hindu Sabha into the Sangh. He inspired others to merge their organizations into the Sangh as well. Once such organization was the 'Mukteshwar Dal' formed in1922-1923 under the leadership of Sant Pachlegaonkar Maharaj. The Dal had the overall welfare of the Hindu nation as its aim. It had taken roots in the Bombay Presidency and Provinces such as Central Provinces and Berar and Khandesh. It had over 100 branches in places such as Pune, Junnar, Nagar, Khed, Sinnar, Nashik, Sangamner, Rahuri, Kopargaon, Belapur, Ambol, Yavatmal, Khamgaon, Yawal and Yewle. Thousands of Hindu youth had rallied under its banner. LB Bhopatkar, Ganpatrao Nalawade, Nanarao Saptarshi counted among its leaders. The programmes of the Dal were organized on a daily basis and included training in lathi, marchpast and shuddhi. After doing laudable work for 5-7 years, the Dal was banned by the Government.

Babarao urged Pachlegaonkar Maharaj to merge his Dal into the Sangh. Babarao told him that instead of having small organizations working locally, they should have a large nation-wide organization. Initially, Pachlegaonkar Maharaj refused to accede to Babarao's suggestion. He feared that if the Dal was dissolved, the work of consolidation and shuddhi would stop. Babarao then asked Dr. Hedgewar to promise Pachlegaonkar Maharaj that the Sangh would continue the work of Hindu consolidation in an effective manner. Pachlegaonkar Maharaj finally relented and merged the Dal into the Sangh. At Babarao's instance, Pachlegaonkar Maharaj himself took the Sangh pledge and toured Bhandara, Wardha and Chandrapur with Dr. Hedgewar for the expansion of the Sangh work. The fledgling Sangh received a boost due to Babarao's efforts.

Babarao and Dr. Hedgewar

Dr. Hedgewar had the highest respect for Babarao. He had great regard for Babarao's selfless service to the motherland. He was also fully aware of Babarao's deep affection for the Sangh. Dr. Hedgewar would speak of Babarao in glowing terms. He would address Babarao with the greatest respect in his letters. "I am arriving as per your command", "I shall spend the month of August in your service" would be the tenor of Dr. Hedgewar's language while addressing Babarao. Dr. Hedgewar would invite Babarao to attend every Officers' Training Camp that would be held in Pune. He would make special arrangements to make Babarao's stay comfortable. Once, there was an Officers' Training Camp in Pune. Babarao happened to be in Pune at that time. However, instead of staying at the Camp, he had put himself up in a guest-house. When Dr. Hedgewar came to know this, he promptly hired a tonga (horse-carriage) and rushed to meet Babarao. Dr. Hedgewar said,

"Baba, when our Sangh Camp is being held in town, it is not proper that you should stay elsewhere. Come, I have brought a tonga to escort you to the Camp." Babarao replied, "Doctor, I would have stayed at the camp but what can I do? My legs ache. I can hardly stand. If come to the Camp, I shall only put others to inconvenience. I require a separate room that is close to the toilet. Hence I do not wish to come. I shall stay here."

But Dr. Hedgewar would have none of it. He lovingly urged Babarao to come with him. Babarao could not refuse Dr. Hedgewar's pure affection. Dr. Hedgewar put Babarao in the tonga and took him to Bhave School (now Garware High School) where the Camp was underway. The Camp was crowded with trainees. Even Dr. Hedgewar had difficulty in finding a room for himself. But, as soon as Babarao arrived, he asked one room to be kept exclusively for Babarao.

He treated Babarao like a king. Such was the boundless love and respect that Dr. Hedgewar had for Babarao! It was this affection that prompted Dr. Hedgewar to once personally nurse Babarao in his illness. This was in 1925 when Babarao had gone to Calcutta (now Kolkata) at the residence of Babu Padmaraj Jain to recuperate from illness. Dr. Hedgewar had stayed with Babarao throughout his stay in Calcutta and had nursed him. The feelings of affection and respect between Babarao and Dr. Hedgewar were mutual. When Dr. Hedgewar passed away in 1940, Babarao was deeply shocked. He deeply mourned the passing away of his dear and personal friend as an irreparable loss to the Hindu Nation.

With Dr. Hedgewar's passing away, Babarao felt deep concern for the future of the Sangh. He prepared a plan for the future functioning of the Sangh and sent it to Advocate Vishwanathrao Kelkar in Nagpur. Babarao had proposed that the reins of the Sangh should pass into the hands of Madhavrao Golwalkar (Guruji) and an advisory committee consisting of Babasaheb Ghatate, Ramchandra Narayan (Babasaheb) Padhye, Vishwanathrao Kelkar and others be formed with Abaji Hedgewar (Dr. Hedgewar's uncle) as its head. Babarao sent his proposal to Nagpur but events were moving in a different direction. M S Golwalkar became Sarsanghchalak (RSS Chief) in tune with Babarao's proposal. The only difference was that no advisory committee was formed. However, the Sangh continued to expand even after Dr. Hedgewar's death. Babarao was happy to note these developments. He was not displeased to see his proposal not being implemented. His only desire was that the Sangh should grow by leaps and bounds. Personal ego meant nothing to him.

Even after Dr. Hedgewar's death, Babarao continued to work for the Sangh. He knew hundreds of Sangh swayamsevaks personally. Many swayamsevaks would look up to him and seek his guidance. Babarao too would answer their queries. Though ill-health prevented Babarao from attending the Sangh shakha, it can be unambiguously said that he was a true and devoted Sangh Swayamsevak.

Babarao's Thoughts on the Sangh:

Babarao's devotion to the Sangh cause was not blind. In his book 'Hindu Rashtra - poorvi, aataa aani pudhe' (Hindu Nation- past, present and future), Babarao has penned the following thoughts on the Sangh, "The birth of the Sangh and the fact that it has taken upon itself the task of securing freedom for the country is an event that signifies the future glory of the Hindu Nation. The Sangh has brought many people together and has organized millions and millions of orderly swayamsevaks in military-like discipline. This contribution of the Sangh is truly remarkable. Future historians will have to record this contribution in letters of gold. The contribution of the Sangh in keeping Hindutva alive is likewise incomparable. It cannot be matched. But henceforth, an organization such as the Sangh cannot remain satisfied with mere numbers of disciplined individuals. The Sangh should gradually find occasions to test its strength. It should create experts in every aspect of the polity so that freedom may be won and maintained. The Sangh followers have taken a pledge to protect 'jati-dharma-samskriti'. To make this pledge meaningful and to serve society and gain its support, the Sangh should protect people from riots and foreign aggression.

Only if this happens will the Sangh progress and expand. Else, the Sangh will shrink and the hopes of the Hindu society will be dashed!" Babarao would never shrink from expressing his views. However, he never crossed the limits of discipline while articulating his views. He never made irresponsible suggestions. His suggestions were those of a sincere and selfless worker.

The Pan-Hindu Flag

The idea of a pan-Hindu flag first struck Tatyarao. In his articles in 'Shraddhanand' dated 02 August 1928, 11 August 1928, 16 August 1928, 08 March 1930 and 15 March 1930, Tatyarao put forth the concept of a pan-Hindu flag. Tatyarao's pan-Hindu flag was Bhagwa (saffron) and had the 'Om' symbol with the kundalini on one side and the kripan (dagger) next to it. The kundalini signified 'nishshreyas' (other-wordly matters) while the kripan signified 'abhyudaya' (material glory). Babarao heartily upheld Tatyarao's concept and asked an artist to draw up a flag as suggested by Tatyarao. He got such a flag prepared for the 1929 session of the Akhil Bharat Hindu Mahasabha that was to be held in Surat. The President of the session, the venerable Ramanand Chatterjee unfurled the pan-Hindu flag for the first time to the prolonged applause of the delegates. Babarao deliberately gave wide publicity to this event and made efforts to popularize the flag. It was mainly through Babarao's efforts that the flag was unfurled at the 1931 Akola session by C. Vijayaraghavachariar and 1932 Delhi session by N.C. Kelkar of the Hindu Mahasabha. When the Moshi taluka (tehsil) Hindu Parishad (Conference) was held in July 1929 at Varud under the Chairmanship of MS Aney, five thousand delegates sang the Hindu Unity Song composed by Tatyarao under the shade of this flag. When the CP and Berar Provincial Hindu Sabha session was held in 1929 under the Chairmanship of Pandit Madan Mohan Malaviya, thousands of delegates led by Pandit Malaviya, Dr. Moonje, Pachlegaonkar Maharaj, MS Aney saluted this flag. Through Babarao's efforts, the pan-Hindu flag became a regular feature at Hindu gatherings.

Pan-Hindu Flag Gets Official sanction:

During the 1933 Ajmer session of the Akhil Bharat Hindu Mahasabha, held under the Chairmanship of Bhai Parmananda, a Flag Committee was constituted to decide the official flag of the Hindu Mahasabha. Babu Padmaraj Jain was the President and Kunwar Chand Kiran Sarda, Sri Anandpriyaji, Babu Narendra Nath Das, Babu Jagat Narain Lal and Babarao were members of this Committee. Babarao had seen to it that the Committee would not have members who would oppose the pan-Hindu flag. For one year before the Committee started its work, Babarao propagated the pan-Hindu flag through letters, pamphlets and articles. He gauged public opinion. No one opposed the pan-Hindu flag. However, some individuals proposed that the image of a cow or some deity should find a place in the flag.

Finally, the Committee met to finalize the flag. As Babarao had expected, only two members namely Kunwar Chand Kiran Sarda and Babu Jagat Narain Lal were present. Sarda wanted a symbol of the Vedas on the flag while Jagat Narain wanted a picture of the cow. As there was no unanimity, the final decision was left to President Babu Padmaraj Jain. Jain was in full agreement with Babarao. In his Presidential capacity, he had Babarao's pamphlets printed and publicized on a large scale.

During the 1936 Lahore session of the Akhil Bharat Hindu Mahasabha, the flag approved by the Committee was accepted to the loud applause from delegates. However, at the last moment, Jugal Kishore Birla insisted that the 'swastik' symbol be incorporated into the flag. Babarao and Babu Padmaraj Jain accepted this suggestion. Finally, the flag was accepted as the official Hindu flag. It is a triangular saffron flag with symbols of 'Om' and 'Swastik' together with the kripan-kundalini. The flag now started being unfurled at every Hindu Mahasabha session as the flag of the Akhil Bharat Hindu Mahasabha.

Revolutionary to the End

Babarao's contact with revolutionaries continued even after his release from prison. Babarao used to stay in the Khar area of Mumbai in 1926. Shivram Hari Rajguru would clandestinely leave Pune and come to Mumbai. He would then meet Babarao and the two would remain engaged in discussion for hours together. Babarao played a major role in introducing Rajguru to Bhagat Singh's 'Hindustan Republican Army'. While at Nagpur, Rajguru had stayed at the house of Babarao's acquaintance. Rajguru used to attend the RSS shakha and even worked as a functionary of the Sangh for some time.

On 17 September 1928, Bhagat Singh, Sukhdev and Rajguru shot dead police officer JP Saunders at Ferozepur to take revenge for the death of veteran leader Lala Lajpat Rai, who died due to excessive police beating. On 07 October 1930, the Special Tribunal gave its verdict and sentenced Bhagat Singh, Sukhdev and Rajguru to be hanged to death. Till 23 March 1931, Babarao made gallant efforts to get this sentence commuted. He kept aside his well-known differences with Gandhi and met him at Wardha in an effort to get a reprieve for the three revolutionaries. Before giving details of the meeting, it is worthwhile mentioning the personal equations between Babarao and Gandhi.

Gandhi for all his much-touted magnanimity disliked Babarao. Once, Babarao had gone to meet Gandhi along with Bhai Parmananda in Mumbai. Bhai Parmananda bowed respectfully before Gandhi. But Babarao merely greeted Gandhi civilly. Gandhi too did not display any special regard for Babarao. When Bhai Parmananda introduced Babarao as Tatyarao's elder brother, they had a long conversation. Babarao had come to know of his meeting with Irwin, the next day. A smart man he was, he could see the need of a pact where political prisoners would be released. He urged Gandhi to strive for Bhagat Singh's release. Though he tried hard, he could not convince Gandhi who kept his ideal of ahimsa above the lives of revolutionaries.

On 14 February 1931, Gandhi had written to Viceroy Lord Irwin asking for a meeting. The meeting between Gandhi and Irwin was scheduled on 16 February 1931. On the previous day, that is 15 February 1931, Babarao went to the Gandhi Ashram in Wardha and sent a note asking for a meeting with Gandhi. The following conversation took place between Babarao and Gandhi:

Babarao: You are going to Delhi tomorrow. When you reach there, you will speak to the Viceroy regarding halting the Civil Disobedience Movement. There will no doubt be a Pact between the two of you. Such pacts have the release of political prisoners as their first pre-condition. I have come to request you to put such a pre-condition before signing any pact.

Gandhi: Fine, but why do you request? I am going to ask for the release of political prisoners.

It is my duty!

Babarao: But there should be no distinction amongst political prisoners as militants and non-militants (atyaachaari and anatyaachaari). My special request is that the pre-condition should cover all political prisoners. Nowhere in the world is a distinction made amongst political prisoners as militant and non-militant. But I fear that you may make such an artificial and unjust distinction.

Gandhi: Look Savarkar, we shall leave aside the question of whether it is proper or not to make such a distinction. My policy is to ask the other party only to the extent that they can possibly give. I do not desire to put hurdles in any agreement. So if it is certain that the Government will not release the militants, what is the use of asking for their release?

Babarao: I do not think that your policy of asking only what the other party can give to be correct. For if such a policy is correct, how can we ask for swaraj (self-rule)? The British are not going to grant it. It means that we should ask for petty rights!

Gandhi kept silent for a moment on hearing Babarao's argument. He then changed the subject and spoke.

Gandhi: Look! It is mean to ask for the release of militants. I shall not do that. How can I go against my ideal of non-violence?

Babarao: You feel that asking for the release of militants is a mean thing! When Abdul Rashid murdered Swami Shraddhanand, how come you told the Hindu society and Swami Shraddhanand's son to 'forgive brother Abdul Rashid'? Was that not mean of you? Can you not display the same meanness for these armed militants?

Gandhi was speechless. But shrewd that he was, he pretended as if someone was calling him. He got up saying, "I am coming" and walked away. He never met Babarao again in his life!

Later, Babarao sent Gandhi a detailed letter by registered post and reiterated his demand for the release of Bhagat Singh and other revolutionaries. Gandhi answered back saying, "I consider it mean to ask for the release of militants."

After this meeting, Gandhi met Lord Irwin in Delhi on 17 February 1931. During the negotiations, Gandhi did ask for the commutation of the sentences served on Bhagat Singh and other revolutionaries. But he was unsuccessful. It is an open question whether Gandhi made all-out sincere efforts towards this end. In Karachi, Gandhi said, "If I had an opportunity to speak to Bhagat Singh and his comrades, I should have told them that the way they pursued was wrong and futile.

We cannot win Swaraj for our famishing millions by sword. The way of violence can only lead to disaster, perdition..." Thus, Gandhi apparently sought reprieve for Bhagat Singh and other revolutionaries due to mounting public opinion rather than any conviction of mind.

Babarao and Chandrashekhar Azad

Chandrashekhar Azad was one of the foremost revolutionaries. He was involved in Kakori Train Robbery (1926), the attempt to blow up the Viceroy's train (1926), and the shooting of John Poyantz Saunders at Lahore (1928) to avenge the killing of Lala Lajpat Rai. He formed Hindustan Socialist Republican Association. He was the guru for revolutionaries such as Bhagat Singh, Sukhdev, Batukeshwar Dutt, and Rajguru. He received his first punishment at the age of fifteen. Chandra Shekhar was caught while indulging in revolutionary activities. When the magistrate asked him his name, he said "Azad" (meaning free). Chandrashekhar Azad was sentenced to fifteen lashes. With each stroke of the whip the young Chandrasekhar shouted "Bharat Mata Ki Jai" ("Hail The Motherland!").

Chandrashekhar Azad was massively built. He was a terror to the British. They announced a prize of ten thousand rupees on his head. It is believed that Azad met Babarao exactly forty-eight hours before his death. Babarao was in Kashi at that time. On 25 February 1931, Babarao went to a small house in a nondescript street in Kashi. The house belonged to a Panda (priest). At the appointed time, a massively built, ferocious looking man arrived to meet Babarao. The family members of the Panda knew that there was something unusual about this man. Both Babarao and this man were closeted for about two and a half hours. Their voices could not be heard outside the room. When their conversation ended, Babarao called the Panda and told him, "Panditji, this gentleman who sits before you is a great man. Your house has been blessed by his feet. Today, he is in difficulty. It is our duty to help him." The Panda went inside, and without saying a word placed a hundred rupee note in the man's hand. He even gave his son's dhoti which was drying in the sun. The stranger thanked him and went away. This man was none other than Chandrashekhar Azad. This incident was told by the Panda himself to Babarao's biographer DN Gokhale.[67]

Writings

As someone who was not much of a writer before his Andaman imprisonment, Babarao yearned to write. He was a voracious reader and kept notes in diaries. He studied Ayurveda along this. One of his best works is Rashtramimansa va Hindusthanche rashtraswaroop (Analysis of the concept of nation and the nature of India's nationhood). It was in two parts where he discusses nationhood and India's nationalist sentiments.

Hindu Rashtra - poorvi, aataa aani pudhe (Hindu nation – past, present and future) was another landmark in literature. This was a purely historical text which threw light on the dangerous circumstances which prevailed back then. The treachery of Congress was detailed in this.

His other works were Shri Shivaraayaanchi aagryaavaril garudjhep, Veeraa-Ratna-Manjusha, Christaparichay arthaat christaache Hindutva, Dharma havaa kashaalaa?, Nepaali aandolanaachaa upakram, Nepaali aandolanaachaa upakram etc. He also wrote articles for periodicals like Kesari, Vande Mataram, Sakaal etc.

Last days

By 1944, Babarao had become weak and had to battle many adversities. His body was already battered with the harsh imprisonment and strain due to his work. On 31st July 1944, Dr. Syama Prasad Mukherjee, President of the Akhil Bharat Hindu Mahasabha came to visit Babarao in hospital.

Babarao Savarkar breathed his last on 16th March 1945. The subsequent events which are part of Indian history would prove how right Ganesh Savarkar was. He could not live to see the light of the day India would become independent India. His brother Veer Savarkar continues to be vilified and attacked by the Congress party and its ecosystem.

Vinayak Damodar Savarkar

Vinayak Damodar Savarkar was born on 28 May 1883, in the Marathi Chitpavan Brahmin Hindu family of Damodar and Radhabai Savarkar in the village of Bhagur, near the city of Nashik, Maharashtra. He had three other siblings namely Ganesh, Narayan, and a sister named Maina. Savarkar began his activism as a high school student.

In 1903, in Nashik, Savarkar and his older brother Ganesh Savarkar founded the Mitra Mela, an underground revolutionary organization, which became Abhinav Bharat Society in 1906. Abhinav Bharat's main objectives were to overthrow British rule and reviving Hindu pride.

One of the most important reasons for V.D. Savarkar's early indoctrination was his exposure to Hindu revivalism that had begun with a reassertion of Hinduism in the 1890s. Bal Gangadhar Tilak was one of the leading lights of the movement which was sweeping across western India and was credited with bringing ritualistic religious practices into the public domain. He began the practice of holding the Ganpati (another name for Lord Ganesha) festival in civic venues which united Hindus across the spectrum on a common religion cultural platform. It was a community celebration of a religious festival.

The decision to pitchfork Lord Ganesha into the forefront of Hindu religiosity in the form of an annual public festival was a well-calculated move, as the Lord Ganesh was neither part of the Holy Trinity-Brahma, Vishnu and Shiva - nor the main deity of any particular community in Maharashtra. The Ganesha festival was therefore one of the first attempts to create a pan-Hindu identity to act as a counter against divergences between different sects and philosophical schools within Hinduism, and more importantly, among various castes. The open display of religious fervour induced a sense of collectiveness and became an occasion for Hindus to not only pray, but also celebrate with gusto.

Buoyed by the success of the Ganesha festival, Tilak launched the Shivaji festival thereafter to arouse nationalistic sentiment amongst Marathi youth. Young Savarkar was attracted to Tilak's initiative. But, what was certain, was that the ten-year-old boy was a ready convert to Tilak's initiative of creating a Hindu collective around a benign god. Savarkar led foreign-clothes bonfire in India with other students in presence of Bal Gangadhar Tilak.[68]

Vinayak Savarkar became an active participant in Mitra Mela, a secret society for young revolutionaries. Later, Savarkar initiated the transformation of this miniscule initiative into the more expansive, Abhinava Bharat Society, or Young India Society, a title inspired by Giuseppe Mazzini's 'Young Italy'. In early twentieth century, Savarkar 'officially' became part of the Indian freedom struggle and played a decisive role in dovetailing Abhinava Bharat Society with Bengal's most formidable revolutionary organisation of the time, the Anushilan Samiti.

In Maharashtra, during this period, Hindus were coming out in large numbers mainly to fight the Colonial rule and the firangee or the much-despised, white man. Amongst other things, the Abhinava Bharat Society fanned aversion towards foreign rule, and which later transmogrified into a sentiment against the 'traitors within', Savarkar became the organisation's chief theoretician.

In 1902, at the age of nineteen, Vinayak enrolled in Fergusson College, Pune, and continued with his revolutionary activities. The young man from Nashik was fast achieving a doughty image and became cause célèbre—the first Indian to be expelled from college for his radical views. Savarkar found support in Bal Gangadhar Tilak who condemned the college administration for its action against a promising student. While this did not force the college administration to revoke the expulsion order, money and sympathy poured in for Savarkar, enabling him to pursue higher studies in Bombay.

The young Vinayak had impressed Tilak to such an extent that the latter recommended his case to a wealthy nationalist, Shyamji Krishna Varma, who had founded the India House in London. Tilak wrote to Krishnavarma that he was fully aware of the rush of applications he would be dealing with, 'but still, I may state, among the applicants there is one Mr Savarkar from Bombay, who graduated last year and whom I know to be a spirited young man very enthusiastic in the Swadeshi cause, so much so that he had to incur the displeasure of the Fergusson College authorities'.

This naturally resulted in the application being cleared promptly, but Krishnavarma had a condition for anyone who wished to take up the scholarship: he or she must pledge not to take up any government job. Savarkar assured him in writing that he had no intention of serving the colonial administration and, in fact, wanted to do a three-year course in law in London so that he could cast a sharper light on the Raj's unjust ways.

The Gujarati patron then sent across the first instalment of the fund Rs 400 to Tilak so that he could hand it over personally to Savarkar. Tilak did that after inviting the young man over to his wada (home) for dinner; the Kaal editor too was present. That was the last time Tilak and his young disciple met. Never again would they come face-to-face over the next sixteen years (Tilak passed away in 1920). In the letter, Tilak wrote that the student was a 'spirited young man very enthusiastic in the swadeshi cause.' This powerful endorsement coupled with V.D. Savarkar's opening sentence in his application letter, which read: 'Independence and Liberty I look upon as the pulse and breath of the nation,' clinched a scholarship for him (named after the Maratha ruler, Shivaji), to study Law in England.[69]

On 9 June 1906, Vinayak Damodar Savarkar set sail on S.S. Persia to London.

At the time of Vinayak Damodar Savarkar's arrival in London, the idea of Hindu nationalism was yet to take root in its soil, and this despite a strong sense of unity amongst resident Hindus. As academics wasn't his sole motive to be in London, Savarkar joined a group of revolutionaries in their mission to liberate India through an armed rebellion. He set up the Abhinava Bharat Society in London, and also began attending the Sunday meetings called by Free India Society, which was founded by the feisty Madame Bhikhaiji Cama. Much like his mentor Tilak, Savarkar introduced Hindu festivals in London, and began commemorating heroic figures from India's ancient history. Within months of his arrival, he wrote a book titled, 'Indian War of Independence 1857', to mark the golden jubilee of the First War of Independence.

Alas, for the young revolutionary-turned-author, the book ran into trouble when a few chapters of the Marathi manuscript had fallen into the hands of the Scotland Yard. An English translation was eventually published a year later in 1909 in Holland, but did not carry Savarkar's name as author, but in its place said: by an 'An Indian Nationalist'. The book was banned in India until 1946, and it was the Congress government in Bombay which had finally rescinded the proscription. However, despite being unavailable in India for almost four decades, several youngsters continued to read it surreptitiously.

Soon, India House became the centre of revolutionary activity in London, and Savarkar came to play a significant role in furthering its cause. He began writing newsletters for a Marathi paper, and took the lead in publishing leaflets, including one in Gurmukhi prodding the Sikhs to revolt against the British, and in 1908, even organised celebrations to mark the birth anniversary of Guru Gobind Singh. His oratory skills saw him gaining popularity among the Indians living in London. India House was a place frequented by revolutionaries from other countries like Russia, Ireland, Turkey, Egypt, and Iran. From India to Europe, and even America, a network of bravehearts guided by him made contacts with Irish, French, Italian, Russian and American leaders, revolutionaries and the press to bring British India and the misery of Indians to the forefront of global discourse. No doubt, the British Government categorised him as one of the most dangerous seditionists. Along with luminaries such as Syamaji Krishna Verma Madame Bhikaji Cama, Sardarsinh Rana, Madan Lal Dhingra, V.V.S. Aiyar, Niranjan Pal, Virendranath Chattopadhyay, Lala Hardayal and M.P.T. Acharya and others, Savarkar spearheaded numerous revolutionary acts ranging from procurement and smuggling to India of bombs, pistols and bomb manuals to orchestrating political assassinations of the British both in India and in the heart of the Empire—London. Savarkar made friends with many British nationals also. One of them was Guy Aldred. Alfred had established some contacts with Russian revolutionary Lenin, who was gaining immense popularity and support across Russia and Europe. Alfred brought Vladimir Lenin to India House to meet VD Savarkar and other revolutionaries in 1909. Lenin is said to have visited India House on four occasions. It is not known what transpired in those meetings but it was well-known that at India House, Savarkar was influenced by Lenin's thoughts and Lenin's methodology to bring change in Tsarist Russia.[70]

Savarkar was influenced by the life and thinking of Italian Nationalist leader, Giuseppe Mazzini. During his stay in London, Savarkar translated Mazzini's biography in Marathi. He also influenced thinking of a fellow student called Madanlal Dhingra. Savarkar met Mohandas Gandhi for the first time in London shortly after Curzon-Wylie's assassination. During his stay, Gandhi debated Savarkar and other nationalists in London on the futility of fighting the colonial state through acts of terrorism and guerilla warfare who was in town to lobby for the rights of Indians living in South Africa. This odd setting for the meeting was significant for two reasons. First, it was a perfect example of the dichotomy which existed, and still does, between the personal lives and political ideologies of Indian politicians. For example, Mohammed Ali Jinnah's political conviction was totally at odds with his fondness for Scotch and ham sandwiches. Second, events of that evening indicated how the two men in the room would strongly disagree on almost everything in the course of their lives. Over time, there was little on which the two would ever agree.

The twenty-three-year-old Vinayak Damodar Savarkar, who was a student of Law in England, cut short Mohandas Karamchand Gandhi mid-sentence, the Indian lawyer who was readying to launch a satyagraha in Johannesburg. He was explaining to Savarkar why his strategy against the British was far too aggressive, almost bordering on militancy.

Their political paths were at sharp variance with each other. Gandhi followed a non-violent or pacifist course which drew strength from India's diversity in fighting Imperialism. In contrast, Savarkar chose aggression, also to target the 'enemy within'. Both wanted to resurrect India's glorious past - Gandhi's idea of a Ram Rajya was at the other end of the spectrum when compared to Savarkar's idea of a Hindu Rashtra. In Gandhi's construct of an ideal State, justice was ensured for the meek. Savarkar believed that as concepts, nationality and citizenship were determined on the basis of one's religious identity, and not just by citizenry.

That cold evening, Gandhi left Savarkar's apartment without securing support for his impending satyagraha. That apart, the meeting had disturbed him immensely, so much so that three years later, he had written to Gopal Krishna Gokhale sharing his remorse; most importantly, about Savarkar's viewpoint of adopting violence as the legitimate political tool to overthrow the British.

Meanwhile, the London branch of Abhinava Bharat Society produced copies of a bomb manual for Indian revolutionaries back in India. Savarkar also despatched pistols back home, one of which was used to assassinate a British magistrate who had sentenced Vinayak's eldest brother, Ganesha (popularly known as Babarao), to six years' imprisonment for writing patriotic songs that were deemed seditious by the Imperial government. But before this, there was yet another violent attack in London which had forced Savarkar to move to Paris.

On 1 July 1909, Madan Lal Dhingra who was one of the regulars at India House and a 'young man inspired by Savarkar,' assassinated Curzon Wyllie, aide-de-camp to the Secretary of State for India. Although the British government had failed to establish Savarkar's direct culpability in Wyllie's assassination, they were not only aware of his close friendship with Madan Lal, but also that Dhingra's 'ringing defence of the killing had been drafted by Savarkar.' Shortly thereafter, India House shut down and Savarkar was forced to shift to a non-descript inn, strictly meant for Indians, in a London borough. On 23 July 1909, on being produced in front of the magistrate at the Old Bailey, Madan Lal Dhingra who had chosen to defend himself, was debarred from reading out the statement, and it was V.D. Savarkar who had it published in a London newspaper with assistance from an aspiring British journalist. However, Madan Lal Dhingra was tried, sentenced and hanged, all in quick succession on 17 August 1909.

Meanwhile, in the aftermath of the British officer's assassination in Nashik, life became tougher for Vinayak Savarkar. In a much-publicized Babarao case, which came to be called the Nasik Conspiracy case, Savarkar was exiled and sent to Cellular Jail in the Andaman and Nicobar Islands. The British knew of Vinayak's association with the assassin, but they had little evidence to establish his firm connection with the conspiracy. However, the British administrators got lucky when the man who had couriered the pistols to India changed sides and became the King's witness.

In anticipation of an impending arrest, Savarkar's associates advised him to take refuge in Paris in the hope that the matter would soon die down. But the lookout for Savarkar continued, and when he returned to London in March 1910, he was arrested the moment he had stepped out of Victoria Station. Initially, the British deliberated over whether Vinayak Savarkar should be prosecuted in London or India, for the reason that while the actual crime was committed in Nashik, Savarkar was at the time residing in England. Moreover, the only charge he could be tried under was incitement to murder, and if convicted, it would've attracted a maximum sentence of two to three years.

Eventually, the Indian authorities pulled out his speeches which he had delivered while in India to examine if they worked as evidence to prosecute him. The British authorities finally concluded that although the speeches were fairly innocuous at the time they were made, they could now be termed subversive.

After being alerted of his imminent arrest, Savarkar hatched a plot to escape from jail. However, after he learnt that the British had got wind of his plans, particularly his pre-emptive escape bid, he told David Garnett, his British 'admirer' who had helped him hatch the original plan that it, 'does not matter whether one wins or is defeated, whether one succeeds or fails. Care nothing about the result so long as you fight. The only thing that matters is the spirit.'

In July 1910, even as the ship which was bringing him back to India docked in Marseilles, Vinayak slipped out through a porthole inside the bathroom. The dramatic escape would have come to fruition, but for the alertness of British police who spotted him swimming in the sea and promptly brought him back. But a slight legal hitch had occurred in his arrest because it was felt that he had actually reached the French waters and was therefore out of bounds for the British. A dispute had ensued between the British and French over jurisdiction, and reached The Hague, but by the time it was adjudicated in his favour, V.D. Savarkar was sentenced to life imprisonment and was on his way to the Cellular Jail in the Andaman and Nicobar Islands.

Overnight, the twenty-seven-year-old V.D. Savarkar was feted as a national hero. He became an international symbol of British repression - several articles in the press condemned the British; the Italian parliament and the Republican Party of Italy demanded his release; in August 1910, a Savarkar Release Committee was established in England; many diplomatic efforts were made to petition the Imperial government for securing his release. At home, stories about his dramatic escape were embellished to the level of a folk-lore and incidents eulogising his patriotic fervour became stuff of legends.

The books he had authored, including those that were banned, came back into circulation which readers and scholars began devouring with renewed vigor. What merits mention here is that Vinayak Damodar Savarkar was among those rare revolutionary nationalists who supplemented his activism with literature. At that particular stage of his life, Savarkar's idea of nationalism wasn't yet integrated with his childhood ambition of restoring Hindu dignity by raising the spectre of 'cultural' Hindus. The codification of Hindu nationalism, which was truly Savarkar's contribution to Indian political thought, occurred at a later stage in his life. However, a careful reading of Indian War of Independence, 1857 provides enough indication of his future postulations because he had clearly focused on Hindu and Maratha exclusivity, and didn't celebrate 'a unified and composite past, present, and future Indian nation.'

Significantly, Savarkar challenged contemporary historiography when it came to the analyses of 1857 and questioned the propensity to emphasise specific incidents as being the principal causes for the war. According to him, the justification behind the First War of Independence was far more serious than the innocuous argument of the use of tallow to grease cartridges, or the poor administrative skills of the British.

Although by no stretch was he advancing the compositeness of the Indian nation-state, he highlighted the 'revolutionary principles of swadharma (acting according to one's nature) and swaraj (self-rule) as being shared by Hindus and Muslims, who fought as Hindi brethren against British

rule.' He was indisputably evolving as a political thinker and often lapsed into 'epic and magisterial explication of battles and strategies, alliances and betrayals, victories and defeats' that had the capacity of inciting passion for revenge. Moreover, he presented a manual-like document for organising a revolution, particularly in a chapter titled, "Secret Organisation", in which he delineated the 'strategies to prepare for and engage in revolutionary warfare.'

On the one hand, Savarkar believed that Indians of different faiths needed to unite against the Imperial forces. He wrote:

"Savarkar's limited acceptance of Bahadur Shah was because the 'old venerable Bahadur Shah was not the old Mogul succeeding to the throne of Akbar or Aurangzeb - for that throne had already been smashed to pieces by the hammer of the Mahrattas."

The Hindu Nationalist

Vinayak Damodar Savarkar's political life can be neatly divided into three phases - the first, when he struck a balance between revolutionary nationalism and Hindu nationalism, which ended when he was sentenced to life imprisonment. His acts of bravado coupled with the jail term earned him the label of the 'brave freedom fighter' or 'swatantra Veer Savarkar'. But the heroism associated with the likes of Mahatma Gandhi, Jawaharlal Nehru and even Tilak wasn't what he desired, Savarkar wanted to go down in history as the 'organiser' of Hindus, in his worldview, to adopt a larger-than-life mantle than merely a soldier sworn to the freedom of the country. In his several articles, books, and essays written during the first phase, the idea of Hindu nationalism was still an ideology in the making.[71]

The second phase of his life began in 1911 with his confinement in the Cellular Jail, his extradition to India, and eventual double life imprisonment sentences to be served at the infamous Kaala Pani prison in the Andaman and Nicobar Islands, christened one of the darkest chapters in Savarkar's life that came to leave deep scars. It was here that Savarkar endured years of inhumane treatment that some have argued, were enough to break his spirit.

He was, reportedly, restrained in chains, flogged, and resigned to months of solitary confinement. Tied to the mill, he was made to extract oil all day, while being denied even basic access to toilets. He was often forced to eat rotten food infested with worms and insects as punishment for his 'crimes' against the government. In 1913, Savarkar, along with a number of other inmates began carrying out hunger strikes to protest against the inhumane treatment of prisoners at the prison. It is true that towards the end of his term in the Andamans, he requested the British to grant him amnesty. This was a routine legal procedure which many Congress leaders and other freedom fighters also requested for. Eventually, his actions received the notice of British government, who granted him permission to issue petitions for his release.

Savarkar's petitions tell of a man that had endured unconscionable suffering that stretched his will to its very limits. In them, he pleads with the government to afford him at least his basic rights, and discusses his unfair and contradictory classification as both, a 'special' and an ordinary prisoner. Following the closure of the prison at Port Blair, his memoirs reveal that he contemplated suicide multiple times as he grappled with the realisation that all his efforts had come to naught. In his petition requesting his release, Savarkar pledges to co-operate fully with the British authorities and refrain from any political acts – something that his critics have often held up as testament to his perceived faltering convictions to the nation's freedom struggle. However, it is worth noting that Savarkar, when questioned of his motive, did, in fact, clarify that he would trade his own freedom for the release of his fellow political prisoners. Veer Savarkar sent a total of 6 mercy petitions to the British government during the punishment of 'Kala Pani' out of which five petitions were sent between 1911 and 1919, while one petition was sent in 1920 on the suggestion of Mahatma Gandhi. But some people are arguing that when Mahatma Gandhi came to India from South Africa in the year 1915, how he advised Veer Savarkar to apologise.

Veer Savarkar was first arrested in London in 1909. One of the charges on Savarkar was the abetment to murder of Nashik Collector Jackson. He was also accused of trying to create a war-like situation by instigating a rebellion against the British government. This proves that the British government at that time considered him to be his biggest enemy and he was one of the biggest revolutionaries of India.

After his arrest, he was sent to the Cellular Jail in Andaman and Nicobar Islands in the year 1911, which was then also known as Kala Pani Jail. During this sentence, Veer Savarkar was subjected to terrible torture, after which he wrote the first letter to the British government on 30th August 1911 and pleaded the British to waive his sentence. But after 3 days, his petition was rejected.

After this, on 14th November 1913, he filed another petition in which he assured not to rebel against the British government. However, there is a difference of opinion among historians about whether this letter should be considered only an apology or a war strategy because Savarkar knew that revolution cannot be brought by being imprisoned in jail and that it was important for him to get out.[72]

He served the terrible punishment for 10 years and, during this time, sent a total of six mercy petitions to the government in 1911, 1913, 1914, 1915, 1918, and 1920.

Mercy Petitions of Savarkar

Savarkar sent mercy petitions to the British to rescue himself; he not only asked for pardon but also surrendered by acknowledging that 'I hereby acknowledge that I had a fair trial and just sentence. I heartily abhor methods of violence resorted to in days gone by, and I feel myself duty-bound to uphold [the] law and the constitution to the best of my powers and am willing to make the reform a success insofar as I may be allowed to do so in future.' Evidence of this is available in the National Archives in New Delhi. This is a very frequent allegation made against Savarkar.

Anyone who has read Savarkar's biography, or at least his autobiography 'Majhi Janmathep' (title in Marathi, meaning 'My Transportation for Life'), would easily understand the lie in this allegation. Written by Savarkar, this book is about his experiences in Andaman's Cellular Jail.

Let's understand that rotting forever in British jails was not Savarkar's concept of patriotism. That was not his goal. According to his British friend, David Garnet - "I could not endure to see a man of such intense vitality spending his life in prison. Obviously, I can serve my motherland in a much better way outside of the prison than inside. Hence, not only as a competitive policy but from the point of view of social interest too, it is important that I should accept every condition to make myself free from the prison. This is my utmost duty." These were Savarkar's thoughts. He strongly believed that real courage lay in making a strong attack on the enemy and still managing to slip away from their clutches. To him, that was bravery and not cowardice.

He never came across any situation wherein he had to take an oath of being loyal towards the British government. However, even if he had, he would have done it for the sake of the nation. What's and how's wrong in giving false assurances to enemy, deceiving, or betraying them? However, we are taught that we should never lie, not even to an enemy. That we should do everything we can to keep our promise given to the enemy, even if that is at the cost of going against our own people. These are distorted concepts of virtues ('Sadgun-Vikruti'- – a word coined by Savarkar in Marathi) that we are being taught. And that's the reason why Savarkar is difficult to understand.

Savarkar's Policy

'Of course, the activities of national interest that I have been doing here in Andaman are of very less importance, than what I could do once I get freedom and go to India. However, for that, one cannot accept something which is against the pride of the religion or the nation, or something which is despicable, lowly and treacherous. Such kind of freedom would be much more harmful to national interest as it would lay an unrighteous and anti-national example in front of others. In case, if I get an opportunity avoiding these conditions, I should try for it. Until get such an opportunity, I should continue to work for the nation in the given conditions. As far as possible, those who are not having furious rage or sharp sight of government over themselves should be used for activities here. In a situation where continuing a public movement is not possible because of reluctant or incapability of others, I should do it myself. Never miss a chance to get released. At the same time, I will not tolerate any atrocities against my fellow countrymen in the prison, fearing that I will not be released.' This is how Savarkar explains his thoughts. In short, he never accepted any anti-national or treacherous conditions while ensuring that he didn't tolerate any atrocities meted out to his fellowmen. He intermittently registered his protest by carrying out hunger strikes, bandhs, no-work days, and so on. He underwent six months of solitary confinement, standing handcuffs seven days, and block chains for ten days for refusing to work. In all, twenty to twenty-two times, he withstood cross bar fetters, standing with chains, handcuffs, confinement in a locked room, starvation, etc. He was put through all this because he conducted various protests. Other prisoners, who were ill were given milk, whereas an ill Savarkar was given only dry rotis, or rice with water.

Do these horrendous punishments indicate that Savarkar tried to compromise with the British?

His morale never diminished in the prison. On the contrary, he wrote an epic poem of 5000 lines called Kamla, that too not with pen and paper, but on the walls of the prison using thorns and nails. This is a truly unique example in all of world history. Is this feat in any way a sign of low morale?

It is always alleged that all freedom fighters who got the death sentence? never sought pardon, while Savarkar did. The death penalty results in martyrdom. The date of the execution is fixed in advanced. This kind of death results in motivating and inspiring millions of other young freedom fighters and people. For example, the death penalty given to the Chapekar brothers was a source of inspiration for many freedom fighters of that time, including Savarkar. But, life imprisonment, which meant languishing and rotting in isolation for years together, would not yield anything. From practical and rationalist Savarkar's point of view, it was foolish to do so. That would neither yield anything of national interest nor would it be an inspiration for young fellow Indians.

No concession in punishment

'Savarkar's identity badge said, Date of imprisonment: 24 December 1910, Date of release: 23 December 1960'. This meant 50 long years. Also, it had a big 'D' embossed on it, which stood for 'Dangerous'. All of Savarkar's property (including his spectacles) was confiscated. During the same period, Bombay University cancelled his B.A. graduation. He was allowed to write only one letter a year-to his younger brother, Narayan Savarkar. While in Andaman, all prisoners undergoing life imprisonment, were not compelled to stay in the prison for the entire length of their term. After five years of imprisonment, they were allowed to stay outside the prison in Andaman. However, both the Savarkar brothers never got this permission.

On 28 October 1916, Savarkar was promoted to second class and it came into effect on 2 November 1916. However, this promotion meant nothing to him as he was not given any concessions. He was not allowed to go outside the prison; he was not given any stationery either. He was not even allowed to talk to his own brother, Babarao Savarkar, who was serving his sentence in the same jail. He was not given any relief in rigorous work. He was never allowed to become warder or to step outside his solitary cell. His family was not allowed to send him anything. Many prisoners were allowed this facility after five years of imprisonment. But Savarkar didn't get this facility even after completion of six years. Which means his promotion to second class was just a pretense. He was not given any kind of facility or concession in his work or punishment. Savarkar met his wife, Maai, after a gap of eight years, on 30 May 1919. In

November 1920, the family members got permission to meet both the Savarkar brothers in Andaman. At that time, the jail authorities did not permit the trunk containing his favourite food items and kerchiefs inside, and forfeited it instead. All these things clearly show that there was no state of compromise between Savarkar and the British.

Strong Opposition to Savarkar Brothers' Release from Prison

The British government strongly opposed the release of the Savarkar brothers. A book titled 'Source Material for History of Freedom Movement in India' published by the government made the following observations in this regard:

1) [The] Bombay Government does not recommend any remission of the sentences passed upon Ganesh Damodar Savarkar and Vinayak Damodar Savarkar.

2) [The] Government of India agrees that the Savarkar brothers should not be released under the Royal Amnesty - 8 December 1919.

3) The Government of Bombay by their letter No 1106/36, Home Department, dated 29 February 1921, informed the Government of India that the Governor in Council was not in favour of the transfer of the Savarkar brothers from [the] Andamans to a jail in the Bombay Presidency, as that would lead to a recrudescence of agitation in their favour.

By the end of 1919, many political prisoners from the Bombay province, including Chandwadkar, Mariwala, Durgadas Advani and Jethamal Parasram, were released. Also, the provincial government of Bengal had agreed to the release of Barindra Kumar Ghosh and his colleagues who were facing life imprisonment in the Alipore bomb blast case. Hence, the demand for Savarkar's release gained momentum. However, the Bombay government was not even ready to transfer them to an Indian prison. 'Indian Jails Committee' had classified the prisoners in various categories, wherein the Savarkar brothers were classified as 'most dangerous criminal', and the committee had recommended against their release from Andaman. British officers were extra cautious about Savarkar and left no stone unturned in torturing him.

In all, Savarkar submitted ten petitions for pardon. These petitions are taken from 'Source Material for History of Freedom Movement in India' published by the government and Samagra Savarkar Wangmay (title in Marathi, meaning 'Complete Works of Savarkar'). No one has tried to hide them. Savarkar himself has mentioned these letters in his autobiography, Majhi Janmathep. So there was no question of seeking pardon secretly. Hence, the claim that the letters of pardon were confidential and were recovered later on from government archives is completely false.

The Rationale Behind the Mercy Petitions

This is quite a common strategy used in war; it is a standard diplomatic tactic to achieve political gains. Those who have no idea what political diplomacy is all about, see these mercy petitions as surrender. Rather, Savarkar's critics got caught in the same trap that he laid for the British. Savarkar's intention behind these letters was to deceive the British and get rid of the imprisonment. The British never fell prey to the ploy; however, the so-called intellectuals seem to remain trapped in it.

Savarkar's firm opinion was that no freedom fighter must give up life unnecessarily, just for the sake of it. He was of the view that no war can be won by embracing death. If need be, to take a big leap forward, a fighter must be ready to retrace his steps. A freedom fighter named Jatindranath (Jatin) Das embraced death on 13 September 1929 due to the hunger strike for 63 days in jail in Lahore. Savarkar wrote an article in Shradhhanand (Marathi periodical), titled 'Laudable!! Venerable! But certainly not imitable!!' On reading this article, it becomes pretty clear why Savarkar accepted various restrictions imposed by the British. He urged the likes of Bhagat Singh and other freedom fighters to refrain from hunger strike till death as Jatindranath did. He writes:

As long as India is not free, we should keep on fighting for our small little rights as and when possible. We should be ready to sacrifice our comforts, if need be. However, as long as the foreign government is powerful, there is a fair chance that whatever rights we gain in the process can be taken back anytime. It is rather foolish to make these petty things so important and lose one's valuable life for that... Martyr Jatindra's sacrifice is an exception. It is definitely laudable and venerable. But it is just that—an exception. It is not at all imitable. When Shivaji was in Aurangzeb's prison in Agra, he didn't starve himself to death. Rather, he smartly escaped from the prison. So, fine-tune your actions according to the situation, but never compromise on the basic strategy. Never forget the larger goal of achieving freedom.

"Hindus no more need mere martyrs. We need to create victorious brave-hearts. It is true that the nation that fails to give martyrs at the need of the hour is a dead nation. However, it is equally true that the nation that only satisfies itself with the laurels of the martyrs and ignores creating victorious warriors is dead as well." This was Savarkar's winning attitude.

"The only aim of a national army is victory and nothing but victory. The minimal loss of our own just side and maximum loss of our enemy's unjust side is true warfare. In real warfare, a martyr is always [an] important and praiseworthy constituent. But it is an exception. Mere martyrdom doesn't guarantee a win."

So says Savarkar, because a defeat is a defeat. Defeat results in long-term physical, mental, financial, social, political and national losses. As per Churchill: "The penalties of defeat are frightful. After the blinding flash of catastrophe, the stunning blow, the gaping wounds, there comes an onset of the diseases of defeat. The central principle of a nation's life is broken, and all healthy normal control vanishes. There are few societies that can withstand the conditions of subjugation."

After World War I began in 1914, Savarkar sent an application to the government. A summary of that letter is as follows:

He demanded colonial self-government. An unconditional majority of Hindu leaders in senior legislature, and in return, Indian freedom fighters would help England in World War I. In this letter, he gave examples, saying that many European nations have released their rebel political prisoners, including Ireland. He also demanded the release of all political prisoners facing their respective imprisonment terms in various jails of India and abroad. In addition, he stated: 'I offered to do without any release for myself personally. Let them release all the political prisoners in the country, leaving me alone in my own cell in the Andamans. I shall rejoice in their freedom as if it was my own.'18 Such a selfless demand it was. This means that Savarkar's demands and letters were not meant for him alone, but for all the freedom fighters of India.

According to his book Andamanchya Andheritun (title in Marathi, meaning 'From the Darkness of the Andamans'), Savarkar says in his letter to his brother, dated 6 July 1920, that he has written a letter to the government on 2 April 1920. In this letter, he said, I pleaded for the further extension of the Royal clemency to those who are yet in Indian jail as well as to the Political exiles abroad. Savarkar writes: 'For although we two have been declared to fall outside the scope of the Amnesty and are still rotting in the cells yet the sight of hundreds of our political comrades and co-sufferers' release makes us feel relieved and repaid for all the agitation that we have been carrying on for the last eight years or so through strikes, letters, petitions, the press, and the platform, here and else where.'

In a letter dated 4 August 1918, Savarkar writes: 'In all my letters to government, I have always demanded unconditional amnesty for all my fellow countrymen. However, if the question of my amnesty is the only thorn in this, then I am happily agree for my continuance in jail.' Most importantly, while giving this selfless consent, his health was deteriorating. In March 1917, his weight was 119 pounds, which decreased to 98 pounds in 1918. 'I am feeling a lot of pain while writing even this small letter... My body is deteriorating every day.' He wrote this heart-wrenching letter to his brother on 4 August 1918.

Rendering of a selfless demand in an unfortunate situation is much more august and difficult to imitate than making a selfless demand in a comfortable situation. Hence, the allegation that he preferred his own freedom over the nation's freedom movement is completely baseless. How can a person take part in a freedom movement if he is imprisoned for life? Therefore, it was most appropriate to deceive the enemy and get out of the prison and when opportunity comes, to once again take part in the freedom movement. Savarkar was demanding a complete release of all prisoners across the nation as well as abroad, hoping to get royal pardon for all. He never put forth any selfish demand; it was never about releasing 'only him' nor 'at least him'.[72]

Savarkar writes: 'I continuously urged all of them to accept much futuristic and nation-friendly condition. It was very any in the nation's interest to accept any such kind of condition. I was trying to give them the examples of [the] Shivaji-Jaisaingh treaty, [the] Shivaji-Afzal Khan incident, Guru Govind Singh in the war of Chamkore and Krishna in [the] Mahabharata in order to convince them of the correctness of the step they were taking. The most obstinately proud among them would not be persuaded even by these parallels from the past. Their stubbornness on [the] subject, after all that they had suffered for the cause, inspired me with great hope for the future of my country. But at last I could convince them of my point of view, and they all signed the pledge without demur, and thus broke open the lock of the Andaman jail.'

Savarkar continually attempted to explain to fellow prisoners his rationale behind sending petitions to the British. He was trying to convince them to get out of the prison at any cost. He didn't limit the idea to getting freedom for oneself, but spread it to others and tried to convince those who didn't agree with the aid of logic and historical references.

Hemchandra Das and Barindra Kumar Ghosh convicted under the Alipore bomb blast case came to the Andamans in 1908. The British then pardoned them in 1920, and they were set free. The accused under Lahore conspiracy, Sachindra Nath Sanyal, pleaded for pardon, saying--'Why would we indulge into underground revolutionary politics if we are allowed to do an open national revolution?' Amnesty given to him, but Savarkar wasn't. Surendranath's son-in-law, Vijay Chandra (V.C.) Chatterjee, was a barrister and a friend of Virendranath Chattopadhyay. When Sachindra Nath met Vijay Chandra, the former said, 'Vinayak Damodar Savarkar said the same thing in his petition - what I said in mine. If you are right, then Savarkar should be released too.'23 This makes it clear that the British did not believe Savarkar at all.

After seeing the examples of Barindra Kumar Ghosh and Sachindra Nath Sanyal, Savarkar-haters change the allegation and say, 'Very few people out of Gadar revolutionaries and Bengali terrorists pleaded for pardon...' Senior revolutionaries, such as V.D. Savarkar and Barindra Kumar Ghosh, pleaded for their release. However, Craddock said about this meet - 'Dhaka gang leader Pulin Bihari didn't say a word.' In 1914, almost all prisoners were granted amnesty, barring Pulin Bihari. In an order dated 6 January 1914, Craddock says - Pulin Bihari will be kept in [the] Andamans as an exception. Savarkar-haters refer to Gadar revolutionaries as 'revolutionaries' and Bengali revolutionaries as 'terrorists'. Here, they indirectly accept that, apart from Savarkar, many other freedom fighters pleaded for pardon. That means they indirectly admit that Savarkar was not the only person who pleaded for pardon. Can sending pardon letters be the only yardstick used to gauge one's patriotism? What was the loss for Indian people in Savarkar sending the letters seeking pardon? What did the British gain out of this? If nothing, then how did sending letters seeking pardon fall under 'betrayal towards the nation'? On the contrary, revolutionaries could have done a lot of work against the British after gaining freedom from imprisonment. Barindra Kumar Ghosh is a perfect example of this. He resumed his revolutionary activities after being released from Andaman.

With the exception of Pulin Bihari, every political prisoner was released from Andaman to Indian jails. However, the point to be noted here is that Savarkar was not released. In an order from 1914, it is said that all political prisoners are being transferred to Indian prisons with an exception of Pulin Bihari as he refused to apologise.

This simply means that all those who were transferred to Indian prisons were offered mercy. Indirectly, this also means that pleading for pardon was the only way to get out of the prisons of Andaman. If most of the prisoners of Andaman pleaded for pardon, why was only Savarkar held guilty of this? Pulin Bihari who never pleaded for mercy, and Savarkar who pleaded for mercy were both kept in Andaman and not released. Savarkar was not given any facilities, comforts or privileges inside the prison. Not even those for which he was eligible as per the rules. How can it be said then that the British gave him any special treatment?

While pleading to the British for mercy, Savarkar put forth the following demands in his letter:

1) Unconditional and comprehensive release of all political prisoners serving imprisonment in and outside India.

2) Responsible governing power, or self-government.

3) Effective majority in legislature.

4) No questions to be asked about our earlier revolutionary activities, conspiracies and persons involved.

Looking at these demands, how one can say that Savarkar offered complete surrender to the British? If he had offered complete surrender, he could easily have named his fellow revolutionaries and got unconditional release from prison. While creating a false illusion of surrender in the eyes of the British, Savarkar never betrayed his fellow revolutionaries or his nation.

In 1919, after the first World War, King George V of Britain issued an order, under which all political prisoners in prisons were pardoned. This was a gift to the people of India because during the war, many leaders, including Mahatma Gandhi, had taken an oath of allegiance to the British.

Under this order, many prisoners were also released from the Cellular Jail in Andaman, but the British government did not pardon Vinayak Savarkar and his elder brother Ganesh Damodar Savarkar.

After this, Savarkar's younger brother, Narayan Rao Savarkar, wrote a letter to Mahatma Gandhi on 18 January 1920.

He asked Gandhi's advice and help in that situation. He wrote that Savarkar had been serving the sentence for almost years and that his health had suffered a lot and his weight has come down to 45 kg.

A week later, Mahatma Gandhi replied to this letter on 25 January 1920. He writes, "I have received your letter. It is difficult to give any advice in this matter. But I will give you a suggestion that you should prepare a detailed petition to prove Vinayak Savarkar to be a political prisoner." Gandhi said that this could generate public support.

It was only after Mahatma Gandhi's suggestion that Veer Savarkar sent his sixth and last mercy petition to the British government, which was later rejected like the rest of the petitions.

Gandhi had also written an article in Young India newspaper on 26 May 1920, titled "Savarkar Brothers", calling for their release.

Veer Savarkar remained in jail for a total of 15 years, out of which he spent 10 years in Kala Pani, which was considered the most dreadful prison. Apart from this, he was also under house arrest for 13 years in Ratnagiri district of Maharashtra.

A freedom fighter, who spent almost 28 years of his life in such terrible situation for the freedom of the country - can his patriotism be doubted? But there are some people in the country who are used to playing politics over it.

Ironically, Savarkar's anti-Gandhi posturing stood him in good stead. When his jail term came up for a review, the British government's leniency combined with a campaign by non-Congress members of the Central Legislative Assembly, resulted in Savarkar being shifted in 1921 from Cellular Jail to Yerawada Jail for two years and eight months. Finally, he was released from prison in January 1924, and permitted to stay with his family within the boundaries of Ratnagiri district. The clincher for the British was when Savarkar promised to 'not engage publicly or privately in any manner of political activities without the consent of Government for a period of five years.'

Vinayak Damodar Savarkar's release was mainly due to the unwavering support of a man called Jamnadas Mehta, who was a Tilakite and member of the Interim government of Bombay. It was

Mehta who had campaigned relentlessly for his release and formed the Savarkar Release Committee. He had also supported his campaign by writing a pamphlet titled, 'Why Savarkar Should Be Released' and had organised a meeting in Bombay with Vithalbhai Patel in the chair. What may come as a surprise to many within the Hindu Right-wing today, Savarkar's release was also courtesy of the Indian National Congress, which had adopted a resolution for his release in its Coconada (now Kakinada) session in 1923.

Unlike numerous political prisoners who were driven to insanity or committed suicide, Savarkar showed remarkable resilience and was ultimately rewarded for it in January 1924 when he was finally released from prison.

For the next thirteen years, his actions were closely monitored, but this did not dissuade him from undertaking a number of local reforms, including actively trying to drown the caste-system in Ratnagiri by promoting inter-caste dining, as well as the construction of a new temple.

It was during this phase when he wrote his seminal work - Hindutva! Who is a Hindu? and became a revered ideologue for future generations of Hindutva votaries.

Savarkar was aware that the British would not believe him and would not allow him to participate in active politics. Hence, in front of the jail commission, he declared that he would not participate in active politics. However, he would want to continue serving society and humanity in some other forms. Also, he said that if, in any way, the government felt that he was not abiding by the promise he had made, they could always put him back behind bars.

Moreover, at the time of discussion with the governor regarding amnesty, he put up the same proposal. He said: 'I will not participate in direct and active politics. In the prison too, there is no such possibility. Outside the prison, apart from politics, there are many ways where[by] I can offer my services, like educational, social, religious and literary contributions, to name a few. As Krishna vowed at the time of [the] Mahabharata, that he will not directly take part in the war, I also urge to be freed with conditions (on parole). Like Krishna, true patriots have no qualms in driving the chariot of other warrior[s], if they are not allowed to participate in the war directly. They take it as their very duty.'

This was his stand. Accordingly, after his conditional release from jail, other than politics, he took part in social reforms, shuddhi (reconversion), scientific temper, language purification, script reforms, etc. Through these varied ways, he did a lot of service to the nation. Numerous leaders and reformers, such as Dr Babasaheb Ambedkar, Maharshi Vitthal Ramaji Shinde, Prabodhankar Thackeray, Satyashodhak Bhai Bagal and Mahatma Gandhi, appreciated his work of social reforms. Social reform is also a kind of service to the nation. Savarkar fought with the same zeal and vitality for social reform as he did for the freedom movement. As eager as he was to break the shackles of British domination, he was equally eager to break the seven Indigenous shackles of social evils, namely prohibition of touch (sparshabandi) of certain castes, prohibition of inter-dining (rotibandi) with certain castes, prohibition of inter-caste marriages (betibandi), prohibition of pursuing certain occupations (vyavasayabandi), prohibition of seafaring (sindhubandi), prohibition of rites sanctioned by the Vedas (Vedoktabandi), prohibition of reconversion (shuddhibandi) to the Hindu fold. He proved that he was a true social revolutionary as well.

All those political prisoners who were freed from prison got release because most of them signed a similar kind of agreement. Most of their promissory notes said - 'I will not take part in active politics or state revolution again (or for some years). If I am found guilty of doing any activities of sedition, I will again be put behind bars and I will serve my remaining term from the previous sentence as well.'

From January 1924 till May 1937, Savarkar was allowed to live with his family, but within the periphery of his hometown, Ratnagiri. During this phase, he pretended to distance himself from all kinds of political activity, and the British authorities took little notice of a campaign that this ex-convict was planning in his village within two weeks of his arrival. Truth be told, it was a seemingly noble, albeit innocuous social reform campaign to eliminate untouchability, but was cleverly dovetailed into his ultimate political goal of uniting Hindus across caste lines. The British were also hoodwinked because campaigns to end social ostracization had been repeatedly conducted in the past by the votaries of Hindutva. It was also during this phase of his life when Savarkar had guided Keshav Baliram Hedgewar in establishing RSS as an organisation to 'supply the Hindu society with power and pillars.'

Gandhi who was extensively touring the country reached Ratnagiri in March 1927. He began his speech making references to Tilak and Savarkar. The Mahatma said, he knew that Savarkar, 'whom he had known well in England and whose sacrifices and patriotism were known, was staying in the same town.' 'We had differences then', he told listeners, and 'we have them now but they have not affected in our friendship, difference of opinion should never mean hostility'.

After the public meeting, Gandhi headed straight to Savarkar's place and two spoke at some length. Savarkar told Gandhi that he was at his place 'not as a political leader but as a friend' and asked him clarify his stance on 2 issues that sharaddanand had laid the greatest emphasis on: Untouchability and Shuddhi,and Gandhi cleared misinterpretation on the same, Gandhi's secretary, Mahadev Desai wrote about this interaction.

The final and third phase, but the least significant in Savarkar's life, was after all the restrictions on him were lifted and he became the President of the Hindu Mahasabha in 1937. He led the Mahasabha to its moment of glory-recognition from British administrators as the sole representative of India's Hindus, as also a coalition partner in the Bengal government.

VD. Savarkar was certainly not the first to expound the idea of Hindu nationalism, but he was indeed the first to codify it and lent coherence to the idea. In the last decades of the nineteenth century, a rudimentary form of Hindu nationalism had emerged, mainly as a reaction to the British response to home-grown social reform movements. As mentioned earlier, apart from Tilak's Hindu revivalist programmes, there were several others which were aimed at 'reforming' the Hindus from 'within', and opposed the introduction of certain laws which threatened to regulate Hindu society.

It is ironic that even though Savarkar was not a member of the Jana Sangh, or the Rashtriya Swayamsevak Sangh (RSS), leaders of the Sangh Parivar, have always held him in great reverence. He was undeniably an iconic figure, because despite his sharp ideological divergences with several leaders of the RSS, his legacy was readily co-opted as history and heritage.

The reason for V.D. Savarkar's indisputable pre-eminence amongst saffron icons is because of his 'first full articulation' of a Hindu nationalist manifesto in the form of his seminal 'prison' treatise - Hindutva! Who is a Hindu?

Those who celebrate the vision of Savarkar also point to his work, 'The History of the War of Indian Independence' as a watershed moment in India's struggle against the British colonialist rule, in the manner in which it challenged an oppressive regime's historiographical narrative, and mobilised the indigenous population. The book came to be banned across the British Empire, but copies inevitably made its way into France, Germany and the Netherlands, as Savarkar's popularity began to grow immensely.

The All India Muslim League was formed in December 1906, and catalysed the formation of the Hindu Mahasabha in the same year in undivided Punjab. However, despite the involvement of senior Congress leaders like, Lala Lajpat Rai, and the founder of the Banaras Hindu University (BHU), Pandit Madan Mohan Malaviya who was its first President, the Mahasabha conclave was restricted to an annual jamboree, and lacked the political reason. It was to the credit of Vinayak Damodar Savarkar that he eventually provided its framework, and established the process of creating a separate and structured channel for Hindu nationalism. Instead of the token alternative presented by revivalists within the Indian National Congress, Savarkar helped the creation of an alternate outfit to the existing nationalist mainstream, in idea as well as structure. The best example of this phenomenon was represented by none other than Dr. Keshav Baliram Hedgewar, who abandoned the Congress and founded the Rashtriya Swayamsevak Sangh, which in time evolved as one of the most ideologically-driven organisations in India.

Meanwhile, Savarkar had an epiphany during his solitary confinement in Cellular Jail - something which had been churning in his mind since childhood, all through his rebellious youth, and finally as a young revolutionary nationalist, it began taking shape. It was in jail that Savarkar noticed how large number of untouchables were converting to Islam because Hindu prisoners were prone to ostracise their low caste brethren. Once, when Savarkar had learnt that an untouchable boy was being converted, he decided to engage with him and earned the terrible epithet of 'Savarkar Bhangi Babu' (meaning, someone who took the low castes under his wing). This was obviously a slur, but Savarkar soldiered on and prevented the boy's conversion.

Emboldened by his first success, Savarkar began the process of 'reverse conversion' by performing the shuddhi ceremony on several others, and although this move was initially met with stiff resistance. He demonstrated that Hindus who had converted to either Islam or Christianity could be brought back into the Hindu fold. Soon it was time for census enumeration in the country, and Savarkar campaigned vigorously amongst Arya Samajis and Sikhs in jail to register their religion as 'at least Hindu', with the words Arya and Sikh in the bracket.

The idea for his best known book, 'Hindutva! Who is a Hindu?' also germinated in the island jail, in which he defined a Hindu as 'a person who regards this land of Bharatvarsh from the Indus to the Seas as his Fatherland as well as his Holy Land, that is the cradle of his religion.' Savarkar distinguished between punyabhoomi (holy land) and pitrubhoomi or matrubhoomi (fatherland or motherland).

It must be mentioned here that the concept of punyabhoomi was first posited by Swami Vivekananda in 1897, as a land where, 'all souls aspiring towards a spiritual quest must attain their last home.' Much like Vivekananda, Savarkar also saw India as a seamless and 'eternal civilisation', but his concept of a nation was different, in that he saw it as being far more exclusive, because he considered that people whose sacred lands were in other countries, meaning Muslims, Christians, Jews and Zoroastrians, were not entitled to refer to India or Bharatvarsh as their own nation. Savarkar's efforts in linking religion and culture with national identity was the genesis of cultural nationalism which eventually became the cornerstone of the virulent phase of Hindutva from the late 1980s. In Savarkar's understanding, Hinduism was not just a religion, but a culture or a way of life - the word Hindutva, as a political construct, did not predate Savarkar's dissertation in the early 1920s.

On his part, Savarkar was often self-contradictory, as we have seen earlier. After his argument on who could consider Bharatvarsh as his or her own land, his formal definition of Hindutva was conspicuous for its exclusivity:

Hindutva is not a word but a history. Not only the spiritual or religious history of our people as at times it is mistaken to be by being confounded with the other cognate term Hinduism, but a history in full. Hinduism is only a derivative, a fraction, a part of Hindutva. Unless it is made clear what is meant by the latter, the first remains unintelligible and vague. Failure to distinguish between these two terms has given rise to much misunderstanding and mutual suspicion between some of those sister communities that have inherited this inestimable and common treasure of our Hindu civilization... Hindutva is not identical with what is vaguely indicated by the term Hinduism... Had not linguistic usage stood in our way then 'Hinduness' (elsewhere, he also used the word Hindudom, italics mine) would have certainly been a better word... Hindutva embraces all the departments of thought and activity of the whole Being of our Hindu race. Therefore, to understand the significance of this term 'Hindutva', we must first understand the essential meaning of the word 'Hindu'...

Savarkar elaborated on his basic premise about other religionists, most importantly, the followers of Islam. His postulation clearly indicated that he precluded them, and the other three, from his idea of who can claim to be Indian: ...although the root-meaning of the word Hindu like the sister epithet Hindi, may mean only an Indian, yet as it is, we would be straining the usage of words too much - we fear, to the point of breaking, if we were to call a Mohammedan a Hindu because of his being a resident of India. It may be that at some future time the word Hindu may come to indicate a citizen of Hindusthan and nothing else; that day can only rise when all cultural and religious bigotry has disbanded its forces pledged to aggressive egoism...

Savarkar further elaborated on that thought as follows

An American may become a citizen of India. He would certainly be entitled, if bona fide, to be treated as our Bharatiya, a countryman and a fellow citizen of ours. But as long as in addition to our country, he has not adopted our culture and our history, inherited our blood and has come to look upon our land not only as the land of his love but even of his worship, he cannot get himself incorporated into the Hindu fold.... Hindus are not merely the citizens of the Indian state because they are united not only by the bonds of the love they bear to a common motherland but also by the bonds of a common blood. They are not only a Nation but also a race – jati. All Hindus claim to have in their veins the blood of the mighty race incorporated with and descended from the Vedic fathers, the Sindhus.

He left no room for ambiguity on what, according to him, should be the future of Muslims, even those who accepted that their forefathers had converted to Islam from Hinduism: The majority of the Indian Mohammedans may, if free from the prejudices born of ignorance, come to love our land as their fatherland, as the patriotic and noble-minded amongst them have always been doing. The story of their conversions, forcible in millions of cases, is too recent to make them forget, even if they like to do so, that they inherit Hindu blood in their veins. But can we, who here are concerned with investigating into facts as they are and not as they should be, recognize these Mohammedans as Hindus?

Savarkar's book not only romanticised the idea of being a Hindu, but also instilled a sense of victimhood among Hindus. There was also this accompanying awe-inspiring story about the method of his writing. According to his biographer, because he was in solitary confinement with no access to either pen or paper, Savarkar had scribbled his initial thoughts on the bare walls of his cell with pebbles. Thereafter, he learnt every word on the walls by rote, and when he was discharged from Cellular Jail and sent to Yerawada in Pune, he continued writing on loose sheets which were either smuggled out, or memorised by his followers who went out and recorded it for him. Eventually, Hindutva: Who is a Hindu? was first published in 1923 under the pseudonym of 'A Maratha' (as prisoners were not allowed to publish any work), and immediately became a manual on Hindutva and Hindu nationalism. The book created a sensation and most importantly because Savarkar steered clear of the 'chaos and confusion created by nearly fifty definitions of the word Hindu including the one made by Tilak.' His choice of words left no scope for any doubt:(You), who by race, by blood, by culture, by nationality possess almost all the essentials of Hindutva and had been forcibly snatched out of our ancestral home by the hand of violence - ye, have only to render wholehearted love to our common Mother and recognize her not only as Fatherland (Pitrubhumi) but even as a Holy Land (Punyabhumi); would be most welcome to the Hindu fold. This is a choice which our countrymen and our old kith and kin (sic), the Bohras, Khojas, Memons and other Mohammedan and Christian communities are free to make a choice again which must be a choice of love. But as long as they are not minded, thus, so long they cannot be recognized as Hindus.

Yet, the above definition does little but confuse when juxtaposed with Savarkar's contradictory views on the same subject, cited previously. However, Hindu nationalists of different hues who emerged in the post-Savarkar era continued to revere him despite the fact that he was never part of any organisation. They readily identified with him not only because he represented a similar socio-religious conundrum, but they found several aspects of his argument closest to their beliefs.

Curiously, Savarkar's repeated efforts to play supplicant to the Colonial regime was accompanied by his criticism of Mahatma Gandhi and his methods. He once dismissed the Mahatma rather unflatteringly and commented about his 'queer definitions of non-violence and truth,' while denouncing the non-cooperation and Khilafat movements. His disagreements with the Congress and Gandhi on administrative reforms were also out in the open: while Gandhi wanted to boycott the Imperial Council, Savarkar was 'sure that many a revolutionist would, like me, cry halt under the circumstances and try to meet England under an honourable truce, even in a half-way house.' Despite the bitter criticism, Gandhi however made a distinction between Savarkar's detention and his political stance. As evidence of fair play, Gandhi wrote in Young India, in 1920, protesting against the imprisonment of both Savarkar and his younger brother, asking that as the charges of violence were not proved against either of them, why the two were still in detention.

He was often subsumed by the thought of Indians' proclivity to be dominated by foreigners, and by the time he was released from jail, he concluded that the primary reason for Hindus' repeated subjugation was a deep-seated psychological shortcoming. He believed that this anomaly could only be rectified by unifying Hindus under the aegis of a sangathan or organisation. Over time, this opinion reflected in his writings influenced K.B. Hedgewar's decision to establish the RSS.

Even while campaigning amongst Sikhs in the Cellular Jail to enlist as Hindus, he had submitted that Hindutva was not identical to Hinduism and that followers of other faiths could also be termed as Hindus (later named as Indian Religionists or IRs). He further convinced his fellow-inmates that Sikhism, Jainism and Buddhism could be treated as IRs because their sacred places (punyabhoomi) lay within the geographical boundaries of India.

Interestingly, as Savarkar was debarred from participating in any kind of political activity during his stay in Ratnagiri, he opted to write fiction - a kind of veneer to conceal its political content from law enforcers. His readers lost no time in inferring the real intent of their favourite author, but the British authorities took the book at its face value and did little else. In January 1927, he also launched a weekly called Shraddhanand and began writing about socio-political issues. The following extract from an article that he wrote on 27 January 1927 was cited:

For a man who was viewed as the votary of reinstating Hindu dignity, his long confinement within a district was a matter of great concern for his followers. For them, his seclusion from political activity was no better than a jail term and they therefore began yet another campaign to end his confinement which was extended periodically by the British. In January 1935, when a review date had loomed ahead, Savarkar was advised to not protest, and appeal for release. In November 1934, this one-time revolutionary who was sworn to his Motherland promised that 'he would be on the right side of law and constitution even if he took to politics.' However, the government concluded that allowing Savarkar to travel and speak publicly was inadvisable, and his internment was extended for two more years.

At the end of the stipulated period, Savarkar petitioned the British yet again and this time, he was advised to route his application through the local administration. By then, a new Savarkar Restrictions Removal Committee had been formed and included former acolytes of Tilak and other social reformers. A signature campaign was initiated, which pleaded for removing restrictions on Savarkar. Mahatma Gandhi was also approached to sign the petition, which he refused while contending that it would be below his dignity to plead with the British while fighting for India's independence. 'You do not beseech adversaries,' the Mahatma is said to have stated emphatically. Jamnadas Mehta played a vital role in Savarkar's release yet again, who it may be recalled had lobbied for his release from prison in 1924. Mehta bargained with the British over the issue when they had approached him to help convince the Congress party to join the provincial governments which had to be mandatorily formed after elections following the agreement on the Government of India Act, 1935. Mehta agreed to plead for the British, but set a precondition: release V.D. Savarkar.

Release and Thereafter

On 10 May 1937, all restrictions on V.D. Savarkar were finally lifted and he was free after twenty-seven years of confinement. The town of Ratnagiri had erupted with several celebratory functions. Savarkar was invited for each as the guest of honour - which was also attended by local Congress leaders. His various speeches and statements during this phase elucidate what he had set to do all his life, but not necessarily in any chronological order; it was more like the pages from his book of life.

For instance, at one of the functions, Savarkar had turned emotional and recalled his agitation against untouchability which he said, pitted one Hindu against the other. He explained that although the movement was met with stiff resistance, he had focused on it considering it to be in the 'best interest of the Country, God, and Man.'

At another public gathering, Savarkar declared that his ultimate goal was the independence of India, and spelt out a three-pronged strategy to achieve it: resistance, alliance, and pressure. However, unlike Mahatma Gandhi or other leaders of the freedom movement, he dwelt little on how to go about achieving these. During the early days of his life out of jail, Savarkar spoke at length about a democratic India which should follow 'one man, one vote,' which was interpreted by some Muslims (when separate electorates existed for the community), as a ploy to establish a government for and by the Hindus.

A few months after settling into life, Vinayak Damodar Savarkar embarked on an extensive tour of Maharashtra and went to Pandharpur, Kolhapur, Pune, and eventually, Bombay. In Pune, Savarkar reached out to a group of untouchables who were considering conversion to Islam or Christianity as an escape route from caste-based discrimination. He counselled them against converting to other religions and suggested that they should join forces with social reformers and fight the malaise within. Even as he went about participating in inter-caste dinners, a long tradition in western India, Savarkar urged the youth to learn to use guns, arguing that drama and poetry were fine hobbies, but not when the 'mother was on her death bed,' a clear allegorical reference to the nation or Motherland. In one public meeting after another, Savarkar kept reiterating about his ultimate political mission, which was to establish a free nation 'on the bedrock of the Hindus, the national majority.' His objective, he said, was to ensure that this 'paper majority' realised its capacity, and 'the fact that they were the bedrock and mainspring of the national life and the State.'

By 1937, V.D. Savarkar had undoubtedly emerged as the greatest icon of the Indian Right-wing, or Hindu nationalist politics. The period of his imprisonment had made him doughtier; this despite the fact of his cosying up to the British and relegating the cause of India's freedom to the backburner in the face of his campaign to build a strong and unified Hindu India, which was viewed by many of his followers as an act of great sacrifice. Two months after restrictions on his free movement were lifted, Vinayak Damodar Savarkar joined the Democratic Swaraj Party (formed in 1933) to propagate the political ideals of Bal Gangadhar Tilak. Yet, within a short period, he concluded that it did not have the potential to evolve into a pan-Indian party and left. Savarkar, finally became a free man in May 1937. Subhas Chandra Bose issued a statement welcoming the return of Savarkar to public life. He hoped that Savarkar would join the Congress. Other congress leaders also welcomed his release and expected he would join Congress. But he had other thoughts. The next logical step for him would have been to join the RSS, and he did visit a branch in Wardha at the request of K.B. Hedgewar, but surprisingly engaged no further with it. There were two reasons for his reluctance - first, despite its subsequent significance in Indian politics, the RSS was a minor organisation at that point of time when compared with the larger-than-life image of V.D. Savarkar. In fact, the RSS would have benefitted greatly from its association with the man. Second, after years of his confinement, Savarkar desired a larger political role for himself and mainly as a counter to the Congress party and its politics.

On the other hand, both Hedgewar and M.S. Golwalkar harboured no such ambitions and were solely devoted to the RSS for which, they felt, falling foul of either the British or Congress, would be counter productive. The dissonance between Savarkar and senior RSS leaders came as a surprise to many because the RSS owed its genesis to Savarkar as an inspirational figure. Despite Savarkar's publicly stated reservations about the RSS, K.B. Hedgewar remained the archetypal dyed-in-the-wool Hindu leader, someone who believed that it was enjoined in the ancient Hindu precepts to show respect towards an elder, and that it was also politically prudent to keep a track open with Savarkar. Consequently, although he treated Savarkar with utmost reverence while remaining conscious of RSS' independent identity, Hedgewar feared that the young cadre may be swept away by Savarkar's political activism and his charismatic personality.

But Savarkar paid no heed to such entreaties, and seven months after being allowed to travel freely and speak without restrictions, he accepted to be president of the Hindu Mahasabha in December 1937 at its nineteenth annual session, aiming to transform it into a national political force and remained at its helm for seven years. As president of the Mahasabha from 1937–1942, Vinayak Damodar Savarkar delivered six presidential lectures, which form part of what is considered to be a major repository of his political thought and ideology. Titled, Hindu-Rashtra Darshan, the Savarkar lectures examine the twin ideas of the Hindu nation, and swaraj (self-governance), a term which was used extensively by nationalists such as Gandhi, Tilak and Sri Aurobindo. But Savarkar's definition of swaraj was different from the others, in that, it did not imply freedom from Colonial rule; independence for him meant, 'as far as the Hindu Nation is concerned, the political independence of the Hindus, the freedom which would enable them to grow to their full height.' [73]

Then in 1938, Savarkar leading the Mahasabha and Arya samaj in an agitation against the atrocities of the Nizam on his state's Hindu population. Significantly, he foresaw the situation which was supporting Kashmiris against their Hindu Rulers as they were in majority refused to follow same logic in the case of Hyderabad. Gandhi even called Dr. Moonje to convince Savarkar and Arya Samaj to End the agitation. Dr. Moonje told Mahatma, Savarkar and Mahasabha know well where to stop. Even as Arya samaj was on the verge of withdrawing the agitation under Congress Pressure, Savarkar gave sent off to Several volunteers who entered Hyderabad to offer resistance.

Eventually over 15000 volunteers, led by Eminent leaders such as Senapati Bapat, L.B Bhopatkar, D.K. Sathe, Dr. L.V. Paranjape and Bapurao Joshi from Maharastra, Pandit Narayan Swami Chandrakiran Sarada from other provinces and Hyderabad Mahasabha Leader, Yashwantrao landed in Jail.

Savarkar and the Two Nation theory

Savarkar is blamed for propagating the two-nation theory in his maiden speech as the president of the Hindu Mahasabha in 1937. But the truth is more complex. The idea of Hindus and Muslims being two separate nations was floated by Sir Syed Ahmed Khan (1888) and Sir 'Allama' Muhammad Iqbal and Choudhary Rahmat Ali (early 1930s). One of the fundamental principles of the Aligarh movement was that the Hindus and Muslims form two separate political entities with a separate outlook and conflicting interests.

"India cannot be assumed today to be a unitarian and homogeneous nation, but on the contrary, there are two nations in the main; the Hindus and the Moslems, in India."

Savarkar made the above statement in his presidential address at the All India Hindu Mahasabha Convention in Karnavati (Ahmedabad) in 1937. From this one sentence, it is ridiculously alleged: 'Savarkar proposed or advocated the two-nation theory and Jinnah demanded Partition by the implementation of these principles.'

Immediately following the above statement, Savarkar adds, "And as it has happened in many countries under [a] similar situation in the world, the utmost that we can do under the circumstances is to form an Indian state in which none is allowed any special weightage of representation and none is paid an extra price to buy his loyalty to the state. The Hindus as a nation are willing to discharge their duty to a common Indian state on equal footing."

Finally, Savarkar says: "We shall ever guarantee protection to the religion, culture and language of the minorities for themselves, but we shall no longer tolerate any aggression on their part on the equal liberty of the Hindus to guard their religion, culture and language as well. If the non-Hindu minorities are to be protected, then surely the Hindu majority also must be protected against any aggressive minority in India."

If Savarkar were to propose the Two Nation Theory, would he have said, 'We shall ever guarantee protection to the religion, culture and language of the minorities?' If he supported the Two Nation Theory, would he have said, 'none is allowed any special weightage of representation?' Why would he have said, 'The Hindus as a nation are willing to discharge their duty to a common Indian state on equal footing,' if he supported the Two Nation Theory?

Most importantly, Savarkar says, 'As it is, there are two antagonistic nations living side by side in India; several infantile politicians commit the serious mistake in supposing that India is already welded into a harmonious nation, or that it could be welded thus for the mere wish to do so'. These well-meaning, but unthinking friends take their dreams for realities... But the solid fact is that the so-called communal questions are merely a legacy handed down to us by centuries of a cultural, religious and national antagonism between the Hindus and the Moslems. When [the] time is ripe, you can solve them; but you cannot suppress them by merely refusing recognition of them.'We must note that poetic-hearted Savarkar was a realist too'. Therefore, when he said, "There are two nations in the main, the Hindus and the Moslems, in India", it was a bitter reality. He was simply expressing an unpleasant truth. It's necessary to first accept the reality, because then only we can find a solution. If a person is diagnosed with cancer, he must admit that he does have cancer. Only then it can be cured.

But how can it be cured if he does have cancer but just won't admit it? How can he get rid of cancer if he continues to take treatment for tuberculosis or heart disease instead of cancer? The primary condition for treatment is to acknowledge that he is infected. That is why Savarkar says, "It is safer to diagnose and treat deep-seated disease than to ignore it. Let us bravely face unpleasant facts as they are."

This part of his speech was criticised even while he was alive. Therefore, Savarkar clarified his statement to journalists on 15 August 1943 in the office of the Marathi weekly Aadesh published from Nagpur. He also clarified his position in an interview given in Mumbai on 23 August 1943. The interview was published in the Aadesh issue dated 28 August 1943. The important part of this interview states: "People still do not understand the important thing that stating the fact of Mussulman and Hindu nations being present in Hindusthan is not to accept the Pakistani adamancy of carving a country of the Mussalmans. While two or two hundred nations that consider themselves separate from the Hindus have presently entered Hindusthan by force and are demanding Partition of Hindusthan, it is not by a woolly-headed and cowardly denial of this fact, but rather by understanding, facing and changing it, [that] an independent, undivided and indivisible Hindu nation alone shall, without doubt, remain in Hindusthan. But, as in our history, when the Hindu nation successfully rallied under the Hindu flag, the Hindus should come forward and rise unitedly. We should not confuse between nation and state. Even if the state goes, the nation remains. When the Mussulmans were ruling over us, the government (state) was theirs. But the existence of the Hindus was most certainly intact. Even so, there is no problem in a common state of Hindus and Mussulmans. In the past, we had nations (Rashtra) such as Maharashtra, Saurashtra, Devrashtra (near Berar). Where are these nations? They mingled with each other. The Shakas and Huns came to Hindusthan as nations. But what is the evidence of their existence today? We digested them. So, if the Mussulmans want, they could amicably stay with Hindus as a minority community. In the end, desire is the most influential and important factor for a nation."

Savarkar was simply expressing the reality. After all, he was merely stating facts. Making a statement of a fact does not mean advocating or propagating it. When a judge in a case of theft, gives verdict after checking the witnesses, evidence, and says, 'You are a thief', it does not mean that the judge is advocating or propagating the act of theft. It simply means that it is required to state the fact of 'You are a thief' while punishing the offender, since the criminal cannot be punished without stating this fact. Hence, when Savarkar was saying, "There are two nations in the main, the Hindus and the Moslems, in India", he was simply stating the fact of it because without accepting the truth, one cannot find the solution.[74]

He argued that the Hindus would be denied freedom if they were governed by non-Hindus, whether from within or without, and therefore, both political and territorial control must rest in their hands. He further recommended 'Sanskritized Hindi' as the lingua franca for the natural inhabitants of such a land and exhorted them to eschew the usage of 'spoken Hindustani', an amalgamation of Hindi-Urdu or what is called in north Indian literature as the Ganga-Jamuni tehzeeb, which he termed as a 'linguistic monstrosity'.

In his lectures, the use of armed violence gained more credence than before, and a rejection of the Gandhian principle of non-violence which he termed as a futile weapon in India's struggle for independence. During the Second World War, Savarkar demanded that Hindus enlist in the war effort and viewed it as an opportunity to militarise them for future conflicts with other communities.

A year after this declaration, Savarkar was approached by the British Viceroy for assistance in the war effort of the Allied powers. Savarkar launched an intensive Mahasabha campaign to militarise Hindus and suggested that Sikh and Gorkha battalions be deployed on the north-western borders of British India. He addressed several public meetings and visited schools, colleges and literary conferences to convince young Hindu men to enlist in the British army.

Besides expanding the political framework of the Mahasabha, Savarkar also travelled far and wide in India to get more people to sign up as members. There was no doubt that at many places, he was treated like a cult figure, but the high point of his tour was when he had met and convinced the iconic Syama Prasad Mukherjee to join the Hindu Mahasabha.

After his release from detention, Savarkar may have been every bit a demagogue while addressing public meetings to draw people into. The Hindu Mahasabha, but he quietly put the spirit of revolutionary nationalism behind him. This obvious change in his strategy was quite simply the result of the loss of freedom he had faced over two and a half decades, and at no cost did he wish to repeat it. Moreover, his political stance had altered dramatically over the years, and anti- Colonialism was no longer central to it. Although he did not state it categorically, but it nevertheless became evident in the most unusual fashion.

After Gandhi's Quit India movement call in 1942 when the Congress had asked its ministers to resign from the provincial government, Mohammed Ali Jinnah saw this as an opportunity to form coalition governments in the Muslim-majority provinces. Meanwhile, Savarkar had already instructed his ministers in the provincial government to remain in office, claiming that if they quit, then Muslim ministers and the British bureaucracy would ride roughshod over them.

Veteran Congressman, NB Khare wrote in 'My Political Memoirs or Autobiography' (Page 64) about the Indian National Army (INA).

"In this enterprise, Subhas Bose took his inspiration from Savarkar's book on the Indian War of Independence of 1857. In one of his speeches, Subhas Bose has freely admitted this. He also distributed copies of this book freely amongst all the army personnel. He named one of his regiments as Rani of Jhansi Regiment and he borrowed the slogan Chalo Delhi from the Indian soldiers in Meerut who marched to Delhi from there on the 10th May of 1857."

Indian revolutionary leader, Rash Behari Bose communicated with Savarkar during the beginning of the Second World War. When the INA was headed and reformed under Netaji Subhas Chandra Bose, all the policies and visions of INA coincided with and were inspired by the ideals of Savarkar.

"After the release of Veer Savarkar from his internment at Ratnagiri in 1937, Sri Rash Behari Bose wrote to him occasionally on the advisability of the Hindu Mahasabha movement and as the result of correspondence between them. Sri Rash Behari Bose started a branch of the Hindu Mahasabha in Japan under his own presidentship," wrote Yukikazu Sakurasawa, author of the book, The Two Great Indians in Japan.

Incidentally, Rash Behari Bose also spoke very highly of Savarkar in a radio address as he said, "In saluting you, I have the joy of doing my duty towards one of my elderly comrades-in-arms. In saluting you, I am saluting the symbol of sacrifice itself."

"The correspondence between them continued right up to the declaration of war by Japan and the formation by Sri Rash Behari Bose of the I. N. A. Indian National Army in Japan even before Netaji Subhas Babu could reach Singapore."

A meeting took place between Bose and Savarkar in Bombay in June 1940. On this occasion, Savarkar is supposed to have suggested to Subhas that he should go to Europe and seek the support. According to an article in the Times of India of June 24, Mr Bose had also talks with Mr V D Savarkar, President of the All India Hindu Mahasabha, at the latter's residence at Dadar on Saturday evening. It is understood that the discussions related to the present political situation in the country, and the steps the Hindu Mahasabha and the 'Forward Bloc' should take in co-operation with other parties. The episode, as always, did not go unnoticed by the police, who gave a brief account of it:

Subhas Chandra Bose arrived in Bombay on June 22nd and had discussions with V D Savarkar at Savarkar Sadan, Bombay with a view of exploring the possibilities of co-operation between the Forward Bloc and the Hindu Mahasabha respectively (MSA, Home Special Department, 1023, 1939-1940, SA dated June 29, 1940, 'Forward Bloc').

The absence of accounts by the Hindu Mahasabha on the meeting can be explained by the fact that, both the leaders being involved in anti-British activities, it would not make sense leaving records of sensitive matters. Not even among Bose's papers and writings is there any reference to the meeting. It is therefore impossible to reconstruct the content of the talks between the two leaders, unless we trust the only source available. This is the speech made by Savarkar on the occasion of the dissolution of the Abhinav Bharat in 1952. Certainly, the meeting did take place, and very possibly the two leaders discussed Bose's intention to go to Europe and seek the support of the axis powers. Savarkar inspired Bose, who, right from 1933, had his own connections with the dictators' governments. The working committee of September 10 decided which steps should be taken in order to prepare the nation to face the emergency provoked by the outbreak of the war.

The preliminary condition was the devolution of full powers to a central Indian government by the British. The committee wished for the realization of the militarisation of Indian society and the Indianisation of the army. It requested a reform of the Arms Act, along the lines prevailing in the UK. It demanded also that territorial forces and paramilitary groups be strengthened, that new military organisations be created in those provinces where they did not exist before.

Savarkar advised Subhas not to waste time in agitating for the removal of British statues like Holwell Monument in Calcutta – only to end up in a British prison during the invaluable war-time. Savarkar was surreptitiously in touch with Rash Behari Bose in Japan. He advocated that Subhas should smuggle himself out of the country and try to reach Germany and Japan (like Indian revolutionaries during World War I) to raise an Indian Army of liberation out of PoWs. In his avatar as Netaji, Subhas Bose's future course of action developed on the prophetic lines of Veer Savarkar. "It was the private and personal meeting between Netaji Subhas Babu and Savarkar at Savarkar Sadan Bombay that a definite suggestion was made to Subhas Babu by

Savarkar that he should try to leave India and undertake the risk of going over to Germany to organise the Indian forces there fallen in German hands as captives and then with the German help should proceed to Japan to join hands with Sri Rash Behari Bose. To impress this point, Savarkar showed to Subhas Babu a letter from Sri Rash Behari Bose to Savarkar written just on the eve of the Japanese declaration of war," wrote Yukikazu Sakurasawa.

After Subhas Chandra Bose's escape from Calcutta, Savarkar had issued a statement, "May the gratitude, sympathy and good wishes of a nation be a source of never-failing solace and inspiration to him. Wherever he happens to be, I have no doubt he will contribute his all, even health and life to the cause of Indian freedom."

Around six months after this meeting, Bose took exactly the same route as was said to have been discussed in the meeting. In January 1941, he disappeared from his house on Elgin Road in Kolkata and eventually joined Rash Behari Bose in Japan.

"Rash Behari Bose was... holding a Tokyo Conference during 28-30 March 1942 where it was resolved to form an Indian National Army under the direct command of Indian officers who would conduct the campaign to liberate India".

Netaji in his speech on Azad Hind Radio (June 25, 1944) acknowledged Savarkar's perspicacity in these words: "When due to misguided political whims and lack of vision, almost all the leaders of Congress party have been decrying all the soldiers in Indian Army as mercenaries, it is heartening to know that Veer Savarkar is fearlessly exhorting the youths of India to enlist in armed forces. These enlisted youths themselves provide us with trained men and soldiers for our Indian National Army."

After INA's campaign came to a close due to the defeat of Japan in World War II, around 250,00 Indian soldiers were taken as prisoners of war by the British.

On September 30, 1943 when Netaji Subhas Chandra Bose toured Andaman as the supreme commander of Azad Hind Fauz, he paid his tributes to the memories of freedom fighters imprisoned in the Cellular Jail.

He got printed thousands of copies of the Tamil version of Savarkar's Indian War of Independence of 1857 and distributed them in public. Andaman and Nicobar islands were re-named as Saheed and Swaraj islands.

While most of the Congress leaders kept a deafening silence on this issue, Savarkar came out openly in defence of these soldiers. He sent a cable to the then British Prime Minister Clement Attlee on 1 December 1945 which read: "In view of general convention of international treatment dealt out to war prisoners and in view of the very deep discontent aroused in the public mind, which could not be easily appeased I implore apart from any question of right that every Indian under arrest of those war prisoners whether they belong to the Subhas Sainiks or outside of it should be released without any humiliating conditions as an act of grace by declaring a general amnesty."

Savarkar reciprocated these noble sentiments, but alas, Subhas was not there to see it. On 10th, 11th, and 12th May 1952, during the dissolution celebration of Abhinav Bharat, the secret revolutionary party Savarkar had founded in 1904 at Pune, the bust of Netaji graced the stage for three days. Hailing Subhas as "deathless", Savarkar said, "Long live deathless Subhas, victory to the goddess of freedom." [75]

Yet, having said all that, in the end, I can't help remembering an illustrious exception. Veteran communist parliamentarian and prolific scholar, Prof. Hiren Mukerjee (who years later penned a study on Netaji Subhas called Bow to the Burning Gold) on February 28, 1966, that is two days after Savarkar passed away, proposed that the Lok Sabha should pay homage to Savarkar, in recognition of his services to the nation. He was supported by U.M. Trivedi of the Jan Sangh. Prof. Hiren Mukerjee said that although Savarkar was not a member of the House, there should still be some way in which the House should register its feelings on the passing away of a great leader. The House had done so in the case of Mahatma Gandhi and Stalin who were not members of the House.

Though, ultimately the House did not formally pay any homage, by observing silence, Speaker Hukum Singh conveyed the sentiments of the House to the bereaved family through the secretary of Lok Sabha. On March 4, 1966, when Union ministers, Opposition leaders, the Speaker of the Lok Sabha paid homage to Savarkar in a condolence meet organised by Delhi's citizen's council, Prof. Hiren Mukerjee, though differing from some of Savarkar's views, had praised the potent brand of nationalism that he championed. Earlier, Mukerjee was the one who had denounced All India Radio for not taking note of Savarkar's Mritunjaya Diwas celebration on December 24, 1960.

Savarkar and Cooperation in World War II

Allegation:

In a meeting with Lord Linlithgow in October 1939, a surprising U-turn was made by Savarkar when he said: 'But if our interests are now so tightly tied together, then Hinduism and Great Britain may now be friends; it is no longer necessary to have old hostility.' Thus, it was a lie that Savarkar didn't participate in the protest held by political prisoners so that he would be able to participate in active politics after his release. This is one of the common allegations made against Savarkar.

On 9 October 1939, Savarkar met Viceroy Lord Linlithgow for an hour between 11 a.m. and 12 noon. This was a purely confidential meeting. But since much news of all kinds was being published in various newspapers relating to this visit, Savarkar released a leaflet and explained about the meeting without breaking protocol. The key points in the leaflet were:

'Different warring nations are fighting for their own good... For Hindusthan, especially while it is in the political control of the British, it is a political illusion that we are fighting for the protection of democracy in the world.'

'Since the war poses danger to the interests and safety of the Hindu Rashtra, the Hindu Mahasabha has to consider this situation.'

For this, there is an urgent need for the British government to declare that Hindusthan has been given the status of an independent colony as an immediate stage of the ultimate goal. In order to convince Hindus that [the] UK is fighting for the independence of Hindusthan, it should be, without any delay, declared that a responsible and Indian majority government is established to take care of central affairs.

'Regardless of caste, religion, class, creed, one man should be given the power of one vote to appoint representatives. This basic democratic principle should be adopted. They will not tolerate deficiency and they do not ask for more. Until a certain period of time, untouchable society has to get more representation or some special rights like that.

'It should be ensured that all citizens of minority and majority societies will not encroach over the rights of others and that they will have complete freedom of language, culture and religion which will nourish public policy and peace.'

"Thus, if the immediate improvement is revealed, the Hindus will want to cooperate with the British government for the sake of protecting Hindusthan in the current European war."

'Protecting Hindusthan from military aggression is the requirement of the British government and us alike. We are unfortunately unable to do this without government assistance, so there is plenty of room for responsive cooperation between Hindusthan and England.'

"The Hindu army is for the people of Hindusthan and the British rulers have nothing to do with it, and the British should create this kind of confidence among the people of Hindusthan. And apart from the protection of Hindusthan, Indian troops should not be sent to any battlefield outside India."

The beauty of this leaflet is described by Shri Goswami Dixitji Maharaj, Bada Mandir, very aptly. He says, "The bitter quinine pill of Hindus' political rights was given to the Viceroy directly, without any sugar-coating of England's interests. The Viceroy must have grimaced while swallowing the bitter pill. This event was unique in the history of the Hindu Rashtra. The Viceroy must have grimaced while swallowing the bitter pill."

Following the meeting with Indian leaders, the Viceroy published a letter stating Britain's policy. In it, he states: 'India's goal is to achieve colonial independence. The 1935 act and the proclamation of the king in 1937 have given India a proper status in the empire. The decision regarding this can be taken at the conference of major political parties in India and Britain.'

Savarkar responded thus to the viceroy's letter: "The Viceroy's letter is disappointing. India has not acknowledged colonial independence as the ultimate goal, but only wants it as the next step. Britain should keep in mind that Hindusthan will not come forward to provide true cooperation unless it is assured that, through responsive cooperation with England, it can achieve the goal of independence."

Savarkar did not take any U-turn in this. It was only after demanding India's complete independence that the hand of friendship was extended to the British. Friendship was a policy. And it was not unconditional. Hitler was more brutal than the British in World War II. Hence, Savarkar called on the British, who were eager to defeat Hitler, and told them that we should forget our hostility and that we should cooperate. That was, of course, not unconditional. It was conditional. Without the help of British assistance, defence of the country from foreign invasion was not possible. This was due to blind and excessive support to non-violence and disarmament. Therefore, it is said that India would cooperate with the British government only for India's security and interest. It was also explicitly stated that Hindusthan troops should not be sent to any battlefield outside India. This is not called a U-turn; rather, it is responsive cooperation.

Between 6 and 13 April 1940, Subhash Chandra Bose's 'Forward Block' party started the Civil Disobedience movement by refusing to cooperate with the British in World War II. The All India Congress Executive Committee too refused to assist the British in the war. But Gandhi and Nehru were of the opinion that we should unconditionally support the British.

On 18 September 1940, Nehru said, 'We do not approach the problem with a view to taking advantage of Britain's difficulties. In a conflict between democracy and freedom on the one side and Fascism and aggression on the other, our sympathies must inevitably lie on the side of democracy. I should like India to play her full part and throw all her resources into the struggle for new order.'

Gandhi said, 'I was sorry to find myself alone in thinking that whatever support was to be given to the British should be given unconditionally... I (Gandhi) know that my views in regard to unconditional co-operation are not shared by the country.'

On 20 May 1940, Nehru said, 'Launching a civil disobedience campaign at a time when Britain is engaged in a life and death struggle would be an act derogatory to India's honour.' Similarly, the Mahatma said, 'We do not seek our independence out of Britain's ruin. That is not the way of non-violence.' It was the definite opinion of Subhash Chandra Bose that the Gandhi wing was doing everything possible in order to arrive at a compromise with Britain.

Gandhi was ready to provide unconditional assistance and service to Britain even during World War I also, which becomes clear from these two letters he wrote. In a secret letter dated 13 August 1914, he says, "We, the undersigned have, after mature deliberation, decided for the sake of the Motherland and the Empire to place our services unconditionally, during this crisis, at the disposal of the Authorities. We advisedly use the word "unconditionally" as we believe that, at a moment like this, no service that can be assigned to us can be considered to be beneath our dignity or inconsistent with our self-respect." This letter had 50 signatures, including those of Mahatma Gandhi, Kasturba Gandhi and Sarojini Naidu. In an open letter on 14 August 1914, he said, "Those Indians who are residing in the United Kingdom and who can at all do so should place themselves unconditionally at the disposal of the Authorities. We beg to offer our services to the Authorities."

When Savarkar was clearly stating that warring nations are fighting for their own interests, especially while Hindusthan is under the British political yoke, it is our political illusion to go to protect the democracy in the world. Gandhi and Nehru were willing to give unconditional support to Britain in World War II. They were more concerned about non-violence, India's reputation and democracy, which was appropriate. However, Savarkar was equally concerned about India's security. Hence, he saw this as one of the best opportunities for India to militarise itself. Foresighted Savarkar recognised this opportunity very well. He insisted on extending help to Britain in World War II based on the important conditions of militarisation and India's independence. Gandhi, Nehru and Savarkar's concerns were different. Gandhi and Nehru extended unconditional support, while Savarkar extended conditional support. Of course, later on, the Congress Working Committee rejected the proposal of supporting the British unconditionally. At that time, Gandhi and Nehru had to change their decisions too. Savarkar clearly warned the

British: 'Britain should note that Hindusthan will not come forward to provide true cooperation unless it is assured that, through responsive cooperation with England, it can achieve the goal of independence.'

On 8 July 1944, Savarkar had an important discussion with Dr Shyama Prasad Mukherjee before the meeting of the Hindu Mahasabha Executive Committee. There, he said, 'If Subhash Babu comes to Bengal with his Indian National Army, then the Bengali leaders, including Dr Mukherjee, should detach the Bengal Hindu Mahasabha from the All India Hindu Mahasabha, and join Subhash Babu's Indian National Army. We will continue to have a strategy of military cooperation here and you may execute different policy there.' That meant, to continue to show military cooperation and pretend to assist the British through it, while at the same time, to take war education on the actual battlefield from the enemy, which was most essential for the security of independent India. As soon as Subhash Chandra Bose and the Indian National Army (INA) attacked the eastern side of India, they should be joined by our local group - this was the kind of strategy Savarkar had designed. However, unfortunately, the tactic was foiled after the INA failed to make the successful march to Bengal due to Japan's refusal to assist it in time, and other such difficulties.[76]

Opinions and analysis behind success or failure of the Quit India Movement

About the Quit India Movement of 1942, historian Ramesh Chandra Majumdar has made the following remark: "The Congress leaders must or should have known all this before they staked everything on this final campaign, as they put it, with a grim resolve to "do or die". They neither did nor died... but left to themselves, without any leadership or plan, programme and organisation... though their courage and sacrifices won them undying fame... The campaign of 1942 would go down in history as an instance of hopeless incompetence and utter mismanagement on the part of the Congress leaders."

A Gandhian and famous author, Y.D. Phadke, further commented: 'For the agitation to be sustained long after the people's anguish has passed, the leaders of the underground agitation need to make definite plans and establish a systematic implementation of the countrywide system... but it didn't have continuity and unity as much as it should have been.'

Journalist and author, Govind Talwalkar also remarked: "The nature of the movement was fierce in Bihar, Uttar Pradesh, and East Bengal. Bengal had lost connection with other provinces for some days, but the movement in Punjab, the North-West Frontier Province, Assam, and Orissa was not very strong. In some parts of the country, the movement was at [a] peak, while in some places, it didn't get any response. Therefore, it cannot be said that the whole country stood up fiercely against British rule... Author of Mahatma, Tendulkar said: "The movement started to slow down in merely fifteen days. There were small resistances here and there for one or two months."[6]

One of the leaders of the underground movement, Nanasaheb Gore, honestly acknowledged in the post-Independence period: "It is said that the socialists were preparing to give a big turn to the 1942 movement. However, they didn't study any such uprisings, let alone the preparations... The attempt was really respectful; however, to be honest, just like our other partners like Achyutrao, none of us were aware about such kind of struggles. It is the bitter truth. It was more like a dream. Lot of colours like rainbow but no substance."

Jaiprakash Narayan, who escaped from Hazaribagh Jail, was an active leader in the underground movement. He explained why the movement faded quickly and why it failed. He says: "There was no efficient organisational machinery of the revolutionary forces that led to the liberation of such enormous powers. The Congress was not in a position to reach the enormous height to which the revolution was supposed to go. The lack of organization was so considerable that even important Congressmen were not aware of the progress of the Revolt, and till late in the course of the rising it remained a matter of debate in many Congress quarters whether what the people were doing was really in accordance with the Congress programme after the first phase of the Rising was over, there was no further programme placed before the people. After they had completely destroyed the British Raj in their areas, the people considered their task fulfilled, and went back to their homes not knowing what more to do. Nor was in their fault. The failure was ours; we should have supplied them with a programme for the next phase. But it did not happen. Hence, the agitation stalled and the low tide started. No movement is successful if it is only destructive. If any movement has to survive, another power should be created immediately in place of the power that was overthrown in the revolution... After destroying the tools and people of foreign power in their area, the people should have established a revolutionary government. And this government should have been given the support of the police and armaments. Had this happened, foreign power would have flowed away under the huge waves of the revolution and the people would have occupied complete power."

The Quit India Movement of 1942 failed due to lack of efficient organisation and programmes. Although Gandhi was against the violence in the movement, there were certain other principles which were responsible for failure of this movement. Gandhi's principle was: 'A struggle which has to be previously planned is not a righteous struggle. In a righteous struggle, God himself plans campaigns and conducts battles.'

As Govind Talwalkar says, "Though the nature of the Quit India Movement was revolutionary, Gandhi did not consciously try to make it go that way, neither he had the capacity to do so. Congress too didn't have any such capacities. Nation was not prepared for this and anyway, any such effort would have been crushed with the help of army."

In a letter sent to historian Dr Majumdar and published in his book History of Bengal, Chief Justice of Calcutta High Court and Governor of West Bengal, P.V. Chakravarty, asked none other than Lord Clement Atlee himself, the British Prime Minster responsible for conceding independence to India, whether Gandhi and his Quit India Movement had led the country to freedom. Chief Justice Chakravarty writes: "When I was the acting governor, Lord Atlee, who had given us independence by withdrawing the British rule from India, spent two days in the governor's palace at Calcutta during his tour of India. At that time, I had a prolonged discussion with him regarding the real factors that had led the British to quit India. My direct question to him was that since Gandhi's Quit India Movement had tapered off quite some time ago and, in 1947, no such new compelling situation had arisen that would necessitate a hasty British departure, why did they have to leave? In his reply, Atlee cited several reasons, the principal among them being the erosion of loyalty to the British Crown among the Indian army and navy personnel as a result of the military activities of Netaji. Toward the end of our discussion, I asked Atlee what the extent of Gandhi's influence upon the British decision to quit India was. Hearing this question, Atlee's lips became twisted in a sarcastic smile as he slowly chewed out the word, 'm-i-n-i-m-a-l!'."

Savarkar's stand Considering all the above, the role of foresighted Savarkar should be understood.

In an article published in Harijan on 5 July 1942, before the Quit India Movement, Gandhi says, 'In vain do I argue that the Allied troops, if they remain, will do so not to exercise authority over the people, or at India's expense, but they will remain under treaty with the Government of free India at the United Nations' expense for the sole purpose of repelling Japanese attack and helping China.' While asking the British to leave India, the All India Congress Committee passed a resolution on 14 July 1942, stating: "The Congress is therefore agreeable to the stationing of the armed forces of the Allies in India, should they so desire, in order to ward off and resist Japanese or other aggression, and to protect and help China."

Speaking to reporters on his visit to Lahore, Savarkar said, 'Hindus want a national government. They will never agree that [the] British Viceroy should stay here. I am happy that now the Congress is gradually coming on the path of the Hindu Mahasabha. I completely understand Gandhi's demand that the British should leave India. However, I cannot reconcile the suggestion that the British should keep their troops here.' 14 British rule in India was completely based on the army. It was ridiculous to tell the British to leave the same army behind and leave India. Also, indirectly, non-violent Gandhi and the Congress acknowledged that weapons and armies are needed for self-defence.

In a speech given in front of Shaniwar Wada in Pune on 2 August 1942, Savarkar said: 'Congress has the word "national" in its name. If [the] Congress really acts like one, [the] Hindu Mahasabha is ready to cooperate with them. We have three demands. The first demand is "The British should leave Hindusthan but their army should remain here." What exactly does this mean? The second demand is "If, say, the British and the Congress come to some compromise, though it is impossible, then [the] Congress should promise that the intactness of Hindusthan will not be compromised". And the third demand is—"No matter what happens in Hindusthan after the compromise, Muslims should not be given any extra rights in the Constitution". If [the] Congress accepts these three demands, we would forget whatever happened in [the] past and [the] Hindu Mahasabha would work hand-in-hand with [the] Congress to achieve Swaraj... If [the] Congress' revolution brings Swaraj, we would, by all means, be happy to have it. Whoever brings Swaraj for Hindusthan is a guru for us. We want freedom. However, there shouldn't be any special rights to minorities in it. No division of country should happen. If [the] Congress gives these assurances by passing a resolution, then we would be willing to sacrifice anything for such struggle for independence.'

This shows that Savarkar was not against the Quit India Movement from the very beginning. He was ready to provide conditional support. The Congress and Gandhi did not take into consideration the relevant and serious conditions that Savarkar put forth in order to gain cooperation.

On the contrary, on 7 August 1942, at the Congress General Assembly convened in Mumbai, the All India Congress Working Committee agreed that 'the Constitution should be a Federal one with the largest measure of autonomy for the Federating Units and with the residuary powers resting in these units'. To top it all, Gandhi wrote a letter to the British saying that, 'the Congress will have no objection to the British Government transferring all the powers it today exercises to the Muslim League on behalf of the whole of India, including the so-called Indian India. And the Congress will not only not obstruct any government that the Muslim League may form on behalf of the people, but will even join the government in running the machinery of the free state'. This is meant in all seriousness and sincerity. Gandhi and the Congress, who were ready to hand over the entire country to the Muslim League, never thought it important to officially meet Savarkar or the Hindu Mahasabha leaders and know their opinion. Nor did they try to express, explain, discuss or negotiate with Savarkar or the Hindu Mahasabha leaders to seek their support for the Quit India Movement.

Savarkar was of the opinion that in respect of tactical questions, the timing, the ways, the means, the methods of revolution and above all, the effectiveness which could depend on sane calculations. There was no elaborate planning in advance by the Congress at all. The truth of this remark was realized by many Congress leaders afterwards. Savarkar was not for mere mass upheaval. The historian-leader wanted a pre-planned revolution which would attempt to gain the support of the military. For, no revolution ever succeeded without the backing of the army.

On 8 August 1942, the Quit India Movement began and the British started their repression, arresting leading Congress leaders, including Gandhi, and invalidating the Congress, Savarkar released a leaflet in August 1942, stating: "The inevitable has happened. The foremost and patriotic leaders of the Congress including Mahatma Gandhi, Pandit Nehru and hundreds of other leaders of the Congress party are arrested and imprisoned. The personal sympathies of the Hindu Sanghatanists go with them in their sufferings for a patriotic cause. We also want the British Government to give India equal status in order to gain India's sympathy. Also, Hindutva supporters should keep in mind that the Congress has yet not brought a resolution to approve the three demands that we suggested in the Pune speech." This means that Savarkar and the Hindu Mahasabha did not participate in the movement as their demands were not fulfilled. However, Savarkar protested against the British repression. He respected the patriotism of Gandhi and the Congress leaders, even though there was disagreement about the path taken, and he expressed it thoroughly in the above letter.

In a leaflet sent to British newspapers on 18 August 1942, Savarkar states:

'India's national unrest will not be stopped with repressive measures. Now, without wasting any time in negotiations, Britain should do the following to get India's cooperation in the war:

1) The British Parliament should declare equal status to Hindusthan.

2) The Viceroy's executive board should be fully nationalised.

3) Indianisation of the army as early as possible.

4) The executive board should be appointed in the provinces, similar to the centre.

5) Appoint a post-war Constitution Committee.'

At the All India Hindu Mahasabha Executive Committee Meeting held in Delhi on 31 August 1942, at Savarkar's initiative, it was proposed that Britain should immediately recognise India as an independent nation and negotiate with all the major parties in India to resolve the current crisis. Additionally, it was suggested that a National Government should be established immediately in India and they should declare war on the common enemy. It was stated that if the British Government does not consider the demands of the Mahasabha, it will have to rethink its current programme and take measures that will show that Britain and its allies cannot suppress self-respecting India. In view of this, the executive board appointed a seven member committee to organise the people, talk to other party leaders, and the British Government. In this committee, Savarkar, Mukherjee, Moonje, Chatterjee, Meherchand Khanna, V.G. Deshpande and Maheshwar Dayal were included. It was decided that the committee should submit its report to the General Committee in Nagpur within a month. The proposal also demanded the release of detained leaders.

Likewise, Dr Shyama Prasad Mukherjee, then Finance Minister of Bengal, visited Lahore on 4 September 1942 and met some ministers. On 9 September 1942, he met Dr Radhakrishnan and the Nawab of Dhaka. In a leaflet dated 26 September 1942, Savarkar says: "There was hype against us that there was no unified demand from India. We have given a suitable reply by submitting a unified demand by the sub-committee of the Hindu Mahasabha." But the realistic Savarkar was aware that Britain would not grant independence to India just because Indians were making a unified demand. On 7 October 1942, Savarkar sent a telegram to British Prime Minister Churchill and made the following demands:

1) British Parliament should immediately declare India's independence.

2) The National Joint Council of Ministers should be formed for the war period. The War Department should be headed by the War Board of the Allies.

3) Other constitutional issues should be decided by the post-war All Party Council. [The] Hindu Mahasabha has been successful in building consensus on that. Also now, as promised earlier, Britain should hand over power to India and give us the opportunity to make sincere efforts to defend ourselves from foreign aggression.

The Hindu Mahasabha was successful in gaining support for these demands from the Sikh community, the Momin and Azad Muslim councils, other Muslim societies, Christian societies, the Liberal Federation, the Hindu Chief Minister of Orissa, the Muslim Chief Ministers of Sindh and Bengal, leaders of the Liberal Party, and many other thinkers. 20 Therefore, looking at the above evidence, the objection that 'Savarkar only worked to oppose Gandhi and the Congress' Quit India Movement but did not create any fight himself against the British or try in that direction' is completely baseless.

Savarkar had predicted the unpleasant fate that 'Quit India will result into split India'. Unfortunately, later on, that came true. Since he did not participate in the agitation, he was severely criticised by the Congress newspapers. Responding to them, Savarkar said, 'While it looks clear that uniting on the wrong question is going to lead to national disaster, I completely disagree to take part in the Congress' fight and to act on the mere assumption that a joint front should be formed. Did the Congress and Gandhi take part in the struggle that the Hindu revolutionaries raised in Bhaganagar and Bhagalpur and the struggle raised by Indian revolutionaries before them? Did he show a tendency to take a united front in that association? At that time, Gandhi and the Congress had a feeling that the path of action adopted by the revolutionaries and the Hindutva union was a hindrance to the national interest. If this is their stand, then the Congress should agree that the same is applicable to the Hindu Mahasabha's policy on this occasion. By becoming a slave of the Congress, we have to adapt to its resolutions and programmes blindly, even in the event where it will eventually result in national disaster. It will never be accepted by real Hindutva soldiers.' This straightforward reply by Savarkar is self-explanatory.[77]

In the summer of 1943, Jinnah invited Savarkar to explore the possibility of forming a government in Muslim-majority provinces, obviously with assistance from the Hindu Mahasabha. Savarkar responded that he was willing to discuss any plan, provided it had nothing to do with the idea of Pakistan. He also declined to visit Jinnah's residence for the meeting, stating that any interaction on the matter should only happen at a venue of his choice. This was unacceptable to Jinnah, and after several deliberations, the two decided to break the stalemate and met at a neutral venue. Unfortunately, even that plan had fizzled out because Savarkar had initially dilly-dallied, and subsequently, as the news of the proposed meeting made it to the press, Savarkar 'outdid Jinnah in resorting to delaying tactics and egoistic gestures.'

The extremists within Muslim organisations were severely critical of Jinnah's plan to collaborate with the Mahasabha, and in accepting Savarkar's demand that his party be allowed to voice its criticism about the idea of Pakistan. In a shocking retaliatory move, a member of the Khaksar Movement, Rafiq Sabir had physically assaulted Jinnah. In his new avatar as a pan-Indian political leader, Savarkar issued a statement which was contrary to his past beliefs and actions: 'Such internecine, unprovoked murderous assault even if the motive be political or fanatical - constituted a stain on public and civic life and should be strongly condemned.'

Despite his unrelenting resolve and fabulous oratorical skills in mobilising large numbers of Hindus across India, V.D. Savarkar was unable to convert the Mahasabha into a mass organisation. A year prior to India's independence, Savarkar had suffered a massive heart attack in January 1946.

After convincing Syama Prasad Mukherjee to join the Hindu Mahasabha, Savarkar also persuaded him to join the coalition government in Bengal in 1940. But unfortunately for Syama Prasad, the Hindu Mahasabha was floundering, even as India was inching closer towards freedom. In the provincial elections of 1946, the Muslim League won several seats in its constituencies, while the Congress won the majority of Hindu seats, leaving the Mahasabha holding little beyond a rump. It may be safe to presume that the political narrative had moved beyond the discourse of the late 1930s and early 1940s. Although a feeling of religious bigotry was on the rise amongst Muslims because of Jinnah's tenacity and the Congress' failure in preventing them from flocking to the Muslim League, large number of Hindus were opposed to communalism, because the Congress had retained its following amongst them.[78]

Syama Prasad Mukherjee took over as President of the Mahasabha. Although he had stepped down as President of the Mahasabha, V.D. Savarkar remained its de facto chief and every crucial decision was run past him. This included Syama Prasad Mukherjee's decision to accept Nehru's offer to join his ministry after independence.

According to Savarkar, "There are many factors, which contributed to the freedom of Bharat. It is wrong to imagine that Congress alone won Independence for Hindusthan. It is equally absurd to think that Non-Cooperation, Charkha and the 1942 Quit India Movement were sorely responsible for the withdrawal of the British power from our country. There were other dynamic and compelling forces, which finally determined the issue of freedom. First, Indian politics was carried to the Army, on whom the British depended entirely to hold down Hindusthan; second, there was a revolt of the Royal Indian Navy and a threat by the Air Force; third, the valiant role of Netaji Subhas Bose and the INA; four, the War of Independence in 1857, which shook the British; five, the terrific sacrifices made by thousands of revolutionaries and patriots in the ranks of the Congress, other groups and parties."

In 1948, Savarkar lost no time in assigning one of his favourite disciples some crucial tasks in the agitation against the Nizam's rule in Hyderabad, Godse was put at the head of the first brigade of protestors. On January 30, 1948, Nathuram Godse shot Mahatma Gandhi three times and killed him in Delhi. Godse was identified as member of the Hindu Mahasabha and former member of RSS. Along with them, police arrested Savarkar. While the trial resulted in convictions and judgments against the others, many leaders including Dr Babasaheb Ambedkar were convinced that Savarkar's arrest was nothing but a political vendetta. The Kapur Commission said, Godse and his accomplices' decision to kill Gandhi was determined by the circumstances of Partition and the death of Hindus in the course of the communal violence of 1947. Around 4000 Marathi brahmins were killed by Congressmen just because the community was more prominent in the Mahasabha-RSS groups. Narayan Savarkar was lynched by Congress mob. He died of the injuries in few days.

The extent of information that Savarkar had regarding Godse's plan to assassinate Gandhi, and his involvement in the conspiracy, remains opens to speculation, but it is noteworthy that unlike Nathuram Godse, Savarkar had pleaded not guilty. He clearly had no intention of being in the dock, and did not want his image of an intellectual and political thinker sullied. Yet, so great was the reverence for him that at the Red Fort trial when the judge had acquitted him, and pronounced Godse and Narayan Apte guilty to be hanged to death, Savarkar was released due to lack of evidence, slogans were 'raised with shouts of "Akhand Hindustan Amar Rahe; Hindu-Hindi-Hindustan, Kabhi Na Hoga Pakistan.

On his release in February 1949, Savarkar remained the votary of Hindu Rashtra, as he always was. This was evidenced in one of his statements made to a Marathi journal, prior to his arrest, in which he had said:

A few months after his release, Savarkar sent a cable to Rajendra Prasad who was then president of the Constituent Assembly. It read. 'I am voicing the sense and sentiment of millions of our countrymen when I beseech the Constituent Assembly to adopt Bharat as the name of our nation, Hindi as national language and Nagari as the national script".

As a practice those days, the Persian script was often used for Hindi alongside Urdu.

The Hindu Mahasabha was in a disarray after Mahatma Gandhi's assassination, and the death of two senior leaders, Bhai Parmanand and B.S. Moonje. Syama Prasad Mukherjee had even suggested that the Mahasabha be converted into a religious-cultural organisation, but it was obviously overturned and after being revived in November 1949. VD. Savarkar presided over its session. Yet again, it became evident that he wasn't sure where he belonged--he was in politics but made distinction by saying that it wasn't 'active politics'.

In April 1950, two years after Mahatma Gandhi's assassination, the government placed Savarkar under detention. This was done as a precautionary measure to maintain peace in the run-up to the visit of the then Pakistani Premier, Liaquat Ali, who was scheduled to meet Prime Minister Nehru. A campaign for Savarkar's release was mounted yet again, but the government stated categorically that he would only be discharged from prison if he took a pledge to not participate in any kind of politics till the first general elections. Despite all the histrionics surrounding the order, Savarkar acquiesced, as he had done on previous occasions in his political life.

During this period, Savarkar busied himself with lecturing on social issues, and campaigned on the need to end the social scourge of untouchability. But he also spoke in favour of what were obviously retrograde ideas--how women must not look at household chores and motherhood as a curse, which clearly reflected his patriarchal outlook.

Eventually, the government allowed him to participate in politics shortly before the first general elections in 1952, and he began seeking votes for the Mahasabha. It however did little in influencing voters and the Hindu Mahasabha performed poorly, winning just three seats in parliament. After the elections, S.P. Mukherjee, who was now the leader of the Bharatiya Jana Sangh, met Savarkar and requested him to join the new party. Savarkar refused the move for merger.

It was clear that Savarkar was now disillusioned with politics, and after failing to find many who would give him their ear, he went back to delivering public lectures on history and culture. But that was only for a short duration, because soon thereafter, he was back to focusing on issues that were part of his larger mission.

As part of his campaign, Savarkar mounted a public and scathing criticism of Christian missionaries in November 1953, accusing them of converting Hindus. He repeated what he had been saying for years the ultimate objective of proselytization was to undermine Hindu nationality. In October 1956, Hindu society was faced with a major challenge when Dr B.R. Ambedkar had led thousands of his supporters for converting to Buddhism. Savarkar's response to the act was guarded, and he commented that the decision did not symbolise a desertion on their part from Hindu ranks, but merely reflected the tardy pace of reforms within Hindu society. Savarkar claimed that despite his 'conversion', Dr Ambedkar remained a Hindu because he had 'embraced a non-Vedic but Indian religious system within the orbit of Hindutva,' and this was not a 'change of faith.' Savarkar's response was indeed consistent with his life-long definition of nationalism - whose pitrubhoomi and punyabhoomi were within the territorial boundaries of India, they were Hindus.

Meanwhile in 1956, preparations were also afoot to celebrate the centenary year of India's First War of Independence. An organising committee was established to steer the celebrations, and V.D. Savarkar was asked to be a speaker at the event, because of his book. Prime Minister Nehru was requested to participate as well, but he had turned down the request after learning that Savarkar had been extended an invitation. Nehru made his objections on the issue rather clear, when he said:

Savarkar is a brave man, a hero, a great man. When I was a student in England, we were inspired by his book on 1857. It is a great book which has inspired many Indians. But it is hardly history.

We have differed on several problems, and it would be embarrassing to him if I were to speak in a different tone on the same platform, would be unjust for both of us.

In contrast with Dayananda Saraswati, Swami Vivekananda and Sri Aurobindo, who were "men of religion", introduced reforms in the society and put Hinduism in front of the world. Savarkar mixed politics and religion, and started an extreme form of Hindu nationalism.

During his incarceration, Savarkar's views began turning increasingly towards Hindu cultural and political nationalism, and the next phase of his life remained dedicated to this cause. In the brief period, he spent at the Ratnagiri jail, Savarkar wrote his ideological treatise – Hindutva: Who is a Hindu? Smuggled out of the prison, it was published by Savarkar's supporters under his alias "Maharatta." In this work, Savarkar promotes a farsighted new vision of Hindu social and political consciousness. Savarkar began describing a "Hindu" as a patriotic inhabitant of Bharatavarsha, venturing beyond a religious identity. While emphasising the need for patriotic and social unity of all Hindu communities, he described Hinduism, Jainism, Sikhism and Buddhism as one and the same. He outlined his vision of a "Hindu Rashtra" (Hindu Nation) as "Akhand Bharat" (United India), purportedly stretching across the entire Indian subcontinent. He defined Hindus as being neither Aryan nor Dravidian but as "People who live as children of a common motherland, adoring a common holyland."[79]

Extract from Hindutva: Who is a Hindu? [80]

What is a Hindu? Although it would be hazardous at the present stage of oriental research to state definitely the period when the foremost band of the intrepid Aryans made it their home and lighted their first sacrificial fire on the banks of the Sindhu, the Indus, yet certain it is that long before the ancient Egyptians, and Babylonians had built their magnificent civilization, the holy waters of the Indus were daily witnessing the lucid and curling columns of the scented sacrificial smokes and the valleys resounding with the chants of Vedic hymns - the spiritual fervour that animated their souls. The adventurous valour that propelled their intrepid enterprises, the sublime heights to which their thoughts rose all these had marked them out as a people destined to lay the foundation of a great and enduring civilization. By the time they had definitely cut themselves aloof from their cognate and neighbouring people especially the Persians, the Aryans had spread out to the farthest of the seven rivers, Sapta Sindhus, and not only had they developed a sense of nationality but had already succeeded in giving it a local habitation and a name!' Out of their gratitude to the genial and perennial network of waterways that ran through the land like a system of nerve-threads and wove them into a Being, they very naturally took to themselves the name of Sapta Sindhus an epithet that was applied to the whole of Vedic India in the oldest records of the world, the Rigveda itself. About Aryans, or the cultivators, as they essentially were, we can well understand the divine love and homage they bore to these seven rivers presided over by the River, 'the Sindhu', which to them were but a visible symbol of the common nationality and culture.

The Indians in their forward march had to meet many a river as genial and as fertilizing as these but never could they forget the attachment they felt and the homage they paid to the Sapta Sindhus which had welded them into a nation and furnished the name which enabled their forefathers to voice forth their sense of national and cultural unity. Down to this day a Sindhu a

Hindu--wherever he may happen to be, will gratefully remember and symbolically invoke the presence of these rivers that they may refresh and purify his soul.

Not only had these people been known to themselves as 'Sindhus' but we have definite records to show that they were known to their surrounding nations—at any rate to one of them—by that very name, 'Sapta Sindhu'. The letter 's' in Sanskrit is at times changed into 'h' in some of the Prakrit languages, both Indian and non-Indian. For example, the word Sapta has become Hapta not only in Indian Prakrits but also in the European languages too; we have Hapta i.e., week, in India and 'Heptarchy' in Europe, Kesari in Sanskrit becomes Kehari in old Hindi, Saraswati becomes Harhvati in Persian and Asur becomes Ahur. And then we actually find that the Vedic name of our nation Sapta Sindhu had been mentioned as Hapta Hindu in the Avesta by the ancient Persian people. Thus in the very dawn of history we find ourselves belonging to the nation of the Sindhus or Hindus and this fact was well known to our learned men even in the Puranic period. In expounding the doctrine that many of the Mlechha tongues had been but the mere offshoots of the Sanskrit language the Bhavishya Puran clearly cites this fact and says—

Thus knowing for certain that the Persians used to designate the Vedic Aryans as Hindus and knowing also the fact that we generally call a foreign and unknown people by the term by which they are known to those through whom we come to know them, we can safely conclude that most of the remoter nations that flourished then must have applied the same epithet 'Hindu' to our land and people as the ancient Persians did. Not only that but even in the very region of the Sapta Sindhus the thinly scattered native tribes too, must have been knowing the Aryans as Hindus in the local dialects in accordance with the same linguistic law. Further on, as the Vedic Sanskrit began to give birth to the Indian Prakrits which became the spoken tongues of the majority of the descendants of these very Sindhus as well as the assimilated and the cross born castes, these too might have called themselves as Hindus without any influence from the foreign people. For the Sanskrit S changes into H as often in Indian Prakrits as in the non-Indian ones. Therefore, so far as definite records are concerned, it is indisputably clear that the first and almost the cradle name chosen by the patriarchs of our race to designate our nation and our people, is Sapta Sindhu or Hapta Hindu and that almost all nations of the then known world seemed to have known us by this very epithet, Sindhus or Hindus.

Name Older Still: So far we have been treading on solid ground of recorded facts, but now we cannot refrain ourselves from making an occasional excursion into the borderland of conjecture. So far we have not pinned our faith to any theory about the original home of the Aryans. But if the most widely accepted theory of their entrance into India be relied on, then a natural curiosity arises as to the origin of the names by which they called the new scenes of their adopted home. Did they coin all those names from their own tongue? Could they have done so? Is it not generally true that when we meet a new scene or enter a new country we call them by the very names—maybe in a slightly changed form so as to suit our vocal ability or taste by which they are known to the native people there? Of course, at times we love to call new scenes by names redolent with the memory of the clear old ones especially when new colonies are being established in a virgin and thinly populated continent. But this explanation could only be satisfactory when it is proved that the name given to the new place already existed in the old country and even then it could not be denied that the other process of calling new scenes by the names which they already bear is more universally followed. Now we know it for certain that the region of the Sapta Sindhus was, though very thinly, populated by scattered tribes. Some of them seem to have been friendly towards the newcomers and it is almost certain that many an individual had served the Aryans as guides and introduced them to the names and nature of the new scenes to which the Aryans could not be but local strangers. The Vidyadharas, Apsaras, Yakshas, Rakshasas, Gandharvas and Kinnaras were not all or altogether inimical to the Aryans as at times they are mentioned as being benevolent and good-natured folks. Thus it is probable that many names given to these great rivers by the original inhabitants of the soil may have been sanskritised and adopted by the Aryans. We have numerous proofs of this nature in the assimilative expansion of those people and their tongues; witness the words Shalankantakata, Malaya, Milind, Alasada (Alexandria), Suluva (Seleucus), etc. If this be true then it is quite probable that the great Indus was known as Hindu to the original inhabitants of our land and owing to vocal peculiarity of the Aryans it got changed into Sindhu when they adopted it by the operation of the same rule that S is the sanskritised equivalent of H. Thus Hindu would be the name that this land and the people that inhabited it bore from time so immemorial that even the Vedic name Sindhu is but a later and secondary form of it. If the epithet Sindhu dates its antiquity in the glimmering twilight of history then the word Hindu dates its antiquity from a period so remoter than the first that even mythology fails to penetrate-to trace it to its source.

Hindus, a Nation: The activities of so intrepid a people as the Sindhus or Hindus could no longer be kept cooped or cabined within the narrow compass of the Panchanad or the Punjab. The vast and fertile plains farther off stood out inviting the efforts of some strong and vigorous race. Tribe after tribe of the Hindus issued forth from the land of their nursery and, led by the consciousness of a great mission and their Sacrificial Fire that was the symbol thereof, they soon re-claimed the vast, waste and very-thinly populated lands. Forests were felled, agriculture flourished, cities rose, kingdoms thrived--the touch of the human hand changed the hole face of the wild and unkempt nature. But while these great deeds were being achieved the Aryans had developed to suit their individualistic tendencies and the demands of their new environments a policy that was but loosely centralised. As time passed on, the distances of their new colonies increased, and different peoples of other highly developed types began to be incorporated into their culture, the different settlements began to lead life politically much centred in themselves. The new attachments thus formed, though they could not efface the old ones, grew more and more pronounced and powerful until the ancient generalizations and names gave way to the new. Some called themselves Kurus, others Kashis or Videhas or Magadhas while the old generic name of the Sindhus or Hindus was first overshadowed and then almost forgotten. Not that the conception of a national and cultural unity vanished, but it assumed other names and other forms, the politically most important of them being the institution of a Chakravartin. At least the great mission which the Sindhus had undertaken of founding a nation and a country, found and reached its geographical limit when the valorous Prince of Ayodhya made a triumphant entry in Ceylon and actually brought the whole land from the Himalayas to the Seas under one sovereign sway. The day when the Horse of Viceroy returned to Ayodhya unchallenged and unchallengeable, the great white Umbrella of Sovereignty was unfurled over that Imperial throne of Ramachandra, the brave, Ramachandra the good, and a loving allegiance to him was sworn, not only by the Princes of Aryan blood but Hanuman, Sugriva, Bibhishana from the south-that day was the real birth-day of our Hindu people. It was truly our national day; for Aryans and Anaryans knitting themselves into a people were born as a nation. It summed up and politically crowned the efforts of all the generations that preceded it and it handed down a new and common mission, a common banner, a common cause which all the generations after it had consciously or unconsciously fought and died to defend.

Foreign Invaders: But as it often happens in history this very undisturbed enjoyment of peace and plenty lulled our Sindhusthan, in a sense of false security and bred a habit of living in the land of dreams. At last she was rudely awakened on the day when Mohammad of Gazni crossed the Indus, the frontier line of Sindhusthan and invaded her. That day the conflict of life and death began. Nothing makes Self-conscious of itself so much as a conflict with non-self. Nothing can weld peoples into a nation and nations into a state as the pressure of a common foe. Hatred separates as well as unites. Never had Sindhus - than a better chance and a more powerful stimulus to be herself forged into an indivisible whole as on that dire day, when the great iconoclast crossed the Indus. The Mohammedans had crossed that stream even under Kasim, but it was a wound only skin-deep, for the heart of our people was not hurt and was not even aimed at. The contest began in grim earnestness with Mohammad and ended, shall we say, with Abdalli? From year to year, decade to decade, century to century, the contest continued. Arabia ceased to be what Arabia was; Iran annihilated; Egypt, Syria, Afghanistan, Baluchistan, Tartary—from Granada to Gazni-nations and civilizations fell in heaps, Vitality of the victim proved stronger than the vitality of the victor. The contrast was not only grim but it was monstrously unequal. It was not a race, a nation of a people.

India had to struggle with. It was nearly all Asia, quickly to be followed by nearly all Europe. The Arabs had entered Sindh and single-handed they could do little else. They soon failed to defend their own independence in their homeland and as a people we hear nothing further about them. But here India alone had to face Arabs, Persians, Pathans, Baluchis, Tartars, Turks, Moguls - a veritable human Sahara whirling and columning up bodily in a furious world storm! Religion is a mighty motive force. So is rapine. But where religion is goaded on by rapine and rapine serves as a handmaiden to religion, the propelling force that is generated by these together is only equalled by the profundity of human misery and devastation they leave behind them in their march. Heaven and hell making a common cause—such were the forces, overwhelmingly furious, that took India by surprise the day Mohammad crossed the Indus and invaded her. Day after day, decade after decade, century after century, the ghastly conflict continued and India single-handed kept up the flight morally and militarily. The moral victory was won when Akbar came to the throne and Darashukoh was born. The frantic efforts of Aurangzeb to retrieve their fortunes lost in the moral field only hastened the loss of the military fortunes on the battlefield as well. At last Bhau, as if symbolically, hammered the ceiling of the Imperial Seat of the Moghals to pieces. The day of Panipat rose, the Hindus lost the battle, but won the war. Never again had an Afghan dared to penetrate to Delhi, while the triumphant Hindu banner that our Marathas had carried to Attock was taken up by our Sikhs and carried across the Indus to the banks of the Kabul.

Hindutva at Work: In this prolonged furious conflict our people became intensely conscious of ourselves as Hindus and were welded into a nation to an extent unknown in our history. It must not be forgotten that we have all along referred to the progress of the Hindu movement as a whole and not to that of any particular creed or religious section thereof of Hindutva and not Hinduism only. Sanatanists, Satnamis, Sikhs, Aryas, Anaryas, Marathas and Madrasis, Brahmins and Panchamas-all suffered as Hindus and triumphed as Hindus. Both friends and foes contributed equally to enable the words Hindu and Hindusthan to supersede all other designations of our land and our people. Aryavartha and Daxinapatha, Jambudweep and Bharatvarsha, none could give so eloquent an expression to the main political and cultural point at issue as the word Hindusthan could do. All those on this side of the Indus who claimed the land from Sindhu to Sindhu, from the Indus to the seas, as the land of their birth, felt that they were directly mentioned by that one single expression, Hindusthan. The enemies hated us as Hindus and the whole family of peoples and races, of sects and creeds that flourished from Attack to Cuttack was suddenly individualised into a single Being. We cannot help dropping the remark that no one has up to this time taken the whole field of Hindu activities from AD 1300 to 1800 into survey from this point of view, mastering the details of the various now parallel, now correlated movements from Kashmir to Ceylon and from Sindh to Bengal and yet rising higher above them all to visualise the whole scene in its proportion as an integral whole. For it was the one great issue to defend the honour and independence of Hindusthan and maintain the cultural unity and civic life of Hindutva and not Hinduism alone, but Hindutva, i.e. Hindudharma that was being fought out on the hundred fields of battle as well as on the floor of the chambers of diplomacy. This one word, Hindutva, ran like a vital spinal cord through our whole body politic and made the Nayars of Malabar weep over the sufferings of the Brahmins of Kashmir. Our bards bewailed the fall of Hindus, our seers roused the feelings of Hindus, our heroes fought the battles of Hindus, our saints blessed the efforts of Hindus, our statesmen moulded the fate of Hindus, our mothers wept over the wounds and gloried over the triumphs of Hindus... no people in the world can more justly claim to get recognized as a racial unit than the Hindus and perhaps the Jews. A Hindu marrying a Hindu may lose his caste but not his Hindutva. A Hindu believing in any theoretical or philosophical or social system, orthodox or heterodox, provided it is unquestionably indigenous and founded by a Hindu may lose his sect but not his Hindutva-his Hinduness-because the most important essential which determines it is the inheritance of the Hindu blood. Therefore all those who love the land that stretches from Sindhu to Sindhu from the Indus to the Seas, as their fatherland consequently claim to inherit the blood of the race that has evolved, by incorporation and adaptation, from the ancient Suptasindhus can be said to possess two of the most essential requisites of Hindutva.

Common Culture: But only two; because a moment's consideration would show that these two qualifications of one nation and one race—of a common fatherland and therefore of a common blood-cannot exhaust all the requisites of Hindutva. The majority of the Indian Mohammedans may, if free from the prejudices born of ignorance, come to love our land as their fatherland, as the patriotic and noble-minded amongst them have always been doing. The story of their conversions, forcible in millions of cases, is too recent to make them forget, even if they like to do so, that they inherit Hindu blood in their veins. But can we, who here are concerned with investigating into facts as they are and not as they should be, recognize these Mohammedans as Hindus? Many a Mohammedan community in Kashmir and other parts of India as well as the Christians in South India observe our caste rules to such an extent as to marry generally within the pale of their castes alone; yet, it is clear that though their original Hindu blood is thus almost unaffected by an alien adulteration, yet they cannot be called Hindus in the sense in which that term is actually understood, because, we Hindus are bound together not only by the tie of the love we bear to a common fatherland and by the common blood that courses through our veins and keeps our hearts throbbing and our affections warm, but also by the tie of the common homage we pay to our great civilization—our Hindu culture, which could not be better rendered than by the word Sanskrit suggestive as it is of that language, Sanskrit, which has been the chosen means of expression and preservation of that culture, of all that was best and worth preserving in the history of our race. We are one because we are a nation, a race and own a common Sanskrit (civilization) in the case of some of our Mohammedan or Christian countrymen who had originally been forcibly converted to a non-Hindu religion and who consequently have inherited along with Hindus, a common Fatherland and a greater part of the wealth of a common culture-language, law, customs, folklore and history—are not and cannot be recognized as Hindus. For though Hindusthan to them is Fatherland as to any other Hindu yet it is not to them a Holyland too. Their Holyland is far off in Arabia or Palestine. Their mythology and God men, ideas and heroes are not the children of this soil. Consequently their names and their outlook smack of a foreign origin. Their love is divided. Nay, if some of them be really believing what they profess to do, then there can be no choice - they must, to a man, set their Holyland above their Fatherland in their love and allegiance. That is but natural. We are not condemning nor are we lamenting. We are simply telling facts as they stand. We have tried to determine the essentials of Hindutva and in doing so we have discovered that the Bohras and such other Mohammedan or Christian communities possess all the essential qualifications of Hindutva but one, and that is that they do not look upon India as their Holyland. It is not a question of embracing any doctrine propounding any new theory of the interpretation of God, Soul and Man, for we honestly believe that the Hindu Thought-we are not speaking of any religion which is dogma-has exhausted the very possibilities of human speculation as to the nature of the Unknown-if not the Unknowable, or the nature of the relation between that and thou. Are you a monist - a monotheist-a pantheist-an atheist - an agnostic? Here is ample room, O soul! Whatever thou art, to love and grow to thy fullest height and satisfaction in this Temple of temples, that stands on no personal foundation of Truth. 'Why goest then to fill thy little pitcher to wells far off, when thoustandest on the banks of the crystal-streamed Ganges herself? Does not the blood in your veins, O brother of our common forefathers, cry aloud with the recollections of the dear old scenes and ties from which they were so cruelly snatched away at the point of the sword? Then come ye back to the fold of your brothers and sisters who with arms extended are standing at the open gate to welcome you their long lost kith and kin. Where can you find more freedom of worship than in this land where a Charvak could preach atheism from the steps of the temple of Mahakal-more freedom of social organisation than in the Hindu society where from the Patnas of Orissa to the Pandits of Benares, from the Santalas to the Sadhus, each can develop a distinct social type of polity or organize a new one? Verily, whatever could be found in the world is found here too. And if anything is not found here it could be found nowhere. Ye, who by race, by blood, by culture, by nationality possess almost all the essentials of Hindutva and had been forcibly snatched out of our ancestral home by the hand of violence-ye, have only to render wholehearted love to our common Mother and recognize her not only as Fatherland (Pitribhumi) but even as a Holyland (Punyabhumi); and ye would be most welcome to the Hindu fold.

This is a choice which our countrymen and our old kith and kin, the Bohras, Khojas, Memons and other Mohammedan and Christian communities are free to make a choice again which must be a choice of love. But as long as they are not minded thus, so long they cannot be recognized as Hindus.

Excerpts from Hindu Rashtra darshan [80]

The definition of the word 'Hindu' As a whole superstructure of the mission and the function of the Hindu Mahasabha rests on the correct definition of the word 'Hindu,' we must first of all make it clear what 'Hindutva' really means. Once the scope and the meaning of the world is defined and understood, a number of misgivings in our own camp are easily removed, a number of misunderstandings and objections raised against us from the camp of our opponents are met and silenced. Fortunately for us, after a lot of wandering in wilderness, a definition of the word Hindu which is not only historically and logically as sound as is possible in the cases of such comprehensive terms, but is also eminently workable is already hit upon when 'Hindutva' was defined as 'Everyone who regards and claims this Bharatbhoomi from, the Indus to the Seas as his Fatherland and Holyland is a Hindu. Here I must point out that it is rather loose to say that any person professing any religion of Indian origin is a Hindu. Because that is only one aspect of Hindutva. The second and equally essential constituent of the concept of Hindutva cannot be ignored if we want to save the definition from getting overlapping and unreal. It is not enough that a person should profess any religion of Indian origin as his Holyland, but he must also recognise it as his Fatherland as well. As this is no place for going into the whole discussion of the pros and cons of the question, all I can do here is to refer to my book 'Hindutva' in which I have set forth all arguments and expounded the proposition at great length. I shall content myself at present by stating that Hindudom is bound and marked out as a people and a nation by themselves not by the only tie of a common Holyland in which their religion took birth but by the ties of a common culture, a common language, a common history and essentially of a common fatherland as well. It is these two constituents taken together that constitute our Hindutva and distinguish us form any other people in the world. That is why the Japanese and the Chinese, for example, do not and cannot regard themselves as fully identified with the Hindus. Both of them regard our Hindusthan as their Holyland, the land which was the cradle of their religion, but they do not and cannot look upon Hindusthan as their fatherland too. They are our co-religionists; but are not and cannot be our countrymen too. We Hindus are not only co-religionists, but even countrymen of each other. The Japanese and the Chinese have a different ancestry, language, culture, history and country of their own, which are not so integrally bound up with us as to constitute a common national life. In a religious assembly of the Hindus, in any Hindu Dharma-Mahasabha they can join with us as our brothers-in-faith having a common Holyland. But they will not and cannot take a common part or have a common interest in a Hindu Mahasabha which unites Hindus together and represent their national life. A definition must in the main respond to reality. Just as by the first constituent of Hindutva, the possession if a common Holyland-the Indian Mahommedans, Jews, Christians, Parsees, etc. are excluded from claiming themselves as Hindus which in reality also they do not,-in spite of their recognising Hindusthan as their fatherland, so also on the other hand the second constituent of the definition that of possessing a common fatherland exclude the Japanese, the Chinese and others from the Hindu fold in spite of the fact of their having a Holyland in common with us. The above definition had already been adopted by number of prominent Hindu-sabhas such as the Nagpur, Poona, Ratnagiri Hindu-sabhas, and others. The Hindu Mahasabha also had in view this very definition when the word Hindu was rather loosely explained in its present constitution as ' one who profess any religion of Indian origin.' I submit that the time has come when we should be more accurate and replace that partial description by regular definition and incorporate in the constitution the full verse itself translating it in the precise terms as rendered above. Avoid the loose and harmful misuse of the word 'Hindu' From this correct definition of Hindutva it necessarily follows that we should take all possible care to restrict the use of the word 'Hindu' to its defined and definite general meaning only and avoid misusing it in any sectarian sense. In common parlance even our esteemed leaders and writers who on the one hand are very particular in emphasizing that our non-Vedic religious schools are also included in the common Hindu brotherhood, commit on the other hand, the serious mistake if using such expressions as 'Hindus and Sikhs', 'Hindus and Jains' denoting thereby unconsciously that the Vaidiks or the Sanatanists only are Hindus and thus quite unawares inculcate the deadly virus of separation in the minds of the different constituents of our religious brotherhood, defeating our own eager desire to consolidate them all into a harmonious and organic whole. Confusion in words leads to confusion in thoughts. If we take good care not to identify the term 'Hindu' with the major Vedic section of our people alone, our non-Vedic brethren such as the Sikhs, the Jains and others will find no just reason to resent the application of the word 'Hindu' in their case also. Those who hold to the opinion that Sikhis, Jainism and such other religion that go to form our Hindu brotherhood are neither the branches of nor originated from the Vedas but are independent religions by themselves need not cherish any fear or suspicion of losing their independence as a religious school by being called Hindus if that application is rightly used only to denote all those who won India, this Bharatbhoomi, as their Holyland and fatherland. Whenever we want to discriminate the constituents of Hindudom as a whole we should designate them as 'Vaidiks and Sikhs', 'Vaidiks and Jains' etc. But to say 'Hindus and Sikhs', 'Hindus and Jains' is as self contradictory and misleading as to say 'Hindus and Brahmins' or 'Jains and Digambers' or 'Sikhs and Akalees.' Such a harmful misuse of the word Hindu should be carefully avoided especially in the speeches, resolutions and records of our Hindu Mahasabha. The word 'Hindu' is of Vaidic origin. We may mention here in passing that the word 'Hindu' is not a denomination which the foreigners applied to us in contempt otherwise but is derived from our Vedic appellation of (Saptasindhus) a fact which is fully dealt with in my book on Hindutva and is borne out by the name of one of our provinces and peoples bordering on the Indus who are being called down to this day as आ संघ and आ संधी. The Hindu Mahasabha is in the main not a religious but a national body. From this above discussion, it necessarily follows that the concept of the term 'Hindutva'-Hinduness - is more comprehensive than the word 'Hinduism'. It was to draw a pointed attention to this distinction that I had coined the words 'Hindutva', 'Pan Hindu' and 'Hindudom' when I framed the definition of the word 'Hindu'. Hinduism concerns with the religious systems of the Hinds, their theology and dogma. But this is precisely a matter which this Hindu Mahasabha leaves entirely to individual or group conscience and faith. The Mahasabha takes its stand on no dogma, no book or school of philosophy whether pantheist, monotheist or atheist. All that it is concerned with, so far as 'ism' is concerned, is the common characteristic, which a Hindu, by the very fact of professing allegiance to a religion or faith of Indian origin necessarily possesses in regarding India as his Holyland - the cradle and the temple of his faith. Thus while only indirectly concerned with Hinduism which is only one of the many aspects of Hindutva resulting from the second constituent of possessing a common Fatherland. The Mahasabha is not in the main a Hindu-Dharma-Sabha but it is pre-eminently a HinduRashtra-Sabha and is a Pan-Hindu organization shaping the destiny of the Hindu Nation in all its social, political and cultural aspects. Those who commit the serious mistake of taking the Hindu Mahasabha for only a religious body would do well to keep thise distinction in mind.

Essential implications of Hindutva [81]

But throughout our inquiry we have been concerning ourselves more with what would have been or what should be. Not that to paint what should be is not a legitimate pursuit; nay, it is as necessary and at times more stimulating; but even that could be better done by first getting a firm hold of what actually is. We must try, therefore, to be on our guard so that in our attempt to determine the essentials of Hindutva we be guided entirely by the actual contents of the word as it stands at present. So although the root-meaning of the word Hindu like the sister epithet Hindi may mean only an Indian, yet as it is we would be straining the usage of words too much—we fear, to the point of breaking-if we call a Mohammedan a Hindu because of his being a resident of India. It may be that at some future time the word Hindu may come to indicate a citizen of Hindusthan and nothing else; that day can only rise when all cultural and religious bigotry has disbanded its forces pledged to aggressive egoism, and religions cease to be 'isms' and become merely the common fundof eternal principles that lie at the root of all that are a common foundation on which the Human State majestically and firmly rests. But as even the first streaks of this consummation, so devoutly to be wished for, are scarcely discernible on the horizon, it would be folly for us to ignore stern realities. As long as every other 'ism' has not disowned its special dogmas, whichever tend into dangerous war cries, so long no cultural or national unit can afford to loosen the bonds, especially those of a common name and a common banner, that are the mighty sources of organic cohesion and strength. An American may become a citizen of India. He would certainly be entitled, if bona fide, to be 'treated as our Bharatiya or Hindi, a countryman and a fellow citizen of ours. But as long as in addition to our country, he has not adopted our culture and our history, inherited our blood and has come to look upon our land not only as the land of his love but even of his worship, he cannot get himself incorporated into the Hindu fold. For although the first requisite of Hindutva is that he be a citizen of Hindusthan either by himself or through his forefathers, yet it is not the only requisite qualification of it, as the term Hindu has come to mean much more than its geographical significance.

Bond of common blood

The reason that explains why the term Hindu cannot be synonymous with Bharatiya or Hindi and mean an Indian only, naturally introduces us to the second essential implication of that term. The Hindus are not merely the citizens of the Indian state because they are united not only by the bonds of the love they bear to a common motherland but also by the bonds of a common blood. They are not only a Nation but also a race-jati. The word jati derived from the root Jan to produce, means a brotherhood, a race determined by a common origin,-possessing a common blood. All Hindus claim to have in their veins the blood of the mighty race incorporated with and descended from the Vedic fathers, the Sindhus. We are well aware of the not unoften interested objection that carpingly questions 'but are you really a race? Can you be said to possess a common blood?' We can only answer by questioning in return, 'Are the English a race? Is there anything as English blood, the French blood, the German blood or the Chinese blood in this world? Do they, who have been freely infusing foreign blood into their race by contracting marriages with other races and peoples possess a common blood and claim to be a race by themselves?' If they do, Hindus also can emphatically do so. For the very castes, which you owing to your colossal failure to understand and view them in the right perspective, assert to have barred the common flow of blood into our race, have done so more truly and more effectively as regards the foreign blood than our own. Nay is not the very presence of these present castes a standing testimony to a common flow of blood from a Brahman to a Chandal? Even a cursory glance at any of our Smritis would conclusively prove that the Anuloma and Pratiloma marriage institutions were the order of the day and have given birth to the majority of the castes that obtain amongst us. If a Kshatriya has a son by a Shudra woman, he gives birth to the Ugra caste; again, if the Kshatriya raises an issue on an Ugra he founds a Shvapacha caste while a Brahman mother and a Shudra father beget the caste, Chandal. From the Vedic story of Satyakama Jabali to Mahadaji Shinde every page of our history shows that the ancient Ganges of our blood has come down from the altitudes of the sublime Vedic heights to the plains of our modern history fertilizing much, incorporating many a noble stream and purifying many a lost soul, increasing in volume and richness, defying the danger of being lost in bogs and sands and flows today refreshed and reinvigorated more than ever. All that the caste system has done is to regulate its noble bood on lines believed and on the whole rightly believed-by our saintly and patriotic law-givers and kings to contribute most to fertilize and enrich all that was barren and poor, without famishing and debasing all that was flourishing and nobly endowed. This is true not only in the case of those that are the outcome of the intermarriages between the chief four castes, or between the chief four castes and the cross-born but also in the case of those tribes or races who somewhere in the dimness of the hoary past were leading a separate and self-centred life. Witness the customs prevalent in Malabar or Nepal where a Hindu of the highest caste is allowed to marry a woman of those who are supposed to be the originally alien tribes but who, even if the suggestion be true, have by their brave and loving defence of the Hindu culture have been incorporated with and bound to us by the dearest of ties—the ties of a common blood. Is the Nagavansha a Dravidian family? Well, then who is who now when the youths of Agnivansha have taken to them the daughters of the Nagas and the Chandravansha and the Suryavansha have bestowed their daughters on the youths of both the families? Down to the day of Harsha-not to mention the partial break-down of the caste-system itself in the centuries of Buddhistic sway— intermarriages were the order of the day. Take for example the case of a single family of the Pandawas. The sage Parashar was a Brahman. He fell in love with the fair maid of a fisherman who gave birth to the world-renowned Vyas, who in his turn raised two sons on the Kshatriya princesses Amba and Ambalika; one of these two sons, Pandu allowed his wives to raise issue by resorting to the Niyoga system and they having solicited the love of men of unknown castes, gave birth to the heroes of our great epic. Without mentioning equally distinguished characters of the same period Kama, Babhruwahana, Ghatotkacha, Vidur and others, we beg to point out to the relatively modern cases of Chandragupta said to have married a Brahman girl who gave birth to the father of Ashok; Ashok who had as a prince married a Vaishya maid; Harsha who being a Vaishya gave his daughter in marriage to a Kshatriya prince; Vyadhakarma who is said to be the son of a Vyadha with whom his mother, a Brahman girl, had fallen in love and who grew to be the ' Yajnacharya of Vikramaditya, Surdas; Krishna Bhatta who being a Brahman fell so desperately in love with a Chandala girl as to lead an open married life with her and subsequently became the founder of the religious sect Matangi Pantha; who nevertheless call themselves and are perfectly entitled to be recognized as Hindus. This is not all. An individual at times by his or her own actions may lose his or her first caste and be relegated to another. A Shudra can become a Brahman and Brahman become a Shudra. The injunction [The family is not really called a family; it is the practices and customs that are called a family. One that does his duties is praised on earth and in heaven] was not always an empty threat. Many a Kshatriya has by taking to agriculture and other occupations of life lost the respect due to a Kshatriya and were classed with some of the other castes; while many a brave man, in cases whole tribes, raised themselves to the position, the rights and titles of the Kshatriyas and were recognized as such. Being outcast from a caste, which is an event of daily occurrence, is only getting incorporated with some other. Not only is this true so far as those Hindus only who believe in the caste system based on the Vedic tenets, are concerned, but even in the case of Avaidik sects of the Hindu people. As it was true in the Buddhistic period that a Buddhist father, a Vaidik mother, a Jain son, could be found in a single joint family, so even to-day Jains and Vaishnavas intermarry in Gujarat, Sikhs and Sanatanis in Punjab and Sind. Moreover, today's Manbhav or Lingayat or Sikh or Satnami is yesterday's Hindu and today's Hindu may be tomorrow's Lingayat or Bramho or Sikh. And no word can give full expression to this racial unity of our people as the epithet, Hindu, does. Some of us were Aryans and some Anaryans; but Ayars and Nayars—we were all Hindus and own a common blood. Some of us are Brahmans and some Namashudras or Panchamas; but Brahmans or Chandalas—we are all Hindus and own a common blood. Some of us are Daxinatyas and some Gauds; but Gauds or Saraswatas—we are all Hindus and own a common blood. Some of us were Rakhasas and some Yakshas; but Rakshasas or Yakshas—we are all Hindus and own a common blood. Some of us were Vanaras and some Kinnaras ; but Vanaras or Naras—we are all Hindus and own a common blood. Some of us are Jains and some Jangamas; but Jains or Jangamas—we are all Hindus and own a common blood. Some of us are monists, some, pantheists; some theists and some atheists. But monotheists or atheists-we are all Hindus and own a common blood. We are not only a nation but a Jati, a born brotherhood. Nothing else counts, it is after all a question of heart. We feel that the same ancient blood that coursed through the veins of Ram and Krishna, Buddha and Mahavir, Nanak and Chaitanya, Basava and Madhava, of Rohidas and Tiruvelluvar courses throughout Hindudom from vein to vein, pulsates from heart to heart. We feel we are a JATI, a race bound together by the dearest ties of blood and therefore it must be so. After all there is throughout this world so far as man is concerned but a single race—the human race kept alive by one common blood, the human blood. All other talk is at best provisional, a makeshift and only relatively true. Nature is constantly trying to overthrow the artificial barriers you raise between race and race. To try to prevent the commingling of blood is to build on sand. Sexual attraction has proved more powerful than all the commands of all the prophets put together. Even as it is, not even the aborigines of the Andamans are without some sprinkling of the so-called Aryan blood in their veins and vice versa. Truly speaking, all that any one of us can claim, all that history entitles one to claim, is that one has the blood of all mankind in one's veins. The fundamental unity of man from pole to pole is true, all else only relatively so. And speaking relatively alone, no people in the world can more justly claim to get recognized as a racial unit than the Hindus and perhaps the Jews. A Hindu marrying a Hindu may lose his caste but not his Hindutva. A Hindu believing in any theoretical or philosophical or social system, orthodox or heterodox, provided it is unquestionably indigenous and founded by a Hindu may lose his sect but not his Hindutva-his Hinduness— because the most important essential which determines it is the inheritance of the Hindu blood.

Therefore all those who love the land that stretches from Sindhu to Sindhu from the Indus to the Seas, as their fatherland consequently claim to inherit the blood of the race that has evolved, by incorporation and adaptation, from the ancient Sapta Sindhus can be said to possess two of the most essential requisites of Hindutva.

As he neared his Eighties, Savarkar was grappling with ill-health, and progressive senility. In many ways, Savarkar's increasing political isolation after he stepped down from the presidentship of the Mahasabha, stemmed from his seclusion during his incarceration in the Cellular Jail. For thirteen long years, he was used to being companionless, and after independence when he realised that his brand of politics had no place in Indian polity, he was yet again reconciled to his own company.

He lived a quiet life with his wife and son. Ironically, for all his frugality, on 27 May 1962, on the eve of entering the eightieth year of his life, Savarkar issued a statement requesting his admirers and well-wishers to not visit him for extending birthday greetings. The next morning, on his eightieth birthday, Savarkar fractured his thigh bone, and was bedridden for a few months.

It can be speculated that for a man like Vinayak Damodar Savarkar, it was imperative that he be recognised as a modernist, for whom religion did not mean adhering to rituals, yet be considered an aspect which defined his nationality, politics, and his culture.

In his role as a social reformer, Savarkar had campaigned relentlessly to secure the right for women to participate in religious ceremonies publicly. There is no doubt that Savarkar fought for women's rights.[82]

On 8 November 1963, Savarkar's wife, Yamunabai, died. On 1 February 1966, Savarkar renounced medicines, food, and water which was termed as prayopavesha (fast until death). Before his death, he had written an article titled "Atmahatya Nahi Atmaarpan" in which he argued that when one's life mission is over and the ability to serve society is left no more, it is better to end the life at will rather than waiting for death. His condition was described to have become as "extremely serious" before his death on 26 February 1966 at his residence in Bombay (now Mumbai), and that he faced difficulty in breathing; efforts to revive him failed, and was declared dead at 11:10 a.m. (IST) that day. The Hindu Mahasabha failed to resurrect itself as a credible political force, while the RSS emerged as the principal organisation advocating Hindu nationalism.

Lokamanya Tilak with Lala Lajpat Rai and Bipin Chandra Pal

Gandhiji with Mahamana Madan Mohan Malviya

Gandhiji with Mahanama M.M.Malviya at Conference

Dharamveer BS Moonje with Rajaji and Other leaders in Congress Conference.

NC Kelkar with Dr S Radhakrishnan.

NC Kelkar with Veer Savarkar.

Mahamana Madan Mohan Malviya with Veer Savarkar and Guruji Golwalkar

Netaji Subhash Chandra Bose and Veer Savarkar.

Veer Savarkar with Dalits who were given Brahman Vidya

Savarkar Brothers: Veer Savarkar(L), Narayan Savarkar(M) and Ganesh Savarkar(R)

Veer Savarkar at All caste inter dining programme

Veer Savarkar with Varadharajulu Naidu

Rashtriya Swayamsevak Sangh

RSS was founded in 1925 on the day of Vijayadashami with an aim to organise Hindu community for its cultural and spiritual regeneration and make it a tool for achieving complete independence for a united India. The initial meeting for the formation of the Sangh on the Vijaya Dashami day of 1925 was held between Dr.Hedgewar and Tilakite & Hindu Mahasabha leaders: Dr. B. S. Moonje, Ganesh Savarkar, Dr.L. V. Paranjape and Dr.B. B. Tholkar. In the 1920 session of Indian National Congress, held in Nagpur, Dr Hedgewar was appointed as the Deputy Chief of volunteers cadre overseeing the whole function. This volunteer organisation was named as Bharat Swayamsevak Mandal which was headed by Dr. Laxman V. Paranjape (Dr. Hedgewar as his Deputy). All volunteers were told to wear a certain uniform (to be made at their own expense) which was later adopted as RSS's official uniform from 1925 to 1940. This could be called as the real beginning of RSS because Dr L. V. Paranjpe had declared the intention of starting such an organisation in future. Dr B. S. Moonje and Dr. L. V. Paranjpe funded and actively supported Hedgewar to start RSS as the Top Senior Leaders of Nagpur region. Hedgewar suggested the term 'Rashtriya' (national) for his Hindu organization, for he wanted to re-assert the Hindu identity with 'Rashtriya'. Hedgewar supported the setting up of a women's wing of the organization in 1936 called Rashtra Sevika Samiti.

Those that participated in the movement were called Swayamsevaks (meaning Volunteers). Early Swayamsevaks included Bhaiyaji Dani, Babasaheb Apte, Balasaheb Deoras, and Madhukar Rao Bhagwat, among others. The Sangh (Community) was growing in Nagpur and the surrounding districts, and it soon began to spread to other provinces. Hedgewar went to a number of places and inspired the youths for taking up Sangh work. Gradually, all his associates had begun to endearingly call him 'Doctor ji.'

Though the RSS was founded on the day of 'Vijayadashami' in 1925, the name of the organization was decided much later.

On 17 April 1926, Hedgewar called for a meeting attended by 26 swayamsevaks. A detailed discussion followed to decide the name of the organisation. Three names were finalised after several rounds of elimination — Rashtriya Swayamsevak Sangh, Jaripataka Mandal and Bhedratoddharak Mandal. There were more deliberations on these three names and finally the name, 'Rashtriya Swayamsevak Sangh', was chosen.

Tilakite ideology

After Tilak's demise in 1920, like other followers of Tilak in Nagpur, Hedgewar was opposed to some of the programmes adopted by Gandhi. Gandhi's stance on the Indian Muslim Khilafat issue was a cause for concern to Hedgewar, and so was the fact that the 'cow protection' was not on the Congress agenda. This led Hedgewar, along with other Tilakities, to part ways with Gandhi. In 1921, Hedgewar delivered a series of lectures in Maharashtra with slogans such as "Freedom within a year" and "boycott". He deliberately broke the law, for which he was imprisoned for a year. After being released in 1922, Hedgewar was distressed at the lack of organisation among the Congress volunteers for the independence struggle. Without proper mobilisation and organisation, he felt that the patriotic youth of India could never get independence for the country. Subsequently, he felt the need to create an independent organisation that was based on the country's traditions and history.

Hindu Mahasabha influence

The Hindu Mahasabha, which was initially a special interest group within the Indian National Congress and later an independent party, was an important influence on the RSS. In 1923, prominent Hindu leaders like Madan Mohan Malaviya met together on this platform and voiced their concerns on the 'division in the Hindu community'. In his presidential speech to Mahasabha, Malaviya wanted the activists 'to educate all boys and girls, establish akharas (gymnasiums), establish a volunteer corps to persuade people to comply with decisions of the Hindu Mahasabha, to accept untouchables as Hindus and grant them the right to use wells, enter temples, get an education.' Later, Hindu Mahasabha leader V. D. Savarkar's 'Hindutva' ideology also had a profound impact on Hedgewar's thinking about the 'Hindu nation'.

RSS took part as a volunteer force in organising the Hindu Mahasabha annual meeting under presidentship C. Vijayaraghavachariar in Akola in 1931. Moonje remained a patron of the RSS throughout his life. Both he and Ganesh Savarkar worked to spread the RSS shakhas in Maharashtra, Punjab, Delhi, and the princely states by initiating contacts with local leaders. Ganesh Savarkar merged his own youth organisation Tarun Hindu Sabha with the RSS and helped its expansion. V. D. Savarkar, after his release in 1937, joined them in spreading the RSS and giving speeches in its support. Officials in the Home Department called the RSS as the "volunteer organisation of the Hindu Mahasabha."

By 1930, the RSS started moving beyond Nagpur and Wardha to Vidarbha region and the Hindi-speaking areas of Central Provinces. The Sangh could muster the active sympathy and support of numerous prominent Hindus of these provinces including Raja Laxmanrao Bhonsle of Nagpur,

Raja Raghoji Rao Bhonsle, Sir Chitnivis, Hon. Tambe (former Governor of C.P. & Berar), Sir Morpant Joshi, Rao Bahadur Kelkar (former Minister of C.P. & Berar). With the patronage of these notables, the RSS increased its membership to 30,000 by 1937 in C.P. & Berar alone.

As early as 1932, the government was getting alarmed over the expansion and programmes of the RSS, whose leaders were 'definitely associated with anti-Government agitation' and it was felt by the authorities that 'this movement will require close attention'.In one confidential reports, the celebration of the Dussehra festival by the RSS at Nagpur in 1932 has been characterized as 'the most important political feature' in the south of C.P. & Berar. On this occasion 1,000 uniformed volunteers headed by Moonje marched past. The important personalities present included the Bhonsla King, G.D. Savarkar, Hedgewar and others.

On December 1932, the Central Provinces Government had issued orders forbidding government employees to join or take part in the activities of the RSS On the occasion of 'Til Sankrant' celebrations on 10 January 1933, Hedgewar asserted that the government had acted on base insinuations made against the Sangh and denied that it was either political or communal. On the other hand, M.V. Joshi, who presided over the same meeting, justified its existence on the ground that the Hindus should be able to defend themselves in times of stress.

Hedgewar adopted two major strategies for the expansion of the RSS in the 1930s. First, he focused his attention on the universities outside Maharashtra and dispatched his trained volunteers to recruit students in the campuses. The RSS started a shakha in the Benaras Hindu University campus with the help of Madan Mohan Malaviya. M.S. Golwalkar, the successor of Hedgewar, was recruited here. Second, Hedgewar requested the prominent members of the Hindu Mahasabha and Congressmen to introduce the RSS pracharaks to the notables of their respective areas and arrange for their stay. The Hindu Mahasabha channel proved to be very useful in the initial stage when the RSS was looking for an entry outside C.P. & Berar.

Between 1937 and 1940, the RSS expanded feverishly amidst deteriorating Hindu-Muslim relations in northern India. The pracharaks were active in Punjab, Delhi, United Provinces and Bihar. In 1939, the RSS entered the southern states of Madras presidency and Karnataka. The first attempt to form a Madras branch of the RSS was made in April 1939 when C.S. Paramarth of Nagpur, 'the Chief Organizer of the Madras Province', visited Madras and recruited about 40 members.

The expansion was steady and impressive. There were only 60 shakhas in 1931. In 1936, the RSS claimed to have 200 branches and 25,000 members. By 1939, there were 500 branches and 40,000 members; in 1940, the RSS had 700 branches and 80,000 members.76 Hedgewar also made his organization financially sound. The income of the Sangh came from subscriptions and donations from volunteers, supporters and well-wishers, usually collected at the annual Guru Purnima festival as Guru Dakshina. A 1939 report stated that Rs. 20,000 was kept as a fixed deposit with two Nagpur money-lenders, Chitnavis and Ghatate. Strict control was maintained over the finances of the Sangh and each branch was normally permitted to retain only a Rs. 200 deposit.

Along with the expansion and a sound financial position, its character also underwent a transformation from being a regional to an all-India organization. Hedgewar was quite pragmatic; he decided to dilute the Maharashtrian emphasis of the RSS to make it acceptable to other regional Hindu traditions. Initially, it did not find an easy acceptance in northern India because of the opposition of the Arya Samaj to the idolatrous rituals and practices of the RSS. Therefore, the worship of Hanuman was given up and insistence on Hindu rituals was less emphasized. The prayer was changed to Sanskrit to break the regional barrier. Thus, Hedgewar's innovative organizational skill, missionary zeal and perseverance helped the RSS to grow considerably in a short time. By 1940, when Hedgewar passed away, the RSS had a nationwide presence except Orissa and Kashmir. 'I see before my eyes today a miniature Hindu Rashtra', Hedgewar reportedly said in his last speech to the trainees of the 1940 Nagpur Officers' Training Camp (OTC).

Congress, Mahasabha and RSS Relationship

Keshav Baliram Hedgewar's primary objective in establishing the RSS was not only to awaken and harness the Hindu consciousness, but also to convert the community into a cohesive group. His lengthy monologues were often directed exclusively towards the Hindus, for he believed that public engagement must be populist with adequate emphasis on the cultural aspects. In his mind's eye, the RSS was not a political 'party' in the tradition of either the Congress or the Hindu Mahasabha.

Dual membership in political organisations was a norm in the 1920s and despite being the RSS chief, Hedgewar had retained his membership of the Congress as well as the Hindu Mahasabha (he was also its secretary between 1926–1931). In 1928, as member of the Congress Working Committee (Central Provinces), he had travelled to Calcutta for the annual session and met with Subhash Chandra Bose who was then Mayor of the city, to seek support for the RSS. Bose had heard him out patiently, but had politely turned down his request citing other commitments. Hedgewar's choice to continue as member of the Indian National Congress and seek an audience with a stalwart of a party that was anathema to his nationalistic brand of politics, as he had precluded active politics from the ambit of the organisation he had created. For instance, the participation of swayamsevaks in the annual session of the Hindu Mahasabha in 1927 was merely symbolic, and their role was restricted to being protectors of public order.

Dr Hedgewar joined the Hindu Mahasabha's activities after its branch in Nagpur was opened in 1923 (the Hindu Mahasabha was founded in 1915). He was nominated as a member of the party's 14-member 'publicity committee'. Raja Laskhmanrao Bhonsale and Dr Moonje were its President and secretary respectively. Dr Hedgewar was made the secretary of the Nagpur unit of the Mahasabha in 1926, a post he served till the following year, i.e., 1927. Yet, he was less active compared to the two earlier secretaries of the Mahasabha, Udaram Pehalwan and Gopalrao Dalvi. In fact, Dr Hedgewar used to be mostly absent from the party's meetings.

Dr Hedgewar's views on the Mahasabha and the Congress were quite clear. He accepted the all-India nature and influence of the Congress and believed that it was the most widely accepted platform for any anti-imperialist struggle. He was against ideological differences leading to the creation of different platforms, which would only weaken the anti-imperialist struggle. He wished that other organizations engaged in the fight against imperialism should utilize the Congress platform without conditions. Dr Hedgewar himself used to participate in agitation or constructive endeavours without any prejudices. He did not expect reciprocity or gratitude from the Congress for this, and wished to see the same sentiment in other organizations too. Dr.Hedgewar did not consider the Hindu Mahasabha to be an alternative of the Congress. He believed the Mahasabha's activities for Hindu interests at various levels to be of rather limited utility.

The Hindu Mahasabha began veering increasingly towards solely political concerns, at the expense of issues of socio-cultural reforms and Hindu unity. It began to propagate itself as the sole representative of Hindus, much along the lines of the Muslim League. As a result, the gulf between Dr Hedgewar and the Mahasabha now began to widen. His ties to the Mahasabha were more or less symbolic from 1927 onwards and in 1930; his links to the party remained confined solely to his personal ties with Mahasabha leaders. The Hindu Mahasabha did receive organizational and manpower support from the Rashtriya Swayamsevak Sangh owing to ideological similarities between the two and Hedgewar's personal regard for the leaders of the Mahasabha.

Confusion regarding relations between the Sangh and the Mahasabha arose because of the fact that during Sangh's early days it had sought and received the cooperation of Mahasabha leaders to set up its organization at new places. Dattopant Thengdi writes in this regard: "Dr Hedgewar had received help from Hindutvawadi leaders when the work of the Sangh began, the purpose of which was to establish the Sangh at newer places. This was his organizational strategy. Many of those Mahasabha leaders whose help he sought were actually made sanghchalaks at various places".

Despite this close relationship, Dr Hedgewar took care to maintain the Sangh's autonomy right from the day of its founding, and did not permit any encroachment upon this particular objective of his. He would arrive at a decision on all important organizational issues only after due consultation with his colleagues. Many instances of this were available. Hedgewar never kept the RSS dependent on the Hindu Mahasabha for policies and programmes, and neither did he involve the Mahasabha leaders in this process. The first instance of this policy approach of Dr Hedgewar became apparent during the Civil Disobedience Movement of 1930. The Hindu Mahasabha itself did not have a single opinion on the issue. A sizeable faction, whose reins were in Bhai Parmanand's hands, was totally opposed to Mahatma Gandhi. Another faction, which included Dr Moonje too, did take part in the movement but kept alive its objections to Gandhi and his policies. Dr Moonje was arrested on July 11, 1930, while offering satyagraha and was soon released on a bail of Rs. 5. The Sangh, however, made its decision after evaluating the national situation. Dr Hedgewar was unaware and unaffected by the doings and dilemmas of the Hindu Mahasabha. The involvement of the RSS in the Civil Disobedience Movement was total and without preconditions.

Mahasabha's Expectations

The Hindu Mahasabha passed a resolution in 1932 under N.C.Kelkar presidency accepting the all-India character of the Rashtriya Swayamsevak Sangh. The resolution praised Dr Hedgewar. The Hindu Mahasabha considered itself to be the axis of all Hindu politics and expected the Sangh to work as its voluntary body and extend help to its growing manpower for the Mahasabha's benefit. The Mahasabha leaders loathed the Sangh's participation in any Congress programme. They envied the Sangh's swayamsevaks and coveted their cadres for their own meetings, conferences programmes and publicity.

The attitude of the Hindu Mahasabha towards the Sangh is evident from this letter of Dr Hedgewar written to Kashinath Limaye, a Sangh leader. Dr Hedgewar wrote that the Mahasabha leaders needed to understand that the Sangh's swayamsevaks were not there to move tables and chairs and carry out other such tasks for the Mahasabha. He further wrote, "Things may continue in their present vein owing to circumstances, for there seems to be little other alternative. I well know that conditions there (i.e. in the Mahasabha) are extremely distressing for our swayamsevaks and this constantly pains my heart".

Dr Moonje's place in the Sangh was the same as that of Bhai Paramanand, Vinayak Damodar Savarkar, Loknayak Aney, M R Jaykar, L. B. Bhopatkar and other Hindu Mahasabha leaders. All of these eminent leaders were invited as guest speakers to the Sangh's programmes. These guest nationalists, however, had no say in the determination of the Sangh's policies or programmes. Dr Hedgewar used to invite both the sympathizers as well as the detractors of the Sangh to its programmes. This was truly a unique example of independent exchange of views. That alone was the reason a person like Balaji Huddar, who had once been the Sarkaryavah (general secretary) of the RSS but later turned Marxist and became the Sangh's bitter critic, still used to be invited to the Sangh programmes. It is evident that Dr Hedgewar was not dependent on outsiders for formulating the Sangh's policies or charting out its programmes or movements.

When Dr Hedgewar drew clear lines between the two organizations, acrimony towards him and the RSS began to arise in the Hindu Mahasabha. This found expression in mutual discussions, which sometimes also spilled over into the public arena. In 1934, Dr Moonje complained to G.V. Deshmukh, one of Dr Hedgewar's close associates that the Sangh was not cooperating in the least with the Hindu Mahasabha. So much so that even a person of Veer Savarkar's stature, criticized the Sangh's 'neutrality' vis-à-vis the Hindu Mahasabha at a public meeting at Panvel. It was at this meeting that Savarkar launched an aside at the Sangh, saying: "The tale of the Sangh's Swayamsevak will be that he was born, enrolled himself in the Sangh and passed away without achieving anything". After Savarkar's quip, the middle and lower rung leaders of the Mahasabha only intensified their verbal attacks on the Sangh. Madhav Bindu Puranik, Nathuram Godse, Veer Yashwantrao Joshi and G.G. Adhikari were prominent among those who vented their ire on the Sangh. Puranik, in fact, in conjunction with Godse, Joshi and the princely house of Solapur even wrote to Savarkar, severely criticizing the Sangh. They especially targeted the Sangh leadership, alleging "they (the Sangh's leaders) deliberately prevent members from working for the Mahasabha. According to them, the Hindu Mahasabha is merely a conglomerate of leaders, who are personally ambitious but disgruntled because they haven't been able to acquire positions or places of respect in the Congress. The Sangh uses us in order to further its own interests". The lukewarm response of the RSS to the Hindu Mahasabha's political agenda led the latter to form its own volunteer organizations - the Ram Sena. The RSS was increasingly seen by many Hindu organizers including Savarkar and Moonje as too ineffectual. Thus, a large number of volunteer organizations, for instance the Mahavir Dal and Agni Dal in UP and Punjab, Hindu Rashtra Dal in Poona, Hindu Rashtra Sena in Bhopal, Mukteshawar Dal and Rashtriya Swayamsevak Mandal in CP, Shakti Dal in Jabalpur and Hindu Rashtriya Sena in Giridih in Bihar were formed.

There were significant ideological differences between Dr Moonje and Dr Hedgewar, but neither ever made these differences public. Hedgewar was not at all in agreement with Moonje's policy as regards British imperialism and the minority communities. Hindu Mahasabha delegations used to meet the Viceroy and other colonial administrative figures. The Mahasabha actually wished to acquire the same political heft in its dealing with the British rulers as the Congress and the Muslim League. Dr Moonje even travelled to London to represent the Hindu Mahasabha in the First and Second Round Table Conferences. The Sangh was the sole all-India organization that never sent any representation to the colonial regime, nor expressed any desire for dialogue. Even when the regime let loose a wave of political and judicial repression in 1934, the Sangh did not put forth any demand or submit any explanation. Dr Hedgewar wished to deal with imperialism in one language that of struggle, whether nonviolent or violent. Like a true yogi, he was engaged in preparing the RSS to be firmly rooted in nationalism against imperialism.

In fact, the RSS used to inspire its workers to participate in Congress movements or agitations too. Hundreds of swayamsevaks of the Central Provinces were active in the Congress network too. But as relations between the two entities soured further in the decade of the thirties, the Congress unit of the Yavatmal district issued a notice with directions that anyone who was linked to the Sangh would not be permitted to be a member of the Congress Committee. This event pained Dr Hedgewar, and he wrote to Yavatmal district sanghchalak Annasaheb Jatkar on July 5, 1937, terming this incident as "an atrocity on the Sangh" by the Congressmen of Yavatmal. Hedgewar wrote, "If this news is true, you may arrange to immediately furnish me with detailed and accurate information regarding the same". The Congress' discriminatory attitude against Hindutva-oriented organizations came to the fore through an event at its Faizpur session. During the flag-raising ceremony at this session, the Congress tricolour was stuck midway on a mast eighty feet high. Many tried unsuccessfully to de-tangle the flag, after which a representative Kisan Singh Pardesi courageously climbed up the mast-pole and freed the fabric. Loud cheers rang out for him as the flag fluttered atop the mast. The Congress session also accepted a proposal to felicitate Pardesi. But no sooner had he revealed that he had mustered courage because of the nationalist spirit of the RSS, the Congressmen developed cold feet. How could they felicitate any swayamsevak of the Sangh?

Dr Hedgewar's joy knew no bounds when he heard about this contribution of a swayamsevak. He departed from the Sangh's tradition of eschewing publicity and called Kishan Singh Pardesi to the Devpur shakha, and publicly felicitated him. Presenting a small goblet of Chanda as a token to him, Dr Hedgewar said, "It is a swayamsevak's natural duty to stake his very life if necessary, to remove any obstacle to the nation's work. This is our national dharma."

Dr Hedgewar invited everyone to attend the programmes of the RSS, without any prejudice or preconceived notions whatsoever towards that individual. Thengdi's book Kritagya Smaran contains a list of all those who were associated with the RSS. These included people of all castes, communities, classes and ideologies. While Congressmen were stirring up opposition to the RSS, Dr Hedgewar invited Prof M.B. Joglekar, a prominent Congress leader in Maharashtra to inaugurate the Sangh's Gondia (Central Provinces) camp in October 1935. In his inaugural speech, Joglekar said, "I am a Congressman. Despite my differences with the Sangh, I do not have an iota of doubt about its dedication and commitment to the nation. The RSS trains the youth for the nation's progress and welfare".

N.V. Gunaji, Dadasaheb Mavlankar, Nanasaheb Sardesai, Govardhandas Gokuldas, R.N. Kanitkar, Nanasaheb Date, Halaji Pant Hirda, Dadasaheb Navre, Balvekar, Kamalabai and other Congress leaders from the Central Provinces and Maharashtra too attended the programmes and ceremonies of the RSS and praised its nationalist character. Congress Leaders from provinces in which the RSS was slated to expand would be invited to preside over the Sangh's ceremonies and events at Nagpur, Wardha, Poona and other established RSS centres. Their relationships would then be used by the Sanghpracharaks to initially expand their network in other provinces. Vitthalbhai Patel had visited the Mohitewada Shakha in Nagpur. M R Jaykar, Jamunadas Mehta, Sergeant Rajiv Kamat, Sergeant B.C. Chatterjee, Gokulchand Narang, Dr P. Varadarajalu Naidu and Pandit Madan Mohan Malviya were among those who not only presided over RSS functions but also helped its efforts.

This in itself is testimony to Dr Hedgewar's organizational acumen. He would obtain the cooperation of everyone in the Sangh's work but would not compromise an inch on the loftiness of his organization's principles nor its work. He once said: "Let no one harbour the arrogance that the Sangh works because of a certain individual. The Sangh is not the endeavour of any single individual, but of the entire community. Young and old alike have to come forward according to their capacity in order to fulfil this task. To those who ask what the Sangh has done, I pose this question what are you prepared to do for the Sangh?"

Apart from its ability to attract support through its own methods, the RSS benefited from the support of local notables in developing its network. The pracharaks sent out on missions were recommended to such patrons by the headquarters in Nagpur, which was skilled in the management of its web of relations. In the RSS's strategic plan, these notables were to become referred to as sanghchalak (lit. directors). They functioned mostly as counsellors or even guides, and by sponsoring the activities of local pracharaks conferred on the movement a certain respectability:

In town after town, the Sangha pracharak would arrive with a few letters of introduction to the local leaders, whether belonging to Congress, Hindu Mahasabha, Arya Samaj or whatever. He would put up in the local Bhavan of any of these organizations or in a temple or with any well-wisher.

The first sanghchalak of the RSS was Hari Krishna (alias Appaji) Joshi, a Congress leader from Wardha, where Gandhi was to have his ashram. As early as 1926, Joshi became sanghchalak for the RSS unit of Wardha district, the first branch to be formed from Nagpur. He then left the Congress in 1931. In fact, most of the public figures patronizing the RSS belonged to the Hindu Mahasabha. In this organization, in addition to M.M. Malaviya and B.S. Moonje, the RSS enjoyed during the 1930s the support of Padam Raj Jain. This Marwari from Calcutta had been impressed by the Nagpur shakha which he visited after the session of the Hindu Mahasabha in Poona in 1935. He told Hedgewar how much he appreciated his 'silent but highly important work'. As General Secretary of the Hindu Mahasabha, he helped Vasant Rao Oke establish the Delhi shakha by authorizing him to set up his general headquarters - and the first shakha - in the central office of the Mahasabha. From the 1940s onwards, the Delhi branch of the RSS benefited from the patronage of a leading industrialist, Hans Raj Gupta, an Arya Samajist who became sanghchalak for the Delhi region in 1947. In the United Provinces, the British secret service believed that the RSS 'owed its growth to Dr Moonje' and his journeys in the region. The RSS also benefited considerably from the influence of local notables such as Narendra Jeet Singh. This patron, who became sanghchalak for the branch of Kanpur division in 1945 and then for the whole province in 1948, was a typical sanghchalak: the son of a reputed lawyer who had been chairman of the Kanpur municipal board, he was himself a leading advocate (he presided over the local Bar Council for many years), and remained prant sanghchalak till his death in 1993.

Having assisted the expansion of the RSS, the Hindu Mahasabha considered itself all the more entitled to ask for the support of its network of swayamsevaks. The Nagpur leadership, however, would not divert their organization from its long-term vocation by becoming involved in political action. Here the RSS showed its divergence from the Hindu Mahasabha since it gave priority to the creation of a Hindu Rashtra as the necessary preliminary for a Hindu Raj (Hindu state), which could not be contemplated at this early stage. The lack of interest shown by the RSS in political activity aimed at winning power in the state reflected the belief that such action would only distract Hindus from the main object, that is, the strengthening of the Hindu nation in socio-psychological and physical terms. At the end of the 1930s, Hedgewar apparently snubbed Jamnalal Bajaj, a Gandhian leader from Wardha, who, according to Appaji Joshi, had designs on the activist network of the RSS and had suggested to Hedgewar that his organization affiliate to Congress. The general stand of the RSS was that the anti-colonial struggle took second place to a Hindu nationalist social reform. When Hedgewar took part in the Civil Disobedience movement which Congress launched in 1930, he took care to emphasize that he was doing so strictly as an individual, and entrusted Dr.L.V.Paranjape with the task of running the RSS, demonstrating thereby his concern to keep the organization aloof from the political arena. However, his old connections with his two mentors, Moonje and Savarkar, made him amenable to doing business with the Hindu Mahasabha. The annual conference of the Mahasabha at Nagpur in 1938 benefited from the presence of RSS volunteers, who helped keep order. After he took over the organization, Golwalkar revoked all these concessions, obliging the Hindu Mahasabha in 1940. [1]

Three years after the birth of the Rashtriya Swayamsevak Sangh, and despite Hedgewar's firm resolve to work exclusively for Hindu consolidation, the British administration kept a vigil over it. This was not only because of Hedgewar's past links with revolutionary groups in Nagpur and Bengal, but the Home Department of Central Provinces had strong suspicion that the RSS had the potential of transforming into a revolutionary outfit. However, the Imperial government's worries were rather unfounded, because Hedgewar's decision to stay aloof from the freedom struggle was not in the least appreciated amongst several of his own peers and 'brought consternation, criticism and disappointment from many Hindu partisans.'

There was no gainsaying the fact that K.B. Hedgewar insisted on retaining the RSS' basic character of a socio-cultural outfit which was devoted to reinforcing Hindu society. But to define it as completely apolitical was erroneous. For Hedgewar, politics at the time was mainly defined by the stance taken by any organisation towards the Colonial regime, and the RSS had chosen ambivalence on this issue. Narayan Subbarao Hardikar, founder of the Hindustani Sewa Dal, who'd worked with Hedgewar during the Nagpur session, denounced this very aspect of the RSS in a scathing speech. Hedgewar, however, ignored every criticism and was unwavering in his standpoint, until it drew the harshest denouncement from a person who had inspired him to establish the RSS in the first place.

The Hindu Mahasabha's narrative was most clearly revealed in its close relations with the Rashtriya Swayamsevak Sangh. The two organisations overlapped in ideology due to an affinity and common commitment to the establishment of a strong and powerful 'Hindu nation'. A 'major influence' on the thinking of Dr Hedgewar, was a 'hand-written manuscript of.... Savarkar's Hindutva which advanced the thesis that the Hindus are a nation'. 'One of the early visitors to Savarkar in Ratnagiri was the great founder of the RSS. The interview took place in [March] 1925 at Shirgaon, a village on the outskirts of Ratnagiri. Before starting the RSS, Hedgewar had a 'long discussion with Savarkar over the faith, form and future of the organization'. The RSS had a vision to infuse the Hindu community with new physical strength. Hedgewar explained that the struggle against British colonialism lacked a 'sense of moral purpose and Hindu nationalism', and that the Indian National Congress had 'no positive vision of a Hindu nation. It is therefore the duty of every Hindu to do his best to consolidate Hindu society. The RSS aimed to re-create a 'nation ruled by Hindus' by uilding a numerically small but devoted and efficient organisation of patriotic men who could provide leadership to the Hindu community in India.

The RSS sought to impart a martial, masculine accent to the spiritual ideals of a good and virtuous behaviour [samskaras] as well as an ideological training [baudhik] through shakhas [branches] in north India. Hedgewar looked to akharas [wrestling gymnasiums] as a source to rally some of his first recruits in shakhas. 'Go to the akharas,' he said, 'but come to the shakhas also.' He introduced the shakhas as the permanent units of the RSS first in Nagpur city in May 1926, and later in the villages and towns of Maharashtra. The shakhas were the centres dedicated to moulding swayamsevaks [RSS cadres] with a spirit of 'devotion to the nation'. They aimed to teach Hindu men the ideals of 'manliness' necessary for the creation of 'true patriotism': discipline, martial prowess, and loyalty to the nation imagined as 'Mother India'. To Hedgewar, a 'total revolution of the Hindu attitudes, thought-processes and behaviour' was required. After all, M.S. Golwalkar explained, 'nations stand only upon the solid foundation of their organized strength.... Then, what are the qualities required of individuals who will form the living limbs of such an organized strength? ... The first thing is invincible physical strength'. The shakhas endeavoured to create new men - 'patriotic selfless individuals loyal to the Hindu nation' who were physically well trained, manly, courageous, self-disciplined and capable of organising Hindus in India. They concentrated on 'physical exercise and cultivation of the mind', besides acting as the 'building blocks' of RSS expansion in the country. The Sangh's principle was that 'only a purification of the self can deliver the ultimate national fullness'. Swayamsevaks, referred to as 'Hedgewar's volunteers', took a life oath initiated in 1928 to consecrate themselves to the RSS with the 'whole body, heart, and money, for in it lies the betterment of Hindus and the country'; and the 'Hindu nation' was viewed as the 'living God'. The outcome of such character-building, Golwalkar emphasised, was a 'dynamic devotion' and 'readiness to sacrifice' our all for the protection of the freedom and honour of India. Hindu society, whole and integrated, should therefore be the single point of devotion for all of us. In effect, the RSS had transformed itself as a cohesive and disciplined body of swayamsevaks and workers on the basis that they would have a 'broad influence' on many areas of Hindu national life in India.

By the 1920s and 1930s, a Hindu characterisation of 'physical culture' by the RSS had largely shaped the formation of armed volunteer groups, which were defined in the framework of Hindu nationalism, in Maharashtra. The shakhas focused on practices such as discussion, exercise and communal eating, but accepted no knowledge of a swayamsevak's 'caste' background. Today, Hedgewar declared, 'we have only one varna and jati, that is Hindu.' The discourse of the shakhas remained an effective method of disseminating the image of a robust 'Hindu nation', focusing on discipline and patriotism built through a militaristic training. Crucially, the RSS emphasised the need for an organised and united India represented by its valorisation of strength, martial power, and national glory - a notion that resulted in an open 'hostility' against Muslims. The Sangh was, Golwalkar explained, a 'Hindu military organisation' and could 'meet and crush Muslim aggressors'. An 'utmost secrecy' was needed so that Muslims, the 'enemies' of the Sangh, could not gauge the organisation's 'physical strength'. In effect, the Sangh represented a more determined organisational effort to rise in self-defence against 'Muslim threats' to Hindu 'life and property' - with a commitment to create a 'Hindu nation' firmly rooted in a militaristic ideology.

The Hindu Mahasabha and the RSS belonged to the same political milieu and militaristic background of the 1920s. The icons of Shivaji, the bhagwa dhwaj [saffron flag], and Shivaji's guru Ramdas were prominent in the rituals of both organisations, suggesting a strong 'militaristic tradition'. Shivaji, the Maratha hero, valued 'strength and force', believing that true religion could flourish only when the Muslim rulers were driven out of Maharashtra. Ramdas popularised the idiom of Maharashtra dharma, interpreted as a call to return to the ancient Vedic 'golden age'. The bhagwa dhwaj - the 'true guru' to which Hedgewar demanded that obeisance be paid – rather than the tricolour was regarded as the true 'national flag' of India. 'Bhagwa [saffron] Flag,' Savarkar explained, 'shall be the Flag of the Hindu Nation. With its Om, the Swastik and the Sword, it appeals to the sentiments cherished by our race since the Vaidik days.' Historical figures such as Maharana Pratap and K.B. Hedgewar were portrayed as the 'ideal Hindus' who had realised the ultimate unity of the 'Hindu nation' and served as role models for Hindu 'reawakening and renewal'. 'Doctor Keshav Baliram Hedgewar', Golwalkar explained, "burned like a steady lamp in the cause of the motherland ... I feel it my proud privilege to worship him as my ideal. The worship of such a soul... becomes the worship of the ideal itself". The Mahasabha and the RSS were centralised command structures, controlled respectively by the President and the sarsanghchalak who had wielded all the powers. To them, the ideal of Hindu nationalism became central as part of a vision to propagate India as a 'Hindu nation' by constructing a 'defensible and militaristic' Hindu community.

There was an organisational unity and ideological consensus between the Hindu Mahasabha and the RSS. The RSS maintained an institutional affinity and continuity with the Mahasabha as a parallel Hindu movement, drawing support from the latter for its expansion and development in north India. In addition to the patronage of M.M. Malaviya, stated the British secret service, the RSS 'owe[d] its growth to Dr Moonje and his journeys in the UP region'. B.S. Moonje, celebrated by the RSS as 'Dharmaveer' [hero in a religious struggle], had a prominent role in the formation of the RSS, being one of its five founding members and Hedgewar' mentor. To Moonje, Hedgewar was perhaps the most loyal follower in Nagpur politics in the 1920s. When the Hindu Sabha was organised in Nagpur in 1923 under the presidentship of Raja Laxmanrao Bhonsle of Nagpur, Moonje became its Vice-President and Hedgewar the secretary. As Mahasabha President, Moonje had played a crucial role in organising the RSS shakhas in Maharashtra and the Central Provinces, even though the organisation's structure was the result of Hedgewar's 'vision and leadership'. Moonje explained:

Our institution, the Rashtriya Swayamsevak Sangh of Nagpur under Dr Hedgewar is of... kind, though quite independently conceived. I shall spend the rest of my life developing and extending this institution of Dr Hedgewar all throughout Maharashtra and other provinces.

Admittedly, the RSS's links to the Mahasabha had served to introduce in the Hindi-speaking areas of north India by the 1920s and 1930s. Ganesh Savarkar had brought the RSS in touch with Mahasabha activists in Delhi and Banaras; and the influence of the Savarkar family enabled the Sangh's expansion among the upper castes of western Maharashtra. Padam Raj Jain, Mahasabha general secretary, helped Vasant Rao Oke establish an RSS shakha in the Mahasabha headquarters in Delhi in 1936. In particular, the RSS attracted new patrons due to its association with the Mahasabha, some of them being Hindu princes and rulers.

The RSS was linked to the Hindu Mahasabha through leadership, even though it remained independent of it. Officials in the Home Department noted that the RSS was the 'volunteer organisation of the Hindu Mahasabha'. Sections of the RSS activists were office-holders in the Mahasabha and vice versa; and a dual membership was common. Lacking in trained youth power, the Mahasabha was anxious to get the support of the RSS cadres. It passed a resolution at its Delhi session in 1932, officially recognising the RSS as the only 'well-disciplined force of Hindus' and encouraging provincial Hindu Sabhas to support its expansion and assist in making it a 'strong organisation of Hindus' in India. In 1937, groups of RSS gathered at public meetings to celebrate Savarkar's release from jail. During the RSS officers' training camp held in Pune on 27-29 May 1943, which was attended by M.S.Golwalkar, G D Savarkar, and B.S.Moonje, Savarkar expressed his admiration for the 'display of march and drills by swayamsevaks in great numbers'. He was 'proud', he declared, 'to see the branches of the Sangh spread throughout India during his visits to various places'. V D Savarkar instructed Hindu Sabhas throughout India to observe a day of mourning for Hedgewar, who passed away on 21st June 1940.Veer Savarkar passed away in 1966; and an honour guard of 2,000 RSS workers attended his funeral procession in Bombay. The RSS stayed outside political campaigns, insisting that it was strictly a 'cultural organisation' concerned with the 'Reorganisation and renewal' of a 'Hindu nation' through character building; but the Mahasabha, a political party, was interested in the 'role of the state'. Nonetheless, both organisations shared an ideological affinity based on Hindu unity.

The growth of volunteer activity transformed politics in UP in the 1940s. It was seen in the last section that there was a visible overlap in new emphases on military-style organisation on the one hand and ideas about community defence on the other: Tandon's Hind Rakshak Dal attracted supporters who combined old allegiances to the Congress with ideas about protection of the 'Hindu race'. This combination revealed other patterns: throughout the 1930s and 1940s, there were not always clear delineations in personnel and training between supposedly Congress-sponsored volunteer organisations and organisations for 'Hindu defence', like the Mahabir Dals, Hanuman Dals, Arya Vir Dal and the Rashtriya Swayamsevak Sangh (RSS). To some extent, the overlap of volunteer activity with religious consciousness was the natural result of the spiritual significance of physical culture in India.

Gandhi, Bhagwan Das, Sri Prakash and Mahabir Tyagi all related their own physical wellbeing to religion, juxtaposing physical with spiritual fitness. It was argued that Congress-led protests could follow ritualistic patterns. The physical culture promoted by the volunteer movements associated with the Congress also incorporated ideas and rituals of individual discipline. These ideas were derived from concepts of individual spiritual strength drawn from an array of sources, the most mainstream being Gandhian 'swaraj', Tilakite philosophies of action, and the physical organisation and discipline connected with the RSS.

From 1938, the UP was at the forefront of Congress-based volunteer organisation. 'Semi-military training' was started in a camp in Ayodhya, with the intention of creating a nucleus for an all-India volunteer corps. The UPPCC issued circulars to all other provincial committees informing them of the inauguration of an All-Indian Central Training Camp at Faizabad in early December, under the organisation of Nand Kumar Deo Vashishta. During a speech at Banaras, Vashishta hinted at the need to build up the capability to take power in the eventuality of a political crisis, or even the need to engineer such a situation. This information suggested the existence of a homogeneous volunteer movement under Congress direction. In reality, the organisation of volunteer activity across UP fell to groups within specific districts, each with varying agendas. Frequently, this undermined any centralised control on the part of the Provincial Congress Committee, allowing organisations in some districts to pool resources with more obviously organisations like the Mahabir Dal and the Arya Vir Dal. For example, at the beginning of September 1938, in Tulsipur, Gonda district, the Hindu Sabha and a selection of Congressmen joined to form a Mahabir Dal and Hanuman Dal. Information on volunteer movements in June 1939 highlighted how the disorganisation and proliferation of volunteer activity could easily feed into other kinds of political allegiance:

The country is full of mushroom organisations, created to meet the exigencies of the moment and then forgotten, seldom properly organized or systematically developed, without central control or financial backing owing allegiance to nobody, or what is worse, to a local faction.The suggestion that at the district levels Congress volunteer activity overlapped with Hindu organisations .

Dr Bhimrao Ambedkar visited an RSS training camp—the Sangh Shiksha Varga—at Pune in 1939. When Dr Ambedkar asked Dr Hedgewar whether there were any untouchables in the camp, the RSS founder replied that there were neither touchables nor untouchables, but only Hindus there.[2]

Ambedkar said, "I am surprised to find the swayamsevaks moving about in absolute equality and brotherhood without even caring to know the caste of the others."

In the 1950s, Ambedkar and RSS pracharak Dattopant Thengadi worked together closely and were constantly in touch.There are quantitative sets of evidence as well as descriptions of activities in certain districts, which support the thesis that Congress volunteer activity sometimes subsumed, included or overlapped with Hindu organisations in terms of personnel and organisation. Firstly, in the early years of 1940, there was a noticeable correlation between the success of Congress's volunteer organisations and the popularity of Muslim League corps. The figures of membership for different districts of UP for the period of January to March 1941 were revealing: Kanpur, Aligarh and Agra districts showed enthusiastic support for Congress-related organisations, with relatively high memberships of 3,465, 1,117 and 1,048 respectively. Muslim League and Muslim National Guards were at the relatively high levels of 670, 1,500 and 385 in these districts. Low Congress volunteer activity in Mainpuri and Bijnor seemed to be reflected by low Muslim League activity. Correlation coefficients have to be handled with care. It is not always possible to derive conclusions from closely related quantitative evidence. Some districts simply had more highly organised volunteer activity for both communities and it should not be particularly surprising that large cities such as Kanpur and Allahabad would be at the forefront of volunteer organisation. However, there were also suggestions that membership of the Congress and Hindu organisations were interrelated: over the year 1941, comment on volunteer figures and activities pointed to the sharing of resources and personnel between the Congress and Hindu communal bodies. For example, in January 1941, the loss of RSS members in Lucknow was apparently offset by increases for Congress organisations. Official assessments of volunteer activity in 1939 also supported this thesis: 'In the United Provinces, Hindu communal organisations are gaining popularity to the detriment of recruitment to the Congress Volunteer Corps.'

More convincing still was the on-going trend, through the late 1930s and 1940s, of regional alliances between organisers and members of Congress and Hindu organisations. In the late 1930s, this was suggested by the often joint activities of Congress and Hindu organisations during Hindu festivals. In Etah, on 16 September 1938, the Congress Swayam Sevak Dal joined with the Mahabir Dal to escort the Ramlila Jhanda procession through the city. By the beginning of October, the two volunteer organisations were seen jointly policing processions. In the same month, Gandhi Day was celebrated in Dehra Dun with the joint activity of Mahabir Dal, Congress Seva Dal and Sikh Guru Dal volunteers. Bahraich was another district which in late 1938 witnessed Mahabir Dal/Congress cooperation at the Kakora Ganges fair. The extent to which the involvement of Congress volunteers with other organisations projected a communal image onto the Congress as a whole was shown in a Hindu-Muslim affray in Dehra Dun. Here, Congress volunteers had worked with Mahabir Dal members in October 1939. Other supposedly non-communal organisations also found themselves embroiled in religious quarrels. On 5 June 1941, a clash between the Nau Yuvak Sangh and the Khaksars at a 'mela' in Bareilly district led to a newly inflated membership of the Sangh for purposes of Hindu communal defence. In other districts and cities, the Congress outwardly relied upon the already existing Hindu organisations to strengthen their own corps. In Allahabad city, in January 1940, Congressmen decided to revive the 'Kesari Dal' to organise the various Hindu communities and parties into one volunteer group. By mid-1940, it was becoming difficult in some districts to differentiate between the Hindu volunteer bodies. In Agra, for example, the Qaumi Raksha Dal could not be distinguished from the regular Congress corps.

The consequences of this overlap between professedly secular and communal volunteer organisations were vital in the on-going ideological relationship between Congress and Hindu institutions in the 1940s. But the reason why such alliances were possible in the first place related to the necessary amorphousness of UP Congress organisation itself. It has already been suggested in the last section that, through the agency of certain leaders, languages of Hindu nationalism became a medium through which increasing militarism could be justified in mainstream nationalist terms. The radical militaristic rejection of Pakistan by communal organisations was also confused with milder Congress activity. At a meeting of the Arya Samaj in Lucknow on 11 February 1943, at which Gandhi was eulogised, Kunwar Sukh Lal declared that volunteer bodies connected to the Samaj would fight a civil war rather than accept Pakistan.

The way in which explicitly aggressive organisations for Hindu defence were associated with cultural organisations which otherwise would have developed little connection to the new upsurge in militarism. Tandon's Hindi Sahitya Sammelan, at its thirty-first meeting between 17 and 19 May 1943, entertained amongst its alumni representatives of the Mahabir Dal and RSS. By the mid-1940s, it also appeared that Congressmen in some districts were moving over to the RSS, or participating in their activities. In Farrukabad, at the end of October 1943, it was reported that several local Congressmen had thrown in their lot with the Sangh. By 1944, the RSS had really taken off in UP. In May, ten training camps had been set up in Budaun and Aligarh. Officer training camps were organised for the summer in Moradabad and Banaras. Muzaffarnagar and Lucknow districts quickly developed as strongholds, the latter under the enthusiastic organisation of Tej Narain. At the new training camps in Aligarh, the importance of Hindi was stressed, and a recruitment drive was started to attract the sons of 'rich' Hindus. In May 1944, again, linkages were found between the Congress and RSS. It was discovered that a few of the volunteers at an RSS volunteer training camp in Banaras retained connections with CSP workers in Banaras and Gorakhpur. The RSS also moved the other way over to the Congress. In August 1945, two RSS workers in Allahabad agreed to help with the training of Congress volunteers at the physical culture training camp, to be convened by Purushottam Das Tandon. By 1946, the relationship had developed further. At an RSS meeting in Kanpur in February, Balkrishna Sharma assured the khaki-clad volunteers of City Congress support. In Etah, a Congress 'shakti Dal' was started on RSS lines at the beginning of March. In Gorakhpur, in the same month, Congressmen were reportedly taking a keen interest in the activities of the RSS. At Allahabad, during the Hindu New Year on 3 April, 50 RSS volunteers attended a meeting at the house of a 'prominent Congressman' and organised the setting- up of two new branches in Jaunpur.

It is difficult to assess the internal activities of the RSS in UP or any other province in the 1930s and 1940s. The organisation went to great lengths to preserve the secrecy of its proceedings - even going so far as to allow police reporters into certain parts of camps to promote conciliation, but preventing non-members from attending lectures. No reporters were allowed to take notes. However, where meetings were more open, it is possible to see some similarities to the rhetoric used in Congress meetings, particularly those of Congress volunteer organisations during civil disobedience. In an RSS officer training camp at Banaras in June 1943, lectures were delivered on subjects such as self-protection and national unity. A sense of national identity was imbued by methods reminiscent of Congress meetings in the early 1930s–examples were used from epics such as the Mahabharata, and volunteers were asked to sacrifice their lives for their country in the manner of Shivaji and Rana Pratap.

As 1946 progressed, it became clear that the association of Congressmen with the RSS in some districts would help to complicate an already tense communal situation. In April, whilst a Congressman was involved in the training of RSS volunteers in drill in Naini Tal, in one district towards the end of the year, it seemed that a Congressman was ready to use the services of the RSS for the purposes of communal defence. In Banda, the Congress Committee President reportedly urged the RSS to take revenge on Muslims for the Pakistan demand during a meeting in the Arya Samaj mandal. In the atmosphere of intense panic and recrimination, volunteer bodies, as well as other political organisations, became aggressively communalised. Congress Hindus were also ensnared in this atmosphere: at Kanpur and Unao rich Hindus raised subscriptions in November 1946 for the financing of a multiplicity of volunteer bodies, including the UP Congress Raksha Dal.

Whilst volunteer movements had been a feature of nationalist politics from the first 'mass movements' in UP, they did not become a regular feature of provincial political life until the late 1930s, with the onset of war in Europe and the growth of the Muslim League. The rapid rise and development of military-style organisations hindered their systematic and ordered development, as did the diverse and often contradictory messages sent out to them by the main political institutions such as the Congress in UP. Although there were province-wide organisations like the Mahabir Dal, Khaksars, Qaumi Seva Dal and Hanuman Dal, their activities and organisation depended upon the specific political context of their district or locality. Even the relatively centralised Congress-related organisations were fluid in their membership and organisation across districts. Given the opportunities for parallel movements for communal defence, Congress volunteer bodies were inevitably confused or allied with Hindu nationalist organisations - sometimes for the very purpose of greater uniformity and organisation. It was perhaps logical, then, that Mahabir Dals, RSS and Congress volunteers should join together to carry out policing activities, or to pool resources for physical training.

The associations of Congress volunteer organisations with Hindu bodies in some districts contributed to Hindu-Muslim cleavages within other organisations. This occurred in Meerut in 1946. The Khaksars had an on-going relationship with the Congress, and fluctuated in their allegiance to that party and the Muslim League on the basis of individual leaders and factions. The Ahrars also joined with Congress volunteer organisations in the late 1930s and early 1940s. But the popularity of the Muslim National Guard, and the force of its communal rhetoric, were inevitably linked to the perception of a Congress-Hindu nationalist alliance, which could be viewed through the apparent Congress-RSS/Mahabir Dal cooperation in some districts. It has already been seen that the philosophical basis of physical culture for individuals like Tandon did not sit comfortably with a cross-communal volunteer effort. Organisations like the Mahabir Dal were more obviously concerned with the policing of Hindu festivals and functions. Congress co-operation with them would have implicated Congressmen as protectors of 'Hindu rights'. Volunteer activity also reflected mainstream political rivalry. Where more obviously communal volunteer bodies were able to throw in their lot with the Congress or the Muslim League, political competition could easily overlap with communal rivalry.

The careers of Algu Rai Shastri, Mahabir Tyagi, Purushottam Das Tandon and Sampurnanand all illustrate the ways in which Hindu nationalist ideologies and languages of politics could have a pervasive effect on political life, alongside and in combination with other forms of political ideology and language. Shastri, Tandon and Sampurnanand were all feted in the mid-1930s for their attachment to socialist principles. The domination of Nehru in all-India politics helped to create an assumption that forms of communal mobilisation necessarily reflected right-wing politics and conservatism. Socialism is considered to be a largely secular ideology in this interpretation of Indian politics. However, in contrast to institutional Hindu nationalism such as the Mahasabha, the more informal connections between communal and non-communal ideologies and languages in UP were not necessarily constrained by socialist ideologies. The Hindu Mahasabha contained a strong Hindu landholding and big-business membership, more likely to be attached to political moderation. But the Hindu Mahasabha in UP was only one thin wedge in the edifice of a range of ideas about community and nation, which manifested themselves in a heteroglossia of languages within mainstream institutions such as the Congress. Hence, institutional connections existed between the Congress at different levels and Hindu Organisations such as Arya Samaj, Hindu Mahasabha and the links of congressmen to institutional Hindu nationalism – the Hindu Sabhas, the Arya Samaj and RSS were complex and regionally diverse. [3]

When the Congress passed the Purna Swaraj resolution in its Lahore session in December 1929, and called upon all Indians to celebrate 26 January 1930 as Independence Day, Hedgewar issued a circular asking all the RSS shakhas to observe the occasion through hoisting and worship of the Bhagwa Dhwaj (saffron flag), rather than the Tricolour (which was, by consensus, considered the flag of the Indian national movement at that time). 1930 was the only year when the RSS celebrated 26 January and it stopped the practice from the next year onwards. However, such celebration became a standard feature of the freedom movement and often came to mean violent confrontation with the official police.

In April 1930, Mahatma Gandhi gave a call for 'Satyagraha' against the British Government. Gandhi himself launched the Salt Satyagraha undertaking his Dandi Yatra. Dr. Hedgewar decided to participate only individually and not let the RSS join the freedom movement officially. He sent information everywhere that the Sangh will not participate in the Satyagraha. However, those wishing to participate individually in it were not prohibited.

Hedgewar emphasized that he participated in the Civil Disobedience movement of 1930 in an individual capacity, and not as a RSS member. His concern was to keep the RSS out of the political arena. According to Hedgewar's biography, when Gandhi launched the Salt Satyagraha in 1930, he sent information everywhere that the RSS will not participate in the Satyagraha. However, those wishing to participate individually in it were not prohibited. RSS' decision to join the Civil Disobedience Movement started by Gandhi in 1930 made HMS furious. Dr. K.B Hedgewar, the founder of RSS, stepped down from the post of sarsanghchalak and led the Forest Satyagraha in Pusad. He, along with 300 RSS workers, was arrested and incarcerated for a year. HMS leader, Dr. B.S. Moonje wrote that RSS workers were being "carried away by Gandhian movement."

For Hedgewar, India was an ancient civilisation, and the freedom struggle was an attempt to re-establish a land for the Hindus after almost 900 years of foreign rule, primarily by the Mughals and then by the British.

Hedgewar insisted that the RSS must only be involved with "man-making". Hedgewar was critical of Hindu society and its degeneration over the centuries with its out-dated and often backward practices. The RSS, he wrote, must be completely devoted to establishing men of character and worthy of respect the world over.

Laxmibai Kelkar was the founder of the Rashtra Sevika Samiti. Before establishing the organization, Kelkar visited Dr. K.B. Hedgewar, in 1936 and had a long discussion to persuade him regarding the need for starting a women's wing in the Rashtriya Swayamsevak Sangh itself. Hedgewar, though, continued to restrict membership of the RSS to men that just as men were being trained in Sangh, women too needed to be trained in nationalism and proper samskars. After many months of discussion, Dr. Hedgewar in the end promised to extend all help to Laxmibai Kelkar (Mauseeji), to found Rashtra Sevika Samiti, an exclusively women's organization, its goal being the same as that of Sangh but which was called upon to operate parallel to the latter and with a different name, prayer and independent structure. Hedgewar advised Laxmibai Kelkar to establish an entirely separate organization that would be autonomous and independent of the RSS, as both groups were ideologically identical. Hedgewar promised Kelkar unconditional solidarity, support, and guidance for the Samithi. Following this, Kelkar established the Rashtra Sevika Samiti at Wardha on 25 October 1936, Vijayadashami day.

As soon as Bharat got Independence, the first challenge was to bring back Hindus safely from Pakistan and rehabilitate them. It may be recalled that in the run-up to Partition, areas falling under Sindh, West Pakistan, and East Bengal were put under the command of a Muslim-dominated army-police combine. The Hindus in these areas were on tenterhooks.

The second RSS Sarsanghchalak, MS Golwalkar, also known as Shri Guruji, took the initiative to reach out to these Hindus and set up the Punjab Relief Committee and the Hindu Sahayata Samiti (Hindu Support Committee) for refugees from West Pakistan. The centre of activity for both of these was initially Lahore. The Punjab state sanghchalak, Raibahadur Badridas, was the chairman and Dr Gokulchand Narang was the treasurer of these committees. Similarly, relief committees were set up for refugees coming from East Pakistan also. The RSS played a major role in rehabilitation of the hapless refugees, when they were left by the ruling dispensation to fend for themselves in pathetically managed government relief camps.

In 1947-1948, when Pakistan attacked Bharat for the first time by sending tribal militia and its regular army in Jammu and Kashmir, the RSS volunteers played an important role in aiding the Bharatiya forces to repel that attack. The RSS swayamsevaks prepared an airstrip within no time in Poonch that helped to land planes carrying Bharatiya soldiers.

After the advent of Independence in 1947, the centuries-long struggle for freedom gave place to the task of nation-building precisely in a literal sense. But the crucial question was what should be the goal and the means to achieve it. It was here that the men then at the helm stumbled. They had all along been. While engaged in the freedom struggle equating the mere transfer of power from the alien rulers, with real independence and hence to some extent, were bewildered at the sudden turn of circumstances in which they were empowered with authority to rule.

In fact, for them, it was a God-given historic opportunity to shape the destiny of the nation, which was as it were taking a new birth altogether. The real need then was to identify the character and the time-tested basic values, which this ancient nation stood for millennia, and to reshape the nation on that basis with any modifications suited for the changing needs of the day. But they deemed economic progress and material welfare as the finality of an independent nation.

They had before them two models, both from the West. While the American one had in it the capitalist economy with all-permissive individual freedom, which in fact was eating into the very vitals of her social life, the Russian socialist alternative with its ambitious five-year plans, presented a facade of heaven on the earth, in which actually the individual was but a cog in the wheel. Being enamoured by both, and material progress alone being made the touchstone, the new rulers opted to simultaneously ape both - an exercise which ultimately tended to make the nation a carbon copy of neither.

The thinking of the Sangh in this regard has all along been of a very basic nature. From its inception, the goal before the Sangh was to attain the "Param Vaibhav" (the pinnacle of glory), the freedom from the alien rule being just a step in that direction. The transfer of power can at the most be "Swaraj" (one's own rule), but definitely not "Swatantrya" (actualization of one's own potential being). The concept of "Param Vaibhav" has ingrained in it the material progress too of the nation, but not with its very identity and interests mortgaged. The Sangh with its total commitment to the actualization of "Swaraj", in other words the Hindu ethos, keeping itself away from the powers-that-be, from 1947 onwards, began on its own to extend its influence to varied fields of social life. The Sangh "Pratijna" (pledge), which until then was for the liberation of the Hindu Rashtra, was amended to indicate "Sarvangeena Unnati" (all-round development) of the nation. The entire gamut of social life was planned to be designed on the rock-bed of Hindu nationalism. The swayamsevaks with the insight and the organizational skill they acquired through the "samskars" on the "sanghasthan" and with the uncompromising urge for the national reassertion gradually began to enter one after another field of national life. The process commenced as early as in the end of forties, and has in these four decades encompassed a vast number of areas that the society is composed of.

In 1948, after the assassination of Gandhiji, when the Sangh was unjustly banned, the exuberant student and youth force, which until then was active in the Shakha work only, was mobilized to contact the public with issues of national interest, particularly the draft constitution which was then being debated in the Constituent Assembly. This movement, the Akhil Bhartiya Vidyarthi Parishad (ABVP), in course of time has grown into a massive nation-wide student organization, successfully harnessing the buoyancy, time, intelligence, talent, and creativity in the students, over and above their educational responsibilities, for nation-building activities. Today ABVP is recognized as the front-rank student organization with a totally nationalist outlook. Earlier, when most of the Sangh functionaries were unjustly incarcerated, and baseless canards against Sangh were let loose by the establishment, to set the record straight, apart from the "Organizer" weekly in English, a series of language periodicals like "Panchajanya", "Yuga Dharma" (both Hindi), Vicrama (Kannada) etc. were started. Nowadays, with regard to this fourth estate of democracy, almost all the provinces have their own vernacular papers all belonging to Sangh school of thought, and command a very wide range of readership.

The educational system initiated by Macaulay with the motive of producing an army of "brown-skinned Englishmen", to serve the imperial administration as "the most obedient servants" was another legacy of the British rule in Bharat. After Independence, there was dire need to reshape the entire system. In 1952, the first "Saraswati Shishu Mandir" (nursery school) was founded in Ghorakhpur, Uttar Pradesh, as an attempt towards inculcating, along with mandatory academic knowledge, discipline, patriotic outlook, love for mother tongue, high moral values and Hindu principles, the thrust of education being based upon a holistic approach to the physical, intellectual, moral, and spiritual growth of the pupil. The small sapling of this "Shishu Mandir" - which it was in fifties - has now grown into, a mighty banyan tree as "Vidya Bharati", an umbrella body for thousands of educational institutions, ranging from nursery to post-graduation level. The system of education being evolved by Vidya Bharati is based on age-old Hindu values, hut having an outer structure in consonance with present-day needs of modern education.

The systematic alienation of the tribals, inhabiting remote forest areas, but who form an inseparable part of the Hindu society through proselytization was another grave challenge that demanded immediate corrective measures. Far away and hence uncontaminated by sophisticated modernity, they are yet, though deprived of literacy, committed to their own rustic cultural moorings and also are very talented. They had all along been a most exploited lot and an easy prey for unscrupulous conversion by Christian missionaries. It is to counter this twin menace of British legacy, that the Bhartiya Vanavasi Kalyan Ashram (BKVA) was founded in early fifties. The BKVA, now spread over a hundred districts in 21 States, has been striving for the all-round development of the vanavasis, in their own natural surroundings, enabling all their latent potentialities and talents to blossom. Over the decades, the Ashram has succeeded not only in putting a stop to conversions in all its areas of operation, but also in bringing the converts back to the Hindu fold.

The trade union movement guided by the alien socialist and Marxist philosophy, started in thirties, was gaining ground by the time and British left the country. This philosophy, with its faith in class conflict and its methodology of anti-production strikes, was in fact, both in theory and practice, a negation of labour and national interests. Bhartiya Majdoor Sangh, a totally new labour movement, apolitical in character, based on Hindu tenets, was started in 1955. The BMS believes in conciliation whenever dispute arises, and considers strike as the last resort. It does fight against exploitation in any form from whichever party, and upholds the all-comprehensive interest of the society as a whole with supreme concern. It is now recognized as a leading labour organization even at the international level and in the home-front, the second biggest one, far ahead of other similar organizations with socialist and Marxist leanings.

The above is a brief, illustrative account of just a few among the vast number of organizations inspired by the Sangh, generally looked upon as "Sangh Parivar". The "Parivar" in fact is very vast, since no field of activity is beyond the reach of Sangh swayamsevaks; and as such a description of each and every activity is beyond the scope of the present book. The swayamsevaks, in whichever field they entered, with their invincible drive to translate the dream of "Sarvangeena Unnati" have made it vibrant with Hindu nationalist ethos. Thus, what was started as a humble man-making activity in the form of Sangh Shakha, in a brief span of seven decades, especially after the advent of Independence, has now assumed the form of a unique and mighty nation-building instrument, with its benign influence pervading each and every field of social life.

Sangh"s March: Some Thrust-Areas

The Sangh has often been misrepresented by its detractors, political or ideological, as having political motives or as a paramilitary organization. The seven-decades-long growth of the Sangh and its ever-growing influence over the society are also sometimes attempted to be evaluated in political terms. But the Sangh, it must be remembered, is for attaining the "Saravangeena Unnati" (all-round development) of Bharat, and for this end only the swayamsevaks pledge to dedicate themselves. They do desire that the political field too needs to be cleansed and reformed, based on Hindu values and ethos, but politics is just one among the many facets of social life. As such, to cast political aspersion on Sangh is, to say the least, baseless, since the concept of all-round development encompasses the entire spectrum of life, including politics. The Sangh has to its credit a few thousands of service projects, covering varied fields of social life. Apart from the projects, the swayamsevaks on their own are rendering service to the society, individually and collectively too, wherever needed, whatever the cause.

The Shakha, in fact, is not an end in itself, but just a means to achieve the end, which in brief is social transformation. The programmes in the Shakha are so structured that while they develop a proper insight and make one aware of the deficiencies and drawbacks in the society, it also instils a sense of pride and intense love for its glorious cultural heritage and, simultaneously, awakens his commitment to work for his emancipation. Thus, through the instrumentality of the Shakha, men are molded, and they in turn enter varied social fields to ennoble them with Hindu fervor. Just as the pure blood flows out of the heart, to reach each and every body-cell, taking along with it oxygen and nourishment, purging it of its dross, making it function properly and then returning back to the heart to get itself once more energized, the swayamsevaks also imbibe proper samskars in the Shakha, and then propel themselves into diverse social activities.

The aim of the Sangh is to organize the entire Hindu society, and not just to have a Hindu organization within the ambit of this society. Had it been the latter, then the Sangh too would have added one more number to the already existing thousands of creeds. Though started as an institution, the aim of the Sangh is to expand so extensively that each and every individual and traditional social institution like family, caste, profession, educational and religious institutions etc., are all to be ultimately engulfed into its system. The goal before the Sangh is to have an organized Hindu society in which all its constituents and institutions function in harmony and co-ordination, just as in the body organs. While this is easily perceived at the conceptual level, the institutional outer form of the Sangh is also necessary for internalization of this habit of organized living, but without making it a creed.

The swayamsevak considers the Hindu society itself as "Janata Janardana"-god incarnate. Any service rendered to this society, accepting nothing in return, is for him the worship of his god, the "Samaja-roopae Parameshwar!" (God in the form of the society). To him, who feels intensely for the good of the society, it provides any number of opportunities of service. The abject poverty, illiteracy, caste barriers, false sense of high and low, untouchability, exploitation, lack of medical facilities, etc., are, to name just a few, the social maladies which call for immediate corrective steps. The prime concern of the swayamsevaks all over the country is now for such service activities. At the Shakha level, a strong orientation is now given for this purpose.

It is but natural that in a self-oblivious society like ours the innate oneness and the fraternal bonds are the first casualty. As such, the poor, the illiterate and the weaker sections in the society become an easy prey for exploitation and conversion to other faiths. While the unsympathetic rich try to suck the blood of the poor, the crafty intelligent exploit the gullible. So, apart from rendering positive service, the swayamsevaks consider it equally important to combat such injustices, on behalf of the weaker sections. Militancy and intolerance become good traits when they are put to use for helping the innocent and the weak in the society. The Bharateeya Vanavasi Kalyan Ashram, the Grahak Panchayat, the BMS, the BKS (Bharateeya Kisan Sangh) etc., are all spearheading such movements for social justice whenever the need arises.

In a society divided on caste, class, and language lines, the greatest service from a social worker to his community will be to keep intact the very social fabric. The oneness of the society being an article of faith with the swayamsevak, it becomes all the more important for him to strive for social consolidation, especially when the self-seeking politicians try to drive a wedge between diverse groups for their own selfish ends, and anti-social elements take advantage of such sensitive situations. The unifying Hindu appeal generated by Sangh has always acted as a powerful antidote to the disintegrating pulls exercised by separatist elements, in many, a trying situation of conflicts born out of casteism, untouchability, and sectarianism. The Rashtriya Sikh Sangat, the Samajik Samarasata Manch of Maharashtra, the "Speak Samskrit" movement of Karnataka, and the like have been rendering yeoman service in this direction.

That the rubric of Dharma should be reflected in all facets of life is a founding principle of Sangh. A constant endeavor of Sangh and all its offshoots has been the propagation of Hindu values as the guiding principles in all sectors ranging from education to labour, sociology to economics.

Obsession with West-originated theories has resulted in blinkered vision in major knowledge-areas like history, science, technology, economies, administration, etc. Thus, mainstream economics as taught and practiced today is blissfully unaware of the fact that such nuances as real commodity prices were comprehensively dealt with by Shukracharya, Kautilya and other sages. The materialist approach, blindly copied from the West, has led the country downhill. While Independent Bharat started with a balance of Rs. 18,000 crores, the Bharat of 1992 is in debt to the tune of Rs. 4,00,000 crores. The so-called "industrial Revolution", supposed to have led to the prosperity of the West, was made possible from the post-Plassey loot from Bharat. With no such plundered capital, Bharat obviously could not reach the heights of material progress scaled in the West. This externally induced impoverishment has been used by the West to make Bharat a debtor country. However, what should cause greater concern is the culturally induced poverty in the psyche of the people through endlessly repeating "you are poor", "you are backward", and 'you are primitive".

A lasting solution to the economic crisis can come only from cultural rejuvenation and re-assertion of Hindu values such as reverence for man and nature, a non-acquisitive and non-exploitative life-pattern, recognizing mutuality rather than individual right as the basis of economy, voluntary austerity in consumption, and a premium on self-reliance. Sangh has been propagating this value-system based on self-knowledge and self-control, not merely because it is necessitated by the present state of the world, but even more basically because it is a source of individual joy, social harmony, cultural richness, spiritual advancement and universal peace.

The Sangh Methodology

Expressed in the simplest terms, the ideal of the Sangh is to carry the nation to the pinnacle of glory, through organizing the entire society and ensuring protection of Hindu Dharma.

Having identified this goal, the Sangh created a method of work in consonance with that ideal. Decades of functioning has confirmed that this is the most effective way of organizing the society. The Sangh's method of working is of the simplest kind, and there is hardly anything esoteric about it. Coming together, every day for an hour is the heart of the technique, and the Sangh has always grown only by personal contact. This is a self-contained mechanism; hence its success.

The daily Shakha is undoubtedly the most visible symbol of the Rashtriya Swayamsevak Sangh. The Shakha is as simple in its structure as it is grand in conception. No better example can be given to prove the truth of the adage that it takes a genius to simplify a mechanical tool, while even a third-rate engineer can complicate a simple mechanism! After nearly 100 years since the inception of the Sangh, people continue to express puzzlement as to how such a simple tool as the daily Shakha can produce idealists and patriots of such sterling worth, willing to dedicate all their energies and talents to the cause of the Motherland, willing even to shed their lives, if need be, to protect the honor of the Motherland. Herein lies the extraordinary vision, skill and foresight of Dr. Hedgewar, the founder of the Sangh.

The RSS took on several features of the Indian organizations such Bharat Swayamsevak Mandal, and Hindustani Seva dal, including a unique style of training recruits and a certain religiosity. However, these features were also reminiscent of older institutions such as the akharas and, at another move, of the Hindu sect.[4]

An ideological akhara, from its inception, the basic unit of the RSS has been the shakha (local branch), which, in the beginning, had a close affinity to the akharas. The term akhara designates a place where the young men of a locality gather daily for body-building, exercise and sports - mainly wrestling and weight-lifting. In this guise, the akhara retains a ritual dimension - even a spiritual one. It includes a temple - when not attached to one - that is generally dedicated to Hanuman; it is placed under the authority of a guru who instructs the members of the akhara in physical and mental discipline, giving them a certain balance (sanyam) that also implies abstinence. Members of an akhara are recruited from all social milieux and develop a strong collective attachment to it.

Before this model was reinterpreted by the RSS, many nationalists had already derived inspiration from it - ideologically and organizationally. The clearest such case was that of the Bengali secret societies, with which Hedgewar was so familiar. These organizations often practiced martial exercises with a religious overtone which found particular expression in the initiation ceremony: the members of the Anushilan Samiti took an oath of allegiance to the organization before an image of Kali, with the Bhagavad Gita in one hand and a revolver in the other, the presence of the goddess serving as a reminder that the movement drew its ethic of violence partly from the ritual of the Shakta sect. Furthermore, the structure of these groups, whose basic cell was a group centered around a dada (lit. 'big brother'), reproduced an important Hindu notion, namely the guru-shishya (master-disciple) relationship, where 'the disciple must render his total loyalty, devotion and respect to his teacher'. The spiritual dimension of the Anushilan-Samiti emerges from its very name since anushilan designates 'the fullest development of all faculties, physical and mental'. Its members kept up, as a means of self-discipline and preparation, the practice of physical culture and of sports such as lathiplay; this was often bound up with religious vows and with a cult of austerity and sexual abstinence drawn from the Hindu tradition of Brahmacharya.

Congress itself drew inspiration from the traditional akhara to develop prabhat pheris (drilling in groups, held each morning) that resembled akhara processions. These prabhat pheris, whose participants sometimes wore uniform and carried batons, were called upon to strengthen the Indian nation both physically and spiritually in the struggle for emancipation. It was in this same spirit that the akharas multiplied, especially between 1890-1910 and particularly in Bengal and Maharashtra, the two regions where, together with the Punjab, the extremist current flowed strongest and the terrorist societies were most active. In the 1920s, the Hindu Mahasabha called for an increase in the number of akharas to protect Hindus in the context of the Khilafat movement. In his presidential address in 1923, M.M. Malaviya recommended the building in each village and mohalla (urban quarter) of a small Hanuman temple and an akhara. Lajpat Rai, as President of the Hindu Mahasabha in 1925, added the formation of 'gymnasiums' to his movement's programme.

Both the political akharas and, subsequently, the RSS were distinguished from the traditional model by their ideological character and style of physical exercise. Physical training and wrestling between individuals gave way to games between opposing teams. This change reflected the influence of the British, for whom 'the development of a healthy body was not as important as playing games of conflict'. The shakha's physical training is 'unambiguously Western' because 'even stave training and other kinds of "Indian exercise" are regimented according to western standards of cadence, formation and discipline'. V.M. Sirsikar, who joined the RSS in 1933 at Nagpur, mentions that the Sunday parade was accompanied by a band playing English music (the orders for the drill were in English) and most of its practices, had been borrowed from the University Training Corps. Again, this phenomenon proceeded from the desire to imitate the cultural traits to which, it was considered, the British rulers owed their strength. As it was, the physical force of the latter had very quickly bred an inferiority complex among the Hindu intelligentsia, whom the British often regarded as puny and effeminate. Here was a clear example of the strategic emulation of which the RSS would be the inheritor. In the case of this organization, however, the process was deeper and more complex.

In the shakhas of the RSS, as in the first political akharas, participants trained in drill with the lathi (a long bamboo stave) and played team games such as kabaddi. Members - swayamsevaks – were selected in small numbers from among the youths attending the shakha. They then pledged to consecrate themselves to the RSS 'with [their] whole body, heart and money, for in it lies the betterment of Hindus and the country' This pledge was uttered before an effigy of Hanuman, who was already the presiding figure in the akharas of the region, where he was known as Maruti. Moreover, in the early years, swayamsevaks were enjoined to remain in their akharas, which multiplied in reaction to rioting, and to attend shakhas only once or twice a week for political education. Vasant Rao Oke, a Chitpavan Brahmin from Nagpur, who joined the RSS in 1927 and was later to occupy high office in the organization, remembers having been attracted to the movement because of the similarity of the atmosphere he found in the shakhas and in the akhara where he practiced every morning: 'I was attracted because I had a natural inclination to have a good physique, a healthy body, a healthy mind and healthy ideals'. Nana Deshmukh, another Maharashtrian, who joined the RSS in 1929 in Akola, and later became a leading figure in the Jana Sangh, points out that he had been going to an akhara, as had most Maharashtrian males, since childhood, but differentiates the two: 'Akhara is for physical strength, shakha for the national cause'. Programmes may be the same but the objectives make the difference. Dr Hedgewar said "Go to the akharas, but come to the shakhas also." Akharas concentrated on physical fitness and shakhas on cultivation of the mind. The physical and intellectual dimensions were gradually integrated as shakhas became a daily occurrence: meetings were held either in the morning or evening and lasted for about one hour.

The resemblance of the RSS to the akhara is only formal, given the ideological overtone of the former. However, it tended to raise Hedgewar, as its founder, to the status of a guru, so much so that from 1927, he subjected his young recruits to weekly sessions of baudhik (ideological education), consisting of simple questions to the novices concerning the Hindu nation, its history and heroes, especially Shivaji. Hedgewar nevertheless refused, as he said repeatedly, to become one of the numerous gurus who sow divisions in Hinduism, and it was only in 1929 that he took the title of sarsanghchalak (supreme leader), a decision that is analyzed below. The true guru to whom he demanded that obeisance be paid was the saffron flag of Shivaji, the Bhagwa Dwaj. Even today, the daily session of the shakhas opens with the volunteers saluting the flag. They are also called upon to render to it each year a guru dakshina which is supposed to finance the movement, and is so named in reference to the traditional offering made by a pupil to his master in recognition of his teaching.

This ceremony occurs in a cycle of six annual festivals which often coincides with those observed in Hindu society, and which Hedgewar inscribed in the ritual calendar of his movement: Varsha Pratipada (the Hindu new year), Shivajirajyarohonastava (the coronation of Shivaji), guru dakshina, Raksha Bandhan (a North Indian festival in which sisters tie ribbons round the wrists of their brothers to remind them of their duty as protectors, a ritual which the RSS has re-interpreted in such a way that the leader of the shakha ties a ribbon around the pole of the saffron flag, after which swayamsevaks carry out this ritual for one another as a mark of brotherhood), Dasahara (when swayamsevaks pay homage to arms), and Makarsankraman (celebrated at the moment when the sun enters Capricorn - in January - to promote the forces of prosperity).

The world-renouncer as an activist. As well as its ritual aspect, the resemblance of the RSS to a religious institution is a function of its emphasis on the merits of renunciation and its social characteristics. In 1927, Hedgewar organized an Officers' Training Camp (OTC) with the task of forming a corps of pracharaks (lit. 'preachers') to constitute the backbone of the RSS. Hedgewar called on the pracharaks to become sadhus first. Following his example, even today these cadres renounce their professions and generally remain celibate in order to devote themselves to the mission of regenerating the Hindu community. They live an austere life of total devotion to the cause, one which professes to be a form of karma yoga, the yoga of action. While karma yoga is expounded in the Bhagavad Gita, where it is described as a matter of inner sacrifice (action, even when it is violent, can constitute a means of renunciation when it is undertaken without regard to personal advantage and in the service of Dharma). Hedgewar embraced this doctrine after it had been re-interpreted by militant nationalists, such as Aurobindo, who were close to the Bengali secret societies. In the RSS, one of the usual ways of honoring pracharaks when they die has been to designate them as Karma Yogis, following the model established by Hedgewar.[5]

Shakha Schedule: Cultivating Continuity, Conviction and Conformity Golwalkar's description of a shakha schedule is worth quoting:

There is an open playground. Under a saffron flag groups of youths and boys are absorbed in a variety of Bharatiya games. Resounding shouts of joyous enthusiasm fill the air. When the rows are assembled, the "bhagwa dhwaj" is hoisted. Then, swayamsevaks offer pranam (salute) to the flag by raising the right hand to the chest, palm parallel to the ground, head down. After the roll call, the swayamsevaks assemble in different areas of the field in gatas or groups. Then starts the sharirik (physical training); the shikshak, assisted by the gatanayak, teach games, Surya pranam, asanas and other yogic exercises. The swayamsevaks play a number of Indian games, the most popular being kabaddi. The sight of the daring young men pressing forward with the cry 'Kabaddi Kabaddi' on their lips thrills the heart. The leader's whistle or order has a magical effect on them; there is instant perfect order or silence. Then, exercises follow - wielding the lathi, Surya namaskar, marching, etc. The spirit of collective effort and spontaneous discipline pervades every programme. They also learn 'defensive' skills in the use of the lathi. The mukhya shikshak blows a whistle after about an hour, to mark the end of the sharirik programme. Then they sit down and sing in chorus songs charged with patriotism. Discussions follow. They delve deep into the problems affecting the national life.

The games are just not meant to build a spirit of cooperation, they also intend to make the swayamsevaks braver and more courageous vis-a-vis opponents. The psychological aspect is no less important than the physical. It is also interesting to note that the leader efficiently integrates both play on the one hand, and authority and discipline on the other.

After the session of physical exercise, the members sit in a circle for discussion. As the RSS claims to aim at 'character-building' and 'man-moulding', the themes of the topics relate to the attributes of 'good' character, e.g., fidelity, fortitude, honesty, hard work, obedience and respect to superiors, personal discipline, etc. But the main thrust is on the ideology of the RSS; the themes of the discussion focus on various aspects of Hindu Rashtra--the plight of Hindus in India and the need for unity among Hindus, etc. The stories on some hero or heroic event in the history of Hindu India are narrated to the swayamsevaks. Occasionally, patriotic songs are sung, glorifying Hindu warriors and heroes or venerating Bharat Mata.

Finally, the swayamsevaks again assemble in rows before the flag to recite the Sangh prayer (prarthana)—Namaste sada vatsale Matrubhume (Salutations to thee oh loving Motherland!). This is followed by the shouting of slogans like Bharat Mata ki Jai (Victory to Mother India) and the shakha comes to an end.

This, in outline, is the Shakha of RSS. The participants are the "Sangh Swayamsevaks".

The Shakha is the most effective and time-tested instrument for the moulding of men on patriotic lines - outreaching by far its physical dimension.The Shakha process is further strengthened by graded training-camps celled "Sangha Shiksha Varga" at provincial and all-Bharat level, at regular intervals.

Meaning of the RSS Prarthana (Namaste sada vatsale Matru Bhoome)

Forever I bow to thee, O Loving Motherland! O Motherland of us Hindus, Thou hast brought me up in happiness. May my life, O great and blessed Holy Land, be laid down in Thy Cause. I bow to Thee again and again.

We the children of the Hindu Nation bow to Thee in reverence, O Almighty God. We have girded up our loins to carry on Thy work. Give us Thy holy blessings for its fulfilment. O Lord! Grant us such might as no power on earth can ever challenge, such purity of character as would command the respect of the whole world and such knowledge as would make easy the thorny path that we have voluntarily chosen.

May we be inspired with the spirit of stern heroism, that is sole and ultimate means of attaining the highest spiritual bliss with the greatest temporal prosperity. May intense and everlasting devotion to our ideal ever enthuse our hearts. May our victorious organised power of action, by Thy Grace, be wholly capable of protecting our dharma and leading this nation of ours to the highest pinnacle of glory.॥ भारत माता की जय ॥

Then, the members disperse after Shakha and have an informal chat. Later, some of them visit the sick and those absent. [6]

The Ekatmata Stotra

(Om sacchidanandrupay Namostu Paramatmane), a collection of 33 verses, is recited in all sangh offices. It is a record of all who distinguished themselves in their service for India. It is a tribute that covers thousands of years of history - Kings, queens, warriors, saints, scholars, philosophers, artists, musicions, poets and all the hallowed geographical sites of India. It is a daily remembrance through which attachment to the nation is instilled. Ekatmata mantra and the mealtime prayer are key elements in daily life of a Swayamsevak. Our social systems are founded on our holistic, spiritual, interconnected Hindu Vision where the standard of life is not determined by economic parameters only, but by one's life values and quality of life.

Hindutva's "Sattva" is augmented by establishing a social value system promoting simple

living, moderate spending, and relinquishment, despite abundance of resources, having socio-centric, multi power centred social systems helps protect Hindutva's "swatva", facilititating the influence of the holistic Hindu world view "satya", bringing happiness and betterment to everyone throughout the world.

"Sarve bhavantu sukhinah sarve santu Niraamayaah

Sarve bhadraani pashyanthu Maa kashchit Duhkhabhagbhavet

Om Shanthi Shanthi Shantih"

May all beings be happy and prosperous, may all remain free from illness. May all see what is auspicious. May no one suffer. Om Peace peace peace. [7]

A few special baudhiks are arranged every month, usually in the evenings. These are mainly the background sessions to acquaint the teachers with issues to be discussed at the shakhas. Occasionally, these meetings are utilized to explain policy-decisions made at central and state levels, to seek opinions on political and social issues, or to draw the attention of the swayamsevaks to major organizational and ideological problems of the RSS.

Golwalkar refers to the activities of a shakha as sadhana. An ideal swayamsevak is expected to practice sadhana in the shakha every day. The purpose of the shakha, as explained by one RSS leader, is "two-fold: continuity and conviction." Regular attendance is a sacred routine of the ideal swayamsevak. He is excused only if he is either ill or has gone out. It gradually becomes a habit for the member to come to the shakha daily. Golwalkar describes a parable on the techniques of habit formation. A rich man, seeing a beautiful peacock in his garden one day, gave it some opium mixed with food. The peacock started coming everyday, and eventually got so habituated that it used to come regularly at that hour, even without the opium. Golwalkar identified three factors in this technique of habit formation: first, constant meditation of the ideal that is to be formed into a samskar, second, constant company of persons devoted to the same ideal; and third, engaging the body in activities congenial to that ideal. Shakhas, therefore, orient the body, the mind, and the immediate surroundings on identical lines.

Golwalkar rightly mentions that the shakha is the 'living practice of principles' and not a bundle of dry preaching. It is described as a process of loka sangraha (collecting the people), loka samparka (mass communication), loka samskara (inculcation of a new spirit), and loka niyojan (deployment of the people). The main purpose of the shakha is to instil in its members the spirit of cohesion, discipline, reverence to organizational authority, and ideological conformity.

Cultural nationalism is nationalism in which the nation is defined by a shared culture and a common language, rather than on the concepts of common ancestry or race. Cultural nationalism is the realization of a nation's identity, history and destiny based on a shared culture. If political nationalism is focused on the achievement of political autonomy, cultural nationalism is focused on the cultivation of a Nation. And since cultivation is a process, the ultimate goal of cultural nationalism is further enrichment of that shared culture of ideas and values. For instance, the cultural nationalism evident in our country is a desirable blending of our rich ancient past, of our common history and certainly of our vision of a bright future of our country. Dismissing the very notion of territorial nationalism, Guruji provides insights into his definition of cultural nationalism in India, and its inherent relation to Hindu civilization. To understand the ideas of any philosopher, Guruji, Hegdewar or even Savarkar in this context, one must shed preconceived notions of morality and consider the circumstantial and contextual references that define a thinker's outlook.Cultural Nationalism as an ideology had votaries even before the formation of RSS - Aurobindo Ghose, Bala Ganagadhar Tilak, Bipin Chandra Pal, Lala Lajpat Rai, M.M. Malviya and others. Those who laid the foundation for the RSS understood that at the time of India's independence consolidating a national identity was critical to protecting the country's newfound sovereignty. It was only natural to them that such an identity be based on the cultural fabric that for many centuries defined ancient India. Whether this fabric was inclusive (or secular) in its outer appearance was inconsequential, as for the very nature of Dharmic (Hindu) thought has been that of non-discrimination and inclusion.

Naturally, perversions to these ideas have occurred: does Hindu Rashtra mean no place for religious minorities, do those with opposing views have no place within the cultural ethos of our nation? Answers to these questions lie again in the fact that Hindu dharma was built on far greater truths of inclusion and acceptance than any other known body of thinking. Dissent is a way of not only allowing for a broad range of views to be accommodated, but also for the expansion of the Hindu way of thinking. Those who truly and genuinely want to criticize, learn and better, this cultural ethos that exists in the country do so with respect and reverence. In return, Hindu Dharma, and therefore our culture, adapt to these course corrections while always nurturing core beliefs.

The organisation above men

RSS volunteers have been dedicated more to an organisation than to one man. In November 1929, the RSS adopted the principle of ekchalak anuvartita (following one leader), and Hedgewar was then appointed sarsanghchalak for life; even so, the organisation remained supreme, and interestingly, his death in 1940 did not affect it.

The routine activities of the RSS are specified and governed by a comprehensive framework of rules, whose strict application ensures that it's intermediate and local units can function without day-to-day guidance from its central authorities. At each level of the organization, the supervision of the prescribed procedures is the responsibility of particular officers, such as the mukhya shikshaks and, most importantly, the pracharaks. The coping stone of this hierarchy is the sarsanghchalak. Charisma is not the basis of his authority. The incumbents of this office are not seen as indispensable and when a new sarsanghchalak is appointed, the basic framework of the organisation is unaffected.

Hedgewar nominated Golwalkar as his successor in 1940, and Golwalkar nominated Deoras as his in 1973, but on neither occasion was it necessary for the new sarsanghchalak to win support from the members of the RSS by presenting himself and his ideas to them. Their legitimacy was derived from the very procedure of nomination, much in the way that the succession of gurus at the head of a sect is endorsed. The cult of personality, which undoubtedly exists within the RSS, is focused on the office rather than the incumbent, who is seen only as the guardian of a wider mission which is beyond the scope of any one individual.

The cohesion of the RSS derives more from its members' respect for a shared ideology than from loyalty to particular individuals, who may hold high office in the organisation. This ideologically based cohesion coincides with a devaluation of individuality in the RSS; the 'new man' must sacrifice his personality to the cause. In 1991, the pracharak of Shivpuri pointed out: 'If there is a position of myself, then it is a wrong process. There must be position of Bhagwa Dwaj, Hindu Rashtra and Bharat Mata. There is no man [in the RSS], but everything is based on men. The fact that the RSS organisation is above men and in particular that the movement does not rely on the authority of a supreme leader, differentiates it from fascist groups.'

The difficulty of using the concept of 'fascism' in the case of the RSS has also been attributed to other aspects of the 'sectarian' dimension that we studied in the previous section. It was recently pointed out by authors not known for their Hindu nationalist sympathies that 'The RSS exaltation of the ascetic model (segregation of shakhas, celibacy of sarsanghchalaks and of most pracharaks and pracharikas) marks an important distinction between itself and other similar patterns for youth organisation. The fascists and the Nazi youth fronts had inculcated a hard macho attitude and an aggressive male sexuality.'

To sum up: since a characteristic of the RSS's Hindu nationalism has been to down-play the role of the state, we cannot classify it straightforwardly as a fascist movement. As distinct from Nazism, the RSS's ideology treats society as an organism with a secular spirit, which is implanted not so much in the race as in a sociocultural system, and which will be regenerated over the course of time by patient work at the grassroots. Finally, in contrast to both Italian fascism and Nazism, the RSS does not rely on the central figure of the leader. Nonetheless, the RSS can be classed as authoritarian in its emphasis on discipline, and in its intention of reforming the Hindu mentality absolutely to prepare the advent of a new man, implying the need to extend the sway of the organisation over the whole of society. [8]

Unique Brotherhood

The shakhas create and cultivate a unique brotherhood among the swayamsevaks. The common observation of rituals and common participation in the physical activities and discussions, a common uniform, the choice of a common set of vocabulary, are all designed to enhance a sense of community and brotherhood. The success of the shakhas largely depends on the extent of brotherhood and kinship they create and sustain among the swayamsevaks. If a swayamsevak does not attend the shakha, the adhikaris (office-bearers) and other members visit his house to find out the reason. In case a swayamsevak is ill, his fellow members of the shakha show necessary concern and care. Even in case of the illness of the family members of a swayamsevak, the organization extends possible help. This humane approach has strengthened the RSS kinship further. While concern for fellow-beings has become a casualty under the pressure of modernization, the RSS has successfully maintained a unique brotherhood among its members. This is one of the main reasons for the growing popularity of the RSS.

The RSS is organized in a hierarchical order: local, district, provincial and all-India bodies. Above the shakha, in the pyramid of authority is the mandal committee, which is composed of representatives from the shakhas of the given locality. Representatives from mandals form a nagar (city) committee. The city committee is very important as most of the day-to-day work takes place at this level. The city committee consists of a sanghchalak, a karyavah and heads of the departments of physical training (sharirik), intellectual training (boudhik), recruitment (sampark), finance (nidhi) and service (seva). The committee meets weekly. The decisions taken along with the orders received from above are transmitted down to the mandal through the karyavah (secretary). The mukhya shikshak and the local pracharak pass on orders and information to the swayamsevaks, the lowest level of the communications circuit. Next to the city committees there may be zilla (district) and vibhag (regional) committees. Above this structure are state and national assemblies.

Provincial

The Prantiya Pratinidhi Sabhas (state assemblies) are deliberative bodies, but exercise no real power. According to the RSS constitution, the sabha consists of one elected delegate for every fifty swayamsevaks entitled to vote. The prant sanghchalak is elected by the state assembly, and he, in consultation with the prant pracharak appoints lower level office bearers. In fact, the sanghchalak, who is the constitutional head at each level, with few exceptions, enjoys little power over the day-to-day activities of the RSS. He is usually an older influential notable, whose participation gives the RSS an aura of respectability as well as important contacts. It is not uncommon for a sanghchalak to have no prior personal experience in RSS activities.[9]

Sangh in independence movement:

Despite strict non-involvement of the RSS in political movements directly, the Sangh was ready to help any political movement indirectly by supplying its cadre and allowing it to give their faculties and facilities, provided it worked for the cause of India's welfare. Trailokyanath Chakravarty (1889–1970) was a Bengali revolutionary and freedom fighter. He met Dr Hedgewar, who promised him that Sangh would provide him with cadre for the future revolution he was planning (Satyavrata Ghosh, Remembering our revolutionaries, Marxist Study Forum, 1994, p.57). Sangh also helped Rajguru when the revolutionary lived underground.

Those in the Congress, who could not rise above the pettiness of sectarian politics had passed the resolution in 1934 that their members could not join the RSS. Eminent historian, Dr.

Kanchanmoy Mojumdar reveals that four years after the resolution of the Congress against the RSS, 'Bose reportedly sent emissaries to Hedgewar in 1939, perhaps seeking his help for an armed uprising.'

The British Intelligence reported that on 27 April 1942, at the training camp of the RSS at Pune, 'Golwalkar condemned those who were selfishly helping the British Government.' On 28 April 1942, he declared that the Sangh has resolved to do its duty even if the whole world goes against it, and impressed on the volunteers that they must be ready to sacrifice their lives for the cause of the country (No. D. Home Pol. (Intelligence) Section F. No. 28 Pol).

Another report of the Home Department, Pol. F. No. 28/3/43-Pol (I) shows the anti-British nature prevailing at the RSS camp at Jubbalpore, where a speaker proclaimed that the aim of the Sangh was to drive the British out of India and the sentiment was repeated by other speakers.

On 16 August 1942, at Chimur in Maharashtra, many RSS workers participated directly in a Quit India agitation which resulted in a brutal suppression by the British. Dada Naik, who was also the head of the Chimur RSS branch, was sentenced to death by the British. The Hindu Mahasabha leader, Dr. N B Khare took up his case with the authorities. Ramdas Rampure, another RSS cadre, was shot dead by the British.

Confidential reports blamed two persons for these uprisings. One was Dada Naik, who, the report said, 'was largely behind the recent disturbances', and the other was Sant Tukdoji Maharaj, who was closely associated with the RSS, and was suspected to have been involved in disturbances at Chimur. Later, Sant Tukdoji Maharaj became one of the co-founders of the Vishva Hindu Parishad (VHP). A report of the CP & Berar Police stated that Hedgewar's participation had invigorated the movement, leading to the first order against the RSS. A report of the Home Department stated, "Of late, the Sangh has started taking interest in political movements of the country, as a result of which the CP government in their circular letter No 2352-2158 IV; dated 15/16 December 1932, was compelled to issue an order warning government servants of the communal and political nature of the Sangh, and forbidding their becoming members or participating in the organisation's activities."

The ban was challenged in the provincial legislature of CP. The government was isolated. The House leader, Raghvendra Rao, when asked about any complaints from the Muslims against the RSS, admitted that there were none. MS Rahman and other members praised the RSS, and the government was forced to withdraw its circular.

When the 2nd World War broke out, the RSS refused to support the government inviting its wrath once again. In June 1939, the Home Department asked the Central Provinces government to ban the RSS using Section 16 of the Criminal Law Amendment Act. When the provincial Chief Secretary, GM Trivedi, insisted that it was not feasible, it resorted to another trick. A new ordinance under the Defence of India Rules was promulgated, prohibiting drills and uniforms. The obvious target was the RSS. Hundreds of RSS volunteers courted arrest against the order.

Quit India was an important, but hastily planned movement. The RSS cadres had dominated the Congress protests during the movement in places where they were strong. In Chimur and Ashti tehsils of CP, the police brutality on RSS volunteers had resulted in killing some while many were sent to jail.

Many in the RSS had their sympathies with Subhash Bose's Indian National Army increasing government's suspicion that together they might incite a revolt in the British Army. A report warned that RSS volunteers had "infiltrated into various departments of the government such as the army, navy, post & telegraphs, railways and administrative services, so that there may be no difficulty in capturing administrative departments when the time comes". It further stated that "the organisation is intensely anti-British, and its tone is increasingly becoming militant."

Orders were issued for banning camps. A Home Department official, GA Ahmed, noted on December 13, 1943, that "This will hit the RSS most". The training camps were raided, and cadres arrested.

Support for Quit India Movement on Principles Set by Dr. Hedgewar

After due discussions with his young colleagues, Golwalkar decided that, "The agitation is being conducted for the freedom of the country. Therefore, swayamsevaks, as citizens, can take part in this agitation in whichever part of the country they are. But, as an organisation, Sangh will keep working for national cause that is organising the society; without getting involved in the agitation directly." This was in line with Dr. Hedgewar's direction during 1930 satyagraha - to work as a common citizen rather than project RSS, as a separate organisation.

Sangh, thus, asked swayamsevaks to take part in this national struggle and extend whole-hearted co-operation to it as patriotic citizens. As a result, many swayamsevaks jumped into this battle and took part in it to the best of their abilities as common citizens.

Rajju Bhaiyya corroborates the Sangh support to 1942 and participation of its swayamsevaks in it - "Sangh told that anybody who wishes to take part in this movement should do it in his personal capacity. It should try to help Congress in every possible way that was looking after Hindu society's interest and also work hard to expand Sangh work at high velocity."

Vidarbha region had strong RSS network. Naturally, the most fierce agitations took place in Bali (Amravati), Ashti (Wardha), and Chimur (Chandrapur). News about Chimur agitation was broadcast from Berlin Radio. This agitation was led by Uddhavrao Korekar of Congress; RSS leaders Dada Naik, Baburao Begade and Annaji. A young Swayamsevak, Balaji Raipurkar was killed brutally in police firing when he was trying to raise the flag to the top. Sangh swayamsevaks took part in Chimur agitation in 1943 alongwith Congress, and Tukdoji Maharaj led Shri Gurudev Seva Mandal.

This encounter became famous in the history of this movement as 'Chimur Ashti episode'. RSS swayamsevaks had established a parallel government in Chimur. 125 satyagrahis were put on trial and handed imprisonment, and thousands of swayamsevaks were imprisoned. Dada Naik was head of RSS Chimur branch. He was sentenced to death. Hindu Mahasabha leader, Dr. N.B. Khare, a member of British Viceroy Council, took up his case with the authorities and got the sentence commuted to imprisonment. Later, Sant Tukdoji Maharaj became one of the co-founders of the Vishwa Hindu Parishad.

There was the heroic story of Hemu Kalani of Sakkhar town in Sindh. He was busy removing fishplates from the railway tracks with his colleagues. Their objective was to frustrate the plans to move forces to suppress the struggle in various areas. Unfortunately, Hemu was arrested while his friends managed to escape the police net. Hemu was given death sentence by the Army Court in 1943. Sindhi brethren in Mumbai celebrate the memory of martyr Hemu Kalani to this day. He has a memorial in his name constructed by local Sindhi swayamsevaks and maintained by 'Hemu Kalani Yadgaar Mandal'. This story is also recounted by late Gobind Motwani in his book '9 years of RSS in Sindh - 1939-1947'. Hemu Kalani remains an unsung hero of freedom struggle because Pakistanis won't recognise him as he was a Hindu, while Indian historians won't recognise his contribution probably because he was a swayamsevak. This writer has visited the memorial and has been fortunate to meet many veteran Sindhis in Mumbai who are witness to those days in Sindh, and still active in RSS.

Swayamsevaks plunged into Quit India agitation wherever they were in India and were imprisoned in many places. Some of the well-known senior swayamsevaks were Dr. Anna Saheb Deshpande (Aarvi, Vidarbh), Ramakant Keshav (Babasaheb) Deshpande in Jashpur (Chhattisgarh), who went on to establish Vanvasi Kalyan Ashram, Shri Vasantrao Oak (Prant pracharak of Delhi), Narayan Singh known as Babuaji in Bihar, who later became Bihar Sanghchaalak, and Shri Chandrakant Bhardwaj (who received bullet in his foot that couldn't be removed). Bhardwaj became a famous poet and wrote many poems sung in RSS. There were Madhavrao in East U.P., who became Prant pracharak later and Dattatreya Gangadhar (aka Bhaiyyaji) Kasture who too became a pracharak later.

On 11th August 1942, Patna saw a successful attempt by young boys to hoist the Tricolour flag on the government secretariat. Six agitators were felled by police firing. Of these six, two - Devipad Chaudhary and Jagatpati Kumar were swayamsevaks. The first Sanghchaalak of Bihar, Babua Ji and

senior journalist Krishnakant Ojha confirmed their RSS connection. A felicitation programme to honour them was organised during 50th anniversary celebrations of Independence in 1997 under the Chairmanship of renowned litterateur and revolutionary Shri Vachnesh Tripathi in the presence of the then regional pracharak, now Sarsanghchaalak, Dr. Mohan Bhagwat. Their kin too were invited in the programme. There are many swayamsevaks in Bihar, who were awarded 'Tamra Patras' as freedom fighters of 1942. Prof. Rajendra Singh (4th Sarsanghachalak), too, is known for having taken part in Quit India. Kailashpati Mishra took part in the Quit India Movement in 1942 and was arrested for the same. While studying in class X, Mishra was arrested for picketing at the main gate of his school at Buxar in support of 1942 Quit India Movement. Till independence, every swayamsevak had to take a pledge with the words 'Desh ko swatantra kar' (free the country). [10]

Safe Houses for Underground Leaders

During 1942, oppression by British was in full force. Therefore, people were uneasy about giving shelter to senior underground Congress leaders. At that time, senior high-profile RSS leaders helped the underground leaders of the movement by providing them safe houses.

House of Sanghchaalak of North-West Lala Hansraj was the secret place of stay for Aruna Asaf Ali and Jayaprakash Narayan. She spoke about it in an interview published in Hindi daily 'Hindustan' in August 1967. She said, "I was underground in 1942 agitation, Delhi Sanghchaalak Lala Hansraj provided me refuge in his house for 10-15 days and arranged for my complete safety. He saw to it that nobody got information about my stay at his house. Since underground workers should not stay for long at the same place, I moved out of his house dancing 'Bhangra' in an embroidered ghagra and chunari in a baraat (marriage procession). This dress was given to me by Lalaji's wife. When I went to return it in due course, she refused to take it back, saying, keep it with our best wishes as our gift to you."

"Famous Vedic scholar Pandit Shripad Damodar Satavalekar was the Sanghchaalak of Aundh. He had given asylum for many days to the revolutionary underground leader Nana Patil who had experimented with the novel idea 'Patri Sarkaar' during this agitation. Nana Patil's colleague Kisanveer had stayed at the house of Satara Sanghchaalak in Wai while working underground there. Famous socialist leader Achyutrao Patwardhan had stayed at many Sangh swayamsevaks' homes when he was working underground and changed places according to circumstances. Not only had these people, but even the life-long bitter critic of Sangh and a follower of Gandhiji, Sane Guruji used to stay secretly in Pune Sanghchaalak Bhausaheb Deshmukh's house."

A very senior RSS leader shared the story of a swayamsevak, Shri Padsalgikar, who was asked by the state Sanghchaalak Kashinath Pant Limaye to help Vasantdada Patil escape from prison in Sangli. He waited at the spot where Vasantdada reached after breaking out of the jail at 12 in the night. He carried him on his shoulders across fields, nullahs and jungles as all the roads and even village lanes were under police watch. He dropped him off at Vishram Bagh railway station at 2 a.m. so he could catch a train and move out of that area. Padsalgikar, who was a wrestler, went on to become the Vice-President of State Kustigir Parishad. He had narrated this story to Dr. Mohan Bhagwat's father at his home, when Mohanji was a child. Later, Dr. Mohan Bhagwat, Sarkaryavaah then, met him twice in Sangli and reconfirmed this incident. There could be scores of such incidents that were never recorded or documented. Since RSS was not keen on documenting or publicising its work as a policy, such inspiring stories are not known outside the local circles. RSS played an important role during the Partition days, which hasn't been discussed much. In the run-up to India being divided, the RSS realised the need to prepare Hindus and Sikhs of undivided Punjab to face the inevitable that had been imposed on them. The second sarsanghchalak (chief), M.S. Golwalkar, Babasaheb Apte, and Balasaheb Deoras, extensively toured the country in the months before Partition.

Golwalkar went to Sialkot and Montgomery after touring Multan in 1946-1947. He entered Sindh from Punjab. The province of Sindh had around 80 shakhas at that time. There were 52 pracharaks that included Lal Krishna Advani.

To implement the plan to Partition India, the British government had divided the army and the police on the basis of religion, a few months prior to the final act.

Thus, areas falling under Sindh, West Pakistan, and East Bengal were put under the command of a Muslim-dominated army-police combine. The Hindus in these areas were on tenterhooks. They were sitting on a powder keg with no one to be their saviours.

Golwalkar took the initiative to reach out to these Hindus and set up the Punjab Relief Committee and the Hindu Sahayata Samiti (Hindu Support Committee). The centre of activity for both of these was initially Lahore. The Punjab state sanghchalak, Raibahadur Badridas, was the chairman and Dr. Gokulchand Narang was the treasurer of these committees. When the entire Punjab was on fire and Congress leaders were sitting helplessly in Delhi, at that time, volunteers of RSS saved the people of Punjab with their discipline, and physical strength, risking their own lives. Partition Days — the fiery saga of RSS, published in 2002, wrote that initially, three RSS pracharaks were sent to Punjab in the mid-1930s, and, within the span of a decade, the RSS had more than 100 pracharaks working in undivided Punjab, with 58 of them coming from Lahore itself.

There were more than 1,500 RSS daily shakhas with a daily attendance of more than one lakh swayamsevaks in undivided Punjab. The three pracharaks who were sent initially from Nagpur to Punjab were K.D. Joshi, Digambar Paturkar, and Moreshwar Moonje.

The RSS activities got a big fillip when Madhav Rao Muley was appointed as the prant pracharak in Punjab around 1940.

It was due to its strong organisational strength in Punjab that RSS was able to save Hindus and Sikhs from communal violence and bring them safely to India. When Government was finding it extremely difficult to stop the bloodshed, it was the RSS that helped organise over 3,000 relief camps for the refugees from Pakistan. As communal frenzy engulfed, the country in the wake of the Partition, the RSS plunged into action saving and safely transporting the Hindus and Sikhs in Pakistan to the Indian side. Golwalkar issued directions to the volunteers that they should leave the villages only after the last of the Hindu and Sikh citizens was escorted out to safety. Many volunteers sacrificed their lives in the process. This also busts the myth that the RSS was an organisation that was mainly supported by Brahmins in Maharashtra, as by 1947, it had reached almost every district from Delhi to Peshawar, involving all sections of the society.

In 1934, when Gandhiji visited a 1500 - strong Swayamsevaks camp at Wardha, he was pleasantly surprised to find that the Swayamsevaks were not even aware of the castes of one another, not to speak of any ideas of untouchability. The incident had left such a deep impression on Gandhiji's mind that he referred to it a full thirteen years later. In his address to the workers of Sangh in Bhangi Colony at Delhi on 16th September 1947, he said, "I visited the RSS camp years ago, when the founder Shri Hedgewar was alive. I was very much impressed by your discipline, the complete absence of untouchability and the rigorous simplicity. Since then the Sangh has grown. I am convinced that any organisation which is inspired by the high ideal of service and self-sacrifice is bound to grow in strength." (The Hindu: 17th September 1947)

When Gandhi came to the refugee camps in Delhi teeming with hapless millions, he was impressed by the work of the RSS volunteers. He called the RSS "a well-organised and well-disciplined body". In the committee formed under Maulana Azad's chairmanship to restore sanity and harmony, leaders of the RSS were also invited to join. India's freedom is the result of the efforts of many such forces.

It would be a good to quote an episode that took place approximately six years later in 1948. Congress committee member of Solapur, Ganesh Bapuji Shinkar took part in the satyagraha to press for the removal of ban on Sangh. He had resigned from Congress on grounds of democratic ethics before joining the satyagraha. He issued a statement clarifying his stand and it was published on 12th December, 1948. He says, "I had participated in Bharat Chhodo (Quit India) movement in 1942. Capitalist and agrarian community was scared of the government at that time. Therefore, we were not offered safe havens in their homes. We had to stay in Sangh workers' homes to work underground. People from Sangh used to help us happily with our underground work. They also took care of all our requirements. Not only this, if someone from amongst us fell sick, Sangh swayamsevak doctors used to treat us. Sangh swayamsevaks, who were advocates, used to fight our cases fearlessly. Their patriotism and value-based living were undisputable."

Sardar Vallabhai Patel, the first Deputy Prime Minister and Home Minister of India, said in early January 1948 that the RSS activists were "patriots who love their country". He asked the Congressmen to 'win over' the RSS by love, instead of trying to 'crush' them. He also appealed to the RSS to join the Congress instead of opposing it, this attitude of Patel can be partly explained by the assistance the RSS gave the Indian administration in maintaining public order in September 1947, and that his expression of 'qualified sympathy' towards RSS reflected the long-standing inclination of several Hindu traditionalists in Congress. However, after Gandhi's assassination on 30 January 1948, Patel changed his view of RSS. In his reply letter to Golwalkar on 11 September 1948, regarding the lifting of ban on RSS, Patel stated that though RSS did service to the Hindu society by helping and protecting the Hindus when in need during partition violence. Patel was also apprehensive of the secrecy in the working manner of RSS.

India's first Prime Minister Jawaharlal Nehru had been vigilant towards RSS since he had taken charge. When Golwalkar wrote to Nehru asking for the lifting of the ban on RSS after Gandhi's assassination, Nehru replied in his letter to the heads of provincial governments in December 1947. Nehru wrote that "we have a great deal of evidence to show that RSS is an organisation which is in the nature of a private army and which is definitely proceeding on the strictest Nazi lines, even following the techniques of the organisation". Nehru tactically used anti-Rssism to consolidate his position in the party and government, it was a tool for him to malign those who differed. His targets included Purushottam Das Tandon, and Govind Ballabh Pant.Nehru rebuked S. Radhakrishnan for addressing a RSS rally at Rewa, and Mukund Malviya, Son of M.M.Malviya for attending a RSS programme.[11]

Sardar Patel, in a letter to Shri Golwalkar, admitted that the RSS undoubtedly served the Hindu society in times of crisis. He said that in such areas where their help was needed, the youths of Sangh protected the women and the children and did a lot for them. But, he expressed his belief that the Sangh-men can do their patriotic works only in association with the Congress.

This admission is contained in the first Home Minister Sardar Patel's reply to the letter that the then Sarsanghchalak Shri Golwalkar wrote him on August 11, 1948.

The weekly `Aakashvani' Journal published from Jalandhar carried a press statement by K. M. Munshi in its issue of October 2, 1949 (p. 6-7). In it Munshi praised the Swayamsevaks of the Sangh and said that during the adverse time of country's partition the young men of Sangh showed unparalleled bravery in Punjab and Sindh. They fought with the tyrant and saved the honour and lives of thousands of women and children. Many of these youngmen layed down their lives in this task.

Manikchandra Vajpayee and Sridhar Paradkar have mentioned in detail these two incidents in their seminal work, 'Partition Days: The Fiery Saga of RSS'. The first attack came on the night of 6 March 1947.

"It was a terrible night of March 6. A formidable, organized mob of Muslims led by National Guards in their uniform was advancing from Sherawala Gate to Chowk Fawara in Amritsar. This time their target was the well-known Krishna Textile market and sacred Darbar Sahib (Golden Temple). But...the moment they reached Chowk Fawara, they saw Swayamsevaks in Khaki shorts,they had taken such fright of the swayamsevaks' that they ran away. Thus, the victory under the leadership of brave swayamsevaks saved both the Krishna market and Darbar Sahib from destruction," Vajpayee and Paradkar wrote.

The RSS posted 75 swayamsevaks (the complete list with names and addresses is available in the appendix of 'Partition Days: The Fiery Saga of RSS') to safeguard the Darbar Sahib at all times from any further onslaught. The RSS' operations to protect the Darbar Sahib were primarily led by Dr Baldev Prakash, the then chief of RSS' evening shakhas in Amritsar, along with the town pracharak (full time worker), Dr Indrapal, and Goverdhan Chopra, incharge of morning shakhas in Amritsar.

The second attack by mobs on Darbar Sahib (Golden temple) began on 9 March. Manikchandra Vajpayee and Paradkar have given a blow-by-blow account of this incident too.

"That day March 9, 1947 troops of uniformed Muslim league National Guards begin to advance towards the Gurudwara from three sides. A big contingent was advancing from the League's stronghold in Katra Karam Singh, the second from Namak Mandi and the third from Sherawala Darwaza. All of them were armed."

"There were a handful of sewadars and they were frightened. Unfortunately, about a hundred unarmed pilgrims were also trapped inside. Because of the curfew they could not leave. Jathas of Sikhs from the rural areas who were coming on receiving information about the situation were stopped outside by armed policemen. This had been done in conspiracy with the League. Phone calls were coming to the Punjab relief committee office from the Gurdwara saying, Muslim mobs were advancing towards the Darbar Sahib and the Golden temple was in danger. 'Would you swayamsevaks not come to our aid?' Durga Das Khanna, in-charge of the Karyalaya (RSS office) kept assuring them — Don't panic, swayamsevaks have reached there and they have taken up positions in every lane. Whatever the cost, we won't let anything happen to the sacred Darbar Sahib." [12]

'RSS played a role in maintaining Hindu-Sikh unity'

In a first-hand account of the riots in Lahore in run-up to partition, Prof. A.N. Bali gives a detailed description of how RSS saved a large number of Sikhs and Hindus. Prof. Bali taught in Panjab University and was a resident of Lahore. The book titled 'Now it can be told' was first published in 1949 and the preface was written by Master Tara Singh, a Sikh stalwart, who played a key role in shaping up of the Akali movement as well as the emergence of SGPC as a key body of Sikhs.

Bali writes: "The police was mostly League minded ... who else came to the rescue of the people at this stage but a band of young selfless Hindus, known as RSS. They organized in every mohalla (area) of every town of the province the evacuation of the Hindu and Sikh women and children from dangerous pockets to comparatively safe centres. They organized for their feeding, medical aid, clothing and care ... even fire brigades were formed in various towns."

"Their (RSS) discipline, their physical fitness and their selflessness in the face of dangers came to the rescue of the people in Punjab when the whole province was burning and when the Congress leaders were helplessly fiddling in New Delhi, not being able to overcome the opposition to the Muslim League and the obstinacy of the governor-general to their proposal for stronger action for the maintenance of law and order."

In his book "Now It Can be Told", A. N. Bali gives a brief account on of the role the Sangh played in those days. He writes ... Non-violence and the advice given by Mrs. Sucheta Kriplani, Mahatma Gandhi and Dr. Rajendra Prasad etc., to stay out where they were with a firm trust in God could only be given from a safe distance. Who else came to the rescue of people at this stage, but a band of young selfless Hindus, popularly known as the R.S.S.? They organised in every Mohalla of every town of the province the work of evacuation of the Hindu and Sikh women and children from dangerous pockets to comparatively safe centres. They organised for their feeding, medical aid, clothing and care. Parties for the protection of institutions were organised. Even fire engine brigades were formed in various towns. Arrangements for transport by lorries and buses and provision of escort on the trains carrying the fleeing Hindus and Sikhs were organised. Day and night vigils in various Hindu and Sikh localities were kept and people were taught how to defend themselves when attacked. When the situation on the eve of Partition became very serious, and Law and Order utterly broke down or it would be more correct to say, was now used only to suppress the Hindus and Sikhs, several members of the R.S.S. showed their proficiency in the use of fire weapons. It almost became a tit for tat. These youngmen were the first to come to the help of the stricken Hindus and Sikhs and were the last to leave their places for safety in the East Punjab. I could name several Congress leaders of note in the various districts of Punjab who openly solicited the help of the R.S.S., even for their own protection and the protection of their kith and kin. No request for help from any quarter was refused and there are cases which came to our notice, where the Muslim women and children were safely escorted out of the Hindu Mohallas and sent to Muslim League refugee centres in Lahore by the R.S.S. men. [13]

While at Lahore I had no means of knowing, what was happening in the East Punjab after partition. I only know this that on my way to Delhi from Amritsar by car, I came across convoys of refugees, several miles long, wending their way peacefully to Wagha border, and even carrying spears with them, unmolested by the Police...

The Post Script to Proclamation of Independent India: Liberation of Forgotten Territories of Goa, Daman, Diu, Dadra and Nagar Haveli, and Pondicherry

Sadly, after independence, the Congress rulers virtually forgot about Portuguese enclaves of Goa, Daman, Diu, Dadra and Nagar Haveli, and French enclave of Pondicherry (now Puducherry). But, RSS did not. Its swayamsevaks took part in liberation of Goa and other Portuguese enclaves with full support from the organisation. These enclaves were finally liberated in 1961 from the Portuguese officially. Since we are talking about events leading to the independence of India from British, I will be brief about this part of history, because without mentioning them, the history of independence cannot be complete. Let us know a little about the role of RSS here in this struggle.

One of the early catalysts for the liberation struggle was Dr. Ram Manohar Lohia. Then, in the early 1954, RSS volunteers Raja Wakankar and Nana Kajrekar visited the area around Dadra and Nagar Haveli, and Daman several times to study the topography and get acquainted with locals who wanted the area to become part of India. In April 1954, the RSS formed a coalition with the National Movement Liberation Organisation (NMLO), and the Azad Gomantak Dal (AGD) for the annexation of Dadra and Nagar Haveli into the Republic of India.

On 2nd August, 1954, a team of 100 swayamsevaks, led by Vinayak Rao Apte, Sanghchaalak of Pune, stormed the enclaves of Dadra and Nagar Haveli. Then, they attacked Silvassa, forcing 175 Portuguese soldiers to surrender, and national tricolour was hoisted and handed over to the Central Government. This were felicitated on 2nd August, 1979 in Silvassa.

In 1955, RSS leaders demanded the end of Portuguese rule in Goa and its integration into India. When Prime Minister Jawaharlal Nehru refused to provide an armed intervention, RSS leader Jagannath Rao Joshi led the satyagraha with a group of around 3,000 members straight into Goa. He was imprisoned with his followers by the Portuguese police. Non-violent protests continued but were met with repression. On 15 August, 1955, the Portuguese police opened fire on the satyagrahis, killing thirty or so civilians. Rajabhau Mahakal of Ujjain led the batch from Ujjain. He died in the police firing while he held the tricolour aloft, even after a bullet had pierced through right eye. Jagannath Rao Joshi was one of the prominent leaders of Jan Sangh later in Karnataka. These freedom fighters were not treated with sincerity and respect they deserved. Mohan Ranade and his friends had led the revolutionary armed struggle in Goa under the banner of Azad Gomantak Dal. Mohan Ranade and his colleague Telu Mescarenus remained imprisoned in Goa and later in various Portuguese jails till 1969. They were released thanks to sustained efforts of Shri Sudhir Phadke, the famous music director and a swayamsevak. Mohan Ranade in his memoirs 'Sarfaroshi ki Tamanna' tells us how badly he suffered due to apathy of Nehru government and subsequent Congress governments. This book also confirms that Nehru disapproved of various patriotic efforts to liberate of these enclaves. He confirms participation of RSS swayamsevaks in this struggle. Indian and French parliaments finally ratified the treaty of cession only on 16th August, 1962, for Pondicherry, when it joined the Indian Union. It is a serious indictment of our political leadership that while India attained freedom in 1947, millions of its inhabitants remained slaves in enclaves surrounded by the mainland India.

On the night of 21 July, United Front of Goans, a group working independently of the coalition, captured the Portuguese police station at Dadra and declared Dadra independent. Subsequently, on 28 July, volunteer teams from the RSS and AGD captured the territories of Naroli and Phiparia, and ultimately the capital of Silvassa. The Portuguese forces that had escaped and moved towards Nagar Haveli, were assaulted at Khandvel and forced to retreat until they surrendered to the Indian border police at Udava on 11 August 1954. A native administration was set up with Appasaheb Karmalkar of the NMLO as the Administrator of Dadra and Nagar Haveli on 11 August 1954.

The capture of Dadra and Nagar Haveli gave a boost to the movement against Portuguese colonial rule in the Indian subcontinent.

Goa was later annexed into the Indian union in 1961 through an army operation, codenamed 'Operation Vijay', that was carried out by the Nehru government.

In fact, a Sarvodaya leader, in appreciation of the service rendered by the swayamsevaks for the cyclone-hit victims of Andhra Pradesh in 1977, meaningfully said that "RSS" stood for "Ready for Selfless Service". Obviously, the real purpose of the Sangh is rightly understood by the unbiased and discerning analyst only.

Golwalkar allowed the RSS to participate in various public activities. It was at the forefront of relief operation among East Bengal refugees and 1950 Assam earthquake victims. It started a campaign against cow-slaughter in 1952. Pracharaks were dispatched to participate in the Bhoodan campaign of Vinoba Bhave. In 1954, the swayamsevaks joined the satyagraha to liberate the Portuguese enclaves of Dadra and Nagar Haveli. The RSS constituted an important element of Goa Vimochan Sahayak Samiti (Goa Liberation Committee). The 1955 Goa agitation further established the Hindu nationalist credentials of the RSS. Along with these public activities, the RSS, by and large, remained preoccupied with its focus on traditional character-building' through regular activities at its shakhas. Golwalkar even temporarily stopped the practice of sending the pracharaks to the affiliates in order to highlight his 'non-political' inclination. This move was, however, reportedly resented by Balasaheb Deoras and his brother Bhaurao Deaoras. Meanwhile the Vishwa Hindu Parishad (VHP) was floated in 1964 and All-India Goraksha Sammelan (Cow-Protection Conference) was held at Vrindavan, in the Mathura district of Uttar Pradesh. Golwalkar inaugurated the sammelan in August 1964 and a deadline was given to the central government to pass legislation to ban cow-slaughter. Although the parliament did not concede this request, many state legislatures, by 1966, adopted appropriate legislations in this direction. However, the RSS organized a massive demonstration outside the parliament on November 1966, demanding a total and comprehensive ban on cow-slaughter. The demonstration turned violent.

Earlier, in the 1960s, a host of leaders visited and appreciated the Vivekananda Rock Memorial at Kanyakumari that was set up under the guidance of RSS pracharak and former sarkaryavah Eknath Ranade.

The then President VV Giri inaugurated the celebrations after the memorial was completed. The then Prime Minister Indira Gandhi visited it after a fortnight of its inauguration. She addressed a meeting of the memorial organising committee, whose secretary was Eknath Ranade. The latter also presented a report after the PM's address.

In the early 1980s, the RSS started a massive campaign to check religious conversions of Hindus after around 800 socially marginalised members of Hindu society got converted into Islam at Meenakshipuram in Tamil Nadu in 1981.

People expressing doubt about the continued survival or growth of an idea like the Rashtriya Swayamsevak Sangh were aplenty in the Twenties and later. However, such doubts have, given place to amazement. Such has been the phenomenal growth of the Sangh. Today, there is not a single major field of life which has remained beyond the purview of the Sangh swayamsevaks.

This does not imply that it has always been smooth-sailing for the Sangh. It has had to pass through many adversities. It was thrice banned officially by the government - in 1948 and in 1975 and again 1992; and each time Sangh came out of the ordeal with redoubled splendor.

War-time activities

During 1962 Chinese Invasion

And two years later, when the Chinese openly invaded our territory in 1962, the Swayamsevaks swung into action mobilising support to the governmental measures in general and to the jawans in particular. Pandit Nehru was so much impressed that he invited a Sangh contingent to take part in the Republic Day Parade of 26th January 1963. At a mere two days' notice, over 3,000 Swayamsevaks smartly turned up at the parade in full Sangh uniform. Their massive march, accompanied by bands, in fact, became the major highlight of the programme. When, later on, some Congressmen raised their eyebrows over the invitation to Sangh, Pandit Nehru brushed aside the objections saying that all patriotic citizens had been invited to join the parade.

During the war, the attitude of labour becomes a crucial factor. When China invaded Bharat, a section of the Communist Party of India proclaimed that Chinese forces were here for liberating' Bharat (from capitalist domination). Their leaders like Basavaponnaiah went to the extent of saying that Bharat was the aggressor and had occupied Chinese territory. Their unions were made tools to sabotage or obstruct our defence efforts. Their water-transporting union in the North-Eastern region served a strike notice. Transport of food and other materials to the jawans at the Front was hampered.

However, the Bharatiya Mazdoor Sangh decided otherwise. At once it withdrew all agitations by its unions. All the pending demands were put off for the time being. A call was given to workers to give top priority to stepping up defence production and assisting all defence efforts.

The BMS did not stop at that. It decided to end the potentiality for mischief in future by such Trojan horses. In strategic sectors such as defence production, transport, power generation, transmission, etc., special efforts were made. Two decades of such persistent efforts have secured for the BMS federation in the defence sector - the Bharatiya Prati Raksha Mazdoor Sangh - a premier position. BMS is now confident that the leftist unions dare not try their 1962 tactics in the future. So also, in other life-lines of the nation like power generation, road and railway transport, the BMS has established a clear lead over others.

Opposing the Surrender on Kutch Front

The Kutch Agreement signed on June 30, 1965, in the wake of Pak-aggression in Kutch, had, in short, recognised the right of Pakistan to patrol Indian territory and a dispute over nearly 9,000 square kilometres of Indian territory in Kutch to be arbitrated by an international tribunal. All this, Pakistan got on a silver platter in lieu of her wanton aggression on our territory. And, what did India get in return? Restoration of status quo as on 1st January 1965 as demanded by the Government of India. But it turned out to be not status quo ante aggression but status quo post aggression. For, later on, our Government confessed that Pakistan had intruded into that area even before 1st January 1965. All this amounted to not only criminal negligence on the part of the Government, but gross betrayal of our national rights and interests.

Among all the political parties, it was the Bharatiya Jana Sangh which came forward to organise a massive public protest against the blatant infringement of national sovereignty implied in the Kutch Agreement. It organised mass rallies, demonstrations and processions in all parts of the country on 4th July 1965 in order to create public awareness about the grave implications of the Agreement and register their protest. In Delhi itself, on 16th August, it organised a mammoth protest rally outside the Parliament House in which MPs of several political parties including the Samyukta Socialist Party and the Republican Party, apart from several independent leaders, joined the Jana Sangh leaders in denouncing the Kutch Agreement. Significantly, a few Congress MPs too came out of the Parliament to join the rally and sat on the dais. While The Statesman described the rally as "by far the biggest ever witnessed in the capital so far," the Dainik Hindustan and BBC put the gathering at half a million. The Broadway Times of Chennai, usually critical of the Jana Sangh, also described the rally as 'the biggest protest march the capital had ever seen'.

During 1965 Pak Aggression

Again, when Pakistan attacked Bharat in 1965, Lal Bahadur Shastri, the Prime Minister, personally rang up Shri Golwalkar who was then touring Maharashtra and requested him to be in New Delhi for the All-Leaders Conference the following day. At the conference, Shri Golwalkar extended complete co-operation on behalf of the Sangh. He also urged that the hands of the Indian army should not be tied down to a defensive posture but allowed to evolve its own offensive strategy. At the conference, when one of the representatives, while addressing Shastriji, kept on saying 'your army', Shri Golwalkar corrected him with a sharp reminder: "Say, 'our army'."

In Delhi, for the entire period of 22 days of war, police duties like traffic control were transferred to Swayamsevaks to free the police for more pressing tasks. Ever since the beginning of war, batches of Swayamsevaks daily reported at the General Military Hospital, Delhi, to offer blood. The military looked upon the Sangh as a friend in need. Whenever they felt the need for any kind of civil assistance they would just ring up the Sangh Karyalaya. When the war was at its peak, a military train carrying wounded jawans arrived in Delhi. Hundreds were urgently in need of blood transfusion. The army officers telephoned to the Delhi Sangh Karyalaya. It was midnight. The very next morning 500 Swayamsevaks reached the military hospital to donate blood. According to the hospital rules, each of them was offered 10 rupees. But the Swayamsevaks returned the amount saying that it could be better used for the wounded jawans.

During 1971 War of Bangladesh Liberation

In 1971, the RSS supported the call of the Prime Minister, Indira Gandhi, to sink political differences and meet the Pakistani challenge unitedly. The Kendriya Karyakarani Mandal of the RSS urged the people to cooperate with the government and the armed forces whole heartedly in the event of an aggression by Pakistan. It also asked the swayamsevaks to remain in the vanguard of the people's efforts in the cause of the nation's defense.

When war with Pakistan broke out again in December 1971, Shri Golwalkar's advice to the Government and the people was clear and crisp: "At least now, we should be shaken out of our illusion that an appeal to the so-called international conscience would work wonders." He also said, "Our war aims should be clear. As our Shastras have declared, no shatru shesh, residue of the enemy, should be allowed to remain." However, the Government, in the wake of the heroic liberation of Bangladesh by our jawans, again relapsed into its old groove. With what results we all know now, with both Pakistan and Bangladesh becoming more and more belligerent all the time.

During the war, as on previous occasions, thousands of Swayamsevaks throughout Rajasthan, North Punjab, Jammu, Uttar Pradesh, Bihar and Bengal pledged their services with the authorities for every kind of mobilisation of civilian support. At several important cities and towns, hundreds of Swayamsevaks enlisted themselves as blood donors as well as volunteers for civil defence and first aid. Patrolling during blackout and undertaking relief works became their normal duties. In Uttar Pradesh, a sustained programme for public awakening was undertaken. Prabhat-pheris (early morning marches) and public contacts were taken up for exhorting the people to remain vigilant about the pro-Pak elements and their possible fifth column activities. In Delhi, the Kingsway Camp police station authorities requisitioned the services of the Swayamsevaks to guard the broadcasting and other vital installations in Radio Colony and the water works at Wazirabad. The Swayamsevaks also looked after the wounded jawans in hospitals at many places. Army hospitals were often flooded with fruits and other consumer articles for the use of the wounded jawans.

On 7th December 1971, when the Barmer railway station in Rajasthan was bombed by Pakistani planes, about 40 to 45 Swayamsevaks rushed to the dangerous spot. A goods train carrying petrol drums was likely to catch fire. The Swayamsevaks, unmindful of the intermittent bombing, removed the drums to safer places. During those critical days, senior defence and government officers insisted that only the Sangh men be permitted to run the canteens in those sensitive border areas.

After the declaration of 1971 Bangladesh War of Independence, RSS provided support to the government, by offering its services to maintain law and order in Delhi and its volunteers were the first to donate blood. RSS Swayamsevaks also helped the Indian Army troops to dig trenches, and after the war helped to repatriate the Bangladeshi refugees back to their newly formed country of Bangladesh. After India's victory, the Akhil Bharatiya Pratinidhi Sabha of the RSS praised 'the unparalleled heroism and acumen of the armed forces and the firm leadership of the Prime Minister',

After the anti-Sikh riots of 1984, noted columnist and author Khushwant Singh had said, "RSS has played an honourable role in maintaining Hindu-Sikh unity before and after the murder of Indira Gandhi in Delhi and in other places. It was the Congress (I) leaders who instigated mobs in 1984 and got more than 3,000 people killed. I must give due credit to RSS and the BJP for showing courage and protecting helpless Sikhs during those difficult days. No less a person than Atal Bihari Vajpayee himself intervened at a couple of places to help poor taxi drivers."

Participation in land reforms

The RSS volunteers participated in the Bhoodan movement organised by Gandhian leader Vinobha Bhave, who had met RSS leader Golwalkar in Meerut in November 1951. Golwalkar had been inspired by the movement that encouraged land reform through voluntary means. He pledged the support of the RSS for this movement. Consequently, many RSS volunteers, led by Nanaji Deshmukh, participated in the movement. But Golwalkar was also critical of the Bhoodan movement on other occasions for being reactionary and for working "merely with a view to counteracting Communism". He believed that the movement should inculcate a faith in the masses that would make them rise above the base appeal of Communism. [14]

Homogenizing Hindus: Caste, Tribe, Woman and Progeny

RSS discourse on community, history and nation leaves no doubt that Hindu Rashtra stands for Hindu hegemony. But Hindus are not a homogeneous entity—there exists a multiplicity of identities among them. Golwalkar recognized this reality, though never admitted so. As Hindu Rashtra aimed at a monolithic Hindu identity, he understandably underplayed these diverse identities under the pretext of one culture, one language and one nation (Hindu, Hindi, Hindustan). Though Golwalkar did not favor any dilution of ideology, he, at the same time, created an array of affiliates to work among various sections of the society with the objective of assimilation and homogenization of these identities into an all-embracing and omnipotent 'Hindu' identity.

In the post-Golwalkar phase, Deoras and other RSS leaders recognized that some of these identities were getting restive and it would be wise to address them with more courage, rather than simply ignoring their existence. They further understood that the RSS would not succeed in its quest for political power without integrating these identities into the framework of Hindutva. An attempt has been made in this chapter to examine how the RSS has made certain strategic shifts in its ideology in order to homogenize different identities like castes, tribes and women into the monolithic framework of Hindu Rashtra. It is also shown how it has modified its strategies in a slow and subtle manner without reversing its original ideological position; new ideas have been incorporated, but not at the cost of the traditional ones.

Integrating Castes

As community politics intensified in early twentieth century, the integration of the depressed classes and tribals into the Hindu fold became a major concern of the then Hindu leaders. Lajpat Rai claimed that 'the depressed classes are Hindus' as 'they worship Hindu Gods, observe Hindu customs, and follow Hindu laws'.' Regarding the 'Santals, Kolis, Bhils, Panchamas, Namashudras and other such [depressed] tribes and classes', V.D. Savarkar argued, this Sindhusthan is as emphatically, the land of their forefathers as of those of the so-called Aryans; they inherit the Hindu blood and the Hindu culture; and even those of them who have not as yet come fully under the influence of any orthodox Hindu sect, do still worship deities and saints and follow a religion however primitive, are still purely attached to this land, which therefore to them is not only a Fatherland, but a Holyland'. Swami Shraddhanand strongly advocated for the abolition of untouchability. The RSS developed its understanding of caste and tribes upon this legacy; it strongly argued that the untouchables and the tribals are very much part and parcel of Hindu society.

RSS' Understanding of Caste

Hedgewar made it clear that in the shakha the identity of the swayamsevak was only Hindu, and nothing else; he should not be conscious of any other identity, especially the caste identity. The shakha was designed to discipline the swayamsevak, reinforce his Hindu identity and impart Hindu sanskar. As most of Hedgewar's recruits belonged to the upper castes, mainly the Brahmins, the swayamsevaks got naturally inclined to imbibe and imitate the values and norms of upper caste Hindus. Despite a significant change in the composition of membership over the years, even today, the imprint of an upper-caste behavioural pattern and value system is unmistakably visible on the swayamsevaks. An upper caste legacy still continues in the organization.

Golwalkar, the ideologue of the RSS, attempts to provide a theoretical formulation of caste, and tries to integrate it into the framework of the Hindu Rashtra. He makes a distinction between varna and caste and explains that while varnas are four, castes are countless. As he proceeds, while the basis of caste is occupation, varna is based on the ancient form of the modern theory of heredity. Varna refers to quality, not to the colour of the skin, argues Golwalkar; therefore, a Brahmin may be dark and a Shudra may be fair. Varna is determined by guna and karma, including that of previous birth, observes Golwalkar. He further contends that when the Brahmin gave up his dharma and started competing for jobs, he knocked out the basis of varna.

Golwalkar rejects the view that caste was an evil institution and was imposed on society by some section which had a vested interest. He does not find any reason to believe that Brahmins exploited other castes and got the benefits. Present RSS writings, in a similar vein, strongly refute that the upper castes are responsible for perpetuating caste oppression for centuries. In Golwalkar's opinion, caste was a great institution, which served society and held it together when everything else seemed to collapse all around. 'It was because caste was weak in West Punjab and East Bengal that these two areas, of all other, succumbed to Invaders, despite the 'positive' contributions of the caste system. Golwalkar, however, feels that this 'ancient armour' is no longer relevant. That is why the RSS does not recognize any caste; it underscores only one identity, i.e. Hindu identity.'

Though caste has lost its relevance, Golwalkar regrets that the caste system still prevails. Then how is it to be abolished? Golwalkar offers a 'natural approach' in contrast to the 'most un-natural approach' of the 'national integration-wallas, who focus on the division of Hindus into various castes, tribes, backward classes, etc. He does not believe in 'cheap attacks on caste' and prefers to abolish it sweetly. . . not by making noises. Obviously, Golwalkar's construction of a unified Hindu identity gets jeopardized if too much stress is laid on the divisive dimensions of Hindu caste system.

Abolishing Untouchability

The major bane of the Hindu caste system is untouchability and Golwalkar pleads for its abolition; 'the Harijan can, and must, enter the temple as a Hindu. Nobody is going to stop him. However, here again, he argues that creating scenes and throwing challenges might create news, but it will not solve the problem. The right approach is to treat the Harijans as equal members of Hindu society and make efforts for their upliftment with the same solicitude with which one works for the recovery of a sick member of the family'. The legal ban is not enough; Golwalkar appeals to religious leaders of various sects to give a religious sanction to the legal ban to make it really effective.

`The VHP, which was entrusted by Golwalkar to strive for the abolition of untouchability, has also made a strident demand in favour of a religious sanction by Shankaracharyas against untouchability: 'For whatever may be said about the correctness of the position of the so-called "Untouchables" in different epochs, the age we live in demands a revision of the obligations and rights on the basis of equality and brotherhood.' The VHP emphasizes the abolition of untouchability to save Hindu society from divisions and puts special responsibility on the Shankaracharyas 'to relegate the inessentials to a back place', so that all the folds and layers, castes, communities and sampradayas could be integrated to turn this society into one huge organism. For this supreme objective of Hindu unity, the VHP does not hesitate to dump the injunctions of the Shastras and modify them as per the need of the present time: 'A healthy and free society need not follow the prescriptions enjoined during adverse times.'

The solution provided by the RSS to eradicate untouchability and caste discrimination appears to be quite simplistic and superficial—the declaration of Shankaracharyas will have very little impact. Its suggestion that a 'beginning can be made to do away with these evils through community festivals, social gatherings and temple worships', hardly makes any headway in getting rid of such an age-old practice. The RSS is yet to address the fundamental questions of untouchability, especially those involving larger social, economic, and political issues. Nevertheless, it is true to a substantial extent that the swayamsevaks do not prefer to be introduced according to their respective castes. They claim that their primary identity is Hindu, not their belongingness to any particular caste. True, once an untouchable becomes part of the RSS brotherhood, he is not treated differently by fellow swayamsevaks.

Dalit intellectuals equate Hindutva with Brahminism. They define Brahminism as a process of fixing finality of relations or human interactions on the basis of the axiom that, 'by birth the Brahmins are superior to all other beings' and as a natural corollary, the Shudras are inferior to them. This is a natural and unalterable arrangement'. They blame Brahminism for perpetuating caste hierarchy, and therefore, equate Hindutva with casteism. They further argue that the stratified Hindu caste based society denies social mobility by the members of each of the caste groups to remain confined within the socio-economic jurisdiction of their respective caste. Brahminism does not grant any right to others to choose their vocation according to their merits, aptitude or active tendencies of character. Merit was made a monopoly of the Brahmins; whatever belonged to the Brahmins was declared to be meritorious. Therefore, Dalit intellectuals argue that 'Hindu society lost potency of both vertical and horizontal mobility'.

But, as per the original and correct interpretation, four Varnas – Brahmanas, Kshatriyas, Vaishyas, and Sudras, and Activities of Brahmanas, Kshatriyas, Vaishyas, and Sudras are well divided on the basis of their qualities shaped by Nature's gunas. Work was divided among people in the society based on their Guna constitution. Each of these social groups took up activities according to their tendencies and skills, and contributed to the welfare of the society. Each of them, by this exclusive dedication to his/her chosen field excelled in it. Same has been quoted in Bhagavad Gita. The Dalit view-point challenges the very definition of Hinduism as the majority religion and the core of Indian tradition.

Integrating Tribals

The RSS also claims that tribals are Hindus. It does not accept the term adivasi as the prefix 'adi' implies that tribals were the original inhabitants and the Aryans came from outside. Instead the RSS has coined the term vanavasi (forest dwellers) to address the tribals. Golwalkar explains that tribals are very much Hindus though they have no knowledge of their religion (Hinduism). He rejects the view that the tribals cannot be called Hindus as they are animists and worship trees and serpents.

He argues that the Hindus throughout the country worship Tulsi, Bilva and Aswattha and also Nag, the cobra.

The RSS does not agree that the Hindu social system was at the root of the neglect of the tribals. Golwalkar tries to convince that in the olden times, when the Panchayat system was the basic unit of society, those forest dwellers had an honoured place in it. Golwalkar applauds the qualities of the tribals, such as courage, intelligence, industry, honesty, warmth of heart, culture and spiritual refinement. 'Probably it was only Maharana Pratap who had established close links with them and made them equal partners with the rest of society. The forest-dwellers in those regions, the Bhills, stood shoulder to shoulder with Rajputs generation after generation in the heroic defence of Swadesha and Swadharma.' Thus, Golwalkar attempts to prove that these tribals fought against the Muslims for the honour of the Hindu religion and a Hindu kingdom.

To bring the tribals into the fold of Hinduism, the RSS encourages them to change their names; instead of 'Oraon' one should write 'Ram' as one's family name. By encouraging the tribals to trace their ancestry to Rajput figure, in fact, strikes at the very roots of the social and cultural history of the tribals.[15]

Integrating the Vanavasis: Sangh Parivar in a Tribal District, Phulbani (Orissa)

Though the RSS is unable to explain adequately the reasons behind the present deplorable socio-economic conditions of the tribals, it recognizes their plight and proposes to adopt such plans by which their primary physical needs could be taken care of. Accordingly, the RSS first created the VHP and then Vanavasi Kalyan Ashram (VKA) for the purpose. It would be useful to examine the method of operation of these affiliates of the RSS in the tribal district of Phulbani, Orissa.

Tribals constitute roughly one-fourth of Orissa's population. The tribal areas, because of the presence of Christian missionaries, offer an ideological advantage to the RSS. The missionaries are active in welfare projects as well as conversion. Therefore, here, the other is clearly identified and resentment amongst Hindus against conversion could be ideally exploited. However, the ideological challenge will not be enough unless the tribals are 'Hinduized and an alternate welfare system is provided to woo them away from the missionary welfare system'. Once this is achieved, the Sangh Parivar will make attempt to bring back 'the lost brothers' to the Hindu fold through reconversion (paravartan). Keeping these objectives in mind, the RSS deputed a Hindu missionary, Laxmanananda Saraswati to Phulbani, a district having a tribal majority and a centre of Christian missionary activities. Raghunath Sethi, a pracharak, was deputed to assist Laxmanananda.

The RSS has advocated the training of Dalits and other backward classes as temple high priests (a position traditionally reserved for Caste Brahmins and denied to lower castes). They argue that the social divisiveness of the caste system is responsible for the lack of adherence to Hindu values and traditions, and that reaching out to the lower castes in this manner will be a remedy to the problem. The RSS has also condemned upper-caste Hindus for preventing Dalits from worshipping at temples, saying that "even God will desert the temple in which Dalits cannot enter"."RSS resorted to instrumentalist techniques of ethnoreligious mobilisation that members of all castes have been welcomed into the organisation and are treated as equals."

During a visit in 1934 to an RSS camp at Wardha, accompanied by Mahadev Desai and Mirabehn, Mahatma Gandhi said, "When I visited the RSS Camp, I was very much surprised by your discipline and absence of untouchablity." He personally inquired about this to Swayamsevaks and found that volunteers were living and eating together in the camp without bothering to know each other's castes.[16]

Aligning with Jayaprakash Narayan against Indira Gandhi

Meanwhile Indira Gandhi's authoritarian style of functioning was getting pronounced day by day. The RSS was quick to understand the nature of her functioning and started opposing it. For example, the RSS took strong objection to the question of supercession of senior judges of the Supreme Court in the appointment of the Chief Justice. An editorial of the Organiser warned that 'the politically conscious elements of the Indian society will have to exert themselves to keep the press free, the judiciary independent and the legislatures responsive - if India is not to drift into the nightmare of a corrupt dictatorship'. Referring to the appeal of the Congress leader Shashi Bhushan for 'limited dictatorship', L.K. Advani cautioned: 'it seems the Congress - is seriously toying with the idea of scuttling democracy, and supplanting it with a totalitarian or a quasi-totalitarian set-up.' Thus, the RSS had started taking a strong position against the authoritarian tendency of Indira Gandhi.

Jayaprakash Narayan launched a protest movement against the corrupt Congress government of Bihar. The ABVP became a part of the Chhatra Sangharsh Samiti (CSS) and joined the JP movement. In late 1974, the movement changed its character by moving beyond Bihar and targeting Indira Gandhi. JP's concept of 'total revolution' was a step endorsed by the RSS.

The ABPS of the RSS took the unusual supporting Narayan's 'total revolution', though it maintained its tradition of keeping aloof from political activities. In a rally at Delhi, Balasaheb Deoras called JP a 'saint', who had 'come to rescue society in dark and critical times',

Jayaprakash reciprocated the compliment by publicly praising the Sangh Parivar. He attended the 20th All-India session of the Jana Sangh and declared, 'If Jana Sangh is fascist, then I, too, am a fascist'. He further complimented the RSS for its efforts to reduce economic inequality and corruption. Both JP and the RSS needed each other. While JP had the leadership, the RSS had a committed cadre. Any struggle against Indira Gandhi demanded a close cooperation between the two. JP's approbation certainly enhanced the public stature of the RSS.

RSS and Anti-Emergency Struggle

On 5 June 1975, the Allahabad High Court declared Indira Gandhi's election to the parliament invalid due to violations of election law. The opposition parties demanded her resignation. They formed the Lok Sangharsh Samiti (LSS) to coordinate the activities of the JP movement. Nana Deshmukh, a former RSS pracharak, and the organizing secretary of the BJS, became its general secretary. On 25 June 1975, JP gave a call to the defense forces not to carry out the 'illegal order'. The next morning a state of Emergency was declared and the political opponents of Indira Gandhi including Balasaheb Deoras were arrested. The RSS was banned on 4 July 1975 under Defence of India Rules, 1971, and a large number of RSS members were arrested.

The initial response of the RSS was cautious. Madhavrao Mulay, the general secretary, declared that the organization had been dissolved. However, the RSS kept alive an effective skeleton organization, although its shakhas, training camps, parades and other activities were stopped. Soon some leading pracharaks, after consulting imprisoned Balasaheb Deoras, met at Bombay in late July to chart out the action plan for their banned organization. They decided that the RSS would work closely with the LSS, thus breaking the RSS tradition of keeping the organization aloof from political movements. The coordinating work of the RSS with the LSS would be carried out by the four zonal pracharaks: Yadavrao Joshi (south), Rajendra Singh (north), Moropant Pingale (west), and Bhaorao Deoras (east). In addition, while Rambahu Godbole was entrusted with the task of contacting the opposition party leaders, Eknath Ranade was to liaison with the government. Incidentally, Ranade was assigned the same job during the previous ban of 1948-1949. This meeting also charted the following course of action for the banned organization: (a) to keep up the morale of the swayamsevaks by arranging some form of congregations; (b) to establish an underground press; (c) prepare for a nationwide satyagraha, establishing contact with significant non-political figures and with prominent representatives of the minority communities; and (d) solicit overseas Indian support for the RSS in the underground activities of the LSS. However, many critics believe that the RSS was keen on a compromise rather than fight Indira Gandhi.

Despite these versions, other evidence suggests that the RSS played a key role in the struggle against Emergency. Its cadre was the backbone of the LSS, which spearheaded the JP movement. After the arrest of JP, Nana Deshmukh assumed the responsibility of leading the LSS. When Deshmukh was arrested, D.B. Thengadi, the general secretary of the BMS, took charge.32 Thus, the RSS contributed its cadres and leaders to the LSS, the instrument of anti-Emergency struggle. Thousands of its members were arrested while offering satyagraha against authoritarian regime of Indira Gandhi. However, it is not to argue that it was only the RSS and its affiliates that participated in the struggle. All the opposition parties like the Samyukta Socialist Party (SSP), the Bharatiya Lok Dal (BLD), the Congress (Organization), the CPI (Marxist), and Naxalites opposed the Emergency. Even many students, teachers, lawyers, doctors, actors, writers, peasants, workers and other professionals, who did not have any party-affiliation, sacrificed their career to join the struggle against dictatorship and authoritarianism. Thus, it was a concerted effort of all individuals, groups and political parties who wanted the restoration of democracy in India. Therefore, the credit goes to the Indian people who participated and sympathized with this struggle.

Post-Emergency Era: Politics of Accommodation and Ideological Flexibility

The Emergency experience greatly exposed the cadres and the leaders of the RSS to the political environment of the country and made them ambitious. They felt proud of having participated in the 'second freedom struggle'. This was badly needed for any political claim in the future as the RSS avoided the fight against colonialism during the freedom struggle. This participation gave them a unique opportunity to feel the political pulse of the people. It also widened their limited political outlook of the Jana Sangh experiment. Their interaction with different political parties, groups and individuals proved to be immensely beneficial.

All these new experiences compelled the RSS leaders to ponder whether they should continue to stick to the old ideological framework of the Hindu Rashtra or should they redefine it in the light of the changed political dynamics. Deoras rightly realized that to remain in the mainstream of national politics, the RSS should opt for a politics of accommodation. Therefore, as the realpolitik demanded, there should be no hesitation to redefine its exclusivist ideological moorings and seek a politics of pragmatism and accommodation. This changing attitude of the RSS leadership helped the formation of the Janata alliance of the opposition parties when general elections were announced. The RSS cadre campaigned vigorously against Indira Gandhi. The Janata alliance won the elections. After the victory, the ban on the RSS was lifted on 4 July 1977.

It was the period of Indira Gandhi's rule, and most importantly the impact of the Emergency (June 1975-February 1977) that determined the fortunes of Hindu nationalism on both the party political and extra-parliamentary, mass cadre front. Indira Gandhi's Congress party had mobilized on an anti-poverty platform during the 1971-1972 national and state elections that resulted in a stunning victory for Congress, reversing its poor showing since 1967. Of additional importance in late 1971 and early 1972 was India's military success against Pakistan which led to the formation of Bangladesh. However, the consequent period of Congress hegemony, opportunism and corruption was seen to signal a dramatic change in India's political culture. Indira Gandhi's political stature after the invasion of east Pakistan was on the wane and her anti-poverty oratory was ineffectual; conversely, the rate of inflation and the prices of fuel and basic foodstuffs continued to rise. Mass protest movements against poverty and political corruption by mainly student groups grew in this period, and were centred around Gujarat and Bihar states. In 1975, a High Court found Indira Gandhi guilty of electoral irregularities. In this year, the 'Gandhian socialist' leader Jayaprakash Narayan launched a people's movement (the Janata Morcha) that called for the dismissal of the Congress government in Bihar state. Jayaprakash, also called for 'total revolution', the latter intended to appeal to both socialist constituencies and to elements who desired a 'revolution' in political ethics and propriety. Previously, in 1973, the student-led Navnirman (reconstruction) movement in Gujarat had similarly demanded the resignation of the governing assembly in the state.

Following the death of Golwalkar in 1973, Balasaheb Deoras became sarsanghchalak of the RSS and oriented the organization towards an activist political direction. Jana Sangh and RSS cadres had participated in both the Gujarat and Bihar movements. In 1975, the Jana Sangh, following Jayaprakash, called for a united people's front of all the non-Congress parties and organizations, which would organize joint actions in parliamentary and extra-parliamentary arenas based on a common program of opposition to Indira Gandhi's Congress government. In the months prior to the declaration of Emergency, the resolutions adopted by the RSS's Akhil Bharatiya Pratinidhi Sabha (its national central assembly) are instructive. In March 1974, the RSS issued a statement that condemned the attacks upon it from Congress and the Communist Party of India following the violence that erupted in the aftermath of the student and public protests in Gujarat and Bihar. This archetypal resolution condemned, and distanced the RSS from, the 'lawlessness and chaos' in those states. It also reflected the paranoid style of RSS politics by claiming that 'foreign loyalties and foreign designs', by which it meant Communists, were aiming to capture state power by instilling nationwide disorder. This resolution called upon its cadres to extend their 'hearty cooperation to every such effort from any direction' that was working for 'patriotism' and against 'the present atmosphere of all-round corruption and selfishness'. A year later, the RSS's Akhil Bharatiya Pratinidhi Sabha (national assembly) issued a statement again condemning Communist 'infiltration' and calling on swayamsevaks 'to exert themselves, with determination, to speed up the expansion of Sangh work throughout the country, heedless of any malicious propaganda indulged in by anti-nationalist and self-seeking elements'. In June, Indira Gandhi, claiming she feared a far right-wing or military coup in India, instructed the president to declare a 'national emergency' and suspend constitutional constraints. This gave Gandhi virtually unlimited powers to undertake actions deemed to be in the 'interests' of the nation. All the leaders of India's opposition parties were arrested and imprisoned or put under house arrest (for up to two years) and northern India's press and media was heavily censored or proscribed.

Aside from the extreme imperatives of political expediency, the RSS's and Jana Sangh's political alliances with Gandhian and socialist organizations before, during, and after the Emergency period require further explanation. Of importance was a strand in Gandhite anti-poverty activist ideology of 'upliftment' that, perhaps in a contradictory way, dovetailed into the Jana Sangh's 'modernizing' strategy. Gandhi's earlier sarvodaya ('upliftment' of rural and village communities out of poverty) strategy was to be followed by Vinoba Bhave's (1895–82) bhoodan yagna (land gift movement) from the early 1950s, which later expanded into the gramdan and jivandan movements. Both the latter emphasized a cooperative sharing of land and labour resources for the collective 'upliftment' of (typically) rural village communities.

Loknayak Jayaprakash Narayana (JP) had started off with a strong prejudice against RSS in the forties. But his contacts with RSS workers and leaders made him understand RSS in a positive way, and he started appreciating its work and ideology. He was very much impressed when he found during Bihar famine of 1966 that, for relief work, RSS workers collected the most, spent the least on collection and distributed the collections the best. After that, his contacts with RSS grew and his misconceptions disappeared. After the emergency, on November 3, 1977, JP addressed a huge RSS training camp in Patna. Following are some excerpts from his speech:

" RSS is a revolutionary organization. No other organization in the country comes anywhere near it. It alone has the capacity to transform society, end casteism and wipe the tears from the eyes of the poor. Its very name is 'Rashtriya', that is national. I am not saying this to flatter you. I believe you have a historic role to play.... I have great expectations from this revolutionary organization which has taken up the challenge of creating a new India. I have welcomed your venture wholeheartedly. Sometimes I have offered you my advice and have even criticized you, but that was as a friend...There is no other organization in the country which can match you The RSS should think over this: how to bring about economic transformation? How to transform the villages? All our leaders, including Mahatma Gandhi, have worked for it. You have included Mahatma Gandhi also in your morning prayers and he is indeed worth remembering every morning. This is very good thing you have done. If he had lived a little longer he would have guided us a little more to remove untouchability and other evils from the Hindu society. But the way is clear now and I think that more than myself you can undertake this mission because you are more competent to do it. You think and deliberate upon the various aspects of our traditions, our culture and Dharma constantly."

"This society, its glorious history and the heritage of our forefathers, the sacrifices of the builders of this country and their achievements and the freedom that we have won - you are the inheritors of it all and it is for you to make the best use of it...Your word has far reaching effect. There is the force of spiritualism and thousands of years of our ancient culture at your back. You are also in the forefront of the transformation that is taking place before our very eyes. The results of this change are also at your disposal...I commend to you the ideals of service, renunciation, sacrifice. I have no doubt that you are already imbued with these ideals and are of self-sacrificing nature and noble conduct. Here is the arena of a vast country open to you. You can accomplish a lot. May God give you strength and may you live up to such expectations."

One can see the unmediated appeal of Jayaprakash's ideology for Jana Sangh and RSS cadres. Golwalkar had also idealized the panchayat system. More importantly, Jayaprakash's vision could result in an ideological shift within the Jana Sangh without committing the latter to abandon its Hindutva foundation. 'Gandhian utopianism' of the kind promoted by Jayaprakash contained progressive and highly conservative resources and crucially both were important for the Jana Sangh. Similarly, the socialist aspects of Jayaprakash's ideology was resonant among the RSS and Jana Sangh cadres' formal commitment to 'equality' and the re-distribution of wealth. In important respects, Deendayal Upadhyaya's ideology of 'Integral Humanism' is awkwardly close to organic-utopian aspects of Gandhi's philosophy; conversely 'Integral Humanism' has had a long-standing appeal for some Gandhians. It is a moot point whether Upadhyaya's ideology can be seen as a direct syncretism of Gandhite-'JP' ideology with the RSS ideal of Hindu rashtra (Of additional significance is that the Janata Party of which the Jana Sangh was a key component, was in principle committed to Jayaprakash's political ideology). Similarly, in 1975, Jayaprakash dismissed charges that the RSS was 'fascist'. It was from such influences that the founding ideology of the Bharatiya Janata Party was determined at its inception to be 'Gandhian socialism'.

The Emergency period was the second time that the RSS had been banned in India. Under Emergency powers, Indira Gandhi also amended the Constitution of India in 1976, making it, allegedly 'for the first time', constitutionally secular (If the unnerving point is that the term 'secular' was inserted into the Preamble to the Constitution under the forty-second amendment during India's most authoritarian period since gaining Independence, article 25 (2) (a) already provided powers to the state to regulate and restrict 'any economic, financial, political or other secular activity associated with religious practice). The RSS and the Jana Sangh leadership were imprisoned, as were the leadership and activists of left and communist parties, and the Jamaati-i-Islami.

The Emergency period, while often considered in popular memory primarily as an attack on the left, was definitive in its impact on the strategy and ideology of the RSS in the late 1970s and into the 1980s. More than anything else, it confirmed for the RSS its own imagination of its centrality, necessity and power in India, as well as its role in rescuing the 'Hindu nation' from totalitarian 'secular' dictatorship. During their incarceration, RSS cadres formed links with organizations that were traditionally political enemies. Aside from socialist, Marxist and communist activists, this also included Jamaati-i-Islami activists. Of 12,986 individuals imprisoned during the Emergency, political affiliation was recorded for 6,346 individuals. Of these, just over 65 percent were members of the RSS or Jana Sangh, about a quarter were members of the Communist Party of India (ML) or the Socialist Party, and a small percentage were members of other parties. The large number of individuals for whom political affiliation was not recorded may confound this interpretation, as indeed might the large number of people arrested and imprisoned during Emergency for allegedly 'non-political' reasons. However, the relatively high percentage of RSS and Jana Sangh activists among those imprisoned during Emergency is salient in understanding both the changed strategy of the RSS during the 1980s and 1990s, and the considerable importance the RSS now attaches to its role during the Emergency period.

In April 1977, the RSS's Akhil Bharatiya Karyakari Mandal issued a statement of tribute to the fighters against the Emergency. Of significance was the absence of criticism of communism and of calls to uphold law and order, both of which were so prominent in its 1974-1975 resolutions. Instead, there was lavish praise for diverse sectors of Indian society, and especially the sangh cadres for their struggles against Indira Gandhi's dictatorship. This was a new political language for the RSS, knitting together its deal of national harmony and social integration with a characteristically non-RSS discourse of liberty, democracy, injustice, tyranny and vigilant struggle.

Perhaps most surprisingly, in 1977 and 1978, the RSS called upon its workers to 'initiate measures to remove the sense of alienation' of Muslims and Christians from the Hindus. Furthermore, the RSS reported that a large number of persons following different ways of worship such as Islam, Christianity, [Zoroastrianism] have participated in the congregations organized for the purpose by the RSS workers at different places, and exchanged views. As result of these get-together, the communication gap among the different followers of different religions has narrowed down, and to an extent mutual goodwill and amity developed.

Following the RSS leader, Deoras' meeting with Christian and Muslim leaders, the RSS's national assembly exhorted 'all citizens in general and R.S.S. Swayamsevaks in particular to further expedite this process of mutual contact by participation in each other's social functions'. Such sentiments can be viewed as consequences of the optimism in Indian public culture in the aftermath of the ending of Emergency, but they nevertheless reflected, though for a very short period, a different orientation to religious minorities, the latter still articulated together with the need for national integration, but with a liberality that perhaps could not be imagined in the Golwalkar period.

The RSS's early 1990s narrative of its role in the Emergency is instructive and its language of heroism emblematic of its bumptious style. The large size of this tome is indicative of the RSS's attempt to place itself, and the anti-Emergency satyagrahas organized by its swayamsevaks as the main and only consistent underground opposition to Indira Gandhi's Emergency. The anti-Emergency satyagrahas were called for by Jayaprakash Narayan in late 1975 and organized under a federation of parties and organizations, the Lok Sangarsh Samiti (LSS). However, the RSS narrative downplays the role of other organizations; even Jayaprakash is barely mentioned.

Instead, the pre-eminent role of sangh workers and volunteers is portrayed as central to and decisive for the struggle against Emergency.

A history of the struggle of the times of Emergency written without referring to the revolutionary work of these underground [mainly Sangh] workers would be like the Mahabharat written without acknowledging the fundamental contribution of Lord Shri Krishna - although it is true that today the common people are more attracted towards political power and Shri Krishna did not ascend the throne of Hastinapur after the Mahabharat war. All his efforts were directed towards the establishment of Dharma Rajya, not for achieving power for himself.

This is characteristic RSS political language. The RSS is said to neither seek nor require any recognition for its selfless, anonymous work for the nation, yet, at the same time, its central heroic role is ceaselessly promoted (indeed compared to that of Krishna) and that of other organizations rebuffed, the latter seen as disorganized and divided. Hence, the RSS claims that of those who participated in the anti-Emergency satyagrahas, over 78 percent (35,310) were associated with the sangh parivar; similarly, of those arrested under the MISA (Maintenance of Internal Security Act) imposed during the Emergency, almost 71 percent (16,373) were associated with the sangh parivar . However, this text is part of deeper and more recent revisionist and vanguardist project aimed at morally rehabilitating the RSS by exclusively identifying it with the history and 'remembrance' of both the anti-colonial and anti-Emergency struggles, significantly extending its own particular ideology to represent or substitute for 'the people'.

RSS during Janata Period

The Janata alliance became Janata Party on 1 May 1977. The RSS approved the merger of the BJS in this new party which formed the first non-Congress government at New Delhi. Three of its swayamsevaks from the Jana Sangh group, A.B. Vajpayee, L.K. Advani and Brij Lal Verma, got cabinet berths in the Morarji government. After the June assembly elections, the Jana Sangh members became the chief ministers in three States, Himachal Pradesh, Madhya Pradesh and Rajasthan and in the Union Territory of Delhi; and shared power in UP, Bihar, Haryana, Gujarat, Maharashtra and Orissa. Again most of them were RSS swayamsevaks.

The other constituents of the Janata Party, particularly the erstwhile socialists, were quick to grasp the growing influence of the RSS. They feared, on the basis of its large disciplined cadres and its influence over the erstwhile Jana Sangh members, that the RSS would soon become too powerful and eclipse other constituents of the Janata Party. Therefore, they devised a strategy to keep the RSS under control. It was suggested that the RSS should merge with the youth wing of the Janata Party to form a united volunteer organization. This was rejected by the RSS.

Balasaheb Deoras did not accept the proposal, which he thought, would certainly adversely affect the long-term objective of his organization. This would not only invite intense political attack from its detractors, but would also bring political culture to the RSS. Therefore, the RSS, as an organization, should never become a part of the government. Even the BMS and the ABVP were not allowed to merge their identities with respective labour and student counterparts of the Janata Party. Besides, being strongly entrenched in the Janata government and with its political affiliate taking care of the RSS interest, Deoras did feel real need for such a merger.

Thus Deoras cleverly avoided the politics of competition and bickering. He rather preferred to concentrate and spend his energy on other areas where there was hardly any competition and the RSS could expand its support base more quietly and effectively. Accordingly, the RSS sought mutual cooperation with the Janata government in the areas of adult education, social welfare, youth affairs, etc. Government patronage, the RSS reasoned, would ensure the flow of resources for these welfare activities.

The Hindu Mahasabha and later the Janata Party wished for the sangh's merger with their youth wings respectively. Perhaps, they were oblivious of its vision. In 1940, a senior RSS functionary had declared in an RSS rally in Pune, "The sangh is over and above all parties. We aim at demonstrating to the world that the sangh, founded on the strong basis of Hinduism, can unite all parties, and thus can face any odds."

The RSS was unmoved by the Congress resolution in 1948, welcoming RSS men into the party fold and subsequently prohibiting them from joining the Congress. The Congress experienced intense quarrels on the issue. It was an ideological shadow of cultural nationalism which was fighting to survive in the face of the Nehruvian onslaught within the Congress. This dilemma led to the formatting of the Bharatiya Jana Sangh. The dilemma of dual membership then led to the formation of the BJP. The Sangh is prepared to face 'odds' and resolve 'dilemmas' if and when they arise.

Relief and Rehabilitation

First aid camp for Earthquake victims in Gujarat. RSS volunteers involved in relief work during floods in North Karnataka and Andhra Pradesh. The RSS was instrumental in relief efforts after the 1971 Odisha cyclone and in the 1984 Bhopal disaster. Two important affiliates were established in 1972, Vivekananda Kendra and Deendayal Research institute. The Vivekananda kendra initiated a sustained effort at social welfare, nutrition, education and community welfare. Deendayal research institute assumed prominence for its rehabilitation efforts after 1977 Andhra Pradesh cyclone. After this cyclone, the RSS had engaged in reconstructing four villages. In Odisha Cyclone in 1982 and 1999 where many villages were destroyed, RSS helped in its reconstruction. They also took care of victims of the Kargil War of 1999.

It assisted in relief efforts during the 2001 Gujarat earthquake, and helped rebuild villages. Approximately 35,000 RSS members in uniform were engaged in the relief efforts, rescue, medical and cremation task and many of their critics acknowledged their role. An RSS-affiliated NGO, Seva Bharati, conducted relief operations in the aftermath of the 2004 Indian Ocean earthquake. Activities included building shelters for the victims and providing food, clothes, and medical necessities. The RSS assisted relief efforts during the 2004 Sumatra-Andaman earthquake and the subsequent Tsunami. Seva Bharati also adopted 57 children (38 Muslims and 19 Hindus) from militancy affected areas of Jammu and Kashmir to provide them education at least up to Higher Secondary level.

At present, the RSS volunteers are running around two lakh welfare projects across the country. The focus is to work for the service of the society, to transform Bharat as a nation and society. Most significantly, the swayamsevaks do this selflessly. There is no urge in the organisation or individual volunteers to win accolades or claim glory for itself. The RSS Swayamsevaks take pride in being the unsung heroes.[17]

Dr. Keshav Baliram Hedgewar

Dr. Keshav Baliram Hedgewar was born on Sunday, April 1, 1889. The Hedgewar family originally hailed from Kandkurti village in Telangana. For better opportunities, many Brahmin families left the Telangana region. Many of them settled down in Nagpur as the Bhonsle Rulers, were known to be patrons of Vedic learning. Among them was Narhari Shastri, whose great grandson was Baliram Pant Hedgewar. In 1853, Nagpur came under the British rule. Vedic learning took a backseat after that as English education took over the former. As a result, many scholars had to resort to priesthood to earn their livelihood. Baliram Pant was one of them, Baliram along with his wife Revatibai, lived a life of contentment. At the age of 13, Keshav lost both his parents to plague. But he continued with his studies amidst quite adverse conditions. He studied in various institutions in Nagpur, Yavatmal and Poona and joined the national movement for freedom. He was greatly influenced by the firebrand nationalism of Lokmanya Tilak. In 1910, he left for Calcutta to study medicine. Trilokynath Chakravariy has written in his book titled 'Thirty Years in Jail' that Keshav Baliram Hedgewar was granted membership of 'Anushilan Samiti', a well-known revolutionary group of freedom fighters at that time. Keshav studied medicine and stayed in Kolkata from 1910 to 1916.[18]

The streak of patriotism was evident in Keshav since his school days. In 1901, when King Edward VII ascended the throne of England, the owners of the Empress Mills in Nagpur had arranged for fireworks. Almost the entire city had gathered to watch this display of fireworks, but Keshav refused to go. Instead he told his young friends, "It is shameful to celebrate the coronation of foreign ruler, and I shall not be party to it." Vaze, one of the Keshav's teachers in the school, used to recount an incident which happened around the same time.[19] During those days, Keshav used to study in the Neil city high school. One day the school inspector was expected to visit the school. Keshav incited students and made a unique plan to welcome him. As soon as he entered, all the students sang in Unison "vande mataram". Inspection came to an End.[20]

It was customary to fly the British Flag (Union Jack) atop the Sitabudi fort in Nagpur. Keshav and his friends decided to replace that flag by theirs. The premises were heavily guarded round the clock. So, this group of boys led by Keshav decided to dig a tunnel to the fort.

"One room in the house of their teacher Vaze had been kept apart for the boys' study. A pick axe, shovel and other implements were brought and they began digging in right earnest, behind closed doors. When the room remained closed for two or three days continuously, Vaze became suspicious and entered the room. A deep pit stared him in the face, beside a corner, anticipating punishment. "What is this you have done?" shouted Vaze. Keshav and his friends explained their intended venture. Vaze patiently advised that boys should not waste their time in such foolhardy activities. However, he could not help admiring the fervent patriotism that had prompted their young minds to undertake the venture."

After finishing his Matriculation examination, Keshav came to Nagpur. He had immersed himself in public activities and developed close relationship with the revolutionaries. He kept himself informed of the activities of the underground activists in various provinces. One such revolutionary from Bengal was Madhavdas Sannyasi. He had been asked to reach Japan by a revolutionary group Krantidal. On his way to Japan, he arrived in Nagpur. Keshav arranged a secret hideout for him in the house of Appaji Halde in the Mohopa village, till his further travel arrangements could be finalised. After spending six months in this secret hideout, Madhavdas left for Japan.

The Nagpur group of revolutionaries had established close contact with the Anushilan Samiti of Calcutta. In fact, funds were collected in Nagpur and sent for activists involved in Alipore Bomb Case. According to Seshadri, "There is documentary evidence showing that Bhayyasaheb Bobade, an advocate, handed a sum of rupees one hundred to Keshav for this purpose."

Amidst these happenings, Keshav's results for the Matriculation examination were announced. He had cleared the examination. The certificate carries the signature of Dr. Rashbehari Ghose, the then President of the National Council of Education (Bengal). It is dated December 1, 1909.

It wasn't a small matter to complete the Matriculation examination in those days. Any other young man who had lived a life of penury would have been tempted to go for a government job with this degree, but Keshav had decided to serve the country and not the colonial government which was ruling India. He decided to join the revolutionaries in Bengal. The revolutionary group in Nagpur also endorsed his decision. They wanted him to go to Calcutta and establish rapport with Pulinbihari Das, a senior leader of the Anushilan Samiti, a revolutionary group which favoured armed revolution to oust the British rule. Ramlal Vajpayee, a US-based revolutionary, has recalled in his autobiography: "With financial help from Shri Dajisaheb Buti, Shri Keshav Hedgewar, was sent to Calcutta - more with the object of receiving training for revoluţionary work under the supervision of Shri Pulinbihari Das, rather than prosecuting higher studies."

In the middle of 1910, Keshav left for Calcutta, carrying a letter of introduction from Dr. Moonje, a leading public figure based in Nagpur and one of his mentors. When Keshav had taken the decision to move to Calcutta, he was staying at the house of Dr. Moonje who had also encouraged him to go there. [21]

After entering the Medical College, Keshav started establishing a network by meeting students from different provinces. Whenever he was not studying, he would visit different hostels. He stayed at Shantiniketan Lodge and ate at his friend's places most of the time. This helped him to strengthen the bond with them. Soon Keshav learnt to speak Bengali language. He frequented the houses of Amulyaratna ghosh, Prafulchand Ganguly , Shyamsundar Chakravorty and Bipin Chandra Pal. Gradually, he became a member of their family. He worked as a volunteer in Swadeshi exhibitions.[22]

As in Nagpur, in Calcutta too, Keshav continued his vigorous physical exercises. He had developed an impressive physique and came across as a fearless patriotic young man.

There were frequent riots in Calcutta. Organising fellow students to rise above provincial separatism, Keshav founded a service unit to serve the victims of these onslaughts, carrying the wounded on stretchers to medical homes, and treating them. Keshavrao kept in touch with many victims even after they recovered and returned home, visiting them in their houses. Keshavrao joined the Ramakrishna Mission relief team sent to work for flood relief in 1913 in Vardhaman District in Bengal. In a team of five, travelling in boats, carrying beaten rice and food for the needy, often wading through waist deep water and mire, avoiding snakes escaping from flood waters, he worked tirelessly, ignoring even the outbreak of cholera. Venkataramana, who was with him, notes in his diary that Keshav's zeal and capacity for work was fantastic.[23]

Despite all these social and political activities, Keshav did not remain behind in studies. He had to deal with great hurdles. He did not have sufficient books. He used to get the books from others, He would read the books at night with utmost concentration and return the same, next morning

Moulvi Liaquat Hussain was a devout follower of Lokmanya Tilak, and had taken the vow of Swadeshi. He himself survived on very less money, but untiringly collected funds for the poor and needy. The funds he collected were used for buying textbooks for the poor students and contributing towards their school fees. He organised early morning processions and public meetings in college squares. Keshav not only participated in these functions with his friends, but also helped in their arrangements.

The British government had realised the potential threat posed by Keshav so ever since he came to Calcutta, he was under constant surveillance. But Keshav was sharp enough to identify the informers.

While staying in Calcutta, Keshav first hand experienced the fragmentation and divisions in the Hindu society as students from one province did not see an eye to eye with students from the other province. He also realised that how disorganised the movement for attaining independence was.

When Lokmanya Tilak had visited Calcutta in 1906, he had initiated the public celebration of Ganeshotsav (festival of Lord Ganesha). Keshav arranged similar celebrations in all the students' hostels. Tilak's incarceration in the Mandalay prison from 1908 to 1914 deeply anguished Keshav.

Aurobindo Ghose who came out of the prison in 1909 aptly described the situation: "Before I moved into the jail, it looked as if the entire nation had been set afire by the resounding cry of 'Vande Mataram! The whole nation had articulated its aspirations and ideals. After I came out of the prison, I longed to hear the same reverberating cry. But there was nothing but muteness everywhere. Quiet and gloom pervaded the entire atmosphere The people appeared benumbed."

Dadasaheb Khaparde, a well-known nationalist, often met Tilak in the Mandalay prison. Whenever he visited Calcutta, Keshav used to invite him to his lodge to talk about Tilak. He also kept himself abreast of Veer Savarkar's condition at the prison in Andamans through letters written by Savarkar to his brother Narayanrao who had become a fellow student of Keshav.

The spurt in the nationalist movement witnessed after the partition of Bengal was met with brutal response from the British government. In the Alipore bomb case, thousands of people were rounded up and a large number of them were imprisoned. The government stopped the publication of weekly 'Yugantar'. It had circulation of more than twenty thousand copies. After completing his education, Hedgewar joined the Anushilan Samiti in Bengal, which was influenced deeply by the writings of Bankim Chandra Chatterjee. Hedgewar's initiation into this group, rooted in Hindu symbolism, was an important step in his path towards creating the RSS.

Led by Pulinbihari, the Anushilan Samiti in Bengal strived hard to bring back the same fierceness to the nationalist movement. One of the tasks taken up by the Samiti was to raise awareness of the public through underground literature. Keshav played an important role in ensuring this literature also reached Nagpur. His friends acted as couriers and whenever he himself went to Nagpur, he would take revolvers for revolutionaries there.

Keshav had become a member of the core group of Anushilan Samiti. His code name was 'Koken'. Trailokyanath Chakravarti had included the photographs of some top members of the Samiti in his book. Keshav's picture also figures in that group. Chakravarti says, "Only those who had taken the ultimate vow were considered full and true members of the Samiti. And only those who had renounced their homes and families were entitled to take that vow." Keshav had met both the conditions. In Anushilan samiti, Hedgewar had first hand knowledge of activities that enabled mass contact and mobilisation, including assisting people during natural disasters which later proved helpful for him.[24]

After completing the five-year course, Dr. Hedgewar returned to Nagpur in early 1916. Dr. Hedgewar resisted pleas to set up practice and get married. Medical practice was lucrative and in great demand, since according to estimates, there were not more than 25 medical practitioners in the whole of Central Provinces and Berar. However, Dr. Hedgewar was not interested in making money or setting up a family.

He was offered a lucrative job in Bangkok after clearing the final examination, but he refused to take up the offer. Many of his fellow students took up offers from the government of the day, but Dr. Hedgewar was quite clear that he would not serve the British government. Instead, he joined Bhauji Kawre in his revolutionary activities in Kranti Dal.

After coming back to Nagpur, Dr. Hedgewar, along with his friend Bhauji Karve, set up revolutionary groups and planned an armed revolution. When marriage proposals came repeatedly, he told his uncle in clear words, " I have vowed to serve the nation for life, so there is no place for family life. God knows how many times may I be jailed while serving the nation, It is quite likely that even my life will be at stake. Therefore, do not think about my marriage at all". [25]

The revolutionary group in Nagpur was also known as Kranti Dal (revolution party). Karve held great influence over the members of the Krantidal. Karve and Dr. Hedgewar had a great equation and they worked in perfect coordination. Both of them also had a strong bond of friendship.

Over the course of several meetings, it was finally decided by both that it was time to plan an armed revolution for India's freedom

It was decided to get fresh recruits and arrange arms and ammunition for the same. Anna Khot started a gymnasium in Nagpur to gather and train fresh recruits. In Wardha and Nagpur, some reading rooms were also started for the same purpose.

Dr. Hedgewar and Karve then went on a tour to Central Provinces and Berar to set the plan in motion. They moved mostly on pretext of attending social gathering on festivals and marriages. With the help of persons who wielded influence at the local level, meetings were arranged in the form of dinners and luncheons where funds were raised to purchase arms. Dr. Hedgewar arranged revolvers and other arms from these funds and sent them to revolutionaries in various parts of the country. Individuals were dispatched to Calcutta, Bhaganagar (Hyderabad) and Goa to purchase the needed arms. Dadasheb Bakshi, a close associate of Dr. Hedgewar, was entrusted with the task of repair and servicing of revolvers.

The duo - Dr. Hedgewar and Karve - successfully established contacts with underground revolutionaries of Bengal and Punjab. A contingent of 20 volunteers from Nagpur and Wardha districts was sent to set up the network of revolutionaries in North India. This contingent was led by a young revolutionary, Gangaprasad Pande.

Pande made Ajmer his headquarters after conducting a survey of Rajasthan. Chandkiran Sarda, a leading public figure of Ajmer, also joined hands with Pande. Dr. Hedgewar coordinated the movement of volunteers and dispatch of funds for activities.

Meanwhile, World War I had begun. Dr. Hedgewar thought it as an opportune moment to openly declare India's independence. He met Dr. Moonje, but couldn't get his approval. He discussed this with few other leaders also, but they too were not forthcoming. With Dr. Moonje's help, he went to meet Lokmanya Tilak at Pune. Both of them discussed the situation arising out of World War and revolutionary activities in Central Provinces and Berar. Apparently, Tilak also thought it was not the right time to make this declaration.

After coming back from Pune, Dr. Hedgewar visited Shivaneri, the birthplace of Shivaji. He came back surcharged with the vibrant memories of Shivaji's childhood and this further strengthened his resolve to dedicate himself to the cause.

One of the volunteers who was recruited by Dr. Hedgewar was Harikrishna (Appaji) Joshi, who remained his lifelong confidant.

Both Karve and Dr. Hedgewar subjected new recruits to close scrutiny and administered them the 'oath of dedication'. The recruits took a vow in front of the portraits of Shivaji and Samarth Ramadas.

The new and old recruits met regularly at Baradwari, Tulsibagh, Sonegaon Mandir, Colonelbagh, Indora Mandir, Mohitewada and other places in Nagpur. At each meeting, the revolutionary literature was distributed. The literature included biographies of foreign revolutionary leaders like Mazzini and Joan of Arc and revolutionaries from Bengal, reports of bomb incidents of Alipore and Manektala, Veer Savarkar's treatise "The 1857 War of independence" under the disarming title of "Two Beauties'. The number of recruits increased to 150 who had enrolled themselves as members of the Krantidal.

An ordinance storehouse of the army was situated at Kamthi near Nagpur. Dr. Hedgewar had established links with some army personnel there for the secret purchase of arms. On one occasion, members of the Krantidal, dressed in army uniforms, carted away a whole consignment of ammunition from the railway clearing house in broad daylight. Plans were afoot for a nationwide uprising. The network created by Karve and Dr. Hedgewar now stretched from Nagpur to distant Punjab.

Now efforts were started to secure ammunition from abroad. Vamanrao Dharmadhikari of Yeotmal recalled, "By 1917-18, Dr. Hedgewar had asked us to be prepared to rise in rebellion." In 1918, Dharmadhikari was sent to Goa as a certain ship with large volumes of ammunition was going to arrive there.

Vamanrao sailed for Goa from Bombay. Another volunteer of the Krantidal, Satara, had already reached Goa. Both of them waited there for eight days, but the ship did not arrive. Then, the news came in that British Navy had intercepted that ship in the high seas. The plan could not be executed. This led to many of the revolutionaries drifting away from Krantidal.

But Dr. Hedgewar's spirits were not dampened. He took a plunge into open public activities. He began with addressing public meetings all over the province on the occasion of 'Ganeshotsava' He also travelled extensively to promote work of the Home League.

Lokmanya Tilak had planned a visit to Berar. Dr. Hedgewar went there before him to look after all the preparations.

"Dr. Hedgewar thus made use of every possible occasion to educate and rouse the people. He addressed gatherings wherever he went, and his speeches were widely acclaimed for their incisiveness. These travels were to meet the Krantidal workers in person and keep up their morale. He had also to decide what was to be done with the funds and ammunition stored already. This was, in fact, his major preoccupation in those days.

Among Dr. Hedgewar's most active colleagues were Ganga Prasad Pande, Appaji Joshi, Baburao Harkare and Nanaji Puranik. By the beginning of 1919, Dr. Hedgewar had received information from Amritsar that the ammunition sent there had been cleverly tucked away. But the workers who had been sent to the North had not yet returned. Appaji Joshi was sent to Amritsar, and he arranged for the return of the workers, making the necessary funds available in some cases. Appaji Joshi also received instructions that Arjunlal Sethi, a revolutionary who had just been released (1919) from jail, should be moved to Wardha. Arjunlal had faced imprisonment for his underground activities and subjected to endless torture. He had, however, stoutly withstood it all, and had not given out the name of even a single colleague.

But the torture he underwent had ruined his health and affected his mental poise, and it was only this that had prompted the police to release him. In accordance with Dr. Hedgewar's instructions, Appaji Joshi brought Arjunlal to Wardha and arranged for his food and lodging.

It took him some three to four years to regain his normal health and mental stability. There was no limit to the caution exercised by Dr. Hedgewar and his co-workers. They knew well that if the government got the slightest scent, not only would their plans be dashed to the ground, but lives and liberty of numerous people would also be endangered. In these circumstances, someone who had returned from Punjab thoughtlessly exploded a bomb at Hingani, and the incident caused grave concern to Dr. Hedgewar and his associates. Government immediately launched a thorough and vigorous investigation followed by arrests.

These episodes made Dr. Hedgewar realise that there was a need to inculcate discipline and patriotism in the society at a much larger scale.

Dr. Hedgewar was also highly influenced by Samarth Ramdas's Dasbodh and Lokamanya Tilak's Geeta Rahasya. His letters often bore quotes from Tukaram, He was deeply influenced by the writings of Lokmanya Bal Gangadhar Tilak, Vinayak Damodar Savarkar, Babarao Savarkar, Sri Aurobindo and B. S. Moonje. He also read Mazzini and other enlightenment philosophers. He considered that the cultural and religious heritage of Hindus should be the basis of Indian nationhood.

Dr. Hedgewar now took a plunge in the public activities and social work. By that time, Dr. Hedgewar had made it clear to his family and friends that he would not follow a normal course of getting married and working for livelihood. Instead, he would spend his life serving the nation.

That was the time when the followers of Lokmanya Tilak were a dominant force in the Nagpur unit of Indian National Congress Party. They had formed the 'Rashtriya Mandal' under which various political activities were organised. Dr. Hedgewar was one of those who pushed for demand of 'Complete Independence' instead the Congress' official demand of an 'Independent Dominion inside of the British Empire'.

The Rashtriya Mandal decided to start a weekly 'Sankalpa' in Hindi. Dr. Hedgewar was at the forefront of this initiative and he went for a hectic four-month tour to popularise the weekly. During the course of his activities, he addressed a number of meetings of students. He developed close contact with many young nationalists. To inspire them through lives of national heroes of India, he founded 'Rashtriya Utsav Mandal'. As the secretary of the Mandal, he played an active role in organising programmes on the birth anniversary of Chattrapati Shivaji, anniversary of Shivaji's coronation, Ganeshotsav, Shastrapooja, Dasanavami, Sankranti and many other Hindu festivals. Several distinguished public personalities addressed the gatherings, which mainly comprised youth, attended these programmes. Dr. Hedgewar often spoke on these programmes and the youth were inspired by this fiery orator.

Meanwhile, Mahatma Gandhi had arrived on the Indian political scenario as a leading figure after the end of the First World War. The Khilafat and non-cooperation movement against the British rule had caught imagination of the masses. Dr. Hedgewar attended the Congress session held in Amritsar in 1919 and went to see the blood-stained site of Jallianwala Bagh. This moved him and further reinforced his commitment to the national cause.

The subsequent Congress session was to be held in Nagpur: There was a strong campaign that this session should be presided over by Lokmanya Tilak - an ambition which had not been fulfilled in 1907. Preparations started in full steam. A reception committee was constituted and an impressive publicity campaign was launched. A news report in the periodical Maharashtra' said, "Accompanied by the leaders, the villagers elaborately decorated the villages and welcomed the guests. The enthusiasm of the peasant folk was unprecedented.

The lectures by Dr. Moonje, Dr. Hedgewar, Ganpathrao Joshi and Babasaheb Deshpande cast a spell over the masses." One of the peculiarities of national politics at the time was the practice of simultaneous membership in multiple organisations. For instance, both Congress and Hindu Mahasabha boasted several common members including stalwarts Lala Lajpat Rai, Madan Mohan Malviya, Dr.Moonje, N C Kelkar and several others. Dr. Hedgewar was in forefront in organising Congress session in his hometown."

In January 1920, Dr. L.V. Paranjpe started the Bharat Swayamsevak Mandal. Dr. Hedgewar was an active member and worked closely with Dr. Paranjpe as his deputy. In July 1920, efforts began to set up a corps of around 1,000-1,500 volunteers for the Congress session. Dr. Hedgewar was on the forefront of organising these corps. In the 1920 session of the Indian National Congress held in Nagpur, which was the biggest conference ever then, a total number of 14583 delegates were present. Bharat Swayamsevak Mandal, under Dr. Paranjape and Dr.Hedgewar had undertaken the arrangements of the conference. All the volunteers were asked to wear a uniform, which was later adopted by the RSS as its own official uniform from 1925 to 1940.

However, even as these efforts were on by enthusiastic supporters of Lokmanya Tilak, tragedy struct. Tilak passed away on the night of July 31, 1920. After Tilak's demise, Dr. Moonje and Dr. Hedgewar went to Pondicherry to invite Aurobindo Ghose to preside over the session. Both of them met Aurobindo Ghose and urged him to come and preside over the Congress session, but he refused.

The Congress session took place in December 1920 under presidentship of C. Vijayaraghavachariar. It was attended by over 3,000 members of the Reception Committee, nearly 15,000 delegates and thousands of common people. Dr. Paranjpe and Dr. Hedgewar were in charge of lodging and food for the delegates. A resolution to support the complete non-cooperation movement was accepted.

Dr. Hedgewar wanted to push it further. He, along with some other leaders from Nagpur, urged to go for a resolution declaring 'Complete Independence'. But their suggestion was not accepted. The Congress accepted a resolution demanding 'Swaraj (Self-Rule)' within one year.

Though Dr. Hedgewar disagreed Gandhi's policy of launching the non-cooperation movement with Khilafat as its major plank, as the Khilafat agitation was aimed at restoring the Caliphate in Turkey, he continued to travel and address meetings, inspiring people to join the freedom struggle.

Dr. Hedgewar sensed danger in Gandhi's slogan of Hindu-Muslim unity, linking Khilafat with non-cooperation. He met Gandhi and argued that it was wrong to reduce to question of unity of different sects in a multi-religious society to a bi-polarity of Hindu-Muslim unity alone. Gandhi replied that this was aimed to secure a friendly attitude of Muslims and their participation in the nationalist struggle. Against this, Dr. Hedgewar argued that leading Muslims like Barrister Jinnah, Dr. Ansari,Hakim Ajmal Khan and others had identified with the nation and worked with Hindus under Tilak's leadership long before Gandhi's slogan of Hindu Muslim unity. He expressed the fear that this new slogan instead of helping unity, might further aggravate the feeling of separateness among the Muslims". Gandhi closed the discussion with the abrupt remark: "I have no such fear".

Unfortunately, Dr. Hedgewar's fears proved to be right. By the time he was released from prison, separatism affected even educated muslims, and Jawaharlal Nehru remarked in his autobiography: "Even western-educated Muslims who had no genuine religious feelings began to grow beards and observe external Islamic rituals." Over 80 lakh rupees collected for the Khilafat movement, to which Hindus had generously contributed, went into the hands of fanatical Muslims. While Hindus burnt foreign clothes, Muslims sought permission to send the foreign clothes to their Turkish brethren. Finally, the Moplahs of Kerala (in the south) rebelled, killing a thousand Hindus, converting twenty thousand, dishonouring and abducting thousands of Hindu women, looting property worth more than Rs. 3 crores (Servants of India Society report). Dr. Moonje, who had toured the area, described it as the biggest Muslim attack on the Hindus after Muslim rule had ended.

Reflecting this view, Mohammad Ali, a leader of the Khilafat movement, declared: "However, pure Mr. Gandhi's character may be, he must appear to be from the point of view of religion, inferior to any mussalman, even though he be without character." Even Gandhi, who supported the Moplahs and the assassin of Swami Shradhananda, finally admitted that the root cause of the riots was Muslim aggression and Hindu weakness. "Before his murder, Swami Shraddhananda testified before the Non-cooperation Enquiry Committee, that Hindus were and stressed the need to organise them."

Dr. Hedgewar toured the rural areas in Central provinces extensively to garner support for the non-cooperation movement. In addition, he also spoke at several public meetings in Bombay and its suburbs. His inspiring speeches drew many young men who dedicated their lives for the country. One of them was Dada Parmarth, who later wrote, "The very mention of the name of the British or their rule set Dr. Hedgewar's mind afire. His works made the audience feel as if the enemy was physically present there and Dr. Hedgewar was pouncing on him in fury! Deep indignation against the foreign domination ran through him like an electric current. Burning eyes, clenched fist, and violently gesticulating arms made him look the very image of Yamaraja (God of Death)."

In May, 1921, he was arrested on charges of 'sedition' for his "objectionable" speeches at Katol and Bharatwada. The hearing of his case began on June 14, 1921, and the court was presided over by Judge Smely. After a few hearings, Dr. Hedgewar decided to use this opportunity in the best possible way and, hence, pleaded his own case.

He read out a written statement on August 5, 1921, which said:

1. It has been charged that my speeches have spread discontent, hatred and feelings of sedition towards the British Empire in the minds of Indians and sown seeds of enmity between Indians and Europeans. And I have been asked to explain. I consider it an affront to the

dignity of my great country that a foreign government should subject a native Indian to inquiry and sit in judgement.

2. I do not recognise that there exists in India today any lawfully established government. It will be surprising if anybody should claim so. What obtains today is a regime of usurped authority and a repressive rule deriving power therefrom. The present laws and courts are but handmaids of this unauthorised regime. In any part of the world, it is only a government of the people constituted for the people that is entitled to administer law. All the other forms of rule are but ruses adopted by deceitful usurpers to loot helpless nations.

3. What I tried to do was to inspire in the hearts of my countrymen an attitude of reverential solicitude for their motherland which at the moment happens to be in a wretched condition. I tried to instill in the people the conviction that India belongs to Indians. If an Indian speaking for his country and spreading the nationalist feeling is regarded as committing sedition, if he cannot speak the truth without promoting hatred between Indians and Europeans, Europeans and those claiming to be the Indian government would do well to bear in mind that the day is not far off when foreigners will be forced to quit this country.

4. The government's version of my speech is neither accurate nor complete. Some stray notes and absurd sentences have been sloppily put together. But that does not bother me. In dealing with British and Europeans, I have borne in mind only the basic principles that ought to govern the relationship between two countries. Whatever I have said has been with a view to asserting the birthright of my countrymen and the inevitability of securing our independence. I am prepared to stand by each word that I have uttered. Though I cannot say anything else concerning the charges against me, I am prepared to justify each word and letter of my speech; and I declare that whatever I have said is lawful.

Dr. Hedgewar gave highly aggressive speeches with Dr. Moonje for 2-3 months in many places like Bhandara, Khapa, Kelwad, Talegaon, Dashasahasra, Deoli, Vardha, Bori, etc. To stop him, the district collector, Cyril James Irwin banned his public speaking and holding meetings for one year, via a notice dated 23 February, 1921. He did not stop his meetings. Finally, he was put on trial in May 1921 for his 'objectionable speeches'. His defence on 5th August was so fiery that the judge Smelly exclaimed, "His statement of defence is more seditious than his speech!" He was given one-year imprisonment on 19th August. 10 Excerpt of his inspiring speech while going to the jail is quoted at the beginning of this chapter:

"Just as it is true that one should always be ready to be imprisoned, or be sent to Kalapani, or get hanged, it is equally true that one should not at all be in confusion that going to prison is like reaching heavens, as if this imprisonment itself means achieving freedom. One should definitely not understand that filling prisons will get us freedom or swarajya. The truth is that one can serve the nation in many ways by being out of prison."

At the time of his statement, the court was filled to the capacity. This statement was followed by a brief speech by Dr. Hedgewar. He said, "India belongs to Indians. We, therefore, demand Independence. This is the content of all my speeches. People have to be told how to secure Independence, and also how to conduct themselves after securing it. Otherwise, it is quite likely that our people may imitate the British in Independent India. The British, though they are aggressing on other nations and governing them through repressive measures, but the very same

British people are ready to shed blood when their own country's independence is threatened. The recent war bears testimony to it. We, are therefore, obliged to advise our people, 'Dear countrymen don't imitate the aggressive ways of the British. Secure independence by peaceful means, and be happy and content with your own country without hungering for others' territories.' In order to explain this idea, I cannot avoid referring to the current political issues. That the British have been carrying on their despotic rule in our beloved country is obvious to everyone. What law is there that gives one country the right to rule over another? I am asking you, the counsel for government, this simple and straight question. Can you answer it? Is it not against natural justice? If it is true that no country has a right to rule over another country, who gave the British the authority to trample the people of India under their feet? Do the British belong to this land? How then can they enslave us and declare that they own this country? Is it not the most blatant murder of justice, morality and dharma?

We have no desire to dispossess Britain and rule over it. Just as the British in Britain and the Germans in Germany rule over themselves, we of this country of India wish to rule over ourselves and carry on our own affairs. Our mind revolts at the thought of remaining the slaves of the British Empire and carrying that stigma for all time. We demand nothing short of 'Complete Independence' Till we achieve it, we cannot be at peace. Is our desire to be free and independent in our own country against morality and law? I believe that law exists not to demolish morality and law? I believe that law exists not to demolish but to enforce it. That ought to be the prime purpose of law."

In his judgement delivered on August 19, the judge ordered him to give an undertaking in writing that he would not deliver seditious speeches in future for a period of one year and furnish bail of 3,000.

Dr. Hedgewar's reaction was:

"My conscience tells me that I am completely innocent. A policy of repression would only add fuel to the fire already raging because of government's vicious policies. I am convinced that the day is not far off for the foreign regime to reap the fruits of its sinful actions. I have faith in the justice of the Omnipresent God. I, therefore, refuse to comply with the order for bail."

As soon as he finished his reply, the judge sentenced him to one year's rigorous imprisonment. Dr. Hedgewar went outside the court where a large number of people had gathered. Addressing them, he said, "As you are aware, I have defended myself in this case of sedition against me. However, these days, there is an impression going round that arguing in one's defence is an act of treachery to the national movement. But I feel it is highly unwise to merely get crushed like a bug when a case is foisted upon us. It is our duty to expose to the whole world the wickedness of the foreign rulers. That would indeed be an act of patriotism. And not to defend ourselves, on the other hand, would be a suicidal policy. You may, if you so choose, refuse to defend yourself, but for God's sake, don't consider those who disagree with you as being less patriotic. If, in the course of our patriotic duty, we are called upon to enter the prison or be transported to Andamans, or even face the gallows, we shall have to willingly do so. But let us not be under the illusion that jail-going is all in all, that it is the only path for achieving freedom. There are, in fact, so many fields of national service awaiting us outside the prison. I would be back amongst you after one year. Till then, of course, I will not be in touch with the national development, but I am confident that by then, the movement for 'Complete Independence' will have gained the added momentum. Now, it is no more possible to keep down Hindustan under the heels of foreign domination. I offer my gratitude to you all and bid you good-bye."

On Friday, August 19, 1921, he was moved into Ajani jail. According to Seshadri, "That very evening, a public meeting to honour him in absentia was convened in the Townhall grounds. Barrister Govindrao Deshmukh presided. Dr. Moonje, Narayanrao Harkare and Vishwanathrao Kelkar - all spoke in a warm strain. "Because of his sacrifice and deep concern for the nation, Dr. Hedgewar will doubtless be the leader of the coming generation,". said Harkare. They all showered unstinted praise on Dr. Hedgewar for his commitment to Complete Independence. Speaking at the end, Vishwanathrao Kelkar recalled the message Dr. Hedgewar had delivered just before proceeding to the prison."

When he came out of prison on 12 July, 1922, he was given a rousing welcome despite a heavy downpour. He was given a huge public reception in the evening in Venkatesh Theatre due to inclement weather. Top national leaders of Congress came to fete him. They included Hakim Ajmal Khan, Pandit Motilal Nehru, Rajagopalachari, Dr. Ansari, Vitthalbhai Patel, and Kasturirangan Iyengar. Pandit Motilal Nehru and Hakim Ajmal Khan too spoke in this programme. In his speech in front of the multitude, Dr. Hedgewar said, "Just being a state guest in a prison for one year does not mean that my qualification has increased, nor has it given me a new identity for the world. If at all, my qualification does seem to have increased, one must thank the government for this. It will not be ideal to have any goal less than full freedom." We find a sense of self-abnegation that was the hallmark of all his acts throughout his life and so also of RSS, viz. keeping social interest above self-interest and keeping away from self-promotion. The weekly 'Maharashtra' wrote an article on Dr. Hedgewar's release from jail saying: "No words can adequately describe Dr. Hedgewar's intense spirit of patriotism and selflessness. These traits of his have now become all the more resplendent after the fire ordeal."

Speaking at the reception to welcome him, Dr. Hedgewar said, "The fact that I was a guest of the government for a year has not in the least added to my merit; and if at all it has increased, the credit for it should go to the government! We have today to place before the country the highest and noblest of ideals. Any ideal short of Complete Independence will take us nowhere. To expound to you the method whereby that goal can be achieved would be an insult to your intelligence as all of you doubtless are aware of lessons of history. Even if death were to stare us in the face, we are not to shirk in our path; we have to keep the ultimate goal constantly burning in our mind and calmly carry on the fight."

One more point which he clarified during the course of his speech, on this occasion as well as at other places, was regarding 'non-violence!' He maintained, "Real non-violence lies in the attitude of the mind. At heart, one should not harbour feelings of violence or hatred.

One may outwardly carry out certain acts which appear to involve physical violence, but if it is done in a spirit of detachment and without any selfish motive or hatred, then the act can no longer be termed violent. This is what Shri Krishna says in the Bhagavad Gita." [26]

After Nagpur, he was felicitated at Yavattmal, Wani, Arvi, Wadhona, Mohopa and several other places. However, these felicitations didn't lessen his concern over the grave situation in the country. Even as Dr. Hedgewar mulled over the need and urgency for organising Hindus to make India a stronger nation once she attains independence, he was appointed as joint secretary of the Provincial Congress in 1922. He was also part of the Hindusthani Seva Dal, a Congress wing of volunteers. The Hindusthani Seva Dal was set up by Dr. N.S. Hardikar of Hubli whom Dr. Hedgewar had known from his student days. Initially, they were politically active together. However, later Hardikar came under the influence of Gandhi, while Hedgewar was under the influence of Lokmanya Tilak. Hedgewar was associated with the Hindustani Seva Dal till he founded RSS. In order to combat indiscipline in Congressmen, to inculcate dedication among them, he tried to organise a volunteer corps in the Congress. He called for four volunteers from each Taluq, but his move ran into difficulties due to the attitude of congressmen who expected volunteers to be merely "charge-free hamals" and assistants to political leaders. Even as Dr.Hardikar's Hindustani Seva Dal (1923) ran into opposition from leading Congressmen, as observed by Nehru.[28]

With such opposition to Hindusthani Seva Dal, Dr. Hedgewar was not very hopeful of infusing discipline amongst Congress cadres. He had been dreaming of building an organisation which had lakhs of people, ready to sacrifice themselves, for the nation.

Allergy to any kind of discipline within Congress, Doctor Hedgewar was against the view that you needed 'yes sir' kind of volunteers only for laying durries and chairs. This strange obsession of dominant section of Congress with non-discipline could be the reason behind the anarchic way our republic and its politics have evolved.

It was time to look out for new options beyond Congress. Dr. Hedgewar invited Gangaprasad Pandey, the revolutionary leader, who had gone to Punjab and Rajasthan to start a wrestling school in Nagpur to attract the youth. But within a year of starting this school, the British government started tailing Pandey. So, he had to be moved from there and the school also closed down.

Dr. Hedgewar never lost a friendship on account of differing viewpoints. Thus, whenever I went to his house, he used to say smilingly, I welcome you, but not your way of thinking!

In 1923, the Nagpur branch of Hindu Mahasabha was set up. Raja Lakshmanrao Bhonsle was its President and Dr. Hedgewar was the Secretary.

In the Deogarh Congress Conference of 1923, over which he presided, when Mahatma Bhagavan Deen, a Gandhian, attempted to leave in protest against go-puja and a cow-protection resolution, Dr. Hedgewar not only prevented Bhagavan Deen from leaving, but gave him the floor to present his views on the subject. Only after Bhagavan Deen spoke, Dr. Hedgewar addressed the Conference. He would not favour estrangement merely because of ideological differences. Hedgewar religiously maintained ties with both Congress and Mahasabha. It remain tradition for him to attend sessions of Congress and Mahasabha regularly.

In 1923, when Savarkar was still in prison, Sardar Vallabhbhai Patel and others pleaded in the Bombay Legislative Council for his release. A public meeting was held in Nagpur also where Dr. Hedgewar mounted a scathing attack on the government demanding release of Savarkar. He said, "In convicting Savarkar, the government has murdered justice, and if the government is interested in washing off this blot, let it forthwith release him. The government will not be bestowing any special favour if it were to release him now, after fourteen years of cruel incarceration. If even now the government does not care to release him, it will only be one more evidence of its evil intentions towards our country."[29]

In the second half of 1923, Dr. Hedgewar with few others launched a daily newspaper called "Swatantrya". Swatantrya began to appear under the editorship of Vishwanathrao Kelkar. However, within a year, due to the financial losses, the publication was struggling. Dr. Hedgewar had to take over the role of the editor.

By then, Dr.Hedgewar had delved deep into the problem of nationalism in India, mulling over the reasons for the floundering of and divisions in the freedom struggle. Patriotism was at the time, mainly an anti-British reaction, and no one seemed to realise the need for constructively arousing the self-confidence of society, building discipline and organisation that would lay foundations for real freedom, and consolidate the patriotic fervour of individuals instead of letting it evaporate after periodic outbursts.[29]

The Non-Cooperation movement gradually died down and a large number of people who participated in it were disillusioned. Meanwhile, even as Mahatma Gandhi championed the cause of Hindu-Muslim unity, riots took place between 1921 and 1923 at several places across the country. Hindus were largely at the receiving end.

There were gruesome assaults by Moplahs in Kerala on Hindus in Malabar region, while Dr. Hedgewar was in prison. The Congress had underplayed this incident and, hence, the rest of the country was not aware of the loot, plunder and the bloodbath targeting Hindus there. According to a report published by the Servants of India Society, "One thousand Hindus were killed. Twenty thousand Hindus were forcibly converted, and thousands of Hindu women dishonoured and abducted. Property to the tune of over 3 crores was looted."

To acquire first-hand knowledge of the happenings, Dr. Moonje personally toured the troubled areas of Malabar. Dr. Hedgewar came to know of the real situation through Dr. Moonje.

In 1923, the Khilafat movement was turned into an anti Hindu hysteria. Bhai Parmanand wrote about the sufferings of Hindus in Saharanpur

"My heart wept at the pitiable condition and hardship of the Hindus. I came to know that the office-bearers of the local Khilafat committee were themselves personally responsible for inciting riots and destroying Hindu life, honour and property. It is clear that the Khilafat movement is the source of all these uprisings."

Riots also broke out in Nagpur, Amethi, Sambhal, Gulbarga, Kohat and other places. The riots at Kohat on 9-10 September resulted in killing of at least 150 Hindus and property worth crores was looted. Congress leader, Sarojini Naidu wrote to Mahatma Gandhi, saying, "We had better put an end to our talks of peace." Mahatma Gandhi began a 21-day fast in Delhi at the house of Maulana Mohammed Ali to end the violence.

Dr. Ambedkar aptly described the end result of this exercise: "Lofty resolutions were passed in Peace Committee sessions. It looked as if each such resolution provided fresh license for violence."[30]

Pt. Madan Mohan Malaviya, in his address, at the Belgaum session of the Hindu Mahasabha in 1923, said, "But for the weakness and fear enveloping the Hindus, many Hindu-Muslim clashes could have been averted. These clashes have driven the country to its present critical situation. It is, therefore, imperative to eradicate the weakness of the Hindus." [31]

Before his murder, Swami Shraddhananda testified before the Non-cooperation Enquiry Committee, that Hindus were divided and not as well organised as Muslims, and stressed the need to organise them

These developments pressed upon Dr. Hedgewar to organise the Hindus. By that time, Savarkar had been able to publish his historical treatise on 'Hindutva'. Savarkar had written it in a prison in Andaman and with great difficulty, it could be smuggled out. Savarkar's treatise defined 'Hindu nationhood' for the first time in recent history.

In 1924, Dr. Hedgewar organised a meeting attended by his close associates including Bhauji Kawre, Appaji Joshi, and Vishwanathrao Kelkar. He discussed the idea of organising Hindus and took the feedback. This could be termed as the turning point where the seeds for setting up Rashtriya Swayamsevak Sangh were sown.

Appaji Joshi recalled what happened at the meeting: "The friends who had assembled that day belonged to different parties. Some had been influenced by Mahatmaji. Some owed allegiance to the Swarajya Party. Seeing their disparateness, Dr. Hedgewar decided early in 1925 to initiate the work of resurrecting the Hindu nation with the help of only like-minded people." Lala Lajpat Rai made the formation of akharas an integral part of the sangathan as Mahasabha president in 1925, which had an impact on Dr. Hedgewar.

After it became clear to Dr. Hedgewar that he would work on organising Hindus, he went to meet Vinayak Damodar Savarkar, popularly known as Veer Savarkar, who was then in detention at Ratnagiri. There was a plague outbreak. So, Savarkar had moved to the house of Vishnu Pant Damle in Sirgaon. Dr. Hedgewar spent two days there and discussed various issues at length with Savarkar.

While being active in freedom movement, one question always bothered Dr. Hedgewar. How could a handful of British coming from 7,000 km across the seas rule over our huge nation? He realised that there was something wrong with us. In his years in public life, he realised that our society had forgotten its own history and was fragmented on lines of caste, language and regionalism. He saw that it was disorganised and stifled by oppressive customs that could be exploited by the British. If we did not change even after gaining independence, history could repeat itself. Therefore, the most important fundamental work seemed to raise the nation above caste and creed, reform it, organise it, help get it rid of its oppressive customs, raise its national consciousness. He could see that it was possible only by keeping away from politics, propaganda and working silently in a sustained manner.

Every movement in this country has had Hindus as its object, whether it was for religious reforms, for social reforms, or for social equality. Thus, the Hindu has been the presiding deity of every major change in this sub-continent. It was therefore on the Hindu that nationalism had to rest. In the body of this country of many peoples, the Hindu was the vital life-force. Hence all the reasons, evils, and weaknesses that made the Hindus effete, dividing them in the name of language, caste, region and class, had to be eliminated in order to rejuvenate nationalism.[32]

With this thought in mind, he founded Sangh in 1925 on Vijayadashami day along with other stalwarts.

The festive day of 'Vijayadashmi', is also known as 'Dussehra'. This festival marks the victory of good over evil as according to the Indian history, this is the day when Lord Rama, who represented the 'Good', killed Ravana, a symbol of 'Evil'.

When Dr. Hedgewar founded the Sangh in this political backdrop, he did not intend to create a Hindu defence force or an army of swayamsevaks (volunteers) to engage in Hindu political activity. Had that been his intention, he could have very well carried out the work of Hindu consolidation from the platform of the Hindu Mahasabha itself. He enjoyed a place of respect in the Mahasabha and also close access to all prominent local and national Mahasabha leaders like Pt. Malviya, Dr Moonje, N.C.Kelkar, Bhai Paramanand, Savarkar brothers and Padmaraj Jain.

Dr. Hedgewar was aware of the need to counter communal events and happenings and political mobilization over attacks on Hindus, and also knew that the Hindu Mahasabha was shouldering the responsibility in this regard. But the national problem required a lasting and permanent solution. The organization that Mahasabha conceived of was based on political imperatives and impulsive behaviour. Actions undertaken at the spur of the moment, or as a reaction to events lose their luster as soon as the immediate impact and potency of those events diminish. Dr. Hedgewar's idea of a Hindu organization was one that was based on positive values, progressive and all-pervading. He therefore, preferred to remain aloof from the prickly issue of the utility or lacunae of existing Hindu organizations and charted his path afresh. No wonder the year 1925 became a milestone in the history of Indian nationalism. It was a unique link to connect the past with the present and that with posterity to nurture the cultural character of modern nation.

Philosophical Background

It is not easy to discern how far Dr Hedgewar agreed with Hindu political thought and activities from Mukherji-Lalchand (1909) to Malviya-Moonje (1923). Studies on the Sangh are of the view that Dr. Hedgewar also belonged to this tradition. This however, is a simplistic, common and rather superficial manner to analyse, define and view the Hindu thought process in a holistic way. Possibly, one reason for this might also be the fact that Dr. Hedgewar never publicly expressed his disapproval or criticism of contemporary Hindu nationalist political streams, organizations or leaders, nor did he ever enter into competition for leadership or chalking out a parallel ideological path. Therefore, he was seen as a link in the chain of Dr Moonje, Malviya, Paramanand and Savarkar, at least on the surface. But a deeper insight showed his outlook to be quite distinct from those of contemporary Hindu political leaders.

Dr. Hedgewar considered the Hindu society, culture and its dharma to be a part of the Indian civilization. The nation takes birth from the womb of civilization, whose flow is strengthened because of the nation it inhabits. Therefore, the Hindu nation is a mirror reflecting its historical consciousness in a cultural manner since time immemorial. Hindu philosophy, literature, culture and history engender a feeling of oneness. Hindu organizations are but means to provide a lasting, dynamic and solid base to nationalism in a cultural perspective. That is the reason Dr. Hedgewar said, "The Sangh's work or its ideology are by no means our invention. Our pristine Sanatan Hindu Dharma, ancient culture, Hindu nation and our highly venerated and timeless saffron flag all these have been presented by the Sanghbefore all in their original conceptual form. The Sangh shall accept whatever methodology is deemed necessary to infuse new dynamism in these concepts in accordance with circumstances".

Hedgewar rejected U.N. Mukherjee's idea that the Hindus were a "dying race". His opinion was that judging Hindus on the basis of their numerical strength alone and imagining the downfall of the Hindu nation of course gives critical direction but did not answer cultural questions. Hindus are a historical race denoting a distinct national identity, which is by nature imbibed with a certain consciousness. The reasons for this nation's weaknesses are the defeats suffered by the Hindu society, dharma and culture. Hindus had lacked the organizational instinct in the past. Dr. Hedgewar was of the clear opinion that "it is the weak society that is the root cause of external aggression. In fact, the blame for disrupting peace in the world is also laid on such weak societies and nations. Therefore, instead of wasting time blaming aggressors, it is the prime duty of the weak society and people to dispel their weakness by every means". Accept only that which stands to your reason. Never accept anything merely because it is preached by some great leader. Test its truth on the touchstone of your intellectual insight.

Dr. Hedgewar's stress was on two important aspects. First, blaming external factors for the weak political and social condition of Hindu society was to turn away from reality. Second, ascendancy is established by one's internal determination and willpower. Therefore, the diagnosis of the present state of affairs was to ceaselessly arouse and strengthen the feeling of nationalism among the Hindus. The reason for Hindus' weaknesses was their fealty to divisive and narrow considerations. Therefore, the foremost responsibility of the organization was to awaken the Hindus' historic role on the basis of their nationalism, which remains embedded in their sublime consciousness. Dr. Hedgewar's vision was both expansive as well as all-encompassing. The Sangh's founding was not a mere reaction to the Moplah riots against Hindus, but on a positive plane. He argued: "Today, Hindus number twenty-five crores in India. The population is thirty-five crores; from where did they come? The other ten crore people at some point of time were our people". His next question denotes his balanced intellect and broad ideological template. Dr. Hedgewar asks: "Why did we lose them? It is because we were lost in deep slumber, which is why we lost them". This self-analysis was an altogether different plane as far as Hindu nationalist thinking, contemplation and reflection were concerned.

He did not approve of the definitions of 'Hindu' and 'Hindu nation', provided by contemporary Hindu nationalists, the fundamental principles of RSS. He knew the meaning of the term Hindu had got constrained and contracted due to steady external and internal aggressions and as a result, was brought down to the level of mere ritualistic practices of worshipping rather than a substantive way of life. He firmly believed and hoped that in course of time, it would regain its original meaning and percept in a civilization culture contest. He knew very well that definitions woven in words were incapable of articulating or manifesting the formless content of emotions, and this limitation would render any principle ineffective. In the Sangh's functioning, Dr. Hedgewar connected intellectualism to activity and principle to practice and turned his attention to those questions that had been hitherto untouched. For instance, what was the practical construct of a Hindu? How national-minded is he and how close is he to nationalism and culture? To which identity of his caste, class, regional, linguistic or national does he attach importance and priority? How much balance does he achieve between personal affiliations and national ones? How much does he feel for his responsibility towards the nation, rising above personal and familial commitments?

The underlying principle of the Sangh is thoughtful activity. In this regard, Dr. Hedgewar said, "Let it be understood clearly that the Sangh is not a gymnasium, a club or a military school. It is a nationalist organization of the Hindus and must be stronger than steel". Undoubtedly Dr. Hedgewar established the Sangh in the same environment in which other Hindu organizations operated, but its character was fully original.

He elicited the views of all of them regarding future activities of the Sangh. "All of us must train ourselves physically, intellectually and in every way so as to be capable of achieving our cherished goal," he declared.

This organisation, RSS, was born not due to political differences with any leader or political party but with a clear positive thought and idea of organising and reforming Hindu society.

Dr. Hedgewar could have stayed back in Congress and become a prominent leader. But, he chose a different path, a more difficult path where he pushed himself beyond very limit of human endurance and dedication to bring up a new organisation based on sacrifice, selfless service and strong sense of brotherly affection. As a fledgling organisation that worked for creating disciplined patriot citizens with character, it was a long haul for RSS. moulding human beings is a slow process.

Interestingly, initially there were no formal preparation for the RSS. The only agenda was to train the young men making them physically, mentally and intellectually strong to serve the country.[33]

The first daily 'Shakha' of RSS actually began from May 28, 1926, which had a regular schedule. The place where daily gathering of the initial volunteers/swayamsevaks of the RSS took place was Mohitewada Ground in Nagpur, which is today art of the sprawling RSS headquarters complex. Initially, some Commands to swayamsevaks were given in Sanskrit. There were some commands given in English also but they were gradually replaced by the commands in Sanskrit or in local Indian languages over a period of time as the RSS grew. There was a conscious effort to repose and rekindle faith in the Indian culture with Sanskrit as its integral part. Even today, this tradition of giving key commands in Sanskrit continues at thousands of daily Shakhas. A Saffron Flag used to be hoisted, which is known as 'Bhagwa Dhwaj' in RSS terminology and the first Shakha used to begin with a salutation to the Saffron Flag. This tradition continues even today with the beginning and end of every daily Shakha happening with a salutation to a Saffron Flag which is designed in such a fashion that it appears to have two flames of fire.

Initially, the first daily 'Shakha' used to end after recitation of a concluding prayer which was a combination of Marathi and Hindi verses. Later on, it was replaced by a Sanskrit prayer. Both these prayers were focussed on promoting nationalistic fervour among the swayamsevaks.

Dr. Hedgewar himself would attend the Shakha daily. After the close of the Shakha, members of each unit met Dr.Hedgewar before departing. Dr. Hedgewar would keenly inquire about absentees, if any, and made it a point to visit their houses to find out the reason for their absence. If he was preoccupied, he sent some other worker to inquire and report. Often, Dr. Hedgewar came to the Shakha earlier than others. He would clean the ground and sprinkle water. He freely joined with the youngsters in various games, as he was convinced that was the surest way to enter into their lives.

Dr. Hedgewar used to say - "We need lakhs and lakhs of young men wholly dedicated to the uplift of the nation. It is they who can bring about the much needed national awakening; and this national consciousness has to be transmitted to successive generations. Then only will the grave problems besetting our country be solved. The Shakha was the instrument he conceived of for realizing this goal of national self-rejuvenation".

It is worthwhile mentioning here that when Dr. Hedgewar was at forefront of the Dindi satyagraha, several people who ran akharas, gyms and bodybuilding clubs, were invited to participate in the campaign, despite no prior experience in politics and Hedgewar promptly invite them yet again to steer the physical activities of the sangh. Dr. Hedgewar also enlisted the assistance of a retired army officer, Martandrao Jog, to conduct weekly parade for the Swayamsevaks. The fact that Jog also involved with Hindustani seva Dal, didn't deter Dr. Hedgewar from involving him in the sangh's activities, as long as the ideological control remained in his hands, he saw no harm in utilising professional expertise from others.

The initial prayer for the first Shakha could be translated as: "Salutations to the Motherland where I am born. Salutations to the Hindu Land where I have been brought up. Salutations to the Land of Dharma for which may my body fall. To Her, I salute again and again."

Currently, the prayer in Sanskrit is also on similar lines. It is interesting to note that the RSS got its present name almost six months after it was founded. On April 17, 1926, Dr. Hedgewar called a meeting at his house in which 26 swayamsevaks participated. A detailed discussion followed to decide the name of the organisation for which everyone contributed their ideas. None of them were aware that the name decided at the meeting would one day find huge resonance across the globe in the years to come. Several names were suggested and each of the names was discussed threadbare. Finally, three names were finalised after several rounds of elimination. They were:

1. Rashtriya Swayamsevak Sangh. 2. Jaripataka Mandal. 3. Bhedra tod dharak Mandal. There were more deliberations on these three names and finally the name 'Rashtriya Swayamsevak Sangh' was chosen.

Initially, activities related to the physical training were entrusted to Anna Sohni. Training in drill and marching was imparted on Sundays by Martandrao Jog. On Thursdays and Sundays, there were discourses on national affairs. These sessions later on came to be known as Bouddhik Varga. Dr. Hedgewar and Vishwanathrao Kelkar addressed these sessions. Amongst others who were also encouraged to speak there were young men like Balaji Huddar, Dada Paramarth and Bhayyaji Dani. Dr. Hedgewar showed keen interest in the welfare of every swayamsevak. The methodology which he had developed to build this organisation was based on personal bonding - one lamp lightens another, one heart kindles another. All the swayamsevaks (volunteers) used to meet once a month to decide upon the activities of the next month.

The report of a meeting (June 21, 1926) recorded by Raghunathrao Bande, who was the Nagpur Karyavaha (in-charge) at that time provides a glimpse of Dr. Hedgewar's style. The report says, "In that session Dr. Hedgewar asked each swayamsevak to state in writing his ideal, the ideal of the Sangh, and how he would organise the Sangh and its activities if he was made the Chalak, i.e., chief. The statements were to be handed over to Dr. Hedgewar before 28th. This indicated the measure of Dr. Hedgewar's concern that the swayamsevaks should themselves think over and imbibe the Sangh ideal and pursue the Sangh activities with self-sustaining zeal and devotion."

In 1926, Dr. Hedgewar asked Martandrao Jog who had retired from the army in 1920 to conduct the weekly parade of the swayamsevaks. Jog was also the chief for the Congress Seva Dal at that time. Martandrao in a letter to Golwalkar later wrote: "I am now totally one with the Sangh. It is the Sangh which has developed my personality. It was Dr. Hedgewar's love which had carved out a place for me in the Sangh."

The setting up of cavalry units wherever it was possible was also encouraged. The wearing of the Sangh uniform during the parade was mandatory. The first route march of swayamsevaks witnessed presence of 30 persons. With great difficulty, money was raised for purchasing the first-ever band instrument.

A special training programme for the selected swayamsevaks was organised in May 1927. It was called the Officers Training Camp (OTC). In the first camp, there were 17 participants. There were physical training sessions from 5 to 9 in the morning and again in the evening. The afternoon hours from 12.30 to 5 were spent in discussion, writing, etc.

The Sangh grew slowly but steadily. However, Dr. Hedgewar was facing a severe financial constraint. Despite that, he refused to take any help from anyone. Raja Lakshmanrao Bhonsle was an admirer of Dr. Hedgewar. He once made a personal effort through his secretary Vasudeva Shastri Sangamkar to ease this financial constraint but Dr. Hedgewar refused.

His reaction was:"I shall ask for it when there is need. Help should not be felt like an obligation, and should not strain the mind. I have no objection to accepting help from people with whom I feel free, but, at present, there is no need for it."

Dr.Hedgewar continued to live in extreme poverty, refusing financial help. At different times, he resisted efforts of Raja Bhonsle, Nanasaheb Talatule, and finally Narayanrao Deshpande and Appaji Joshi to help him. Around this time, some friends of Dr.Hedgewar set up a company called the "Ideal Insurance Company", and persuaded Dr.Hedgewar to become the chief medical examiner. This arrangement which brought him an annual remuneration of a few hundred rupees continued till 1935-36 helped to meet his basic needs.. Much later, Bhai Paramanand observed on Dr.Hedgewar: "For the past few years Doctorji has been devoting all his time and energy to the Sangh work, totally unmindful of the needs of his home. He does not ask for funds, and he shuns publicity." [34]

In 1926, on the occasion of Ramnavami festival, Dr. Hedgewar took for the first time RSS swayamsevaks in full uniform to Ramtek where they helped in organising the worshipping of deity by thousands of worshippers.

Dr. Hedgewar was designated as the RSS Chief in a meeting held on December 19, 1926. The resolution read: "In order to carry on the activities of the Sangh in a regular, smooth and disciplined manner, it is essential that there should be one chief person at the helm. For this reason, this meeting unanimously appoints Dr. Hedgewar as the chief organiser (Chalak)."

Within one-and-a-half year of its inception, the RSS had established a strong base in Nagpur and Wardha.

The RSS soon spread its activities to the Central Provinces. Whenever and wherever Dr. Hedgewar travelled, he carried with himself a saffron flag. He would gather the prominent citizens of a town, city or locality and explain to them the ideology of the RSS passionately and lucidly. He was a great orator and was able to convince most of the people in the meetings he addressed. At the end of every such meeting, he would administer those present in the presence of the saffron flag and a new RSS Shakha would start. This is how the RSS founder set up hundreds of RSS Shakhas across the country.

With the spread of the organisation, it also required funds. Dr. Hedgewar didn't want to take anyone's obligation and wanted to keep the organisation also free of any such obligation.

Thus, the RSS founder decided to introduce the practice of Guru-Dakshina (the humble offering to the Guru) before the sacred Bhagwa Dhwaja on the occasion of Vyas-Puja (a Hindu festival of worshipping Saint Vyas, who is the creator of 'Mahabharat') in 1928.

A day prior to the first Guru-Dakshina, Dr. Hedgewar addressed the swayamsevaks: "Guru-Pooja is to be observed tomorrow. All of you should bring your offerings to the best of your ability, and flowers for worship of the Guru."

On the day of Guru Dakshina, the RSS founder informed the swayamsevaks: "The Rashtriya Swayamsevak Sangh does not recognise any individual as its Guru. The sacred Bhagwa Dhwaja (saffron flag) alone is our Guru. An individual, however great, is after all temporal and imperfect. The individual is conditioned by time; it is the principle alone which is timeless. The Bhagaw Dhwaja symbolises that timeless principle. The very sight of this Flag brings before our eyes the entire history, the glorious culture and tradition of our land; inspiration wells up in our mind. That is our true preceptor. Seeing the Saffron Flag (Bhagwa Dhwaj),. The mind rises and special motivation comes in it. Only this Saffron Flag (Bhagwa Dhwaj) we consider as our Guru, as a symbol of our Tattva i.e. principle. It is the embodiment of all basic elements of our nationhood. Bhagwa Dhwaj is not Sangh's own creation. Nor, it has any intention of creating a separate flag. Sangh has only accepted the Bhagwa Dhwaj, which for thousands of years has been the flag of our Rashtra Dharma. Bhagwa Dhwaj has a long history and tradition and it is an embodiment of Hindu culture.The Rashtriya Swayamsevak Sangh, therefore, accords the place of Guru to none else, and has accepted the Bhagwa Dhwaja as its Guru." If we keep Chhatrapati Shivaji Maharaj as our ideal, we will remember his heroics for the cause of defending Hindudom. The samarthya i.e. power of Shivaji is as much as that of the Saffron Flag. The history we remember looking at the saffron flag, and the motivation we get from it, the same is got from Shivaji Maharaj's life. Shivaji lifted the saffron flag which was truly in the dust, re-established Hindu Pad-padshahi and rejuvenated the dying Hindutva.

Then he worshipped the sacred Bhagwa Dhwaja. He was followed by the swayamsevaks.The amount offered on the first Guru-Dakshina by all the swayamsevaks was in total 84 Rupees.

Dr. Hedgewar took special pains to evolve a suitable technique to see that the Swayamsevaks are kept above all such personal lures. Systems like keeping apart at least one hour a day for service of the Motherland, the collective prayer to Bharat Mata invoking in oneself the spirit of total surrender at Her altar, and praying for virtues of invincible strength, character, knowledge, heroism and dedication to the ideal, offering Guru Dakshina in a spirit of selfless service to the society, practice of spending from one's own pocket while taking part in camps and other special programmes, and not going in for public funds for organisational expenses and much less seeking any kind of governmental favours - all these have helped in planting an unshakable spirit of self-reliance and self-sacrifice in the Swayamsevaks and steeling their character. The trust and confidence the Swayamsevaks enjoy in the public eye because of this strict training is in ample evidence all over the country. The secret of the overwhelming response the Swayamsevaks receive from the people and the growing number of projects and programmes coming up with public participation lies precisely in this.

One of the main reasons for the continuous growth of the Sangh - without deflecting from its chosen path for over 100 years - can be directly traced to the tradition of 'organisation-oriented' instead of personality-oriented' working style built into its technique. Dr. Hedgewar's farsightedness in this regard was evident when he placed the Bhagawā Dhwaj, the eternal symbol of our national culture and traditions, as the supreme ideal - the Guru - and considered himself as one among the Swayamsevaks devoted to that Guru. The tragedy of organisations and parties built around personalities in our country is now too apparent to need any elaboration. The phenomenon of Rashtriya Swayamsevak Sangh, on the other hand, is truly remarkable.[35]

Building a Young Dedicated Team for Expansion

To expand the Sangh outside Vidarbha, Dr. Hedgewar encouraged the youth to go for studies outside their state. He also encouraged well educated youth to go out for jobs. He would send out young boys to go to other villages to start Sangh work during holidays. Some would work full-time. Arrangement for their stays would be made at homes of people known personally to Dr. Hedgewar. These families would take care of their basic day-to-day requirements. He would keep a tab on their work and behaviour by writing letters to the hosts and locals Sangh contacts. He was highly conscious of his swayamsevaks' behaviour, both at a personal and organizational level, and cautioned them where required.

Dr Hedgewar used to keep in touch with people through letters. While recuperating from a sickness in Indore, he wrote five letters to his young colleagues - most of whom were students – about his grand vision about Hindusthan and the RSS. Most of them were hardly twenty-five years old. The first to act on his appeal for giving more time to the Sangh was Krishnarao Mohril who gave his entire life to the organization after completing his B.A. The next was Govind Sitaram Paramarth alias Dadarao Paramarth, and the third was Babasaheb Apte, the senior-most. While Dadarao was hardly twenty-five at that time, Babasaheb was twenty-six years old. This was the first team of the RSS that worked full-time for the Sangh till their last breath. This was the team that laid the foundation of the institution of pracharak within RSS.[36]

Till date, all the activities of RSS are funded by the money collected through Guru-Dakshina. The organisation does not accept any other private or government funds in any form.

By the end of 1928, the number of Shakhas had increased to 18 in Vidarbha area. Dr. Hedgewar encouraged students who had finished their matriculation examination to go to other parts of the country for higher education and spread the activities of the Sangh along with their studies. He was of the firm view that the RSS swayamsevaks should be well qualified as this would enhance their credibility also. That tradition still continues. Most of the RSS functionaries, especially at the senior level, are educationally well qualified. A large number of pracharaks are equipped with professional degrees from prestigious institutions. Though, this is not a criterion which guides the distribution of work and responsibilities within the organisation, but the organisation encourages its volunteers to excel in their respective fields so that they can be role models for the society.

In October 1928, Vijaya Dashami was celebrated with great enthusiasm as a contingent of swayamsevaks in full uniform marched in Nagpur. There were around 600 swayamsevaks in that contingent. Those who attended this function included national leaders like Vitthalbhai Patel who was immensely pleased with the impressive display of discipline.

Towards the end of 1928, Dr. Hedgewar met Subhash Chandra Bose in Calcutta. Dr. Hedgewar was, at that time, member of the Working Committee of the Central Provinces Unit of All-India Congress. He had gone to attend the annual session of Congress in Calcutta and Bose was the Mayor of the city. Initially, the meeting between two was scheduled for ten minutes, but it went on for a couple of hours. There was exchange of ideas and a freewheeling conversation. Dr. Hedgewar regarded independence and national unity as complimentary, like two sides of the same coin. Therefore, even after embarking upon the work for national unity he did not abandon working for independence. In the year 1928, he took part in the Congress convention held in Calcutta. There he discussed about the Sangh mission and about the national situation with Netaji Subhash Chandra Bose. Both the leaders exchanged views on the number of subjects concerning the Indian nation and appreciated each other's point of view and Dr.Hedgewar briefed Subhash Babu on the long term significance of the work of the Sangh. Subhash Babu appreciated his work, but expressed his inability to do more due to prior political commitments, saying: "Dr.Hedgewar, There is no doubt that yours is the only effective method of emancipating the nation. But I am already too much engrossed in the work of a purely political kind, and am not in a position to venture anew in another direction ..."

With the same objectives, Dr.Hedgewar met Ketkar the famous Marathi encyclopaedist, and introduced the work of the Sangh to the leaders of Akhil Maharashtra Taruna Hindu Parishad: Masurkar Maharaj, Loknayak Bapuji Ane, Swami Sivananda, Dr.Shivajirao Patwardhan, Pachlegaonkar Maharaj, and others. Pandit Madan Mohan Malaviya also visited the Shakha in this period.[37]

During those years, Pandit Madan Mohan Malaviya also visited the Nagpur. Malaviya offered financial assistance to Sangh as he said to Dr. Hedgewar, "People call me a royal beggar. If you consent, I shall be happy to collect some funds for you also." The latter replied, "Panditji, I am not in need of money. Blessings of elderly people like you are enough for me." Malaviya responded, "Many institutions first think of money, and then only about men. You are the very opposite of this! You place the heart above everything else. In future, I shall make it a point to mention this speciality of yours wherever I go."

When in 1928, the Congress invited Dr. Ansari for the unveiling of the Tilak statue, while excluding Dr. Hedgewar and the Moonje group from the function, Dr. Hedgewar not only participated, but arranged a guard of honour for the statue by the Swayamsevaks.

The first winter camp of the RSS was held in 1928. The RSS was spreading its wings faster than anyone had expected. The British government had started getting wary of the organisation. The police and intelligence corps often interrogated the swayamsevaks.

Dr. Hedgewar's connections with the revolutionary underground continued. When Avare wanted to protest the government ban on carrying weapons by taking out a procession with weapons, Dr. Hedgewar dissuaded him arguing that the weapons would simply be seized by the government and would thus become unavailable for a national uprising. Instead, he suggested that dummy weapons should be used for the Satyagraha.

Not only arms, but also the Sangh had to be preserved for the eventual uprising. Gangaprasad's hideout contained the arsenal of the revolution as well as information on the revolutionaries. Thus, when Gangaprasad Pandey's revolver was inadvertently used for committing a dacoity, taking great personal risk, Dr. Hedgewar went with Appaji Joshi, then Provincial Secretary and member of AICC, to Gangaprasad's hideout, and recovered the revolver. His and Appaji's involvement came to be known to the British through their informer, but could not be conclusively proved. When forced to drop proceedings by local gentry, the District Collector lamented: "What can we do, if even such respectable people take to dacoity."

In 1929, after assassinating Saunders at Lahore in December 1928, Rajguru escaped to Nagpur. As a student of Bhonsle Vedashala, Nagpur, he used to attend the Shakha at Mohitewada in 1927-28 and was acquainted with Dr. Hedgewar. Dr.Hedgewar arranged for a safe house for him at the farmhouse of Bhaiyaji Dani at Umred, and specially warned him not to go to Poona. Unfortunately, Rajguru disregarded this advice and went to Poona, and was arrested.

In 1929, a crucial meeting of the Sanghchalaks was held at Nagpur on 9-10 November. The agenda of the meeting was explained in the circular sent by Dr. Hedgewar, "Amidst the political and social storm that is about to engulf the country, how do we row the boat of the Sangh to safety? What should be the policy of the Sangh? What programmes should be undertaken to accelerate the growth of the Sangh? To discuss these and other momentous issues, it has been decided to call a meeting of the Sanghchalaks at Nagpur on 9th and 10th November."

In April 1930, Mahatma Gandhi launched the 'Salt Satyagraha!' Dr. Hedgewar supported the movement whole-heartedly. Many swayamsevaks were also keen to participate in this and sought permission from Dr. Hedgewar. As the organisation was young and not sufficiently strong, so Dr. Hedgewar chose a middle path. He sent a direction to all the RSS Shakhas, "...The Sangh as such has so far not resolved to participate in this movement. However, those who would like to participate in their personal capacity are free to do so after obtaining permission from their Sanghchalaks."

In view of the ongoing needs of various mass movements as well as the RSS programmes, a medicare unit of 100 swayamsevaks was set up and imparted training to provide medical care. This unit provided immediate relief to the victims of the police's brutal violence in the wake of the Salt Satyagraha. The participants in Satygraha who bore the brunt of this brutality were immediately treated in Nagpur and the adjoining areas.

Meanwhile, Dr. Hedgewar himself decided to take part in this Satyagraha. Appaji Joshi also decided to join the movement. The arrest by British authorities was imminent. So, the task of running the organisation, in Dr. Hedgewar's absence, was entrusted to Dr. L.V. Paranjpe by nominating him as the new Sarsanghchalak.

A new agitation - Non-cooperation Movement (Savinay Avagyaa Andolan) was launched in 1930 by Mahatma Gandhi in the form of 'Daandi March' or Salt satyagraha. The agitation began in Akola on 2nd April, 1930. In Madhya prant, it was decided by Congress to add Jungle Satyagraha to this Salt Satyagraha since there were no salt pans there, and British had put in a law to curtail people's rights over jungles.

Many swayamsevaks had begun taking part in this agitation from its very inception. In November 1929, senior RSS workers had a 3-day-long meeting to decide what should be RSS's role in this agitation. It was decided that RSS would give unconditional support to it. By 1929, there were Sangh shakhas in 37 villages in Vidarbha. In Wardha, there were 12 shakhas. By 1930, this number had risen to 30. Once Dr. Hedgewar decided to take part in it, there was a huge backing to it from all around.

On 12th July, the Guru Purnima festival day in RSS shakha, Dr. Hedgewar shared his decision to participate in the satyagraha and resigned as the Sarsanghchaalak or Chief of the RSS, as his view was that freedom struggle must be fought under one organisation that was Congress at that time. He handed over the reins of RSS to Dr. L.V. Paranjape. In his speech, Dr. Paranjape said, "Those who wish to participate in the agitation must do so. Others should work for this young organisation. This current movement is to take our nation forward, there is no doubt. But, this is just one step towards freedom. The real work is to organise such people who will give their lives for the freedom of this nation." One can see that the RSS leaders had no delusion that this agitation would be the last. Their goal was to create dedicated swayamsevaks who would be able to stand for the nation for times to come. It was also an option for the young members to choose satyagraha or to keep working for strengthening the organisation that had long-term goals of freedom and reforming the Hindu society.

Dr. Hedgewar left for Pusad on 14th July satyagraha from Nagpur. Speaking to hundreds of people who had gathered to see him off, Dr. Hedgewar said, "Please don't be under the impression that this current agitation is the last battle for independence. Real battle will start after this. And be ready to jump into this coming battle fully prepared to sacrifice your all. We are taking part in this satyagraha because we believe that this will take us one more step towards independence." He was received in every town on way by hundreds of people. Of prominent leaders, Congress leader and Sanghchaalak of Vidarbh Appaji Joshi, editor of Maharashtra's evening edition Balasaheb Dhawle, Dadarao Paramarth, Vitthalrao Dev, Wankhede, Gharote, Bhaiyyaji Kumbalwar, Ambade, Narayanrao Deshpande, Trayambakeswhar Deshpande, Palewar, etc. also went to prison with him. Dr. Hedgewar offered satyagraha in Yavatmal on 21st July. He was handed a nine-month imprisonment with hard labour. Other 11 in that batch received 4 months' imprisonment. There were 100s of swayamsevaks in Akola jail with Dr. Hedgewar. Thousands of swayamsevaks offered satyagraha in other places. Many other prominent RSS leaders offered satyagraha too. Many of these names are mentioned in the biography of Dr. Hedgewar written by N.H. Palkar quoted here, but space doesn't permit me to give all the names and more details.

These satyagrahas by RSS swayamsevaks were also reported in Kesari newspaper dated 20, 22 July, 1930 and 2 August, 1930. 24 After Dr. Hedgewar was imprisoned, number of satyagrahis only increased. This was possible because Dr. Hedgewar was an organiser and motivator par excellence; and organisation he built didn't depend on any leader to deliver. He had set in motion a process of creating a truly cadre based self-driven organisation. We also note that he didn't wish to give false hopes to swayamsevaks after the experience of fizzling out of Non-Cooperation movement of 1920.

An important decision by Dr. Hedgewar at that time led to a convention followed by RSS till now. He instructed to work as an organisation of the society, not an organisation within a society. And, RSS members should take part in public programmes as citizens and not as members of RSS. A circular was sent to all the shakhas that 'ordinary swayamsevak can take part in the satyagraha in his personal capacity after taking permission from the local Sanghchalak'. On November 10, a full-fledged organisational meeting was held at Mohitewada in which all the swayamsevaks of Nagpur as well as those from mofussil areas who had come for the meeting participated. The practice of 'Sarsanghchalak Pranam' (Bowing to the RSS chief) was initiated that day for the first time with Appaji Joshi issuing the command.

The Sarsanghchalaks and other workers stood with their back to the stone wall, which has survived to this day. Dr. Hedgewar was standing next to the saffron flag and was visibly moved by an impressive gathering of the swayamsevaks.

Appaji Joshi, who had already briefed the workers, gave the command in a raised voice, "Sarsanghchalak Pranam - Ek, Do, Teen." All the swayamsevaks offered Pranam to Sarsanghchalak Dr. Hedgewar. This was followed by a talk by Vishwanathrao Kelkar who explained the unique concept of 'chalak' in Sangh, as being the 'head of a wider family'.

After the ceremony, Dr. Hedgewar told Appaji Joshi: "Appaji, today you have done something unplanned. I do not approve of it. It is not proper for me to accept salutation from my own colleagues, many of whom are senior to me and entitled to my veneration." Appaji replied, "All of us have decided on this procedure unanimously in the interest of efficient organisation, even though you might not personally relish it."

The idea behind having this ceremony was to establish the role of Sarsanghchalak on the lines of head of the family in Hindu society. The swayamsevaks are like children in the family and together the whole family works together for the betterment of the society. The Sarsanghchalak, as head of the family, has to protect and nourish it.

As the Sangh expanded, there were some reports about opposition from Congress and Hindusthani Seva Dal. In a letter to Dada Paramarth and Krishnarao Mohrir, Dr. Hedgewar said:

"In your letter, you have informed me of a significant development. Let us pray to God that He guide these critics. As far as we are concerned, we work with faith in God and heeding to the dictates of our conscience. If in this process we fail to please some sections, or if some are inclined to oppose us, what can we do? All this has its root in politics. We need not be afraid of these expressions of others born out of malice."

In fact, when Congress adopted a resolution proclaiming Complete Independence - Sampurna Swatantrya - as its goal, Dr. Hedgewar immediately sent out a circular to all the Shakhas: "This year the Congress has passed a resolution declaring Complete Independence as its goal. The Congress Working Committee has called upon the entire nation to celebrate Sunday, the 26th of January, 1930 as Independence Day. We of the Sangh are naturally immensely happy that the All-India Congress has endorsed our goal of Complete Independence. It is our duty to co-operate with any organisation working towards that goal... It is, therefore, suggested that all the swayamsevaks of each Shakha meet at 6 p.m. on Sunday, 26th January, 1930, at the respective Sanghasthans. After offering salutation to the National Flag, i.e., the Bhagawa Dhwaj, the concept of Independence and the reason why this ideal alone should be kept before everyone should be explained. The function should conclude with an expression of congratulations to the Congress for having accepted the ideal of Complete Independence."

As a result of this circular, all the RSS shakhas observed Independence Day. It would be interesting to go through the notes jotted down by the RSS founder regarding this development: "The Hindu culture is the life-breath of Hindusthan. It is, therefore, clear that if Hindusthan is to be protected, we should first nourish the Hindu culture. If the Hindu culture perishes in Hindusthan itself, and if the Hindu society ceases to exist, it will hardly be appropriate to refer to the mere geographical entity that remains as Hindusthan. Mere geographical lumps do not make a nation. Unfortunately, the Congress organisation has given no thought to protecting the Hindu Dharma and Hindu culture. The organisation keeps its eyes closed to the daily onslaughts by outsiders on the Hindu society. It is to fulfil this duty of protecting the Hindu society that the Rashtriya Swayamsevak Sangh has come into existence. But the Sangh harbours no ill-will towards the Congress. The Sangh will co-operate with the Congress in the efforts to secure freedom, as long as these efforts do not come in the way of preserving our national culture. The Sangh has indeed been co-operating with the Congress all along."

The workers were informed about this change on July 12. Dr. Hedgewar explained the reason for this move on the occasion of Guru Puja on July 12, "After I tender the vote of thanks in a few moments, I shall cease to be the Sarsanghchalak. Dr. Paranjpe has agreed to accept the stewardship of the Sangh. I express my gratitude to him on behalf of the Sangh. All of us are participating in this movement (Salt Satyagraha) in our personal capacity. There has been no change either in our policy or in our way of working, nor has our faith in the Sangh suffered in the least because of these developments. It is the duty of all organisations working towards the country's independence to keep themselves abreast of all such movements in the country. All those swayamsevaks who have already jumped into the Satyagraha movement, and we who are doing so presently, have been inspired by these considerations."

He further added, "Going to jail is today considered a sign of true patriotism. However, a person who would willingly court a two-year prison term hesitates when he is asked to come out of his house and work for organising the freedom movement. Why should this be so? Is six months or a year enough to secure the country's Independence? However, the people are not yet prepared to realise the simple truth that organised work for several years alone can take us to our cherished goal. There can be no salvation for the country until this type of fleeting emotion gives place to positive and lasting feelings of devotion and sustained efforts. Preparedness to lay down one's life for the country is the essence of such lasting patriotism. The present fate of the country cannot be changed unless lakhs of young men dedicate their entire lifetime for that cause. To mould the minds of our youth towards that end is the supreme aim of the Sangh."

After this speech, Dr. Hedgewar and the swayamsevaks participating in Satyagraha were garlanded. The group left Nagpur on July 14 as hundreds of people came to bid them farewell at the Nagpur railway station.

According to the information available with the RSS archives, the group led by Dr. Hedgewar reached the Satyagraha centre at Pusad, after receiving felicitations on the way at Wardha and other places. Loknayak Ane had already initiated the Satyagraha at the Pusad centre. Organisers of that centre, therefore, felt that a leader of the stature of Dr. Hedgewar should inaugurate the Satyagraha movement at another important place, Yeotmal. It was decided that Dr. Hedgewar should proceed to Yeotmal and sound the clarion call there....

Dr. Hedgewar and his batch had announced the breaking of the Jungle Law on July 21. Over 10,000 people had assembled to witness the Satyagraha. As the Satyagrahis registered their defiance of authority by entering the reserve forest, the police officers promptly arrested them. Dr. Hedgewar, before getting into the police van, gave a farewell message to the people to carry on the movement with ever greater momentum. Dr. Hedgewar was awarded six months' rigorous imprisonment and three months' simple imprisonment. He and others were shifted to Akola Jail.

The RSS founder started an RSS shakha in the Akola Jail premises also. In fact, the Vidarbha unit of the RSS was born in the jail itself!

While in jail, Dada Paramarth contracted tuberculosis. Dr. Hedgewar personally nursed him for months. He read Lokmanya Tilak's famous treatise on Bhagavad Gita 'Gitarahasya' whenever he had time during the prison term.

He was released from prison on February 14, 1931. After his release, he stayed for a couple of days in Akola and Wardha, where he was felicitated in public functions. He reached Nagpur on February 17. A massive crowd had gathered to welcome him at the railway station. He was taken in a procession from there. After coming back, he resumed the responsibility of the RSS as Sarsanghchalak.

Dr. Hedgewar first went to Bombay to press for expansion of Sangh there and then moved to Banaras where Hindus were feeling threatened. It was decided to start a regular RSS Shakha there. With the blessings of Pandit Madan Mohan Malaviya, a regular Shakha was started in the Banaras Hindu University Campus. Another Shakha was started in Banaras city.

The Banaras visit of Dr. Hedgewar proved to be a boon for the organisation also as the beginning of the Sangh work led to the RSS finding its second Sarsanghchalak there.

"While at Kashi (Banaras), Dr. Hedgewar had learnt that one Madhavrao Golwalkar, called 'Guruji', a lecturer in the Banaras Hindu University, was taking interest in the Sangh activities. During the next summer vacation, in 1932, Golwalkar had returned to Nagpur. Dr. Hedgewar invited him to his house. Accordingly, Golwalkar went and met Dr. Hedgewar."

Hedgewar adopted two major strategies for the expansion of the RSS in the 1930s. First, he focused his attention on the universities outside Maharashtra and dispatched his trained volunteers to recruit students in the campuses. The RSS started a shakha in the Benaras Hindu University campus with the help of Madan Mohan Malaviya. Second, Hedgewar requested the prominent members of the Hindu Mahasabha to introduce the RSS pracharaks to the notables of their respective areas and arrange for their stay. The Hindu Mahasabha channel proved to be very useful in the initial stage when the RSS was looking for an entry outside C.P. &. Berar.

Between 1937 and 1940, the RSS expanded feverishly amidst deteriorating Hindu-Muslim relations in northern India. The pracharaks were active in Punjab, Delhi, United Provinces and Bihar. In 1939, the RSS entered the southern states of Madras and Karnataka. The first attempt to form a Madras branch of the RSS was made in April 1939 when C.S. Paramarth of Nagpur, 'the Chief Organizer of the Madras Province', visited Madras and recruited about 40 members.

In 1931, the Congress appointed a seven-member committee to decide about India's national flag. The members of the committee included Sardar Patel, Pandit Nehru, Pattabhi Seetaramayya, Dr. N.S. Hardikar, Acharya Kaka Kalelkar, Master Tara Singh and Maulana Azad.

The committee members unanimously said in its report, "Our National Flag should be of one single colour and it is the saffron colour which can represent to the maximum extent the entire populace of India. This colour has a speciality of its own over the other colours and reflects the ancient tradition of India."

Dr. Hedgewar was quite pleased with the report and he met several Congress leaders in Delhi to press for accepting this report. But the policy of appeasement led to the rejection of this report.

Even as the RSS founder continued to engage with various public personalities from different walks of life for issues of national importance, his relentless efforts to expand the outreach of the organisation started bearing fruits.

In a letter dated September 1931, Dr. Hedgewar reported to the RSS headquarters in Nagpur: "Many leading advocates and doctors have joined the Sangh. However, it is not easy to work in Vidarbha; we have to press forward through hard and difficult terrain. Our efforts are succeeding only because this is a divine work and carries God's blessings. The responsibility of the Nagpur Shakha is correspondingly increasing. And, swayamsevaks of all ages in Nagpur must realise this responsibility. It is only my complete trust in you which has prompted me to expand the Sangh activities outside Nagpur."

RSS and Hindu Mahasabha had their differences from early days. Dr. B.S. Moonje wanted RSS to keep away from Non-Cooperation movement. He had been like a mentor of Dr. Hedgewar since his young days. He had helped him a lot in his studies too. But, Dr. Hedgewar politely refused to toe Hindu Mahasabha line and chose his own path in this struggle. Inspite of these differences, Dr. Hedgewar maintained excellent relations with Dr. Moonje till last.

In the heated atmosphere of 1931 Non-Cooperation movement, Dr. Moonje accepted the invitation for Round Table Conference and got ready for travelling to England. There was strong and bitter reaction to it from supporters of Non-Cooperation movement. Dr. Hedgewar, who was in jail at that time, said, "There can be political differences. But, they should not be exhibited bitterly or cheaply. Inspite of differences, the right way is that each side should respect their patriotism and commitment to the cause and keep working in their own way."

After the Vijayadashmi festival, he started touring Chhattisgarh and other Hindi-speaking areas of Central Provinces. His tour was briefly reported in Maharashtra (December 9, 1931): "Dr. Hedgewar, the founder of Rashtriya Swayamsevak Sangh, toured the Chhattisgarh area for three weeks to popularise the Sangh ideals. Branches of the Sangh have now been started in all the district headquarters of that area."

In 1932, Bhai Parmanand, a leader of the reformist Arya Samaj and HMS, held an All India Hindu youth conference in Karachi and used Babarao Savarkar's influence to invite Dr.Hedgewar. Dr. Hedgewar went to Karachi and spent around six days there, trying to set up as many new RSS Shakhas as he could. He met a number of workers from Sindh and Punjab. As the tensions ran high in this area and with Hindus constantly being under onslaught, a number of youth got attracted towards Sangh as they found it be saviour of Hindus.

D.D. Chowdhary was appointed as the first Sanghchalak in Sindh. Dr. Hedgewar wrote from Karachi:

"This city is definitely far better than Bombay or Calcutta. It excels all other cities in beauty, cleanliness, broad and well tarred roads, electrical illumination, gardens and parks."

After the summer training camp (1932), he set out for another tour of Maharashtra with Babarao Savarkar. The duo visited Bombay, Pune, Satara, Sangli, Kolhapur, Karhad amongst other cities, which resulted in Sangh finding roots at several new places. During his month-long tour of Maharashtra, Dr. Hedgewar also visited Jamkhandi in North Karnataka and started the first Shakha there. By this time - several workers decided to become full-time workers of Sangh, leaving their families and dropping their lucrative careers. They further expanded the reach of the RSS and also helped it in consolidating its presence wherever it had reached so far.

In 1933, invitations were sent by the Sarsanghchalak, Dr. Hedgewar, to a large number of prominent personalities to attend the Vijyadashmi (Dussehra) function.

In a letter dated September 1, 1933, he explained to the swayamsevaks, "Our Dasara festival at Nagpur is the measuring rod for the people to gauge our strength and vitality. The enthusing sight of these celebrations is bound to instil a sense of pride and joy in the minds of our well-wishers. We should ever remember that it is such countless sympathetic hearts that are the pillars of strength for us. Not only from our province, but even from distant provinces distinguished people come to attend the function. Since it is our desire that branches of the Sangh should sprout in all the provinces of the country, we should see to it that these functions leave a lasting impression on the minds of those who attend."

As expected, the Vijyadashami festival was celebrated by the RSS in an impressive way. Over 1,200 swayamsevaks participated in the parade in full uniform. Golwalkar, who later became the second RSS chief, was also present there. He had come from Banaras to attend the event.

With the rapid expansion of the RSS, there were certain reports that the British government might ban the organisation. Dr. Hedgewar made an interesting observation in his diary on January 29, 1934: "It is only a worthless individual who puts the blame on circumstances."

While offering his guidance to the swayamsevaks as to how they should face the looming challenge of the government, Dr. Hedgewar said: "Granted that government is planning to ban the Sangh, but how can they stop its functioning? Shakhas will spring up many-fold. At the most, government can stop the external activities, but how can they efface the feelings surging in the heart? I am sure the number of Shakhas will then become the same as the number of swayamsevaks! If this is so, then, why not we expand the Shakhas now itself to the same extent? That would be the fitting reply to the government's challenge."

By mid-1930s, Nagpur city alone had atleast 17 Shakhas. In 1934, the RSS held its training camps at two places - Nagpur and Mehkar. This was an indication of the growing strength of the organisation. By then, the number of Shakhas had crossed the three-digit mark and they were spread across the country. The number of swayamsevaks in the RSS was more than 10,000.

The Government of Central Provinces and Berar issued a circular in 1932, prohibiting government servants from joining the Sangh. Within a few days, government pressurised even local self-government institutions to pass similar orders.

To counter the government orders against the RSS, Dr. Hedgewar adopted the strategy of inviting more and more prominent people to the RSS functions.

Noted industrialist and philanthropist Jamnalal Bajaj came to Nagpur on the morning of January 31, 1934. He met Dr. Moonje and Dr. Hedgewar separately. Dr. Hedgewar's stand was clear, which he shared with Bajaj also: "The Sangh is aloof from politics. It has no hatred for any other institution. Nor is it opposed to Khadi. And it totally disapproves of the practice of untouchability."

The RSS pracharaks, during all this, were quietly working on the ground to build the organisation. Gopalrao Yerkuntvar went to Sangli, Dadarao Paramarth to Pune and Babasaheb Apte to Khandesh districts. Thus began the practice of sending out pracharaks.

The C.P. Legislative Council was to meet in March 1934. Dr. Hedgewar met several legislators and urged them to oppose the government orders regarding the Sangh.

The Akola District Board and the Municipalities of Wardha, Umred, Savaner, Katol, Bhandara, etc. had already passed resolutions demanding revocation of the order.

Babasaheb Kolte of Bhandara, who had been Dr. Hedgewar's teacher, moved a resolution on March 7, condemning the government's order. Several members of the assembly supported the resolution. The discussion on the resolution continued for three days.

At last, the motion was put to vote, and was carried. It was an unprecedented defeat for the government. However, the government refused to act on this resolution and, hence, did not annul the order officially, though it refrained from enforcing it also. For all practical purposes, it became a dead order. These developments gave a further fillip to expansion of the RSS. Golwalkar who was in Banaras till now, also came back to Nagpur in 1933 and remained in close contact with Dr. Hedgewar.

"In 1934, Sant Panchlegaonkar Maharaj merged his Mukteswar Dal in the Sangh. The Dal had been formed for the protection of the Hindus during the periods of Muslim onslaughts. The Dal had 25 branches in Yeotmal, Khamgaon, Washim, Nagpur and other places. They all now became part of the Sangh."

Ironically, while the RSS was facing a threat from the British rulers, the Congress also passed a resolution in June 1934, prohibiting its members from associating with RSS apart from Hindu Mahasabha and the Muslim League.[38]

When Hardikar, Chief of the Hindustani Seva Dal, impressed with the successful organisation of the Sangh, wished to meet him in 1934, he was welcomed to study the Sangh at close quarters.

Replying to Dr. N.S. Hardikar, the chief of Hindusthani Seva Dal, Dr. Hedgewar said, "Your letter of 10th December, 1934 has reached me. Reading it has given me much pleasure. I am indeed very happy that you are desirous of studying the Sangh activities at close quarters. I shall be out of town for a few days after the Akola Parishat. It might, therefore, be useful for you to go over to Nagpur, a couple of days prior to the Parishat, so that you may familiarise yourself with the working of the Sangh." Dr. Hardikar, however, could not go to Nagpur on account of his indisposition. But he spent two days with Gopalrao Yerkuntvar, the pracharak at Bombay, and closely studied the Sangh activities. In 1934, Mahatma Gandhi visited the RSS camp at Wardha and met with Dr. Hedgewar. Seshadri gives an authentic account of this memorable event, "Gandhiji was then camping at the Sevagram Ashram near Wardha. The Sangh camp was right opposite that house. Near about 1,500 swayamsevaks of Wardha district were camping. Gandhiji had seen the preparations for setting up the camp. He also observed the camp activities from his residence and felt like seeing the camp from close quarters. He spoke to Mahadev Desai who, in turn, wrote to Appaji Joshi. Appaji immediately went and met Gandhiji and invited him: "Please do come whenever it is convenient for you. You will be most welcome." That was the day of silence for Gandhiji. He wrote on a slip of paper: "I shall come at 6 tomorrow morning and shall spend an hour-and-a-half there."

The next day, i.e., on 25th December, 1934, Gandhiji arrived at the Sangh camp punctually at 6 a.m. All the swayamsevaks offered their pranam to him. Gandhiji was accompanied by Mahadev Desai, Miraben and a few others. After seeing the camp in its impressive set-up, Gandhiji patted Appaji on his back and said: "I am really delighted. I have not witnessed such a sight anywhere in the country before." He then inspected the kitchen. Food was prepared and served to over 1,500 people without the least fuss or confusion; the cost to each swayamsevak came to just one rupee and a certain quantity of grain, and all the expenses of the camp were met by this; the swayamsevaks themselves made up the shortfalls, if any. All this information astonished Gandhiji.

He later visited the sick ward and the tents of the swayamsevaks. He saw people of all castes and classes harmoniously engaged in work without any reservations. In order to confirm his observation, he enquired the swayamsevaks themselves. Their response was uniform:

"There are no differences like Brahmin, Maratha, Asprishyas (untouchables), etc, in the Sangh. We are, in fact, not even aware of what castes many of our swayamsevak brethren belong to; nor are we interested in knowing it. It is enough for us that we are all Hindus." Gandhiji asked Appaji, "It appears almost impossible to ward off the evil of untouchability from our society. How has this phenomenon been made possible in the Sangh?" Appaji replied, "Feelings of high and low, touchability and untouchability can be abolished only by emphasising the inherent oneness of all Hindus. Then only will the spirit of fraternity be reflected in their sincere behaviour, and not merely in words. The credit for this achievement goes to Dr. Keshav Hedgewar."

By then, it was time for the general assembly. The bugle was sounded. All the swayamsevaks stood to attention. Flag was hoisted. In accordance with the Sangh custom, Gandhiji also joined Appaji in offering pranam to the Bhagawa Flag.

Gandhiji then visited the stores. Provisions and various requisites had been neatly arranged. There was a decorated portrait prominently displayed. Mahatmaji looked at it intently and enquired, "Whose portrait is this?"

"That portrait is of Dr. Hedgewar," replied Appaji.

"Is that the same Dr. Keshav Hedgewar you mentioned when we were talking about untouchability? How is he connected with the Sangh?"

"He is the Chief of the Sangh. We call him the Sarsanghchalak. All the activities of the Sangh are carried on under his guidance. It is he who has started the Sangh."

"Will it be possible to meet Dr. Hedgewar? If possible, I want to hear about the Sangh from him directly."

"He is due to visit the camp tomorrow. If you desire, we shall bring him to you."

Gandhiji then returned to his Ashram.

Next morning, Dr. Hedgewar arrived at the camp. That evening, the valedictory function was held under the presidentship of Laxman Bhopatkar of Pune. Afterwards, at Gandhiji's invitation, Dr. Hedgewar went to meet him, accompanied by Appaji Joshi and Bhopatkar. The discussion between Dr. Hedgewar and Gandhiji extended for over an hour. The general trend of discussion was as follows:

After preliminary exchange of courtesies, Gandhiji turned to a point uppermost in his mind:

Dr. Hedgewar, your organisation is admirable. I am aware of the fact that you were for many years a Congress worker. That being so, why did you not build such a volunteer cadre under the aegis of a popular organisation like the Congress itself? Why did you float a separate organisation?"

"It is true that I worked in the Congress. I was also the Secretary of the Swayamsevak Dal at the time of the 1920 session of the Congress, when my friend Dr. Paranjpe was the Mandal President. Subsequently, the two of us tried to build such a volunteer cadre inside the Congress. But our efforts were not successful, hence, this independent venture," he replied.

"Why did your attempt fail? Was it for want of financial assistance?"

"No, no! There was no dearth of funds. Money can be a great help, no doubt. But money alone cannot accomplish everything. The problem that faced us was not one of money but of attitudes."

"Is it your opinion that noble-hearted people were not there in the Congress, or that they are not there now?"

"That isn't what I meant. There are many well-meaning people in the Congress. What is at issue is certain basic attitudes. The Congress has been formed primarily with a view to achieving a political end. Its programmes have also been drawn up accordingly, and it needs volunteers to arrange for these programmes. The Congress leaders are, therefore, used to looking upon volunteers as unpaid servants who arrange chairs and benches during meetings and conferences. The Congress does not seem to believe that the problems of the nation can effectively be solved only when there is a large and disciplined body of dedicated swayamsevaks who are eager to serve the country of their own accord and without waiting for inspiration from elsewhere."

"What exactly is your conception of a swayamsevak?"

"A swayamsevak is one who would lovingly lay down his life for the all-round upliftment of the nation. To create and mould such swayamsevaks is the aim of the Sangh. There is no distinction between a 'swayamsevak and a 'leader' in Sangh. All of us are swayamsevaks and are, therefore, equal. We love and respect everybody equally. We give no room for any differences in status. This is, in fact, the secret of the remarkable growth of the Sangh in such a short period without any outside help, money or publicity."

"I am indeed very glad. The country will certainly be benefited by the success of your efforts.

I have heard of the vast following the Sangh has acquired in the Wardha district How do you meet the expenses of such a huge organisation?"

"The swayamsevaks themselves bear the burden, each offering his mite as Guru-dakshina." "It looks as if your entire time is consumed by this work, how do you carry on your medical profession?"

"I have not taken to medicine as a profession." "How then are you supporting your family?" "I am not married."

Gandhiji was evidently taken by surprise. In the same surprised tone, he said, "I see! you are not married! Very good. That explains the remarkable degree of success you have achieved in such a short duration!":

At the end, Dr. Hedgewar said, "I have probably taken too much of your time. I have no doubt that, with your blessings, our efforts will succeed. Permit us to take your leave now."

Gandhiji came up to the door to bid farewell, and said, "Dr. Hedgewar, with your character and sincerity, there is no doubt you will succeed."

Dr. Hedgewar offered his pranam to Gandhiji and returned to the camp."

The RSS continued to take big strides. A new Officers Training Camp was held in Pune in the year 1935.

Babu Padmaraj Jain, a prominent public personality, wrote several letters to Dr. Hedgewar, urging him to undertake a tour of Punjab and United Provinces. Dharmaveer, son-in-law of Bhai Paramanand, wrote to the RSS chief from Lahore on October 3, 1935: "The position of the Hindus here is precarious. I want to spend a few days with you to train myself in the art of organising mass self-protection of the Hindus. Another friend will be accompanying me."

Dr. Hedgewar was constantly encouraging young students to move to different provinces, learn the local language and expand the RSS network.

From the organisational perspective, he ensured there was uniformity in division of work and conducting the daily Shakha. He defined the responsibilities of the office-bearers of the Sangh and the conventions to be followed in the daily Shakha.

In October 1935, the RSS expanded further in Karnataka as Dr. Hedgewar visited Chikkodi, Nipani and Sadalga in Belgaum district. This was his second visit to Karnataka. A patha sanchalana - route march – was held in Sadalga. He also addressed a meeting at Chikkodi. A Shakha was started there on October 23, 1935. That marked the beginning of the RSS' activites in Karnataka.

Inspite of differences with Hindu Mahasabha, Dr. Hedgewar organised a march past of 500 smartly uniformed RSS swayamsevaks on 30th December, 1935, when HMS held their session under Madan mohan Malviya in Pune. Dr. Moonje himself briefed the delegates about RSS's work as Dr. Hedgewar was not well and had travelled to Pune inspite of strict 'bed rest' instructions from his doctors. It is difficult to think of such affection between organisations holding differing viewpoints in today's fractious politics.

In March 1936, Krishnarao Wadekar went to the Dhule Jalgaon area in Maharashtra to start Shakhas there.[39]

On March 24, 1936, Dr. Hedgewar gave him a written aide memoire - 'Sangha-sthapna Vidhi'. That document clearly set down the conduct expected of a swayamsevak. Its salient features included the following:

"Just as every officer under Shivaji was an expert strategist, every officer of the Sangh should be well versed in all aspects of the Sangh training... The swayamsevak may, with the Sanghachalak's permission, participate in any activity not inimical to the welfare of the Hindus, on their personal responsibility. Swadeshi should be cultivated, inspired by a patriotic attitude. Keeping one's self aloof from the extremes of lack of any code of conduct on the one hand, and meaningless rituals on the other, the Sangh activities should strike a golden mean to energise the entire society. The Sangh must stay away from programmes born out of momentary, enthusiasm, and outbursts of mercurial emotion. Association with such programmes will only harm the stability of the Sangh."

In response to the requests from Punjab, Janardan Chinchalkar, Rajabhau Paturkar and Narayanrao Puranik were part of the group of workers which was sent there.

Along with their studies, they set up the RSS' Shakhas in Lahore.

Babasaheb Apte and Dadarao Paramarth had started touring Maharashtra, Mahakoshal, Punjab and Uttar Pradesh regularly.

Later in 1936, he explicitly pointed out the limits of Ahimsa, stating that it should not result in "Atma-Himsa". Observing that while the precept "Ahimsa Paramo Dharma", was well rooted in the Hindu mind, it had to be taught to other communities as well, and others would learn it only if it was taught on the basis of strength" since predatory communities would not listen to weakness. Also in 1936, Dr. Hedgewar participated in the Temple Satyagraha in Pune against the Government ban on ringing of bells in Sonya Maruti temple, and playing of music on public roads. He explained that such agitations were like external bandages to boils on the body, serving to provide relief without correcting the internal impurity that would cause the problems to re-surface. They were necessary but short term remedies. For long term remedy, Hindu society would have to be united, and become robust.

A new chapter was set to begin in 1936 when Lakshmibai Kelkar, mother of a swayamsevak in Wardha, met Dr. Hedgewar at Appaji Joshi's house. In her own words, "Dr. Hedgewar asked me about the purpose of my visit. "Why don't you impart this training and idealism to women also?" I asked. 'Well,' he replied, 'for the present, we have restricted the activities to men.' I said, 'If you can permit my son to teach me the techniques, I shall in my turn teach them to other women of the town'".

Dr. Hedgewar did not agree. I persisted, "Just as women are part of the family, they are part of the nation too. If your message reaches women at home, that will certainly strengthen the Sangh."

Seeing my insistence, Dr. Hedgewar finally agreed and said, "If you are prepared to take up the entire responsibility, Appaji Joshi will offer you the necessary help."

In 1937, Dr. Hedgewar sent a team of 10 swayamsevaks to northern India to expand the RSS work. Their efforts resulted in the spread of the shakhas in Punjab, Delhi, Uttar Pradesh and Central India. Dadarao Paramarth and Babasaheb Apte supervised these efforts touring these areas extensively.

Golwalkar also returned from Saragachi Ashram around this time. That was a great relief for Dr. Hedgewar, who later chose him as his successor. After his return, Golwalkar closely worked with Dr. Hedgewar.

By this time, winter camps had become a regular feature in a number of provinces where RSS had set up its shakhas.

An interesting incident happened in Nagpur when the training camp there at Nagpur was inaugurated by the Raja of Audh. He was so impressed by the event where more than 1,000 young swayamsevaks were participating that he asked his cameraperson to shoot the scene. Dr. Hedgewar noticed it after a few moments and stopped him, as it was against the convention in the Sangh. However, the cameraperson was able to capture on film, Dr. Hedgewar hoisting the saffron flag. It remains one of the very few pictures of Dr. Hedgewar, arguably the only one, of Dr. Hedgewar at an RSS event.

People keep accusing RSS of disrespecting the tricolour. Here is another example of swayamsevaks' loyalty to the tricolour. During the flag-raising ceremony at the Congress Faizpur session of 1936 December, the Congress tricolour was stuck midway on an 80-feet-high mast when Nehruji was unfurling it. Many tried unsuccessfully to untangle the flag, after which a delegate, Kishan Singh Pardesi courageously climbed up the mast-pole and freed the flag. People carried him on their shoulders and many people literally showered him with currency notes. The Congress session accepted a proposal to felicitate Pardesi. But no sooner did he reveal that he was a swayamsevak of RSS from Shirpur, Congressmen developed cold feet. When Dr. Hedgewar heard about this contribution of a swayamsevak, he was very happy. While returning from his tour from Nasik, he invited Pardesi to Dhule and publicly felicitated him, presenting a small silver bowl as a token of appreciation and patted him on his back. Dr. Hedgewar said, "When any act for the nation hits a hurdle, and we have the ability to take it forward, then we should rush forward without thinking about the party, etc."

Similarly, when in 1937, Seth Jugal Kishore Birla, impressed with the ideology and method of working of the Sangh offered a donation of Rs. 500, Dr. Hedgewar said, "The Sangh wants you, and not your donation!".

Hedgewar's Conceptualization of Women

Hedgewar's RSS was designed to be an exclusively male organization. Lakshmibai Kelkar approached Hedgewar with an appeal to admit women as members. Though Hedgewar believed that women had a definite role to indoctrinate the young minds in 'proper' directions, he refused their entry into the RSS as the Sangh leaders have taken the vow of 'brahmacharya'. However, he helped her to set up a parallel but separate organization called the Rashtra Sevika Samiti. Thus, this first affiliate of the RSS was started on the Vijayadashami day of 1936. Delivering a boudhik on 24 June 1938, organized by the Wardha shakha of the samiti, Hedgewar spoke: 'Time and again there have been suggestions to start Sangh work among women. But it was not feasible. Nor was it correct to ignore it. Therefore, a decision was taken to start an independent organization for women working along the aims and objects of the Sangh and encourage it to grow.' Therefore, despite making it formally independent, the RSS very much designed and controlled the course it would charter. It is also important to note a small yet significant difference in name: the members of the RSS are rashtriya swayamsevaks while the members of the women's wing are rashtra sevikas. This partly explains Hedgewar's conceptualization of woman.[40]

Subsequently, Lakshmibai met Dr. Hedgewar three to four times. She recalled later:

"Dr. Hedgewar suggested that the name of the organisation should be different from the Sangh, though conveying the same meaning; the two organisations should work parallel to each other, though independently. He also explained the peculiar problems that would confront a women's organisation. At each meeting, he was minutely observing and assessing my firmness in the matter. I remained steadfast and told him, 'With your blessing and by the Grace of Almighty, I shall not waver in my effort.' I think I passed in Dr. Hedgewar's test. At last, he agreed to give all possible help. On the Vijaya Dashami day, 25th October, 1936, the 'Rashtra Sevika Samiti' was born."

Dr. Hedgewar was well aware that service to the nation required a deepening of the self into a state of selflessness. Speaking in 1938, he said: "While thinking of offering our service to Hindu Rashtra we have to remove from our minds all thoughts of the 'self'. A real servant of the nation is one who identifies himself totally with the nation. There are some who take pride in proclaiming their 'sacrifices for the sake of the nation'. Any service offered to our broader national family does not amount to sacrifice. It is just a sacred duty to be performed by us."

Hedgewar's revolutionary past and the paramilitary nature of the RSS convinced the Central Provinces Home Department that the RSS could develop into a dangerous revolutionary group, and this suspicion continued throughout the pre-Independence period. In fact, the RSS remained scrupulously non-political and it was not until after Independence that it began seriously to consider political activities. People who knew the RSS well, such as Dr. Hardikar, the leader of the Hindustan Seva Dal, criticized the RSS for its refusal to get politically involved. V. D.

Savarkar, the President of the Hindu Mahasabha, after 1937, frequently denounced the RSS for its 'purely cultural' orientation.

Hedgewar's stress on the educational role of the RSS - referred to as character building - led some of his senior colleagues, who wanted it to take a more activist stance, to leave the organization. Anna Sohani, one of his closest colleagues, withdrew from the RSS in 1928. Hedgewar, in 1931, condemned the RSS general secretary G. M. Huddar for participating in an armed robbery, even though the money was intended to fund anti-British activities. Huddar drifted away from the RSS after his release from prison.

By 1938, the RSS started its work in Andhra also. The Central Provinces alone had more than 35,000 swayamsevaks. Dr. Hedgewar visited Lahore in August, 1938 but fell ill there and could address the Swayamevaks for half an hour. He was accompanied by Golwalkar who also spoke there.

Referring to Dr. Hedgewar's brief speech, Golwalkar later wrote: "It was a unique privilege to listen to such a logical, coherent and comprehensive exposition of the Sangh ideal. What a forceful and attractive address it was! When it was over, everybody wished it had continued for another half an hour or more."

Dr. Hedgewar arrived in Delhi on August 30. His health had deteriorated further. The relentless pursuit to expand the RSS had taken its toll on the body. His Gujarat and Maharashtra tours were cancelled. Aware of his failing health, Dr. Hedgewar started entrusting more and more responsibilities to Golwalkar. He was made in-charge of the training camp at Nagpur in 1938.

The Vijaya Dashami celebrations of 1938 at Nagpur had Dr. Gokulchand Narang from Punjab, who presided over the programme. More than 3,000 swayamsevaks in RSS uniform participated in the parade.

Dr. Hedgewar, in his address to Maharashtra Hindu Yuvak Parishat at Pune in 1938, had stated:

"A real servant of the nation is one who identifies himself totally with the nation. There are some who take pride in proclaiming their sacrifice for the sake of the nation. Such an expression only betrays their feeling of being something distinct from the nation. Just as a person never says that he has made sacrifices for the sake of his son, so also any service offered to our broader national family does not amount to sacrifice. It is just a sacred duty to be performed by us."

A mass agitation against the Nizam of Hyderabad began in 1938. About 1,500-2,000 swayamsevaks also took part in the agitation led ably by Bhayyaji Dani. Dr. Hedgewar had, though, clarified quite early about such political agitations: "Whoever wants to take part in the Satyagraha may do so in his personal capacity." The same policy was observed with respect to this Satyagraha also.

Veer Savarkar started a mass agitation against the Nizam of Hyderabad in 1938, and thousands of Swayamsevaks participated in their personal capacity. Sangh shakhas multiplied rapidly in Punjab, Uttar Pradesh, Bihar and other provinces. To suit the spreading influence of the Sangh, a new prayer and some new conventions were set in place. Bhaurao Deoras set up an impressive network of shakhas in Uttar Pradesh. Shakhas spread to princely states under different names, such as "Rajaram Swayamsevak Sangh" in Kolhapar, "Ramoji Swayasevak Sangh" in Gwalior etc. Dr. Hedgewar started paying special attention to the qualities of the Swayamsevaks. In 1939, in order to test the readiness of the Swayamsevaks, he called for a meet at two-hour notice in Pune.[41]

Explaining, he pointed out that quick mobilisation was one of the reasons why the British could rule India from 5000 miles away. He himself had witnessed its effectiveness during his jail life, given a signal, the entire jail staff assembled to bear arms.

In 1935, Dr Ambedkar had made his famous statement that he was born a Hindu but would not die as a Hindu. In 1939, Dr Hedgewar had called Dr Ambedkar to preside the Makar Sankranti function at the RSS camp. A knee jerk reaction would be to brand Dr Ambedkar as an anti-Hindu and a colonial stooge. But Dr Hedgewar was able to see the real reason and pain behind the words of Dr Ambedkar. Gangadhar Bagul, one of the swayamsevaks present in that training camp and a witness to the interaction between Dr Ambedkar and Dr Hedgewar had given a complete description of the event in his autobiography. Dr Ambedkar asked Hedgewar if there were any scheduled community members in the sangh camp. Dr Hedgewar replied that there were no touchables and untouchables in the camp but only Hindus. Dr Ambedkar, however, did go on to inquire the cadre in the camp and found that not only were there many Scheduled Community members but also there was an absolute sense of equality among them and no caste consciousness.[42]

The Sangh Shakhas multiplied rapidly in Punjab, Uttar Pradesh, Bihar and some other provinces. It was time to take a relook at the commands given at the Shakha in Marathi and Sanskrit. Dr. Hedgewar called for a meeting of prominent workers at Sindi in February 1939. The meeting was attended by M S Golwalkar, Appaji Joshi, Balasaheb Deoras, Tatyarao Telang, Vitthalrao Patki, Babaji Salodkar, Nanasaheb Talatule and Krishnarao Mohrir. The Sindi Chintan baitak is recalled as a unique phenomenon because it was only when three men who presided over the RSS for almost seven decades (from 1925 to 1994) were huddled together to deliberate on its past, present and future. The deliberations went on for ten days. The discussions were held on constitution, commands, prayer technique of the Sangh, the pledge and all other organisational aspects.

When language became a barrier for reciting the prayer, the shakha heads in different regions requested that the first stanza be translated into the local language. Finally, Dr. Hedgewar came up with a solution for tackling cultural and linguistic differences and his proposal to change the prayer endorsed at the Sindi Chintan baitak. It was decided that the Sangh prayer and the commands should be in Sanskrit. Dr. Hedgewar outlined the ideological content of the prayer, and Nanasaheb Talatule wrote it down in prose. This was later put into verse. Some operational and procedural changes were also decided upon. 'Namaste sada vatsale' written by Narahari Narayan bhide was first sung by pracharak named Yadavrao joshi on April 23,1940. It continues to be recited every day in shakhas across the country. Sangh prarthana ends with a salutation to the nation – Bharat mata ki jai. The construct of a nation as motherland or fatherland is undoubtedly a universal tradition, but in India, the deification of the nation as a Hindu goddess was a twentieth century phenomenon. It is to the credit of the RSS which lent it a political dimension.

It was a path-breaking meeting as the conventions of the Sangh were revised in detail. What we witness today in RSS is largely an outcome of that meeting.

There was rapid expansion of the RSS during that era. "After the meeting (at Sindi), Golwalkar and Vitthalrao Patki were sent to Calcutta for establishing the Shakhas there. Reports of expansion of Shakhas were pouring in from everywhere. Bhaurao Deoras, who had gone to Uttar Pradesh for studies, had built up a formidable network of Shakhas in that area."

"The conditions in United Provinces are now very congenial for the growth of Sangh," he wrote in a letter of 29th April. Bapurao Bhishikar, who had gone to Karachi to take up a job in an educational institution gave a strong push to Sangh activities in that area. Punjab was throbbing with enthusiasm. Appreciative letters from local workers and sympathisers poured in from Rawalpindi, Sialkot and other far-flung places. Those letters invariably showered praise on the workers who had gone there from Nagpur, and urged Dr. Hedgewar to enable the workers to continue in those areas... By then, some workers had been deputed to Bihar also. Swayamsevaks, from some northern provinces had come to participate in the Officers Training Camp at Nagpur that year in 1939. Dr. Hedgewar personally supervised the arrangements for their board and lodging. To suit the differing food habits of participants, Dr. Hedgewar had arranged for two or three different Courses.

On the Guru-Poornima day in 1939 (August 13), Dr. Hedgewar announced the appointment of Golwalkar as the Sarkaryavah, and Babasaheb Ghatate as the Nagpur Sanghchalak.

In a letter to Dadarao Paramarth, Dr. Hedgewar wrote: "Encouraging reports have started coming from Punjab, United Provinces, Bihar, Bengal and Karachi. More than 150 swayamsevaks have come from about 50 Shakhas in Lahore. It has been decided to give a special thrust to the Sangh activities in Punjab this year.

As the session of the Aryan League was held at Nagpur this year, we had an opportunity of meeting many all-India leaders from Punjab and United Provinces. All of them have offered support to spread the Sangh activities in their respective regions. They seem deeply impressed by the successful working of the Sangh. As you are aware, four of our Pracharaks have gone to Bihar. In a short while, Shri Madhav Golwalkar will also join them. I am fully confident that you will manage the work entrusted to you in the Madras province quite competently."

Throughout the year 1939, Dr. Hedgewar asked Golwalkar to speak on all public occasions.

Dr. Hedgewar had spent the last few months of his life suffering from extremely poor health. Despite that, he continued with the RSS work. Finally, Gopalrao Ogale, Editor of Maharashtra and some other prominent people convinced him to go to Rajgir in Bihar in January 1940 for his treatment. He was accompanied by Appaji Joshi amongst others. The warm-water springs at that place are well known for their curative properties.

Dr. Hedgewar stayed there for two months. In April, he again had to return there. Even while being so unwell, one day a batch of students came to meet him. He met them and motivated them to start a Shakha in Rajgir. He again came back from Rajgir to Nagpur on May 16, 1940 to attend the RSS training camp at Pune. But he remained quite unwell and was suffering from high fever for the next 24 days, i.e., the whole duration of the camp. On June 2, Golwalkar addressed the swayamsevaks in his presence. By that time, his health had deteriorated so much that he could barely sit. On June 4, he made a short speech with great effort and addressed the Swayamsevaks. That proved to be his last message to the swayamseveks:

"I do not feel that I am today in a fit condition to say even a few words to you. As all of you know, I have been confined to bed for the last twenty-four days. From the point of view of the Sangh, the last one year has been a glorious period. Today, I am seeing before me the Hindustan in miniature. Because of my illness, it has not been possible for me to get acquainted with each one of you individually, even though I have been in Nagpur for so many days. I spent a fortnight at the Officers Training Camp in Pune. I was able to get acquainted with every Swayamsevak there. I was hoping to be able to do so here also, but I found myself unable to be of even the slightest service to you. I have come today to have your darshan.

Though you and I are not acquainted with each other, what is it that draws my heart towards you and your hearts towards me? That is surely the result of the philosophy imbued in the Rashtriya Swayamsevak Sangh. Even if there is no previous contact, Swayamsevaks warmly take to one another even at the first meeting. And even before they talk to each other, they become mutual friends! The smile on the face itself is enough for them to identify one another."

Such is the result of the incessant penance of the Sangh. Shri Sanjiv Kamath of Madras who spoke here a few days ago exclaimed, "Well, I came here as a stranger, but am returning as one of your brethren." In a matter of four days, he became like a brother to all of us and has returned with profound fraternal feelings. The credit for all this does not belong to any one individual, but to the Sangh. How did the swayamsevaks from Punjab, Bengal, Madras, Bombay, Sind, etc., with differing behavioural backgrounds, come to love one another? It was possible because they all belong to the Rashtriya Swayamsevak Sangh.

All the swayamsevaks of the Sangh love one another as they love their own brethren. Even, children of the same mother sometimes quarrel among themselves in regard to property. But, such quarrels can never take place among swayamsevaks.

You are all leaving for your respective places today. I bid you all a loving farewell. Though the parting is painful, there is no cause for sadness. You are all returning to fulfil the very purpose for which you came here. I want you to take the vow that you will not forget the Sangh till your last breath. Let nothing distract you. May there never come an unfortunate moment in your lifetime when you will be obliged to say, "I was a swayamsevak of the Sangh some five years ago." Let us all remain swayamsevaks till the very last breath of our life. Let us keep ever aglow our resolve to work for the Sangh ideal through body, mind and soul. Everyday, before going to bed, let us ask ourselves, 'How much Sangh work did I do today?'"

Mere execution of the routine programmes of Sangh or daily physical presence at Sanghasthan is not enough for achieving our goal. Remember, we have to organise the entire Hindu society from Kanyakumari to the Himalayas. In fact, our main area of operation is the vast Hindu world outside the Sangh. The Sangh should not be the preserve of only the swayamsevaks, but must cover the entire Hindu people outside the Sangh fold. Our object should be to show to the people the true path of national salvation. The true path is none other than Organisation. The Hindu race can save itself only through such an organisation.

Rashtriya Swayamsevak Sangh is not interested in any other work. To ask what the Sangh is going to do in future is meaningless. The Sangh will strive on to accelerate the pace of organisation. As we continue our efforts, a golden moment will arrive when the entire Bharat will stand as one, undivided and indivisible entity. No power on earth will then cast its malicious eyes on Hindusthan. We have not set out to assault anybody. But we must always be vigilant and resist any outsiders' efforts to assault us. I am not telling you anything new. Every swayamsevak must regard the Sangh work as his sole mission in life. I am confident that you will all depart from here with the firm conviction ingrained in the depths of your hearts that the Sangh work alone has the utmost priority in your lives. I bid you all farewell with this assurance.[43]

Second World War and Final Effort at Armed Uprising

Trailokyanath Chakravarti of the Anushilan Samiti also visited Nagpur to discuss plans of armed revolt with Dr.Hedgewar. Dr.Hedgewar felt that although the time was ripe, the organisation was not yet ready. His anxiety to prepare the organisation for the expected armed uprising was often seen in his questions to Swayamsevaks : "How many Swayamsevaks would be needed for achieving the freedom of the country?" Indicating his own calculations, he said: "I should like to place before you a plan that could make the Sangh most effective. In the course of the next three years, at least three per cent of the population of cities and one per cent in villages should become Swayamsevaks equipped with full uniform."

Shyama Prasad Mukherji and the Move to Bengal In 1940, Dr.Shyama Prasad Mukherji called on Dr.Hedgewar, then sick, with an appeal from Bengal. Hindu properties were being looted, their women molested. The condition of widows was most pitiable. Dr.Hedgewar noted that the Muslim government of Bengal which had British support would not allow a militia to come up. He suggested that organisation and an intense feeling of oneness was the only answer. "Whether it is Punjab or Bengal or any other province – the chief cause for the pitiable plight of the Hindus is want of organization among themselves. As long as this is not set right, no solution is possible. Hindus will continue to undergo such travails at one place or the other. The situation cannot be transformed by half-baked or retaliatory measures. The Hindus must be made to feel intensely that they are one single cohesive society. The concept of one nationhood must be deeply engraved in their hearts. They must love one another and share the common goal of raising up our country. This is the only way, the only positive and enduring way of national resurrection. And this is what the Sangh is doing." Dr.Shyama Prasad Mukherji returned to Calcutta and decided to set up a six-week training camp there. He asked for trained instructors and assistance from Nagpur. Dr.Hedgewar made the necessary arrangements.

The outbreak of the Second World War threw England into turmoil. Veer Savarkar, now President of Hindu Mahasabha, wanted to exploit the situation, and even planned to start a Hindu army. Subhash Chandra Bose who had left the Congress, wanted to attack the British. Naturally, both thought of Dr. Hedgewar. Balaji Huddar and Dr.V. R. Sanjgiri came to Dr. Hedgewar carrying a brief from Subhas Bose. Dr. Hedgewar was at that time undergoing treatment at Deolali, having suffered a severe attack of double pneumonia. The message from Subhas Babu was conveyed to him. It related to formulating a plan for a countrywide revolt against the British, with help from such countries as were opposed to Britain.

After attentively listening to the narration by the two emissaries, Dr. Hedgewar said: "It is a fact that the situation is ripening for a national uprising. But the crucial question is: How far has your preparation progressed? To start with, at least fifty per cent of preparation should be complete.

How many people are there at present under the command of Subhas Babu? Without a corresponding preparation on our part, mere dependence upon foreign help would be of no avail." It was then decided that Subhas Babu himself would shortly come to Nagpur to meet Dr. Hedgewar. However, Subhas Babu could not come. Doctor Sanigiri then wrote to Dr. Hedgewar to come over for the meeting. However, Dr. Hedgewar was then convalescing. In 1940, accompanied by the late R.S. Ruikar, Subhash Chandra Bose himself came to meet Dr. Hedgewar to discuss the question of an armed uprising. Unfortunately, Dr. Hedgewar was terminally ill. He could barely exchange pleasantries.[44]

With deteriorating health, he was taken to the Mayo Hospital on June 15 for a special check-up. After a series of tests at the Mayo Hospital, he was shifted to the residence of Babasaheb Ghatate.

The doctors got ready to give him the lumber puncture. Dr. Hedgewar had realised that the end was near.

He called Golwalkar near him and told him, in the presence of all, "Well, hereafter you have to shoulder the responsibility of the Sangh." On Friday, June 21, 1940, the founder of the RSS, Dr. Keshav Baliram Hedgewar took his last breath.

His last journey was a tribute to his life's work. It was the biggest procession that Nagpur had ever witnessed. Bicycle-riders led the procession. Behind them followed in four rows several thousand Swayamsevaks in plain clothes, and thousands of residents of Nagpur. At the centre was Dr. Hedgewar's mortal body and the Bhagwa Dhwaj. Behind these were prominent citizens, followed by another long contingent of Swayamsevaks and bicycle-riders. Workers belonging to Congress, Hindu Mahasabha, Forward Bloc, Socialist Party, Mazdoor Sangh, Harijan organizations, Women's organizations and numerous other bodies joined in the procession to pay their last respects. Almost every prominent person of Nagpur could be seen there.

Madhav Sadashiv Golwalkar

Madhav Sadashivrao Golwalkar (19 February 1906 – 5 June 1973), popularly known as Guruji, was the second Sarsanghchalak of the Rashtriya Swayamsevak Sangh (RSS). Golwalkar is considered one of the most influential and prominent figures among Rashtriya Swayamsevak Sangh.He took over this responsibility in 1940, and worked in the same capacity till 1973.

The RSS expanded rapidly from 1940 to 1973 under his leadership, As RSS' leader for more than 30 years, Golwalkar made it one of the strongest religious-cultural organisations in India; its membership expanded from 100,000 to over one million, and it branched out into the political, social, religious, educational and labour fields through 50 front organisations. [45]

Golwalkar is known to have travelled the whole country more than 65 times. His extensive travelling, even at the cost of his health, and a gruelling schedule for 33 years resulted in the RSS inspired organisations coming up in every field and sector ranging from tribal welfare to student politics.Golwalkar has remained one of the most revered figures in RSS, also because he was spiritually quite advanced. In fact, Golwalkar's spiritual master once told him that the long hair he had kept as a young sannyasi looked good upon him. Golwalkar never cut his hair after that. He had taken formal 'diksha' as a sannyasi at Ramakrishna Mission in 1930s.[46]

Golwalkar was born to Sadashivrao and Lakshmibai Golwalkar in a Marathi Karhade Brahmin family at Ramtek, near Nagpur in Maharashtra. Sadashivrao was commonly known as Bhauji and Laxmibai as Tai. His family was prosperous and supported him in his studies and activities. Sadashivrao, a former clerk in the Posts and Telegraphs Department, became a teacher in the Central Provinces and Berar and ended his career as headmaster of a high school. Golwalkar was the only surviving son of nine children. Since his father was frequently transferred around the country, he attended a number of schools. Golwalkar studied science and was apt and apolitical as a student. As an adolescent, he developed a deep interest in religion and spiritual meditation.

Recalling his childhood, Golwalkar said in one of his speeches (at Pune) as Sarsanghchalak, "When I remember my childhood, my mind is filled with many sweet memories. All those events pass in succession before the mind's eye. I used to be woken up early in the mornings. My mother used to busy herself with household chores, but at the same time, chant stotras and the names of God. Tai's melodious voice would fill my ears and heart. What a deep and noble impact those melodious tunes sung in the peaceful and elevating moments of the morning must have made on my young mind!".

When Madhav was around eleven years old, the sacred thread ceremony (upanayan samskara) was held at Khandwa (presently in Madhya Pradesh). Madhav started doing 'Trikal Sandhya (regular ritual of prayers)' since that day and never missed it since his last breath.

While speaking at a conference of young brahmachaaris (celibates) in Pune's Narad Temple, he recounted his experience "Nurturing inner and physical strength through Gayatri Mantra and Surya Namaskar and through sandhya has given me a healthy body as well as a healthy mind."

Madhav was a brilliant student. In 1919, he entered the English High School. He got a scholarship of four rupees per month on winning the 'high school entrance and scholarship exam' after class seventh.

He had already read the entire Ramcharitmanas and memorised parts of it before completing higher secondary education. Madhav was a voracious reader. He was equally enthusiastic about sports, especially hockey and the malkhamb exercise.

At the age of 16 years, Madhav passed his matriculation in 1922 from the Jubilee High School at Chanda (now Chandrapur). Madhav took admission at Hislop College in the Science stream. He passed Intermediate Examination in 1924 from the same college and his name appeared in the list of meritorious students. At the college, he was reportedly incensed at the Open Advocacy of Christianity and the Disparagement of Hinduism; much of his concern for the defence of Hinduism is traceable to this experience.[47]

Once his Professor Gardiner made a reference to the Bible in the class. As it was a missionary college, study of the Bible was compulsory. Madhav had made a deep study of the Bible also. Even in his speeches as a Sarsanghchalak and during conversations, sometimes he used to make references to the Bible as well as to the life of Jesus Christ. When he saw that Prof. Gardiner was wrong in giving that particular reference, he stood up and said, "Sir, you are giving the wrong reference' and quoted the right reference from his memory. The professor was amazed, but how could he stand a student being more knowledgeable about the Bible than him? So, he called for a copy of the Bible to check up and found that Madhav was right. The book contained the reference exactly as Madhav had quoted it. The professor accepted his mistake sportingly and patted Madhav on his back."

After passing the Intermediate Examination, Madhav took admission in the Banaras Hindu University (BHU). Founded by Pt. Madan Mohan Malaviya in 1916, this institution was a hub of nationalism and attracted the best talent across the country.

Madhav got himself admitted in the Bachelor of Science Course. The University had a library stocked with more than one lakh books, the surroundings were scenic, the laboratories were well equipped and the playgrounds were huge. Madhav spent a lot of time in reading books in the library as well as in sports.

In 1926, he took his B.Sc. degree, in 1928, a master's degree in biology, and in 1929, he passed the M.Sc. examination with a First Class. During the four years at the University, he started his spiritual journey too. At the University library, he spent more time than probably anyone else. He read on a wide variety of subjects, such as Sanskrit Western philosophy, inspiring thoughts of Ramakrishna Paramhansa and Swami Vivekananda, the main scriptures of various religions and sects in addition to many books on scientific subjects. He was deeply influenced by Madan Mohan Malaviya, a nationalist leader and founder of the university.

"Madhavrao was such a voracious reader that even during a prolonged illness in the final year of B.Sc., he always had a book in his hands. Many a time, he returned from the college in the evening, took his meal and settled down to his reading-books and continued till the early hours of the morning. Then he was again ready, fresh as ever, for the next day's activities. Books always lay scattered all over his room. As he had a spiritual bent of mind, even while he was a student at Hislop College in Nagpur, he used to go to the headmaster of the City High School, Shri Muley, to study the Hindu scriptures. While in Banaras, spiritual discussions, study of Vedic treatises and contact with Pandit Madan Mohan Malaviya too had left a deep impact upon him, which became visible in his life in various ways like worship, meditation, asanas, Pranayama, indifference to mundane individual life, and a sense of identification with the joys and sorrows of the society. It is possibly during this same period that he might have started thinking about his future course of life. As a student at the University, he had to undergo great financial hardships, but his face never betrayed them."

After doing his Masters in Science, Golwalkar went to Madras to pursue a doctorate in marine biology, but could not complete it because of his father's retirement and due to financial constraints, and left it half way to come back to Nagpur. Golwalkar later obtained a law degree in 1937 in Nagpur.

"Studies apart, the thought raging in Madhavrao's mind in those days finds a reflection in the letters he wrote from Madras. They reveal the sanskars imbibed in Kashi, the natural impact of the happenings in the country on a highly sensitive young mind and the mental struggle in deciding his future goal in life. This was indeed a very crucial period in Madhavrao's life. The storm raging in his mind gives a clue to the direction his future life took. The important point to be borne in mind is that although this young man was engaged in scientific research and was standing on the threshold of a conventional family life after completing his education, thoughts like personal ambitions of a happy personal life never so much crossed his mind."

During the freedom struggle at that time, three revolutionaries - Bhagat Singh, Sukhdeo and Rajguru - had assassinated a notorious British officer Saunders for his atrocities. Madhav wrote to his friend Baburao Telang in the first week of January 1929:

"Heard about the explosion at Lahore. Felt highly gratified. It is a matter of satisfaction that, although to a small extent, the insult meted out to the nation by the power-crazy foreign rulers was avenged. I have often discussed with you, ideas such as of universal brotherhood, equality, peace, and so on. I have denounced violence, hatred, the attitude of revenge, etc., and held you guilty, quarreled with you. You will be surprised that it is the same me who is writing like this."

In the same letter, he writes, "There has to be a new national awakening among the people. The Brahmin-non-Brahmin controversy will have to be ended. I am not a big leader nor a worker or any group. But everyone must contribute his might to this task."

After leaving the University, Madhav was trying to decide whether he should become a hermit and move to Himalayas to attain the goal of self-realisation or whether he should stay back and work for the society.

In a letter to his friend Telang, written on March 20, 1929, he talks about this, "I have no desire to attune myself to a mundane human life. What I want is to stretch this string of life to create a still purer tune. While doing so, mental strain cannot be avoided. This means it does not matter if one has to live apart from the common world. The important thing is that the string of life must not be out of tune with that heavenly music."[48]

What initiated Madhav to dedicate his life for the RSS can be gauged from another letter written to Telang in 1929, where he says: "I have already accepted initiation into Sannyasa, but it is not yet complete. Perhaps my original idea of going to the Himalayas was faulty. Now I am trying to cultivate a sense of renunciation in every atom of my being even while living in the ordinary world, sharing in the sorrows of a common man's life and discharging all its responsibilities with diligence. Now I shall not go to the Himalayas, rather Himalayas shall come to me, its serene silence will dwell within me. Now it is not necessary to go anywhere for attaining that serenity."

In 1930, he got an opportunity to work as a lecturer in Zoology at the same Banaras Hindu University where he had studied. He spent around three years there. These three years played an important role in deciding the future course of his life. His students called him 'Guruji' because of his beard, long hair, and simple robe like a sanyasi, a practice later continued in a reverential manner by his RSS followers.

Although young Madhav was a lecturer in Zoology, he also taught his students and friends subjects like English, Economics, Mathematics and Philosophy. A majority of his salary was spent on supporting the poor students. This earned him the love and respect of his students. Doing all this, Madhavarao had no expectation in return at all. Pandit Madan Mohan Malaviya noticed his talent as well as his deep affection for the students, and grew fond of him.[49]

The most significant development during this period was Madhav coming into direct contact with the Rashtriya Swayamsevak Sangh. Bhayyaji Dani, who had arrived in Kashi in 1928 for further studies, had started a Shakha there. Dani established close contact with Golwalkar and the latter started visiting the Shakha occasionally.

Interestingly, around a decade later, when Golwalkar became Sarsanghchalak, Bhayyaji Dani was Sarkaryawah (General Secretary), for some years. It was Golwalkar who used to take swayamsevaks to meet Pandit Madan Mohan Malaviya at the BHU campus.

Malaviya was impressed about the RSS. Later, he gave the organisation open space for Shakha and a small building for its office within the University campus.

In 1932, the then RSS chief Dr. Hedgewar invited Shri Golwalkar, who was still teaching at the University, along with another lecturer friend Sadgopal, to Nagpur for the Vijaya Dashami function. This personal contact with Dr. Hedgewar gave clearer picture of the Sangh work to Golwalkar. After this visit, when he returned back to the BHU campus to resume his teaching assignment, he started taking more interest in the RSS work.

In 1933, Golwalkar returned to Nagpur after completing the three-year teaching assignment at BHU. His parents were staying at Ramtek, around 25 miles from Nagpur, where they had bought a house after retirement. So, he started living with his maternal uncle. He visited them quite often. To support them financially, he started working as a teacher in his Uncle's coaching classes. Simultaneously, he enrolled himself in a Law College. Meanwhile, he was also entrusted with a greater responsibility in the RSS, as in 1934, he was appointed Karyawaha (Secretary in-charge) of the Sangh's main Shakha, which was being held at Tulsibagh at that time. He was also sent to Mumbai in 1934 by Dr. Hedgewar to spread the organisation's work there. In 1935, he was appointed as the Sarvadhikari (the overall chief) of the RSS training camp held at Akola. In 1935, Golwalkar passed his Law examination as a meritorious student. Those were the days when his parents asked him to get married. However, he told his parents that he had no desire to get married. He told his mother, "Tai, please do not talk about the family coming to an end. Even like many families like ours come to an end for the good of the society, it would be very much necessary in its present-day condition. I am not in the least worried about the end of our family." Tai never broached the topic of marriage again.

While carrying out the Sangh work, Golwalkar also developed a strong leaning towards becoming a hermit. He leaned more and more towards the Ramakrishna Ashram located in the Dhamtoli area of the Nagpur city and developed a close relationship with the head of the Ashram, Swami Bhaskareshwarananda. He started spending more and more time at the Ashram in his quest for spirituality.

This quest became so strong that in the summer of 1936, he abandoned his law practice and RSS work, left Nagpur for Ramakrishna Mission Ashram at Sargachhi in West Bengal to renounce the world and become a sanyasi. He took formal 'deeksha (initiation into the life of asceticism)' from Swami Akhandananda, who was a disciple of Shri Ramakrishna Paramahansa and brother monk of Swami Vivekananda. He became a disciple of Swami Akhandananda.

Golwalkar had received initiation on January 13, 1937 on the auspicious occasion of Makar Sankranti. He later recalled these moments: "Red-letter day for me to be noted down in words of gold. For did not the fortune of countless millions of births smile upon me and confer upon me the bliss of being graced by the Master? Indeed, the experiences of that day are very sacred, too sacred for words. I can never forget the touch, the love, the whole bearing of the master as he conferred upon me this favour of the blessed, and all the time I trembled. I feel changed. I was not what I was a minute ago."

Golwalkar returned to Nagpur in March 1937. Here, he stayed with Amitabh Maharaj at Ramakrishna Ashram for a month. During this period, the latter asked Golwalkar to translate Swami Vivekananda's Chicago address into Marathi. He also called Golwalkar's maternal uncle and asked him to take Golwalkar to Dr. Hedgewar.

Both Dr. Hedgewar and Golwalkar had a series of meetings after that. It took some time before Golwalkar decided to dedicate his life for the society through the RSS. During this period, he also translated Babarao Savarkar's 'Rashtra Mimansa' in Marathi in a single day and presented it to Nagpur's reputed lawyer Vishwanath Kelkar.

Dr. Hedgewar gave him responsibility of Sarvadhikari (the overall chief) of the Sangh training camp in Nagpur in 1939.

In 1939, Golwalkar had a detailed discussion with the Bhausaheb Madkholkar, a well-known Marathi author and editor of the daily 'Tarun Bharat', Nagpur. Dr. Hedgewar also was present at this meeting. After the demise of Golwalkar, three-and-a-half decades later, Madkholkar wrote a detailed account of this meeting in an article titled 'Trikoni Sangam' in 'Tarun Bharat' (16.6.73).

Madkholkar wrote, "I asked Shri Golwalkar, "I have heard that for some time, you had left the Sangh work here and had gone to the Ramakrishna Ashram in Bengal, where you received initiation from Swami Vivekananda's Guru Bandhu, but later, you left the Ashram and rejoined the Sangh. How was that? Don't you think that the Sangh's stand is quite different from that of the Ashram?" On listening to my question, Shri Golwalkar fell silent and with eyes half closed, he thought for a few moments. It was as if he had gone into a trance. After some time, he began to speak slowly."

He said: "This is a totally unexpected question. But whether there was or was not a difference in the stands of the Ashram and the Sangh, Dr. Hedgewar would be able to say with greater authority, because during the period of revolutionary movement, he was in Calcutta and was closely connected with their activities. You must have read Bhagini Nivedita's book titled 'Aggressive Hinduism! I am sure you also know how closely she was connected with the revolutionaries. Right from the beginning, my inclination was towards both – spirituality on the one hand and the task of national regeneration on the other. During my stay in Banaras, Nagpur and Calcutta, I realised that if I stayed with the Sangh, I would be able to do this work more effectively. So, I dedicated myself to that Sangh work. I think what I am doing is in consonance with Swami Vivekananda's philosophy, guidance, and method of work. Golwalkar worked for the nationalistic awakening by following the philosophy of Swami Vivekanand, Ramakrishna Paramhansa and Sri Aurobindo.

No other great personality's life or teaching has influenced me so much. I believe by doing the Sangh work, I shall be carrying out only his work."

Madkholkar added, "I shall never forget the light of self realisation that shone in Shri

Golwalkar's eyes as he explained this to me. Doctor saheb had also fallen silent, lost in thought."

The RSS training camp in 1939 proved to be a turning point for Golwalkar as he got himself totally immersed in the organisational work and emerged as a role model for people around him in the organisation. Now, Dr. Hedgewar and Golwalkar started working closely, relentlessly to build the organisation. In February 1939, an important meeting was held at Sindi in which the top brass of the organisation took several crucial decisions after having a threadbare discussion which had a permanent impact on the direction which RSS took in the years to come. This meeting had lasted for 10 days. The current prayer of the RSS, the commands at the daily Shakha, etc. were adopted in this meeting breaking away from earlier tradition. Golwalkar was a part of this meeting, too. Along with others, Appaji Joshi, a close confidante of Dr. Hedgewar and Balasaheb Deoras, who later became the third RSS chief, were also present in this meeting.

Once, while talking about this meeting, Appaji Joshi recalled a particular incident: "After bowing to the Flag on the Sanghasthan (the place where daily Shakha is held) to whom should the swayamsevak bow next? I and Shri Golwalkar differed on setting up a definite system for this. While Shri Golwalkar forcefully argued in favour of constitutional norms, I emphasised upon a system that was in accord with the family spirit of the Sangh. Finally, Dr. Hedgewar decided in my favour. At that time, I was closely watching Shri Golwalkar, but there was not a trace of resentment on his face. There was also no bitterness in his words at any time thereafter. We were all impressed with his mental balance and faith in the leader."

Appaji also recounted another incident at the meeting, "In this meeting at Sindi, Dr. Hedgewar once asked me, 'What do you think of Shri Golwalkar as the future Sarsanghchalak?' On the basis of my observation during the discussions in the meeting, I unhesitatingly replied, 'Excellent! the most proper choice.'"

Since 1932, Dr. Hedgewar's health had started deteriorating. It was only his strong will that kept him going but it was clear that he had started looking for a successor to lead the organisation and he had found one in Golwalkar.

After the Sindi meeting, Golwalkar was sent to Calcutta to start the Sangh work in Bengal. He used to walk 25 miles a day as there was hardly money for transportation. With his efforts, the first Sangh Shakha started in Calcutta on the Varsha Pratipada (The Hindu New Year Day) of 1939. In April 1939, he was called back to Nagpur to look after the RSS training camp as 'Sarvadhikari'.

Meanwhile, Dr. Hedgewar went to Deolali to recuperate for a few days, but his condition worsened. Golwalkar personally nursed Dr. Hedgewar.

When the temperature rose very high, Dr. Hedgewar would become delirious. But even in this state, he would talk about the RSS work. Golwalkar was constantly by his side, taking care of him all the time. Finally, Dr. Hedgewar recovered and returned to Nagpur with Golwalkar on August 7, 1939. At a function, to celebrate the festival of Raksha Bandhan in 1939, he announced Shri Golwalkar's appointment as the Sarkaryawah (General Secretary) of Sangh.

Golwalkar was on the Sarkaryawah post for only ten months. During this time, the RSS work continued to expand rapidly as several new Shakhas were started in Madhya Pradesh, Maharashtra and even in distant places, like Punjab, Delhi, Karachi, Patna, Calcutta, Lucknow, etc. The RSS had assumed a national character with expanding its outreach to most parts of the undivided India within a short span of time.

Meanwhile, Dr. Hedgewar's health continued to deteriorate and he had to go to Rajgir (Bihar) to take some rest. In his absence, Golwalkar ably looked after the work of the organisation.

The treatment at Rajgir was not of much help, but Dr. Hedgewar came back and resumed organisational work. In April 1940, Dr. Hedgewar went to Pune for an RSS training camp and his health deteriorated dramatically. He had realised that the end was near. So, he sent for Golwalkar and said to him in the presence of several RSS functionaries, "Now the entire Sangh's responsibility is entrusted to you. Accept this first, and then you may do whatever you want to my body."

Golwalkar said, "Why do you say so? You are going to get well soon."

Dr. Hedgewar replied back with a smile despite being in great pain, "May be, but don't forget what I have said." That was the moment when Golwalkar was appointed as Dr. Hedgewar's successor and he was handed over the complete charge as Sarsanghchalak. Dr. Hedgewar had to suffer two more days of pain before he left for the heavenly abode on Friday, June 21, at 9:27 am.

After a few days of Dr. Hedgewar's demise, a meeting of five Sanghchalaks took place in Akola, attended among others by Appaji Joshi, Babasaheb Ghatate, Maharashtra Sanghchalak, and Kashinathrao Limaye. Babarao Savarkar had proposed that the reins of the Sangh should pass into the hands of Madhavrao Golwalkar and an advisory committee consisting of Babasaheb Ghatate, Ramchandra Narayan (Babasaheb) Padhye, Vishwanathrao Kelkar and others be formed with Abaji Hedgewar (Dr.Hedgewar's uncle) as its head. The meeting reviewed the situation and everyone agreed that Golwalkar is the right successor.

This laid the foundation of a permanent system of appointing successors by subsequent Sarsanghchalaks as followed in a religious mutt. "After this unanimous conclusion, they all (the five Sangchalaks at Akola meeting) expressed their confidence in Shri Golwalkar's leadership and decided that in the homage offering meeting on the thirteenth day of his demise, Shri Golwalkar's name should be officially announced as the new Sarsanghchalak. Accordingly, a function was held on the appointed day at Dr. Hedgewar's samadhi at Reshimbagh to pay homage to his hallowed memory and to make the public announcement of Shri Golwalkar's name as the new Sarsanghchalak.

Accordingly, Nagpur District Sanghchalak, Babasaheb Padhye announced Shri Golwalkar as the new Sarsanghchalak. The first to speak at this function was Babasaheb Padhye, who announced Shri Golwalkar's appointment as the new Sarsanghchalak.

Explaining the Sangh's one leader' system 'Ekachalakanuvartitva' and Dr. Hedgewar's own arrangement for the future, he said in his speech, "In accordance with the final wish of our first Sarsanghchalak, respected Shri Madhavrao Golwalkar has been appointed our new Sarsanghchalak, and now he is for all of us in the place of Dr. Hedgewar. I offer him my first Pranam (salutation) as my new Sarsanghchalak.

Dr. Hedgewar's aged uncle, Abaji Hedgewar also spoke on that occasion. In his brief but inspiring speech, he said, "Indeed, our Dr. Hedgewar has not left us at all; we still see him in the form of Madhavrao Golwalkar. Now onwards, every directive from him is to be obeyed as if it was from Dr. Hedgewar himself."

Golwalkar also spoke on the occasion as the new Sarsanghchalak. His speech served as a telling index to his supreme self-confidence, humility and his deeply felt reverence for Dr. Hedgewar. This was his very first speech as the new Sarsanghchalak.

Golwalkar was rather new in the Sangh as compared to other associates. He was also not very well known in the country. This obviously raised doubts in the minds of quite a few well-wishers and others regarding the future of the Sangh. Many of them started commenting and advising too.

But Golwalkar silenced everybody in his very first preliminary speech as the Sarsanghachalak, "Doctorji was a synthesis of an affectionate mother, a responsible father and an able Guru. He has entrusted me with this tough job of Sarsanghachalak, but then this is the throne of Vikramaditya (a king of ancient Bharat known for his benevolence and justice); even if a rustic boy would sit on it, he would but dispense justice..... The meritorious deeds of our great leader would ensure that I will always do the rightful things. Our great leader's hallowed merit will make me do only the right things. Now let us set ourselves to the task with full faith and confidence and take it forward with redoubled vigour and enthusiasm.", he further said, "Our organization is like an impregnable fort; those who would attack it would only receive its brunt." Golwalkar's self-confident utterances boosted the morale of the Swayamsevaks and silenced his critics.[50]

Thus, he made the work of the Sangh the sole purpose of his life. A most important aspect lay in his concentrated efforts to orient his daily routine, life-style and nature as per needs of the Sangh. He also gradually tried to overcome his weaknesses. The aggressiveness in his tone due to his strict disciplinary nature also started to soften. He was always alert about all these aspects. He had totally imbibed the ideal of Hindu nationhood. For him, Dr.Hedgewar served as a living example in all such respects. [51]

Before his death on 21 June 1940, Hedgewar had nominated Madhav Sadashiv Golwalkar as the next sarsanghchalak, thereby setting the precedent that the top leadership position would not be open to democratic election. The choice of Golwalkar surprised many of the RSS members, as senior and experienced stalwarts like Appaji Joshi, Keshav Apte and Dadarao Parmarth were bypassed. The RSS members had speculated that Appaji Joshi, the senior most leader, would be the likely successor. However, according to the RSS sources, there was no dispute over the issue of succession. Hedgewar's grooming including encouragement to obtain a law degree is seen as key to Golwalkar's later success.

Why was Golwalkar preferred to others? What was his special quality? In fact, Golwalkar had greater inclination towards personal salvation than national resurrection. In contrast to Hedgewar, who was an extrovert and an outright political activist, Golwalkar was more inward-looking and inclined to spiritualism. Then why did Hedgewar choose such a person as his successor? The reason for this choice remains in the sphere of speculation. One possible explanation is that Hedgewar was frustrated by the endless bickering among Hindu Mahasabha stalwarts - between Moonje and Savarkar, Bhai Parmanand and Savarkar. Therefore, he was keen to detach the RSS from the Hindu Mahasabha, despite their ideological proximity and wanted a successor who would effectively keep his organization away from the influence of these Mahasabha leaders. Golwalkar ideally fitted into this criterion as he was not close to any of the Mahasabha leaders and he was thought likely to maintain RSS independence, otherwise liable to be regarded as a youth front of the Hindu Mahasabha. Moreover, he had other advantages vis-a-vis his competitors: educational and intellectual background, and young age.[52]

In June 1940, the Sangh began its journey under the extraordinary ideological and organisational stewardship of Golwalkar. Although Sangh had spread out to some provinces outside Maharashtra, several parts of the country still remained untouched.

Till now, the RSS volunteers started shakhas wherever they went as students. There were only a handful of Pracharaks. Golwalkar started the system of having full-time workers (Pracharaks) exclusively to expand the organisation's work. The result was phenomenal growth in the organisation's network across the country.[53]

Meanwhile the RSS encouraged its volunteers to participate in the freedom movement. The organisation itself was at a nascent stage. So, it adopted a strategy that instead of getting involved as an organisation in struggle against Britishers, its volunteers should participate in this movement as individuals. A large number of RSS swayamsevaks participated in the freedom struggle. Many of them lost their lives too, many served long sentences in jail.

Golwalkar's saintly style and his apparent disinterest in politics convinced some swayamsevaks that the RSS had become more concerned with other-worldly implications of character building than with its national political implications. Links between the Hindu Mahasabha and the RSS were virtually severed: the military department of the RSS was dismantled; the RSS remained aloof from the anti-British agitations during World War II, and it refused to assist the various militarization and paramilitary schemes advocated by many other Hindu nationalists. Golwalkar, unlike Hedgewar, showed no public interest in the movement to enlist Hindus in the armed forces of British India.

Golwalkar took over, when the Second World War was looming large. The new leadership got preoccupied with two major considerations: first, the protection of the Hindu community against a possible Japanese invasion of India, and second, the handling of communal conflicts at the end of the War. Keeping this perspective, Golwalkar was shrewd enough to understand the disadvantage of an open conflict with the government. Therefore, the RSS withdrew from the political arena. Accordingly, it did not support the Hindu Mahasabha's call to the Hindus to get enrolled in the British army. Golwalkar also refused Moonje's invitation to the Sangh volunteers to attend the guerilla warfare classes at Bhonsle Military School, Nasik. He instructed all the RSS branches to comply with the government order of 5 August 1940, which prohibited military drill and wearing of military uniform. He also stopped the military training and abolished the Military Department of the Sangh. Some militant swayamsevaks, including Nathuram Godse, disagreed with this policy and deserted the RSS to join the Mahasabha.[54]

A significant part of the RSS establishment in Bombay province, particularly in the Marathi-speaking districts where the Hindu Mahasabha had a firm base, was disturbed by the reorientation of the RSS under Golwalkar. K. B. Limaye, sanghchalak of the province, resigned, underscoring the depth of the discontent there. A number of swayamsevaks defected in 1942, and formed the Hindu Rashtra Dal the next year. Nathuram Godse, the founder of the paramilitary organization, intended to use it to fight against British rule.

Despite the apprehensions regarding Golwalkar's leadership, there was no large-scale defection. He moved quickly to consolidate his position by creating a new position-provincial pracharak (organizer) - responsible directly to him rather than to the provincial sanghchalaks. He convinced several local Congress figures to preside over RSS functions, which offered convincing public proof that the RSS was not the youth front of the Hindu Mahasabha.

Golwalkar himself briskly travelled through the country to expand the RSS' work. In 1941, he made a highly emotional appeal that touched the hearts of many youth and they decided to dedicate their lives of the RSS' work as Pracharaks.

In 1942, he delivered a historic speech which spelled his outlook towards national issues and the RSS' future. In this speech delivered on the occasion of Hindu New Year (Varsh Pratipadi), Golwalkar said:

"It is our great good fortune that we are born in these dangerous times which we must view as the most auspicious. The golden moment that arrives in the history of the nation after centuries is coming our way. If we sleep at such a crucial hour, no one would be more unfortunate than us. He only achieves immortal fame who stands up in the face of adversities. Let us, therefore, face the present adversity with serenity and determination. Consider it as an excellent opportunity to bring out the best in us....

Rejuvenation of a fallen nation should be possible at the most within one generation. But what is our condition today? Even after 17 long years of strenuous efforts, our work has remained far too limited. The Sangh stands by the Truth and so it will certainly succeed and redeem its pledge. Once we give our word, we shall have to prove its worth even if we have to sacrifice ourselves in the process.

So, keep aside all your thoughts about family and your personal fortunes for a period of at least one year. Adopt this life of treading on a razor's edge. Be prepared to be hard to yourself. Concentrate all your time, all your thoughts and all your energy on this very task. We have to be vigilant about this and steel ourselves for achieving the success of our Cause."

His appeal to young swayamsevaks in 1941 and 1942 was, "We need Pracharaks. we need Pracharaks. This is the demand arising from all directions. We must fulfil this demand." He further said, "Karyakartas don't fall from heaven. For this, we will have to make efforts ourselves and create Karyakartas from amongst ourselves. We will have to walk the path of duty with firm resolve and austerity by giving up all thoughts about our personal lives. The mission before us is enormous with very little time in hand. But, do not worry. If we decide even now, we can do as much work as we wish and create as many Karyakartas as we want. The question is of just bringing about a little revolution within our hearts. Just one revolution of hearts and our lives will see unprecedented changes and we shall see the gateway of hope Let us close all the doors of our personal lives and take a pledge to put in concerted effort. Let us become sannyasis for one year."

The impact of Golwalkar's clarion call was phenomenal. Forty-Eight Pracharaks came out just from Lahore in 1942. Of these, 10 were M.A., two doctors and others were B.A. and above matric. Similarly, 52 Pracharaks came out from the Amritsar city and out of these, there were four doctors amongst them.

From June 1942 onwards, a large number of Pracharaks began to be sent to various provinces, and the RSS expansion acquired a new momentum.

Meanwhile, the British government in India had become wary of the growing popularity of the RSS. They tried to crack down on the organisation by putting restrictions on the government employees to attend the Shakha. The RSS under the guidance of Golwalkar adapted itself to the situation by making certain changes in nomenclature (shedding words like 'Commander') and by ensuring that its physical drills are not compared with military training.

A report sent by the Central Police Intelligence Department on December 13, 1943 says, "It is not possible to create a case for banning the Sangh. But, it is equally clear that Golwalkar is creating a strong organisation at a rapid pace, so that they would obey the orders, maintaining confidentiality and jump into any activity of sabotage or of any other type whenever required as per their leader's orders. The structure of this organisation looks superficially like that of khaaksaars. But, the fundamental difference between the two is that the leader of Khaaksaar, Inayatullah, is a big-mouthed imbalanced lunatic, while Golwalkar is a very cautious, crafty and much more capable leader."

Golwalkar is known to have propagated Dharmic teachings. A book based on extracts of his writings, includes a chapter titled "Hindu—the Son of this Motherland", which claims that 'Bhartiya' includes only those who have followed faiths rooted in pluralism, and that Indic faith followers represent this in India, since it accepts all approaches towards spirituality. In another chapter, titled "Our Identity and Nationality", he wrote, "All the elements required to develop as a great nation are present in this Hindu society in their entirety. This is why we say that in this nation of Bharat, living principles of the Hindu society are the living systems of this nation."[55]

Support for Quit India Movement on Principles Set by Dr. Hedgewar

After due discussions with his young colleagues, Golwalkar decided that, "The agitation is being conducted for the freedom of the country. Therefore, swayamsevaks, as citizens, can take part in this agitation in whichever part of the country they are. But, as an organisation, Sangh will keep working for national cause, that is organising the society; without getting involved in the agitation directly." This was in line with Dr. Hedgewar's direction during 1930 satyagraha - to work as a common citizen rather than project RSS as a separate organisation.

Sangh, thus, asked swayamsevaks to take part in this national struggle and extend whole-hearted co-operation to it as patriotic citizens. As a result, many swayamsevaks jumped into this battle and took part in it to the best of their abilities as common citizens.

Rajju Bhaiyya corroborates the Sangh support to 1942 and participation of its swayamsevaks in it - "Sangh told that anybody who wishes to take part in this movement should do it in his personal capacity. It should try to help Congress in every possible way that was looking after Hindu society's interest and also work hard to expand Sangh work at high velocity."

Vidarbha region had strong RSS network. Naturally, the most fierce agitations took place in Bali (Amravati), Ashti (Wardha) and Chimur (Chandrapur). News about Chimur agitation was broadcast from Berlin Radio. This agitation was led by Uddhavrao Korekar of Congress; RSS leaders Dada Naik, Baburao Begade and Annaji. A young Swayamsevak, Balaji Raipurkar, was killed brutally in police firing when he was trying to raise the flag to the top. Sangh swayamsevaks took part in Chimur agitation in 1943 along with Congress and Tukdoji Maharaj-led Shri Gurudev Seva Mandal.

This encounter became famous in the history of this movement as 'Chimur Ashti episode'. RSS swayamsevaks had established a parallel government in Chimur. 125 satyagrahis were put on trial and handed imprisonment and thousands of swayamsevaks were imprisoned. Dada Naik was head of RSS Chimur branch. He was sentenced to death. Hindu Mahasabha leader Dr. N.B. Khare, a member of British Viceroy Council, took up his case with the authorities and got the sentence commuted to imprisonment. Later, Sant Tukdoji Maharaj became one of the co-founders of the Vishwa Hindu Parishad.

There was the heroic story of Hemu Kalani of Sakkhar town in Sindh. He was busy removing fishplates from the railway tracks with his colleagues. Their objective was to frustrate the plans to move forces to suppress the struggle in various areas. Unfortunately, Hemu was arrested while his friends managed to escape the police net. Hemu was given death sentence by the Army Court in 1943. Sindhi brethren in Mumbai celebrate the memory of martyr Hemu Kalani to this day. He has a memorial in his name constructed by local Sindhi swayamsevaks and maintained by 'Hemu Kalani Yadgaar Mandal'. This story is also recounted by late Gobind Motwani in his book '9 years of RSS in Sindh - 1939-1947'. Hemu Kalani remains an unsung hero of freedom struggle because Pakistanis won't recognise him as he was a Hindu, while Indian historians won't recognise his contribution probably because he was a swayamsevak. This writer has visited the memorial and has been fortunate to meet many veteran Sindhis in Mumbai who are witness to those days in Sindh, and still active in RSS.

Swayamsevaks plunged into Quit India agitation wherever they were in India and were imprisoned in many places. Some of the well-known senior swayamsevaks were Dr. Anna Saheb Deshpande (Aarvi, Vidarbh), Ramakant Keshav (Babasaheb) Deshpande in Jashpur (Chhattisgarh) who went on to establish Vanvasi Kalyan Ashram, Shri Vasantrao Oak (Prant pracharak of Delhi), Narayan Singh known as Babuaji in Bihar who later became Bihar Sanghchalak, and Shri Chandrakant Bhardwaj (who received bullet in his foot that couldn't be removed). Bhardwaj became a famous poet and wrote many poems sung in RSS. There were Madhavrao in East U.P. who became Prant pracharak later and Dattatreya Gangadhar (aka Bhaiyyaji) Kasture who too became a pracharak later."[56]

On 11th August 1942, Patna saw a successful attempt by young boys to hoist the Tricolour flag on the government secretariat. Six agitators were felled by police firing. Of these six, two - Devipad Chaudhary and Jagatpati Kumar were swayamsevaks. The first Sanghchalak of Bihar, Babua ji and senior journalist Krishnakant Ojha confirmed their RSS connection. A felicitation programme to honour them was organised during 50th anniversary celebrations of Independence in 1997 under the Chairmanship of renowned litterateur and revolutionary Shri Vachnesh Tripathi in the presence of the then regional pracharak, now Sarsanghchalak, Dr. Mohan Bhagwat. Their kin too were invited in the programme. There are many swayamsevaks in Bihar who were awarded "Tamra Patras' as freedom fighters of 1942.

The "Quit India" movement had started in 1942. The RSS swayamsevaks took part in this national struggle as patriotic citizens. In Vidarbha, swayamsevaks of Chimur launched an agitation under the leadership of Ramakant Deshpande. Breaking the bounds of non-violence, it turned violent. A few Britishers were also killed in an encounter. This encounter became famous in the history of this movement as 'Chimur Ashti episode!'

During 1942, oppression by British was in full force. Therefore, people were uneasy about giving shelter to senior underground Congress leaders. At that time, senior high-profile RSS leaders helped the underground leaders of the movement by providing them safe houses.

House of Sanghchaalak of North-West Lala Hansraj was the secret place of stay for Aruna Asaf Ali. She spoke about it in an interview published in Hindi daily 'Hindustan' in August 1967. She said, "I was underground in 1942 agitation, Delhi Sanghchaalak Lala Hansraj provided me refuge in his house for 10-15 days and arranged for my complete safety. He saw to it that nobody got information about my stay at his house. Since underground workers should not stay for long at the same place, I moved out of his house dancing 'Bhangra' in an embroidered ghagra and chunari in a baraat (marriage procession). This dress was given to me by Lalaji's wife. When I went to return it in due course, she refused to take it back, saying, keep it with our best wishes as our gift to you"7

"Famous Vedic scholar Pandit Shripad Damodar Satavalekar was the Sanghchaalak of Aundh. He had given asylum for many days to the revolutionary underground leader Nana Patil who had experimented with the novel idea 'Patri Sarkaar' during this agitation. Nana Patil's colleague Kisanveer had stayed at the house of Satara Sanghchaalak in Wai while working underground there. Famous socialist leader Achyutrao Patwardhan had stayed at many Sangh swayamsevaks' homes when he was working underground and changed places according to circumstances. Not only had these people, but even the life-long bitter critic of Sangh and a follower of Gandhiji, Sane Golwalkar used to stay secretly in Pune Sanghchaalak Bhausaheb Deshmukh's house."[57]

A very senior RSS leader shared the story of a swayamsevak, Shri Padsalgikar, who was asked by the state Sanghchaalak Kashinath Pant Limaye to help Vasantdada Patil escape from prison in Sangli. He waited at the spot where Vasantdada reached after breaking out of the jail at 12 in the night. He carried him on his shoulders across fields, nullahs and jungles as all the roads and even village lanes were under police watch. He dropped him off at Vishram Bagh railway station at 2 a.m. so he could catch a train and move out of that area. Padsalgikar, who was a wrestler, went on to become the vice-president of State Kustigir Parishad. There could be scores of such incidents that were never recorded or documented. Since RSS was not keen on documenting or publicising its work as a policy, such inspiring stories are not known outside the local circles.

It would be a good to quote an episode that took place approximately six years later in 1948. Congress committee member of Solapur, Ganesh Bapuji Shinkar took part in the satyagraha to press for the removal of ban on Sangh. He had resigned from Congress on grounds of democratic ethics before joining the satyagraha. He issued a statement clarifying his stand and it was published on 12th December, 1948. He says, "I had participated in Bharat Chhodo (Quit India) movement in 1942. Capitalist and agrarian community was scared of the government at that time. Therefore, we were not offered safe havens in their homes. We had to stay in Sangh workers' homes to work underground. People from Sangh used to help us happily with our underground work. They also took care of all our requirements. Not only this, if someone from amongst us fell sick, Sangh swayamsevak doctors used to treat us. Sangh swayamsevaks, who were advocates, used to fight our cases fearlessly. Their patriotism and value- based living were undisputable."

When anti-national Communists were acting like fifth columnists and getting agitating patriots arrested, Sangh was doing its bit for the struggle. Eventually, the agitation cooled down after 75 days by the end of October. Scattered and weak leadership and disorganised agitation on one side and highly well-entrenched ruling set up of British on the other led to death of a well-intentioned movement in its infancy.

Rajju Bhaiyya, who later on became RSS Chief, noted about 1942 - "I came into Sangh very late. Therefore, there was not much discussion whether Sangh contributed to 1942 movement or not. But, it seems whatever decisions Sangh took was correct. Congress leaders passed the 'Quit India' resolution. All the leaders were caught and put into jail. Not one leader remained out of jail who could guide the nation, the society or the people about the next step. All the big leaders like Nehru ji, Tandon ji and Kripalani ji were members of the working committee. To imagine that the British wouldn't ban Congress or would not send people involved to jails could be excused only as a thinking of a common person with limited short-term thinking. There was no plan for the people who may not have been arrested and were out of prison. Only Ram Manohar Lohia ji and Jayaprakash ji did something outside."

To give a bit of a background, as a young student, Rajju Bhaiyya had very good connections with Congress leaders of that time and as a young man, he would visit Anand Bhavan in Allahabad regularly and seek guidance. Anand Bhavan was the residence of Nehru family and centre of Congress activities in Prayag during 1942 Quit India movement. Lack of long-term planning and organisation resulted in its failure. All the Congress leaders sat back at home, dejected. Rajju bhaiyya met many leaders and asked them about future plans. But, nobody had any clue. He was very disappointed to see this lack of direction in an organisation like Congress. He was studying in final year of M.Sc. It was during this time that he was introduced to Sangh. Rajju bhaiyya confirmed this fact with Shridhar Damle in 1982 when he had gone to America and stayed with him. Two of his friends, Shantaram and Shyamnarayan Shrivastav, introduced him to the divisional pracharak Bapurao Moghe at that time, who was just 5-6 years elder to him. This introduction turned into friendship and Rajju Bhaiyya became a regular Swayamsevak of Bhardwaj sayam shakha. We can, thus, witness a sense of dissatisfaction in the youth of that time about planning and handling of 1942.

We note that wherever RSS had a decent base, its swayamsevaks took part in the 1942 movement enthusiastically. Wherever they could, they helped other participants, thus strengthening the movement in every possible way.

Apart from such activities, many swayamsevaks also helped the underground leaders of the movement. The house of Sanghchalak of Delhi, Lala Hansraj, was the secret place of stay for Aruna Asaf Ali. She herself spoke about it in an interview published in Hindi daily, Hindustan in August 1967. She said, "I was underground in 1942 agitation, Delhi Sanghchalak, Lala Hansraj provided me refuge in his house for 10-15 days and arranged for my complete safety. He saw to it that nobody got information about my stay at his house. Since underground workers should not stay for long at the same place, I moved out of his house dancing 'Bhangra' in an embroidered ghagra and chunari in a baraat (marriage procession). This dress was given to me by Lalaji's wife. When I went to return it in due course, she refused to take it back, saying, keep it with you as our gift with our best wishes."

"When the famous Vedic scholar, Pandit Shripad Damodar Satavalekar was the Sanghchalak of Aundh, he had given asylum for many days to the revolutionary underground leader, Nana Patil who had experimented with the novel idea 'Patri Sarkar'. Nana Patil's colleague, Kisanveer had stayed at the house of Satara Sanghchalak while working underground there. Famous socialist leader, Achyutrao Patwardhan had stayed at many Sangh swayamsevaks' homes when he used to work underground and change places according to circumstances. Not only these people, but even the life-long bitter opponent of the Sangh and follower of Gandhiji, Saane Golwalkar used to stay at Pune Sanghchalak Bhausaheb Deshmukh's house secretly."

To give more clarity to this subject, it would be a good idea to quote an episode that took place about six years later. The Congress Committee member of Solapur, Ganesh Bapuji Shinkar had taken part in the satyagraha press for the removal of ban on the Sangh in 1948. He had resigned from the Congress on grounds of democratic ethics before joining the satyagraha. He issued a statement clarifying his stand and it was published on 12th December, 1948. He says, "I had participated in Quit India movement in 1942. The capitalist and agrarian community was scared of the government at that time. Therefore, we were not offered safe haven in their homes. We had to stay in Sangh workers' homes to work underground. People from the Sangh used to help us happily with our underground work. They also took care of all our requirements. Not only this, if someone from amongst us fell sick, the Sangh swayamsevak doctors used to treat us. Sangh swayamsevaks, who were advocates, used to fight our cases fearlessly. Their patriotism and value-based lifestyle was undisputable."

The CID kept sending reports about him regularly. The report of 30th December, 1943 says, "Rashtriya Swayamsevak Sangh is moving ahead rapidly towards building a highly significant all-India organisation. Spokesmen of the Sangh keep saying that the basic goal of the Sangh is to achieve Hindu unity... In a programme in November 1943 at Lahore, M.S. Golwalkar declared that the Sangh's objective is to remove the feeling of untouchability and weave together all sections of Hindu society in a single unifying thread.

It is clear that the Sangh is bent upon expanding its area of influence and this year, it has been able to bring on board the famous religious saint Sant Tukadoji Maharaj from Central Provinces for spreading its message...

Membership of the Sangh is swelling continuously. In Central Provinces, membership has increased from thirty-two thousand to thirty-three thousand three hundred forty-four. It has reached twenty thousand four hundred seventy-six from eighteen thousand twenty-nine in Mumbai and fourteen thousand from ten thousand in Punjab.

A new dimension to their growth is their efforts to gain entry in the villages. M.S. Golwalkar laid a lot of stress on this aspect in the winter camp of Wardha - that the Sangh should expand into villages.

The Sangh office-bearers from its head office are touring the Shakhas in remote areas continuously, so that they can heighten interest of the swayamsevaks in Sangh work, give them secret directions and strengthen the local organisation. We can see the recent well spread out tour of the present chief of the Sangh, M.S. Golwalkar as an example of such efforts. In the last month of April, he was in Ahmedabad; in May, he was at Amravati and Pune. In June, he was at Nasik and Benaras. He toured Chanda in August, Pune in September, Madras and Central Provinces in October, and Rawalpindi in November.

Golwalkar's religiosity and apparent disinterest in politics disillusioned some RSS members that the organization was no longer relevant to the nationalist struggle, and connections with the Hindu Mahasabha were severed. The RSS membership in the Marathi-speaking districts of Bombay became disillusioned and the Bombay sanghchalak, K. B. Limaye, resigned. Several swayamsevaks defected and formed the Hindu Rashtra Dal in 1943, with an agenda of a paramilitary struggle against British rule; Nathuram Godse was a leader of that group.

However, Golwalkar moved quickly to consolidate his position. He created a network of prant pracharaks (provincial organisers). Golwalkar invited local Congress leaders to preside over RSS functions, demonstrating the organisation's independence from the Hindu Mahasabha. The RSS continued to expand during the Second World War, especially in North India and present-day Pakistan. Many new members were religious, small-scale entrepreneurs interested in consolidating their positions with the RSS' Hindu symbols. Organisation policy during the war years was influenced by potential threats to Hinduism, with the RSS expected to be prepared to defend Hindu interests in the event of a possible Japanese invasion.[58]

Partition

In run-up to the partition of India, the RSS realised the need to prepare the Hindus to face the inevitable that had been imposed on them by the Congress leadership. Golwalkar, Babasaheb Apte and Balasaheb Deoras extensively toured the country. Hundreds of young men and middle-aged people began joining the Sangh, especially in cities and villages of Punjab like Rawalpindi, Lahore, Peshawar, Amritsar, Jalandhar, Ambala, etc. He visited all the districts from Amritsar to Multan. During this period, he would travel on damaged railway tracks, on goods trains or sometimes in the train engine. There was a bridge at Chahedu on way, and it seemed impossible to proceed any further, as the railway-track was hanging down from the bridge and below the bridge, flood-waters were gushing in tremendous speed. The Swayamsevaks were clueless as to how to proceed further, but when Shri Guruji reached there he unhesitatingly briskly walked over the broken track and crossed the bridge in no time. The rest of the Swayamsevaks also gathered courage and followed him. People were wonder-struck to receive them at the other end (Ludhiana).

Golwalkar went to Sialkot and Montgomery after touring Multan in 1946-47. He entered Sindh from Punjab. The province of Sindh had around 80 Shakhas at that time.

To implement the plan to partition India, the British government had divided the Army and Police on the basis of religion few months prior to the final act. Thus, areas falling under Sindh, West Pakistan and East Bengal were put under the command of Muslim League-Police combine. The Hindus in these areas were on tenterhooks. They were sitting on a powder keg with no one to look up to as the saviour. Golwalkar took the initiative to reach out to these Hindus and set up the Punjab Relief Committee and Hindu Sahayata Samiti (Hindu Support Committee). The centre of activity for both of these was Lahore. The Punjab state Sanghchalak, Raibahadur Badridas was the Chairman and Dr. Gokulchand Narang was the Treasurer of these committees.

When the entire Punjab was on fire and Congress leaders were sitting helplessly in Delhi, at that time, volunteers of RSS saved the people of Punjab with their discipline, and physical strength, risking their own lives. Now, if somebody from outside Punjab was to tell the Hindus and Sikhs to forget those Sikhs and the brave heroes of Rashtriya Swayamsevak Sangh who put their lives at risk to defend them, then their calls would go unheeded.

"Each and every person from amongst the refugees who came from West Pakistan is indebted to the Sangh. When everybody had abandoned them, only the Sangh stood by them." Nearly a year later, the Golwalkar-led RSS took up major relief and rehabilitation effort in West Bengal to address the issue of Hindu refugees from East Pakistan.

In his book, 'The Incomparable Golwalkar', Ranga Hari recounted an important incident which indicated that the Golwalkar also played a role in integration of the then Jammu-Kashmir with India. The then Maharaja of Kashmir was not very forthcoming on signing the treaty of accession unlike most other princely states.

"Golwalkar reached by air on 17th October, 1947, with Delhi state Pracharak, Vasantrao Oke and Barrister Narendrajeet Singh. The regional Pracharak of that area, Madhavrao Muley and four to five state-level workers of Jammu & Kashmir waited for them. Under Sangh's arrangement, Golwalkar and his colleagues stayed in barrister's in-laws' home in Divaniyat Bhavan. Next day, on 18th October, Golwalkar went in a private car to Karan Mahal to meet the Maharaja. The Maharaja and Maharani had great reverence for Golwalkar. So, both of them were there at the palace gates to receive and welcome him. Just as the Maharaja bent down to touch Golwalkar's feet, Golwalkar caught hold of his hands. After an initial informal chat, formal discussions began at 10.30 a.m. Nobody was present from either side during these discussions. So, nobody knows what transpired during the discussion, what kind of subjects or suggestions came up. When the Maharaja came out to bid farewell to Golwalkar after the discussions, he went near Golwalkar's car and said, "I will definitely weigh your suggestions carefully." At the moment of seeing him off, the royal couple presented two highly valuable shawls to Golwalkar. Before leaving, Golwalkar urged the Maharaja, "It may be a good idea to send the Prince to Jammu and you should remain in Srinagar so that the people's morale does not dip." Golwalkar and his colleagues reached their lodging before lunch.

That same evening, a pre-planned get-together (saanghik) of senior swayamsevaks was held at DAV College in Mangal Bagh near Lal Chowk. It was attended by more than 500 volunteers. Golwalkar delivered his Bouddhik or discourse. He did not speak anything about his meeting with the Maharaja. He returned to Delhi on 19th October.

Golwalkar met Home Minister Sardar Patel in Delhi and apprised him of the favourable attitude of Maharaja. Fortunately, Meharchand Mahajan had become the 'Prime Minister' by that time in place of Ramchandra Kak. The next step was taken by the strategist, Sardar. As a result, Jammu & Kashmir merged with the rest of the country."

Such was Golwalkar's influence that he could directly reach out to Deputy PM, Sardar Vallabhbhai Patel, when some RSS workers were missing from Sindh. Infact, after the Partition, even the Mahatma Gandhi had met Golwalkar to discuss RSS role in Running refugee camps.

The occasion for the dialogue had come up during Gandhi's address to a gathering of RSS volunteers in a Delhi Colony. He later spoke with Golwalkar who said that the organisation had no intention formenting trouble and added that 'the policy of the sangh was purely service of the Hindus and Hinduism and that too not at the cost of any one else. The sangh did not believe in aggression. It did not believe in ahimsa. It taught the art of self defence. It never taught retaliation.' At Golwalkar's behest, the Vastuhara Sahaayata Samiti (Displaced People's Relief Committee) was constituted under the chairmanship of Ranadev Chaudhary.

Golwalkar resumed his nationwide tours to expand the organisational work within months of partition. He addressed a meeting attended by more than one lakh people in Pune on October 30. For a state-level training camp of the RSS, he reached Akola on December 6. The camp was attended by 10,000 swayamsevaks. More than 75,000 people attended his public meeting at

Shivaji Park in Mumbai. His meetings drew huge crowds in Madhya Pradesh and the Mahakoshal region. The latter alone had 600 Shakhas.

The RSS outreach had gone beyond the Vindhyas and the organisation started consolidating its footprint in the southern parts of the country also. The Guntur district in Andhra Pradesh had 31 Shakhas and 3,000 swayamsevaks when Sarsanghchalak arrived there. The Nizam of Hyderabad did not allow activities of the RSS in his state. Karnataka had been a fertile ground for the organisation since its inception. In January 1948, more than 8,000 swayamsevaks attended the state-level winter camp in the state. They were present in full uniform of the RSS at Bengaluru.

In Kerala, the Leftists tried to disrupt a meeting of Golwalkar held in the month of January 1948, but they did not succeed. In Madras also, the RSS had been able to start building its base.[59]

Ban on RSS

On January 30, 1948, Mahatma Gandhi was assassinated in New Delhi. Golwalkar was in Madras. On the same day, he passed instructions to all the Shakhas, "To express our grief due to the sad demise of respected Mahatmaji, Shakhas will observe a condolence period for 13 days and all daily programmes will be put on hold." He left for Nagpur on January 31 by air.

In Delhi, the state Sanghchalak Lala Hansraj Gupta, city Sanghchalak Harishchandra Gupta and state Pracharak Vasantrao Oke - all the three went to Birla Bhavan and met many Congress leaders to express their grief and offer condolences.

But a section of Congress, which was probably getting uncomfortable about the growing influence of the RSS, saw an opportunity to finish off the organisation. The then Prime Minister, Pandit Jawahar Lal Nehru, declared in Amritsar, "RSS is responsible for the murder of the Father of the Nation."

Golwalkar wrote two letters to Nehru and Sardar Patel (the then Home Minister). The contents of both the letters were largely same. He wrote: "I was in Madras yesterday when I heard about the tragic news that has shaken the entire humanity. Such an evil and condemnable incident would never have taken place in history. The heart is distressed with unbearable pain."

It is difficult to find the right words to condemn the person who has carried out this despicable act. One cannot even think of such a senseless evil act. What can one say of a person who has stunned the whole world into silence?

But, let us all carry out the responsibilities that have come upon us due to the untimely demise of a great leader by remembering that noble soul who could weave together people of different nature into a unifying thread and take them along on a common path, and let us all arise with renewed strength in this terrible time of a catastrophe with reasoned emotions, compassionate behaviour, controlled speech and fill the nation with a perennial sense of unity.

This will be a true and pious remembrance of that great personality. I pray to the ever-benign Supreme Being on behalf of our organisation that treads the path of unity with reverence that he may guide them on to the path that may inspire all the people of this nation to generate pure sublime patriotism.

In reaction to the false allegations on the RSS about Mahatma's assassination, homes and properties of thousands of swayamsevaks were burnt down.[60] Government machinery incessantly spewed venom against the Sangh. As Godse, the assassin of Gandhiji was a Brahmin, the Brahmins of Maharashtra and neighboring areas were targeted and arson and looting followed. In northern Karnataka, in a village named Terdaal nine people were burnt alive in one such incident. A violent mob also attacked the house of Golwalkar. In order to maintain harmony throughout the country in such testing times, the Sangh appealed to all the Swayamsevaks to "be calm, at all costs." He also issued a detailed statement, directing how things were to be taken in a composed, rational and sublime spirit. He also asked the alert and armed (with lathis) Swayamsevaks outside his office, who had come to disperse the attacking mob, to go back peacefully and retired for his evening prayers. He told the Swayamsevaks nearby, "the service of the society has been my life-motto and I would never allow myself to be the cause of shedding of a single drop of its blood."[61]

Golwalkar was arrested on February 2 and the RSS was banned on February 4 through a central government notification. The Sarsanghchalak while being arrested in Nagpur said, "The cloud of suspicion will melt away and we shall come out of this unblemished. Till that time, there will be lots of atrocities, but we should bear them with fortitude. I firmly believe that Sangh swayamsevaks will pass this test successfully." He was sent to Nagpur Central Jail.

Dwarika Prasad Mishra, who was Home Minister of Central Provinces at that time, writes in his autobiography, 'Living in An Era', "That Mahatma Gandhi's assassination gave a handle to unscrupulous politicians to defame and, if possible, to pull down their rivals is difficult to deny" (P. 59 of the original English version).

Major points of this notification banning the RSS were:

- ➤ It has been resolved to uproot and wipe out all inimical forces that are putting the country's Independence at risk and blemishing its bright reputation. Under this policy, Government of India has decided to declare Rashtriya Swayamsevak Sangh an unlawful organisation.

- ➤ The declared objective of Rashtriya Swayamsevak Sangh is 'to develop Hindus physically, intellectually and mentally and bring about a feeling of brotherhood and spirit of service in them'. But it is a matter of regret the that members of Rashtriya Swayamsevak Sangh do not conduct themselves according to this declared objective.

- ➤ The government accepts it as its duty to take strict steps to crush this extreme expression of violence. As a first step in this direction, the Sangh is being declared an unlawful organisation.

Reacting to the ban on the RSS, Golwalkar issued a brief statement saying:

"It has been Rashtriya Swayamsevak Sangh's policy to conduct its activities within the rules and regulations of the government. The present government has declared Sangh illegal. Thus, I deem it fit to disband the Sangh till this ban is taken back. However, I completely refuse to accept the allegations levelled against the Sangh."

Nearly 20,000 swayamsevaks were arrested across the country. On August 6, Golwalkar was released from the jail but with several conditions including restricting his movements within the municipal limit of Nagpur. On August 11, Golwalkar wrote to Sardar Patel asking him to restore the democratic rights of the RSS to function.

Patel wrote a long letter to the Prime Minister on February 27, 1948 (Collection of Nehru-Gandhi Correspondence, Volume VI, page no. 56 and 57). Excerpts from this document are as follows:

> All the materials received through known-unknown, true-untrue, named and unnamed sources have been sifted thoroughly. Ninety per cent of these are baseless speculative reports. Most of the allegations are about the activities of the RSS - that they distributed sweets, held celebrations. All this was found to be false upon investigation.

> Confessions of the conspirators prove that the RSS was not a party, in any way, to this conspiracy.

Meanwhile, Golwalkar continued his correspondence with Sardar Patel as well as the Prime Minister seeking to lift the ban from the RSS. Nehru reacted even more aggressively and Golwalkar was arrested at the midnight of November 12, 1948 at Barakhamba Road, Delhi under the Bengal State Criminal Procedure Act of 1818. This 130-year-old Act gave absolute power to arrest anybody anywhere without any proof or reason. Golwalkar was brought to Nagpur on November 15. The government tried to keep this arrest as quiet as it could. He was first taken to Nagpur Central Jail from the airport and then after couple of days shifted to Sivni sub-jail.[62]

The letters which Golwalkar wrote in those days were written to Gopalswamy Iyengar and Shyama Prasad Mukherjee in English, to Sardar Patel and Purushottamdas Tandon in Hindi and to Ambedkar and Khaparde in Marathi. He reached out to various other national leaders.

To put an end to unnecessary animosity, Golwalkar himself went and met Pandit Nehru and Sardar Patel in the first week of August. He wrote to Pandit Nehru, "I am trying hard as it requires uncommon efforts to wipe away bitter memories from the hearts of my co-workers. There is no sense in remaining lost in the memories of the past. I am doubtlessly sure about receiving co-operation from the government that will help generate a healthy atmosphere based on mutual affection, respect and co-operation, which would result in a helpful environment of goodwill."

Sardar Patel wrote back to Golwalkar (within three days of receiving his letter) on July 21, "As you have said in your public address, situation in the country is such and things are happening in such a manner that we should all look at the present and the future rather than into the past."

Golwalkar wrote to Babasaheb Ambedkar, "The duty of meeting well-wishers like you is getting postponed due to my busy schedule to set up Sangh work properly again."

Both the men replied back, and although Vallabhbhai Patel in his letter dated 11 September 1948, acknowledged the work done by the RSS in protecting the women and children who had arrived as refugees from across the border after Partition.

In the same letter, Patel had touched upon a sensitive issue and said that he was 'convinced that the RSS men can carry on their patriotic endeavour only by joining the Congress and not by keeping separate (identity) or by opposing.' Opening the doors for swayamsevaks barely a few days after Gandhi's assassination and without prior discussion with members of the Congress, was not appreciated within certain sections of the party, including the prime minister. In a way, Patel's letter to Golwalkar had brought into sharp focus the divergent views held by two Congress stalwarts with regard to the RSS.

A few days later, an officer in the Prime Minister's Office or PMO, A.V. Pai, wrote to Golwalkar that the RSS, 'was engaged in activities which were antinational, prejudicial from the point of view of public good.' Nehru also said that the objectives of the RSS were, completely opposed to the decisions of the Indian Parliament and the provisions of the proposed Constitution of India. The activities (of the RSS), according to our information, are anti-national and often subversive and violent.

One wonders if it was the beauty of democracy and therefore the respect accorded to a stalwart of a leader like Patel, but in October 1948, Madhav Sadashiv Golwalkar was allowed to travel to Delhi to discuss the lifting of the ban. He first met Patel, after Nehru had declined to meet him as the Prime Minister had felt that it would not 'serve any useful purpose.' Unfortunately, Golwalkar's meetings (he had two by now) with Patel too came to naught and the RSS remained on the proscribed list. Patel also asked his office to issue instructions to Golwalkar to 'make immediate arrangements to return to Nagpur,' as restrictions on his travel which had been kept in abeyance, were now re-imposed.

The official order from the government of India stated that M.S. Golwalkar had committed to the RSS' agreement, 'entirely in the conception of a Secular State for India and that it accepts the National Flag of the country,' which however did not suffice to end the ban because Golwalkar's commitment was 'inconsistent with the practice of his followers.'

Golwalkar was extremely disappointed with Sardar Patel's response and in a letter dated 5 November 1948, he openly expressed his bitterness as follows:

I tried my utmost to see that between the Congress and the Rashtriya Swayamsevak Sangh...there be no bad blood, there be only everlasting mutual love, one supplementing and complementing the other, both meeting in a sacred confluence. I extended my hand of cooperation. With utmost regrets, I have to say that you have chosen to ignore my best intentions. My heart's desire to see the converging of both the streams has remained unfulfilled.

However, his impassioned plea proved to be futile and after his subsequent requests to meet Patel were turned down, Golwalkar decided to defy the order, and stayed put in Delhi. There was a midnight knock on the door of a RSS functionary for the second time that year, the difference being that this time around, the posse of police had landed up at Delhi's RSS chief and industrialist, Lala Hansraj Gupta's bungalow on Barakhamba Road. Golwalkar was spared the ignominy of an arrest, but was put on the earliest flight to Nagpur. It was obvious that the door had been slammed shut on the RSS at Nehru's insistence. Patel's proposal of merging the RSS with the Congress was not only rejected by the prime minister, but also by the sarsanghchalak, who wanted the RSS to henceforth dedicate itself towards establishing Hindu hegemony in the country. He was also doubtful about Patel exerting his influence over the Prime Minister, and after virtually being hounded out of Delhi, Golwalkar had little option but to revive the spirit of his cadre.

He began by writing an open letter to the swayamsevaks contending that the ban was 'an insult to the honour of the citizens of free Bharat,' and suggested that shakhas be made operational despite the governmental order. In many ways, the letter was symbolic of Golwalkar's assertiveness in independent India, and the stage was readied for a head-on confrontation with the government. It was rather ironical that in December 1948, eleven months after Gandhi's assassination, the RSS launched its first mass agitation using the Mahatma's principles of non-violence and non-cooperation, demanding the lifting of the ban. A massive all-India signature campaign was launched for the cause and amongst the nine lakh signatories, there were also several Congress leaders like Acharya Kripalani who had been Gandhi's inmate at the Sabarmati Ashram.

Although M. S. Golwalkar was lodged in Seoni Jail (in what is now Madhya Pradesh) where he was confined in anticipation of the agitation, the protest was a great success—an estimated eighty to sixty thousand supporters were put into jail for violating prohibitory orders. The 'satyagraha' had succeeded in rejuvenating the sagging spirits of the swayamsevaks and there was an all-round condemnation of police action against hapless citizens in a newly independent India.

The government swung into action to quell the rebellion and decided to resume its dialogue with the RSS. The process had already been initiated, albeit secretly, during the RSS' 'satyagraha', when the mediators had convinced Golwalkar to withdraw the agitation.

As Golwalkar was in prison, D.P. Mishra, then Home minister of the Central Provinces (father of the late Brajesh Mishra), had acted as an interlocutor between him and Sardar Patel in yet another effort to rescind the ban after the failed bid made between August-November 1948.

While Sardar Patel acquiesced to Mishra's suggestion about finding a legitimate method to lift the ban on the RSS, Mishra convinced Golwalkar of the need to suspend the satyagraha. Yet, another man, who had played a crucial role in aiding Golwalkar to adopt a reconciliatory posture was G.V. Ketkar, editor of the Marathi newspaper, Kesari, which was started by his illustrious grandfather, Bal Gangadhar Tilak. A few weeks after Golwalkar suspended the 'satyagraha', a new interlocutor arrived on the scene - T.R. Venkatarama Sastri, the former Advocate General of Madras and a leader of the Liberal Party, who had past experience of mediating between Mahatma Gandhi and the British. On 13 February 1949, Sastri met Golwalkar at Seoni Jail and discussed several issues, including steps to rescind the ban. Although the Tamil leader had discharged his duties, he found Golwalkar, 'a blunt man, innocent of the etiquette required in a correspondence with Government. The soft word that turneth away wrath is not among his gifts,' and that 'Golwalkar's reply is said to have been such as to give offence to the Government of India. I can well believe it.' According to a report by a member of the jail staff, Golwalkar had given Sastri, a 'blank cheque to make any decision they like and assured them that he would honour the decision they arrive at.' During the meeting, it was also decided that the RSS adopts a draft constitution, and the task was delegated to two experienced hands, Bhaiyaji Dani and Balasaheb Deoras.

Over the next few months, several letters were exchanged between Golwalkar and representatives of the government (compiled later as Justice on Trial: Historic Document of Golwalkar-Govt Correspondence). Despite what was essentially seen to be an effort to accommodate the RSS to function within the ambit of the Constitution, the dialogue had run into several problems. First, Home Secretary, H.V.R. Iyengar informed Golwalkar that despite all the pledges to abide by the rule of law, including being peaceful and legitimate, this was 'in practice been systematically violated by your followers.' Second, the government sought a specific declaration of allegiance from the RSS to both the Constitution of India and the Tricolour. And finally, the government ordered a close scrutiny of RSS' account books; an end to the practise of functionaries being 'nominated from above,'; and that the RSS should 'unequivocally recognise and act upon the democratic elective principle. The government was particularly wary of the functions of the head (sarsanghchalak) which had not been defined with any degree of precision, and wanted that all vestiges of a dictatorial character should be removed.'

As was expected, the government reached an impasse, Golwalkar accused the government of misinterpreting the clauses in the draft constitution and applying different yardsticks to the RSS, in comparison to other 'cultural' organisations. The stalemate continued for a while before the government sought the assistance of one Mauli Chandra Sharma, a former Congress leader-turned - President of the Jana Sangh. He, along with Deendayal Upadhyaya reworked the draft and, amongst several other things, emphasised on two crucial points--the first was to acknowledge the organisation as democratic, and second, that while Keshav Baliram Hedgewar had nominated Madhav Sadashiv Golwalkar as his successor, the latter would choose the next chief with the consent of the Kendriya Karyakarini Mandal. On the other issue, which had been brought up during Sastri's intervention regarding the entry of minors into the fold, the reworked draft mentioned that while admissions would remain open for fourteen-year-old boys, but if the parents or guardians had any objections, the child could leave the RSS at any given time.[63]

Golwalkar gave a call to the RSS swayamsevaks to launch a non-violent protest ('Satyagraha') to protest the high handedness of the Nehru government.

The satyagraha was carried out for 45 days from December 9, 1948 to January 22, 1949. More than 77,000 swayamsevaks courted arrest and were sent to prison. Later, Golwalkar was shifted to Baitul prison.

The communication with the government to lift the ban on the RSS continued with some hiccups. The government wanted the RSS to give its Constitution, which it did. Finally, the ban on the RSS was lifted on, midnight of July 11, 1949.

Golwalkar was released on July 13, 1949 from Baitul prison. He went straight to Nagpur from there. During the ban, the government had confiscated Dr. Hedgewar Bhavan. It was given back to the RSS on July 17. The RSS shakha at Mohite Ground was started the next day. Golwalkar, while addressing the swayamsevaks, on this occasion said,

"Our work is beginning again today. A person waking up from sleep feels refreshed and energetic. We too have to get down to work with the same enthusiasm. We have to make this work magnificent by developing it. Purity of the work depends on the purity of heart. The heart cannot be pure without the pure emotion of love. Whether one is a friend or an enemy, our approach should always be 'maa vidvishaav hai' (animosity towards none). Immersing ourselves with utmost pure emotions, that Bharatvarsh represents the colossal form of our nation and we are all arms, limbs and parts of this body, we have to develop this gigantic magnificent work, winning over everybody with allegiance to the goal and our affectionate behaviour."

By July 20, Golwalkar had resumed a punishing schedule travelling across the country. But before that, he sent written replies to all those who had sent their good wishes after the ban was lifted. Amongst those, who had sent the wishes was Dr. Shyama Prasad Mukherjee also. He had sent a written message to the Sarsanghchalak saying, "I am sure that now an atmosphere can be created to bring together all positive spiritual forces of the nation." Mukherjee later founded Bharatiya Jana sangh.[64]

Despite the month-long negotiations that had necessitated several compromises, Golwalkar claimed that the RSS had 'given up nothing.' In his address to a gathering in Nagpur, he declared, there was no compromise. There was no undertaking of any kind given to the Government. At another meeting in Madras, he clarified that he did not 'want any of them (new members) to bring politics into the Sangh,' before he was asked the inevitable question by a reporter: Was Nathuram Godse a member of the RSS? Golwalkar accepted that the assassin was a member years ago, but had since left, and even had major disagreements with the RSS. He was also asked another pointed question--did the RSS subscribe to secularism? Henceforth, it was this reply by the iconic chief of the RSS that would be adopted by several Right-wing leaders to obfuscate the crucial question of secularism vis-a-vis the organisation, which Golwalkar articulated as follows, 'To a Hindu, the state is always secular.'

A number of felicitation functions were held across the country for Golwalkar. The idea behind organising these functions was to also revive the Sangh work as early as possible. The training camps were started by the end of 1949. Golwalkar was travelling from one city to another in an untiring manner. Young Pracharaks and more than 77,000 swayamsevaks, who were arrested during the 8-month ban ensured that within a short span of few months, the organisation emerged even much stronger than before.

On 7 October 1949, while Nehru was abroad, the Congress party's working committee voted that RSS members could join the Congress as primary members. The decision immediately set off a controversy within the ruling party, with Patel's supporters generally supporting the action and Nehru's supporters opposed to it. A. G. Kher, Minister for local self-government in the United Provinces, and a staunch supporter of Patel, responded to the critics of the 7th October decision by predicting that an adverse decision regarding the participation of RSS members in the Congress might force the RSS into politics.

The members of that organization [RSS] cannot take part in politics unless they join some political organization. The main political parties are the Congress, the Socialists, the Communists, the Hindu Mahasabha, the Muslim League, and the RSPI. Do we desire that RSS youths should join other groups which are opposed to Congress, or should we desire they should join us? Let those who desire that RSS should not be admitted even as primary members of Congress understand the implications of their attitude. They are compelling RSS men to join the opponents of Congress if they have to take part in politics.

This was reflected in the 1949 Congress working committee resolution. Passed soon after the ban on the RSS was lifted, it allowed RSS members to join the Congress.

The sangh continued to influence Congress politics. A.G. Kher, United Provinces Minister for local self-government, wrote an article in Mahratta called "Admit the RSS into Congress fold." Urging his party to cooperate with the RSS, he warned partymen that "Calling them fascist, abusing and insulting them, and again and again repeating old charges does not serve any purpose." An example of this, of course, was Purushottam Das Tandon's resignation from the party presidency after being accused by Nehru of representing the reactionary ideology of the RSS.

Kher's warning to the Congress proved prophetic, as RSS leaders began to consider seriously the question of political involvement. Nehru reversed the decision a month later.

On 17 November 1949, the Congress Working Committee rescinded its earlier decision. It ruled that RSS members could join the Congress as primary members, but only if they first gave up their RSS membership. This decision virtually guaranteed that the RSS would assume some role in the political process.

Even before the ban, RSS leaders were reassessing the organization's role in an independent India. By RSS standards, Hindu society was far from united. A large part of 'Mother India' had been 'lost,' and the RSS was not reconciled to it. Some believed that the leadership of the Congress had neither the commitment nor the capacity to inspire the sacrifices needed for national rejuvenation. Many felt that the new political order rested on foreign concepts which not only undermined India's Hindu identity but also were contrary to India's historical, social, and political legacies, and they were not prepared to admit that the ancient wisdom was irrelevant in the contemporary period.

The negotiations between Patel and various RSS leaders during the ban period reveal that, Golwalkar, at the beginning of these negotiations, was ready to accept some kind of relationship between the RSS and the Congress in which the RSS would be entrusted with character building and the Congress with politics. The evidence also suggests that Golwalkar did not want the RSS itself to become directly involved in political matters. With the Congress closing all doors to even minimal political involvement, Golwalkar was forced to deal with the RSS activists, who wanted the RSS to play a direct role in the political process, and in other areas as well. The RSS experienced an internally divisive debate on the question, which involved fundamental questions of strategy and goals. The end result was a decision to get far more deeply involved in politics than Golwalkar had originally anticipated. Another outcome of the debate was the decision to sanction the establishment of affiliated organizations around the RSS. [65]

However, even as Golwalkar was focussing on the organisational work, a large number of persecuted refugees began pouring in from Pakistani Bengal to Bharatiya Bengal. Though the RSS did not have a very strong presence there, but at the behest of Golwalkar, Vastuhara Sahaayata Samiti (Displaced People's Relief Committee) was constituted under the chairmanship of Barrister Ranadev Chaudhary on February 8, 1950. Many Pracharaks were deputed from the nearby states to help these refugees. Eknath Ranade was entrusted to drive this initiative. Golwalkar himself visited Kolkata to assess the situation and then after coming back to Delhi, he issued an appeal to the people of the country, "I have recently come back from Bengal and after getting information from various sources about the conditions in East Bengal, I believe it is of utmost importance to help Hindus there. It is not possible to describe the horrible condition of the people there. Piercing the steel wall put over East Bengal, we are getting news regularly about inhuman killings, robbery, arson, rapes and religious conversions."

He further said, "It would not serve any purpose if we forget that the atrocious condition of these people is a result of our leaders' acceptance of religion-based division of our country. It is paramount that our leaders should free themselves and the people of this delusion that Partition is not based on religion but on geography. The reality is clear and we should face it. It will not do any good if people who control the reins of power do not accept this truth."

"This confused thinking about Partition along with distorted ideas about secular (vidharmee) state being presented before the nation on and off are proving to be a major hurdle in resolving the problems faced by the nation. What will you call these one and-a-half crore unfortunate brethren - foreigners or locals? The rehabilitation minister has concluded that they are foreigners and they have become an unnecessary burden on us. But, is this view right? Using the softest possible words, one can only say that this view is absolutely inhuman. Not only is this view condemnable, but also an insult because of which they are being deprived of their right of Bharatiya nationality and being sacrificed at the altar of Pakistani cruelty."

Appealing to the government, he said, "It is my request to the government and especially to the Prime Minister that he should find a solution to stop these bestial atrocities of Pakistan and rescue our brothers and sisters on the other side of the border. If our policy is going to be vague, confused and weak, then the government will be accused of sin of complete devastation of one-and-a-half crore innocent Bharatiyas and its esteem will be reduced to dust. This may take police action or mean sending Muslims to Pakistan and getting Hindus back to Bharat in exchange. Any stern action must be initiated immediately, so that our one-and-a-half crore brethren of our own flesh and blood should be able to lead a secure life."

More than 5,000 swayamsevaks joined the relief work. Golwalkar wrote a letter to Sardar Patel on April 5, sharing information and insights about the gravity of the situation. He also met him on April 12 and apprised him of the RSS' efforts.

Meanwhile, on January 26, 1950, India had been declared a Republic and it adopted a new Constitution. Golwalkar sent Sangh's congratulations and wishes to the President, Dr. Rajendra Prasad. On January 25, he wrote to him, "I greet you with great pleasure on the occasion of your election as the President of the republic of independent Bharat... May the merciful God bestow you with strong health and long life to help you succeed in this immense job."

In 1950, the RSS training camps were restarted in the months of May-June after a gap of two years. Golwalkar went to all the camps and spoke to swayamsevaks at length.

These camps were important as they were the maiden camps in independent India. The last camps were held in May-June 1947, prior to Independence.

Even as the country was getting ready to celebrate its first Independence Day as a republic, a disastrous earthquake struck Assam. Golwalkar reached there immediately and set up a Relief Committee with its centre at Dibrugarh under the chairmanship of retired Justice Kamakhya Ram Baruah. After returning to Kolkata, he sent out an appeal to help the victims of the earthquake.[66]

When the ban was lifted in 1949, it appears that Golwalkar expected some kind of agreement with the Congress which would allow individual RSS members to join the Congress and its affiliated front organizations, leaving the RSS free to pursue its more traditional character-building activities. This option was eliminated on 17 November 1949, when the Congress

Working Committee decided to exclude RSS members. Several other options now faced the RSS leadership. It could (1) transform itself into a political party, (2) form a political affiliate, (3) make some kind of arrangement with the Hindu Mahasabha or another compatible political group, (4) abstain from any political involvement, (5) continue to negotiate with the Congress. The activists tended to support the first two options, and the traditionalists the last two. The possibility of cooperation with the Hindu Mahasabha was never seriously considered. The Mahasabha had performed very poorly in the post-war Central Legislative Assembly elections.

Rashtriya Swayamsevak Sangh (RSS) began to contemplate the formation of a political party to continue their work, begun in the days of the British Raj, and take their ideology further. Around the same time, Syama Prasad Mukherjee left the Hindu Mahasabha political party that he had once led because of a disagreement with that party over permitting non-Hindu membership. Dr. Shyama Prasad Mukherjee had resigned from Pandit Nehru's cabinet in protest against his policies. The former was thinking of setting up a new political party. He met Golwalkar, Balasaheb Deoras and Bhaurao Deoras in early 1951 at the home of Nagpur Sanghchalak Babasaheb Ghatate. It was decided to launch Bharatiya Jansangh after the discussions. The RSS loaned out some of its Pracharaks to help the cause of setting up a nationalist party while making it clear that the RSS would not be involved directly in any political activity. So, Pracharaks like Deendayal Upadhyaya, Balraj Madhok, Atal Bihari Vajpayee and Nanaji Deshmukh got associated with the Bharatiya Jansangh with Dr. Mukherjee at the helm of affairs.

The BJS was subsequently started by Mukherjee in consultation with MS Golwalkar on 21 October 1951 in Delhi, with the collaboration of the RSS, as a "nationalistic alternative" to the Congress Party. In 1952, India witnessed its first General Elections, BJS made impressive start as a National party.

Golwalkar had a clear vision of the ideal conditions in every sphere of national life. Guided by the firm faith that it was impossible for Bharat to become strong and confident enough to fulfil its destiny unless every aspect of the nation's life was informed with the pure and inspiring ideology of the Sangh, he pioneered the formation of many fields of such activity. It was Golwalkar's tremendous drive and initiative that lay behind various nation-wide organisations like Akhila Bharatiya Vidyarthi Parishad, Bharatiya Mazdoor Sangh, Vanavasi Kalyan Ashram and the Shishu Mandir educational institutions. The year 1952 saw the RSS inspiring its swayamsevaks to move into the field of education by setting up a model of Swadeshi education and later the Vishwa Hindu Parishad, Vivekananda Rock Memorial, There were detailed discussions between Golwalkar and Professor Rajendra Singh, Nanaji Deshmukh, Pandit Deendayal Upadhyaya and Bhaurao Deoras on this issue.[67]

As a result, the first Saraswati Shishu Mandir came into existence under the leadership of Nanaji Deshmukh at Gorakhpur. All its teachers were graduates, who had retired from their Pracharak life. Golwalkar laid the foundation stone of the building. Today, this movement has the largest number of schools in the country educating millions of students.

In 1952, the RSS also launched the Cow protection movement. The Akhil Bharatiya Pratinidhi Sabha (the higest decision-making body of the RSS) passed a resolution in Nagpur in September 1952 about banning cow slaughter across the country.

A massive nationwide campaign was launched. Golwalkar issued a statement: "The main objective of this signature collection is to submit a gigantic request containing crores of signatures to the President. This is an act of fiery patriotism. It is my request that each citizen of this country should rise above the differences of religion, sect, caste, party, etc. and participate in this sacred work." He wrote letters to political leaders, editors and religious heads individually. The signature campaign was formally launched by Sarkaryavah Bhayyaji Dani and by Golwalkar in Mumbai. The RSS volunteers collected signatures from 94,459 villages and towns. Total count of signatures was one crore seventy-nine lakh eighty-nine thousand three hundred thirty-two (1,79,89,332)!

Next day, on December 8, Golwalkar met the President to hand him over the signatures with an appeal to ban cow slaughter across the country.

One of the key impacts of the cow protection campaign was that it galvanised the RSS at an organisational level and increased its organisational reach significantly.

The RSS was now getting increasingly involved in the relief and rehabilitation efforts wherever a disaster or calamity struck in the country. This resulted in setting up of the 'Seva Vibhag' (a wing for Social Services).

As the poll fever gripped the country, Golwalkar and a few senior Sangh functionaries such as Bhayyaji Dani, Balasaheb Deoras, went to the famous Simhagarh Fort for reviewing the organisational situation and chalking out the future course of action. He stayed there from December 25, 1951 to January 18, 1952 at Lokmanya Tilak's bungalow.

In 1952, the Bharatiya Jansangh (BJS) had not done well in the General Elections. Golwalkar wrote to one of the BJS workers, "During the campaigning, it is not unnatural that much acrimony and bitterness is let loose. But I feel that all these undesirable feelings should be completely washed away and the correct understanding that we are all children of our Motherland and of our nation, should be assiduously cultivated and all, irrespective of party affiliations, should determine to work in co-operation for the good of all our people. Properly seen, it will be found that the area of agreement is extensive and of differences negligible. With this attitude, our democratic system will survive any onslaughts by elements desirous of wrecking it and bringing about chaos in the country."

Even as Golwalkar continued to work towards strengthening the organisation, on June 23, 1953, a disaster struck as the founder of Bharatiya Jan Sangh died in a prison in Kashmir under suspicious circumstances. Golwalkar had a premonition about this probably, as he had indicated to Dr. Shyama Prasad Mukherjee to not to go to Kashmir. He was in Secunderabad when the news reached him. As soon as he received this news, Golwalkar went inside a room and shut the door. The RSS Pracharak Bapurao Moghe who was with Golwalkar at that time, summed up his reaction when he recalled later, "It was a disaster that shook the Himalayas."

The Golwalkar wrote to Dr. Mukherjee's son Ashutosh after reaching Nagpur: "We had been in touch for the last 10-12 years and our affection and relations were becoming stronger over time. I am very distressed to note that nobody would be able to fill the void left by his death."

In another statement issued in Nagpur, he said, "Shyama Prasad Mukherjee has sacrificed his life on the battlefield of the struggle waged to press for complete merger of Kashmir in Bharat, that

Kashmir should remain an indivisible part of Bharat. The news about the demise of Shri Shyambabu in Srinagar has hurt me grievously. I could not even have his last darshan. The wound left by this incident in my heart will never heal. A scholar of the highest order, skilled organiser, an impressive speaker, incomparable parliamentarian, a servant of the people, who dedicated his life to the sacred motherland, a fearless crusader for pure nationalism and civil rights, and most importantly, a rare idealistic, cultured individual in today's times with unblemished character has gone from amongst us. Imprisonment of Dr. Mukherjee, his death in prison - it is difficult to forget all these things. If nothing else, responsibility of leaders of the so-called government for the people for the fatal lack of care definitely lies at their doorsteps."

In March 1954, a brainstorming session of the key RSS functionaries was organised at Sindi (Maharashtra). In addition to the daily Shakha, Golwalkar would address the participant's everyday under the shadow of a great banyan tree and it was followed by the Questions and Answers session.

Golwalkar reminded the participants in this brainstorming session, "I just wish to say one thing - that we are conducting this programme at a place where highly revered Doctor Saheb had finalised different aspects of our protocols, our prayer and orders, etc. It is an occasion to remember and revise our thoughts about our work once again at the place where we had sat together for a week to plan out our work. If we ever get some doubts in our heart due to any situation around us, we should resolve that we shall not let any weakness develop within us, and working day and night with all our energy, we shall spread our work in all fields to such an extent that nobody would remain untouched in that environment."[68]

After the Sindi meeting, the RSS training camps were organised all over the country according to the usual schedule even as Golwalkar travelled and addressed thousands of swayamsevaks attending these camps.

During this period, The New York Times carried an interview of Golwalkar by its reporter Lucas that throws light on relations between the RSS and Jan Sangh as he perceived it. He suggested that they should not publish interviews and articles on the BJS and the RSS together in the same issue as that would create further confusion. His response to the question about Sangh and Bharatiya Jan Sangh was,

Sangh swayamsevaks are free to join any political party. Till 1937-38, our swayamsevaks used to be in Congress and Hindu Mahasabha. Whatever be their political differences, they could work together quite well in Sangh. Congress shut its door on Sangh swayamsevaks later on. Hindu Mahasabha has become very weak and it does not even have presence in many places. Therefore, those who wish to join politics, seem to get into Jan Sangh. But, number of swayamsevaks who are not in any political party is substantially higher. It is our belief that our nation can progress only if the society is unified and organized in a thread of unity, and its ethical and spiritual association remains unbroken.[69]

In 1951, Golwalkar expressed his views in newspapers thus, "China is expansionist by nature and is very likely to attack Bharat soon." The point of reference was that of the military activities of China in Tibet. Those days Shri Guruji many a times warned, "It has been a terribly blunderous act to gift away Tibet to China. This is one governmental blunder which even the British did not commit." Those very days, Pt. Nehru was busy visiting the country with Chau-en-lai and harping hand-in-hand the slogans of Hindi-Chini Bhai-Bhai and the doctrine of Panchsheel. It was quite natural for the common man to be carried away by these slogans. But in those days, Shri Guruji was the only leader who sounded the alarm about an impending attack. Later in November 1962, China openly attacked Bharat along the borders in Arunachal Pradesh and occupied 64,000 sq. km of our land along the borders.

Meanwhile, the demand for formation of state on linguistic basis was gaining momentum across the nation and there was a growing buzz about regionalism. On May 23, 1954, Golwalkar, as the chief guest at a conference against regionalism in Mumbai, said, *"Due to the wicked strategy of the British, we have begun to believe that difference in language leads to difference in culture, but this assumption is wrong. This thinking has even forced its way into the Bharatiya Constitution. We have called our country a 'Union' in our Constitution, which is incorrect. 'Union' actually means sticking together some fragmented pieces to make them stand together. Ours is a nation with a unified soul, and it is not fragmented. Some people call themselves supporters of 'united India! But,from where has this term 'united India' come? This idea itself contains an unconscious thought of differences, which is spreading like an epidemic across the nation."* "This may in future lead to fanatic instances in the name of languages. This may well become an issue of friction and ill-will amongst neighboring states." He wrote an impressive article on this issue in which he appealed to the leaders of the country to 'have guts and accept a unitary state for the entire nation.' In this context, he had reminded the historic role of Abraham Lincoln in shaping the unified America. Unfortunately, the then leadership did not have the nerve to take this vital decision in the cause of the unity of the country.

He asked the supporters of linguistic states a question, "Why should those people, who talk of the whole world being one single state, be afraid in their hearts about making Bharat into one state?"[70]

In July 1954, when Golwalkar reached Bhopal by train, the station master told him that his father had passed away the previous night at Nagpur. It wasn't possible to travel a distance of 400 kms and reach in time. So, a message was conveyed to maternal nephew, Dinkar Tikekar to perform the final rites. Golwalkar came back to Nagpur and stayed with his mother for five days and carried out the last rites of his father on the banks of the holy River, Godavari in Nasik. He went back to Nagpur on August 3.

Golwalkar took time out amidst even this personal tragedy to write a letter to station master of Bhopal, "The pure sympathetic emotions, with which you conveyed to me the unhappy news you had received from Nagpur, has resulted in deep faith and respect for you in my heart. News being unexpected, I forgot to convey my gratitude to you while I was trying to recover from this grief. You obliged me by conveying this news to me promptly in a gentlemanly manner. I am sending mine and my colleagues' heartfelt thanks to you through this letter. I hope I would get a chance in future to know you better by meeting you personally and offering my respects to you in person."

In 1955, an agitation for freedom of 450-year-old Portuguese colony, Goa had started. The previous state Pracharak of Delhi, Vasantrao Oke, was leading one of the groups for 'Satyagraha', as Bharatiya Jansangh took a leading part in this agitation. Golwalkar sent his letter personally to Oke: "All my good wishes are with you for this great task. I pray to the Supreme Lord from the bottom of my heart that He may bless this programme with success. Whatever pious deeds I may have accumulated with God's blessings in my life, I offer them to you for your success and protection."

One of the stalwarts and leading ideologues of the RSS, Dattopant Thengadi, who also founded the Bharatiya Mazdoor Sangh (the largest trade union in India at present), received an invitation from the president of INTUC (an organisation backed by Congress Party), P.Y. Deshpande, in 1950, to work for that organisation. Interestingly, despite Congress being a detractor of the RSS, Golwalkar told Thengadi, "Follow the discipline of the organisation you are going to work for. When its discipline and your ethical intellect lead to any conflict, it would be ideal to resign at that time. But, as long as you are in that organisation, you should always consider its discipline your yardstick."

This decision to send Thengadi to INTUC helped the RSS to breach one of the strongest bastions of the Communists in India - the labour movement. After his initiation into the labour movement and whatever he had learnt with his work in INTUC, Thengadi helped in founding the Bharatiya Mazdoor Sangh on July 23, 1955.

Prior to the 1957 elections, Shri Golwalkar said, "I address myself to the great Hindu people, to strive for whom has become my Dharma, the hoary immortal Hindu people whom I worship as the veritable manifestation of Eternal Divine. I pray that they rouse themselves to their consciousness and freely and boldly exercise their right of vote without being misled, without being distracted or frightened into upholding any individual or party. Let them be alert and... resolutely vote for men and parties dedicated to the Hindu people and Hindu cause, free from narrow-minded parochialism, progressive, free from unseemly hatred and uncalled-for antagonism to people of differing views, dominantly and essentially Hindu, possessing sterling character, individual and national, determined to serve the people and the country with devotion who know the value and method of homogeneous coordinated action and possess faith and devotion to the Motherland, the Nation and the people and who can shoulder the heaviest and most onerous task completely, disregarding all personal comfort, and the voters will not have voted in vain. They will have chosen rightly, and helped in laying unshakable foundations of a flourishing and honourable national life with all that it connotes in our dear Motherland - our Bharat Mata."[71]

Golwalkar's commitment to democracy and democratic norms was not superficial or based on convenience; nor did it depend on the politics of the time. It can be seen from a little known episode of Kerala in 1959 when the first democratically elected Communist government in the world was sought to be thrown out by Indira Gandhi and other opposition parties by hook or by crook.

Panchjanya had planned a 'Kerala special' issue in the light of anti-Communist agitation, led by Congress under Indira Gandhi to dismiss the Communist government there. Devendra Swaroop was editor of the weekly. He thought Guruji will give his support to the efforts to bring down the Communist government. Guruji sent him a long confidential letter, not for publication, dated 29 June 1959. He disclosed this letter much later in his book. Extract of relevant portions of the letter say:

"Friend, Pandit Deendayal Upadhyaya and others are discussing this issue. You would have received analysis from them. So, it would not be right for me to present my views. But, one thing is clear that if we consider democratic system and consider our constitution then it may be said that the agitation going on there should not be supported. If someone is trying to remove a ruling party using forms of satyagrah, but basically use of muscle power seems incorrect, it would be disrespect for the constitution. People who believe in the principle that might is right, for them all these activities are right. Unless the Centre and Constitution declare the current government as anti-national, people who believe in the constitution cannot support this agitation, I believe."

One notes that though Golwalkar considered Communist ideology as non-Indian and inspired from outside and Communist movement as anti-national, he was not ready to support an agitation that was inspired only by party politics. In the same letter in the first para he had noted that themeeting will be held under the directions of the Sarkaryavaah and he will follow the tour plans and decision that was to be decided in that meeting on 11 July. The letter also shows that though people believed that he was the all-in-all, the supreme leader of the RSS, he considered himself only an obedient member of the organization, when he clearly indicated that the decision would be taken by Deendayal Upadhyaya and his colleagues, his juniors, showing his belief in internal organizational democracy. Those who raise doubts about his commitment to the Indian constitution and democratic values would do well to study this incident.

Devendra Swaroop goes on the note that Jan Sangh and Panchjanya didn't go by his advice and celebrated 18 July as 'Kerala Divas' as per decision taken in all-India meeting of Jan Sangh on 8 July and supported the agitation. Golwalkar did not reprimand the people involved in Kerala matter about this, but he just let his views be known. This incident illustrates the democratic nature of collective decision-making in the RSS and Jan Sangh. Against this backdrop, it is ridiculous to keep calling him a supporter of Nazis and Hitler, for years without a shred of evidence. Critics quote 'We - Our-Nationhood defined; a 1938 publication which we noted above, he had disowned as no longer valid. He took over as Sarsanghchaalak in 1940. His views on minorities were enunciated well in his last interview published in 1972. Even if taken at face value, the horrors of gas chambers had not yet reached the world. World War II ended around 1942 and horrific facts came into public domain around 1945. There were many politicians who appreciated Hitler till these horrors burst upon the world. The worst charge against him, was he advocated that no group should have any special privileges (which the Leftists translate as the minorities being given a status of second-class citizens). This is the basic premise of a secular polity.'

'Even if this view is taken at its full face value, it is not in any way different from the stated Islamic rule (evident in all Muslim majority states) that gives status of second class citizens to non-believers - claiming it to be as per 'The Book. If this is acceptable to supporters of Semitic religions, will critics accept that Islamic rule is fascist?'

When people try to relate Nazism or Fascism to Hindu organizations, they forget that both the Hindu Mahasabha (founded in 1906) and the RSS (founded in 1925) came into existence before anyone in India knew of Hitler. Savarkar's Hindutva (1923) was published three years before Hitler's Mein Kampf. RSS was founded on the lines of Bharat Swayamsevak Mandal and Hindustani Seva Dal. The Communists opposed the British in 1940 (under Stalin's pact with Hitler) and supported them after 1941, yet after independence they have not been branded as collaborators with either fascism or colonialism. But calumny continues. Contrary to Congress and Left propaganda, Dr. Hedgewar never went out of India and never met Mussolini or Hitler.

As we have seen earlier that he had basic differences with the HMS leader Dr, Moonje and did not follow Moonje or Savarkar's advice many times. Another extract often quoted by the critics is from the chapter titled 'Internal challenges: Christians, Muslims and Communists' from Bunch of Thoughts, is mentioned. Dr. Manmohan Vaidya, analyses Golwalkar's views in the present context in a recent article. He says, in today's context, it should be interpreted as Christian evangelism, jihadi Muslim fundamentalism and Naxalism or Maoism. Their activities are a threat to the very idea of Bharat envisaged by the Constitution makers.[72]

Golwalkar's Vision of a Secular Hindu Nation is misrepresented (often deliberately) as a 'Hindu State', a Hindu Nation does not strive to make India a theocracy, much less variant of Saudi Arabia. Ideologically, Golwalkar's vision is poles apart from both Nazism and fascism that called for totalitarian state and for the subservence of the individual to the state control. Golwalkar repeatedly said, each action of the state had to be judged with the welfare of all Indian in mind. He was also against state sponsored violence perpetrated upon citizens. There is no force of sanction behind the disciplined physical training, the swayamsevaks undergo voluntarily. But such a perception of the sangh is rampant among most academics.

After Sindi, another important camp of key RSS functionaries was held at Indore (Madhya Pradesh) in March 1960. It was a bigger camp than the one at Sindi in 1954. The objective was to review the Sangh work over the previous six years, and to chalk out future plans. The camp was more of a brainstorming session and Golwalkar was present throughout all the sittings. He spoke at several Questions and Answers sessions. Golwalkar clearly said at this Camp that if the Varna and the Caste system in Hindu society has lost its utility, it should be done away with.

In the year 1960, Golwalkar warned the government of the day about a possible foreign aggression and, in 1962, China attacked India. The RSS came out in full force to defend the nation and help the government to fight this aggression.

The then Prime Minister Pandit Nehru had to recognise the value of the efforts made by the RSS and he invited an RSS contingent to participate in the Republic Day Parade in 1963. Around 3,000 RSS swayamsevaks participated in that march.

In January 1963, Golwalkar went to Nepal. He called on the King of Nepal, Mahendra Vikram Shah and met the then Prime Minister of Nepal, Tulsi Giri.

Immediately after his return, Golwalkar wrote to Pandit Nehru and Lal Bahadur Shastri: "If we improve our relations with Nepal, accord it due to respect, strengthen our friendly ties with it and take into consideration its educational, economic and other requirements, that country could indeed become our strong and dependable ally and a defender of our borders. As all our interests are closely interrelated, it is also necessary from our own security point of view to establish sincere and friendly ties between the two. The bitterness that has developed between the two countries, because of the apathetic and insensitive attitude, either deliberate or unintended, of Bharatiya officials should be removed, and if necessary, such officials be replaced by more sensitive officials. I have no doubt you will take all these factors into consideration and succeed in putting Bharat-Nepal relations on a firm and friendly footing."

In 1965, when Pakistan attacked India by invading Chamb area in Jammu and Kashmir, Lal Bahadur Shastri, as a Prime Minister, invited Golwalkar for an all-party consultative committee meeting in Delhi, even though the RSS was a non-political entity. Golwalkar was touring Maharashtra and was in Sangli when he was given the Prime Minister's message about the meeting. He immediately flew to Delhi and attended the meeting.

Golwalkar made a suggestion in this meeting that in order to halt Pakistan's advance on the borders of Jammu-Kashmir and Kutch, the Indian armed forces should march on to Lahore. The RSS played a stellar role during the war as it extended complete support to the government. Disagreeing with the way, the ceasefire had been declared suddenly as Indian defence forces pummeled Pakistan's army. Golwalkar said, "In fact, our war of independence would not reach a successful conclusion until we liberate the whole of Pakistan. There is no meaning whatever in raising the bogey of what the world would say."

He argued that at least the cease fire line should be fixed at the point up to which the Indian army had penetrated into Pakistan, and the same rule be applied to Bharat that UN had applied to Kashmir in 1949. Golwalkar was also of the opinion that it was not desirable for Shastriji to go to Tashkent for negotiations. Shastriji died under mysterious circumstances in Tashkent.

Under the guidance of Golwalkar, the swayamsevaks inspired by the RSS had started working in various fields setting up a number of organizations. In one such initiative, the VHP was founded in 1964 by RSS leaders in collaboration with the Hindu spiritual leader: Chinmayananda Saraswati, and S.S. Apte. According to Chinmayananda, the objective of the VHP was to awaken Hindus to their place in the comity of nations.

Chinmayananda was nominated as its founding President, while Apte was nominated as its founding General Secretary. It was decided at the meeting that the name of the proposed organisation would be "Vishva Hindu Parishad" and that a world convention of Hindus was to be held at Prayag (Allahabad) during the Kumbh Mela of 1966 for its launch. It was further decided that it would be a non-political organisation and that no office bearer of any political party shall be simultaneously an office bearer in the Parishad. The delegation of the founders also included Bharatiya Vidya Bhavan founder - K. M. Munshi, Gujarati scholar - Keshavram Kashiram Shastri, Sikh leader - Tara Singh, Namdhari Sikh leader - Satguru Jagjit Singh and eminent politicians such as C. P. Ramaswami Iyer. Its stated objective is "to organise, consolidate the Hindu society and to serve and protect the Hindu Dharma". It was established to construct and renovate Hindu temples, Chinmayananda was nominated as its founding President, while Apte was nominated as its founding General Secretary. Formally, the organisation was set up in 1966 at a convention held in Prayag (Allahabad) on the auspicious occasion of Kumbha in 1966. This three-day global Hindu convention took place on January 22, 23, 24 on a grand scale. Prior to this convention, a senior RSS Pracharak Dadasaheb Apte had gone on a world tour to garner support for setting up this organisation at the behest of Golwalkar. Golwalkar made the following points in his speech at Prayag:

1. Owing to the prolonged slavery, lack of self-confidence, aping of others and an inferiority complex, the Hindu diaspora has been reduced to a state of being neither a Hindu nor a non-Hindu ("Na Hindur, na Yavanah"). They should now be progressively acquainted with the unique greatness of Hinduism, the all-encompassing Hindu philosophy and the Hindu code of noble conduct, and, thus, establish the true content of Dharma once again.

Initially, arrangements should be made to impart only the minimum sanskaras. What these should, be, it was for the scholars and savants to decide.

2. Doubtless Hindu brethren settled abroad intensely desire to live as Hindus. But proper arrangements for imparting the necessary knowledge and sanskaras of our Dharma and Sanskriti are not available to them. Consequently, there is a danger of their succumbing to undesirable modes of Western civilization. So, arrangements for the imparting of such knowledge and sanskaras need to be urgently made for their families.

3. In our own country, we often hesitate to call ourselves Hindus. We have become victims of a sense of inferiority complex. It is essential, therefore, to awaken intense pride in being a Hindu within ourselves and also the missionary zeal to promote our sacred Bharatiya traditions throughout the world. Hindus settled abroad should be made to feel confident to declare proudly that the Hindu society in Bharat is there as their great bulwark. But for this to happen, the right congenial atmosphere should be created in Bharat itself. All of us, whether in Bharat or abroad, should take pride in being Hindus and move all over the world with our heads held upright as Hindus.

4. We are not against any other faith. So, our work will have to be based on honesty, love and purity of character, and a sense of affection for the entire mankind. It would not be right to promote any kind of narrow-minded or selfish attitude in the name of any sect or religion. Let us not forget that Hindutva is all-encompassing in its spiritual sweep.

5. Sanatana Dharma implies the eternal, sublime code of highly principled human conduct, applicable to all human beings of all claims and times. It embodies all the various persuasions like Buddhism, Sikhism, etc., born out of the same Dharmic traditions. An eminent Jain Muni has truly said, "How can he who does not call himself a Hindu also be a Jain?" All our different sects, in fact, share the same holy traditions and values of life. It is our duty to evolve harmonious accord among all of them and take the whole society to the heights of spiritual eminence. Our Vanavasi brethren, living in hills and forests, are in great distress. In fact, it is our so-called high-caste society which is responsible for their present-day miserable plight. For long years, these Vanavasis have been subjected to grave injustice. As they are indeed an integral part of our society, we should help them in all possible ways and, thus, atone for our past mistakes.[73]

"In his valedictory address, he said:

"This event of two-and-a-half days is worth written in golden letters. This indeed is a great and fortunate occasion for all of us. Our good fortune, which was asleep for the past many years, has now awakened. Now it will resound the world over and its banner will fly high. Swami Vivekananda had said that the day is not far when our flag will fly on top of the world. We have absolutely no doubt this will happen." The 1966 meet at Prayag during the Kumbh Mela was of great historical significance in yet another aspect also. For centuries there was this misconception in the Hindu society that once a person leaves the Hindu Dharma and embraces Christianity or Islam, he cannot come back to the Hindu fold. The misconception proved to be a breach in the dam of Hindu society, resulting in a one-sided exodus of the Hindus from Hinduism with no way to return. The Hindu population was getting thinner and that of non-Hindus bigger. From the platform of VHP, all the religious leaders including Shankaracharya pronounced, unequivocally.

"It is the sacred religious duty of all the Hindus to bring back all the converts to their original Hindu Dharma." At that time, the word coming back (Paravartan) replaced the word purification (Shuddhi). Later Shri Pejawar gave it as a mantra 'na Hindu patito bhavet' i.e. the Hindus can never become fallen. The main objective of this mantra was to dispel the false notion that 'converted Hindu is fallen forever and cannot be accepted back as a Hindu.'

After Prayag, provincial conferences of the Vishwa Hindu Parishad were held in Gujarat, Maharashtra, Assam and some other states. Golwalkar was present at all these conferences.

Golwalkar's Cultural Nationalism

Golwalkar points out that 'the climax in the process of denationalization was the propagation by the foreign ruler . . . of the amazing doctrine that the Nation is composed of all those who, for one reason or the other happen to live at the time in the country'. He completely rejects the idea of territorial nationalism, which, according to him, had deprived us of the positive and inspiring content of our real nationhood. He regrets that in the early days of our 'so-called freedom struggle', the leaders used to propagate falsely that we were a nation in the making, thus ignoring the fact that 'there was a full-fledged ancient nation of the Hindus, and the various communities which were living in the country were here either as guests, the Jews and Parsis, or invaders, the Muslims and Christians'. Savarkar had kept a certain link with territorial nationalism through his concept of pitrubhoomi, but had then shifted his emphasis towards Hindu 'sentiments' or 'culture' by arguing that pitrubhoomi and punyabhoomi could be identical only among the Hindus. But Golwalkar brought out the implications, in all their totalitarian fullness.

Golwalkar prefers to call his theory of nationalism 'cultural nationalism'. The cultural nationalist sees the nation as inherent in the group of people who possess certain common cultural traits. While the territorial nationalist gives priority to the direct relationship of the individual to the territorial defined nation-state, the cultural nationalist gives priority to collective cultural realization through nationalism. Golwalkar argues that the concept of a Hindu Nation is not a mere bundle of political and economic rights. 'It is essentially cultural. Our ancient and sublime cultural values of life form its life breath. And it is only an intense rejuvenation of the spirit of our culture that can give us the true vision of our national life.'

Then how does he define culture? Cultural values are not something mysterious and out-worldly as perceived by the Western-influenced elite, writes Golwalkar. He regrets that sometimes culture becomes another name for cheap entertainment; the so-called men of culture associate themselves with 'Miss India' beauty contests. Golwalkar admits that though the term 'culture' defies definition, it has left an indelible stamp on all walks of life. Giving the example of Jawaharlal Nehru's decision to offer the sacred relics of his wife in the bosom of Gangamata, Golwalkar states: "This is samskar, the imprint of culture."

Apart from the philosophical framework of the Hindu approach to life and its problems, Shri Golwalkar had expressed his views on almost all aspects and problems confronting the contemporary world. They are too numerous to be included in the compass of a small book of this size. We shall only try to select some from among them, which are illustrative in character. Regarding the much-misunderstood word "Hindu", Shri Golwalkar was of the view that 'the Hindu' denotes a society. It is a word that is found in our Shastras. It is formed with the letter

'Hi' from the Himalayas and Indu Sarovar, conveying the entire stretch of our Motherland. Shri Golwalkar quotes from the Bruhaspati Aagama. Himaalayam samaarabhya yaavad-indu-sarovaram Tam devanirmitam desam Hindusthaanam prachakshate. Though the word 'Arya' is an old and proud name, Shri Golwalkar was not in favour of using that word in view of the "Cooked-up Aryan-Dravidian controversy". The word Bharateeya, though very ancient and normally unobjectionable, it has acquired a connotation slightly different and ambivalent and as such cannot be a substitute or equivalent to the word Hindu. Hindu Rashtra, according to Shri Golwalkar, is not merely a religious concept. He defines Hindu Rashtra in the following terms. "Let me try to clear, at the very outset, one misconception about 'Hindu Rashtra'. The word Hindu is not merely 'religious'. It denotes a 'people' and their highest values of life. We, therefore, in our concept of nation, emphasize a few basic things: unqualified devotion to the motherland and our cultural ideals, pride in our history which is very ancient, respect for our great forefathers, and lastly, a determination in every one of us to build up a common life of prosperity and security. All this comes under the one caption: 'Hindu Rashtra'. We are not concerned with an individual's mode of worship". When he was asked the question whether he opted for a Hindu state, Shri Golwalkar explained his concept in very simple terms, "The word Hindu state is unnecessarily misinterpreted as a theocratic one which would wipe out all other sects. Our present state is in a way a Hindu State. When the vast majority of people are Hindus, the State is democratically Hindu. It is also a secular state and all those who are now non-Hindus have also equal rights to live here. The State does not exclude any one who lives here from occupying any position of honour in the State. It is unnecessary to call ours a Hindu State or a secular state". Many people, supposed to be very intelligent and highly learned are confused about the fundamental unity of Hindu society on account of the multitude of faiths, sects, castes, languages, customs and habits. They look upon Hindu society as a conglomerate of disparate and even conflicting elements. But Shri Golwalkar disagrees. He says, "Well, this question stems from a superficial view of our Hindu life. A tree, for example, appears to be full of heterogeneous parts like the branches, leaves, flowers and fruits. The trunk differs from the branches, the branches from the leaves - all as if entirely different from one another. But we know that all these apparent diversities are only the varied manifestations of the same tree. The same sap runs through and nourishes all those parts. So is the case with the diversities of our social life, which have been evolved down these millennia. They are no more a source of dissension and disruption than a leaf or a flower is in the case of a tree. This kind of natural evolution has been a unique feature of our social life". Shri Golwalkar's views about the role of war in settling conflicts among nations and place of violence in society are clear and specific. According to Hindu Dharma war is the last resort, not to be undertaken lightly at the very first provocation. "It should be used as a surgeon's knife. Even as a surgeon uses his knife to perform an operation to get rid of an infected portion to save the patient, so also violence in certain extraordinary circumstances can be used to cure the society of any malady that needs such a surgical intervention. Further, certain other conditions should be fulfilled.

One who applies violence should have perfect control over it, should know when, where, to what extent and how far to apply it, when to end it and how to repair the damage caused, if any" He was absolutely non-dogmatic about certain things, which people very often consider to be basic to Hindu Dharma. On the question of vegetarianism, Shri Golwalkar is of the view that our Shastras have taken the comprehensive nature of the world into consideration and made rules for different living being to suit their different tastes, attitudes etc. They have not made a flat rule applicable to one and all.

As human life evolves, the concept of mother also takes a wider and more sublime form. When a man looks around with his discerning intellect, he sees so many things to which he owes a debt of gratitude. He begins to look upon them also as mother. He sees a river as mother which gives him food and water. And then he reaches the state of understanding that it is the mother-soil which nourishes him, protects him and takes him in her bosom after he breathes his last. Thus, Golwalkar invoked one's land not only as mother matribhoomi, which, to him is a sign of a high state of human evolution but also as pitrabhoomi and punyabhoomi - the father land and the holy land. Therefore, he says, 'It is upto us to keep aglow that highly evolved divine sentiment of mother towards our land.' Now, how are we to express our devotion to her? Our people have been doing this even today in a spirit of religious devotion. They go round the country on pilgrimages, follow the religious injunctions, recite hymns, worship and offer flowers and, take bath in various holy waters. In Golwalkar's view, this emotional bond between the masses and the motherland was the most important ingredient of nationhood. He felt that the country ranging from Hindu Mahasagar (Indian Ocean) to all the branches and sub-branches of Himalayas along with the island in the Hind Mahasagar constitute one homogeneous geographical unit and the society has been living on thisland since time immemorial. The seers and saints who were forefathers of Hindu society, through their conduct and life which was full of devotion and adhered to values, created certain ideals and traditions for the society. Because of the climatic conditions, the dress habits were different in different parts of the country. Because of social life confined to a certain region, different languages also thrived in different parts of the country. Golwalkar held that the sacred land Bharat—a land visualised by Mahayogi Aurobindo as the living manifestation of the Divine Mother of the Universe--has assumed concrete form to enable us to see her and worship her. Philosopher poet Rabindranath Tagore described as:

- *"a land worshipped by all our seers and sages as Matrubhumi, Dharmabhoomi, Karmabhoomi and Punyabhoomi, a veritable Devabhoomi and Mokshabhoomi.*

- *a land which has been to us since hoary times the beloved and sacred Bharat Mata, whose very name floods our hearts with waves of pure and sublime devotion to her;*

- *well, this is the mother of us all, our glorious Motherland."*

Golwalkar was very touchy if any one treated the feeling of nationalism as dry intellectualism alone. He used to say that mere intellect was not enough. Man must be capable of experiencing the nobler sentiment of the heart. To the question: "What is the so-called motherland, except stones and clay!", he counters questioned: "The human body is after all material. The body of one's mother also is as much material as any other woman's body. Then, why should anyone consider his mother as different from other woman? Why have devotion for her? An intellectual has no answer for this. He used to cite another instance, "after all, biologically, man is nothing but flesh, blood and bones. So, why not eat up our neighbour? But if a person says this, he may be called a scholarly logician, but certainly not a civilised human being. Such intellectualism leads only to cannibalism. Ravana was a scholar but a barbarian all the same."

The name of the nation, Bharat, according to him, originates from king Bharata who was noble, virtuous, victorious king and shining model of Hindu manhood. When a woman has more than one child, we call her by the name of her eldest or most well-known among her children. Bharat was well known and this land was called as his mother, Bharat the mother of all Hindus. Golwalkar contended that India was one nation, one people, one culture, since earliest time in human annals. "He used to quote the trumpet cry of Vedas:

(The land to the north of the oceans and south of the Himalayas is called Bharatavarsha, and Bharatis are her children)."[74]

Golwalkar had a gruelling schedule and he continued with them relentlessly, not bothering too much about his health. In 1969, it was suspected that he was suffering from cancer, but Golwalkar did not allow his scheduled programme to be altered. In May 1970, the RSS workers at Mumbai compelled him to have a diagnosis done by Dr. Prafull Desai, the well-known cancer specialist at the Tata Memorial Hospital. After a detailed examination, Dr. Desai confirmed the diagnosis that Golwalkar had cancer. Golwalkar was informed but he remained as undisturbed as ever. He asked Dr. Desai, "How much has the cancer spread, and can it be cured?" Dr. Desai replied, "That can be known only after an operation. Not to operate would be to invite danger. I sincerely wish that you should agree for the operation."

Golwalkar agreed to this on a condition that it would be done after he was finished with visiting the RSS training camps according to his pre-decided schedule. Very few people knew as he travelled and interacted with swayamsevaks at the training camps that he was suffering from such a serious disease. In fact, he also held a press conference in Delhi on June 11, 1970, during the course of the tour, to respond to the RSSs detractors who had been trying to malign the organisation.

After the press conference in Delhi, he went to Calcutta to address the swayamsevaks at a training camp. He went to Mumbai from there and was admitted on June 30 to Tata Memorial Hospital for surgery.

On July 1, he underwent a three-hour surgery. While being at hospital, he started visiting a nearby RSS Shakha. He also attended the annual meeting of the RSS' Central Executive Committee at Mumbai from July 10 to 12. On July 26, he left the hospital and on August 3, he left for Nagpur by train.

On August 13, Golwalkar addressed an RSS programme on the occasion of Raksha Bandhan. He stood for 45 minutes and addressed those who were present without displaying any discomfort.

In September, he again returned to Nagpur on September 26 and resumed his old routine. Addressing the Vijaya Dashami function in 1970, where V. Shankar, retired Secretary to Sardar Vallabhbhai Patel, was the chief guest, Golwalkar warned against the possible foreign aggression and emphasised on the need to build up the internal strength of the nation. He left for a countrywide tour on the 23rd of October. Golwalkar had told Dr. Desai, "Mortal that man is, he should not worry too much about his physical well being. Every living being has to depart some time or the other. So, what is important is not how long a man lives, but how he lives. I have a mission to live for before me and I have to fulfill it. So, I only pray to the almighty to keep me fit till the end." The final phase of Golwalkar's life had begun. He knew he was not well, and yet he continued with a schedule which didn't give him time to take rest. Immediately after his surgery, he toured extensively from October 23 to December 7, three days each in Mumbai, and at

Bangalore, for a meeting of Prant Pracharaks, in Nashik and in Pune, followed by four days in Mumbai and a short halt in Nagpur, then Delhi, then Mumbai, enroute to Karnataka for a provincial Sangh conference. From there he went to Pandharpur, then to Solapur, again Mumbai, and back to Nagpur. At all these places, the schedule used to be crowded and the pace hectic - meetings for guidance to workers, public speeches, and planning for the future.

Dr. Desai had given Golwalkar around three years. So, till 1973, he immersed himself in the organisational work. In the later half of 1972, his tour of Mahakoshal, Maharashtra and Vidarbha had to be cancelled. He developed intense pain in the throat; he could neither eat nor drink nor even speak.

In December 1971, general elections were announced. The Congress (I) swept the polls. Golwalkar, in every one of his speeches at Sangh's training camps in 1971, warned of the dangerous consequences of the explosive situation observing in East Pakistan.

On June, 28, 1971, he completed his tour and returned to Nagpur. By this time, the situation had turned critical. The number of Hindu refugees had swollen to over three million. The Sangh hadalready launched relief operations through the Vastuhara Sahaayata Samiti. A country-wide campaign was also launched for collecting relief materials, and foodgrains, clothing and medicines were distributed at the refugee camps on a very large scale.

The RSS' Central Executive met at Nagpur from 8-10 July, 1971, and passed a resolution on the situation in Bangladesh, calling upon the Government to keep its solemn promise given to the Hindus of Pakistan at the time of partition, assuring them of safety and security. The demand was growing louder every day to liberate East Pakistan from Yahya Khan's strong hold by taking recourse to military action in support of the Awami League and to send the refugees back home. Golwalkar called upon the swayamsevaks to be vigilant, extend all the required assistance and also keep the public morale high.

On December 3, 1971, Pakistan attacked India. "At that time, a training camp for youth swayamsevaks was in progress in Nagpur. Golwalkar immediately issued a statement regarding the aggression and the corresponding responsibility of the citizens. Lakhs of copies of his statement were distributed from door to door by the swayamsevaks."

In his statement, issued on December 4, 1971, Golwalkar appealed to the countrymen, "The unity inspired by genuine love for the motherland alone can lead us to victory."

"Pakistan is openly at war with us. Our Government and the army are quite capable of meeting the challenge, but it is essential to keep the morale of the people high and maintain the highest levels of production in fields and factories. Besides, our Jawans on the front must feel that the entire nation is behind them. Civil defence, blood donations, nursing of wounded personnel, etc., are some of the essential services to be organised forthwith."

The RSS, as desired by Golwalkar, lent its full support to the defence efforts. Bangladesh was liberated after an emphatic victory of Indian defence forces in December 1971.

He sent a letter to the then Prime Minister, Indira Gandhi on December 22, saying, "May the unity of the country be a realistic assessment of the situation, and the determination to preserve the honour and prestige of the country continue like this.

This is necessary not only in times of danger but for all time and for all activities of national renaissance. In the creation of the strength of national unity infused with national pride, the Rashtriya Swayamsevak Sangh is and will always be with you. I have confidence that as the representative of the country, you will take all these factors into consideration while determining our domestic and foreign policies. May the prestige of Bharat grow like this under your leadership."

After the war, Golwalkar expressed his deep reservations about the Shimla Accord.

In 1972, Golwalkar's health deteriorated very fast. From October 28 to November 3, a brainstorming session was organised at Thane (Maharashtra). It was attended by key RSS functionaries. He continued his travels even after the Thane Camp. On 4th February 1973, in Bangalore, he delivered a public address in fluent English, for one-long hour and that too, standing. None in the audience of thousands of Swayamsevaks and other citizens felt that he was about to leave this mortal world so soon. On 25th March, he delivered what was to be his last speech to the important workers from all over the country in Nagpur, on the occasion of Akhil Bharatiya Pratinidhi Sabha. The Swayamsevaks listening to him were wishing that he should finish his lecture soon as he had to struggle to speak every word. But even in this state of failing health, he spoke for 40 minutes. He said, "The single aim of all our different endeavors should be to make our nation stand high commanding worldwide respect for our country." He emphasized, "Whatever be the atmosphere, tread on your path with this faith that the word 'Hindu' will be recognized all over one day." And he concluded his speech saying, "Vijay hi vijay hai" (ever victorious).[75]

On his return to Nagpur, medical treatment was resumed afresh. In 1973, he spoke at the concluding session of the RSS' highest decision-making body, known as Akhil Bharatiya Pratinidhi Sabha, which was arranged at Nagpur.

It was clear there that he was unwell as he had to make a herculean effort to speak.

In March 1973, his health deteriorated further and he was confined to the RSS headquarters at Nagpur. From March 26 onwards, he could not even bathe with his own hands. On April 2, 1973, he wrote three letters in his own hand and handed them over to the office secretary, Pandurang Kshirasagar. Dr. Sujit Dhar of Calcutta used to visit him once a fortnight to examine him.

Golwalkar asked him, "Why are you trying to sustain this body?" For how many more days would you be able to save it?"

"On the night of June 4, Shri Baburao Chouthaiwale came to massage him with his usual bottle of oil. But no oil came out of it. Shri Golwalkar saw this, smiled, and said, "The oil is finished? That is all right. Anyway, who's going to need it tomorrow?" The agonising significance of the words was not lost on Chouthaiwale. The whole day Golwalkar sat in his chair facing north. He looked like a Yogi, his eyes half-closed, probably contemplating the Divine. That night also he did not lie in bed, but On 5th June in the morning, he took his bath and meditated sitting on his usual seat. Later at 9.30 in the night, he breathed his last and his soul got liberated from the shackles of the mortal body.

The Moment of Inexpressible Grief

His body was kept at the front of Mahal Karyalaya in Nagpur. On the morning of 6th of June, grief-stricken people thronged the place. The three letters, written and sealed by Shri Guruji were opened and read. The Sanghachalak of Maharashtra province Shri. Babasaheb Bhide read the first letter wherein Shri Balasaheb Deoras was given the charge of Sarsanghachalak. The other two letters were read by Shri Balasaheb Deoras. In the second letter, Shri Guruji had indicated that it was not desirable that a memorial be erected for anyone other than that of the founder of the Sangh, Dr. Hedgewar. In the third, he had humbly written, "If I have ever knowingly or unknowingly caused hurt to anyone, to all of them I tender my apologies with folded hands." This deeply moved the thousands of people who had gathered there who burst into tears. Shri Balasaheb himself felt choked. An Abhanga (composition) of Saint Tukaram was also mentioned in this letter, the meaning of which is –

O Saints! Please forward my last request

To the God that He might not forget me.

He knows everything; what may I say more.

Tukaram says his head placed on His feet

I may always remain under the shadow of His grace.

His body was given Mantra-agni (fire sanctified by sacred mantra) and cremated by the side of the Samadhi of Doctorji in Reshambag, (Nagpur) on a pyre made of sandalwood. The fire soon consumed his body, which like the sandalwood dissolved into the five elements. Later Bhagwadwaj was hoisted and the gathered thousands sang the prayer of the Sangh in grief-struck tones. And after the utterance of Bharat Mata Ki Jai all the Swayamsevaks returned home, with heavy hearts.

Now Reshambag is home to two great personalities in their chaitanya form Dr. Hedgewar sitting in the form of his image is on the upper floor of Smriti-Mandir and Shri Guruji, like the sage Dadhichi (who sacrificed his body for the welfare of gods and mankind.), as a smriti chinha (a symbolic memory). Many of his followers found Golwalkar's leadership authoritarian at times, but in the end, Golwalkar knitted the organization while also expanding it to various field.[76]

Dr. Hedgewar with Guru ji M.S Golwalkar and other Swayamsevaks

Dr. Hedgewar in 1930 Satyagraha

[Left]: 'Guruji' Golwalkar with Ram Manohar Lohia: Photo courtesy Tapan Gosh. [Right] 'Guruji' Golwalkar with Sant   Tukdoji Maharaj during the founding of the VHP

Swayamsevaks in 1963 Replublic day Parade

Syama Prasad Mukherjee with Pandit Jawaharlal Nehru

Syama Prasad Mukherjee with Veer Savarkar

Syama Prasad Mukherjee with B.R. Ambedkar

बी.सी. रॉय, डॉ. श्यामा प्रसाद मुखर्जी, मनीबेन पटेल, के. एन. काटजू और सरदार वल्लभभाई पटेल
B.C. Roy, Dr. Syama Prasad Mookerjee, Maniben Patel, K.N. Katju and Sardar Vallabhbhai Patel

एम. एस. गोलवलकर के साथ डॉ. मुखर्जी
Dr. Mookerjee with M.S. Golwalkar

Guruji M.S. Golwalkar with Pandit Deendayal Upadhyaya and Atal Bihari Vajpayee

Initial Swayamsevaks deputed to BJS: (LtoR) Jaganath Rao Joshi, Pandit Deendayal Upadhayay, Atal Bihari Vajpayee, Sunder Singh Bhandari, Nanaji Deshmukh, Jagdish Prasad, Balraj Madhok, Yagyadutt Sharma and Kedarnath Sahni.

Bharatiya Jana Sangh

Many members of the right-wing Hindu nationalist Rashtriya Swayamsevak Sangh (RSS) began to contemplate the formation of a political party to continue their work, begun in the days of the British Raj, and to further their ideology. Around the same time, Syama Prasad Mukherjee left the Hindu Mahasabha, the political party that he had once led, because of a disagreement with that party over permitting non-Hindu membership.

Precursors of the Bharatiya Jana Sangh

In the aftermath of Independence and during its banning in 1948 and 1949, the senior leaders of the RSS conducted several re-evaluations of its relationship to formal party politics, that it had often disowned as detracting from its main mission of 'character-building' for the 'Hindus'. Several senior RSS pracharaks, who had established a degree of regional and national organizational independence during the ban, argued for the RSS to acquire a direct role in the political environment of the Lok Sabha, which, at the time, was dominated by Nehru's Congress but also included Communist, Socialist, and Hindu Mahasabha as representatives. Aside from the Mahasabha, which had withered in the intervening period, the RSS considered each of the other main parties as vigorously opposed to its Hindu nationalist aims; conversely, the RSS was strongly attacked by Nehru, Congress, and the left parties. Key proponents of an increasingly political orientation for the RSS included Balraj Madhok, Dadarao Paramarth, Vasantrao Oke, and K. R. Malkani.

Golwalkar opposed the transformation of the RSS into a political party but apparently considered the involvement of RSS pracharaks in the formal political process both problematic and politically expedient. This particular orientation of Golwalkar's is difficult to explain. It has often been argued that Golwalkar had to agree to the political participation in an individual capacity of senior RSS members in order to offset organizational and ideological tensions among sections of the senior RSS leadership while also retaining his different non-political' vision of the RSS. However, Golwalkar's evasive orientation regarding the political involvement of RSS pracharaks and his decision to loan RSS workers for Jana Sangh activities should be noted. Of additional relevance are two related issues: whether Hindu nationalist ideology proffered a coherent theory of political power, and whether the substantive content of Hindu nationalist ideology betrayed a considerable intellectual paucity from which no philosophical or transcendental vision, let alone a political theory of government, governance, and administration, could be realized. With some exceptions noted below, Hindu nationalism has, perhaps until recently, been unable to articulate a coherent theory of political power or 'Hindu government' which moves beyond an eclectic melange of militant religious- nationalist symbolism and an inexperienced politics of expediency and pragmatism.

From a broader perspective, other factors also seem important in explaining the RSS's entry into politics. The decline of the Mahasabha during the 1940s had created a political vacuum during a critical period when Nehruvianism represented not just a non communal orientation but one determined to 'secularize' the Indian state and make India's post-Partition Muslim minorities feel secure and integrated into Indian civil society. The 1950s represented a period of secular nation building and an attempt to forge a nationalist ideology reliant on the memory of the anti-colonial struggle and leaning towards distinctly programmatic, socialist directions. It has been argued that during this formative period, Nehruvianism failed to instigate a nationwide, deep-seated cultural policy that supplemented, and hegemonically articulated, its vision of secular nationalism for Hindus, Muslims, and other groups. A cultural politics of secularism was hence radically underdeveloped. The importance of cultural politics in civil society, seen from a Nehruvian perspective as potentially capable of stirring Hindu communal interests, was elided in favor of a belief that a strong secularism of a federal state and an 'equal', benevolent orientation to India's religious traditions would suffice. In Nehru, one can perhaps see an attempt at merging a federated civic nationalism with a hesitant religious pluralism under a broader framework of planned, democratic, 'secular', socialist governance. What the ideological inculcation from the center of an Indian nationalism reliant on anti-colonialism could have meant for the plurality of Indian civil societies that were not simply suffused with religious sentiment but deeply organized through divergent religious affiliations was therefore unclear. Of importance were not Nehruvian techniques of governance but the elision of the public and private institutions of a potentially differentiable civil society in the making and of the alternative communitarian, religious-public spheres that were arising from the latter.

During the 1950s, the institutionalization of the political power of nationalist elites was underway, the latter process both reflecting and creating new centers of regional and national Congress power during a period of invigorated nation-building. Congress foreign policy leaned towards, and later allied itself with, the communist Soviet Union. Conversely, the US forged links with Pakistan, its main anti-communist ally in south Asia during the Cold War period. Nehru referred the settlement of the Kashmir issue to the United Nations, whereas Hindu nationalists demanded its immediate occupation, the expulsion of Pakistani forces, and the integration of Kashmir with India. Later border clashes with China and Pakistan (in the early and mid-1960s respectively), combined with the perception held by Hindu nationalists that Nehruvian foreign policy favoured peaceful resolution over war, fed their belief that their new "Hindu Rashtra," post-Independence India, was in threat from a military perspective. Hence, they called for aggressive militarization, including the nuclearization of India. The various sweeping social and political changes in the Nehruvian period, reflecting the heyday of Indian nationalism and social reform, were characteristically grating for Hindu nationalist sensibilities. In this respect, some form of Hindu nationalist political emergence can be seen as inevitable, though not necessarily predetermined in form or content, especially after the death of Nehru in 1964.

During the period of the RSS ban, Golwalkar had indicated strongly to Nehru the potential 'non-political' role of the RSS in forming a bulwark against communist influence among India's youth. This was to be a central ideological plank during the initial stages of the formation of the Bharatiya Jana Sangh. In his 'program for a new political party', formulated in 1950 by RSS activist K. R. Malkani, the RSS's political role was pitted against the threat of communism to India, a threat that could only be countered by Hindus through the mobilization of Hindutva. The early discussions within RSS Pracharak networks about the basis for a new political party were to dovetail into attempts by Shyamaprasad Mookherjee to establish initially a regional and then a national political platform outside and in opposition to the ruling Congress Party.

Mookherjee had been president of the Hindu Mahasabha (after Savarkar) but was given a Cabinet post as Minister of Industries and Supplies in Nehru's government. However, he resigned his Cabinet position following the agreement between Liaquat Ali (Pakistan's Prime Minister) and Nehru regarding procedures for addressing the grievances of minorities and provisions for the return of refugees to their respective countries. The 'Liaquat-Nehru pact' stipulated that neither country could make 'extraterritorial claims' on behalf of minorities in the other country. Mookherjee viewed this as a betrayal of the Hindus of East Bengal, many of whom had arrived in India claiming persecution by the Muslim majority. Nehru's granting of limited autonomy to Kashmir was similarly opposed by Mookherjee. In the following year, while senior RSS activists were creating Jana Sangh political groupings in various regional centers, Mookherjee, although supporting the latter, launched first his own 'People's Party', centered in Bengal, and subsequently (in 1952) the National Democratic Party, aimed as a federation of various smaller parties. In October 1951, Mookherjee was elected president of the Bharatiya Jana Sangh at its founding convention held in Delhi, which launched it as a national party. The general secretary of the Bharatiya Jana Sangh was Deendayal Upadhyaya, an RSS pracharak (depicted as an 'ideal swayamsevak') whose ideology of 'integralism' and 'Integral Humanism' became considerably influential within the RSS and the Jana Sangh. The BJS was subsequently started by Mukherjee on 21 October 1951 in Delhi, with the collaboration of the RSS, as a "nationalistic alternative" to the Congress Party. The symbol of the party in Indian elections was an oil lamp and, like the RSS, its ideology was centred on Hindutva. In the 1952 general elections to the Parliament of India, 94 candidates contested on the Bharatiya Jana Sangh ticket and its election symbol.Three Jana Sangh MPs were elected for the first time in 1952; two from West Bengal and one from Rajasthan. The three elected representatives were Syama Prasad Mukherjee (from Kolkata South-East seat), Durga Charan Banerjee (from Midnapore-Jhargram seat), and Umashankar Trivedi (from Chittor, Rajasthan). The BJS would often link up on issues and debates with the center-right Swatantra Party of Chakravarti Rajagopalachari,Rama Rajya parishad, and Hindu

Mahasabha. The strongest election performance of the BJS came in the 1967 Lok Sabha election in which it won 35 seats, when the Congress majority was its thinnest ever.

The Jana Sangh contested the 1951-2 elections and secured just over three percent of the votes for the Lok Sabha and 2.76 percent of the votes in the state legislative elections. This was to rise to almost 9.5 percent by the 1967 general elections, and almost 9 percent in the state legislative elections. However, it was not until the critical period of the mid-to-late-1970s that the Jana Sangh emerged as a major national political force. Nor can one understand the emergence and the political direction of the BJP without consideration of the political experience gained by the Jana Sangh and the RSS during and in the aftermath of Indira Gandhi's Emergency period.

From its inception, the Jana Sangh advocated its fundamental principle of 'one nation, one culture, one people', a political sentiment that continues to be strongly articulated by the contemporary BJP. The Jana Sangh mobilized this view both in opposition to the partition of India, which it believed should be 're-united', and in its vision of post-Independence nationalism, the latter based on the consolidation of 'Bharat' through sanskriti culture and maryada ('political rectitude', or 'righteousness' as conceived in Hindu tradition). Similarly, the Jana Sangh opposed the idea that India constituted a composite nationality, the latter conceived as a policy of 'appeasement' or 'special treatment' of India's religious or regional minorities. Consequently, the Jana Sangh robustly opposed Nehruvian secularism, the latter seen as equivalent to a policy of 'appeasement' of Indian Muslims. The application of the war metaphor of 'appeasement' to describe both Nehruvian foreign policy towards Pakistan and domestic secular policy towards India's Muslims is instructive and continues to resonate in both senses today. The Jana Sangh initially conceived of post-Independence India as 'Bharatiya Rashtra' (or 'Indian nation', as conceived in Hindu usage.) This was to change to 'Hindu Rashtra' in 1956, the Jana Sangh claiming that the two were equivalent and coextensive with 'Indian' nationalism,[1]

Main Issues of Jana Sangh

The Jana Sangh sought a Uniform Civil Code for the country, a complete ban on cow slaughter, and the abrogation of Article 370 in Jammu and Kashmir. The first manifesto of the BJS, released at its founding convention, underlined the key issues that find resonance in the present BJP government's plans and policies. Some of the key issues were promoting Swadeshi economics, ensuring cow protection, decentralisation of power, a strong policy on Pakistan, making Kashmir an integral part of India, promotion of Indian languages, but most importantly, doing away with the western framework of decision making at the policy level. The BJS kept its stance largely unchanged on all these issues in subsequent years and continued to focus on them.

The BJS's ideological approach to addressing any issue, which is reflected in today's BJP too, was outlined in the first manifesto of the BJS in 1951 itself, where it stated: "The mistaken policies and 'Abharatiya' and unrealistic approach to the national problems by the party in power is primarily responsible for this state of affairs in the country. In their anxiety to make Bharat a carbon copy of the West, they have ignored and neglected the best in Bharatiya life and ideals."

When the BJS was formed, the party adopted an eight-point program that largely formed its ideological core over the next few decades. These were: united Bharat; reciprocity instead of appeasement towards Pakistan; an independent foreign policy consistent with Bharat's paramount self-interest; rehabilitation of refugees with suitable compensation from Pakistan; increased production of goods, especially food and cloth, and decentralization of industry; development of a single Bharatiya culture; equal rights for all citizens regardless of caste, community, or creed, and improvement of the backward classes' standard; and readjustment of West Bengal's boundary with Bihar.

In 1953, the Jana Sangh launched its first major campaign regarding Jammu and Kashmir, supporting the complete integration of Kashmir with India, without any unique status, in line with the integration of other states. At the time, a permit was required to enter Jammu and Kashmir, and instead of a chief minister, there was an office of the prime minister.

Mukherjee saw this as a policy hindering the unity of the country and staunchly opposed it. On May 8, 1953, Mukherjee started his journey to Jammu and Kashmir without a permit. After he entered Jammu, he was arrested by the Sheikh Abdullah government on May 11.

The Evolution of the Jana Sangh

The Jana Sangh, from its inception, comprised 'sangathanist' political strategies in the early to mid-1950s based on RSS ideology and organization, a 'hybridization' of its sangathanist strategy from the early 1960s, a strategy of integration into the political mainstream and 'moderation' of its Hindu nationalism during the 1960s, and finally the 'mixed strategy' during the troubled period of the 1970s. In the early to mid-1950s, Jana Sangh goals were based on the strategic and long-term consolidation of 'Hindu society' through the creation of a network dedicated, like the RSS, to patiently imposing its vision of the world over a long period by working at the grassroots. Up to the early 1960s, the Jana Sangh's leaders considered that they had to resist any drift into propaganda or alliances that would be counter to party ideology.

However, the Jana Sangh was entering a public sphere of representative politics in which they had little experience. Most Jana Sangh activists only had knowledge of local Arya Samaj and RSS agitations. Hence, there were contending pressures on the Jana Sangh during the 1950s: one pushing towards constitutional politics and the other towards local activism, the pressures reflecting a sociological divergence between constitutional politics and social movements. Both directions would involve working with politicians and organizations that had not arisen from within the RSS nor shared its ideology or discipline. Perhaps an additional pressure was the affiliation with RSS itself.

The Jana Sangh's involvement in the Kashmir agitation (satyagraha) during 1952-53 illustrated these various tendencies. The Jana Sangh worked with the Jammu-based Praja Parishad, the Ram Rajya Parishad and the Hindu Mahasabha in opposition to Sheikh Abdullah's attempts to 'constitutionally' consolidate the special status of Jammu and Kashmir. The aim of the satyagraha was to demand full integration of Jammu and Kashmir into the Indian Union, rescind its special status, and disallow its constitutional autonomy. The Praja Parishad, however, defended the power of feudal landlords (mainly Dogras) against land reforms that would give greater economic power to small tillers; the Hindu Mahasabha allied feudal power and Hindu itself with and depended on the support of princely states and orthodoxy; the Ram Rajya Parishad defended Hindu 'upper' caste orthodoxy and opposed reforms in untouchability.

In each instance, the orientation of these three bodies went against the RSS and Jana Sangh goals of organic economic cooperation, 'anti-feudal modernization' and opposition to untouchability. Attempts at mergers between the Mahasabha, the Praja Parishad and the Jana Sangh hence failed, as the Jana Sangh had (at this stage of its development) few qualms about alienating the princes, the zamindars, or Hindu orthodoxy. The futility of the Kashmir agitation (and the arrest and deposing of Sheikh Abdullah by Nehru in 1953), the incarceration of Jana Sangh leaders by the Jammu and Kashmir government, and the death of Mookherjee, a recognized national political figure, while in detention led to a crisis of leadership and strategy in the Jana Sangh under its president Mauli Chandra Sharma and general secretary Deendayal Upadhyaya. This led to furtherfailed attempts during the early 1950s to merge with the newly formed Praja Socialist Party and the Hindu Mahasabha. Into the 1960s, this led to a reorientation in its political strategy that indicated both a pragmatic and an ideological shift away from the RSS's 'sangathanist' strategy.

During the early 1960s, in the face of massive Congress presence in the Lok Sabha and state legislatures, in comparison with its own very poor political representation, the Jana Sangh turned towards social and economic issues. The Jana Sangh appealed to the urban and rural middle classes and their economic interests, rather than simply rehearsing issues which would guarantee a small Hindu nationalist constituency (such as Kashmir or cow protection). It also demonstrated a willingness to negotiate alliances with non-RSS sympathizers, especially the non-Communist parties. Its organizational strength was centred primarily in Madhya Pradesh and the 'Hindi belt' in northern India. Hindu 'traditionalism' and 'orthodoxy' had allied itself with the ruling Congress power, and in this sense, Congress, while remaining a 'secular' party in national government, could secure or procure the interests of Hindu 'traditionalists' at state and local level. The 'Congress system,' for example, could allow political space for those like K. M. Munshi, who could otherwise be viewed as Hindu nationalists. This also left the Jana Sangh little room for ideological or political maneuver.

Hence, an instructive and perhaps surprising set of alliances was formed with socialist leaders such as Ram Manohar Lohia and Jayaprakash Narayan. It has been argued that it was precisely the influence of socialist leaders such as Lohia and (in the early 1970s) Jayaprakash that dragged the rightist Jana Sangh out of its marginal position and allowed its entrance into the political mainstream. The attraction of the Jana Sangh for the smaller socialist parties was often related to the organized and disciplined cadre that the Jana Sangh brought to any coalition. Leaving aside the question of opposition to Congress hegemony, there were important ideological ambiguities in Jana Sangh and RSS visions of nationalist, indigenous, corporatist economic and social policy which could be sutured with economic socialism based on 'anti-imperialist', 'self-reliance' or Swadeshi precepts.

Furthermore, following the death of Nehru in 1964, the 1965 war with Pakistan, the consequent devaluation of the rupee, and the poor performance of Indira Gandhi's Congress during the 1967 elections (Congress' majority in the Lok Sabha was reduced from about 200 to less than 50 seats; it also lost about 3,400 state legislative seats), there emerged from the late 1960s the so-called 'multi-party system' at national as well as state levels. The Jana Sangh hence became an important component in the arithmetic logic of state coalition governments. After the 1966-1967 elections, the Jana Sangh entered coalition governments in Madhya Pradesh, Uttar Pradesh, Haryana, Bihar, and Punjab state. The Jana Sangh gained experience of coalition electoral strategies with minor parties and formed long-term associations with Hindu 'royalty' (such as Vijaya Raje Scindia) and sections of India's industrial capitalist class. It cultivated a militant Hindu nationalist constituency through campaigns against Urdu, for the banning of cow slaughter, and for a militarily strong India. But while it appealed to a selective northern Indian Hindu electoral constituency, it could also be portrayed as a responsible party that attempted to reflect broad Indian interests.

The BJS was ideologically close to the RSS and derived most of its political activist base and candidates from the RSS ranks. It also attracted many economically conservative members of Congress who were disenchanted with the more socialist policies and politics of Jawaharlal Nehru and the Congress Party. The BJS's strongest constituencies were in Rajasthan, Gujarat, Maharashtra, Madhya Pradesh, Bihar, and Uttar Pradesh.

The BJS leadership strongly supported a stringent policy against Pakistan and China and were averse to the USSR and communism. Many BJS leaders also inaugurated the drive to ban cow slaughter nationwide in the early 1960s.[2]

The Jana Sangh, a replica and auxiliary of the RSS

From 1954 onwards, leaders of the Jana Sangh with an RSS background reshaped the political program and organization of the party in conformity with those of the mother organization. The main architect of this transformation was D. Upadhyaya, who was to remain the party's General Secretary till 1967 with the full support of Golwalkar. In the eyes of his peers and of those in charge in Nagpur, he represented the 'ideal swayamsevak'.

Upadhyaya abandoned his studies after completing the first year of a MA in English literature in order to dedicate himself entirely to the RSS, which he had first joined while in college at Kanpur in 1937. He worked for the organization first as pracharak in Lakhimpur district, then as joint prant pracharak he was the first non-Maharashtrian to hold this responsibility between 1947 and 1951 and finally as an editor, launching a weekly publication, Panchjanya, which subsequently became a Pan-Indian journal. Obliged to operate underground after Gandhi's assassination, he was one of the leading instigators of the satyagraha of 1949 in his province. He then went on to help frame the RSS's constitution and in effect founded the Jana Sangh in Uttar Pradesh. Upadhyaya 'was considered the ideal swayamsevak not only because, with humility and discipline, he had consecrated his whole life to the cause, to the extent of refusing marriage, but also because, in the opinion of RSS veterans, 'his discourse reflected the pure thought current of the Sangh'. It was therefore not surprising that he should have progressively taken on the task of endowing the Jana Sangh with a doctrine of its own, although one that seemed to be a variant of the ideology of the RSS.

The two principal texts in which he set out his political thought are "The Two Plans" (1958) and "Integral Humanism" (1965); these were to provide the bases of the Jana Sangh's foundation of its 'Principles and Policies' in 1965. The salient point here was the diminution in importance of the state by comparison with society. This may have been in conformity with the ideology of the RSS, but it was paradoxical in the case of a political party whose vocation was, in theory, the conquest of power.

For Upadhyaya, the 'basic cause of the problems facing Bharat is the neglect of its national identity' shown by westernized and unprincipled politicians. However, his model of the nation was the Western one, and he recognized that 'nationalism is the oldest and strongest of the 'isms' invented in the West. By means of reference to the so-called 'historical' varnas, he tried in his turn to affirm the existence of a Hindu nation. His thought process thus remained within the framework that stigmatized and emulated the Other through a reinterpretation of tradition.

Following in the footsteps of Golwalkar, he rejected the theory of a social contract, explaining that "society is "self-born"" as an "organic entity":"

In our socio-political set-up, the king and the State were never considered supreme. The mightiest of the kings did not ever disturb the Panchayats. Similarly, there were associations on the basis of trade. These two were never disturbed by the State; on the contrary, their autonomy was recognized. Thus, the State was concerned only with some aspects of life of the Society.

The ideology of the Jana Sangh, codified by Upadhyaya, followed the RSS in the value it accorded to the society-nation in comparison to the state. Certainly, the reference to the varnas contrasted with the egalitarian mission of the RSS, but this difference was logical: it was this which separated the world of the sect from that of the actual society in which conflict had to be eliminated, a task that the RSS entrusted, in particular, to its affiliates.[3]

The complementarity of the RSS and its affiliates

The RSS and the Jana Sangh were complementary in two respects. First, the existence of the Jana Sangh enabled the RSS to be represented in party politics without being directly affected by the rules and workings of this milieu. Secondly, and more importantly, the task of promoting a kind of social harmony relying on intermediate institutions, such as villages or corporations, could be undertaken by the Jana Sangh while the RSS concentrated on its long-term mission of preparing Indian society for its final transformation, when individuals would accept direct involvement and even fusion in the life of the nation. Two speeches made by Golwalkar between 1947 and 1952 can be usefully compared to illustrate this point.

The plan, conceived by Dr.Hedgewar, of an ideological brotherhood with a vocation to absorb the whole of Hindu society, was central in Golwalkar's speech to the ABPS at the end of 1947.

Continuously expanding amongst the Hindu society, we hope to reach a stage where the Sangh and the entire Hindu society will be completely identical. This is bound to happen in the course of time, for there is no escape.

These words have the millenarian emphasis inherent in the mission of the RSS. Five years later, in a speech that opened with a eulogy to the 'scientific' nature of the varna system, Golwalkar declared:

Today, there is talk of a classless society. Such a society would be possible of achievement only if all persons in the society were seers who have realized the Soul and have transcended worldly bonds. As long, however, as social development does not reach this stage, a classless social structure is a danger. If a developed society realize that the existing differences are due to the scientific social structure and that they indicate the different limbs of the body social, the diversity would not be constructed as a blemish.

In principle, RSS leaders perceived the shakhas as the crucible of a nation of individuals 'liberated' from their original personality and social characteristics (such as their caste), who have 'transcended worldly bonds', in Golwalkar's words. As a preliminary stage towards this organicism based on the sacrifice of the individual, the RSS affiliates are expected to promote the 'restoration' of a certain holistic organicism referring metaphorically to a varna system located in an idealised past. The RSS was therefore prepared to coexist for a lengthy period of transition with a society based on corporate groups in the same way as sects might coexist with a caste system. Indeed, Golwalkar himself proposed a theory of social reform that presupposes the state would rely on institutions mediating between itself and individuals. His project would combine territorial representation (election by constituencies, as already practised) with 'functional' representation, where in each corporation would nominate delegates at the request of both its local branches and the central organization. This mechanism was described as merely giving concrete form to what was already practiced in ancient India, where each of the varnas chose its representative for its village councils (Gram panchayat) and thence to the royal council. Golwalkar did not hesitate to demand, if necessary, a revision of the Constitution to put this plan into action.

In its work of reforming society, the RSS relied not only on its own efforts but also on those of the Jana Sangh and its other affiliated organizations, particularly its trade unions. While the RSS's shakhas formed a special world where egalitarian values could develop, the organization's affiliates worked in the real world and were faced with organized groups in conflict - hence their mission of promoting a harmonious society based on an organicist scheme.

Unions were quickly developed by the RSS to resist Communist influence, which was heavily attacked because of its anti-national bias and the risk that the Communists' scheme of class struggle would provoke division in Hindu society. In July 1948, Madhok – a teacher who argued that the infiltration of student organizations was a vital task founded in Delhi, with approval from Nagpur, the Akhil Bharatiya Vidyarthi Parishad (ABVP). In conformity to RSS philosophy, the task of this organization was to bring about collaboration between all those involved in university education, since 'the teachers and the taught are both wheels of the same car'. It would be a rival to the All-India Students' Federation, which was described as being dominated by "Communist agitators".

The front organization of labour unions was developed above all by Datto Pant Thengadi, a swayamsevak from Nagpur who began his service as a pracharak in Kerala and then served in Bengal and Assam from 1942 to 1948 before establishing the ABVP branch in Nagpur. After Independence, Golwalkar, who was extremely worried by the 'Communist threat', asked Thengadi to infiltrate 'red' labour unions in order to gain the experience that he would need in order to found his own workers' branch of the RSS. Thengadi directed his activities towards the INTUC (the labour union affiliated to Congress), whose Madhya Pradesh branch he revived in 1950, before finally setting up the RSS's own labour union. Significantly, this new body, the Bharatiya Mazdoor Sangh (BMS), was established in July 1955 with the approval of the preceding annual session of the Jana Sangh at Jodhpur. The Jana Sangh functioned on this occasion more like a social movement than a political party since it released one of its own cadres, Thengadi, who was the Organising Secretary of the party in Madhya Pradesh, to take charge of the BMS, a task different from normal party work but conforming to Hindu nationalist plans. Thengadi, who declared Communism to be 'enemy number one' at the inaugural conference of the BMS in Bhopal on 23 July 1955, Tilak Jayanti Day, entrusted his trade union with the task of rehabilitating Hindu social organicism. He wanted to substitute family for class in political discourse and proposed a corporatist scheme inspired by the 'functional' ordering of the representational system suggested by Golwalkar.

The apparent division of the Jana Sangh's forces to assist other offshoots of the RSS was perfectly in accord with the task assigned to the latter's affiliates: to work in society in order to 'restore' its supposedly lost harmony. This decision also followed from the conviction that the Jana Sangh should achieve political power only after society became deeply imbued with its ideals, as Upadhyaya himself pointed out:

As a matter of fact, electoral success is only a means to achieve the realisation of our ideals. We do have to amass popular support, but only from those who can follow our ideals and become one with our organization. We do not simply want popular support; it must be an idealistic popular support.

Hence, the party's truly political involvement was both progressive and selective. Electoral success could wait; first, the Jana Sangh had to acquire a network of propagandists of the Sangathanist type who would work upon society in such a way that, in the end, political power would fall into its lap like a ripe fruit. Although the Jana Sangh, like any other affiliate of the RSS, had been assigned a definite role to play within the division of labour of the 'Sangh parivar', this did not mean that it was expected to develop ideals and a structure different from the RSS. The Jana Sangh accepted that it was more important to concentrate on the long-term process of building the nation than on short-term methods of gaining control of the government. Thus, it also adopted organizational principles that conformed to those of the RSS.

Mukherjee's leadership acted as a constraint on the Nagpur movement in other ways too. Despite Golwalkar's initial caution, the Jana Sangh leaders, both during and after the election campaign, expected the activists of the RSS to be at the service of their political cause. In August 1952, Mukherjee exhorted the swayamsevaks to abandon their 'isolationist policy'. But the RSS's priority remained, now more than ever, the development of its Sangathanist network, which had been adversely affected by the ban of 1948-49, rather than political activism, for which there had been such high demand during the election campaign. The resolutions passed by the Jana Sangh Working Committee after the election in February 1952 further reveal the determination of the RSS men within the party to steer it towards social issues. Resolution No. 8 declared:

The Working Committee feels that now that the General Elections are over, the workers of the Jana Sangh should take up more important work for organizing a network of Jana Sangh bodies all over the country and carrying through them, constructive programs for the cultural, social, and economic regeneration of our society and for the building of a sound and stable political structure based on democracy. The constructive program shall be carried on particularly among those sections of society that need help because they have been lacking in opportunities, resources, education, leadership, or organization.

There followed a detailed list of 'target' groups: workers, students, women, refugees, peasants, and above all, Scheduled Castes.

This position was restated in the form of a resolution entitled 'A Massive Constructive Programme' at the first plenary session of the party, held at Kanpur in December 1952. Represented at the top level of the party by D. Upadhyaya, who had succeeded Bhai Mahavir as General Secretary, it came to be imposed by force in the months following the premature disappearance of Mukherjee. The latter's death in 1953 during a campaign of protest against 'Kashmiri separatism' led to an

intervention by the RSS in the internal affairs of the Jana Sangh, doubtless because of fears that the party would fall into the hands of another politician who would be less reliable than Mukherjee.

M.C. Sharma was the logical successor to Mukherjee as head of the party, but he had only a small support network concentrated in Delhi.Its key figures were two RSS workers, Vasant Rao Oke and Kunwar Lal Gupta, a lawyer and merchant in the Old City linked to the Hindi Sahitya Sammelan. Above all, Sharma was the very personification of a politician in the Mukherjee mould. The son of Din Dayal Sharma, one of the promoters of the Hindu Mahasabha in the 1920s who was close toM.M. Malaviya, M.C. Sharma had remained in the Congress without showing any great activism up to Independence. Like a number of Hindu traditionalists, he became chief minister of a princely state. But at Partition he was particularly impressed by the help given to Hindu refugees by the RSS and by the movement's internal solidarity, which seemed well placed to promote Hindu interests. He had acted as an intermediary with the authorities when the RSS was bannedand then appeared to play an active role in the setting-up of the Jana Sangh. These qualifications were still not significant enough to make the party cadres who had come from the RSS regard him as a legitimate president, and they were not slow to show their defiance in Organizer. Sharma immediately had to compromise with the RSS over the composition of the Working Committee. Among its twenty-nine members were a number of RSS men: D. Upadhyaya, Bapusaheb Sohni, Bhai Mahavir, Nana Deshmukh, A.B. Vajpayee, B. Madhok, S.S. Bhandari, Bhairon Singh Shekhawat, and Jagannath Rao Joshi.

Sharma attempted to reinforce his position during a meeting of the All-India General Council (AIGC- the full authority of which the Working Committee was an offshoot) was held at Indore in August 1953. But, this move only served to provoke the hostility of the AIGC. Consequently, he resigned in November, denouncing the increasing interference of the RSS in party affairs. The leaders of the Delhi branch followed suit. The Working Committee merely took note of these defections and appointed Sohni as interim president until the session at Jodhpur (30 December 1954 -- 1 January 1955), when Prem Nath Dogra, the RSS sanghchalak of Jammu and head of the Praja Parishad, was named president, and the Delhi branch was dissolved. Dogra reappointed twenty-three of the twenty-nine retiring members of the Working Committee, indication the extent to which the RSS had already penetrated the party apparatus.

The main conclusion to be drawn from this episode is that, although the RSS leaders were willing to become involved in the work of setting up a political party because they were persuaded to agree with certain of their own 'activists' that party politics could not be ignored, they were not prepared to allow the Jana Sangh to be taken over by politicians who would ignore their organization and make policy compromises to attract support rapidly. To prevent such an outcome, they virtually converted the Jana Sangh into a front organization and thus kept it within the framework of the other groups affiliated with the RSS.[4]

BJS Leadership:

Bharatiya Jana sangh was led by many leaders until Shri Deendayal upadhaya took over in 1967. All the years from its formation, he served as General secretary, making important decisions.

M. C. Sharma is the son of Pandit Din Dayal Sharma, a sanathanist Sanskrit scholar, promoter of the Hindu Mahasabha in the 1920s and an associate of Madan Mohan Malaviya. Mauli Chandra grew up in Delhi and attended the Hindu College. He went on to study law, but gave that up in 1923 to join political activity.

Sharma had been a member of the Indian National Congress and Hindu Mahasabha up to the time of independence. He worked as the Chief Minister of a princely state and as the Secretary to the Chancellor of the Chamber of Princes. He attended the Round Table Conference in London in 1930 and 1931 as a member of the States delegation.

After 1947, he was active in the politics of Delhi and the surrounding areas. He had close ties with the Delhi unit of the Rashtriya Swayamsevak Sangh (RSS), including its pracharak Vasantrao Oak. He was impressed with the work of the RSS in rehabilitating the refugees of the Partition. When RSS was banned after the assassination of Mahatma Gandhi, he organized a civil rights group, Janadhikar Samiti, to campaign for lifting the ban. He was arrested for this activism under the Public Safety Act. He later acted as a mediator between the Home Minister, Vallabhbhai Patel and the RSS chief, M. S. Golwalkar to help reach an agreement on the constitution of the RSS.

Towards the end of 1950, Shyama Prasad Mukherjee gathered in Delhi, a core group of activists including M. C. Sharma for forming a new political party, the future Bharatiya Jana Sangh. Several other members of the core group were RSS pracharaks. Sharma played an active part in forming the Punjab-Delhi branch of Jana Sangh on 27 May 1951, which later became part of the nationwide `Bharatiya' Jana Sangh. He was named as a General Secretary of the nation-wide party, with the RSS pracharak Bhai Mahavir being the other General Secretary.This indicated an equitable sharing of influence in the Jana Sangh by the Hindu traditionalist politicians and the Hindu nationalist RSS. Once the decision was taken, Guruji deputed some of the best pracharaks to Jan Sangh. They included Nanaji Deshmukh, Balraj Madhok, Dharmavir, Sunder Singh Bhandari, Jagannathrao Joshi, Atal Bihari Vajpayee, and L.K. Advani. A B Vajpayee was appointed secretary to Dr Mukherjee. Deendayal Upadhyaya was chosen to take on the onerous responsibility of organizing the party and he was made the general secretary of the party. He held this post till he was persuaded to take up the responsibility of party President in 1968.

Jana Sangh had been formed on the eve of the first General Elections of 1951-52. The party won only 3 seats in the Lok Sabha, including that of Mukherjee. Sharma contested for the Lok Sabha seat from Outer Delhi, but lost. He secured 74,077 votes or 16 percent of the votes cast.

When Mukherjee died in June 1953, Sharma was appointed as the Acting President of the Jana Sangh. By this time, Deendayal Upadhyaya, had firm control of its RSS faction, enjoying the full confidence of the RSS chief, M. S. Golwalkar. Sharma found his position weak even within the party's central office. There were discussions to merge Jana Sangh with the Hindu Mahasabha and Ram Rajya Parishad to form a single party representing the Hindu interests. A statement of

Sharma calling the Hindu Mahasabha, a 'communal body' is said to have broken off the negotiations. However,

According to N. C. Chatterjee, the President of the Hindu Mahasabha, V. D. Savarkar blocked the merger proposals.

Balraj Madhok, a member of the RSS faction in the Working Committee, warned in the RSS magazine Organiser that whoever became the next President of Jana Sangh would need to secure the "willing cooperation" of the RSS swayamsevaks in the Party. Being the Acting President, Sharma was a natural candidate for the Presidency. However, at the party's second plenary session in Bombay in 1953, Sharma was told upon his arrival that the RSS headquarters at Nagpur had decided in favour of another person and he was asked to stand down. Some party leaders threatened to take the matter to the open meeting, forcing the RSS faction to relent. Sharma was then given a full slate of the Working Committee members that he was asked to appoint, which also became a matter of contention. Despite his resistance, the eventual composition of the Working Committee was heavily weighted in favour of the RSS faction, including such RSS leaders as Bhai Mahavir, Jagannathrao Joshi, Nana Deshmukh, Atal Bihari Vajpayee, Balraj Madhok, Bhairon Singh Shekhawat, and Sunder Singh Bhandari. Vasanthrao Oke, who was also an RSS pracharak, was not in the original list because he was seen by the RSS leadership as having become too close to the politicians. He was included upon Sharma's insistence.

Sharma and Oke made efforts to recruit party workers and also to raise funds from businesses to finance the expansion of the party. These efforts were thwarted by the RSS faction because they saw it as an effort to reduce the party's dependence on the RSS. At the Indore session of the Central General Council in August, Sharma's Presidential address emphasized the principles laid down in the Party constitution, namely, "secular nationalism and unflinching faith in democracy." However, a fuss was raised that he was too uncritical of the Government. A delegate from Punjab brought forward a resolution condemning the interference of the RSS in party affairs, and it was decided to refer it to a further session of the Council.

However, Upadhyaya, as the General Secretary, refused to a call a second meeting of the Council and maintained that the decision belonged to the Working Committee, not the President. In response, Sharma resigned. According to Andersen and Damle, he anticipated the purge of the non-RSS party workers and tried to avert it. In a statement to The Statesman, Sharma stated that differences of opinion regarding interference by the RSS had been persistent for over a year. He confided that Shyama Prasad Mukherjee was "seriously perturbed" by the demands of the RSS leaders in the appointment of office-bearers, nomination of candidates, and matters of policy. "A vigorous and calculated drive was launched to turn the Jana Sangh in the mould of the RSS.

Sharma hoped that his resignation and revelations about interference by the RSS would rally the party members. He also expected a meeting of the General Council to be called, as it alone had the constitutional power to accept his resignation. However, the Working Committee accepted his resignation on its own and appointed Bapu Saheb Sohni, the RSS sanghchalak from Berar, as the Acting President. The Working Committee condemned what it described as Sharma's attempt "to abuse the Jana Sangh forum to try to run down the RSS." It called his actions undemocratic and unfair to the members of the Working Committee. Sharma was expelled from the party and the Delhi

unit that backed him was summarily dissolved. Organiser informed its readers that Sharma suffered from "insufferable self-aggrandisement", and he was hardly the man to lead the great and growing organisation of the Jana Sangh. Subsequently, Sharma rejoined the Congress Party.

In a 1974 interview, Sharma clarified that he and his supporters were in sympathy of the basic aims of the RSS, and that he greatly admired the work of the RSS in its efforts to strengthen the Hindu community. The main concerns were about the RSS domination of the Jana Sangh. He, like Mukherjee, wanted Jana Sangh to remain open to other influences and to use them for further growth. The young RSS organizers, on the other hand, were intent upon making the Jana Sangh more centralized and more disciplined, very much in the image of the RSS itself.[5]

Prem Nath Dogra succeeded Sharma as president of the party, also known as Pandit Prem Nath Dogra, was a leader from Jammu and Kashmir, who worked for total integration of the state with India [He is commonly referred to as Sher e Duggar]. He was instrumental in forming the Jammu Praja Parishad party in 1947 along with Balraj Madhok and opposed the policies of Sheikh Abdullah. He was later elected the President of Bharatiya Jana Sangh in 1955 for a brief period. He dedicated himself to the service of downtrodden poor, and proletariat part of society. As president of the Jammu and Kashmir Praja Parishad in 1949, Dogra was arrested along with hundreds of members of the party for demanding that only the Indian flag remain official. He was arrested again on November 26, 1952, during a demonstration against the hoisting of both the state and Indian flags in Jammu. The arrest and further developments led to the Praja Parishad agitation spreading to other parts of Jammu and Kashmir.[6]

Acharya Debaprasad Ghosh succeeded Premnath Dogra as President. Ghosh was an Indian mathematician, politician, lawyer, journalist and educationist. He started his career at the age of 21 as a professor of mathematics at the Ripon College. He was actively involved in politics as the President of Bharatiya Jana Sangh from 1956 to 1965, except for the period between 1960 and 1962. Debaprasad was born in a Bengali Hindu Kayastha family on 15 March 1894 in the village of Gava, in the district of Barisal, in eastern Bengal, now in Bangladesh. Debaprasad ranked first in the Entrance Examination in 1908 from Brajamohan School in Barisal. In 1910, he again ranked first in the I.A. from Brajamohan College. In spite of that he was denied scholarship as both his school and college were connected with the Swadeshi Movement. In 1912, Debaprasad stood first in B.A. (Mathematics) from City College, Kolkata and obtained the Ishan scholarship. He completed M.A. in Mathematics in the year 1914. He was also conferred with the title, " Ramanujan of modern times". His impeccable academic record says that he has never stood second ever in his life. His brother, Satyavrata Ghosh and his sister, Shantisudha Ghosh were prominent freedom fighters. He was associated with Hindu Mahasabha. He was actively involved in politics as the President of Bharatiya Jana Sangh from 1956 to 1965, except for the period between 1960 and 1962.[7]

Pitamber Das was president in 1960. He was the President of the Bharatiya Jana Sangh. He was a Member of Parliament, representing Uttar Pradesh in the Rajya Sabha, the upper house of India's Parliament, as a member of the Bharatiya Jana Sangh. He was known for his upliftment of the poor and depressed class. He worked towards providing opportunities to the poor. He has time and again been associated with social justice and managed to raise their issues at different platforms.[8]

Avasarala Rama Rao was the President of the Bharatiya Jana Sangh in 1961 and succeeded by Ghosh.[9]

Raghu vira succeeded Ghosh as President. Raghu Vira was born in Rawalpindi (West Punjab) on 30 December 1902. After gaining an MA from Punjab University, he received a Ph.D. from London and a D. Litt. from Leiden (Netherlands). He was in close touch with most of the Indologists of Europe during and after his three visits there. His early center of work after his three study trips of Europe was Lahore, where he became Head of the Sanskrit Department of the Sanatan Dharma College. At that time, his reputation as Head of the Department of Sanskrit of S.D. College was great. He was offered principalship of the college under the condition that he would not take part in politics. He turned down the offer.

He was elected first to the Constituent Assembly in 1948 and then to the Rajya Sabha in 1952 and 1957 by Indian National Congress. He left the party in 1961 because of differences with Jawaharlal Nehru over the China policy. His contribution to parliamentary and inner party debates with inside knowledge of China and South-East Asia was unique. He pleaded for a large anti-China, anti-communist front with the Buddhist countries of South-East Asia. After his return from a three-month cultural research tour of China in 1956, he told Nehru that China as a once 'cultural brother' of India, was dead, and that it was now an expansionist, materialist country. He had many skirmishes with Nehru in party meetings and ultimately resigned in December 1960 when the Chinese danger loomed large as the Government of India just watched aimlessly. Soon after his resignation, he was invited to the Jana Sangh and joined, as it was the only major party close to his views, with a strong network of cadres.

Raghu Vira's linguistic mission - Raghu Vira was a linguist and nationalist. He tried to organize Indian leaders against the imperialist monopoly of English. He had mastered many languages including Hindi, Sanskrit, Persian, Arabic, English, Urdu, Bengali, Marathi, Tamil, Telugu, and Punjabi.

He coined approximately 1.50 lakh (150,000) scientific and parliamentary terms with Sanskrit as the common base, just like Latin is for European languages. His Greater English-Hindi Dictionary remains his fundamental contribution to the cause of Indian languages. He was in touch with leading Tamil and Telugu scholars too for his research work.

Apart from his work of creating a scientific, technical and legal vocabulary for Hindi based upon Sanskrit, his reputation as a scholar will rest mainly on many editions of ancient Sanskrit texts, either his own direct work or inspired by him.

Raghu Vira aimed to re-establish India as Jagat Guru by researching, excavating, and collecting an estimated three lakh Sanskrit manuscripts spread worldwide. These are considered as the relics of the glorious work of the Hindu and Buddhist missionaries who served as cultural colonisers of Mongolia, China, Central Asia, South-East Asia and Indonesia.

As a result of his visits to many countries, huge number of relics and manuscripts were collected. These impressed leaders like Nehru, Chou En-lai, and Sukarno who extended personal encouragement, and appreciation to him for excavatory missions in search of Indian artifacts and manuscripts in those countries. When he came back from China after a three-month tour in 1956, he had a baggage of 300 wooden boxes with him containing rarest of finds, antiques and manuscripts, bearing on the deep cultural contacts between China and India. He established International Academy of Indian Culture (Saraswati Vihar). The Vihar was as Acharya Raghuvira's personal centre of research work in Indian culture, literature and religion, with studies in its widespread impact and proliferation from Mongolia to Indonesia, China, Russia, and Central Asia. It was established first at Ichhra near Lahore in 1932, and sensing trouble in 1946, he shifted to Nagpur a year before Partition. The State Government of Pt. Ravi Shankar Shukla provided him all the facilities for the rehabilitation of his research network.

The Vihar was later shifted to Delhi in 1956 and is still functioning under the stewardship of his son, Dr Lokesh Chandra. Prime Minister Jawaharlal Nehru, President Rajendra Prasad and ambassadors of nearly all South-East Asian countries used to visit it to see the progress of his work and his latest collections. Before embarking on his last fatal journey to Kanpur, he had divided his cultural mission among his son, daughter-in-law, two daughters, and a son-in-law.

The Indian National Congress recognized Raghu Vira's linguistic expertise and elected him first to Constituent Assembly in 1948, and then to Rajya Sabha in 1952 and 1957. In 1948, he clashed with Congress Party bosses on the question of Sheikh Abdullah's repressive policies against people of Jammu represented by Praja Parishad. Along with another Congress member, M.L. Chattopadhyay, he visited Jammu to see things for himself and issued a blistering report against Sheikh Abdullah's policies, which later on turned into the Sheikh's Azadi mongering Islamiat.

Even before RSS work began in Lahore, he started his Hindu Rakshak Sangh, and used to hold daily drills in DAV College grounds. There were great expectations when such a luminary with a grand Hindu cultural vision joined the Jana Sangh in early 1961. His gloomy prophecies about China came true within a year in the Chinese attack. His address at the Bhopal session of Jana Sangh in December 1962, a month after the attack, was a wonderful analysis of India's defense problems, foreign affairs, and economic policies.

Apart from being a scholar, he was also a man of great energy and the highest ideas, that he sometimes put into practice by working among the untouchables in villages and spending some time in Gandhiji's Sabarmati Ashram. His interest in politics came from Lala Lajpat Rai's ideas. In Delhi, he found time from his studies to work for improving the living conditions of people living in slums. His life ended in a car accident near Kanpur when, as Jana Sangh President, he was going to do election propaganda work for his socialist friend Ram Manohar Lohia's by-election in the Farrukhabad Lok Sabha constituency in UP in May 1963.[10]

Bachhraj Vyas was the President of the Bharatiya Jana Sangh in 1965. He was a member of the Maharashtra Legislative Council from 1958 to 1962. As its President, he was instrumental in grooming young firebrands who were ready to sacrifice their lives for the cause of the Nation.[11]

Balraj Madhok came from a Jammu-based Khatri family with Arya Samaj leanings. His father Jagannath Madhok was from Jallen in the Gujranwala district of West Punjab, and worked as an official in the Government of Jammu and Kashmir in the Ladakh division. Balraj Madhok was born in Skardu, Baltistan and spent early childhood at Jallen. He studied in Srinagar, the Prince of Wales College in Jammu and the Dayanand Anglo-Vedic College (DAV College) in Lahore, graduating with B. A. Honours in History in 1940.

While studying in Jammu, Madhok joined the Rashtriya Swayamsevak Sangh (RSS) in 1938, which he found to be close to the Arya Samaj way of thinking. He became a pracharak (full-time worker) for the RSS in 1942 and was appointed as a worker for Jammu. He is said to have worked in this position for about eight months, building up the RSS network. He then moved to Srinagar in 1944 as a lecturer in history at the DAV College and continued to work as an RSS organiser. He established the RSS network in the Kashmir Valley. When the Hindu refugees started arriving in Srinagar after the Partition, they also joined the RSS branches. Mehr Chand Mahajan, the Prime Minister of Jammu & Kashmir from 15 October 1947, was the Chairman of the managing society of the DAV College.

After the state joined India, and Sheikh Abdullah was appointed as the Head of Emergency Administration in the Kashmir Valley, Madhok moved back to Jammu. He worked to form the Praja Parishad party, founded in November 1947, in collaboration with Hari Wazir. Prem Nath Dogra also joined later. The party demanded the complete unification of Jammu and Kashmir with India, in opposition to the loose autonomy negotiated between Abdullah and Nehru (later embodied in the Article 370). Madhok was extended from Jammu and Kashmir by Sheikh Abdullah as a result of his political stance.

Madhok moved to Delhi in 1948 and started teaching at the Panjab University College, which was established for the education of refugees from West Punjab. Later, he was a lecturer of history at the DAV College in Delhi affiliated to the Delhi University.

In 1951, Madhok launched the student union of the Sangh Parivar, viz., the Akhil Bharatiya Vidyarthi Parishad. The Jana Sangh won only three seats in the Lok Sabha - two of them in Bengal, thanks to the influence of Mukherjee - and thirty-five in the Vidhan. But despite this reverse, Mukherjee contrived to become the main leader of the opposition in the new Lok Sabha by virtue of his eloquence and by gathering some forty members from the Jana Sangh and Ganatantra Parishad (a landowners' party in Orissa) into a single parliamentary group, called the National Democratic Party. This group was the third largest after the Communists. For Mukherjee, it was 'the beginning of the inter-communal, conservative, all-India party he had hoped to found'. Fueled as it was by Mukherjee's political ambition, this prospect was likely to displease the RSS since it implied a dilution of Hindu nationalist identity.[12]

The Jana Sangh and the Demand for the Abolition of Cow-Slaughter: The Cow Protection Movement

Indira Gandhi's inexperience and the Hindu traditionalism of certain Congress bosses help to explain why the Jana Sangh felt able to take up the issue of cow protection to build up the Hindu vote in 1966-67. The cow, as a symbol of Hindu identity, holds sacred character in Hinduism. This status, which has numerous explanations, "is recognized by all currents of Hinduism This was treated as a legitimate theme by a major body of opinion in Congress; Gandhi expressed his veneration for the cow on several occasions."

In 1949-50, there were prolonged debates in the Constituent Assembly between secularists, such as Nehru, and Hindu nationalists and Congress traditionalists, which resulted in an ambiguous compromise over cow slaughter. Its prohibition was recommended by Article 48 of the Constitution, i.e. at the level of the 'Directive Principles' to guide the states of the Union. Nehru had insisted on the fact that legislation against cow slaughter had to be a matter of relevance solely to the states. But apart from the refusal of certain states like Kerala, to restrict the practice, a judgement of the Supreme Court in 1958 limited the scope of laws passed against cow slaughter in the other states to draught animals.

There had already been protests against these restrictions from the RSS (in 1952 and 1954, in association with Prabhu Datt Brahmachari). In 1962, the Chief Minister of Madhya Pradesh, Kailash Nath Katju, and Nehru were denounced by Hindu nationalists as non-believers. This contributed to the success of LaxmiNarayan Pandey, a medical practitioner and member of the RSS, who defeated Katju, and was symptomatic of a political symbols that attained a new dimension during the 1960s.

The Bharat Gosevak Samaj (BGS, or Society to Serve the Cow) - whose patrons in Delhi, its base, were Hans Raj Gupta, Vasant Rao Oke and the businessman, Jai Dayal Dalmia - organized a conference in August 1964 to demand that the government should take upon itself the task of banning cow slaughter. Officially, the initiative for this came from the BGS, but the fact that Golwalkar opened the conference, that Prabhu Datt Brahmachari was there to give the event his blessing, and that D. Upadhyaya delivered an address. Furthermore, the date of the conference coincided with the launching of the VHP.

The question of the prohibition of cow slaughter was put decisively to the test in August 1966 by Jana Sangh MPs, including. Swami Rameshwaranand, an Arya Samajist from Haryana. The response of the Minister of Agriculture was to exhort the governments of the states, where the prohibition was only partial, to intervene, an approach that found favour with many Congress traditionalists. On 5th September, a delegation led by Seth Govind Das, sent a memorandum on the subject to G. Nanda, the Home Minister, who was reputed to support it. Meanwhile in Parliament, Swami Rameshwaranand had exclaimed, 'Glory to our mother the cow!', despite calls to order from the Speaker, as the result of which he was suspended for ten days.

A few days after the demonstration, according to the Sarvadaliya Goraksha Maha-Abhiyan Samiti (SGMS)'s plan, the Shankaracharya of Puri and Prabhu Datt Brahmachari began their fast; they were quickly arrested, which, as anticipated, aroused public ire. The RSS expressed its satisfaction at seeing the Shankaracharya continue his fast after being released, and members of the Jana Sangh fasts in solidarity and as acts of protest, which spread throughout the country. On the one hand, the Jana Sangh's national leaders busied themselves defending a liberal image. In parliament, Vajpayee denied that Swami Rameshwaranand was representative of the Jana Sangh's policy, and Trivedi accused the government of having encouraged the violence by its inadequate security measures. He even went on to support the demand of the Swatantra Party for a commission of inquiry. These efforts resulted from the desire to pursue a strategy of integration. On the other hand, instrumentalist practices prevailed at the local level. In addition to the cow, the Hindu nationalists also sought to exploit another universal symbol of Hinduism. The police's ruthless handling of these allegedly non-violent individuals led to the very public resignation of some MLAs from Uttar Pradesh.[13]

Although the Punjab crisis of 1966 had been a difficult one for the Jana Sangh, it had accomplished its retreat in good order and had not lost touch with its most valuable non-partisan ally, the Arya Samaj. At every stage in the conflict, the party had known what issues were at stake, and what penalties and rewards attached to different courses of action. After a suitable interval, it was able to come to terms with its old rival, the Akali Dal. Having redefined its goals in Punjabi politics, it was less likely to be committed to campaigns of high principle in defense of Hindu nationalism. This pattern and this outcome stand in sharp contrast to that which formed around the campaign for the abolition of cow-slaughter at the end of 1966, when the Jana Sangh was once again called upon to honour a commitment to one of the oldest and most emotional causes of Hindu politics. However, on this occasion, it found itself working with a range of relatively unknown and politically inexperienced pressure groups, groups capable of stimulating an agitational movement, which could sweep the Jana Sangh into an outright and damaging confrontation with organized authority.

In legal terms, the call for the abolition of cow-slaughter had been reduced to the demand that the central government should give effect to Article 48 of the Constitution of India, which stated that the state should, amongst other things, take steps for 'prohibiting the slaughter, of cows and calves and other milch and draught cattle'. Although this Article belonged to the Directive Principles, and was therefore intended only to provide guidance to the states in the making of laws, there had been several attempts to persuade the central government to prohibit cow-slaughter through an Act of Parliament.

The Jana Sangh consistently referred to the need for a ban on cow-slaughter in its manifestos, implying that it would serve both economic and religious ends; for example, the 1954 manifesto stated:

Cow is our point of honour, and the eternal symbol of our culture. Since immemorial times, it has been protected and worshipped. Our economy too, is based on the cow. Cow protection, therefore, is not only a pious duty but an indispensable need. It is impossible to protect and improve cattle so long, as its slaughter continues. The only way to stay the rapid decline of cattle is to ban its slaughter forthwith. Jana Sangh will impose complete ban on cow slaughter and, with the cooperation of public and administration, improve its quality.

When the 1958 judgement of the Supreme Court was announced, the Jana Sangh's Central Working Committee claimed that it had made 'the values and objectives which prompted the States to ban cow-slaughter ineffective in practice' and it therefore called for an amendment of Article 48 of the Constitution and demanded that those states which had not instituted bans should do so 'at the earliest'.

However, in spite of its rhetoric, the Jana Sangh left it to various other non-party groups to organize lobbying campaigns and demonstrations. In the mid-sixties, the initiative for a new national campaign came from the Bharat Gosevak Samaj (India Cow-Servant Society), which organized a two-day session of the All-India Goraksha Sammelan (Cow-Protection Conference) at Vrindavan, in the Mathura district of Uttar Pradesh, in August 1964. The Sammelan decided to ask the central government to pass legislation to ban cow-slaughter completely by Gopashtami (a day in the Hindu-calendar month of Kartik, which usually falls in October or November) in 1965, and to send a deputation to meet the President, the Prime Minister and other ministers and to place the demand before them. The session was blessed by Prabhu Datt Brahmachari, known as the Sant of Jhusi, who suggested that if the central government had not imposed a ban by a given date, a peaceful and nation-wide agitation should begin. The organizers of this session had canvassed the support of as many interests as possible, and the list of people who sent their good wishes included the Jagatguru Shankaracharyas (the heads of the four principal monasteries of Hinduism), three state governors and three central ministers. Golwalkar, the RSS leader, had inaugurated the Sammelan, and Upadhyaya of the Jana Sangh had been one of the speakers, but the extent of their commitment to this venture was not clear. In the following month, the Jagatguru Shankaracharya of Goverdhan monastery, located at Puri in Orissa, presided over a convention at Amritsar, which also demanded a ban on cow-slaughter by parliamentary legislation.

Although Parliament did not accede to these requests, the fact remained that many of the state legislatures had already adopted appropriate measures by 1966; a total ban on cow-slaughter, as interpreted by the Supreme Court, had been imposed by this date in all the northern states and in Gujarat, the Vidarbha region of Maharashtra, Bihar, Orissa and parts of Mysore, and a partial ban, on the slaughter of young and useful cows only, had been imposed in several other states and regions, including Assam, West Bengal and Madras. Only Kerala and the coastal regions of Andhra Pradesh had not imposed any ban. However, the Government of India decided that more progress was required, and on 23 August 1966, the Union Food Minister, Subramaniam, stated that the centre would once again draw the attention of the states to Article 48 of the Constitution. Meanwhile, the cow-protection groups were mobilizing their resources for another attempt to bring about a total and comprehensive ban, and on 5 September, they held a large demonstration outside Parliament House in New Delhi to make clear their views. A deputation led by Govind Das, a Congress MP, submitted a memorandum to the Home Minister, Gulzarilal Nanda, asking for central legislation to provide a ban. Inside the chamber of the Lok Sabha, Swami Rameshwaranand, a Jana Sangh member, raised a commotion by trying to draw attention to the demonstration outside and was eventually suspended from the house for the remainder of the session. Later in the month, an organization known as the Sarvadaliya Goraksha Maha-Abhiyan Samiti (SGMS, literally, the All-Party Cow-Protection Great-Campaign Committee) was established under the presidency of Prabhu Datt Brahmachari, who announced that if no agreement for banning cow-slaughter had been reached by 20 November, a 'mass satyagraha' would be launched, in which about 100,000 persons would court arrest. He warned that he and others would begin fasts unto death on that day, and that one-day hunger strikes would be held at district and tahsil levels.

Indirectly, the SGMS represented a wide range of Hindu religious institutions and Hindu nationalist associations. But, as its campaign gathered momentum, the responsibility for its decisions fell increasingly on a small group of leaders, which included Swami Karpatriji Maharaj (a prominent Ram Rajya Parishad figure), Swami Gurucharan Dassji Maharaj (President of the Bharat Sadhu Samaj), Muni Sushil Kumar (a leader of the Jain community), and Golwalkar of the RSS. The formal and spiritual leadership was provided by Prabhu Datt Brahmachari and by the Jagatguru Shankaracharya of Puri.

The central government was still endeavouring to influence the policies of those few state governments which had not yet imposed a total ban on cow-slaughter. Following Subramaniam's announcement on 23 August, the central Ministry of Food and Agriculture had communicated with state governments about the subject, and on 8 October, the Union Home Minister had written to the Chief Ministers of states in which only partial bans were in force, and to the governments of union territories, to remind them of Article 48 and of the 'widespread sentiments' in favour of a ban. He also pointed out that the central government was considering the formation of a committee on cow protection. On 29 October, acting on a directive from the central cabinet, he sent out another set of letters to the Chief Ministers concerned and requested them to consider this question further with a view to preparing legislations on the subject of cow slaughter for introduction in your state legislatures. I propose to announce that I have addressed the states concerned in this matter and that it is my expectation that they would consider this matter urgently.

Then, on 2 November, the Congress Working Committee advised the central government to impose a ban on cow-slaughter in centrally administered areas and union territories and to ask states where this had not been done 'to take similar action as soon as possible'.

It was thus quite clear that the central government and the Congress leaders were working together to place pressure on the states to adopt further measures against cow-slaughter and, had the SGMS been more politically aware, it would have realized that there was less to be gained from agitational methods than from negotiations with the central ministers concerned. However, its programme of demonstrations had already become a series of individual and group actions which were intended to culminate in a large procession through the streets of Delhi on 7 November. At its meeting at Nagpur early in that month, the Jana Sangh's Central General Council noted what was being done and assured the SGMS 'of complete co-operation'. It warned the central government that what it saw as its apathy was 'increasing public resentment':

The people have very deep feelings on the matter of the cow. If on any occasion this widespread public resentment goes out of control, the consequences would be serious and their responsibility will be completely on the Government. Hence the General Council strongly urges the Government to think seriously of the matter and ban cow-slaughter by amending the Constitution in the present session of Parliament.

On 6 November, the central executive of the Bharat Sadhu Samaj also warned that unless the government took such a decision before the 20th, the movement would be continued with 'full strength'.

The demonstration in Delhi on 7 November was organized by a number of associations, including the Hindu Mahasabha, the Jana Sangh, the Arya Samaj, and the Sanatana Dharma Sabha. Groups of demonstrators assembled in different parts of the city in the morning and then went in procession to Parliament Street, where the leading members of the SGMS and some parliamentarians, including Vajpayee, were seated on a large improvised platform. There were women and children in the crowd, many saffron robes were in evidence, and flags bearing the cow emblem were held aloft. The leaders on the platform rose in turn to make speeches, and the affair looked as though it would take a peaceful course until about 1.30 p.m. when, according to a later statement by the Home Minister, Swami Rameshwaranand stood up. Evidently referring to his suspension at the time of the previous demonstration in September, he asked those around him:

"why are you sitting here? I am driven out of this Parliament? Why don't you go and force this Parliament to close down? Why are you merely sitting here? Better go and surround this Parliament and see that Members and Ministers do not come out of the Parliament House."

From this point onwards the crowd became disorderly. In his account of what happened, Vajpayee said that Seth Govind Das and Prakash Vir Shastri spoke after Swami Rameshwaranand but that when he, Vajpayee, started to address the crowd, a sadhu had snatched the microphone away from him.

Now, the violent incidents began. Groups in the crowd pushed forward and tried to break through the police cordons protecting Parliament House. Sadhus armed with spears, and tridents were in the vanguard. The police tried lathi charges, and then tear-gas, but the rioting had spread well out of control. The police were forced to open fire and eight people (including one constable) were killed. Some people rampaged through government buildings, others overturned vehicles and set fire to them; the house of the Congress Party's President, Kamaraj, was attacked; and buildings and property were damaged in adjacent localities, including Connaught Place. A thick layer of smoke lay over the scene. Troops were brought into the city to assist in keeping order and a curfew was imposed. By the 9th, the police had arrested more than 1,450 people belonging to organizations connected with the SGMS, and Balraj Madhok, the national President of the Jana Sangh, was among them.

Aware that their party's reputation for moderation was now at stake, the Jana Sangh's spokesmen tried to argue that the violence had been instigated by trouble-makers who had succeeded in infiltrating an otherwise peaceful demonstration and that the authorities were at fault for not having dealt more firmly with the disturbances. Speaking in the Lok Sabha immediately after the demonstration, U.M. Trivedi claimed that from the very beginning 'it was noticeable that some unruly elements had got in and it was the Government's duty to see.' At this point, he was interrupted but he insisted that it was the duty of the Government to see that the situation would not go out of hand. Proper precautions ought to have been taken.

However, there was no denying the party's close association with the SGMS. In an editorial, the National Herald commented:

Swami Rameshwaranand, who is known to have incited a mob of unhinged minds with an inflammatory speech, has achieved temporary notoriety. In Parliament, Mr. Trivedi, leader of the Jan Sangh Party, had shown courage and decency in repudiating an unreasonably defiant swami. The more prominent of the Jan Sangh leaders, who were also parties to the demonstration, may have intended it to be peaceful, but they should not have associated themselves with others whom they must have known they could not manage.

Then came the news that it had been Kedarnath Sahni, the General Secretary of the Delhi State Jana Sangh unit, who had applied to the Delhi administration for permission to hold the procession on the 7th.

The most detailed and considered defence of the Jana Sangh's position was offered by Vajpayee to the Rajya Sabha on the 16th. He insisted that the procession on the 7th had been organized by the SGMS and that the Jana Sangh was not included in that body. In his vivid description of the events of the afternoon, he implied that groups of provocateurs, including a number of sadhus, had been planted in the crowd to stir up trouble and he demanded a full investigation of the incidents by a judge of either the Supreme Court or a High Court. Protesting against the number of arrests which had been made, he warned that the Jana Sangh would resist any attempt to use the incidents to attack the party: why are these people being arrested? Again, why are those opposed to the Jana Sangh defaming us? Is it because the leaders of the Congress are disturbed by the increasing popularity of the Jana Sangh?

Gulzarilal Nanda was backed Kamaraj for the important home affairs. The support of Kamaraj for Nanda is important in its own way because he was one of the openly pro-Hindu Congressmen. In 1956, he had been active in Hindu Sanghathan work through creating social institutions and goshalas. Indira Gandhi would later ensure that this reason would cause the downfall of Nanda. The unexpected police firing at the unarmed but highly agitated sadhus, demonstrating against the government demanding protection for cows, led to the sacking of Nanda by Indira Gandhi.

Some people evidently allowed mischief makers, and perhaps even goonda elements, to become part of the procession consisting mainly of sadhus. These elements forced their way into the precincts of Parliament House. The police naturally took action. Also, it appears, some of the mischievous elements even forced their way into the house of the Congress President. It was in the guise of Sadhus that some mischief makers were able to bring about violence, which ultimately created a problem for the Home Ministry that Nanda had to leave. The whole matter appears to have been engineered. Nanda's enemies won the day. Interestingly, this episode was twisted into an anti-Rashtriya Swayamsevak Sangh (RSS) urban legend in Tamil Nadu, which said that the RSS tried to kill Kamaraj in Delhi. In reality, it was a diabolically choreographed ploy in which Nanda and Kamaraj were on one side and Indira Gandhi and the leftists on the other. Nanda, who had the support of Kamaraj, was for cow protection.

Y. B. Chavan, who had succeeded Gulzarilal Nanda as Home Minister on the 13th, had this to say about the issue of responsibility when the incidents were discussed in the Rajya Sabha on the 17th:

"It was such a big demonstration; it cannot be undertaken by one person. There must have been many persons, organizations, their goodwill, their strength and their aid and it is their entire collective effort that really speaking can undertake a very huge demonstration of this type. Then out of the parties mentioned here, Jana Sangh was certainly one of the major participants in this. Highlighting the effects of Swami Rameshwaranand's remarks to the demonstrators just before the violence," he said:

"it cannot be denied that he is a representative of the Jana Sangh in Parliament. I am only referring to the minimum facts. That was the beginning of the whole trouble."

Vajpayee interrupted to say that Rameshwaranand 'did not speak as a representative of the Jana Sangh' but the Home Minister insisted on his point:

"Now, naturally when such a thing happens, people will try to hold responsible those who led the movement, who participated in it, who organized it, who gave all support, moral, material and manpower support. Can the Jan Sangh deny that they did not do that?" Interrupting once more, Vajpayee replied: 'We only deny that we indulged in violence'.

In spite of all the arrests, the campaign to ban cow-slaughter carried on; the Jagatguru Shankaracharya of Puri and Prabhu Datt Brahmachari, who began fasting on the 20th, were taken into custody, but they continued to fast, and by January 1967, their health was causing serious concern. Then, on 2nd January, the Working Committee and the General Council of the SGMS met together at Vrindavan and resolved to continue the movement; they requested the Jagatguru

Shankaracharya of Jyotirmath to postpone a fast he had decided to undertake and appointed him, alongside Swami Karpatriji Maharaj and Swami Gurucharan Dassji Maharaj, to see to the conduct of the agitation. In an effort to find a solution, the Union Home Minister offered to establish a committee representing central and state authorities, the SGMS and expert opinion to examine the subject of cow-protection. But, the representatives of the SGMS insisted that as a precondition, the central government should agree to a ban on the slaughter of 'all progeny of the cow'. Realizing that the campaign had now become a liability, however, the Jana Sangh's leaders began appealing for the fasts to be given up. "The Jana Sangh's posture is understandable", wrote the special representative of the Statesman.[14]

In 1963, Balraj Madhok, who had served as a Jana Sangh member of parliament from Delhi in 1961- 62, even proposed that the Jana Sangh unite with the conservative Swatantra Party to form a new party. While the Swatantra Party may have agreed, General Secretary Upadhyaya did not want the Jana Sangh to become transformed into a party of the right. In his view, anti-communism was not a sufficient justification for the step proposed by Madhok. The Jana Sangh working committee rejected the notion ostensibly because of the ambiguous attitude of the Swatantra towards Indian control of Jammu and Kashmir. Upadhyaya was then seeking to give a more populist orientation to the Jana Sangh, and a union with a political organization representing the interests of private capital and large landholders was unacceptable. Moreover, the RSS brotherhood could not have relished the prospect of a significant diffusion of its power for the uncertain benefits of the new party.

Even prior to the Jana Sangh's electoral understanding of the early 1960s, the party leadership was under some pressure to formulate a set of principles that would distinguish the Jana Sangh from other political parties. Perhaps prompted by the Jana Sangh's growing collaboration with some of the opposition parties following the deterioration in Sino-Indian relations, Upadhyaya responded to the demand for a distinct ideological statement by drafting a set of principles he referred to as Integral Humanism. He introduced the concept at the January 1965 meeting of the party's working committee, which adopted Integral Humanism as the Jana Sangh's official statement of fundamental principles. Upadhyaya gave greater substance to the notion in a series of lectures later that year in Bombay.

In 1966–67, Madhok rose to become the President of the Jana Sangh.He led the party in the general election of 1967, when the party won 35 seats in the Lok Sabha, its highest tally. Madhok tried to create a coalition of rightist forces along with the Swatantra Party. He saw the split in the Congress party in 1969 as an opportunity to expand the role of Jana Sangh. On 12 November 1969, the Prime Minister of India, Indira Gandhi, was expelled from the Congress party for violating the party discipline. The party finally split, with Indira Gandhi setting up a rival organization, Indian National Congress (Requisitionists), which came to be known as Congress (R) or Indicate/New Congress. In the All India Congress Committee, 446 of its 705 members walked over to Indira's side. K Kamaraj and later Morarji Desai were the leaders of the INC(O).[15]

Unofficial talks took place in March and April 1969 between leaders of the Jana Sangh, the Bharatiya Kranti Dal, the Swatantra Party, and the Praja Socialist party, at a meeting convened by Prakash Vir Shastri, a member of parliament from Uttar Pradesh. In those talks, Vajpayee, who had become party president following Upadhyaya's death in early 1968, insisted that any merger or electoral alliance must be preceded by a commonly accepted set of principles. The mysterious circumstances surrounding Upadhyaya's death on 11 February 1968 led many Jana Sanghis to conclude that he had been murdered. The wave of sympathy aroused by his death probably helped establish, among the cadre, the legitimacy of Atal Bihari Vajpayee, Upadhyaya's protege and member of parliament since 1957. Vajpayee had already become the party's parliamentary leader and its most articulate orator and public spokesman. Following Upadhyaya's death, he had considerable freedom to formulate policy and, as the opposition parties manoeuvred for alliance partners in the late 1960s, Vajpayee's preference was to avoid a relationship unless there had been a prior agreement on principles.

After the Jana Sangh's 1969 annual session at Bombay, the leaders of the Jana Sangh, Swatantra Party, and Bharatiya Kranti Dal resumed their talks. Because the Jana Sangh representatives ruled out the option of merger, and because they continued to insist on a consensus regarding principles, the Swatantra Party and the Bharatiya Kranti Dal leaders decided to continue their talks without the Jana Sangh. While Vajpayee and most of the working committee members were moving away from participation in any 'grand alliances', Madhok, and his supporters argued for a merger with other conservative parties. Political polarization was, in their view, the wave of the future. The Jana Sangh, being neither 'fish nor fowl', would became isolated from the voters unless it committed itself to one or the other of the developing ideological configurations. They pressed for a merger between the Jana Sangh and the Swatantra Party, and even coined a name for the projected party - the Nationalist Democratic Conservative Party. Madhok was infuriated by the leadership's refusal to heed his advice. In public speeches, he insinuated that the leftward tilt was due to some kind of collusion between the leadership and Prime Minister Indira Gandhi. He compared his differences inside the Jana Sangh to the disagreements between Jawaharlal Nehru and Vallabhbhai Patel. Madhok identified himself with the 'nationalist', 'democratic', and 'conservative' Patel; and he compared his opponents to Nehru. The Jana Sangh parliamentary board met in Delhi in September 1969 and censured Madhok for his remarks. Madhok denounced what he called the party's `leftist' leanings and the influence of the RSS on its functioning. His stand led to his marginalisation in the party. In 1973, L. K. Advani, who became the president, expelled Madhok from the party for three years.[16]

Despite pressure from the right, Vajpayee was reluctant to change the ground rules for negotiations on political alliances. However, the situation changed drastically when, on 27 December 1970, leaders of the Congress (O) led by Kamaraj and Morarji Desai, Swatantra Party, and the Jana Sangh met in Delhi to consider an electoral alliance. On 3rd January, party leaders announced that they were considering a national electoral alliance. About a week later, the Samyukta Socialist party (SSP) joined the discussions. The state units of the four parties were instructed to set up committees to allocate the seats among candidates of the four parties. On 25th January, the coordinating committee of the 'grand alliance', as it was called in the press, reached an agreement on 300 of the 520 parliamentary seats. Despite the public show of harmony, the allies were still deeply divided; the one issue on which they all agreed was their opposition to Prime Minister Gandhi.

The split can, in some ways, be seen as a left-wing/right-wing division. Indira wanted to use a populist agenda in order to mobilize popular support for the party. The Old guards led by K. Kamaraj, Morarji Desai, S. Nijalingappa, C. M. Poonacha, Neelam Sanjiva Reddy, Atulya Ghosh, S. K. Patil, Hitendra K Desai, Satyendra Narayan Sinha, Chandra Bhanu Gupta, Veerendra Patil,

P. M. Nadagouda, Ashoka Mehta, Tribhuvan Narain Singh, Ram Subhag Singh, and B. D. Sharma, who formed the INC(O), stood for a more right-wing agenda, and distrusted Soviet help.[17]

For the 1971 Indian general election, the Congress (O) under K.Kamaraj, Samyukta Socialist Party, and the Bharatiya Jana Sangh had formed a coalition called the "Grand Alliance" to oppose Indira Gandhi and the Congress (R), but failed to have an impact. Indira's Congress (R) won a large majority in the 1971 elections, and her popularity increased significantly after India's victory in the war of 1971 against Pakistan. However, Gandhi's subsequent inability to address serious issues such as unemployment, poverty, inflation, and shortages eroded her popularity.In the 1971 general election, the INC(O) won about 10% of the vote and 16 Lok Sabha seats, against 44% of the vote and 352 seats for Indira's Congress.[18]

In Bihar, the Vidyarthi Parishad participated in a statewide protest that accepted the Total Revolution concept of Jaya Prakash Narayan, a respected social reformer. Narayan advocated the replacement of a political system dominated by professional politicians with a form of participatory democracy. He initially directed his criticism at the Bihar state government, but in late 1974 concluded that no fundamental changes could take place unless the Total Revolution was broadened to include the centre on the grounds that Prime Minister Indira Gandhi controlled the policies of the state governments dominated by her Congress party. Thus the stage was set for a confrontation between the RSS, which supported Narayan's Total Revolution, and Prime Minister Indira Gandhi.

The Government of India in 1975 charged that the RSS 'family' of organizations was a force in the movement supporting Total Revolution, and with some justification. From late 1974, the Jana Sangh was closely involved in Narayan's activities. On 25 and 26 November 1974, Jana Sangh leaders met in Delhi with their counterparts from other opposition parties to establish a national coordination committee that would back Narayan's movement of Total Revolution. Organiser, the unofficial mouthpiece of the RSS, reported that the Jana Sangh leaders were considering a 'prolonged war of attrition in which civil disobedience and no-tax campaigns would play their due role'. Balasaheb Deoras, at a rally in Delhi on 1 December 1974, called Narayan a 'saint' who had 'come to rescue society in dark and critical times'. The Vidyarthi Parishad was already deeply and directly associated with Total Revolution.

While the central assembly of the RSS took the unusual step of supporting Narayan's Total Revolution, the RSS leadership did not deviate from the organization's traditional policy of keeping the RSS itself aloof from political activities, and it continued to do so until after the July 1975 ban on the RSS. However, RSS leaders certainly encouraged swayamsevaks 'in their individual capacity' to get involved.

Narayan for his part publicly praised the RSS (and other members of the 'family'). At the annual Jana Sangh session in March 1975, he dismissed charges that the Jana Sangh was 'fascist'. At an RSS camp, two months later, he complimented the RSS for its efforts to reduce economic inequality and corruption. Such praise from a respected national figure like Narayan was a major achievement for the RSS, as it reached out for public acceptance and for political protection.

INC(O) led governments in Bihar under Bhola Paswan Shastri, Karnataka under Veerendra Patil, and in Gujarat under Hitendra K Desai. It was also a part of the Janata Morcha that ruled Gujarat under Babubhai J. Patel from 1975–1976 during the emergency era.

The Janata Morcha ("People's Front") was a coalition of Indian political parties formed in 1974 to oppose the government of Indian Prime Minister, Indira Gandhi, and her Congress (R) party.

The grass-roots structure of the LSS included many RSS workers, which presented the RSS cadre with an unprecedented opportunity to gain political experience and to establish a working relationship with political leaders. This RSS activism promoted the careers of dynamic pracharaks, such as Rajendra Singh and H. V. Sheshadri.

RSS activism reached a high point during the 1975-77 Emergency and set the stage for a more dynamic organization in the post-1977 period. Regarding the Emergency period itself, RSS publications claim that the swayamsevaks played the key role in the underground movement, constituting the 'backbone' of the LSS, according to one senior RSS official. The RSS had also mobilized its extensive support network among overseas Indians to publicize the anti-Emergency effort internationally and to smuggle literature into the country. Whatever the extent of the cadre's role, no one doubts that it was significant. Even Prime Minister Indira Gandhi admitted in late 1975 that 'there has been no letup in its [RSS] activity. They are now functioning in an organized underground manner. Even in a region like Kerala, the RSS has established a foothold.' RSS sources claim that over 25,000 of its members were arrested under the Defense of India rules and an equal number under the Maintenance of Internal Security Act, many of them during the November 1975-January 1976 satyagraha organized by the underground RSS. Nana Deshmukh, a former RSS pracharak, with close ties to the top RSS leadership, was asked by Narayan to assume 'full powers' of the LSS when Narayan was arrested. Deshmukh had earlier been selected by Narayan to be the secretary of the LSS, perhaps because of the major involvement of the RSS 'family' of organizations in the movement of Total Revolution. Following Deshmukh's arrest in October 1975, Ravindra Varma, a Congress (O) politician, took charge. He was succeeded in November 1976 by D. B. Thengadi, a former RSS pracharak, who was then general secretary of the Bharatiya Mazdoor Sangh.

The Janata Morcha was formed by Jayaprakash Narayan and Morarji Desai as an alliance of political parties opposed to the Congress (R) and Indira Gandhi. The constituents included the Congress (O) led by Morarji desai and Kamaraj, Bharatiya Jana Sangh, Samyukta Socialist Party, and the BLD. The Janata Morcha won a surprising victory in the elections held for the Vidhan Sabha (Legislative Assembly) of the Indian state of Gujarat on 11 June 1975. The next day, the Allahabad High Court judged Indira Gandhi guilty of electoral malpractices, invalidated her 1971 election victory and barred her from elective office for six years. This led Indira to impose a state of emergency on 26 June 1975 and threw many major opposition politicians in jail including the leaders of the BJS. Indira's government used the state of emergency to clamp down on opposition and dissolved the newly elected assembly, preventing the Morcha from forming the government and taking power. During the emergency, the leaders and activists of the Janata Morcha were imprisoned. Kamaraj was among the few Congress (O) leaders who were not arrested, partly because he helped get her elected as PM, and because through their alliances in Tamil Nadu and Puducherry, they were well on their way to unite the two Congresses. C Subramaniam, a prominent Ruling Congress leader then, said Kamaraj wanted to take the plunge for a merger, but the Emergency happened. "My impression was that Kamaraj would have taken the plunge for a merger but he fell ill. Then Emergency was declared. He then became allergic to any decision taken during the Emergency, when his colleagues were in jail."[19]

On June 27, 1975, Kamaraj, at a public meeting in Sholingur, said, "I was shocked to hear that leaders have been arrested throughout the country. This state of affairs is not good for the nation. The country is lost ".

In 1977, the Emergency was withdrawn, and elections were announced. After the 1977 elections were called, the constituents of the Janata Morcha formally launched the Janata Party on 18 January 1977. Later the same year, INC(O) formally merged with the Bharatiya Lok Dal, Bharatiya Jan Sangh, Socialist Party of India, Swatantra Party, and others to form the Janata Party, determined to forge a united front of all opposition political parties. The Janata party replicated the success of the Morcha in Gujarat by winning the 1977 elections, and forming the first non-Congress government of India. In March 1977, the party fought the post-Emergency election under the banner of Janata Party.[20]

The Janata Party alliance inflicted crushing defeat to Indira's Congress Party. Nevertheless, the total vote share of Congress (O) in 1977 was almost halved from 1971 and they lost three seats. Congress (O)'s leader Morarji Desai served as the fourth Prime Minister of India from 1977 to 1979. The Janata Party became the first Indian government not led by what was by then called the Indian National Congress. Former BJS leaders, Atal Bihari Vajpayee and L. K. Advani became the External Affairs (Foreign), and Information and Broadcasting Ministers respectively.

Madhok was arrested during the Emergency and was imprisoned for 18 months (1975–1977). He joined the Janata Party, into which Jana Sangh merged, but resigned in 1979 and tried to revive Jana Sangh under the name Akhil Bharatiya Jana Sangh. However, the party was not successful.

Bhartiya Jana Sangh (BJS), the precursor to BJP, fought the general elections of 1977 as part of Janata Party group, though there was no formal merger of the two. The Janata Party won 299 seats out of 405 it fought. Interesting part was that the BJS emerged as the largest constituent of the Janata Party, with 93 seats, but BJS leaders Atal and Advani, never claimed for the Prime Minister's post. BJS selflessly sacrificed the whole party in the Janata Party Experiment, emerged as the biggest faction in the Janata Party and did not even claim for the Prime Minister's post, as for them the nation's interest was supreme.

1977 Janata Party experiment failed due to Prime Ministerial ambitions of Chaudhary Charan Singh and a few others, and country had to face fresh elections. In 1980 elections, the Janata Party managed to win only 31 seats out of 432 it contested, and again BJS contributed almost half of it – 15 seats. At this moment, factions started to re-surface within the Janata Party group. Threatened by the electoral successes of BJS section in the Janata Party in 1977 and 1980 elections, many socialist leaders within the Janata Party again raised the issue of 'dual membership' – meaning members of the Janata Party, cannot be a member of Rashtriya Swamsevak Sangh (RSS).[21]

The ousted PM, Morarji Desai, did try to work out a compromise to keep the former BJS members within the Janata Party fold. But, the national executive of the Janata Party on 4th April 1980, rejected the 'compromise' and, instead, resolved to expel all former BJS leaders from the party. This came both as a jolt and a relief to Vajpayee, Advani, and their followers. It was a jolt because they had made the 'supreme sacrifice' of merging the BJS with the Janata Party in 1977, following a call by Jayaprakash Narayan, with the hope of giving the nation a firm political alternative. And it was a relief because it was 'good riddance and finally, liberation', though they were 'proud to have been associated' with the party.

On 5–6 April 1980, at a two-day national convention, the erstwhile BJS members met in Delhi and resolved to form a new political outfit—the BJP, with Vajpayee as its founding President. It turned out to be a milestone in its journey as the party came into its own, and Vajpayee established himself as the undisputed leader of the Indian political spectrum. Vajpayee was of the opinion that the party should not look back but forward.

'We look to the future, and not to the past, as we begin our endeavour to rebuild our party. We shall move ahead on the strength of our original thinking and principles," Vajpayee said in his inaugural presidential speech. His speech, delivered in Hindi, was a typical example of his oratory excellence and his hope and confidence about the future. 'Andhera chhatega, suraj nikalega aur kamal khilega [Darkness will subside, the sun will rise and the lotus shall bloom],' he thundered. His speech was appreciated by leaders and journalists alike.

Today the BJP formed by Atal Bihari Vajpayee and Lal Krishna Advani is the world's largest party by membership size, with more than 18 crore members. It has formed the government in the center, the 5th time in its history in 2019, with last two governments under PM Narendra Modi having absolute majority in the Lok Sabha. It's ruling in 18 states, directly or through its partners. It's getting good vote share even in states like Kerala and West Bengal. It is no more a party of north India or the cow belt. The President of India, the Vice President of India, the Prime Minister, and the Lok Sabha Speaker are all from the BJP. At no other time in history has any non-Congress party been this dominant in India's polity. In many ways, the BJP today is where the Congress used to be in the 1950s.

Though the BJP was formally founded in 1980, its political journey started with the formation of the BJS in 1951. The BJS has his roots in the RSS and in other dharmic, cultural, and nationalist movements before it. So to understand, we have to go to the roots, the formations, the ideas, the leaders, and the ideological frameworks of the BJS, the RSS and the other movements before them, right back to the Arya Samaj & Hindu Mahasabha.

The understanding of the BJS and its leaders like Deen Dayal Upadhyay, Atal Bihari Vajpayee, and Balraj Madhok, added to this post-Independence discourse on nationalism. This discourse was clearly inspired by the ideas of freedom fighters like Lokmanya Tilak, Lajpat Rai, Bipin Chandra Pal, Madan Mohan Malviya, Aurobindo Ghosh, Savarkar, as well as spiritual gurus like Dayanand, Ramakrishna Paramahamsa, and Swami Vivekanand. The idea of cultural nationalism propagated by BJS and BJP leaders like Vajpayee and Advani appeared in continuation to the ideas practiced and propagated by Mukherjee, who believed in the age-old civilizational ethos of India.

Today is the day, when we should reflect back that current Ghar Wapsi debates have their roots in the Shudhi Andolan of Arya Samaj, in which Swami Sharaddhanand lost his life. Today's Hindutva and nationalist doctrine has its roots in the ideas of Savarkar. Debates around cow find its history in the cow protection movements of 1881. Today's political tactic of appeasement has its roots in the divisive ideas of Sir Syed Ahmed (Founder of today's Aligarh Muslim University). Today's corrections, like removing article 370, implementing National Citizen Register (NRC), and Ram Janm Bhoomi Verdict, have their history in major political blunders of the Congress Party in the past. Today's dissolution of centralized top-down governance structure of Planning Commission finds its roots in BJS' initial manifestos. It's noteworthy that Prime Minister Narendra Modi, captured this core essence of BJS and gave the motto of 'Nation First' and 'Sabka Sath, Sabka Vikas, Sabka Vishwas' to lead the aspirational India.

The BJP of today is the latest political manifestation of the years of nationalist movements that India has seen. As the Congress ruled the government for decades after Independence and the left ruled the academia, the story of the nationalist movement—from the Arya Samaj to the Hindu Mahasabha to the Rashtriya Swayamsevak Sangh (RSS) to the Bharatiya Jana Sangh (the BJS) to the Bharatiya Janata Party (BJP)—never got narrated in its entirety and purity.

Syama Prasad Mukherjee

Syama Prasad Mukherjee was born in a Bengali Brahmin family on 6 July 1901 in Calcutta (Kolkata).West Bengal. His grandfather, Ganga Prasad Mukherjee, was born in Jirat and he was the first in the family to move to Calcutta and settl there.

Syama Prasad's father, Ashutosh Mukharjee, was a judge of the High Court of Calcutta, Bengal, who was also Vice-Chancellor of the University of Calcutta. His mother was Jogamaya Devi Mukherjee. He was a very meritorious student, and he came to Calcutta to study in Medical College with the help of the wealthy people of Jirat. At sixteen years of age, Syama Prasad cleared his matriculation examination, and in 1921, he graduated with Honours in English from the prestigious Presidency College, Calcutta. When it was time for him to pursue his Masters, he chose Bengali instead of English, in deference to his father, who, as Vice Chancellor of Calcutta University, had introduced the language as a subject in 1906.

He enrolled in Bhawanipur's Mitra Institution in 1906, and his behavior in school was later described favorably by his teachers. In 1914, he passed his matriculation examination and was admitted to Presidency College. He stood seventeenth in the Inter Arts Examination in 1916 and graduated in English, securing the first position in first class in 1921. He was married to Sudha Devi on 16 April 1922. Mukherjee also completed an MA in Bengali, being graded as first class in 1923, and became a fellow of the Senate of the University of Calcutta in 1923. He completed his BL in 1924.

He enrolled as an advocate in the Calcutta High Court in 1924, the same year his father passed away. Subsequently, he left for England in 1926 to study at Lincoln's Inn and was called to the English Bar in the same year. In 1934, at the age of 33, he became the youngest Vice-Chancellor of the University of Calcutta; he held the office until 1938. During his term as Vice-Chancellor, Rabindranath Tagore delivered the University Convocation Address in Bengali for the first time, and the Indian vernacular languages were introduced as a subject for the highest examination. On 10 September 1938, the Senate of Calcutta University resolved to confer an honorary D.Litt. on the ex-Vice Chancellor, considering him "by reason of eminent position and attainments, a fit and proper person to receive such a degree." Mukherjee received the D.Litt. from Calcutta University on 26 November 1938. He was also the 15th President of the Association of Indian Universities during 1941-42.[22]

As a twenty-year-old man in 1921, Syama Prasad wasn't even half as politically aware as his father was at that age. According to Tathagata Roy in 'The Life and Times of Shyama Prasad Mukherjee', he very probably had designs on following in his father's footsteps to become an educationist and a lawyer. His philosophy of life seemed to be contained in the oft-quoted Sanskrit saying, "Chattranam

Adhyanam Tapah", meaning for a student, study is worship. Mookerjee was inspired by the ideologies of Swami Pranavananda, founder of Bharat Sevashram Sangha and considered him as his guru.

At the time of his death, the sixty-year-old Sir Ashutosh Mukherjee had quit as Vice Chancellor of Calcutta University due to a 'heated controversy' with the Governor of Bengal, Lord Lytton, over the funding of the institute. Prior to his stint with the University, he had retired as a judge of the Calcutta High Court and was regarded as one of the most deserving candidates for a career in public life.

A few months after his father's death, Syama Prasad Mukherjee was nominated to the Senate and Syndicate of the university; in 1934, he was appointed as Vice Chancellor of Calcutta University; and at thirty-three, he became the youngest in the history of the institute to preside over its affairs.

Despite all his outstanding achievements at a young age, he decided in the interim to firm up a career path that he felt was most suitable for him. According to several accounts, he was initially disinclined to be a full-time career educationist and consequently set sail for England in 1926 to study Law at Lincoln's Inn. He also represented Calcutta University at a Conference of Universities. A year later, the young barrister returned home, but instead of pursuing a legal career, he entered a field thought to be tailor-made for his late father: politics. In 1929, Syama Prasad was elected to the Bengal Legislative Council from the Calcutta University constituency as a member of the Indian National Congress.

Regardless of what was obviously a conscious political choice, Syama Prasad Mukherjee was beginning to feel constrained in the Congress party, most importantly, with what was its most potent weapon against the British: Mahatma Gandhi's mass mobilization movements, particularly the Dandi or Salt March which he had undertaken in 1930. Ironically, it was Gandhi who had eventually come to his rescue when at his insistence, all the Indian members of Legislative Councils were instructed to give up their seats throughout British India, facilitating Syama Prasad Mukherjee to resign from the Congress because he was opposed to the Civil Disobedience movement.

In retrospect, several writers have justified Mukherjee's decision to quit the Congress, propelled as he was, according to them, by a greater political insight than even Gandhi. But, the fact of the matter was that, apart from his discomfort with Gandhi, Syama Prasad strongly believed that mass agitations and resignations gave space for toadies, to play mischief. He felt it necessary that the interests of the university be safeguarded in the legislatures, particularly because education had become a transferred subject under the Montagu- Chelmsford Reforms of 1921.

In the aftermath of the mass resignations, although the legislative bodies were left with little or no credibility, Mukherjee decided to fight the impending elections from the same university constituency, but as an independent candidate. At a time when India was in ferment over the arrest of top Congress leaders, Mukherjee consciously shunned political campaigns and plunged head long into the job at hand by becoming an assistant to Hassan Suhrawardy, the Vice Chancellor of Calcutta University.

There was no doubt that Syama Prasad was an efficient administrator, but his vision for the university was no different from that of the British. On the one hand, if his parting with the Congress party in 1930 had given rise to his two decades-long opposition to its policies, it had also enabled his rise in the pecking order of the university. In 1934, he became the youngest Vice Chancellor of Calcutta University, a position that handed him 'the right to talk on just a little less than equal terms with the governor.'

Vice Chancellor Syama Prasad Mukherjee was insistent on producing a class of English-speaking 'brown sahibs' in the university. In his presidential address to the All-India Educational Conference in Nagpur in 1935, he said that educational institutions should be geared towards producing

'Students who are capable of providing leadership to our self-governing institutions, such as municipal corporations, provincial, and central legislatures'. In 1937, the poet-litterateur Rabindranath Tagore arrived in Calcutta University to deliver the annual convocation lecture and it was his endorsement of the institution under Syama Prasad's baton-introducing Bengali medium for several subjects; compilation of technical terms in Bengali, and most significantly, standardizing Bengali spellings—which had catapulted him from being the son of Banglar Bagh to an eminent educationist in his own right. In 1938, the thirty-seven-year-old Syama Prasad Mukherjee retired as Vice Chancellor of Calcutta University, and three months later, in recognition for his achievements, Viceroy Lord Brabourne conferred an Honorary Doctorate of Law upon him. In his address, the Viceroy said:

Nobody can say that Syama Prasad Mukherjee is being honored by this Honorary Degree because he is the son of a great father. It is because he is himself. He has earned every bit of it.

He was now his own master and was raring to go in the next decade and even further. Politics is My Destiny.

Syama Prasad had set sail for England in 1926 to study for Bar-at-Law. Although several students' groups were politically active in London at the time, Mukherjee steered clear of them. In the two years that he spent in London, he 'pursued his studies single-mindedly' and had no time for 'soapbox oratory at Hyde Park,' a fine tradition in the city since the 1870s when people gathered to hear speeches on religion, politics etc. The platform was also used by young Indian Communists and Congress supporters to protest against the British, but Mukherjee had little interest in such pursuits.

It may be recalled that when he had set sail for England, Syama Prasad Mukherjee was already a Senate member of the prestigious Calcutta University, and therefore, it seems logical to infer that his intention was less to acquire 'legal distinction' than to obtain knowledge about the workings of English and French universities. According to his roommate, Surendra Nath Sen, Syama Prasad was 'anxious to do the Bar Examination as quickly as possible', so that he could spend the rest of his time studying Western systems of education.

Within a few weeks of his arrival, he had to sit for the preliminary Bar exams in which his performance was anything but noteworthy. 'Under ordinary circumstances the result could be considered satisfactory if not creditable,' wrote Surendra Nath Sen and further added, 'but the tongue of calumny soon got busy.' The news of his average performance eventually travelled to India and was discussed at great length and with great delight by his detractors, including the then Vice Chancellor of Calcutta University, the renowned historian, Sir Jadunath Sarkar.

From August 1932 onwards, there was a palpable change in Bengal politics, and despite the anti-Imperialistic fervour across the region, religious identities were slowly beginning to occupy centre stage. For instance, the Colonial administration had introduced a separate electorate for Muslims under the Morley-Minto Reforms in 1909; in Bengal there were forty-six Hindu seats to thirty-nine Muslim seats and after the Communal Award of 1932, the Bengal Council had eighty seats for Hindus, while the number of Muslim seats had gone up to. Considering a large number of Hindu seats were allocated to the Depressed Classes (as the Dalits were then known) under the September 1932 Poona

Pact signed between Mahatma Gandhi and Dr B. R. Ambedkar; this had further angered the upper caste Bengali elite.

Syama Prasad Mukherjee, as part of a 'stunning array of Bengalis or bhadraloks (gentle, elite Bengalis), including Rabindranath Tagore, Sarat Chandra Chattopadhyay, Brajendra Nath Seal, and Dr P.C. Ray, petitioned the government, claiming that the 'Hindus of Bengal, though numerically a minority, are overwhelmingly superior culturally' because of which they were objecting to the 'unfair and unprecedented provision to protect a majority community.' Although group of erudite Bengali men exhorted people to hold meetings and pass resolutions protesting against the Award, the movement had failed to take off, because the arguments put forth by the petitioners were deemed 'too technical to draw the sympathy of newly enfranchised individuals' in rural Bengal. Although, Syama Prasad Mukherjee cut his teeth in politics by opposing the contentious Communal Award, albeit in a limited fashion, the kernel of the protest stayed with him ever since and later shaped his brand of politics.

Following his protest against the Communal Award, Syama Prasad began pursuing legislative activism, but soon realised the limitation of such interventions. He, therefore, shifted focus and became an understudy to his predecessor, Hassan Suhrawardy, who was the first Muslim Vice Chancellor of Calcutta University.

In 1934, as Vice Chancellor of Calcutta University, Syama Prasad was presented with his maiden opportunity to engage in student politics, when a few of his students began to involve themselves with European leaders. He encouraged the young academics and assured them of forging a 'close relationship' between the Italian Institute for the Middle and Far East and Calcutta University.

For a major part of the 1930s, Mukherjee's experiments with politics revealed a deep-seated desire to involve with non-Congress political groups. However, owing to his limited understanding of politics, save antagonism towards the Congress party, Syama Prasad committed blunders that he would come to regret later. For instance, in August 1936, the students of Calcutta University had invited Mohammed Ali Jinnah to address a meeting which was presided over by the Vice Chancellor. While introducing Jinnah, Syama Prasad had referred to him as 'an Indian nationalist...one of those fighters who knows how to fight stubbornly for the attainment of the ideal which they have made their own.' In response, Jinnah, who at the time was keen to showcase his nationalist credentials, was overtly pleased with the endorsement and thanked Mukherjee profusely.

The event at the university was held barely a few months prior to the 1936-37 elections to the Provincial Assemblies. Jinnah had arrived in Calcutta after addressing a series of meetings in several cities as part of his electoral campaign, and the captive students' community was just what he had needed to kick-start his campaign in Bengal.

In the impending elections to the Bengal Legislative Council, none of the political parties secured an absolute majority, because of members who happened to be independents. The Congress was indeed the largest party, but with an unimpressive tally of just fifty-four seats, followed by the Muslim League with thirty-seven seats, and the Krishak Praja Party (KPP) with one seat less at thirty-six. However, despite the lowest number of seats in the Council, the fledgling KPP stood out amongst the rest because it was headed by a distinguished lawyer and an extremely astute man called Abul Kasem Fazlul Huq, popularly known as Sher-e-Bangla (Tiger of Bengal). It may be recalled that Huq and Sir Ashutosh Mukherjee's monikers were the same, while Banglar Bagh was in Bengali, Sher-e-Bangla was more Hindustani. This so-called 'appropriate' reference in the language was, however, incongruous, given that Huq, or even his colleagues in his party, were Bengalis first and Muslims later. Even this small detail was indicative of the latent communal divide in Bengal, where even languages were segregated based on religious identities.

Meanwhile, the British were aware of Huq's facility for politics. The Governor of Bengal, Sir John Anderson wrote to Viceroy Lord Linlithgow about the man most succinctly as, 'the most certain quantity in Muslim politics, completely devoid of principle and trust of nobody.'

In April 1937, at the head of a fractious coalition, backed by the Muslim League, a few Europeans and members from the Depressed Classes, Fazlul Huq was sworn in as the Premier of Bengal. Despite the British's mistrust of him, the primary reason for his ascendance was the common objective of keeping the Congress out of the government, and in their collective pursuit, not only did they allow the Muslim League to become part of the ruling coalition, but allotted four ministerial berths to its members.

With Huq becoming Bengal's Premier, Syama Prasad Mukherjee began exploring other political avenues, and was gradually drawn to the Hindu Mahasabha. Surprisingly, he wasn't the only one to politically realign with another party, even Premier Huq was moving closer to joining the Muslim League. In fact, in 1940, Huq had moved the controversial Lahore or Pakistan Resolution which demanded the creation of a separate state from the Muslim-majority areas in India. Syama Prasad was quick to respond to what he viewed as a major transgression and declared that the Premier was essentially anti-Hindu. He quoted the Bengal Secondary Education Bill and the

University Bill in the context, which he felt had jeopardised the 'existence of Hindus as equal and self-respecting sons of the soil,' because it undermined an educational system, which was designed by the Mukherjees 'mainly with the cooperation and help of Hindu philanthropists.' His objections to the twin bills stemmed from the fact that they proposed to shift secondary education from Calcutta University (which was dominated by upper caste Bengali bhadraloks) to a Board of Secondary Education comprising fifty members drawn from Hindus, Muslims, Europeans, as also members of the government. In 1939, at the annual conference of All Bengal Teachers Association, Syama Prasad Mukherjee declared that if such a Board was ever established, 'we shall sever all connections with such anti-educational board and shall, if necessary, seek affiliation for our schools with an outside university.' He found ready support from several Hindus for what was perceived as a bold move, and even as Huq was forced to relegate the proposal to the back burner, it was Mukherjee's first major political victory against the Muslims.

In August 1938, Syama Prasad's resignation as Vice Chancellor of Calcutta University coincided with a No-Confidence motion against Fazlul Huq's government, which was eventually overcome but not before eroding the Bengal Premier's reputation both inside and outside the legislature.[23]

The Hindu Leader

In the midst of a severely polarised Bengal, made worse by a tottering Legislative Council, Syama Prasad Mukherjee met Vinayak Damodar Savarkar, in early 1939. The two men met in Calcutta in the course of Savarkar's 'whirlwind tour' of India, which he had commenced in 1938 after his release from the Cellular Jail in the Andaman and Nicobar Islands. To borrow Balraj Madhok's phrase, V.D. Savarkar had 'raised a hornet's nest' by joining the Hindu Mahasabha instead of the RSS.

Veer Savarkar came to Bengal again in August/September 1939, and Dr. Mukherjee was brought in close contact with him. Dr Mukherjee toured different parts of Bengal in September 1939 and was greatly perturbed at the helpless position of Bengali Hindus, whom the Congress, in my opinion, failed to rouse and protect. While touring eastern Bengal, he realized, how desperate the position of Hindus had become and how the spirit of resistance against an outrageously communal aggression was dying out - slowly but surely. This was how Dr Mukherjee, along with some others, were drawn to Savarkar's influence that gradually took root. Nirmal Chandra Chatterjee, a renowned barrister of the Calcutta High Court and Veer Savarkar's host in Calcutta, invited several prominent men of the city, including Dr. Mukherjee, for meeting him. Incidentally, Chatterjee was also the father of Somnath Chatterjee, the erstwhile leader of the Communist Party of India.

Dr. Mukherjee, who was deeply impressed by Savarkar's analysis of the Indian political situation and his gospel of unalloyed nationalism to checkmate the anti-national policies of the League and the 'cowardly passivity' of the Congress party, was pressed to join the Mahasabha by Nirmal Chatterjee, S.N. Banerjee, Asutosh Lahiri and others. Thus, circumstances inevitably led him to the Hindu Mahasabha, which took up precisely those issues that worried the bhadralok, many of whom despaired of any effective remedies from a Congress party led by the Bose brothers. His entry into the Mahasabha and his quick rise to the position of its working president marked the beginning of his active political career.

Dr. Mukherjee's entry was welcomed by Gandhi, who was greatly impressed by his thoroughly nationalistic outlook and told him, "Somebody was needed to lead the Hindus after Malviyaji [Pandit Madan Mohan Malviya]. Patel is a Congressman with a Hindu mind, you be a Hindu Sabhaite with a Congress mind. " Dr Mukherjee had quipped, 'But then you will dub me as communal.' Gandhi had replied, 'Like Shiva who drank the poison after churning the sea, somebody must be there to drink the poison of Indian politics. It can be you.' In fact, Gandhi, without ever saying so in so many words except as above, appears to have had a deep appreciation of Dr. Mukherjee's abilities. It was at his insistence that Nehru was induced to include him as the minister for industries in the first Indian cabinet in 1947.

At that time, there were two Hindu sabhas in Bengal, one that owed allegiance to the all-India body, and the other which functioned under B.C. Chatterjee's leadership. An agreement was reached between the two sabhas and they came together under the presidency of Sir Manmatha Nath Mukherjee. On 27 December 1939, Veer Savarkar launched the Mahasabha conference in Calcutta, flying its saffron flag over Deshbandhu Park. Nalini Ranjan Sarker, the astute but unprincipled politician, who had engineered the Haq-Muslim League coalition, claimed that the Mahasabha leaders had been 'attempting to win him over' for some time. According to Dr. Mukherjee, "This was a great beginning of a great struggle." This also heralded a new stage in his career. He came out of 'academic seclusion' and became an active political leader, although he continued to give much of his time and attention to university affairs.

Dr. Mukherjee found formidable obstacles when he started organizing the Hindu Mahasabha. Any nationalist Hindu consolidation was bound to be disliked by the British. He and his associates also had to encounter bitter opposition from the fanatical elements gradually gaining force under the banner of the Muslim League. Additionally, they had to meet resistance from the three important elements within the Hindu community—one being the Congress. Dr. Mukherjee's diary says, "Subhas [Bose] once warned me in a friendly spirit, adding significantly, that if we proceeded to create a rival political body in Bengal, he would see to it, by force [emphasis added] if need be, that it was broken before it was really born. This I considered to be a most unfair and unreasonable attitude to take up."

During his conversation with several members of the Bengali elite, Savarkar espoused 'his gospel of unalloyed nationalism as the only effective antidote to Muslim separatism and divide-and-rule policy of the alien rulers.' Mukherjee was already a convert, considering he had raised the anti-Hindu bogey against Fazlul Huq, and by the end of Savarkar's visit, he had become a devout loyalist. In his biography of V.D. Savarkar, Dhananjay Keer wrote, 'Indeed, Dr. Mukherjee was a discovery of Savarkar's tour of Bengal.'

On 9th October 1939, Lord Linlithgow invited Savarkar and some of his associates for a meeting to discuss Indians enlisting in the Second World War as part of the Imperial army. Prior to the meeting, Savarkar had conferred with Syama Prasad Mukherjee and informed the British that he was, 'prepared to cooperate in the policy of militarisation.' In turn, Linlithgow impressed upon Secretary of State for India, Lord Zetland that the British 'must now turn to the Hindus and work with their support', and although the colonial administration and Hindus had 'had a good deal of difficulty with one another in the past,' their 'interests were now the same, and we must therefore work together.'

In December 1939, Savarkar's 'find' played a stellar role in organising the annual convention of the All India Hindu Mahasabha in Calcutta and was rewarded with the post of Vice President. At the convention, the Mahasabha's main thrust was on addressing the insecurities faced by upper caste Hindus, and it even passed a resolution to this end which claimed that the Hindus' 'situation as a community is deteriorating day by day,' and how 'Hindu women are oppressed, Hindu boys and girls are kidnapped...Hindu temples are polluted and Hindu idols are destroyed.'

The Viceroy happened to be in Calcutta that day, and in his report to the government, he described the convention as a 'monster meeting from which has emerged a series of resolutions highly communal in character and condemnatory of the Congress.' Linlithgow further added that it wouldn't surprise him if the Mahasabha stole 'a certain amount of the Congress thunder.'

Within a few months of the convention, Syama Prasad Mukherjee was elevated as the Hindu Mahasabha's acting President, primarily because of V.D. Savarkar's failing health. Finally, three years later, in 1944, Syama Prasad became the President of the Hindu Mahasabha.

Apart from the common ideological plank that he shared with the Hindu Mahasabha, Mukherjee's decision to join the outfit in 1939 was clearly part of a carefully-orchestrated plan.

He had ably elicited the support of several members of Calcutta society, including influential Marwari businessmen (the list of donors for the Calcutta convention included the Birlas, Goenkas, Jalans, Kanodias, and the Khaitans), and even members of the Congress party.

It was more than evident that Syama Prasad had joined the Mahasabha with a definite objective and which was to 'make it an effective instrument for checkmating the anti-national policies of the Muslim League and the cowardly passivity of the Congress.' Within months, Mukherjee not only began to target M.A. Jinnah, whom he had once described as a 'nationalist', but also sharpened his criticism against Fazlul Huq's regime.

The Premier of Bengal was already combating the sudden and large exodus of ministers from his government, including his Finance Minister Nalini Ranjan Sarkar, who was one of the founding members of the Krishak Praja Party. A prominent Hindu leader, Nalini Ranjan was inducted into the Huq Cabinet with an aim to soften the anti-Hindu rhetoric, which obviously came to naught after he quit the party. The impact of his resignation was such that no Hindu legislator thereafter considered joining the Huq government until the jinx was broken by Syama Prasad Mukherjee in 1941, but more of which later.

In 1940, during the local body elections in Bengal, Syama Prasad Mukherjee led the Hindu Mahasabha in forging an alliance with Subhash Chandra Bose. Although the two men were bitterly opposed to each other's ideologies, Bose and Mukherjee decided that a three-way split between the Congress, Hindu Mahasabha and Muslim League would ultimately benefit the latter.

Dr. Mukherjee had mean whise been impelled to enter the political arena to save Bengali Hindus from their miserable plight, as a result of being systematically humiliated and persecuted by the Muslim League with the connivance of the British. The task that faced him in Bengal was twofold. He had to establish his position vis-à-vis the Congress leadership which had come to regard the Hindus as their own flock, who could be fleeced by them at will. He also had to meet the challenge of the Muslim League. The main figure on the Congress side in Bengal at that time was Subhas Chandra Bose, whose stand against Gandhi at the Tripuri Congress, and subsequent exit from the Congress presidency had made him a hero in Bengal. He was planning to hold Bengal, and particularly Calcutta, as his own citadel, to demonstrate his strength to the Congress high command by winning its corporation election that was scheduled to be held in March 1940. While the official Congressmen found themselves totally unprepared to fight against Subhas, the Bengal Hindu Mahasabha, which wanted a strong Hindu Sabha party in the Calcutta corporation, decided to contest the elections.

This pitted the two stalwarts directly against each other in their bid to win the loyalties of Bengali Hindus. The Mahasabha was prepared to work with Subhas and run elections jointly, provided they also worked as a team in the corporation later on. Subhas agreed to this but the situation soon made him realize that in a tripartite contest between the Hindu Mahasabha, the Muslim League and his men in the name of the Congress, the League might secure a majority. Dr. Mukherjee and Bose then agreed that the Mahasabha and Subhas's Congress should contest an agreed number of seats to be determined by mutual consultation. A selection board was formed, Subhas, Sarat Bose, and Rajendra Chandra Deb representing Subhas's Congress, and Dr. Mukherjee, S.N. Banerjee, and Sanat Kumar Roy Chaudhury representing the Hindu Sabha.

Then began an unfortunate mutual game of attrition. Constituencies were accordingly selected and candidates approved, but in respect of just two constituencies, the two groups could not arrive at any agreed decision about the candidates to be set up. One night after a long and heated discussion, Sarat Bose broke the joint front.[24]

The Muslim League, on its part, was clearly intent on playing the communal card and shortly before the polls, passed the Lahore Resolution demanding a separate country for Muslims. As a man who had mooted the resolution in the first place, Fazlul Huq now unequivocally asserted that he was a 'Muslim first and Bengalee afterwards.'

Despite gaining support amongst his community, Fazlul Huq was losing his grip over Bengal with each passing day. In contrast, Syama Prasad Mukherjee had succeeded in gaining credence and won the trust of upper caste Hindus. In early 1940, he was invited by the RSS to attend a meeting in Lahore and said that, 'the one silver lining in the cloudy sky of India,' was none other than the Rashtriya Swayamsevak Sangh.

Political Options

As was evident, Mukherjee and Huq had sharp public differences, but Bengal's political demography was such that it compelled them to work together. The reason: since Hindus made up for almost forty-four per cent of the total population of the province, 'no Muslim ruler could feel secure without some Hindu support.'

The wily administrator that he was, Fazlul Huq was cognisant of the fact that getting the Hindus to support his endeavours would become an impossibility if he remained associated with the Muslim League, and he therefore parted ways with M.A. Jinnah. On 17 December 1941, Syama Prasad achieved the near-impossible and began a new phase in his political career as Finance Minister in the Fazlul Huq-led Progressive Coalition government. This classic case of a politically convenient marriage required no analysis—while Mukherjee's political ambition took flight. Huq described himself to be 'the best defender of Hindu interests and Mukherjee (of)... Muslim interests.'

By 1941, Bengal had plunged deep into a communal abyss. Syama Prasad was somehow completely oblivious of its portent and was guided by the belief that by joining the Huq ministry, he would succeed in keeping the 'Muslim League's communalism, British's divisive policies and the Congress's browbeating at bay.' In one of his interviews to a local newspaper, Mukherjee had quoted the Secretary of State for India, Leo Amery, that despite several differences, Bengal could 'combine for the good of the country.'

With the passing of Rabindranath Tagore in August 1941, it was left to the other cultural icon of Bengal, the poet Qazi Nazrul Islam to hail the Huq-Mukherjee partnership as a big step in forging Hindu-Muslim unity. The poet's association with the warring duo-turned-allies rekindled hope in the people of Bengal that together they would overcome the communal fault lines. The endorsement by an eminence grise of the Bengali literary world was based on the enthusiasm manifest in the initial days of the alliance when not 'a single instance of communal rioting' was reported, and the generous allocation of one lakh rupees by Finance Minister Mukherjee for promoting communal harmony in the state.

One of the reasons for this was due to the Muslim League's sustained campaign against Fazlul Huq for 'betraying' Muslim interests. Finance Minister Syama Prasad had immediately sprung to Premier's Huq's defence and voiced his protest against the 'dirty calumny' spread by leaders of the League, mainly M.A. Jinnah. But in actual terms, despite the camaraderie, neither could Mukherjee aid Huq's cause amongst his Muslim brethren, nor secure support for himself amongst Hindus. In his book, Rajmohan Gandhi argues, how the experiment had failed in bridging the gap between the Hindus and Muslims of Bengal:

Though apparently successful, the bud was four years too late. Hindu and Muslim legislators should have been combined in 1937. The opportune moment was missed by Bose and others in the Congress. The November 1941 exercise did not bring Hindus and Muslims together. Haq's exercise was seen by Bengal's Muslims as a Hindu manoeuvre.

As mentioned earlier, after the initial euphoria of having joined hands with Fazlul Huq, Finance Minister Mukherjee swiftly began losing support amongst his constituency. His credibility was further eroded after the Congress launched the Quit India movement in August 1942. Even as leaders such as, Subhash Chandra Bose were escalating the anti-Imperialist struggle in the face of repressive measures, the Hindu Mahasabha, Muslim League, and the Communists opposed the Quit India movement, albeit for different reasons.

Unlike Congress ministers in other provinces, who had resigned in protest against the oppressive measures of the British in the aftermath of the Quit India movement, Syama Prasad Mukherjee was faced with a difficult choice - 'to defend Congress's rebellion during a war would invite dismissal, but to defend the Raj's repression when India's freedom movement was at its climax would invite the public's censure. At a time when there existed no middle path, Mukherjee attempted to find one. The Governor of Bengal asked Mukherjee and other ministers to either resign or endorse British policies. In response, Mukherjee appealed to the Viceroy to declare India independent and initiate steps to form a transitional government. He further added that if the demand was overturned, and the administration allowed the 'present impasse to continue, I must regretfully ask my governor to relieve me of my duties as a minister so that I may have the full freedom to help mobilise public opinion.'[25]

We can now return to the Quit India movement. Gandhi finally gave the call of 'Quit India' from the Gowalia Tank Maidan (now called August Kranti Maidan) in Bombay on 8th August 1942, when the All-India Congress Committee approved the resolution. The British almost instantly retaliated by throwing all the principal Congress leaders in jail the very next day and, as a result, the movement became a disjointed one, led mainly by second or third-rung leaders with local followings.

The other political parties also did not follow the Congress in the movement. The communists openly sided with the British and made efforts to derail the movement. The previous year, Hitler had launched his Operation Barbarossa, or the attack on Soviet Russia. Until this point, the Indian communists had dubbed the war an 'Imperialist War' and opposed it. With the attack on the Soviets, they changed their line overnight, and what was the Imperialist War now became the 'People's War'. From this point onwards, the Indian communists totally sided with the British and indulged in abject hypocrisy to whitewash the misdeeds of the British. The Muslim League and the Hindu Mahasabha both distanced themselves from the movement. Dr Mukherjee, a Hindu Mahasabhaite since 1939, toed his party line and continued with parliamentary politics. Dr B.R. Ambedkar, the leader of the scheduled castes, was also bitterly critical of the movement, saying that it was a mad venture which took the most diabolical form and proved to be a complete failure.

Haq told Dr. Mukherjee upon his return to Calcutta that important secret instructions had arrived from the Government of India and he had requested the Governor to place the whole matter before a cabinet meeting. The Governor declined to do so and replied to Haq that the cabinet would meet later. Herbert expected any minister who disagreed with the Government of India's policy would forthwith resign. The ministers met to consider the unprecedented situation. Responsible ministers were to be treated with suspicion and refused access to important documents which were being secretly discussed with ICS officers—this was a real mockery of provincial autonomy. On the morning of 9th August, the Governor summoned the cabinet, but the meeting could not proceed and had to be adjourned. This is because all the ministers insisted that they would not proceed without seeing the documents. As the ministers were about to leave the Government House, Additional Home Secretary Porter came with the file and handed it over to the Chief Minister who gave it to Dr Mukherjee. He took the file home and read it very carefully. It was clear that long before the Congress could give any provocation, the government had decided to start its campaign of repression, and all the details for this purpose were elaborately outlined in the letter. It was tersely put that 'prevention was better than cure' and this time, the government was determined to anticipate a possible revolt and sternly deal with the situation from the beginning. The government appeared to have a clear foreknowledge of the phase of the freedom struggle, namely the 'Quit India' phase that was coming, and was quite adequately prepared for it. Or could it have been an insider who had passed on advance information on it? We shall never know.

It was clear that the government envisaged running Bengal through the Governor and the ICS coterie, keeping the ministers as figureheads. Dr. Mukherjee felt very uneasy about the whole thing, as it was useless to function as a minister when they would become mere tools at the hands of the bureaucracy. The ministers met at the house of the Nawab of Dacca to decide a course of action, but the meeting broke up without a final decision. It was clear that none of the ministers was willing to resign. All of Dr. Mukherjee's colleagues begged him not to resign and precipitate the matter. The Governor, on the other hand, felt that Dr. Mukherjee would most likely quit office. Herbert reminded the ministers that the policy was that of the Government of India, and that was unchangeable. If any minister disagreed with it, he would be glad if he offered his resignation at a time when India was threatened with a dangerous war.

Dr. Mukherjee's personal views on the Quit India resolution were, however, balanced and not completely in line with that of the Mahasabha. He was in complete agreement with the patriotic content of the resolution, but had serious reservations as to the technicalities, and these points to his eye for detail and his political foresight. Before the adoption of the resolution by the AICC, it had been approved by the Congress Working Committee meeting at Wardha in July 1942, and about this, Dr Mukherjee, was wary and watchful. [26]

Dr. Mukherjee, on 8 September 1942, requested the viceroy for an interview, especially to obtain his permission to meet Gandhi at Poona. He was granted such an interview the next day. Among other things, Sikandar Hyat Khan was proved absolutely right. The interview did not go well for Dr. Mukherjee who had to face a lot of uncomfortable questions which could not be answered - neither by him nor anyone else.

Linlithgow told Dr. Mukherjee that he had ruined his chances of acting as a mediator by insisting on prior repudiation of Pakistan by His Majesty's Government as a condition of any settlement. He then asked him to explain what he meant by 'national government', to which Dr. Mukherjee had to confess that he really had no clear idea. He said that national government was national only if it was really representative. Linlithgow asked if Dr. Mukherjee expected to get the Congress and the League to support his national government, to which Dr. Mukherjee had to reply that he had little hope of either. Secondly, Dr. Mukherjee could give no answer to the question whether he expected that a government based essentially on the Mahasabha, without either Congress or the League, could be described as 'national' in a true sense. Thirdly, he admitted that the risk of severe communal trouble in the event of a completely Hindu political government at the Centre was not negligible. Finally, the viceroy added that any alternative to his existing executive council must be able to deliver the goods in terms of popular support and give full support to the war. Dr Mukherjee's argument was the usual one--that if the Muslim League would not play, and the Congress could not play, the British ought to give the vacant seats to the Mahasabha. Linlithgow warned him that if he was thinking of a government based essentially on the Mahasabha, with odd sections of the Muslims, he could hardly hope for much success if both Congress and the Muslim League were out in opposition.

Dr. Mukherjee found the viceroy very bitter. He said that the Hindus were doomed, as Jinnah was made great not by the government but by the Congress who made the mistake of taking him seriously about Pakistan. He frankly admitted in his diary: 'However much I disagree with the viceroy on other matters, there was a good deal of truth in what he said.' Anyway, Linlithgow did not say that the door was closed to any constitutional progress. He clearly told Dr. Mukherjee about the practical objections likely to operate against his scheme. When the latter asked if he could go and see Gandhi, the viceroy replied in the negative. He then asked if he could come back in a few days. The viceroy said not unless there were some really substantial changes in the position. Dr. Mukherjee merely told the press that he had a 'full and frank' discussion with the viceroy but his diary records his disappointment: "Thus our efforts failed. But we demonstrated that in spite of tremendous odds, an agreement between the Hindus and Muslims and also other communities could [be reached] only if the British Government took a rational view of things."

Then, Dr. Mukherjee met Jinnah. Here were two people, politically at two opposite poles, completely convinced of their positions, and not prepared to concede anything to the other without a real struggle, and without solid political logic behind. They met as resolute, self-respecting equals no brotherly business here, no coaxing, no genuflections. This meeting was in Delhi and lasted for three hours. Dr. Mukherjee records that they spoke very frankly to each other. According to V.P. Menon, the principal idea which he had put to Jinnah was that representatives of the two communities should meet and that each should explain in what respect it expects protection from the other. The Mahasabha would be willing to concede the fullest measure of autonomy to the provinces and would give the minorities the maximum protection in respect of their religion, language, and customs. On the question of Pakistan, however, Jinnah was as adamant as Dr. Mukherjee was against it and they could not discover a point of contact. Dr. Mukherjee reminded Jinnah that before Cripps came out to India, all that Jinnah wanted was that his Pakistan should not be tabooed, but considered dispassionately at the time of constitution-making. Dr. Mukherjee asked why, on that basis, should they not agree to demand from the viceroy the immediate establishment of an interim national government, followed by the release of Congress leaders. Jinnah's reply was immediate. He said that the situation had changed since Cripps gave him something like Pakistan, though it was not exactly what he wanted. His basis for settlement would now, therefore, be the acceptance of the principle of Pakistan here and now, and only then could he talk of an interim settlement. Dr. Mukherjee exposed to him the utter fallacy of his Pakistan logic, but it made no impression on him. In any case, as Dr. Mukherjee notes in his diary, there was no acrimony between the two, and they agreed that they should not issue statements accusing each other, but would consider themselves happy that they had tried to explore each other's point of view, respecting each other's sentiments. He served as the Finance Minister of Bengal Province in 1941–42 under A.K. Fazlul Haq's Progressive Coalition government which was formed on 12 December 1941 after the resignations of the Congress government.During his tenure, his statements against the government were censored and his movements were restricted. He was also prevented from visiting the Midnapore district in 1942 when severe floods caused a heavy loss of life and property. He resigned on 20 November 1942 accusing the British government of trying to hold on to India under any cost and criticised its repressive policies against the Quit India Movement. After resigning, he mobilised support and organised relief with the help of Mahabodhi Society, Ramakrishna Mission and Marwari Relief Society.[27]

The Viceroy deigned to not reply, and Syama Prasad bought time and postponed his resignation. Yet, he was well aware of the rising tide of opposition against the British, and in order to regain lost ground, he used the ruse of inadequate relief measures in cyclone- struck Midnapore as the reason for his quitting. His resignation letter of 20 November 1942 listed two main reasons - first, in a classic instance of doublespeak, he expressed his opposition to the coercive steps taken by the British administration after the Quit India call, and secondly, the Governor's bid to convert the principle of 'provincial autonomy into a meaningless farce.' Mukherjee and Huq parted, but not as bitter rivals, for they remained cordial even after Partition when the latter became a leader of some significance in East Pakistan.

The British government, on its part, suppressed Syama Prasad Mukherjee's resignation letter, as a result of which he paraphrased it in a speech to the Bengal assembly in February 1943. This was indeed a clever ploy, as the Defence of India rules were not applicable to disclosures in legislatures! With that one single tactical act of defiance, Mukherjee had succeeded in proving his patriotic credentials. He explained why he had become part of Fazlul's ministry in the first place and as mentioned earlier, said that 'this way he would be able to keep Muslim League's communalism, British divisive policies and Congress's browbeating at bay.' But it was indeed doubtful if he had managed to accomplish any of these objectives. In 1943 during Bengal Famine, Around 50 lakhs people died of hunger. Mukherjee - Organised large scale relief work during the famine of Bengal.

After his resignation as Finance Minister, Syama Prasad Mukherjee set about the task of re-positioning himself as an effectual Opposition leader in the Bengal Council under the newly-installed Muslim League dispensation. It may be recalled that he had also bolstered his image by playing a pivotal role in the Bengal Relief Committee, which was set up in response to British apathy towards the famine. During a debate in the Legislative Council in July 1943, Mukherjee said that the government was fiddling while the villagers in Bengal were crying for a morsel, They (British) want to first provide for their troops... forgetting their responsibilities to the people.' Meanwhile, he also campaigned against the Secondary Education Bill introduced by the Muslim League government, terming it anti-Hindu. In response, the Muslim League declared that the Bill was 'for the Muslims, and that was why it was being attacked by Hindus.' Finally in May 1944, when it was felt that there shall not be any let-up in the barrage of provocative statements from both sides, Mukherjee demanded the setting up of a non-communal and autonomous board for secondary education.

The controversy over the secondary educational board had not even subsided, when the Hindu Mahasabha picked up yet another issue to agitate about: the revival of the Chakravarti Rajagopalachari Formula, popularly known as the C.R. Formula. The idea was first mooted by the Congress stalwart in 1941 and was widely denounced, for it had ratified the idea of Pakistan. Three years later, in September 1944, Mahatma Gandhi and Jinnah met to discuss the issue yet again.

The Mahasabha, led by V.D. Savarkar criticised the meeting in strong words and claimed that it was the beginning of a 'downward course of Gandhi's monopoly of power as a leader.'

However, Syama Prasad disagreed with Savarkar's postulation, and proceeded to meet Gandhi, who reiterated that while there was no room for abandoning a dialogue on the issue, he also gave Mukherjee an assurance that he would reject the idea of Partition. Thereafter, Gandhi met Jinnah yet again and turned down the proposal of partitioning the country. The second meeting between Gandhi and Jinnah provided Mukherjee an opportunity to raise the 'irrelevant' issue of Partition, and he was catapulted to the centre stage yet again. In 1944 Presided over the Bilaspur session of the All-India Hindu Mahasabha and Founded an English daily, "Nationalist."[28]

Dr. Mukherjee followed this letter by a personal meeting with Gandhi at Wardha on his way back from Poona early in August 1944. C. Rajagopalachari was also at Wardha at that time. Dr. Mukherjee placed before them both the inherent dangers in any scheme of partition of India on the basis of religion. With a prophetic vision, he told Gandhi that if Pakistan was created it was bound to have a foreign policy opposite to that of India, which would endanger India's security and create very many new and unseen problems.

Gandhi, in reply, told him that he was committed to meet Jinnah and that he could not go back on it. But he assured him that he would never accept partition of India so long as he was alive.

This gave some consolation to Dr. Mukherjee. But his fears were not wholly allayed. He gave expression to his fear and anxiety in his presidential address to the 26th session of All-India Hindu Mahasabha held at Bilaspur in the last week of December 1944. "Mr. Jinnah's dream of Pakistan," he said, "was fading away even from the minds of a section of his own followers. His prestige and that of the Moslem League were on the wane when Gandhiji came forward to give his blessings to what is called the C.R. Formula and thus gave the League a fresh lease of life. Mr. Jinnah has rejected even this scheme and asks for further surrender. Gandhiji's commitment however remains... Once we allow religious considerations to determine the sovereignty of particular areas in India, which will by no means be confined to one single community following one religion, there will be no peace and progress for us. Again self-determination for provincial units will create warring zones within the country and completely shatter its central authority."

"Pakistan," he went on, "is no solution of the communal problems. It will rather make them more pronounced and can only end in civil war. Let us not delude ourselves by ignoring the fact that the urge for Pakistan is to see Islam re-established in India as the sovereign power. To placate it is to let loose the worst type of fanatical zeal."

He suggested a cessation of hostilities between the Indian political parties and creation of a common platform for the formulation of a common demand on the most fundamental problems of India's liberation and reconstruction. "It may be," he added, "that Muslim League will not join in such a demand, but there will be other Muslims who have been stabbed in the back by the C.R. Formula, who are prepared to stand for Indian Nationalism with rights of minorities duly protected. It will be an act of the finest Indian statesmanship if today there can be a combination of all the nationalist elements in the public life of India for the preparation of an invulnerable national opposition to the continuance of the imperialistic designs of Britain."[29]

As mentioned earlier, Savarkar was ailing by the time Syama Prasad became President of the Hindu Mahasabha and more importantly, Mukherjee's perceived success in getting Gandhi to reject the idea of partition had further weakened his grasp on the party. Finally, in 1944, V.D. Savarkar bowed out and made way for Syama Prasad to take complete control of the Hindu Mahasabha.

Syama Prasad Mukherjee got down to work immediately and 'initiated a campaign to reorient the Hindu Mahasabha, from a class-based organisation to one for the masses.' He further ensured that it maintained sufficient distance from the Imperial government and forged closer ties with the Indian National Congress 'in the fight against the Raj and Pakistan.'

But all his strategies, mostly overtly political, to win back the support of Hindus failed, as was proven in the elections to the Bengal Legislative Assembly in March 1946. The Hindu Mahasabha was decimated, and while Mukherjee won the party's lone seat, it was only the non-elective special seat in the University.

The setback notwithstanding, there was a pending political task which required Syama Prasad's attention after the British government sent the Cabinet Mission in March 1946 to begin negotiations for the setting up of an Interim government. As head of the Mahasabha delegation, he demanded that 'the integrity and indivisibility of the country should be maintained...and that Partition would be economically unsound, disastrous, politically unwise and suicidal.' He also refused to 'agree to any suggestion that Hindus and Muslims should be represented in the central government on the basis of equality.' In his deliberations with the Cabinet Mission, Mukherjee reiterated what he had once discussed with Jinnah - that Hindu and Muslim representatives should meet to discuss issues on which they required protection from each other. Insofar as granting complete protection to minorities in respect of language, religion and customs was concerned, Mukherjee was willing to acquiesce, but he was unwilling to grant them equal rights.

In June 1946, the Cabinet Mission returned to England after failing to make any headway in the negotiations. Within a span of two months, Jinnah called for Direct Action Day (also known as the Great Calcutta Killings) on 16 August 1946 and with that, the partition of the subcontinent became an inevitable reality. Muslim League under the instruction of Jinnah and guidance of Mr. H.S.Suhrawardy, launched "direct action" against the Hindus in Calcutta on 16th August,1946. Rampant looting, killing & aron went on for 4 days, Mukherjee stood firmly behind the people during the great Calcutta killing ,raping and widespread communal riots organised by the Muslim League in Nookhali district under the leadershp of Suhrawardy. Mukherjee saved the affected people during the communal disturbances. The initial leg-work on cleaving parts of the nation had begun, except Bengal, for it was still undecided whether it would go the Punjab way and be partitioned, or merge with Pakistan, because of its Muslim-majority population.

After the horrific killings in his native city, Syama Prasad Mukherjee proclaimed during a debate in the Legislative Assembly that the deliberations were essentially over a 'no-confidence motion against the Ministry under circumstances, which perhaps, has no parallel in the deliberations of any legislature in any part of the civilised world. What happened in Calcutta was without a parallel in modern history'. In the aftermath of the Great Calcutta Killings and the riots in Noakhali in October-November 1946, the Hindu Mahasabha witnessed an exponential growth in its base numbers. In 1943-44, for instance, the Mahasabha had just about ten branches in Noakhali district, but in a period of three years, this number rose dramatically to one hundred and forty-three. The deteriorating communal situation in the country had brought the Mahasabha, which went into political hibernation after its electoral defeat, back on the political scene. The event that influenced Shyama Prasad Mukherjee's ideology, one was the Noakhali riots, that occured in 1946 during months of October and November. Occuring primarily in Chittagong division of East Bengal (now in Bangladesh), it was one of the worst genocides of Hindus, by Muslim League mobs, that involved forced conversions, arson, mass rapes and looting. Beginning on Durga Puja, it was a series of planned forced attacks on the Hindu population in that region, which at the last count led to 5000 dead. Another was the Kolkata riots of 1946, carried out by the Muslim League leader Suhrawady, in response to Direct Action Day.

On 20 October 1946, precisely twenty days after the Noakhali riots, Mukherjee formed the Hindu National Guards; in order to forge unity amongst Hindus, irrespective of caste, he also set up the Hindu Society Board; in addition, he also established the Hindu Sangathan Society. From here on, he was not only 'heard' in the Bengal legislature, but was seen to be acting with great alacrity in restoring the dignity of his Hindu brethren.

Though he was opposed to partition initially, after Noakhali and the Direct Action Day riots in Kolkata, he was convinced that it would be equally wise to partition Bengal too, with the Hindu population living in the Western part, that would be a part of the Indian Union.

Fight for Partition of Pakistan

Punjab and Bengal were the two key provinces on which the edifice of Pakistan as conceived by the Muslim League rested. Both these provinces had slight Muslim majority. The Communal Award put them in commanding position in both these provinces. The zonal scheme which had been put forth as an alternative to partition by the Cabinet Mission had put these provinces as a whole in the two Muslim majority zones to be constituted in the east and west of the country. The Muslim League, therefore, took it for granted that both of these provinces as a whole would be included in Pakistan. But the redeeming feature in the situation of these provinces was that the Hindu population in both the provinces was concentrated in districts adjoining the neighbouring Hindu majority provinces. These compact Hindu majority parts of Bengal and Punjab could logically demand their inclusion in India in the event of partition of the country on communal basis. The British plan to create a large geography in the eastern part of India consisting of Assam and Bengal as an 'independent country', not joining either the Dominion of India or Dominion of Pakistan was mooted by Lord Mountbatten on April 26, 1947, during his discussions with Suhrawardy and later with Jinnah.

Mohammad Ali Jinnah reportedly told Mountbatten, "...what is the use of (divided) Bengal (as East Pakistan) without Calcutta? They had much better remain united and independent; I am sure they would be on friendly terms with us."

But Hindu leaders, including Shyama Prasad Mukherjee, K.C. Neogy and Binoy Kumar Roy strongly opposed the idea of an "independent country of Bengal". "Hindus will not be safe in a 'united but independent Bengal'" appeared to be the general consensus, as riots broke out and the communal situation turned volatile. Both Sardar Patel and Jawaharlal Nehru assured these leaders that they were both against "a sovereign Bengal unconnected with the Union".

The Muslim League leadership was conscious of this fact. It therefore decided to take advantage of the situation created by its electoral success, the Congress' nervousness and favourable change in the British attitude, to terrify the Hindus of these areas into submission to their will. The Muslim League leaders and their British patrons were particularly interested in annexing Calcutta to Pakistan. To that end, a planned orgy of loot and massacre was let loose on Calcutta on 16 August. Thousands of innocent Hindus were butchered, their houses, and shops looted and burnt in broad daylight with the direct connivance of the Muslim League administration.

But the League plan to terrify Hindus out of Calcutta was foiled by the determined resistance put up by the Calcutta Hindus under Dr. Mukherjee's fearless leadership, to the organised goondaism of the Muslim League. The Hindustan National Guards - a volunteer organisation that had been started by Dr. Mukherjee to checkmate the goondaism of the Muslim National Guards of the Muslim League - gave a good account of itself in this crisis. Dr. Mukherjee himself moved about the riot-affected areas, with sheer indifference to his own safety, to give courage and consolation to the afflicted people.

Later, the same story was repeated in Noakhali and its surrounding villages. Dr. Mukherjee was again the first to rush to the affected areas at great personal risk to give succour to the victims of the bestial persecution at the hands of soldiers of Islam.

These happenings sent a wave of indignation all over the country. To the Hindus of Bengal, they gave a taste of Pakistan. The prospect of utter humiliation and annihilation in their own land for the freedom of which they had made the greatest sacrifices, began to assail their hearts. The Congress leadership, in which they had put their faith, lacked both realism and courage to appreciate the situation and take up its challenge. The eyes of nationalist Bengal were, therefore, once again turned towards Dr. Mukherjee.

He then decided upon a bold move which partitioned Pakistan of Jinnah's conception and saved half of Bengal for India. He realised that the only way of saving Bengali Hindus from sure annihilation under perpetual Muslim domination was to divide Bengal, so as to separate its Hindu majority western part from the Muslim majority eastern part. It was a painful idea for a patriot of Bengal, who was conscious of the great sacrifices his predecessors had made to annul the earlier partition of Bengal. It demanded exceptional courage to put forth a proposal which was sure to give a great emotional shock to the patriotic Bengalis - none but Dr. Mukherjee could have done it.

Once he had made up his mind, he put in all his resources to educate and mobilise public opinion accordingly. He undertook a whirlwind tour of the whole of Bengal, particularly East Bengal, addressed mass rallies, wherein he boldly put forth his plan of partitioning Bengal. This was followed by a two-day conference of Hindu representatives from all parts of Bengal in the middle of March, which unanimously resolved that a separate province must be created comprising the Hindu majority areas in Bengal.

As this move gained momentum and strength, it began to be subjected to severe attacks both by the Muslim League and the Congress. The Congress critics who were perturbed more by the growing influence of Dr. Mukherjee on the Hindu masses than by the move itself, began to shift the onus of accepting partition of the country on Dr. Mukherjee. They asserted that the creation of the new province as visualised by Dr. Mukherjee would support the cause of Pakistan.

Dr. Mukherjee replied to the criticism through a detailed statement issued on March 9, 1947. "It is wrong," he said, "that this move supported the cause of Pakistan. We are against Pakistan in any shape or form. It does not, however, depend on Bengali Hindus alone whether division of India will be prevented or not. If Hindus and other nationalist forces throughout India are really determined not to allow any portion of India to go out of the Indian Union, they will get the largest measure of support from Bengali Hindus. If, on the other hand, an attempt is made to place Bengal out of the Indian Union due to commitments with which the British Government, the Muslim League and the Congress are closely associated, we shall, at any rate, break the solidarity of Eastern Pakistan, save one area of Bengal and link it up with the Indian Union."

To those who criticised his scheme on the ground that division of Bengal on religious basis would be against the fundamental principle of nationalism, he retorted, "No one desires religion to be introduced into politics. But why must we hide our head ostrich-like and ignore present realities? It is not we who want division of India or any part thereof merely on religious considerations. But if we find that the whole of Bengal is going to be dominated by communal frenzy and 45% of its population reduced to a state of slavery only because they follow a particular religious faith, is it a crime on our part to demand that we must have our own territory where we can live as free men? And was not", he asked, "Sind carved out from Bombay only to placate communal whims and did not many of our present Congress opportunists quietly acquiesce in such division much to the detriment of the Hindus of Sind?"

Referring to the criticism that his scheme would be stoutly opposed by the Muslim League, he said that he expected that because "if this scheme succeeds Eastern Pakistan would virtually finish. It is all the more reason", he added, "why all Hindus in Bengal should sink their differences and stand united on this great issue in spite of all the isms that divide them." He urged upon his compatriots to look at the problems facing them with complete realism, and not allow themselves to be carried away by emotions. He concluded his momentous statement with an appeal to the Congress party in Bengal to rise to the occasion and support his move in the wider interest of nationalist Bengal and India.

His well-reasoned and forceful advocacy of the scheme for partition of Bengal did succeed in winning a large number of Congressmen over to his side, and soon it became the universal demand of Bengal Hindus.

The Muslim League leadership in Bengal was naturally perturbed over it. It could not logically deny the right of the Hindu majority areas of Bengal to determine their own future when it was demanding the same right for Muslim majority areas. But it realised that the success of Dr. Mukherjee's move would truncate East Pakistan, deprive it of Calcutta and leave it "moth-eaten".

H.S. Suharawardy, the brain of Muslim League in Bengal, then put forth the scheme for United Sovereign Bengal mainly to counteract the move of Dr. Mukherjee. He feigned to be a Bengali first and appealed to the Bengali sentiment of the Congress-minded intelligentsia, which had an emotional antipathy for any idea of partitioning Bengal once again. Some top Congress leaders like Sarat Chandra Bose fell into his trap.

He was reported to have obtained Gandhi's blessings as well for his scheme.

But, Dr. Mukherjee was not one to be deflected from his resolve by these manoeuvres. He met Gandhi at Sadpur on 13 May 1947, to ascertain his views on the Suharawardy scheme of United Sovereign Bengal. Gandhi told Dr. Mukherjee that he had not yet made up his mind but was trying to ascertain what the proposal really meant. He then asked Dr. Mukherjee his own opinion about it. The latter replied that though apparently Suharawardy was the author of his scheme, it was really being sponsored by British commercial interests and that Lord Mountbatten had personally asked him to give the proposal careful consideration. But, Dr. Mukherjee questioned as to what there was to prevent this United Sovereign Bengal from seeking voluntary alliance with Pakistan? Suharawardy, he feared, could surely manipulate a decision of this kind with the help of the majority of Muslim votes. "Can you contemplate Bengal lying separate from the rest of India?" he asked Gandhi, to which he had no reply.[30]

Then Suhrawardy, with a few other Muslim Leaguers, hatched a novel scheme. Suhrawardy would claim to be an ardent Bengali first, then a Muslim, and with a few gullible Hindu associates clamour for a 'sovereign independent undivided Bengal'. He would shout from the rooftops that Bengal and Bengalis were one, no matter what religion they followed, and they just could not be divided. He would, of course, have to sweep under the carpet the fact that only a few months ago, he had tried mass murder on fellow Bengalis who happened to be Hindu. If he managed to get independent Bengal, with Calcutta of course, he would always have the power to decide policy because of their numerical superiority. After that, joining Pakistan (if he preferred that it remained sovereign) would merely be a matter of time. In fact, Suhrawardy had this gambit up his sleeve quite early, even before his Direct Action was launched. In a very significant public statement on 9th August 1946, he threatened to declare Bengal's complete independence from the Centre which the Hindu press interpreted as a threat to 'Pakistanize' the whole of Bengal forthwith. His personal focus was all along very strongly on Calcutta, for a variety of reasons, ranging from his West Bengali origin to his love for the city that had given him so many pleasures, not excluding those of the flesh. However, there are strong grounds to believe that he allegedly owned a huge lot of benami property in the city.

This is the reason why the person who had fought so hard for Pakistan was not in Dacca or Karachi on 14 August 1947, but in Calcutta, hanging on to the tail of Mahatma Gandhi's shawl for dear life, not leaving the city. He was trying to dispose of the property before going to Pakistan, and he eventually moved only in 1948.

Dr Mukherjee, who had so long campaigned so indefatigably to prevent the partition of the country, by this time realized that dreaded partition was inevitable, a certainty. He had no doubt in his mind that if the whole of Bengal went to Pakistan then the condition of the 47 per cent Hindus of the undivided province would be worse than miserable (as was proved to be true from the treatment of the Hindus of East Pakistan. He therefore decided to make partition of the province a necessary corollary to partition of the country, presumably following the ancient Sanskrit maxim, sarvanashe samutpanne ardham tyajati panditah (when total disaster is imminent, a wise man relinquishes half). He therefore started mobilizing Bengali Hindus across party lines in support of partition of the province. he managed to salvage a large territory for India through his efforts. Today, the state of Bengal is an integral part of India.

The partition movement was already well under way before the end of 1946, with the establishment of the 'Bengal Partition League'. Its declared object was to demand a separate province to safeguard Hindu interests in the Hindu-majority districts of western Bengal. The promoters of the Bengal Partition League were the Hindu bhadralok, who were determined to be once again masters in their own house and formed the core of the movement. In the months that followed the Calcutta Killings, Bengali Hindus of Calcutta and the surrounding districts were mobilized by being asked not to forget Direct Action Day, and demand partition of the province to create a separate 'West Bengal Province' within the independent Indian federation to save them from the unacceptable humiliations of living under Muslim raj. Zamindars, professionals, respectable white-collar clerks and business groups dominated the movement, and the petitions were addressed to either Congress President J.B. Kripalani or sent to Dr Mukherjee and the Mahasabha. After giving him a humiliating election defeat less than two years back, the Bengali Hindus suddenly realized who their best hope for emancipation from League rule was.

As soon as Dr. Mukherjee realized that the only way of saving Bengali Hindus from certain and sure annihilation under perpetual Muslim rule was to divide Bengal, he put in all his resources to educate and mobilize public opinion accordingly. As this move gained momentum, there was criticism that the creation of the new province would support the cause of Pakistan. He replied by issuing a detailed statement on 9 March 1947. In this, he asserted that the move was meant to save one area of Bengal from Pakistan, which was repugnant in any shape or form, and not to support its cause. Referring to the criticism that his scheme would be stoutly opposed by the Muslim League, he said that he expected that because if the scheme succeeded, 'Eastern Pakistan would virtually finish'. It was all the more reason why all Hindus in Bengal should look at this great issue with complete realism instead of emotion and stand united. He concluded his momentous statement with an appeal to the Congress party in Bengal to support his move in the wider interest of nationalist Bengal and India.

Dr. Mukherjee's well-reasoned and forceful advocacy of the scheme for partition of Bengal succeeded in winning many Congressmen over to his side. At a meeting in Delhi on 9 March 1947, Bengali Hindu members of the Central Assembly adopted, with the approval of N.C. Chatterjee of the Mahasabha and General A.C. Chatterji of the INA, a resolution demanding partition. This was followed by a well-attended two-day conference of Hindu representatives from all parts of Bengal that started in Calcutta on 15 March 1947 under the auspices of the Bengal Provincial Hindu Mahasabha with Dr. Mukherjee as President. The large number of invitees, apart from the Mahasabha members, included prominent persons like Lord Sinha, Dr R.C. Majumdar, Dr Suniti Kumar Chatterji, Bhabatosh Ghatak, Iswardas Jalan, and Hemendra Prasad Ghosh. The conference unanimously resolved that a separate province must be created comprising the Hindu-majority areas in Bengal, and appointed a committee to frame a memorandum to be placed before the next scheduled conference.

In a statement on 19 March, Dr. Mukherjee asserted that their current proposal for Hindu Bengal was aimed at saving Bengali Hindus and also the cause of nationalism, which was their lifeblood. It had absolutely no similarity to Curzon's Partition Plan of 1905 that was aimed at giving a death blow to the 'seditionist' Bengali Hindus. Even then, Hindu (Congress) opinion was very divided. On the one hand, or 10 March, Nehru was telling Wavell in private that though 'the Cabinet Mission Plan was the best solution if it could be carried through, the only real alternative was the partition of the Punjab and Bengal'. On the other hand, Sarat Bose condemned and Gandhiji did not approve of the Bengal partition movement, though he did not seem to have very strong feelings on the matter, and had many other things to worry about. Bose had lost the bulk of his credibility after he had refused to lead the students' movement on 22 November 1945.

Meanwhile, Dr. Mukherjee, through his adroit stewardship of the partition movement managed to bring about what he had tried for so long-to make the Congress work for Hindu interests in tandem with the Mahasabha. When the Working Committee of the Mahasabha decided on 17 April to observe a one-day strike to protest the misbehaviour of Punjabi Muslim policemen, the Mahasabha leaders consulted the Congress leaders to chalk out a joint plan of action. While the demand for the creation of a separate province of West Bengal was endorsed by the provincial Congress and the Mahasabha, in the opinion poll held by the Amrita Bazar Patrika on 22 April 1947, partition gained a virtually unanimous vote of confidence, 98.6 percent voting yea, with only 0.6 percent favouring a united Bengal. Dr. Mukherjee held a 'top secret' interview with

Viceroy Mountbatten on 23 April, in which he explained that the main purpose of his visit was to convince the viceroy of the necessity for partitioning Bengal, if the Cabinet Mission Plan were to fail. He went into matters at great length using many plans and papers, which were left with the viceroy's chief of staff Lord Ismay. A mammoth public meeting, jointly convened by the Mahasabha and the Congress in Calcutta, was held in May 1947 to press for partition. It was presided over by the historian Sir Jadunath Sarkar, by no means a friend of the Mukherjees, but now an ardent supporter of the cause. The meeting set the pattern for as many as seventy-six subsequent public meetings that were organized by the twoparties working closely together for the cause of partition until it became clear in July that Bengal would, indeed, be partitioned.[31]

In spite of the opposition of some top Congress leaders, the move for partition of Bengal, in case the demand for Pakistan was to be conceded, became so popular and powerful that it became impossible for the British Government, the Congress and the Muslim League to resist it. The announcement made by the British Government on 3rd June, which laid down the blueprint for India's independence after its partition into two States of Bharat and Pakistan, conceded the right of Hindu majority areas of Bengal and Punjab to opt out of Pakistan. A Boundary Commission under the chairmanship of Radcliffe was appointed to demarcate such areas.

In hindsight, once the deed was done, it seems obvious that Bengal (and Punjab) would have to be partitioned. But it was by no means obvious then, and an undivided Muslim majority (even if the majority was thin) landing up with Pakistan might well have become a fait accompli. Once partition was accepted for Bengal, by logical extension, it followed for Punjab. Yet, another detail for a proper retelling of history needs to be mentioned.

Even here, Dr. Mukherjee intervened and convinced Radcliffe that while deciding the population balance for deciding whether to award a particular unit of area to India or Pakistan, the unit to be considered should be the thana, the police station area, and not the district or subdivision. It is on this basis that a number of districts themselves came to be partitioned; and the Krishnanagar and Ranaghat subdivisions of the Nadia district, the bulk of Malda district, the Balurghat and Raiganj subdivisions of Dinajpur district, the Bongaon subdivision of Jessore district and many other parts came to India.

The terms of reference under which the Radcliffe Commission was to work gave it large scope to play havoc with the boundary line that was to divide Hindu Bengal from the Muslim Bengal that was to go to Pakistan. Dr. Mukherjee, therefore, took up the task of preparing and presenting the case of Hindu Bengal before the Boundary Commission. A Committee of leading jurists was set up for the purpose, and a detailed plan showing the areas that should constitute West Bengal on the basis of their being Hindu majority was drawn up. According to it, the whole of Khulna district, which had over sixty percent Hindu majority should have come to West Bengal.

But the Congress spokesmen, in their anxiety to see East Pakistan grow up as a viable unit, were prepared to forgo Indian Bengalis' claim to Khulna to appease their Pakistani counterparts. As a result, the Radcliffe Award proved to be very unfair to West Bengal. A large tract of land containing over two million Hindus which should have legitimately formed a part of West Bengal was awarded to Pakistan.

As the plan for partition began to be given effect, the Hindu minority in East Bengal, which had already got a bitter taste of Muslim dominated administration, began to feel nervous. The leaders of East Bengal Hindus had supported the demand for partition of Bengal in the hope and on the understanding that their co-patriots of West Bengal and the rest of India will look to their welfare. They wanted to be assured that they would not be left at the mercy of Pakistan. Dr. Mukherjee, therefore, undertook another tour of East Bengal. He persuaded top Congress leaders like Gandhi and Sardar Patel also to visit East Bengal and authoritatively reassure its Hindu population, which had always remained in the forefront in the fight for India's independence. At numerous places, he told large audiences that he was conscious of the great sacrifices they had made for the wider interests of India and their Hindu brethren of West Bengal. He also assured them that he would watch their interests and stand them in all their difficulties. He remained dutifully conscious of this pledge ever after and did all he could to redeem it.

At the same time, his performance in the Constituent Assembly of India, his political acumen, oratorical skill, and mastery of parliamentary procedure were winning new laurels for him. His position as one of the topmost public figures, whose record of service in the cause of the country's independence could be surpassed by few, was universally recognised.

So far as Bengal was concerned, he had become its undisputed leader and spokesman. No wonder, therefore, that his name readily occurred to the Congress leaders who were then engaged in selecting personnel for the national government to be formed on 15 August 1947.

Syama Prasad Mukherjee's stance on Partition has undoubtedly been one of the most significant aspects of his political career. It is interesting to note that he disagreed with most of the Mahasabha leaders on the issue, especially his mentor, V.D. Savarkar.[32]

On the eve of the Viceroy's departure (to London on 18 May 1947), Dr. Mukherjee had put his demand for a separate Hindu Province in the West of Bengal. However, in less than a year, political pragmatism had forced a change in Mukherjee's standpoint on this vital issue. Yet, within days of Mukherjee's volte-face, Savarkar launched a fresh campaign for India's unity. On 27 May 1947, he made a 'fervent and forlorn appeal' to Congress leaders 'not to betray the electorates and India by agreeing to a scheme involving vivisection of the Motherland.' This stark divergence in thought between the two Mahasabha stalwarts indicated that while Syama Prasad Mukherjee had come to terms with the inevitability of Partition, V.D. Savarkar was relentless in his pursuit of keeping the nation united.

Several academics, has maintained that Syama Prasad Mukherjee had indeed supported India's partition. Then there were others like the writer, Subrata Mukherjee who argued that his 'most important achievement was the creation of West Bengal.' According to Subrata, the Hindu Mahasabha leader had come to the realisation that a united Bengal would limit the role of the Hindu community, and hence proposed that the state be partitioned into a Hindu-majority West Bengal, and a Muslim-dominated East Bengal (later East Pakistan).

Even Prime Minister Nehru didn't spare Syama Prasad for endorsing the division of the country and said as much during a debate in the Lok Sabha. In response to the Prime Minister, Syama Prasad had retorted as follows: 'You have divided India, I have divided Pakistan.'

Minister Mukherjee

Despite strong ideological differences between the two men, Prime Minister Nehru invited Syama Prasad Mukherjee to join independent India's first Cabinet. In retrospect, it would be safe to surmise that his government, which was formed after the terrible Partition, was most ideologically balanced. On one side were conservatives like Morarji Desai, K.M. Munshi and S.K. Patil, who clearly did not share Nehru's enthusiasm for Socialism. On the other was an assorted of non-Congress leaders - Syama Prasad Mukherjee, B.R. Ambedkar, John Mathai's group, and C.D. Deshmukh.

One of the primary reasons for Syama Prasad Mukherjee's inclusion in Nehru's Cabinet over several other leaders from Bengal was because he was backed by none other than Sardar Vallabhbhai Patel, who had proposed his name after he had demanded 'Bengal's partition in March 1947 and (refused) to join an abortive bid for a united and independent Bengal that Sarat Bose and Suhrawardy made in April and May (1947). Several academics have argued that Mukherjee's decision was a strategic ploy and back it with the theory that he, as well as other Mahasabha leaders, were 'unsure about what their role should be. In particular, they were uncertain how to react to the Congress at the centre. Some of them, Dr. Mukherjee prominent among them, thought they would do best by joining the national government as partners of the Congress,' but hadn't risked initiating the process. Although they had differed with each other on the issue of Partition barely three months ago in August 1947, when Jawaharlal Nehru had requested Syama Prasad Mukherjee to join his Cabinet, V.D. Savarkar had endorsed the proposal.

In his book, Balraj Madhok provides a wonderful insight into the Mahasabha leadership--how they launched a public broadside against the Congress in public, yet remained sympathetic in private. According to him, Mukherjee's colleagues 'had always stood for responsive cooperation...and, wanted to give the Congress leaders a fair chance to show their worth (and) advised him to accept the invitation.' Despite the oath of secrecy, there was no corroboration of the fact if Mukherjee had discussed the issues relating to Nehru's policies with Savarkar.

In September 1947, Prime Minister Nehru forwarded an internal report to his Cabinet colleagues which stated that his Minister of Industry and Supplies, Syama Prasad, flew the Mahasabha flag at his official residence instead of the Tricolour. Mukherjee responded to the Prime Minister, saying that although he hoisted the Indian flag regularly, he also flew the Mahasabha's flag on a few occasions.

Evidently, even after becoming a Central Minister, Mukherjee continued to confer with the Mahasabha leaders on several political and policy matters. Mahatma Gandhi's secretary, Pyarelal, reported one such instance as follows - shortly before his assassination, Gandhi had sent his secretary to meet with Syama Prasad to register his protest against the virulent rhetoric adopted by some his party associates, including incitement to assassinate a few Congress leaders. According to British author, Keith Meadowcroft 'when informed on Mukherjee's "halting and unsatisfactory" reply, the Mahatma's brow darkened.'

It was clear that Syama Prasad was caught in a cleft stick between his commitment to the Hindu Mahasabha and his duties as a minister in Nehru's Cabinet. As he had accepted Nehru, while he hoisted the Mahasabha flag, reiterating his allegiance to the party, he also tried convincing his mentor, V.D. Savarkar, that the Mahasabha must restrict its political character and metamorphose into a social, cultural, and religious organization.

In so far as the Congress party was concerned, despite the inclusion of a Hindu Mahasabha member as a minister in the government, the antagonistic views apropos Hindu nationalists persisted amongst most of its members. However, one group led by Sardar Patel in the Congress wished closer ties with the Mahasabha, even suggesting a merger with the party, for it felt that it was Syama Prasad Mukherjee who was instrumental in making the Mahasabha 'less aggressive than the (Muslim) League and less irresponsible." But Jawaharlal Nehru, much like several times before, opposed the move and, in a letter to Mukherjee dated 28 January 1948 (exactly two days prior to Gandhi's assassination), wrote that the Mahasabha was the 'main opposition' to both the Congress and his government. The prime minister also wrote to the Director of Intelligence Bureau (IB) and drew his attention to the 'increasingly aggressive and offensive activities' of the Mahasabha.

Considering Syama Prasad Mukherjee's stature, which preceded even his Hindu Mahasabha phase, there was speculation over why Prime Minister Nehru had allocated the ministry of industry and supplies to him, which of course came with his Home Minister's strong recommendation of his candidature. It was rather well known that if he had had his way, Mukherjee would have 'personally preferred education, which had been his special field since his early youth,' a sound foundation for a truly national, for he could have then 'laid education policy. However, Nehru was well aware of the fact that a man who led an organization like the Hindu Mahasabha should be precluded from any decision-making involving social policies and hence put in charge of a suitable portfolio.

It must be mentioned that Syama Prasad Mukherjee was an efficient minister. Mukherjee was a great minister, and many important projects like the Hindustan Aircraft Factory (Today's Hindustan Aeronautics Limited), the Sindri Fertilizer Plant, and the Chittaranjan Locomotive Works started during his tenure as Minister of Industry and Supply. Nearly five decades later, President R. Venkataraman, while unveiling Syama Prasad Mukherjee's bust at a function in Kolkata on 23 February 2001 had remarked how he had 'handled the portfolio of industries with a rare felicity,' and laid the foundation for a mixed economy in the country. 'Despite being an ardent believer in the private sector,' the former President added that Mukherjee had 'established outstanding public sector undertakings. Pragmatism and not dogmatism informed his industrial policy.'

As Industry and Supplies Minister, although Syama Prasad had few disagreements with Prime Minister Nehru, there were several other issues apart from ideological principles that the two bitterly disagreed on. For instance, in the aftermath of the partition, the extent to which India could exert pressure on Pakistan to protect the rights of Hindus in East Pakistan which was, diplomatically speaking, an internal matter of India's new neighbor.

While Prime Minister Nehru was committed to running his government based on constitutional propriety and not succumbing to majoritarianism, Mukherjee was of the view that India must intervene in Pakistan and provide succor to Hindus who were seeking refuge in the country. The prime minister refused to budge and repeatedly insisted that 'protection in Pakistan can be given only by Pakistan. We cannot give protection to Pakistan.'

The other contentious issue between the men was Kashmir, and Mukherjee was severely critical of Nehru's handling of the state's integration with the Union of India.

Meanwhile, in the aftermath of Mahatma Gandhi's assassination on 30 January 1948, the RSS was banned, and some of its top leaders were arrested. Although the Hindu Mahasabha wasn't proscribed,

V.D. Savarkar was taken into custody days after the murder. As a senior member of the Hindu Mahasabha, Syama Prasad could have, on a matter of principle, resigned from Nehru's Cabinet, but he chose to stay on and cleverly strategized to secure a reprieve for his party. At an extraordinary meeting of the Mahasabha convened a day after Savarkar's arrest, Mukherjee reasoned with its members that the party either ceases 'its political activities and limits itself to social, cultural, and religious problems,' or abandons 'its communalist composition (...) and opens its doors to every citizen, regardless of religion, '

On 15 February 1948, the proposal was discussed in the Hindu Mahasabha's Working Committee, and it was decided to go with the first option in order to avoid censure from the government. Even in a moment of great crisis, when their iconic leader was thrown into jail, the traditionalists within the Mahasabha stuck to their stand of not admitting non-Hindus into their fold. In the first place, the reason for Mukherjee's suggestion stemmed from his strong conviction that the 'Muslim problem...could be solved in free India' permanently, provided 'their outlook on cultural, social, and political problems of the country was Hinduized or nationalized while leaving them free, in keeping with the Hindu tradition of absolute tolerance, to carry their religion and way of worship as they pleased.' His position on this issue was similar to the RSS' theory that the Muslims were originally Hindus and could be brought back into the 'nationalist' mainstream.

Meanwhile, the traditionalists within the Mahasabha had no intentions of ceasing political activism. Three months after agreeing to put a halt on every kind of political activity, the Mahasabha conservatives succeeded in convincing the Working Committee to reverse its decision. Syama Prasad did not take well to this rebellion, and on 23 November 1948, he resigned from the Hindu Mahasabha. For a man who was at the forefront of consolidating its position and had worked tirelessly for its expansion even as a Cabinet minister, his resignation from the Hindu Mahasabha had raised several questions, and foremost being whether it would survive thereafter.

But Syama Prasad Mukherjee was resolute in his belief that the Mahasabha had run its course and needed an overhaul as an expansive Hindu nationalist party. While recommending that Muslims be made part of the organization, Mukherjee had not only encouraged a form of assimilation but had also taken cognizance of the fact that after Partition, barring the state of Jammu & Kashmir, their numbers had come down drastically across the country. As expected, the Mahasabha thought otherwise, which gave rise to questions about the political path that he would henceforth follow and those he would eventually partner with.

Mukherjee's so-called political conundrum was not impossible to comprehend because, as a national leader, he lacked both party and cause, and there seemed little chance of his finding a place in West Bengal. For instance, after his move to Delhi in the late Forties, he was also quick to recognize that Dr. B.C. Roy was well ensconced as chief minister of West Bengal and would brook no threat to his political preeminence either within the Congress or from the right.

Differences with Nehru

Unlike the norm in contemporary politics, when seldom does a leader of repute sit out of the system for long, Syama Prasad Mukherjee kept his counsel after resigning from the Hindu Mahasabha and did not jump into any other right-wing bandwagon. It should be mentioned here that this was also a time when the nation had been spliced into two, and as a votary of Hindutva, he could have used his political clout to push the Muslims deep into the abyss.

There is no denying the fact that it was also him who had mooted the idea of assimilating them by offering them membership in the Mahasabha.

He particularly took Nehru to task on two accounts. One was his foreign policy, and the other was his countercharge against Nehru's charge of communalism. Nehru's foreign policy was based, as it seems in retrospect, on what is termed today as mere 'lofty moral posturing'. Dr. Mukherjee particularly lambasted Nehru on two of his grand follies: first, welcoming the Chinese annexation of Tibet and thereby removing this very important buffer state between the two great powers; and secondly, giving a long rope to Pakistan during the Kashmir war through his declaration of the unilateral ceasefire. Posterity has amply proved his foresight in these matters, as it has in regard to several other policies of the government mentioned earlier, though pro-Congress and pro Nehru– Gandhi family historians have deftly tried to gloss over these 'Himalayan Blunders' of Nehru. Jawaharlal Nehru who positioned himself as an internationalist and humanitarian. When the simplest route to resolve the Kashmir issue could have been either use of force or bilateral talks, he dragged the issue to the United Nations which at that point was still in an early phase and building legitimacy. Nehru remained the External Affairs Minister for 18 years during which period India witnessed several diplomatic fiascos and lost territories.

Dr. Mukherjee further argued, 'If it is communalist to love one's community and not think ill of other communities, if we feel that an attempt should be made to unite 40 crores of Hindus living in India that have been liberated after 1000 years, if we try to recover our lost position in a manner that is one hundred percent consistent with the dynamic principles of Hinduism, which Swami Vivekananda said, I am proud to be a communalist.'

About Nehru, he further said in a meeting with the elite of Punjab in Simla, 'Pandit Nehru claims that he has discovered India, but he is yet to discover his own mind that has a heavy overcoating of what is un-Indian and un-Hindu.' In the course of his electioneering, Dr Mukherjee also got an opportunity to watch at close quarters the men, young and old, who constituted the Jana Sangh at the town, district, and provincial levels. He could see the problems between young cadres drawn mainly from the RSS and the older people with diverse social and political backgrounds drawn from elsewhere. He was quick to grasp the untiring zeal, humility, and hard work of the young workers drawn from the RSS which impressed him. As an educator, he understood the workings of young minds. He also realized that it was not easy for older people who had grown up in a different atmosphere to reconcile with the young swayamsevaks. He, therefore, started training the young leaders with a view to building a second line of leaders. Madhok has remarked that this act was fundamentally different from Nehru, who took deliberate steps to ensure that no individual, whether young or old, however capable and deserving, came anywhere close to him so as to jeopardize his unchallenged hold over the Congress party and the government.

As mentioned earlier, Mukherjee and Nehru had severe differences over the extent of India's intervention in Pakistan to protect the rights of Hindus. These differences were not only limited to the magnitude and form of exerting pressure on Pakistan but also pertained to adherence to the basic principles of democracy. Syama Prasad Mukherjee considered his standpoint as more logical, according to which it was obligatory on India's part to intervene and rescue Hindus from being persecuted in East Pakistan.

Gradually, the growing dissent between the two spilled over to two Inter-Dominion Agreements signed with Pakistan in 1948, which addressed the problems faced by Hindus in West and East Pakistan. Despite Mukherjee's relentless campaign and the steady stream of Hindu refugees into West Bengal, Nehru refused to go past the diplomatic route.

In April 1950, the Liaquat-Nehru Pact (also known as the Delhi Pact) to secure the safety of life and property of minorities was readied to be inked. Exactly a week before the Pact was to be formalized, Syama Prasad Mukherjee resigned from the government on 1 April 1950. A few days later, on 19 April 1950, he delivered what many consider to be 'one of the greatest political speeches in the annals of independent India.' While highlighting the attacks on Hindus in Pakistan, he said:

We saw the gradual extermination of Hindus from North Western Frontier Province and Baluchistan ,and latterly from Sind as well. In East Bengal, about 13 million Hindus were squeezed out. There were no major incidents as such, but circumstances so shaped themselves that they got no protection from the Government of Pakistan and were forced to come away to West Bengal for shelter. In the course of 1949, we witnessed a further deterioration of conditions in East Bengal and an exodus of a far larger number of helpless people. The Pioneer, dated May 22, 1950, reported that 8,60,000 Hindus came to India as refugees. Between February 10, 1950 and February 20, 1950, 10,000 Hindus were killed. Some reports suggested that 13 lakh Hindu refugees entered West Bengal between April 9, 1950 and July 25, 1950. Stories of brutal atrocities and persecutions came to light...

Just a year before he quit the government, Syama Prasad had also raised the issue of police atrocities against Hindus in the Khulna district of East Pakistan. However, it also needs to be highlighted that there was yet another significant issue involving the rights of Hindus about which Syama Prasad Mukherjee had vacillated for a considerable period of time. Since 1941, the question of codifying and modernizing Hindu legal tradition has surfaced periodically, and eventually, the Constituent Assembly formulated a Draft Code Bill in 1944. However, the deliberations on the Bill had led to a virtual split in the Congress party between the conservatives, led by India's first President Rajendra Prasad, and the modernists or reformists led, by Jawaharlal Nehru.

During the period when the Bill was being evaluated by both groups, Syama Prasad Mukherjee had chosen to be on the side of the conservatives in Congress and had opposed the codification of Hindu laws. But after joining Nehru's cabinet, he preferred to remain silent during debates. The veteran journalist, Inder Malhotra, had commented about Mukherjee's studied silence in The Indian Express dated 1 May 2009, and wrote that the industries minister hadn't said a word against the Hindu Code while he was a member of Jawaharlal Nehru's cabinet. He thundered in 1951 that the Bill would 'shatter the magnificent architecture of the Hindu culture'.

We should never tolerate any criticism from any quarter, especially from a foreign quarter, when they say that Hindu civilization or Hindu culture has been of a static nature or of stagnant nature, or decadent nature.

This was also the same speech during which Mukherjee was at his vituperative best in criticizing Nehru's government and said how the government did not dare to touch the Muslim community.'

A New Innings

After breaking all ties with the Hindu Mahasabha and virtually stepping out of V.D. Savarkar's shadow, Syama Prasad was now on the lookout for a credible platform to further his political mission.

Meanwhile, the ban on the RSS was lifted in July 1949 and its leaders felt an 'urgent need for a political organization that could reflect the ideology and ideas of the RSS in the political sphere.' In the December 1949 issue of the Organiser, its then editor, K.R. Malkani, wrote that the RSS must have a political presence, not only to protect itself...but to stop the anti-Bharatiya policies of the government and to advance and expedite the cause of Bharatiya through state machinery.

Syama Prasad Mukherjee was well 'aware of this stream of thought in the RSS circles and made several trips to Nagpur between November 1949 and early 1950 to meet the RSS sarsanghchalak, Madhav Sadashiv Golwalkar.

Although Syama Prasad had in the past endorsed RSS for its commitment to nationalism, he knew little about its internal dynamics. But after giving the idea some thought, he was somehow convinced that he could be its potential leader in the absence of a 'logical political mentor,' as the organization was in need of 'an ideological shepherd.[33]

After excluding the Hindu Mahasabha from consideration, some RSS activists, especially Vasantrao Krishna Oke, the Delhi state pracharak, and Balraj Madhok, a young pracharak from Kashmir, met Dr. Mukherjee and proposed the formation of a new nationalist party. The initial contact with him was probably not with the clearance of the top RSS leadership, which was even then somewhat apprehensive about its pracharaks hobnobbing with politicians. However, the mention of the 'RSS mind' mentioned in the interview with Balraj Madhok (unless he had the dates totally mixed up) shows that collaborating with the organization was never far away from Dr. Mukherjee's mind, even before the informal approach by Oke was made.

It is not as if Dr. Mukherjee was a total stranger to the RSS. In April 1940, he attended an RSS shakha at Raja Dinendra Street in Calcutta and was impressed by the soldierly discipline of the swayamsevaks. Balasaheb Deoras, who later became the third Sarsanghchalak of the RSS, was present at that meeting. Dr. Mukherjee was aware that it was the most organized, trained, disciplined and efficient non-political national organization of the Hindus in the country, and its approach to the problems of culture, nationalism and partition had his fullest approval. The very next month, he was returning from a Hindu Mahasabha meeting in Bombay en route to Calcutta when he came to know that Dr. Hedgewar, founder of the RSS, had fallen seriously ill and was bedridden at the home of Babasaheb Ghatate at Nagpur. Golwalkar at the time was running an Adhikari Shiksha Varg (Officer Training Camp for RSS functionaries) at Nagpur, and Dr. Mukherjee decided to stop by at Nagpur and meet them. But at the time, Dr. Hedgewar was so ill that he could not do much more than exchange pleasantries and died soon afterwards. Dr. Mukherjee did, however, query whether the RSS could help the Hindu Mahasabha in its task, and Dr. Hedgewar affirmed that the RSS had to stay away from politics. There had been contacts between the two organizations before Dr. Mukherjee had joined the Mahasabha, and Dr. Hedgewar had maintained close ties with Vinayak Damodar Savarkar and Dr. Balkrishna Shivaram Moonje of the Mahasabha. The same year, Dr. Mukherjee addressed a rally of swayamsevaks in Lahore in the Punjab. By then, the RSS had become a powerful force in the Punjab, and he described the organization as the 'only silver lining in the cloudy sky of India'. It was, therefore, almost divinely ordained that the leader and the organization would meet, and meet they did, shortly after Dr. Mukherjee's resignation.

In the summer of 1950, a meeting was arranged between Dr Mukherjee and Golwalkar at the residence of a swayamsevak in Calcutta. The late Bansi Lal Sonce, then a young pracharak, who later served in the Bharatiya Janata Party for a long time, had been present at the meeting and had recalled that Dr. Mukherjee was trying to speak in halting Hindi. During the meeting, they had differences, but they tried to iron them out with a frankness rarely seen among political leaders in India. Dr. Mukherjee had earlier stated at a press conference that the Hindu Mahasabha was 'communal' inasmuch as it believed in Hindu Rashtra (Hindu state). Golwalkar told him that the RSS also believed in the Bharatiya Rashtra being Hindu Rashtra, though perhaps not so strongly as the Hindu Mahasabha. As such, would he like to keep the RSS too at arm's length? If he did that he would not be able to secure the cooperation of swayamsevaks, all of whom believed in this idea. However, Dr. Mukherjee acknowledged that he had made an inadvertent remark and expressed full agreement on the Hindu Rashtra ideal. Golwalkar, in turn, agreed to assist him and promised to lend him some of his best swayamsevaks, staunch and tried workers, for setting up his party. Also, Golwalkar had later stated in an article by him in the Hindi weekly Panchjanya that Dr. Mukherjee agreed with him that restoration of the Hindu Rashtra was in no way inconsistent with the establishment of a modern democracy.[34]

While exploring the prospect of joining the RSS, Mukherjee had firmed up his mind that his engagement with it should have political ramifications in the history of Indian politics. Meanwhile, even as he held his final plan close to his chest, he decided to reach out to his former Mahasabha colleagues. In early 1949, he met its then President, N.B. Khare and invited him to be part of the plan, but to no avail. However, a few well-known businessmen who had previously backed the Hindu Mahasabha chose to support Mukherjee, which proved that despite the ignominy faced in the aftermath of the Mahatma's assassination, his brand of politics still held good amongst certain sections of society.

However, it would be grossly erroneous in presuming that Syama Prasad Mukherjee was the only leader to have recommended that the RSS assumes a political avatar. As mentioned earlier, on 7 October 1949, in a critical development, the Congress Working Committee had given permission to RSS workers to join the party as primary members. The decision was taken in the absence of Prime Minister Nehru, who was travelling at the time. Although on his return, the move was reversed forthwith, pointed towards the fact that the RSS was not a pariah even for the Congress party, and this was just one year after the killing of Mahatma Gandhi. Even as Syama Prasad went about finalising his plans, the RSS found an ally in him (Mukherjee), and over the next few months, the details of the Jana Sangh were worked out between Mukherjee and the RSS leadership. The decision of the RSS to allow Mukherjee to be the leader of the new political formation was an extension of Golwalkar's well-known view that the interests of the RSS would be best served if it could utilise either existing organisations, or well known leaders to propagate their views.

Despite a common ideological plank, both sides treaded with utmost caution - Mukherjee kept an eye on the ongoing power struggle within the Congress party, while the top brass of the RSS was busy evaluating the pros and cons of the arrangement. After Sardar Patel's death in December 1950, Mukherjee realised that the doors of the Congress party were permanently shut for him, as it was for any other Right-wing leader. In what was construed as presenting MS Golwalkar and company with a fait accompli, while on a tour to Punjab, Syama Prasad announced the birth of a new party called the Bharatiya Jana Sangh, which was way in advance of its formal launch in October 1951. The move to hasten the decision was a direct fall out of the first general elections which had kicked off on 25 October 1951 in the Chini and Pangi assembly constituencies in Himachal Pradesh where voting had to be mandatorily completed before snowfall.

The all-India convention finally took place on 21 October 1951 in Raghomal Arya Kanya Higher Secondary School, New Delhi. About 1000 special invitees from among the citizens of Delhi and another 500 delegates from different parts of India attended the convention. The All-India Bharatiya Jana Sangh was formally launched by a unanimous vote at the convention.

He founded a political party named Bhartiya Jana Sangh (BJS). He had the choice to form a party with 'Hindu' in its title or even to simply continue with Hindu Mahasabha, but he chose to form a party with a nationalist vision. He was an unequivocal supporter of the idea that the civilisational identity of India has a continuity which can be best defined in terms of being Hindu. He was clear that there should be no compromise with Hindu interests and Hindu population should not be treated as secondary subjects as done for more than 900 years by different foreign rulers.

Similarly, the constitution and the manifesto of the party were also adopted by a unanimous vote. And finally, the name of Dr. Mukherjee was proposed as President by Lala Balraj Bhalla of Punjab and seconded by a number of prominent delegates from different parts of India, and similarly carried by a unanimous vote.

In his presidential address, before the historic gathering, Dr. Mukherjee said:

"Our party must continue to function [even after the forthcoming general election] carrying a message of hope and goodwill to all classes of people and try to draw out from them their best efforts in rebuilding a happier and more prosperous free India... One of the chief reasons for the manifestation of dictatorship in Congress rule is the absence of well-organized opposition parties which alone can act as a healthy check on the majority party... Bharatiya Jana Sangh emerges today as an all-India political party which will function as the principal party in opposition, we have thrown our party open to all citizens of India irrespective of caste, creed or community. While we recognize that in matters of customs, habit, religion and language, Bharat presents a unique diversity, the people must be united by a bond of fellowship and understanding inspired by deep devotion and loyalty to the support of a common motherland While it will be dangerous to encourage growth of political minorities on the basis of caste and religion, it is obviously for the vast majority of Bharat's population to assure all classes of people who are truly loyal to their motherland that they will be entitled to full protection under the law and to build equality of treatment in all matters - social, economic and political. Our party gives this assurance unreservedly ...Our party believes that the future of Bharat lies in the proper appreciation and application of Bharatiya sanskriti and maryada."[35]

"The RSS leadership with its greater stress on organisational working and its keen desire to have the real control of the new party in its own hands wanted to take its time to usher it into existence. The delay irritated Dr. Mukherjee who, at one stage, even thought of going alone. His impatience was understandable.

Although Upadhyaya had been 'loaned' as a temporary source to the new party, this soon became a routine practise over a period of time, and many pracharaks were regularly sent on deputation to the Jana Sangh. This resulted in periodic conflicts, and according to Mauli Chandra Sharma, Mukherjee was, often seriously perturbed by the demands of the RSS leaders for a decisive say in matters like appointment of office-bearers, nomination of candidates for elections, and matters of policy."[36]

For all his talk about establishing a Right-wing party with a difference, at the time of the first general elections in 1952, Mukherjee informed:

In fact, in West Bengal, the party was called People's Party of India and it had later merged with the Jana Sangh. The campaign committee decided that the party should be projected as being open to all citizens who owed unalloyed allegiance to India and her great culture and heritage, which is essentially Hindu in character. However, not only had his strategy backfired, even his projections were grossly exaggerated. The Jana Sangh managed to win only three seats, although Mukherjee himself did well and was elected from Calcutta, while the Congress had performed spectacularly by winning 364 of the 489 seats. It wasn't as if there was a strong Opposition in parliament either; the Communists with sixteen members were the largest non-Congress' party.

Despite the poor show of numbers, Syama Prasad converted the moment of adversity into an opportunity and cobbled together a parliamentary forum called the National Democratic Front comprising thirty-two Lok Sabha members. The real intent behind the initiative was already manifest in Mukherjee's speech at the Jana Sangh's inaugural convention in Delhi on 21 October 1951, in which he had said, 'One of the chief reasons for the manifestation of dictatorship in Congress rule is the absence of well-organised opposition parties which alone can act as a healthy check.'68 He had succeeded in convincing other political parties that in the absence of requisite numbers, they could act as a united front against the Congress party in the Lok Sabha.

Although he was not accorded the formal status of Leader of Opposition, Mukherjee strode the floor like a colossus, obviously because of his stature and knowledge of parliamentary affairs. He soon earned the epithet of 'Lion of Parliament' and was respected across party lines for his speeches and informed interventions.

The seasoned parliamentarian that he was, Mukherjee used every opportunity to attack Nehru's government and went back to the same issues that had driven a wedge between him and the Prime Minister in the past - the government's policy on Hindu settlers from Pakistan, the Kashmir issue; and the Hindu Code Bills. But Mukherjee was at his acerbic best when it came to trading personal charges with Nehru. In 1953, he alleged that he 'saw with my own eyes how government resources can be made to operate for the purpose of winning the elections. I can tell the Prime

Minister sometime later. He does not know that money and wine played their part in many a sphere.' Nehru was furious at the allegation, because he had heard Mukherjee declare openly that the Congress party had used 'wine and women' to win elections.

Yet, getting the better of Nehru in parliament was no solace for Mukherjee for he wished for a greater and deeper political involvement at the juncture. During the campaign for the first general elections, Mukherjee had claimed that he could 'set this man (Nehru) right if I can take even ten members of Parliament with me.' But this was easier said than done.

However, the wheel of fortune soon turned in his favour and the Jana Sangh bagged four seats in the by-elections to the Delhi assembly. The reason: his party's campaign in the capital, which was then swarming with refugees, had cleverly highlighted the government's alleged indecision on Kashmir's integration with the Union.

The Kashmir Conundrum: Syama Prasad Mukherjee was a member of the Nehru Cabinet when, on 17 October 1949, the Constituent Assembly had adopted the resolution to provide special status to the state of Jammu & Kashmir. When N. Gopalaswami Ayyangar, a ministerial colleague and member of the drafting committee, in a reply to a query from Maulana Hasrat Mohani, the Urdu poet and member of the House, had stated that Article 370 in the Constitution was being inserted 'due to the special conditions of Kashmir. That particular State is not yet ripe for this kind of integration. It is the hope of everybody here that in due course even Jammu and Kashmir will become ripe for the same sort of integration as has taken place in the case of other States.' Syama Prasad Mukherjee had acquiesced to the formulation.

Yet, within a year, his party's election manifesto had proclaimed ambitiously that it would 'end the uncertainty about Kashmir's future, it should be integrated with Bharat like other acceding states and not be given special position.'

It was hereafter crystal-clear that Kashmir, especially 'the problem of (its) relationship' with the 'rest of India,' and the Hindus of Jammu, had come to occupy central space in Mukherjee's politics. This was indeed paradoxical because Mukherjee's interest in the Kashmir problem only 'grew casually71", and although he was consulted by the state leaders on the issue from the time of India's independence, Kashmir was hitherto not the kernel of his larger political mission. In February 1952, Mukherjee criticised the government for having mismanaged the state's integration under the Instrument of Accession and committing India to plebiscite. He had also protested against the state's Constituent Assembly's decision to adopt a separate flag, and it is in this context that he had raised the iconic slogan which later became a clarion call for several Right-wing parties in the country:

Ek desh mein do vidhan, Ek desh mein do nishan ,Ek desh mein do pradhan, Nahin chalenge, nahin chalenge

In his maiden speech in Lok Sabha as President of the Jana Sangh in May 1952, Syama Prasad Mukherjee had posed a sharp question to next Prime Minister, Nehru: 'Are Kashmiris Indians first and Kashmiris or are they Kashmiris first and Indian next, or are they Kashmiris first second, and third and not Indians at all?' As a veteran and respected parliamentarian, he was well aware that parliamentary decorum did not require the Prime Minister to give an immediate reply, but Syama

Prasad was relentless in his assertion and resorted to a barb that underscored his deep dislike for the Prime Minister, 'Nehru claims to have discovered India. But he has yet to discover his mind.'

Meanwhile, in the Hindu-majority Jammu, the RSS had discovered a great opportunity for mobilising the community, and at the behest of Balraj Madhok, they chose to back a well-known local leader called Prem Nath Dogra to form a party called the Jammu Praja Parishad in November 1947. When a few members of the fledgling party were subjected to police atrocities during a protest march, it was Syama Prasad Mukherjee who had come to their rescue and suggested that they storm their way into the Constituent Assembly of Jammu and Kashmir.

Mukherjee's continuing pursuit of Hindu-centric politics raised the hackles of the Prime Minister yet again, and he accused both the Jana Sangh and the Praja Parishad of pursuing communal politics. In response, Mukherjee said that he was, 'getting quite sick of this charge which is unfounded, if we want to consider whether communalism exists in the country or whether it is openly advocated as a plank by any political organisation, let us fix a date for debate and let us discuss the matter. Let government bring forward its charges. Let us have a chance of replying.'

Despite such rhetoric and overt posturing, by the end of 1952, Mukherjee decided to firm up his party's position on Kashmir and adopted a resolution to this effect. At its All India Session in Kanpur in December 1952, the Jana Sangh demanded a round table conference between the representatives of Praja Parishad, the Sheikh Abdullah government, and a few 'recognised leaders of India'. Mukherjee was also instrumental in the Jana Sangh's decison to partner with other Hindu organisations like the Hindu Mahasabha, RSS, and the Jammu Praja Parishad in launching an 'agitation from Jammu into the Punjab and up to Delhi and beyond, on the three issues of Kashmir, refugees from East Bengal, and the banning of cow-slaughter.' The resolution authorised the party's Working Committee (Mukherjee was re-elected as president at the first plenary session) to 'prepare whatever is necessary for an all-India agitation for the complete integration of the State of Jammu and Kashmir.'

After the drubbing that the Jana Sangh received in the first general elections, Mukherjee set his eyes on the next, which was scheduled in 1957. Planning to calibrate mass agitations, he arrived in Kashmir in 1952-53. He 'took up cudgels', insisting on his right to travel anywhere in India. He strode across the state border without a permit and was promptly jailed. Unlike Mahatma Gandhi, Mukherjee had little or no expertise in launching and managing mass movements and felt severely hamstrung.[37]

Dr Syama Prasad Mukherjee, unknown to himself, set out on his last and fateful journey from Delhi railway station at 6.30 a.m. on 8 May 1953. The passenger train, carrying him and his entourage to Punjab on their way to Jammu, steamed out of the station. The compartment in which he sat had been bedecked with flowers and Jana Sangh flags. Guru Datt Vaid, Atal Bihari Vajpayee, Tek Chand, Balraj Madhok and a few pressmen were there with him. Shortly before his departure, he issued a statement explaining his purpose for going to Jammu: to find out for himself the extent and depth of the Praja Parishad agitation and the repression let loose on the citizens of Jammu by Abdullah.

Explaining why he had not applied for an entry permit; the statement said:

Mr Nehru has repeatedly declared that the accession of the State of Jammu and Kashmir to India has been hundred percent complete. Yet it is strange to find that one cannot enter the state without a prior permit from the Government of India. This permit is granted even to Communists who are playing their usual role in Jammu and Kashmir, but entry is barred to those who think or act in terms of Indian unity and nationhood.

Regarding his aim in going to Jammu, the statement said:

My object in going to Jammu is solely to acquaint myself with what exactly has happened there and the present state of affairs. I would also come into contact with available local leaders representing various interests, outside the Praja Parishad. It will be my endeavour to ascertain the intentions of the people of Jammu and to find out if there is any possibility of the movement being brought to a peaceful and honourable end, which will be fair and just not only to the people of the state but also to the whole of India.

He was thus, contrary to what Nehru and Abdullah had sought to project, not out to provoke the agitators and lead them further into confrontation with Abdullah's government. Ever the constitutional politician, he wished to bring the agitation to an end whereby both warring parties could be able to save face. However, in entering the Indian state of Jammu and Kashmir, he had refused to take the permit issued by the Government of India.

The first stop on his itinerary was nearby Ambala, in Punjab (now Haryana). While on the train, Dr. Mukherjee remembered that before leaving Delhi, he had promised Professor Walter Johnson, a visiting American dignitary, that he would send him papers on the Jana Sangh. More importantly, he realized he ought to send some official intimation to Abdullah about his entering the state. In fact, he had scheduled a meeting with Johnson on 13 May, but possibly on the apprehension that he might be arrested, he also told him that he might not be able to keep the appointment. In any case, he shot off a telegram to Abdullah which read, 'I am proceeding to Jammu. My object in going there is to study the situation myself and to explore the possibilities of creating conditions leading to a peaceful settlement. I would like to see you also if possible.' He sent a copy of the telegram to Nehru.

The train reached Ambala at about 2 p.m., and there was such huge crowd on the platform that Dr. Mukherjee had a hard time getting down. Even before he alighted, the president of Ambala Town Jana Sangh, advocate Raghbir Saran, showed him the latest issue of the Illustrated Weekly of India, which carried on its cover the pictures of Dr. Mukherjee and Jayaprakash Narayan with the caption, 'After Nehru, Who? Mukherjee or J.P.?'

From Ambala, he drove down to Karnal via Shahabad and Nilokheri, where he had to make unscheduled stops and give speeches. From Karnal, he sent a short letter to his sister-in-law, Tara Devi, describing the reception he had received so far. He also expressed his worry about his dear Hasu, his younger daughter, whom he had left back in Delhi. He had a special soft corner for her, the quiet, withdrawn girl who had never known a mother's love and had recently recovered from a bout of tuberculosis. He spent the night in Karnal and the next day drove to Panipat, where he addressed a huge meeting. Then he took a train to Phagwara, where he received a reply to the telegram he had sent to Abdullah. It read, "Thanks for your telegram. I am afraid your proposed visit to the State at the present juncture is inopportune and will not serve any useful purpose.' Nehru did not bother to send a reply or even an acknowledgement.

After Phagwara, the next stop was Jullundur, where he addressed a press conference. He also sent Madhok back from Jullundur and boarded a train for Amritsar. On the train, an elderly person introduced himself as the deputy commissioner of Gurdaspur (the district in which Pathankot is situated) and informed him that the Punjab government had decided not to allow him to reach Pathankot. Upon hearing this, Dr. Mukherjee proceeded to make arrangements for his arrest and decided, after consultations, that Guru Datt Vaid, the well-known Ayurvedic physician and author who was then president of Delhi state Jana Sangh, and Tek Chand, a young, energetic worker from Dehra Dun, would accompany him and court arrest with him.

But strangely, he was not arrested, neither at Amritsar nor at Pathankot nor anywhere on the way. A huge crowd of over 20,000 people received him at the Amritsar railway station, where he halted for the night. He met the local workers and talked to them. He was emphatic that he would go to Jammu whether Abdullah liked it or not. The journey from Amritsar to Pathankot was yet another triumphant march. Thousands of people greeted him at every station. He arrived to an unbelievable reception at Pathankot. A sea of people with folded hands stood on both sides of the bazaar through which his jeep passed. Just before his departure, a ninety-year-old lady blessed him in Punjabi with the following words: 'Oye Puttar! Jit ke avin, aiwan na avin (My Son! Do not return until you are victorious).'

Soon after his arrival at Pathankot, the deputy commissioner of Gurdaspur, who seemed to have preceded him, sought an interview with him. He informed Dr. Mukherjee that he had been instructed by his government to allow him and his companions to proceed and enter Jammu and Kashmir state without a permit. He himself appeared quite surprised that the orders he was due to receive had been reversed. Little did he, or anyone else present, know that the diabolical scheme that had been hatched intended for Dr. Mukherjee to be arrested in Jammu and Kashmir state and not in Punjab, so that he would remain outside the jurisdiction of the Indian Supreme Court.

The next stop was the border check post at Madhopur on the River Ravi, one of the five great rivers of Punjab, marking the boundary between the states of Punjab and Jammu and Kashmir. There was a bridge across the river, and the boundary lay at the midpoint of the bridge. Dr Mukherjee and his companions reached the check post at 4 p.m. The deputy commissioner of Gurdaspur and other officers present there saw them off at the bridge. However, as soon as the jeep reached the centre of the bridge, they found the road blocked by a posse of the Jammu and Kashmir state police. The jeep stopped, and a police officer who identified himself as the superintendent of police, Kathua, handed over to him an order from the chief secretary of the state, dated May 10, 1953, banning his entry into the state.

'But I intend to go to Jammu,' Dr.Mukherjee declared.

Thereupon, the police officer took out an order of arrest under the Public Safety Act of the state, signed by Prithvinandan Singh, inspector-general of police, dated May 10, which stated that Dr. Mukherjee 'has acted, is acting, or is about to act in a manner prejudicial to public safety and peace'," and that 'in order to prevent him from so acting... Captain A. Azeez, Superintendent of Police, Kathua' was being directed to arrest Dr Mukherjee and remove him under custody to the Central Jail at Srinagar. 'All right,' said Dr Mukherjee upon reading the order and got down from the jeep. Guru Datt Vaid, Tek Chand and others also got down. Atal Bihari Vajpayee, his private secretary, had been with him up to this point. In his last message as a free person, Dr Mukherjee told Vajpayee and others to tell the country that he had at last entered the state of Jammu and Kashmir, though as a prisoner, and to carry on his work in his absence.

The police jeep halted for a short while at Lakhanpur. The threesome was put in another closed jeep which rushed towards Srinagar through Tawi bridge and Jammu city. Thousands of people had assembled near Tawi bridge in Jammu to receive their hero. They waited for him until nightfall, but did not notice a closed jeep passing the bridge at dusk. They reached Udhampur around 10 p.m. and Batote around 2 a.m., where they spent the night. They finally arrived at Srinagar Central Jail around 3 p.m.

From there, he and his two companions were escorted by the superintendent of the jail, Pandit Siri Kanth Sapru, to a small cottage near the Dal Lake. There, one of the most prominent members of the Indian Parliament, the president of one of India's national parties, was to spend the last forty days of his life as a prisoner of Sheikh Abdullah, ostensibly just for having committed the offence of acting 'in a manner prejudicial to public safety and peace'.

It is important to note here that many are under the impression that Dr Mukherjee was imprisoned for entering Jammu and Kashmir state without a permit. This is a canard deliberately spread by Sheikh Abdullah himself, as he had done in a broadcast, for reasons best known to him. Dr Mukherjee mentioned this in a handwritten note to his counsel, U.M. Trivedi for the drafting of his habeas corpus petition. In fact, on May 11, the state government of Jammu and Kashmir issued an ordinance through the Sadri-Riyasat stating that it is an offence to enter the state without a state permit. But, as the order of Prithvinandan Singh, inspector-general of police, reveals, Dr Mukherjee was not (and could not have been) arrested under that ordinance. On the day of the arrest, the only permit that could have been issued was one by the Government of India and not by the government of Jammu and Kashmir. But as we have already seen, the deputy commissioner of Gurdaspur told him that the Government of India had already decided to allow Dr Mukherjee to enter Jammu and Kashmir state without a permit. This reveals a very strange and suspicious chain of circumstances unfolded.

Meanwhile, Madhok had been arrested and put in Ambala Central Jail. A habeas corpus petition was moved on his behalf and he was freed. When he came to know that Dr. Mukherjee had been arrested and imprisoned in Jammu and Kashmir, he lost his nerve and ran to the one person from whom he thought he could always seek advice. That person was Justice Mehr Chand Mahajan, erstwhile Prime Minister of Jammu and Kashmir and then a judge of the Indian Supreme Court. He was from Kangra and spoke Dogri, the language of Jammu. Madhok unthinkingly rushed to him, little realizing that as a sitting judge of the highest court of the country, his powers were severely circumscribed by the canons of judicial conduct. Mahajan was understandably flabbergasted. He said in Dogri,' 'Balraj, please have some regard for my position. I am a judge of the Supreme Court! Just one week back, I released you on a habeas corpus, and now here you are at my residence, asking me to do something!' Madhok said, 'Sir, what can I do, you are the only man whom I can see.' Then Mahajan told Madhok, 'Had he been arrested in Gurdaspur district, Pathankot or anywhere else, the Supreme Court could have released him within a week, maybe earlier; but the Supreme Court has no jurisdiction over the Jammu and Kashmir state. What will happen, I can't say. My only advice is to send some advocate immediately and have habeas corpus application made.'

The news of the arrest created a stir all over the country. Protests, meetings and hartals took place in Delhi and other places, giving new impetus and direction to the satyagraha. Satyagrahis began to proceed to Jammu without a permit and court arrest. But neither Abdullah nor Nehru was moved. Whether with or without the consent or knowledge of Nehru, Abdullah had a scheme up his sleeve which he was determined to follow.[38]

Dr. Mukherjee was incarcerated in a small cottage converted into a sub-jail, located near Nishat Bagh, far away from Srinagar city. The cottage was situated on the slope of the mountain range flanking the Dal Lake. It could be reached only by climbing a steep flight of stairs, which must have been a hard task for Dr Mukherjee with his bad leg and proved to be much harder later. The cottage had one main room, about 10 feet by 11, in which Dr Mukherjee was lodged and two small side rooms that accommodated his co-detenues, Guru Datt Vaid and Tek Chand.

In the annals of the Indian Right, the last forty-odd days of Mukherjee's life are eulogized, reminiscent of tragic stories of leaders who faced grave injustices at the hands of a cruel dispensation, and ended up as martyrs. But another view often suggests that these events reflect the failed manoeuvres of a politically naïve man. Mukherjee was transferred to a cottage outside the city, where his condition started deteriorating. He started feeling back pain and high temperature on the night of June 19-20. He was diagnosed with dry pleurisy, a condition he had suffered from in 1937 and 1944.

The doctor prescribed him a streptomycin injection and powders, but Mukherjee informed him that his family physician had told him that streptomycin did not suit his system. The doctor, however, assured him that new information about the drug had come to light and that he would be fine. On June 22, Mukherjee felt pain in the heart region, began perspiring and felt like he was fainting. He was later shifted to a hospital and provisionally diagnosed with a heart attack. He died a day later. The state government declared that he had died on June 23 at 3:40 a.m. due to a heart attack.

Syama Prasad Mukherjee's death at fifty-two, along with the circumstances leading up to his end, hung like the proverbial albatross around the BJS's neck and caused significant discomfort within the Jana Sangh. It required the political gumption of a man whose credentials within the party remains unchallenged to take a step that appeared as if he wanted to emerge from Syama Prasad's shadows.

On June 23, 1953, Prime Minister Jawaharlal Nehru was in Geneva, en route to Cairo after attending the coronation of Queen Elizabeth II, when he received the news of a bereavement from India. He immediately dispatched a condolence letter through the diplomatic post to Lady Jogmaya Mukherjee, stating: "Though we may have differed in politics, I respected him and had great affection for him.' However, for the mother, who believed her son had died a mysterious death in faraway Srinagar, the prime minister's commiseration was inadequate. In her reply, Lady Mukherjee demanded 'justice' and condemned the condolence message as being of little value because 'it comes from people who themselves should stand trial.' She further concluded:

A fearless son of free India has met his death while in detention without trial under the most tragic and mysterious circumstances. I....demand an absolutely impartial and open inquiry.

The anguish of a mother notwithstanding, it was against contemporary wisdom that the woman in question had 'Lady' prefixed to her name, while her son-the fifty-two-year-old Syama Prasad Mukherjee- had died defending the principles of a Hindu nation in the cold confines of a jail. The 24th of June of 1953 was indeed a sad day. More than a lakh of people awaiting the arrival of Mukherjee's body at Dum Dum Airport, Calcutta. The body had been flown from Kashmir to Calcutta. Slogans were raised.

Jahan hue balidaan Mukherjee, woh Kashmir hamara hai (The Kashmir where Mukherjee laid down his life, is ours)

Equally, whenever the perennially contentious and unresolved issue of Kashmir's special status was brought into focus, Mukherjee was recalled for his famous slogan:

Ek desh mein do vidhan, ek desh mein do nishan, ek desh mein do pradhan

Nahin chalenge, nahin challenge (In a nation which is one entity, there can be no room for two constitutions, two heads, nor two flags)

A fortnight after his death, the Jana Sangh's Central Working Committee passed a resolution stating that India was 'stunned by the mysterious circumstances' of Syama Prasad Mukherjee's passing and alleged 'criminal medical negligence.' His death in custody raised widespread suspicion across the country and demands for an independent inquiry were raised.

Ever since its formation in 1951, first the Jana Sangh's, and later the BJP's, stand on Kashmir hinged on two basic premises: first, that the Hindu-majority region of Jammu was neglected in preference for the Muslim-majority Kashmir Valley; and second, that the integration of the state with the rest of India was impossible until Article 370 of the Constitution (which grants a special autonomous status to the state) was not abrogated. Syama Prasad Mukherjee was a modern, conservative, nationalist who not only worked for the idea of 'territorial nationalism' but also played an important role in popularising the idea of 'cultural nationalism' which later become the bedrock for BJS and BJP and showed a new path to the youth in post-independence India.

Meanwhile, after returning to India, Prime Minister Nehru rose up in parliament to pay homage to the departed leader: "In any event, his passing away would have been sad and a great blow to this house and the country, but in the peculiar circumstances in which it took place, naturally this added to our sorrow. Later, the BJS claimed that the arrest and death of Mukherjee in Jammu and Kashmir was an "Abdullah - Nehru conspiracy" and that Mukherjee's death remains "even now an impervious mystery".

Deendayal Upadhyaya

Deendayal Upadhyaya was born in 1916 in the village of Nagla Chandraban, now called Deendayal Dham, near the town of Farah in the Mathura District, 26 km (16 mi) from Mathura, into a Brahmin family. His father, Bhagwati Prasad Upadhyaya, was an astrologer who worked as an assistant station master in the Indian Railways and was posted in Jalesar, in the United Provinces (now Uttar Pradesh). His mother, Rampyari Upadhyaya, was a homemaker and observant Hindu. Both his parents died when he was eight years old and he was brought up by his maternal uncle.

Under the guardianship of his maternal uncle and aunt, he attended high school in Sikar. The Maharaja of Sikar presented him a gold medal, Rs 250 to buy books and a monthly scholarship of Rs 10. He did his Intermediate in Pilani, Rajasthan, (Now Birla School, Pilani). The frequent tragedies in young Deendayal's life impacted his academic journey, forcing him to change several schools, from Gangapur to Kota in Rajasthan, and attend different colleges in Pilani, Agra, Kanpur and Allahabad. Finally at the age of twenty-five, he earned a degree in Bachelor of Education. He also took a BA degree at the Sanatan Dharma College, Kanpur.

In 1939, he moved over to Agra and joined St. John's College, Agra to pursue a master's degree in English literature but could not continue his studies due to family and financial issues. Although he was a promising student and expected to sit for the civil services exams, he rejected the idea and later completed a Master's in English literature.

Upadhyaya came into contact with the RSS through a classmate, Baluji Mahashabde, while studying at Sanatan Dharma College in 1937. He met the founder of the RSS, K. B. Hedgewar, who engaged with him in an intellectual discussion at one of the shakhas. Sunder Singh Bhandari was also one of his classmates at Kanpur when he passed his B.T. from Prayag. However, he did not enter a job nor did he marry. Instead, he started full-time work in the RSS from 1942.

He had come to Kanpur with Balwant and stayed at a hostel, joining the RSS shakha of the hostel under Balwant influence. In 1937, he formally took the oath and started hoisting the Sangh flag in the shakha, eventually becoming the gatnayak of the hostel gat. He attended the 40-day summer vacation RSS camp at Nagpur, where he underwent training in Sangh Education. As a swayamsevak in Kanpur, he participated in 40-day Officers Training Camps (OTC) of the Sangh in 1939 and 1942. These camps used to be held only in Nagpur in those times.

After spending time at these camps, he became more convinced and dedicated to the nationalist cause. Following his second-year training in the RSS Education Wing, Upadhyaya became a lifelong pracharak of the RSS. He worked as the pracharak for the Lakhimpur district and, from 1955, as the joint Prant Pracharak (regional organiser) for Uttar Pradesh. He was regarded as an ideal swayamsevak of the RSS because 'his discourse reflected the pure thought-current of the Sangh'. Deendayal was convinced of his future, and even though his extended family wanted to see him married, this desire was relegated to the backburner, particularly after his meeting with K.B. Hedgewar in Kanpur.[39]

By now, it was abundantly clear that Deendayal had chosen politics over the life of a householder. In his reply to a letter from a cousin who had requested him to return to the family fold, he wrote sensitively:

"I am torn between affection (for you and the family) and duty (towards the nation). I have been assigned to work in a district to awaken the slumbering Hindu society and raise a volunteer corps. I will (not) be allowed to take up a stable job. The society and the country are the first priority for an RSS worker. His individual duties come later. You are apprehensive because you do not know much about the Sangh. It is in no way associated with the Congress (Gandhi had already announced the Quit India movement leading to its repression; emphasis mine). Nor is it part of any political organisation. It is not involved in politics. RSS does not resort to satyagraha or going to jail"[40]

Deendayalji, however, could not withstand the physical rigour of the training, but he stood out in its educational segment. Babasaheb Apte writes in this connection: "Pandit Deendayalji versified several parts of his answers. It was not merely versification, nor was it a flight of imagination. He simply adopted the medium of verse instead of prose in writing his answers. It was balanced and logical. I could not help being impressed by hill.

After completing his education and second-year training in the RSS Education Wing, Pandit Deendayal Upadhyaya ji became a lifelong pracharak of the Sangh and he lived this life till the very end. He entered politics through the Rashtriya Swayamsevak Sangh, became the General Secretary of the Bharatiya Jan Sangh, and later its President. His life was thus an embodiment of a thorough political thought process.

Early days in RSS

He was determined and strong-willed. While everyone was impressed with his intellectual abilities, he concerned himself with analyzing the problems that the Indian society faced and was convinced of the need for disciplined and dedicated swayamsevaks in society. Completely convinced of the ideas and methods of the RSS, he decided to dedicate his life to serve the nation through the Sangh work. While it was a decision that had far-reaching implications for his personal life, the nation was to see the emergence of a thinker karmayogi who would lay the foundation of future politics in the country.

Deendayal decided to become a lifelong pracharak in 1942. It was a very tough decision. A pracharak is supposed to live a life like a sanyasi, without marrying and work full-time to serve the nation by strengthening the Sangh's work. In a letter to his uncle on 21 July 1942, he expressed his deep desire to work as a pracharak of the RSS: 'Can we not forgo a few worthless ambitions for the benefit and protection of the society and for the faith for which Rama suffered exile, Krishna bore innumerable hardships, Rana Pratap roamed from forest to forest, Shivaji staked his all and Guru Gobind Singh allowed his little sons to be buried alive?"

He started his work as a pracharak from a Tehsil in the Lakhimpur district of Uttar Pradesh. His commitment to the cause, ability to mix with everyone, humility, intellectual capacity and dedication helped him win the hearts of people. From the rich and educated to the poor, destitute and deprived sections of society, everyone was fascinated by his personality and started drawing closer to Sangh activities. His tireless efforts and organizational abilities helped him win the support of both the rural and urban masses.

His organizational abilities and talent did not escape the notice of his seniors in the Sangh. He was given the responsibility of Sahprant Pracharak of Uttar Pradesh in 1945. At that time, Shri Bhaurao Deoras was the Prant Pracharak of the Sangh in Uttar Pradesh. Deendayal's responsibilities increased with every passing day and he proved himself efficient on a number of occasions, taking initiatives and implementing them successfully.

Deendayal faced a testing time when the Sangh was banned in 1948 by the Congress government. The RSS decided to launch satyagraha in response to the ban. Deendayal organized the satyagraha, employing his effective organizational capabilities and strategic acumen. The Congress, which had become weary of the growing popularity of the RSS and took the extreme step of banning the Sangh, was stunned by the discipline and dedication of the RSS satyagrahis, who never resorted to violence even in the face of extreme provocation by the police.

The attempt to crush the satyagraha with an iron hand resulted in strengthening the voices in support of the RSS. Thousands of swayamsevaks participated in the satyagraha, and while the police resorted to violent suppression of the movement, the satyagrahis remained committed to the principles of non-violence. Not a single incident of violence by the satyagrahis was reported. Deendayal, who was organizing and planning the satyagraha, never lost his cool.

Appreciating Deendayal's qualities, Guruji Golwalkar said that he was adept in the art of keeping the mind cool while having a burning fire in the heart. The fire in his heart could never reach his mind to disturb his mental balance and neither could the coolness of his mind come down to extinguish the fire that his heart. This quality was fully displayed during the satyagraha when Deendayal maintained his composure and allowed the movement to keep its momentum.

He not only kept the movement on the ground alive, but also found out a way to keep the ideological struggle active and uninterrupted. As a result of the ban on the RSS, the magazine set up by Deendayal, Rashtradharma, was also banned. But Deendayal's pen could not be reined in; he immediately started another publication, Panchjanya. Himalaya came out the same day Panchjanya was banned. As soon as Himalaya was attacked, Desh Bhakta was started. In this way, he maintained the continuity of the ideological struggle through his relentless efforts and skills.

Bhaurao Deoras wrote about the tireless efforts, dedication and organizational skills of Deendayal in strengthening RSS work in Uttar Pradesh: 'In the early days of your Sangh work, when your path was strewn with thorns, you set out on this difficult task. No one was familiar with the Sangh activities in Uttar Pradesh at that time. You took over the onerous responsibility on your shoulders as an ordinary swayamsevak. You truly laid the foundation of the Sangh work in Uttar Pradesh. Today, the RSS work in the province is a result of your hard work and sense of duty. Many of our volunteers have been inspired by the examples set by you. You have been a constant source of inspiration to all of them. You are an ideal swayamsevak. We had heard of the ideal swayamsevak from our founder; you embody all these qualities in yourself. A brilliant intellect, an unequalled sense of duty, modesty and humility-you symbolize all of them in your person.

Another remarkable contribution of Deendayal was the development of a think-tank in the RSS called the Education Cell. It was formed by Bhaurao Deoras, Deendayal Upadhyaya and Nanaji Deshmukh.[41]

WRITER AND THINKER

Apart from his organizational capabilities, skills and dedication, Deendayal was a writer par excellence. He was an original thinker and philosopher. He believed in the intellectual awakening of the nation, and for this, he wielded strong writing on almost every issue. He wrote two literary pieces: Samrat Chandragupta in 1946 and Jagadguru Shri Shankaracharya in 1947. Bharatiya Artha Niti: Vikas Ki Ek Disha (Indian Economic Policy: A Direction of Development) is a brilliant work that captured his economic thinking. Rashtra Chintan and Rashtra Jivanki Disha are collections of his articles written on the issues related to nation, society, politics, dharma and culture.

In Bharatiya Artha Niti: Vikas Ki Ek Disha, he pointed out the main malady in policy-making. He wrote that the direction for the future was not based on thinking about the present with an understanding of the past, which resulted in different theories by historians, economists and politicians. He called for a coordinated effort, which he tried to present by emphasizing economic ideas, including those in Indian traditions; fundamental priorities; demand and industrial priorities; small and big industries; trade; transport; and social service.[42]

Upadhyaya started the monthly Rashtra Dharma publication from Lucknow in the 1940s, using it to spread Hindutva ideology. Later he started the weekly Panchjanya and the daily Swadesh.

Although Deendayal Upadhyaya was a contemporary of Balasaheb Deoras, he joined the RSS more than a decade after his colleague, because it was yet to be established in the United Provinces.

Interestingly, Upadhyaya's trajectory was very similar to the RSS at the time-the organisation was yet to plunge into mass-based politics either like the Congress or the Hindu Mahasabha, neither was Deendayal aiming to be a people's leader, as he was more inclined towards understanding the ideological underpinning of the outfit. He was often seen in the company of students and scholars in universities, and later began indoctrinating them into the Sangh's philosophy.

Once he had settled into his job as sah-prant pracharak in 1945, Upadhyaya took the lead in establishing the education cell for the RSS in UP, which was a crucial arm for the organisation for communicating its ideology and programmes amongst families of its volunteers. In time, Deendayal's initiative on education was taken forward and the activities by these multiple cells were consolidated by Balasaheb Deoras under the umbrella of a new affiliate, Vidya Bharti.

He also set up a publishing house in Lucknow called the Rashtra Dharam Prakashan, which brought out books and other literature to propagate the RSS' ideology. But of all his endeavours, Deendayal's most significant contribution was the setting up of the Panchjanya magazine in 1945, which is since acknowledged as the official mouthpiece of the RSS, and a platform for furthering its ideology (It must be mentioned here that the magazine was later re-launched with much fanfare on 14 January 1948, with the late Atal Bihari Vajpayee as its first editor). Meanwhile, it was Deendayal Upadhyaya's engagement with the written word which came in handy in 1949 during the drafting of the RSS constitution. As was obvious, Deendayal's initial years in the RSS were spent more on intellectual pursuits than furthering his career prospects, and it was his proclivity towards academics and pedagogy which later made it difficult for him to be a hard-nosed political animal, but more of which later.

Meanwhile, in April 1946, Bhaurao Deoras decided to put Deendayal's literary talent to better use and requested him to write historical fiction for children. The larger intent of the project was based on the premise that not only was there a dearth of suitable literature for the young minds, but a version of history that was biased when viewed from the prism of ancient Indian precepts. In 1946, Deendayal wrote a novella titled, Samrat Chandragupta on the life of a king who was said to have unified the country. In what was ostensibly a children's book, Deendayal inserted a bit of polemic in its preface, acknowledging that the events in the book 'are true despite the concerted efforts of European scholars and their blind followers among Indian historians (sic), to distort them to serve their own purpose and vested interests.'

The sangh parivar's objections to the distortion of Indian history, particularly by Left-leaning historians is well documented. However, the first red flag in the context was raised by Deendayal Upadhyaya, who had perceptively blurred the lines between folklore and history, and wrote in Samrat Chandragupta that the, 'readers of this book need not (sic) be told everything about the maze of historical facts.'

After the great success of his maiden book, Deendayal Upadhyaya took on a more challenging subject in 1947 and began writing about Adi Shankaracharya, the saint-philosopher from Kerala, who is revered amongst other things for lending a definitive form to Hinduism. Titled eponymously as Jagat Guru: Adi Shankaracharya, Deendayal perhaps intended his readers to go beyond the philosophical contents of the book and said that his "objective was to inspire the youth to look back to the country's glorious past, take pride in it and dedicate their lives to the revival of the ancient glory." This idea of invoking India's 'glorious' past and exhorting the youth to 'revive' it as part of their duty to the nation is what the RSS and its political affiliates have held on to for years.

In 1951, when Syama Prasad Mukherjee founded the BJS, Deendayal was seconded to the party by the RSS, tasked with moulding it into a genuine member of the Sangh Parivar. He was appointed as General Secretary of its Uttar Pradesh branch, and later the all-India general secretary. For 15 years, he remained the outfit's general secretary.

During the publishing of Rashtradharm, the journalist within Pandit ji first came to light with publication of monthly "Rashtradharm" from Lucknow in 1940s. The publication was meant for spreading the ideology of nationalism. Though he did not have his name printed as editor in any of the issues of this publication, there was hardly any issue which did not have his long lasting impression due to his thought provoking writings. He chose to publish those items which had a positive side. He never had a problem with the criticism of anti-people thoughts or movements unless the language was balanced and the criticism was healthy. Later on, Panchjanya weekly and Daily Swadesh also started getting published from there, where the present Prime Minister, Mr. Atal Bihari Vajpayee, was appointed as an editor. After sometime, Deendayal ji was asked to work in the political field. There, he had regular interaction with scribes and he had to issue statements quite frequently.

He had a column in "the Organiser", a weekly. The name of the column was "Political Diary". While reading this column, one realized that despite being critical of several policies of Nehru era, his language was always decently balanced. In 1959, I was asked to edit Panchjanya.

Annoyed over the Nehru government's policy about China and Tibet, I wrote a strong editorial in the first issue of the weekly itself. After reading it, Deendayal ji said, "your piece was excellent but perhaps you should be little more cautious with the heading as Pandit Nehru is after all the Prime Minister of the Country." We should not be careless in using words while criticizing him. His message was clear and worthwhile. 'Don't Distort the News' was his mantra. Once, he gave a statement which was quite out of context to one of the English dailies.

When he met the journalist concerned, he told him in a polite manner and with a personal touch, "I know you just cannot do this, but kindly tell your news editor not to publish statements out of context as it just not seems right to mislead the readers? It is the responsibility of a journalist to report the facts correctly and if he does not agree with somebody's views then that should also be published." A mature journalist always has his own perception about a problem. He himself is also motivated by an ideology. Sometimes, he is also a follower of a particular Party or Organization.

The natural question is that as a journalist, he should be loyal to whom? To his ideology? To the Party or Organization, he is related to? Or to the wider interest of Country and the common people? In a similar situation, I received a directive about publication of one of my edits. It was 1961. The Country was facing a distinct threat of Chinese invasion. At that time, a number of political parties and trade unions called for a nation wide strike to support certain demands of Railway employees. In view of the elections in 1962, Bharatiya Jansangh had also supported the call. Most of its leaders were expecting that Panchjanya will obviously support the strike. But then, I consulted my editorial colleagues and took the stand that the strike is not in the interest of the nation. "Navjivan" of ruling Congress Party used this ploy to mount attack on Jansangh. A number of Jansangh leaders, quite naturally, were not happy. They complained to Deendayal ji, who was General Secretary of the Party at that time, that whether it is appropriate for Panchjanya to criticize the policies and programmes of Jansangh? In the evening, he called me and these leaders to his residence. He told me why these leaders were unhappy.

Then he himself asked, "If something is in interest of Party but not in the interest of Party but not in the interest of nation, then what should be done?" The answer was inherent in the question. Then he said, "The Party might have certain compulsions to support the strike but Panchjanya should not have any such compulsion. I think everybody has taken right decision in their position. Parties can not be larger than the society or the country. The national interest should get top priority. A journalist should be loyal to the country." Why English News Papers have an anti-Indian attitude? In our conversations, several issues related to journalists and journalism used to come up. Once I asked him, Why English newspapers take a negative stand when it comes to Indianisation while the Hindi and regional newspapers always have a positive approach on this issue? His answer was - "Almost all the major English newspapers were run by the Englishmen. Though after independence, the ownership came into hands of Indians, the scribes and the editors were the same and so was their psyche. They were no more with the Britishers but the attitude was same. They remained alienated from the culture, civilization and tradition of this country. There are certain exceptions to this too. Generally, the English journalist was from the highly educated class and he was overawed by the old attitude."

Going further deep into the issue he said, "Even after the Britishers have left, India has failed to develop an education system according to its traditions. Physically Indian but intellectually English oriented Macualay oriented education system according to its traditions. Physically Indian but intellectually English oriented Macualay oriented education system is still prevalent with minor changes. How could the journalists coming out of this system be not alienated?"

Alternative of Congress

As mentioned earlier, in November 1949, the Congress Working Committee had adopted a resolution, backed by Deputy Prime Minister Sardar Vallabhbhai Patel, proposing the entry of RSS members into the party. This was recommended not only after the ban on the RSS, but also in the absence of Prime Minister Nehru, who was away on an official tour to the US. On his return from America, Jawaharlal had promptly reversed the proposal and said that the Congress could only admit members who were part of its volunteer bodies like the Sewa Dal. With the hope of the so-called grand alliance dissipating, Syama Prasad Mukherjee, leader of the Hindu Mahasabha and part of Nehru's interim Cabinet as Minister of Industry and Supplies (who resigned in April 1950), urged the RSS' sarsanghchalak Golwalkar to grant him permission to establish a political party forthwith, which was turned down. Eventually, after Sardar Vallabhbhai Patel's death in December 1950 and with the impending general elections, Mukherjee took the plunge and established in early May 1951 what he called a 'People's Party' in West Bengal.

Despite Golwalkar's scepticism towards mainstream politics, the move by Mukherjee was like a shot in the arm for the cadre, and it was planned that prior to launching the party at a national level, the state units be first established. Subsequently by September 1951, the Bharatiya Jana Sangh's state units were set up in UP, Punjab, PEPSU, Karnataka, Bihar, Rajasthan, Orissa (now Odisha), Madhya Bharat (now Madhya Pradesh), and Delhi. Deendayal Upadhyaya was sent on deputation to the Jana Sangh in UP, where he had begun his career as an RSS pracharak.

In less than a year, he became one of the most trusted lieutenants of Syama Prasad Mukherjee, and by the time of the Jana Sangh's first plenary session in Kanpur in December 1952, he was elevated as the general secretary of the party with the additional responsibility of piloting seven of its fifteen resolutions.

One of the first and most significant resolutions drafted by Deendayal was on the 'cultural revival', which redefined the RSS' philosophy while emphasising on the following: education must be based on national (read Hindu, emphasis mine) culture; the revival of Sanskrit and the acceptance of Devanagari script 'for all languages of the country rewriting of history on the right lines, so that it is the history of the people of India and not of those who committed aggression on her; and launching a campaign amongst Hindus to take up the noble task of Indianisation of general life and of those sections of the Indian national being which were shaken out of national moorings and were made to look outside the country for inspiration.'

In a way, the resolution was a precursor to his booklet, Akhand Bharat Kyon? and was viewed by many as a counter to the Congress' emphasis on India's compositeness. In his introduction to the resolution, Upadhyaya proclaimed that in the recent centuries, India's unity was often tested because of the constant reiteration of its diversity which prevented its citizens from being knitted into one nation on the basis of a single or homogenous cultural tradition. Unlike the Hindu Mahasabha, which rejected Muslims as part of the Indian mainstream, Upadhyaya referred to them and the Christians as 'different parts of the same body.'

Yet another resolution which bore Deendayal's unmistakable stamp at the Kanpur plenary was one which laid greater emphasis on organisation-building and social issues, as opposed to political activism. As mentioned earlier, unlike Syama Prasad Mukherjee, who was insistent that the Jana Sangh plunges into electoral politics, Upadhyaya took a long-term view and pressed for building a robust network of cadre.

The first plenary session of the Jana Sangh was a great success as evidenced by the thunderous applause for Dr Mukherjee's proclamation: 'Give me two Deendayals, and I will completely change the face of this nation.'

The public endorsement by the Jana Sangh chief guaranteed Deendayal Upadhyaya's unhindered rise in the party thereafter. During these initial five years, despite being busy with the first general elections and organizing a mass movement in Kashmir, Upadhyaya and his associates were able to provide a framework of the Bharatiya Jan Sangh. By 1957, the Jan Sangh had 243 regional and 889 local committees, and its membership rose to 74,863. The first general elections in 1952 were not particularly encouraging. Only Dr. Mukherjee and two of his friends were elected to Lok Sabha. The organisation was not very helpful in this, but the Jan Sangh, on the basis of its scoring 3.06% of the votes; was recognised as a national political party. In his address at the January 1954 session in Mumbai, encouraging the party workers to have faith in the party and be enthusiastic, Upadhyaya said: "Adult franchise is a big step towards educating the electorate politically. We will have to cate the public appropriately for the success of democracy. Our attitude has been vitiated as a result of over a thousand years of slavery... Narrow-mindedness and blind tradition have harmed our progress. Discrimination on the basis of caste and untouchability have shaken the foundations of our society. English education has given us wrong values of life. There is lack of discipline and self-restraint. We no longer believe in the dignity of labour. We must establish the right values for educating our countrymen. We must make them aware of the oneness of this country, spread from Kashmir to Kanyakumari...Awareness is the guarantee of a nation's bright future.... There is lack of wealth everywhere but this cannot be met from outside. We must assimilate all our resources, save and spend less. We must concentrate on our ultimate objective and move ahead with self-confidence and dedications."[43]

Instead of showing his co-workers and volunteers a short cut to win elections, Upadhyaya inspired them to move on to the long path of basic principles. Instead of asking them to work enthusiastically for short-term gain, he asked them to work with devotion and dedication.

The concept of a cultural nation that the Jan Sangh had propounded resulted in the setting up of a number of cultural centres in the first year of its inception. Chiefs of local municipal bodies were elected. Upadhyaya's initial area of work was Uttar Pradesh. He particularly inspired and enthused the workers there. In his address, he said: "By God's grace, the Jan Sangh representatives have been elected in Ayodhya, Mathura, Vrindavan, Gokul, Haridwar, Rishikesh and other pilgrim centres. Without tomtoming the slogan of non-violence, the Jan Sangh chief succeeded in banning not only cow slaughter but slaughter of all animals at Mathura. "Although the state government has announced putting roadblocks in our path, the people at large have given the Jan Sangh's elected representatives an opportunity to serve them. They will firmly move on this path of service to the people, failing which they will quit and join the people in their tight for civic rights."

Many local units were successful in Uttar Pradesh. In particular, out of the 970 contestants, 581 were successful there. The Jan Sangh workers had just entered politics, they also had to work as an opposition. The opposition has its own duty to perform, the chief being to tight for peoples' rights with the government. Communists exercised influence over the opposition at that time. Upadhyaya did not like their attitude, nor did he favour their methodology. He remained in office as general secretary for fifteen years until December 1967, when he was elevated as Jana Sangh president which was at variance with RSS' philosophy that pracharaks should remain as general secretaries with overall responsibility of the organisation and not take up the role of a titular head. Comparatively, the Jan Sangh was better organised in North India by 1957. Upadhyaya proposed to organise the 1958 annual session of the party at Bangalore. This was because he wanted to give an all-India outlook to the organisation. In the North, Jan Sangh workers emphatically connected Hindi with nationalism and National Language. Why was the session being held in Bangalore? Upadhyaya replied;

"Some delegates from Punjab told me after the session that this journey down south has pacified their feelings that Hindi was being hastily imposed on them. This also led to nullifying the exaggerated anti-Hindi feelings that were emanating from there."

In his address at the Bangalore session, Upadhyaya dwelled at length on the essential point of his party's programme for development. The Jan Sangh workers were emotionally involved with countrywide and national issues naturally. Ban on cow slaughter, undivided India, Kashmir, Berubari etc., were issues that agitated and enthused the party cadres. But the party had its own limits in trying to convince local forces and make them think of party lines. He, therefore, directed his workers; "Although no political party can exclude countrywide issues from its mass movement, we should largely concentrate on local issues." Explaining the process underlying a democratic movement, he said: "A movement in democracy does not mean opposition or fighting; it is an expression of people's sentiments. The state suppression may benefit political parties that play the role of a mediator for a short while between the state and the people, but it does not bode any good for the nation. Some political parties have adopted such an irresponsible attitude as a part of their programme. I feel we must give serious thought to this issue and fix limits for all political parties as well as the state."

A good political worker must have positive capabilities. Any developing party must be ready to take over the reins of the country's administration. A political worker must, therefore, be conversant with administrative processes and various laws. While we must make the state aware of people's reaction over its wrong policies, represent the electorate and influence the administration, it is our duty to attempt to know their problems and try to resolve them sympathetically by adopting a positive approach. We must study all the issues accordingly. We must constantly strive to properly understand the viewpoint of the administration.

Integrity of the nation and its security were the favourite subjects of the Jan Sangh. It had a different approach from that of other political parties, towards Pakistan. Upadhyaya said: "Pakistan's aggressive designs are clear. Its violation of our territory are a challenge to our sovereignty, and are disgraceful. No other political party, except the Jan Sangh, speaks on this issue. They are scared of losing the support of pro-Pak Muslims in elections. They are mum not only on this issue but also on the communally explosive and fifth columnist activities of Muslim fanatics. This is a wrong and condemnable incident of party self-interests."

Here it must also be mentioned that, through his speeches, Upadhyaya introduced some new things in the organization every year. The Jan Sangh had sent its elected representatives to various state legislatures, in the 1957 general elections. This strength was likely to rise in 1962. There was an urgent need to prepare a model code for legislators so that their conduct was in line with the democratic norms and dignity, and so that they received adequate training in this respect. A training camp for legislators was organised at Poona from June 28 to July 7, 1959. At the eighth annual session held in 1960 at Nagpur, Upadhyaya moved a resolution: "The base of Jan Sangh being basically principled, we urgently require such training camps and workshops. Without these, we shall not be able to assess the different approaches of other political parties." The various points of the legislators' code of conduct were decided in 1960 at Poona. "Walking out of the House and a tendency of create chaos through shouting or sloganeering, which are always aimed at capturing newspaper space, are not considered right by the Jan Sangh. We have advised our members to keep away from such a conduct; they should not protest in this unbecoming manner during the Governor's and the President's address to the House in order to register their protest. Dedication to democracy means that we must observe the parliamentary form of government scrupulously. Democracy cannot function without such conventions."

In 1960, Deendayal Updhyay started polarisation against congress. He actualised it by 1965 and by 1967, there was anti-congress regime. He is called architect of non-congress movement along with Ram Manohar Lohiya. In 1967 election, for the first time after independence, in the hindi belt of India, a political non-congress government was formed. It was Lohia's tactical prescription of anti-Congressism that became the basis of Samyukta Vidhayak Dal governments that were formed in nine states in 1967.

The seeds of destruction of the monolithic power of Congress were sown and within a decade, the first non-Congress government came into being. Lohia's dream came true, but he did not live to see its fruition.

Lohia's politics of anti-Congressism was essentially spearheaded against Jawaharlal Nehru during his twilight years. He was defeated by Nehru in the Phulpur Lok Sabha constituency by a margin of 64,671 votes (33.45 percent of the total votes counted).

But the maverick, albeit an erudite socialist, did not give up. The then Jana Sangh President, Deen Dayal Upadhyay, a staunch adherent of the Rashtriya Swayamsevak Sangh (RSS)

A few months later, bye-election was due at Farukkabad, also in UP. Lohia came in, followed by Upadhyaya as a campaigner. He was victorious. The two cashed in on India's humiliating defeat by China in 1962 and targeted Nehru.

The Sangh Parivar sensed Lohia's impulse. RSS ideologue Nanaji Deshmukh entered the scene and managed to bring Lohia at an RSS camp in Kanpur. Chaturvedi wrote, "When reporters asked Lohia why did you go there, Lohia's answer was, 'I went to turn sanyasis into homemakers'."

Thus, Deendayal Upadhyaya paved a way for non-congress alternative in India. It was not opportunism. According to him, there should be diversity in democracy. There shouldn't be one leader-one party-one policy. This is detrimental for democracy. He believed in India's tradition and culture and was not against modern tech, but he wanted policies which suited Indian requirements and conditions. His approach was also constructive but at the same time he was not soft when it came to principles. For example, in Rajasthan, he had expelled 6 MLAs of Jan Sangh out of 8 MLAs because they were opposing Zamindari abolition act. For him, quality mattered than quantity.

He was a Philosopher, journalist, sociologist, economist, thinker, and worked dedicatedly for organisation and with principles. For him, morality in public life was important.

In 1950s, there was a proposal to merge Jan Sangh and Swatantra party, Hindu Mahasahba and Ram Rajya Parishad as these parties constituted 16% vote. But, Deendaayal Updhyay objected the merger. The reason was that Shyama Prasad Mukherjee had asked Hindu Mahasabha to open its door for all religions but it didn't agree. So, Deendayal Updhyay objected to it. According to him, Ram Rajya Karpatri Maharaj's cottage was run from palaces which was not acceptable to Deendayal Upadhyaya in politics. He believed in purity in politics and principle. This is the difference between contemporary politics and Upadhyaya ji. He sacrificed LS seat for values in politics. His message should be spread across the political parties for casteless politics, communalism less politics. He stood for politics which should be value based. This is why Jan Sangh got credibility due to his value based politics.[44]

Upadhyaya analysed the gains and losses of each party. He also discussed the new emerging factors. Regarding the maintenance of democratic norms and expressing his concerns about new realities, he said:

"Bharatrya Jan Sangh washes to give a constitutional shape to politics. Its publicity and mass movements have always adopted constitutional norms. We maintained our standards in these elections also. Our speakers chiefly presented their own viewpoint and criticised other parties only in the background of our own convictions and beliefs. It is time that since we have alternate policy and programme and we have differences with the Congress and other parties which are its offshoots, our criticism is basic and penetrating. Because of our fearless and selfless nature, such criticism might have been sharp at places but Jan Sangh has nowhere resorted to personal allegations or roused communal or casteist feelings, nor has it ever resorted to regional and class conflicts. How far this statement of Upadhyaya can be true at a lower level is difficult to say, but he always tried to establish an organisation and educate his workers towards the creation of such an environment, can be easily understood by his deep-rooted beliefs. There were several untoward incidents during the elections that involved the Congress, the Communists, and the Jan Sangh. In this context, Upadhyaya said: "I demand that the administration should investigate the election publicity of various political parties impartially. It is essential not only to put an end to the prevailing malpractices but also to raise the standard of electioneering in the future."

A historic training camp of the executive committee of the Jan Sangh was organised at Gwalior from August 11 to 15, 1964. The resolution Upadhyaya had prepared on its principles and policies was given the final touches at his camp. Jan Sangh had come into being on the basis of the cultural resurgence thinking in 1952. The 1964 document was the culmination of such thinking. The Jan Sangh declared its concept of Integrated Humanism authoritatively, to elaborate which Upadhyaya delivered four historic addresses in Mumbai.

The Vijayawada session on January 23-24, 1965 marked a new beginning in the history of Jan Sangh. It was the first session held on a large scale in the South. The Jan Sangh manifesto on its policies and programmes was formally presented at this session. Its acceptance marked the beginning of a new chapter in Jan Sangh history. So far, the President of the party had been a reputed elderly, affluent and eminent personality. This was the first occasion when a seasoned Jan Sangh worker, Bachhraj Vyas, was elected President.

Comparatively, he was younger and belonged to the first generation of Jan Sangh leaders; he was among those workers who had been trained by Dr. Mukherjee and Golwalkar. His entire political life had been shaped and developed by Jan Sangh, and he was its first worker-President, who had risen from the ranks. Upadhyaya had prepared a list of workers for Jan Sangh's political leadership, which had now come to take over the organisation completely.

All-India President Bachhraj Vyas, Organisational Secretary Sunder Singh Bhandari, Secretary Jagannathrao Joshi, and Election Organiser Nanaji Deshmukh were all first-generation Jan Sangh pracharaks, who had come up from the ranks. Upadhyaya mentioned these names with a great deal of satisfaction in his address. By this time, Atal Bihari Vajpayee had become a leader of note, he was leader of the party in Parliament. The second important leader was Balraj Madhok. Both of them did not attend the Vijaywada session. Their conspicuous absence was another notable feature because they were not in favour of Bachhraj Vyas' election as President.

In the 1967 general elections, the Jana Sangh got 35 seats and became the 3rd largest party in the Lok Sabha. The Jan Sangh also went onto be a part of the Samyukta Vidhayak Dal, an experiment of having non-Congress opposition parties as a coalition to form governments in multiple states. This brought the right and the left of the Indian political spectrum on one single platform. He became President of the Jana Sangh in December 1967 in the Calicut session of the party. His presidential speech in that session focused on multiple aspects right from the formation of coalition government to language. No major events happened in the party during his tenure as the President that ended in 2 months in February 1968 due to his untimely death. Deendayal's elevation as Bharatiya Jana Sangh President in 1967 and set in motion his centennial, a former editor of Organiser commented, "Upadhyaya is to BJP what Mohandas Karamchand Gandhi was to Congress." Deendayal, though at the helm only for a brief three-month period (he became party chief in December 1967; died under mysterious circumstances in February 1968) was the main organiser of the Bharatiya Jana Sangh, the party sans an umbilical link to the Congress movement, pre and post Independence by Shyama Prasad Mukherjee in 1952. His contribution to the formation and growth of the party which is the precursor of present day BJP is best summed up by a statement by Shyama Prasad in 1953: "If I had two Deendayals, I could transform the face of India."

Upadhyaya edited Panchjanya (weekly) and Swadesh (daily) from Lucknow. In Hindi, he wrote a drama on 'Chandragupta Maurya', and later wrote a biography of 'Shankaracharya'. He translated a Marathi biography of Hedgewar.

Gradually, his political views began to take firm shape and were sharpened over the next few years.

That Upadhyaya idolised Adi Shankaracharya was not in doubt and it was manifest in the book that the author drew inspiration from the saint-philosopher's attempt at countering the spread of Buddhism. It was therefore not surprising when it was argued that the 'methodology adopted by Shankaracharya to counter the Buddhist threat resembled to a large extent the methodology of the RSS and its thinking.

Although Jagat Guru was a novel in Hindi, it's still considered authentic 'history' within the sangh parivar and treated as an important treatise on one of Hinduism's greatest thinkers. Meanwhile, the book had such an impact on its author that Deendayal was guided by the belief that 'action does not lie in mere sermonising, but in truly inspiring and motivating one's emotions; it must appeal to the heart and not to the barren intellect.'10 It was perhaps from here on that he began rejecting everything which had an association with the materialistic world, and was drawn more towards character-building of the RSS and its cadre.

Upadhyaya was constantly endeavoring to make Jan Sangh dignified, cultured, disciplined and democratic in its conduct. A member of his party, Pandharirao Kridant, threw a shoe at the Deputy Speaker of Madhya Pradesh Assembly. This was painful for Upadhyaya. He made a mention of this incident in this address and said: "Whatever the reasons for the member's agitation and frustration, this conduct is against all parliamentary conventions and against the Jan Sangh code of conduct. None of our workers should resort to this. We must exercise self-discipline."

The social set-up does not become democratic merely by accepting democracy as a form of government. By 1965-66, it had become clear that all constituents of the system were lacking in democratic functioning. While describing this in his address, Upadhyaya suggested: "The Prime Minister should convene a meeting of all parties and try to constitute a body on the lines similar to the National Integration Council which should make efforts to work for democratic norms. There should be a model code of conduct for the state, the political parties and the press. The

State must itself accept a process through which it should change its policies in accordance with public opinion between one general election and the next. Democracy and stubbornness cannot go together. It would have been better if such a council was formed to deliberate over what Upadhyaya had proposed.' Changing policies on the basis of public opinion' can be the starting point of a constructive debate. It is still left to a democratic society to find a practical approach to the powers of the legislature that is affected by party politics and an inefficient executive."

Under its young leadership, Jan Sangh had made adequate preparations for the 1967 general elections. The Jan Sangh emerged as the largest political party after the Congress in the 1967 polls. The resolution regarding these elections is Upadhyaya's last most important document. The era of non-Congress parties started after these elections, and Deendayal Upadhyaya was a respected leader of India's second largest political party in the opposition. Dr. Rammanohar Lohia was the leader who had given this idea; the age of a single-party monopoly in Indian politics was gradually coming to an end.

"The five years from 1962 to 1967 were so eventful and mass-based that there were many apprehensions in the public mind. But they proved to be baseless. The public participated peacefully and judiciously in these elections and this gave proof of the strength of democracy in Indian".

There was an attempt at bringing together the non-Congress parties on the same platform. But Upadhyaya did not agree with the suggestion. He said in his address: "There was an atmosphere of weakness and lack of strength in the Congress which led the non-Congress parties to think of coming together to fight elections. Their justification was that they could defeat the Congress as one entity. Bharatiya Jan Sangh's experience has been that such a compromise has no value because when it comes to a direct contest, the other non-Congress parties prefer to join the Congress instead of Jan Sangh in such contests. These elections have justified our contention."

Regarding the formation of an alternative to the Congress, he opined: "Since there is a gradual decline in the influence of the Congress and it is slowly losing its effectiveness, it is of paramount importance that there should be a national and democratic party as an alternative, but this task is not possible through manipulation. We require a clear policy, a well-defined programme, the right principles and a strong organisation for this." Jan Sangh won 35 seats in the 1967 general elections.Besides, there were 75 constituencies where the Jan Sangh contestants directly faced the winners. Out of these, it lost in 15 constituencies by a margin of 200 to 5,000 votes. Upadhyaya was not dissatisfied with his party's performance: "It is clear that the Jan Sangh is not only ahead of all the other non-Congress parties but it has secured more votes than both the Communist parties, Socialist Party, and the Praja Socialist Party put together." He presented a detailed assessment of the parliamentary and state legislature party positions in this address.

Widening the Horizons

In the mid-Forties, the idea of independence and with it the partition of the subcontinent, was fast becoming a reality. Despite its apolitical underpinning, the RSS was bitterly opposed to the cleaving of the nation, which was best explained by Deendayal Upadhyaya who said that an,

"undivided India is not only a symbol of geographical oneness, but it manifests the oneness of Indian life.... Undivided India is not just a political slogan...it is the basis of our life."

The premise formed part of a booklet that he wrote five years after Partition, titled 'Akhand Bharat Kyon?' or 'Why Undivided India?' His essential argument being that India was more a cultural entity than a geo-political unit, and that Muslims and Christians were essentially part of this 'oneness' that was unequivocally Hindu in nature. Most importantly, Upadhyaya analysed the very idea of India's freedom that was obtained after a long struggle on 15 August 1947, and bemoaned the fact that,

"independence was announced by unfurling the tricolour from the ramparts of Red Fort, but Ravi (the river), at whose banks we had adopted a resolution of complete freedom, had been snatched away from us."

In a bitter indictment of the Two-Nation theory, which had unfolded at the time of his political initiation, Upadhyaya wrote in the booklet that, by calling the Khilafat movement a nationalist movement, we not only put a blot on our nationalism, we also generated a feeling in the Muslims that they need not give up following the external forces for continuing to remain Indian nationals.

Akhand Bharat Kyon? is considered to be the first comprehensive analysis of inter-community relations by the sangh in post-Independent India. 'Hindu-Muslim problem remains what it was,' wrote Upadhyaya in the booklet, and how, political parties have adopted the mixed culture and heritage as the basis of their operations and separatism and secessionism are on the rise, providing justification for the creation of Pakistan.

Upadhyaya was of the view that adherence to a unitary concept of the nation could have prevented Partition, and 'if the Congress leaders had stood their ground and helped the awakening among the rank and file of Indians.' He criticised the Indian National Congress for its lack of resolve when presented with the partition plan, 'British could have been forced to leave behind an undivided India by handing power to the Congress.'[45]

Indo-Pak Confederation Concept Mooted

Another example of Deendayalji's creative and non-doctrinaire approach is the following important joint statement for the Indo-Pak confederation that he signed, on 12 April 1964, with Dr. Lohia. They were both good friends, despite differences on certain ideological issues. Their friendship became stronger after the Chinese aggression of 1962, when Dr. Lohia endorsed the Jana Sangh's demand for India to produce its own nuclear weapon. Their joint statement said:

"Large-scale riots in East Pakistan have compelled over two lakh Hindus and other minorities to come over to India. Indians naturally feel incensed by the happenings in East Bengal. To bring the situation under control and to prescribe the right remedy for the situation, it is essential that the malady be properly diagnosed. And even in this state of mental agony, the basic values of our national life must never be forgotten. It is our firm conviction that guaranteeing the protection of the life and property of Hindus and other minorities in Pakistan is the responsibility of the Government of India.

To take a nice legalistic view about the matter that Hindus in Pakistan are Pakistani nationals would be dangerous and can only result in killings and reprisals in the two countries, in greater or lesser measure. When the Government of India fails to fulfill this obligation towards the minorities in Pakistan, the people understandably become indignant. Our appeal to the people is that this indignation should be directed against the Government and should in no case be given vent to against the Indian Muslims.

If the latter thing happens, it only provides the Government with a cloak to cover its own inertia and failure, and an opportunity to malign the people and repress them. So far as the Indian Muslims are concerned, it is our definite view that, like all other citizens, their lives and property must be protected in all circumstances.

No incident and no logic can justify any compromise with truth in this regard. A state, which cannot guarantee the right of living to its citizens, and citizens who cannot assure safety of their neighbours, would belong to the barbaric age.

Freedom and security to every citizen irrespective of his faith has indeed been India's sacred tradition. We would like to reassure every Indian Muslim in this regard and would wish this message to reach every Hindu home that it is their civic and national duty to ensure the fulfillment of this assurance.

"We hold that the existence of India and Pakistan as two separate entities is an artificial situation. The estrangement of relations between the two Governments is the result of lopsided attitudes and the tendency to indulge in piecemeal talks. Let the dialogue carried on by the two Governments be candid and not just piecemeal. It is out of such frank talk that solutions to various problems can emerge, goodwill created and a beginning made towards the formation of some sort of Indo-Pak Confederation."

The idea of an Indo-Pak Confederation was born out of an intensive discussion between Deendayalji and Dr. Lohia. It had its origin in the latter's concern that the Jana Sangh's and RSS's belief in the concept of 'Akhand Bharat' (India Undivided) put people in Pakistan at unease and posed a hurdle in the progress of Indo-Pak relations. Dr. Lohia told Deendayalji: 'Many Pakistanis believe that if the Jana Sangh came to power in New Delhi, it would forcibly reunify Pakistan with India.' Deendayalji replied: 'We have no such intentions. And we are willing to put to rest Pakistani people's concerns on this score.[46]

He was also unsparing in his denunciation of the Muslims in their insistence on maintaining a distinct identity:

War (with Pakistan) is not a means to bring about an undivided India. War can only bring about geographic oneness, not national integration.... We have to work for an undivided India...Muslims who are backward as compared to our national parameters will associate themselves with us (sic) if we give up this policy of compromise and appeasement...If we want unity, we must adopt the yardstick of Indian nationalism, which is Hindu nationalism, and Indian culture, which is Hindu culture. Let us allow all other streams to merge with this mainstream Bhagirathi. Yamuna will merge with it. So will Ganga, shedding all its pollution. And one continuous Bhagirathi will flow throughout India.

What is particularly telling in the above passage is the usage of the as a tool for cultural integration, and how 'Ganga', rivers' analogy invoked as the holiest river in India, shall shed 'all its pollution' to transform into a single national stream.

The overt politicization of the Sangh ideology as evidenced in his writings occurred after the RSS was proscribed following Mahatma Gandhi's assassination in January 1948. As mentioned previously, Deendayal was Bhaurao Deoras' 'discovery', and after setting up a unit in the United Provinces, he become part of a group of pracharaks that advocated mass contact programs to ensure that the RSS remained relevant even during the ban. Yet, unlike Balasaheb Deoras, Upadhyaya didn't conform to the view that the RSS needed to formally set up a political wing. He along with several others agreed with MS. Golwalkar's view of keeping a close watch on the developments within the Congress, which was in the midst of a churn.

While Jan Sangh's fight for power was with the Congress, it considered the Communist Party more dangerous for the country. Upadhyaya called upon his workers to counter the influence of the Communists . "We must go deep into society in order to shake them from their roots. People, who only understand the language of community, regionalism, and their own selfish interests, must be taught the real meaning of nation and 'dharma'.

The same year (1959) the Swantantra Party was formed. It welcomed several regional parties, rulers, landlords, capitalists, and defectors from other political parties in its fold. Consequently, it was perceived as an effective political party right at its inception. Upadhyaya warned of the dangers arising out of this short cut to power: "We must be more disciplined and organized as a party. A single instance of indiscipline weakens our party, and people lose faith in us. If we are self-disciplined, we can train the people to be disciplined. People must identify themselves with principles and party today. People who change parties today give rise to a loss of faith in democracy. The center of their interest is not society but the individual...Society has been shocked by this betrayal. We must try to re-establish this faith through hard work and sacrifice, and commit ourselves to the service of society."

Upadhyaya issued a manifesto to elaborate his thoughts: "The Jan Sangh has to work for the defense of the nation, nationalism of the masses, democratization of administration, and decentralization of democracy. We should be so effective that our work is not misguided and misunderstood. The truth must be complemented with strength." Upadhyaya used to conclude his remarks with inspiring and emotional expressions.

The third general elections were held in 1962. Jawaharlal Nehru's charisma was gradually on the wane. The Jan Sangh had been warning the people of Pakistan's and China's designs for long. The public started taking the Jan Sangh's voice seriously. On the other hand, because of lack of Nehru's clout, indiscipline and groupism were on the rise. The opposition parties were waiting for a break up of the Congress because they obviously stood to gain from its disintegration. However, Upadhyaya did not think that it was in the nation's interest. To come to power by defeating a disorganized Congress was evidence of negative thinking. Internecine fights in any party, as well as indiscipline in any party weakened democracy. Upadhyaya wanted to defeat a united and capable Congress through the efforts of Jan Sangh legislators. He, therefore, cautioned his workers: "Groupism in Congress is assuming serious proportions. In view of the 1962 elections, every group in the party in adopting its own strategy. It is certain that many people will leave Congress on the matter of distribution of tickets. Many political parties, which believe that Congress dissidents will help them win elections, are keenly looking forward to this. But we should strengthen our own organization and establish intimate contacts with society." He outlines a plan to implement this.

After the 1962 general elections, Upadhyaya analyzed the gains and losses of each party. He also discussed the new emerging factors. Regarding the maintenance of democratic norms and expressing his concerns about new realities, he said:

"Bharatiya Jan Sangh washes to give a constitutional shape to politics. Its publicity and mass movements have always adopted constitutional norms. We maintained our standards in these elections also Our speakers chiefly presented, their own viewpoint and criticized other parties only in the background of our own convictions and beliefs. It is time that since we have alternate policies and programs and we have differences with the Congress and other parties, which are its offshoots, our criticism is basic and penetrating. Because of our fearless and selfless nature, such criticism might have been sharp in places but Jan Sangh has nowhere resorted to personal allegations or roused communal or casteist feelings, nor has it ever resorted to regional and class conflicts.

How far this statement of Upadhyaya can be true at a lower level is difficult to say. But he always tried to establish an organization and educate his workers towards the creation of such an environment, which can be easily understood by his deep-rooted beliefs. There were several untoward incidents during the elections that involved the Congress, the Communists, and the Jan Sangh. In this context, Upadhyaya said: "I demand that the administration should investigate the election publicity of various political parties impartially. It is essential not only to put an end to the prevailing malpractices but also to raise the standard of electioneering in the future."

Upadhyaya assessed the performance of the various political parties thus': "The Congress, the Communists, and the Praja Socialist Party-all these three, in their quest for garnering Muslim votes, encouraged the forces of communalism and separatism... They raised the Jan Sangh bogey in their minds so as to create a scare and tried that they should not exercise their franchise independently because of the threat posed by Jan Sangh."

The various alliances that the political parties entered into were not only surprising but also painful. This gave rise to the speculation that in their lust for power, they can go to any extent. The Communist Party had decided to support the Congress in order to defeat the Jan Sangh. They proposed such an arrangement in Kerala. In West Bengal, they adopted their old leftist leanings and raised the slogan of an alternative government. This time, the Praja Socialist Party did not join them. In Punjab, they entered into an informal agreement with the Akali Dal and in Andhra with the Swatantara Party. Probably, they did so because of the prevailing caste equations there. In Maharashtra, they contested the elections in the name of Republican Party and Shetkari Kamgar Paksh ".

"The Swatantara Party entered into alliances with practically every party other than the Congress including, the Akali Dal, Dravida Munnetra Kazhagam, and the Communists. Hindu Mahasabha and Ram Rajya Parishad entered into a compromise and contested the elections. The Republican Party contested with two groups: the Praja Socialist Party, which supported Vidharbha, and the Communists. In Uttar Pradesh there was an agreement between the old Muslim League elements and the Republican Party. The Congress tried to enter into an alliance with the Jharkhand Party, but it was not successful. The Bharatiya Jan Sangh and the Socialist Party are the only parties that contested the elections on the basis of their policies."

"The Congress is disintegrating rapidly. Defeated in their bastions, the communists have slightly increased their tally by picking up in other parts of the country. The beginning of the end of the Praja Socialist Party has started. The Bharatiya Jan Sangh has taken a step forward, but it still lags behind in fulfilling the historic mission with which it was formed."

Upadhyaya considered shortcuts and opportunistic alliances for winning elections a social weakness. He favored principled policies. He, therefore, attempted to analyze the third elections on the basis of principles and healthy political norms. According to him, "it is difficult to arrive at Indian politics's principled stand on the basis of these election results because a voter's decision is based on several factors. Principles have a very small role to play in this. Probably this is why eminent leaders of various political parties did not feel any need to define their ideals in these elections. The Congress staked its claim to power because it is the largest political party, and no other party has a leader of Jawaharlal Nehru's stature. The other political parties have been saying that the Congress has failed on all fronts or that they have given tickets to people who have tried to be different from the Congress candidates on the basis of their communal or regional view points. It is difficult for me to say what success they have achieved in this. If we say that the people became victims of greed or

fear or were swept by communal and casteist forces, it implies that we have failed to prepare them for their democratic rights." He formed a sub-committee of his party to go into this issue and arrive at its resolution.

The 1962 general elections had transformed the Bharatiya Jan Sangh into an important force, and the person who contributed to it, largely through his efforts and talents, was Deendayal Upadhyaya. This is becoming increasingly clear now. It was not easily transparent because Upadhyaya always worked in the background; he was not easily seen, and the RSS and the Bharatiya Jan Sangh were his outward reflections.

Strengthening the organization enthuses the workers, but it can also mislead them through enhanced self-esteem; They come to consider it their birthright to violate all rules under the guise of their commitment. Many political parties encourage this tendency in their workers in order to create a radical and agitational image for themselves. Upadhyaya was constantly on guard against this danger. He made Jan Sangh's planned and disciplined movement a part of political functioning: "Rail fares were to be linked from July 1, 1962. It was decided to stage demonstrations against this hike and generally against the imposition of new taxes at railway stations. It was also decided that the demonstrations should be peaceful, that the railway employees were not to be put to any inconvenience, and that no law was to be violated. Accordingly, demonstrations were organized at all stations, and the public was made aware of the new taxes through the distribution of leaflets all over the country. Barring a few places, where the railway employees did not issue platform tickets and the police arrested a few demonstrators who had platform tickets, there was no untoward incident anywhere." In his resolution, Upadhyaya generally took care to include these factors so that no one violated it at lower levels. Also, people must remember, where they had gone wrong, and the newly recruited workers understood the doctrine of protest and discharged their responsibilities positively.

While Deendayal Upadhyaya opposed opportunistic political alliances, he considered political untouchability undesirable. He wanted the different political parties to work together for the resolution of national problems. "Communist China's aggression on India and the declaration of a state of emergency by the President have not led to stable conditions in the country. The dormant nationalist sentiment of the people has been awakened; there is an atmosphere of unity. It has given a golden opportunity to the various political parties to come together on a common platform to understand one another and put an end to their prejudices. If this atmosphere of cooperation and goodwill continues, it will certainly healthy for the nation's political development".

There was a sort of unity among the non-communist parties, especially the Bharatiya Jan Sangh and Dr. Lohia's Socialist Party, against the Chinese aggression and in support of Hindi as the national language. The two parties fought the 1963 elections in Uttar Pradesh on a common platform. The goodwill between the two parties increased, and there was a move to launch a permanent anti Congress front. But Upadhyaya did not see anything concrete emerg out of such a move. He, therefore, suggested that both parties should work separately on the basis of their programs and policies: "Different parties have different viewpoints. People do not have any opinions about their thoughts. Sometimes they think of the basis of goodwill that all political parties should come together, but there are certain basic points to justify separate existence. For that, only goodwill is not enough. That is why we have decided that we won't live in an imaginary world and enter into some alliance, the success of which is doubtful. It would be better to work together on issues where we reach a consensus; otherwise, we should operate from our own platforms."

The year 1964 was a milestone in Indian history. Jawaharlal Nehru died this year. This was a shock to the Congress; it was the end of an era. It was a testing time from an organizational and policy point of view. A historic training camp of the executive committee of the Jan Sangh was organized at Gwalior from August 11 to 15, 1964. The resolution Upadhyaya had prepared on its principles and policies was given the final touches at his camp. Jan Sangh had come into being on the basis of cultural resurgence thinking in 1952. The 1964 document was the culmination of such thinking. The Jan Sangh declared its concept of integrated humanism authoritatively, to elaborate on which Upadhyaya delivered four historic addresses in Mumbai.

The Vijayawada session on January 23-24, 1965 marked a new beginning in the history of Jan Sangh. It was the first session held on a large scale in the South. The Jan Sangh manifesto on its policies and programs was formally presented at this session. Its acceptance marked the beginning of a new chapter in Jan Sangh history. So far, the president of the party has been a reputedly elderly, affluent, and eminent personality. This was the first occasion when a seasoned Jan Sangh worker, Bachhraj Vyas, was elected president. Comparatively, he was younger and belonged to the first generation of Jan Sangh leaders; he was among those workers who had been trained by Dr. Mukherjee and Golwalkar. His entire political life had been shaped and developed by Jan Sangh, and he was its first worker-President who had risen from the ranks. Upadhyaya had prepared a list of workers for Jan Sangh's political leadership, which had now come to take over the organization completely. All-India President Bachhraj Vyas, organizational secretary. Sunder Singh Bhandari, Secretary Jagannathrao Joshi and Election Organiser Nanaji Deshmukh were all first-generation Jan Sangh pracharaks who had come up from the ranks. Upadhyaya mentioned these names with a great deal of satisfaction in his address. By this time, Atal Behari Vajpayee had become a leader of note; he was the leader of the party in Parliament. The second important leader was Balraj Madhok. Both of them did not attend the Vijaywada session. Their conspicuous absence was another notable feature because they were not in favor of Bachhraj Vyas' election as president.

The conditional deadline for English as the official language of the Center was January 26, 1965; its place was to be taken by Hindi. Around this time, there were protests and demonstrations for the further continuance of English and opposition to Hindi in the South. Shri Aurobindo Ashram, Pondicherry, and Dr. Radhakrishana's library in Tirupati were set on fire. There was widespread violence in Tamil Nadu. Upadhyaya said in Jalandhar, "The root cause of the movement was not language, but politics. Chakrawarty Rajagopalachari and the Dravida Munnetra Kazhagam inflamed public passions and adopted all means to incite them. The Congress's infighting also contributed to this. What added fuel to the fire was the Madras Chief Minister's intransigence and the Congress President's call to throw all papers in Hindi in the wastepaper basket. After the movement was launched, it soon slipped into the hands of the leftists and old Muslim Leaguers. Some foreign missionaries also encouraged it." Upadhyaya wished to convey through this statement that the Tamilians were really against Hindi. The occasion was exploited by vested interests. The statement may appeal to those who subscribe to Upadhyaya's and Jan Sangh's views on Hindi as the national language, but it is not easy to simplify the issue of Indian languages in this manner. Deendayal also conceded the inability of his own party to meet the challenge. "The Jan Sangh influence in Madras State is new and limited. We could not, therefore, be effective there."

Upadhyaya was constantly endeavoring to make Jan Sangh dignified, cultured, disciplined, and democratic in its conduct. A member of his party, Pandharirao Kridant, threw a shoe at the Deputy Speaker of the Madhya Pradesh Assembly. This was painful for Upadhyaya. He made a mention of this incident in this address and said: "Whatever the reasons for the member's agitation and frustration, this conduct is against all parliamentary conventions and against the Jan Sangh code of conduct. None of our workers should resort to this. We must exercise self-discipline."

The social set-up does not become democratic merely by accepting democracy as a form of government. By 1965-66, it had become clear that all constituents of the system were lacking in democratic functioning. While describing this in his address, Upadhyaya suggested: "The Prime Minister should convene a meeting of all parties and try to constitute a body on the lines similar to the National Integration Council, which should make efforts to work for democratic norms. There should be a model code of conduct for the state, the political parties, and the press. The state must itself accept a process through which it should change its policies in accordance with public opinion between one general election and the next. Democracy and stubbornness cannot go together. "It would have been better if such a council was formed to deliberate over what Upadhyaya had proposed. "Changing policies on the basis of public opinion" can be the starting point of a constructive debate. It is still left to a democratic society to find a practical approach to the powers of the legislature that are affected by party politics and an inefficient executive.

Under its young leadership, Jan Sangh had made adequate preparations for the 1967 general elections. The Jan Sangh emerged as the largest political party after the Congress in the 1967 polls. The resolution regarding these elections is Upadhyaya's last and most important document. The era of non-Congress parties started after these elections, and Deendayal Upadhyaya was a respected leader of India's second largest political party in the opposition. Dr. Rammanohar Lohia was the leader who had given this idea; the age of a single-party monopoly in Indian politics was gradually coming to an end.

"The five years from 1962 to 1967 were so eventful and mass-based that there were many apprehensions in the public mind. But they proved to be baseless. The public participated peacefully and judiciously in these elections, and this gave proof of the strength of democracy in Indian".

There was an attempt at bringing together the non-Congress parties on the same platform. But Upadhyaya did not agree with the suggestion. He said in his address: "There was an atmosphere of weakness and lack of strength in the Congress, which led the non-Congress parties to think of coming together to fight elections. Their justification was that they could defeat the Congress as one entity. Bharatiya Jan Sangh's experience has been that such a compromise has no value because, when it comes to a direct contest, the other non-Congress parties prefer to join the Congress instead of Jan Sangh in such contests. These elections have justified our contention."

Regarding the formation of an alternative to the Congress, he opined: "Since there is a gradual decline in the influence of the Congress and it is slowly losing its effectiveness, it is of paramount importance that there should be a national and democratic party as an alternative, but this task is not possible through manipulation.

We require a clear policy, a well-defined program, the right principles, and a strong organization for this." Jan Sangh won 35 seats in the 1967 general elections. Besides, there were 75 constituencies where the Jan Sangh contestants directly faced the winners. Out of these, it lost in 15 constituencies by a margin of 200 to 5,000 votes. Upadhyaya was not dissatisfied with his party's performance: "It is clear that the Jan Sangh is not only ahead of all the other non-Congress parties, but it has secured more votes than both the Communist parties, the Socialist Party, and the Praja Socialist Party put together." He presented a detailed assessment of the parliamentary and state legislature party positions in this address.

After interpreting and analysing data in these elections, Upadhyaya commented on the newly-emerged realities and tendencies: "The Muslims have voted against the Congress at most places, but it is not appropriate to say at this juncture, that they are veering to other parties on the basis on economic, political and other issues. Obviously, the Majlis-e-Mushawwarat-e-Musalman has been organised on communal basis and it has voted on these lines. The Mushawwarat leaders are definitely using this party for political bargaining. In Andhra, Ittehadul-Musalmeen has also been formed on communal lines... The Muslim league has added to its clout through a united front in Madras and Kerala. The influence and expansion of these parties is a stumbling block in the way of Indian Muslims joining the national mainstream."

However, Upadhyaya, who had prior experience setting up the organization in UP, managed to circumvent every objection that may have come in his way and discharged the twin duties of pracharak and president of the Jana Sangh. In his memoirs, L.K. Advani wrote that although there were several party presidents from 1953 (after Syama Prasad's death) to 1967, everybody knew that 'Deendayalji, its General Secretary in charge of the organization, was the mind, heart, and soul of the party. As a matter of fact, he was more than the organisational head of the party. He was its philosopher, guide, and motivator, all rolled into one.'

However, if it wasn't for certain extraneous reasons, and most importantly, if history hadn't been unkind to certain men, then Deendayal Upadhyaya may not have become the president of the Jana Sangh. Almost a decade after Deendayal became the axis of the Jana Sangh, the one-time Congress President Purushottam Das Tandon, who'd locked horns with Nehru over the 1949 resolution to admit members of the RSS into the Congress party, died in 1962, almost a forgotten man. Deendayal wrote an evocative obituary in the Organiser, mentioning that if Tandon had not resigned as Congress president in 1951 (under pressure from Prime Minister Nehru), 'probably the Bharatiya Jana Sangh would not have come into existence. It was ironical that the internecine squabbles within the Congress over the proposed role of the RSS in the party and Nehru's striking down of any such suggestion had indirectly resulted in the birth of the Jana Sangh.

Similarly, but for Deendayal Upadhyaya, the Jana Sangh would have either folded up or lurched from one crisis to another post Mukherjee's tragic death in June 1953. As per its constitution, not only did the Jana Sangh restrict the tenure of its president to one year, but there was no succession plan for any eventuality in case the founder- president either left the party or as was proven later, died. Although there were several claimants to the post of president, including NC. Chatterjee, who was one of the founders of the Hindu Mahasabha, nobody came close to S.P. Mukherjee, either in stature or erudition.

After a few months of his death, the proposal to merge the Jana Sangh with the Hindu Mahasabha was revived yet again, but Deendayal Upadhyaya had rejected it outright. His ideological commitment to the RSS notwithstanding, there were three other reasons which had made the merger impossible-first, there were major differences, albeit nuanced, in their definitions of what constituted Hindu nationalism; second, certain influential RSS leaders, especially M.S. Golwalkar, were sceptical about V.D. Savarkar's overt opposition to the RSS' continuous efforts in organization- building. It was precisely for these reasons that Upadhyaya had openly declared his opposition to the viewpoint that, 'since the Hindu Mahasbha has a galaxy of leaders and the Jana Sangh none, the two organizations should merge into one.'

Finally, a couple of months after Syama Prasad Mukherjee's death, Mauli Chandra Sharma, a one- time Congress leader-turned-RSS supporter, was appointed the acting president of the Jana Sangh. The new president was familiar with the internal dynamics of the Jana Sangh, which was largely dominated by RSS pracharaks with whom he had once worked closely in Delhi after Partition. Yet, in what was deemed to be unwise, he attempted to seize control of the party for instance, his open defiance of Deendayal's move to nominate an executive council which was to function as an independent authority of the party. The power struggle between the two continued for of 1954, until Sharma was shown the door and Deendayal inducted the low-profile S.A. Sohoni, who was the sanghchalak of Bihar, as president of the Jana Sangh. With this unusual or rather out-of-turn appointment, Deendayal had ensured the end to the last vestiges of an external influence over the Jana Sangh. In retaliation, several members of the Jana Sangh had decided to quit, but Upadhyaya had paid no heed and remained resolute in ensuring the continuance of the RSS' influence over the party.

However, this wasn't the only instance of Upadhyaya forcing his hand on the party. In the decade and a half of managing party affairs, he had handpicked a team of new generation Pracharaks. In 1965, at Jana Sangh's landmark plenary session in Vijayawadaas it was here that Upadhyaya had unveiled his philosophy of Integral Humanism, which has since then been the official doctrine of the BJP-he'd ensured Bachhraj Vyas' elevation as party president. Two of Jana Sangh's senior leaders at the time, Atal Bihari Vajpayee and Balraj Madhok, had vehemently opposed the decision and boycotted the session. Yet Deendayal was undeterred because it was a matter of principle for him, which carried more weight than an individual's brilliance, clout, and capacity to sway the public.

Upadhyaya's insistence on retaining Jana Sangh's distinct identity resurfaced in 1962, when yet another proposal for its merger with the Swatantra Party and Ram Rajya Party (both right-wing entities) was suggested, and obviously rejected. It may be recalled that in the late 1980s, L.K. Advani used the phrase 'splendid isolation' while describing the BJP's loneliness in Indian politics. In a way, the genesis of this long period of isolation could be attributed to Deendayal, who had ensured that every external voice was silenced to protect the distinct ideological base of his party.

It wasn't just the ideas which he had rejected; but Upadhyaya was strongly against forging political alliances for electoral gains. In an article in the Seminar magazine, he wrote that all such arrangements 'degenerate into a struggle for power by opportunist elements coming together in the interest of expediency.' From the time he took charge of the Jana Sangh, Deendayal was guided by the principle of building a 'party with a difference'-another phrase which was resurrected by L.K. Advani in the 1990s. As an aside, it may be worthwhile to mention that when Advani was elected Jana Sangh president in 1973, the Organiser headlined its report on the Kanpur plenary session as: 'Second Deendayal at Helm of BJS.'

Upadhyaya was loathe to the idea of fighting elections and grabbing political power as the means to an end of a political party's existence-social transformation was the kernel of Deendayal's political philosophy, which he viewed as the ultimate objective. He was not only exacting towards party colleagues who were obsessed with the pursuit of power but, curiously, even towards ordinary voters. In 1955, he wrote in the Organiser:

We do not have to amass popular support but only that of those who can follow our ideals...we do not simply want popular support; it must be an idealistic popular support.

His obduracy towards accepting the realities of electoral politics notwithstanding, Deendayal considered even political movements or agitations as deterrents for coercing the State into accepting sundry demands, however unfair. He recommended that dissent of such nature should act as tools for furthering a party's ideology and for securing greater support, rather than merely as issue-based endorsements. His recommendation of avoiding confrontational politics also extended to Opposition parties, who he felt were perennially in conflict with the government of the day. This was strange, considering the Congress was in power at the Centre and was bitterly opposed to everything that the Jana Sangh stood for.

Deendayal attributed the genesis of agitational politics to the Indian freedom struggle, which he felt had encouraged 'negative' patriotism, and which needed to be replaced with constructive nation-building in which the government and people could forge a partnership. Amongst all his postulations, what was most significant was his curious belief that a democracy should function in a somewhat 'controlled' manner:

State suppression may benefit political parties that play the role of political mediator for a short while between the State and the People, but it does not bode good for the nation.

As is obvious, this viewpoint was contradictory to his proposal for a collaboration between the people and the State. It was left to his senior colleagues in the Sangh to convince him to view the situation pragmatically in the ongoing tussle between politics and ideology.

Upadhyaya considered shortcut and opportunistic alliances for winning elections a social weakness. He favoured principled policies. He, therefore, attempted to analyse the third elections on the basis of principles and healthy political norms. According to him,

"It is difficult to arrive at Indian polity's principled stand on the basis of these election results because a voter's decision is based on several factors. Principles have a very small role to play in this. Probably this is why eminent leaders of various political parties did not feel any need to define their ideals in these elections. The Congress staked its claim to power because it is the largest political party and no other party has a leader of Jawaharlal Nehru's stature. The other political parties have been saying that the Congress has failed on all fronts or they have given tickets to such people who have tried to be different from the Congress candidates on the basis of their communal or regional viewpoints. It is difficult for me to say what success they have achieved in this... If we say that the people became victims to greed or fear or were swept by communal and casteist forces, it implies that we have failed to prepare them for their democratic rights."

He formed a sub-committee of his party to investigate this issue and arrive at its resolution.

The decade of the 1960s saw a major upsurge in mass protests in various parts of the country. This was due to the Congress governments' failure to fulfil people's legitimate expectations. There was a minority view within the Jana Sangh that the party should not get associated with agitational politics. Deendayalji refuted this view in his Presidential speech by saying,

'People's agitations are natural and necessary in a rapidly changing social system. As a matter of fact, they are a manifestation of a new awareness in society. Hence, we have to go along with them and provide leadership to them. Those who want to perpetuate the status quo in the political, economic and social fields are fearful of people's agitations. I am afraid we cannot cooperate with them. They want to stop the wheel of time, they want to halt India's predestined march, which is not possible.'

In his inspirational address, Deendayalji gave another proof of his forward-looking vision.

'We are energised by the glory of India's past, but we do not regard it as the pinnacle of our national life. We have a realistic understanding of the present, but we are not tied to the present. Our eyes are entranced by the golden dreams about India's future, but we are not given to sleep and sloth; we are karmayogis who are determined to translate those dreams into reality. We are worshippers of India's timeless past, dynamic present and eternal future. Confident of victory, let us pledge to endeavour in this direction.

The 1962 general elections had transformed the Bharatiya Jan Sangh into an important force and the person who contributed to this largely through his efforts and talents was Deendayal Upadhyaya. This was becoming increasingly clear now. It was not easily apparent because

Upadhyaya always worked in the background; he was not easily seen and the RSS and the Bharatiya Jan Sangh were his outward reflections.

Strengthening of the organisation enthuses the workers, but it can also mislead them through enhanced self-esteem; They come to consider it their birthright to violate all rules under the guise of their commitment. Many political parties encourage this tendency in their workers in order to create a radical and agitational image for themselves. Upadhyaya was constantly on his guard against this danger. He made the Jan Sangh's planned and disciplined movement a part of political functioning:

"Rail fares were to be linked from July 1, 1962. It was decided to stage demonstrations against this hike and generally against the imposition of new taxes at railway stations. It was also decided that the demonstrations should be peaceful and the railway employees were not to be put to any inconvenience and no law was to be violated. Accordingly, demonstrations were organised at all stations and the public was made aware of the new taxes through the distribution of leaflets all over the country. Barring a few places where the railway employees did not issue platform tickets and the police arrested a few demonstrators who had platform tickets, there was no untoward incident anywhere."

In his resolution, Upadhyaya generally took care to include these factors so that no one violated them at lower levels. Also, people must remember where they had gone wrong and the newly-recruited workers understood the doctrine of protest and discharged their responsibilities positively,

In the May 1963 by-elections for the four Lok Sabha seats, three in Uttar Pradesh and one in Gujarat, Deendayal finally agreed to contest his maiden election from Jaunpur (UP) after the seat had fallen vacant following the sudden death of a Jana Sangh leader, Thakur Bhramjeet Singh.

Meanwhile, Deendayal found a perfect ally in M.S.Golwalkar, whose antipathy towards conventional politics was well known. Golwalkar believed that pracharaks should 'organise the organization', and maintain a distance from power politics, which might result in any form of gain. On the other hand, there was Balasaheb Deoras, who not only patronised Upadhyaya but also openly challenged Golwalkar. Deoras stepped in at this crucial juncture to forge an understanding between several non-Congress parties to jointly put-up consensus candidates in the elections.

Deendayal Upadhyaya lost the by-election by a substantial margin and for two reasons. First, Deoras had 'not counted on an uncharacteristic pulling together of the factionalized Uttar Pradesh Congress Party'; second, the Jana Sangh had failed to notice that all the previous winners from this constituency were local Rajputs, while Deendayal was a Brahmin and thus did not garner enough votes.

The third and possibly most important reason was that the combined-Opposition candidates from UP were stalwarts in their own right, including Acharya J.B. Kripalani from Amroha, and the Socialist leader Dr. Ram Manohar Lohia, who had contested from Farrukhabad. The fourth seat in Gujarat was being contested by a leader of considerable repute, the Swatantra Party general secretary, Minoo Masani.

There was a sort of unity among the non-Communist parties, especially the Bharatiya Jan Sangh and Dr. Lohia's Socialist Party, against Chinese aggression and in support of Hindi as the National Language. The two parties fought the 1963 by-elections in Uttar Pradesh on a common platform. The goodwill between the two parties increased leading to a move to launch a permanent anti- Congress front. However, Upadbyaya did not see anything concrete emerging from such a move. He therefore suggested that both parties should work separately on the basis of their programs and policies:

"Different parties have different viewpoints. People do not have any opinion about their thoughts. Sometimes they think on the basis of goodwill that all political parties should come together, but there are certain basic points to justify separate existence. For that, only goodwill is not enough. That is why we have decided that we won't live in an imaginary world and enter into some alliance the success of which is doubtful. It would be better to work together on issues where we reach a consensus; otherwise, we should operate from our own platforms."

Importance of being Deendayal Upadhyaya

Upadhyaya had a very short innings in politics-less than two decades. However, his creative politics has left a legacy for the present as well as posterity. His contribution began with his efforts to moralise politics. Of the many instances, the most relevant is his candidature for the Jaunpur Lok Sabha constituency by-election in 1963. Three other opposition veterans - J.B. Kripalani, Minoo Masani and Ram Manohar Lohia - were in the fray.

Nehru had used the Muslim card to defeat Kripalani in the Amroha constituency by inserting a Muslim candidate at the eleventh hour. Earlier, the party had selected a committed local leader, Ramsaran.

Upadhyaya did something worthy of being regarded as the epitome in politics. The seat, vacant due to a sitting Bharatiya Jana Sangh (BJS) MP, was seen as 'safe' for Upadhyaya. But he invited his defeat by opposing any caste affiliation and identity to garner votes, infuriating his own caste-men. Yet, he celebrated his own defeat, saying he lost but the Jan Sangh's ideology won. Even Lohia's constituency selection was guided by the caste factor. While others preached idealism, Upadhyaya practiced it. He is, therefore, the seed for future transformative forces.

Upadhyaya engendered a new political discourse by challenging Western categorisation of political parties as Left and Right. Beyond fostering a false ego, this categorisation entails rigidity on certain positions for the sake of identity. Upadhyaya argued that parties share many commonalities on economic issues but differ on social philosophy and vice versa. His new classification was "pro-changers" and "no-changers" parties.

There were two important events in the history of Jan Sangh and the country in 1963. First, three parliamentary elections were held, which gained national importance for two reasons. One, there was a polarisation of the political parties between the Congress-Communist and the non-Congress, non-Communist parties. Important political leaders contested these by-elections. They were Acharya Kripalani, Dr. Ram Manohar Lohia and Pandit Deendayal Upadhyaya which were the joint candidates of the opposition.

The second important incident of the year was the death of Dr. Raghuvira, a reputed linguist and National President of Bharatiya Jan Sangh, in a car accident. After the death of Dr. Mukherjee in

1953, this was the second occasion when the Jan Sangh had lost such a person of eminence as Dr. Raghuvira as its President. His death was an irreparable loss to Jan Sangh. Upadhyaya remembered him with pride and gratitude at the annual session. It was also the first time that the party General Secretary did not present an analysis and assessment of the parliamentary by-elections, perhaps because he was himself a contestant in those elections. Whatever the reason, the absence of an analysts and assessment of the year's parliamentary by-elections was jarring.

The year 1964 was a milestone in Indian history. Jawaharlal Nehru died this year. This was a shock to the Congress; it marked the end of an era. It was a testing time from the organisational and policy point of view.

A historic training camp of the executive committee of the Jan Sangh was organised at Gwalior from August 11 to 15, 1964. The resolution Upadhyaya had prepared on its principles and policies was given the final touches at his camp. Jan Sangh had come into being on the cultural resurgence thinking in 1952. The 1964 document was the culmination of such thinking. The Jan Sangh authoritatively declared its concept of Integrated Humanism, which Upadhyaya elaborated on in four historic addresses in Mumbai.

The Vijayawada session on January 23-24, 1965, marked a new beginning in the history of Jan Sangh. It was the first session held on a large scale in the South. The Jan Sangh manifesto on its policies and programs was formally presented at this session. Its acceptance marked the beginning of a new chapter in Jan Sangh history.

So far, the President of the party had been a reputed, elderly, affluent and eminent personality. This was the first occasion when a seasoned Jan Sangh worker, Bachhraj Vyas, was elected President.

When viewed from the surface, it was a failure for the Jana Sangh, but it also revealed that sixteen years after independence and a year before his death in 1964, Pandit Nehru was perhaps losing his grip over politics. However, Upadhyaya's candidature was the crucial first step in forming an anti- Congress alliance in post-Independent India, which later crystallised into the Janata Party in 1977. Despite the coalition (of which Jana Sangh was a part) becoming a necessity post the Emergency, Deendayal resisted the inevitability of alliances. Even when he acquiesced, as he had done in 1967-68 with the Jana Sangh joining coalition governments in several states, he viewed it as a transitory phenomenon. In contrast, active practitioners of parliamentary politics like his colleague Atal Bihari Vajpayee viewed them as essential agents of change.

A year after his failed bid to enter the Lok Sabha, Deendayal Upadhyaya, unbeknownst to himself, realised the advantage of political alliances. In April 1964, ironically just six weeks prior to Nehru's demise on 27 May, he had issued a joint statement with the iconic Socialist leader, Dr. Ram Manohar Lohia. This revolutionary, albeit unimaginable coming together of two leaders who represented opposing ideological spectrums, was not only the result of their concurrence on a significant issue, but their joint opposition to the ruling Congress party's stand on nuclear disarmament.

The sworn nationalist that Deendayal Upadhyaya was, he strongly demanded that India seeks US' assistance in developing a nuclear bomb, and obtained Dr. Lohia's endorsement. In 1964, the two issued a joint statement in favour of the 'formation of some sort of Indo-Pak Confederation.' Even today, the joint declaration is cited as one of Upadhyaya's major political successes, after he had secured Lohia's backing on what was, till then, two extremely contentious arguments put out by the sangh. First, 'guaranteeing the protection of life and property of Hindus in Pakistan is the responsibility of the government of India,'; second, the assertion that 'the existence of India and Pakistan as two separate entities is an artificial situation.'

While the second point in the declaration was a de facto ratification of the idea of Akhand Bharat, because it questioned the reality of Partition which had happened a decade-and-a-half earlier, the first statement was a geo-political disaster.

Deendayal Upadhyaya supplements Golwalkar's cultural nationalism with his theory of integral humanism (Ekatma Manavavad). This new theory adds some sophistication to the RSS concept of Hindu Rashtra and enriches its ideological underpinnings.

Though essentially, he shares Golwalkar's formulations, Deendayal adds some innovative dimensions to it. Despite Golwalkar's talk of India's spiritual mission in the world, he very rarely went beyond the confines of nation. Upadhyaya, on the contrary, talked of integration of the nation with the rest of humanity, universe and the Almighty (Paramesthi). But this integration is more emotional and philosophical rather than political. The central idea of integral humanism is that 'while the humanity and the entire animate and inanimate nature around man are full of almost infinite diversity, it has got a common Atma (nearest English rendering is Ethos or Soul).' The diversity is superficial. Because of the common Atma, all things naturally are cooperative and complementary. This is expressed by the word Ekatmata.

The logic of this philosophy not only intends to obviate the conflict between various entities, but also desires the merger of the smaller into the bigger one in the process of development. Thus the individual merges into the family, the family into nation, and nation-state into world state on the basis of integral humanism. In the realm of thought, the highest level would be the principle of non- dualism, Advait.

Individual and Society

Deendayal writes that the individual is a conglomerate of body, mind, intellect and soul. These are all integrated. Confusion has arisen in the West because they have treated each of the above aspects of human being separately and without any relation to the rest. But in Bharat, he proceeds, we have placed before ourselves the ideal of the four-fold responsibilities of catering to the needs of body, mind, intellect and soul with a view to achieving the integrated progress of man. Dharma, artha, kama and moksha are the four kinds of purushartha or human efforts. Purushartha means, efforts which befit a man. These four efforts are thought to be integrated.

Elaborating the relation of this integrated individual with the society, Deendayal explains that the individual is not limited to a singular 'I' but is also inseparably related to the plural 'We', i.e. the society. He categorically rejects the social contract theory and believes that society is an organic entity with its own self and life. Society too has its body, mind, intellect and soul. It also has four purusharthas (objectives) in its life. But since the individual and the society are ekatma, there is no conflict in their interests; they are mutually complementary.

He admits that classes and castes do exist in society. But the conflict is not fundamental. He explains that the entire Western-thought stream has presumed a conflict between the individual and society. The main theme around which the conflict is woven is the concept of rights. Indian thinking, on the other hand, lays emphasis on cooperation and synthesis. The emphasis is on duties, not on rights.

Nation and Culture

Deendayal explains that a nation too has a soul. There is a technical name for it - chiti, which is analogous to that of an individual. Chiti determines the direction in which the nation is to advance culturally. Whatever is in accordance with chiti is included in the culture. These things are to be cultivated. Whatever is against chiti is discarded as a perversion, undesirable and is to be avoided. He concludes that the soul of Bharat could be properly understood only from a cultural point of view. To him the nation is not a political but a cultural concept. Elaborating further, he writes, the basis of our nationalism is not simply Bharat but Bharat Mata; Bharat would remain just a piece of land if the word Mata is taken away. The first characteristic of a Bharatiya culture is that it looks upon life as an integrated whole. However, to him, 'there can be only one culture in India. The slogans of many cultures can break this country into pieces and destroy it.' This very much reflects Golwalkar's ideas.

Deendayal makes a critique of both Western materialism and Marxism contrasting them with the Hindu/Bharatiya culture. Upadhyaya's integral humanism does not take into consideration the divergent social, political and philosophical crosscurrents of Western countries, and club them under one monolithic 'West'. Similarly, the diversities of Indian life and thinking are ignored by putting them under a monolithic Bharatiya culture. Though in his discourse he emphasizes more on the term Bharatiya than Hindu, he certainly believes that both are synonymous.

However, Upadhyaya's innovation lies in outlining a new economic blueprint that he believed 'would suit our national genius'. In his opinion, both Marxism and capitalism are unsuitable; while the former denies individual freedom, the later encourages profit motives and aggrandizement. He categorically rejects the Nehruvian model of economic development as it does not conform to our cultural and spiritual heritage. He strongly believes that swadeshi and decentralization would constitute the essence of an alternate economic system. In this respect, Upadhyaya identifies more with Gandhian economic philosophy.[47]

A Political Theorist

As an RSS ideologue, Deendayal Upadhyaya continuously stressed on the need to Indianize 'western concepts of the nation, western secularism, western democracy.' For instance, he was sceptical about ushering in adult franchise prior to increasing literacy levels - curiously, a typical elitist argument that links political judgement with formal education, thereby serving as a tool for exclusion. Deendayal viewed Indian democracy as a system which made it imperative for government to be run through mutual discussion, as enshrined in ancient Indian traditions, but reasoned thereafter that, 'if we carry it to the other extreme, it could prove troublesome.'

His unusual views on mass awareness programmes were, however, in perfect sync with the division of labour that he proposed that the government must be entrusted with building democracy; campaigns for moulding public opinion should be the preserve of 'selfless' ascetics; and governance was the prerogative of an elected government. Of the lot, the suggestion to entrust renunciates with the responsibility of creating mass awareness programmes was most telling, because that in turn minimised the onus on a particular government in case its policies didn't find favour with the group and vice-versa. The principle of integrating ascetics or sadhus in official programmes was clearly driven by the intent to provide official sanctity to pursuits of faith and evolved from the idea of creating a system based on the 'fusion of both materialism and spiritualism', in contrast to 'Western culture (which) is materialistic.'

While pontificating about the electoral system, Deendayal argued that for it to succeed, good candidates, good parties, and finally good voters were mandatory. While political parties must be principled, and shun casteism, Upadhyaya held an odd viewpoint about ex-royals as electoral candidates in a democracy, who he said, 'must be active in the country's politics, but he contradicted it by saying that political parties should avoid nominating them solely for their princely status and wealth.'

For voters, Deendayal had a long list of suggestions as follows: do not vote for a party, but for its ideals; don't support an individual, but opt for the party; and opt for an individual, and not for his or her money power, or be 'misled by hype.'

Of all his theories, what stood out prominently was his rejection of India's federal system and as a natural corollary, its administrative and governance structure. His recommendation was for a centralised system, and he objected to India being defined as a Union of States, and protested against the enactment of Reorganisation of States on linguistic principles (He demanded the setting up of a commission to reorganise states, which was eventually established by the Nehru government in 1954).

While he was in favour of centralisation, Upadhyaya also opposed a 'unitary constitution' and suggested that we should 'decentralise our fiscal and other resources.' It must be mentioned here that the idea of cooperative federalism, which forms a significant part of Prime Minister Narendra Modi's governance module, is an expansion of the premise.

Deendayal Upadhyaya shall be best remembered in history for the two seminal texts that he wrote within a span of seven years - *The Two Plans: Promises, Performance and Prospects* (1958), and *Integral Humanism* (1965). However, of the two, the latter which is essentially a detailed hypothesis on philosophical issues with a bearing on the larger economic vision, merits greater attention because it has survived for more than half a century as the 'official' philosophy of the Jana Sangh, and later, the BJP.

At one level, the theory of Integral Humanism which was adopted as the 'Principles and Policies of the Jana Sangh' at the plenary session in Vijayawada in February 1965, was considered by the party to be self-sufficient in terms of a well-argued political thought. But according to Deendayal's detractors, one of the biggest shortcomings of the theory was in its assumption that India is a civilisational concept, and not an idea which had evolved over centuries. It was felt that the text reflected Deendayal's very own idea of his party's raison d'être vis-à-vis his position in it. While at a personal level, there was often an overlap and confusion over what he was first and foremost, a swayamsevak or general secretary, there was a complete lack of clarity over whether the party's primary objective was to be part of active politics, or consolidate Hindu society.

Upadhyaya was a Bharatiya Jana Sangh (BJS) leader who enjoyed the confidence of the RSS and has been held in high esteem for his idealism. In a rare gesture, the second Sarsanghchalak of the RSS, Golwalkar, described him as "100 per cent Swayamsevak." His perspective and thought have become a foundation stone to the socio-economic philosophy of the Sangh Parivar and current PM Narendra Modi's pro-poor commitment has the obvious imprint of Upadhyaya's life and mission. Upadhyaya, however, played a larger role in India's thought process and political life.

His impact on contemporary political actors can be gauged by his acceptance as an original thinker who transcended party affiliations: Veteran Congressman and a former chief minister of Uttar Pradesh, Sampoornanand, wrote the preface of Upadhyaya's Political Diary, which contains social, cultural and political insights. He described Upadhyaya as "One of the most notable political leaders of our time, a man devoted to the good of his country, a person of unimpeachable character, a leader whose weighty words swayed thousands of educated men", and considered Political Diary essential reading for future political workers.

As mentioned earlier, Golwalkar had a distaste for politics and considered it an immoral influence on his cadre. Similarly, the RSS was unequivocal in its opinion that a society or nation had greater value than the State, but it was paradoxical for a political party like Jana Sangh to have endorsed such a view. Just as the other affiliates of the RSS—the Bharatiya Mazdoor Sangh (BMS) or Vishwa Hindu Parishad (VHP)—are primarily committed to their respective agendas which are dovetailed into the overall framework of the sangh, the Jana Sangh needed to be more independent than what an organisation driven by a pracharak as organising secretary desired it to be.

As the largest cadre-based party in the world, with more than a dozen ideological arms, initially, the RSS wasn't known to micro-manage the affairs of its affiliates. However, since the mid-forties, it began a trend of holding annual meetings with its agencies to ensure adherence to a broad code of conduct. Deendayal attended these meetings regularly, but if one analyses the events of the period, it does appear that there was far greater concurrence between him and RSS. Upadhyaya also required clarity regarding his twin roles, and was gradually found wanting in his ability to balance between ideology and active politics.

There is no doubt that it was the theory of Integral Humanism which established the theory of Hindu political philosophy in post-Independent India. Upadhyaya began work on it in 1964–65 and after presenting it at the Jana Sangh's Vijayawada plenary session where it was accepted as the party's core philosophy, he elaborated on it in a series of four lectures in Bombay in April 1965.

According to L.K. Advani, Upadhyaya's choice of the title was with the intent of contrasting his party's ideological premise with that of M.N. Roy's philosophical theory of Radical Humanism. For instance, Integral Humanism rejected the class theory primarily because it was espoused by the Communists. Instead, Upadhyaya's theory recommended that different sections of society should work together, and in this context, he referred to a peculiar analogy to elucidate the relationship between the oppressor and the oppressed: 'A flower is what it is because of its petals, and the worth of the petals lies in remaining with the flower and adding to its beauty.' In Upadhyaya's political construct, associations or loyalties were either civilisational, cultural or religious. People were inter-connected not because of class interests, but because of a common religious and cultural heritage. In effect, this meant that a Hindu factory worker would have greater.

According to him, 'dharma was neither a religion nor sect and also not an entirely personal matter as his detractors had contended. Dharma for him was much wider term with extensive connotation.' Deendayal argued that dharma was 'our chiti, the inner spirit that pervades all of us. He further introduced the idea of virat (shakti), which, according to him, was the power that energises a nation. While chiti, which is Fundamental and is central to the nation from its very beginning... the soul determines the direction in which the nation is to advance culturally. Whatever is in accordance with chiti is included in culture.'

In conclusion, the core objective of Integral Humanism was to 'create a Bharat which will excel...to achieve through a sense of unity with the entire creation, a state even higher than that of a complete human being, to become Narayan (god) from nar (man).' The theory is therefore primarily addressed to a Hindu faithful, and as a result of which it remains an exclusionist philosophy which may not appeal to the adherents of cultural and religious pluralism.

According to him, dharma rajya has and should be the ideal of the Indian state. In such a state, "tolerance of and respect for all faiths and creeds is an essential feature". Further, in a dharma rajya, "freedom of worship and conscience is guaranteed to all and the state does not discriminate against any one on grounds of religion, either in the formation of policy or in its implementation. It is a non-sectarian state and not a theocracy".

He said this Indian concept was quite distinct from what is available elsewhere in the world, but the nearest English equivalent of dharma rajya would be the rule of law. In such a state, no individual or body is recognised as sovereign. Every individual is subject to certain obligations and regulations, and the rights of all institutions and individuals, be it the legislature or the executive or the people at large, are all regulated by dharma, and "licentious conduct is not permitted".

On the one hand, dharma rajya would curb arbitrariness and totalitarianism and on the other, it would prevent democracy from degenerating into mobocracy. Significantly, he noted that while other concepts of the state propounded elsewhere in the world were oriented towards the rights of the individual, the Indian concept of dharma rajya was duty-oriented.

The Economist

In contrast to the philosophical nature of Integral Humanism, *The Two Plans: Promises, Performance and Prospects* was a general critique of Nehruvian economics, focusing on the First (1951-56) and Second (1956-61) Five Year Plans of the erstwhile Planning Commission, respectively. Interestingly, the assessment while intrinsically economic in nature, was an amalgamation of the four ancient Indian principles or purusbarthas—artha or wealth, kama or bodily desire, dharma which is righteousness, and finally, moksha, denoting a release from all worldly pleasures or the attainment of salvation. Although the meanings of these four goals have by and large remained constant through centuries, its interpretation and significance in a human being's life have often depended on varying philosophical schools.

Deendayal Upadhyaya placed 'Artha and Kama bracketed between Dharma on the left and Moksha on the right side of the axis. That raised the thesis that the limits of creating and enjoying Artha and Kama should be governed by Dharma and aimed at Moksha.' Therefore, he didn't think that the pursuit of wealth was in anyway unethical, although he did elaborate that both the paucity or excess of it had a negative impact on society. While Deendayal's economic theory was heavily protectionist and had similarities with some of Gandhi's principles, especially his emphasis on encouraging cottage industries to help rural Indian achieve self-sufficiency, his rejection of what he envisaged as the principles governing a 'modern world' were at variance with the Mahatma. Upadhyaya had fundamental disagreements with Nehru's idea of development and in all likelihood wouldn't have seen large dams as the 'temples of modern India'. He argued that it was 'wrong to accept industrialisation as our ultimate objective.' Contrary to his political vision of centralisation of authority in a non-federal set up, the two mainstays of Upadhyaya's economic theory were, decentralisation and the use of technology, which were principally dichotomous in nature. On the one hand, if he encouraged the use of technology for production, he was against mechanisation and not in favour of using as a mere tool for speeding up economic progress, which was yet again at variance with Nehru's vision of stepping up growth and infrastructure. His *Two Plans* had a romantic idealism about it, evoking India of the yore in which progress unfolded organically.As someone who hailed the indigenous sector as a significant element in furthering India's economy, Upadhyaya was not a great votary of the public sector, and criticised the government for constraining the growth of the private sector. His argument being that social justice shall continue to elude India till 'the private sector is encouraged to develop along with the expansion of the public sector and there should be a mechanism to effectively bring this about.' As he was bitterly opposed to Socialism, he recommended the system to encourage individual initiative and enterprise, and wrote that just as 'dictatorship destroys man's creativity in politics, large-scale industrialisation destroys individual enterprise.' Clearly, Upadhyaya did not take into account the factor of individual enterprise in massive industrial projects, and appeared myopically focused on small-scale enterprises.

As one of the earliest votaries of the constitutionally granted, right to Work, Upadhyaya was of the view that under-employment was bad for society besides of course being detrimental to economic security of an individual, artha as essential for dharma, being his primary belief.

The centrality of village as the engine for economic growth was evident in the first election manifesto of the Jana Sangh in 1951. A short document compared to a long list of promises as is the norm now, it mentioned how villages have been the 'centre of Bharat's life in all times,' and that the 'ideal of Sarvodaya cannot be achieved until and unless the village is restored to its original position as the basic economic unit.' The manifesto promised that the Jana Sangh if voted to power, shall usher in gramtantra or the hegemony of villages over urban India, which alas didn't come to fruition. Upadhyaya's opposition to Nehruvian economic policies were also evident in his criticism of the Planning Commission, which he said was trying to 'build a pyramid from top.'38

Towards the end of his political career, Deendayal Upadhyaya who had made his criticism of public agitations more than evident (yet again) in his seminal Integral Humanism theory, did a volte-face in his maiden presidential speech in 1967. He made a direct reference to 'those who are trying to preserve the status quo in the economic and social spheres, are unnerved by popular movement.' Compared to his earlier stance in the early 1950s, Deendayal had now cast his lot with his mentor, Balasaheb Deoras who had a more egalitarian approach to public life in comparison to M.S. Golwalkar. This in effect was the beginning of the 'Leftward turn' that the Jana Sangh was seen to have taken, but the major part of it unfolded after Deendayal's unfortunate death.

The Tragedy

In December 1967, Deendayal Upadhyaya became the President of the Jana Sangh. However, as mentioned earlier, his elevation was fraught with controversy as his colleague and senior member of the party, Balraj Madhok had also thrown his hat in the ring. But the RSS pressed on and besides elevating Deendayal, it also nominated Sunder Singh Bhandari, the lawyer-turned-RSS worker from Rajasthan as Vice President of Jana Sangh. Upadhyaya's presidentship coincided with the 1967 general elections in which the Jana Sangh won thirty-five Lok Sabha seats, and 257 seats in the state assemblies. This was up from fourteen and 119 in 1962, and the credit for this was largely attributed to the Deoras-Upadhyaya combine, who had eventually chosen the path of political pragmatism over ideological purity. It would be safe to surmise that much like the personal battle that he had waged throughout the initial years of his career, Deendayal Upadhyaya was once again at the crossroads.

The encouraging results during the elections had forced a debate within the Jana Sangh whether it should join the coalition governments in some states of north India, like Haryana. Finally, Deendayal had sided with the likes of Atal Bihari Vajpayee who was in favour of becoming part of the coalition, but certain voices within the RSS made their protestations loud and clear. As mentioned earlier, Deendayal had past experience of having worked in the United Provinces and had instilled the ideal of bolstering and transforming Hindu society as the sangh's primary objective amongst its members. For most of his fifteen-year-long tenure as a revered member of the Jana Sangh, Deendayal Upadhyaya continued to be viewed as an avowed pracharak, but post 1967 when he had become non-theoretical, his devoted followers who had been nurtured by him on a diet of ideological puritanism, raised objections against his quest for political power.

His presidential address in Calicut (now, Kozhikode) in December 1967 was a clinching evidence of how he was torn between running a party, keeping his core ideological beliefs intact, and facing up to the emerging challenges in Indian politics. Upadhyaya confessed that, although with the 1967 general elections, 'the process has started for Congress's gradual withering away,' the 'results left much to be desired.' His reasoning was that it had led to several post-election problems, which he classified into three broad categories. First, the 'problems pertaining to the politics of the transition, inter-party relations instability of coalition ministries and floor-crossing.' Second, how the emerging situation was testing the Indian 'constitutional set-up as such scenarios were hitherto unknown.' Third, how the resultant instability was aiding the 'problems relating to economic, defence home and foreign affairs, which he attributed to mishandling by the Congress party.' Upadhyaya was of the view that although the first set of concerns were immediate and 'evoke the maximum of public comment and debate,' the other two also required immediate attention.

Despite the absence of political morality, which had willy-nilly become incumbent on ensuring political stability, Upadhyaya took no initiative in diluting his party's idealism. It merits mentioning that in 1960, he had ensured the passing of a resolution at the party's annual session that acted as a code of conduct for parliamentarians and legislators. Sadly, in recent years, the BJP has also abandoned certain set of rules like, 'walking out of the House and a tendency to create chaos through shouting or sloganeering.'

Deendayal's most innovative and lasting contribution to the Indian political discourse was his proposal to confront the problem of political defection or 'floor-crossing' as he had termed it. The issue had merited focus as a result of the fragmented verdicts in 1967 in Punjab, Bihar, West Bengal, Kerala, Madhya Pradesh, Uttar Pradesh, and Rajasthan. The respective state governments were dismissed by the Governors because of the number of defections from a clutch of non-Congress parties. Meanwhile, the Constitution was silent on how Governors should conduct themselves in order to be seen as non-partisan while dismissing a government.

In 1967, during his presidential address, Upadhyaya had drawn attention to the 'arbitrary conduct' of Governors and had demanded that the process of their appointment be made transparent.

He had also added that, although India had opted for the Westminster model, we should try to mould this to suit our changing politics. A convention can be accepted that no government would resign except on the adoption of a no-confidence vote against it by the legislature. Another convention which may be evolved...is that if a majority of members of a legislature request the Speaker that the House be convened, a meeting of the legislature would be invariably summoned.

Preceding the famous S.R. Bommai judgement by almost three decades, Deendayal's suggestions were brilliantly precedent. Absence of transparent guidelines for Governors over crucial issues following a hung verdict had resulted in questions being raised about the sanctity of such a constitutional position.

Meanwhile, in 1967, Deendayal was faced with a challenge of dealing with members who had joined the Jana Sangh from other political parties and were, therefore, alien to the culture of the RSS. In order to keep them under check, and confined to the acceptable ideological framework, Upadhyaya came up with a two-pronged strategy: first, he inducted large number of pracharaks into the party and second, he decided to 'place the legislative members more closely under the direct support of the organisation.'

He also entrusted the 'party cadre' with the task of taking forward the 'programmes of the party or government to people, translate them into realities for the people.' These programmes...become the vehicle to continue to build and take the organisation from strength to strength. This was in continuation of the process that he had initiated in 1960, when he had spelt out his goal of appointing one pracharak for every district unit of the party.

Although it happened after he was long gone, it was one of Deendayal's initiatives which was at the root of the dual membership controversy in the Janata Party in 1978-79. The dispute which had triggered the collapse of India's first non-Congress government at the Centre, was chiefly due to Upadhyaya mandating that the 'party cadre' be entrusted with the task of taking the 'programmes of the party or government to people, translate them into realities for the people.'[48]

In the eyes of his peers and those in charge in Nagpur, Deendayal Upadhyaya represented the 'ideal swayamsevak'. This was because he had devoted his whole life to the RSS, to the extent of refusing marriage, and also because, in the opinion of RSS veterans, 'his discourse reflected the pure thought-current of the Sangh'.

This doctrine found its main expression in Integral Humanism, a text which provided the bases of the Jana Sangh's 'Principles and Policies' . As in Upadhyaya's first text, Two Plans, which targeted Nehru's economic policy, the salient point of Integral Humanism lies in its promotion of society vis-à-vis the state which, by comparison, is shown to be a secondary institution. This approach was in conformity with RSS ideology, which focused on groundwork at the local level, but paradoxical in the case of a political party whose vocation was, in theory at least, the conquest of power. Upadhyaya advocated decentralization of power to the village level and the rehabilitation of the old varna system in an organic vein, so much so that his thought had some affinities with Gandhian notions. Though he ran for office only once during a by-election, Deendayal Upadhyaya remained the Jana Sangh's general secretary from 1953 to 1967. He then became party President but was mysteriously assassinated in 1968. In the 1970s, the RSS named its think tank, the Deendayal Research Institute, after Upadhyaya and he has remained a reference point for the official programme of the Jana Sangh, and later the BJP - as is evident from the frequent deployment of Integral Humanism in the election manifestos of these parties.

Deendayal Upadhyaya wanted to base India's independence on its culture. He was, therefore, not prepared to accept any widely-accepted notion in this regard blindly. A western concept of the nation, western secularism, western democracy, and various other western issues came up for comment; Deendayal was for Indianizing all these concepts.

He enthusiastically accepted the concept of democracy. Although it was established in India immediately after independence, and universal franchise was introduced through the Constitution of India, Deendayal was slightly apprehensive of this move in view of India's long years of slavery. He reached the conclusion that universal adult franchise should come after proper education. He believed that democracy was not a gift of the West to India. Indian nationhood is naturally democratic.

He wrote:

"Vedic Sabhas and Samitis were also organised on the basis of democracy, and many medieval states in India were completely democratic. We have confined the powers and privileges of kings and made them cater to the demands of the public. We may find instances of kings violating the code of public welfare and public good, but people's protest against them and their not being considered ideal rulers justify our democratic sentiments... The way democracy has been defined, it is a government to be run through mutual discussion. Continuous consultation and discussion is an old Indian adage. But... if we carry it to the other extreme, it would prove to be troublesome. Voltaire has said, "If I do not consider your viewpoint right, I would fight with all my strength for your right of self-expression." 'He has, therefore, accepted men's ability to discuss and argue. The Indian culture goes beyond this and views democratic discussion as something through which we arrive at the essence of thought.' Deendayal comments on the rise of democracy in the West, its deterioration into Capitalism and Karl Mark's dictatorial reaction as under."

"After nationalism... the second radical concept is democracy, which has deeply affected European polity. In the beginning, nations were ruled by monarchs, but their tyranny led to an awakening among the people. In the wake of the Industrial Revolution and development of international commerce, the trading community became a demanding force. Naturally, the traders came into conflict with the nobility and the monarchy. This conflict sowed the seeds of democracy. Roots of this form of government have been traced to the nation-states of ancient Greece. Liberty, equality and fraternity were the slogans of the French Revolution. Ruling dynasties were either put an end to or their rights and privileges were limited to make way for constitutional rule. Today, democracy is an accepted form of government in Europe. Those who ignored democracy, today subscribe to this form of government. Even dictators like Hitler, Mussolini and Stalin did not go against democratic principles." Democracy was developed in the West as an idealistic and popular concept, but the newly-created traders and the modern Industrial Revolution made it a tool of capitalistic exploitation. Upadhyaya, therefore, says further:

"Although democracy has granted the franchise to every citizen, its leadership was confined to the people who expounded this concept. A new method of production was introduced after the Industrial Revolution. The worker who stayed at home and worked, became an employee of a factory owner. He left his home in the country side and came to live in the city. There were proper arrangements for his living there. There were no rules in the factory where he worked. The organization of labour was weak and ill-defined. The worker become a victim of torture and exploitation. Those who had the right to govern were the very people who exploited the workers. The workers, therefore, could not look up to the government for the redressal of their grievances.

Many people raised their voice to protest against the prevailing situation and worked for bringing about an improvement in it. They called themselves socialists. Karl Marx was one of them. He commented on the economy and history in order to bring about a transformation. It was on the basis of his thought that socialism assumed a scientific standing. The later socialists may or may not have subscribed to his views, but he has left a deep imprint on their thinking"

Deendayal Upadhyaya, while agreeing with the basic tenets of democracy in the west that were a reaction to oligarchy, exploitations and capitalism, wanted to Indianise the concept of democracy. He gave a call for Indianising the democratic set-up of government.

Indianisation of Democracy

Elections are an important constituent of democracy in the west. Constitution executive, legislature and judiciary are its byproducts, but they are a mere formality in any democracy. Its soul consists of reflecting the opinion of the people rightly. Democracy is not dependent on any outward manifestations. Adult franchise and the electoral process are important parts of any democracy, but they do not alone lead to its establishment. Both these are present in Russia, but experts do not accept it as a democracy. Another feature is required for democracy besides adult franchise and the electoral process.... Democracy is not merely the rule of the majority... In such a government, at least one segment of the public will be there whose voice is stifled even though it may be right. This form of democracy cannot work for everyone's welfare and everyone's good.... Therefore, in any form of democracy for India, elections, majority and minority etc., all must be combined and harmonized at one place. Anyone who has a different opinion from the majority, even if he a single individual, his viewpoint must be respected and incorporated into governance. In England, where democracy has achieved the maximum success, the leader of the opposition is paid his salary from the National Exchequer. In any democracy, there must be two political parties in Parliament. The Opposition always comments upon and criticise the policies of the Government.

Two Extracts from Integral Humanism Bharatiya Culture is Integrated

The first characteristic of Bharatiya culture is that it looks upon life as an integrated whole. It has an integrated view point. To think of parts may be proper for a specialist but it is not useful from the practical standpoint. The confusion in the West arises primarily from its tendency to think of life in sections and then to attempt to put them together by patch work. We do admit that there is diversity and plurality in life but we have always attempted to discover the unity behind them. This attempt is thoroughly scientific. The scientists always attempt to discover order in the apparent disorder in the universe, to find out the principles governing the universe and frame practical rules on the basis of these principles. Chemists discovered that a few elements comprise the entire physical world. Physicists went one step further and showed that even these elements consist only of energy. Today we know that the entire universe is only a form of energy.

Philosophers are also basically scientists. The Western philosophers reached up to the principle of duality; Hegel put forward the principle of thesis, anti-thesis and synthesis; Karl Marx used this principle as a basis and presented his analysis of history and economics. Darwin considered the principle of survival of the fittest as the sole basis of life. But, we, in this country saw the basic unity of all life. Even the dualists have believed the nature and the spirit to be complementary to each other than conflicting. The diversity in life is merely an expression of the internal unity. There is complementarity underlying the diversity. The unit of seed finds expression in various forms - the roots, the trunk, the branches, the leaves, the flowers and the fruits of the tree. All these have different forms and colours and even to some extent different properties. Still we recognise their relation of unity with each other through the seed... It is a simple truth that society is a group of men. But how did society come into being? Many views have been put forward by philosophers. Those propounded in the West and on which the western socio-political structure is based can be broadly summarised as 'society is a group of individuals brought into being by he individuals by an agreement among themselves.' This view is known as 'Social Contract Theory'. Individual is given greater importance in this view. If there are differences in different western views, these pertain only to the questions, namely, 'If the individual produced a society, then in whom the residual power remains vested, in the society or in the individual? Does the individual have the right to change the society? Can the society impose a variety of regulations on the individual and claim a right to the allegiance of the individual to itself? Or the individual is free as regards these questions?'

Extracts from Integral Humanism:

Basic Needs to Be Met

Really speaking, our slogan should be that the one who earns will feed, and every person will have enough to eat. The right to food is a birthright. The ability to earn is a result of education and training. In a society, even those who do not earn must have food. The children and the old, the diseased and the invalids, all must be cared for by society. Every society generally fulfils this responsibility. The social and cultural progress of mankind lies in its readiness to fulfil this responsibility. The economic system must provide for this responsibility. The economic system must provide for this task. Economics as a science does not account for this responsibility. A man works not for bread alone, but also to shoulder this responsibility. Otherwise, those who have had their meals would no longer work. Any economic system must provide for the minimum basic necessities of human life to everyone. Food, clothing and shelter constitute, broadly speaking, these basic necessities. Similarly, society must enable the individual to carry out his obligations to society by educating him properly. Lastly, in the event of an individual falling prey to any disease, society must arrange for his treatment and maintenance. If a government provides these minimum requirements, then only it is a rule of Dharma. Otherwise, it is a rule of adharma. Describing King Dilip, Kalidas had said in Raghuvansha, "Being responsible for the maintenance, protection and education of his subjects, he was their true father. Others were merely instrumental in giving them their birth". The description of King Bharat after whom our country has been named Bharat, also runs similarly, i.e. "By maintaining and protecting his subjects, he was called Bharat". This is his country, Bharat. If in this country, maintenance and protection are not guaranteed, then the name Bharat is meaningless.

Western Versus Bharatiya View

Yesterday we had seen that even after 17 years of independence we have still to decide what direction we should adopt to realise our cherished dream of all-round development in the lives of our countrymen. Normally, people are not prepared to seriously consider this question. They think only of the problems which they face from time to time. Sometimes, economic problems are viewed with concern and an attempt is made to resolve them, and at other times, social or political problems come to the forefront claiming attention. Not knowing fundamentally, the direction in which we all are to go, these efforts are not accompanied by sufficient enthusiasm, nor do they give a feeling of satisfaction to the people engaged in these efforts. These efforts produce only a fraction of the results that they ought to have produced. Modern Versus Ancient, however, there are two distinct types of people who do suggest some definite direction. There are some who suggest that we must go back to the position when we lost our independence and restart from there. On the other hand, there are people who would like to discard all that has originated here in Bharat and they are not ready to give a second thought to it. They seem to think that Western life and thoughts are the last word in progress and all of them should be imported here if we are to develop. Both these lines of thought are incorrect, though they do represent partial truths and it will not be proper to reject them altogether. They, who advocate starting from where we left off a thousand years ago, forget that whether it may or may not be desirable, it is definitely impossible. The flow of time cannot be reversed. In the past one thousand years, whatever we assimilated, whether it was forced on us or we took it with willingness, cannot be discarded now. Besides, we too have original creations in the life of our society. We did not always remain mere passive witness to whatever new challenging situations arose, nor did we merely react to every alien action. We too, have attempted to reshape our life as was required to face the new situations. Therefore, we cannot afford to shut our eyes to all that has happened in the past one thousand years. Similarly, those who would like to make Western ideologies the basis of our progress, forget that these ideologies have arisen in certain special situations and times. They are not necessarily universal. They cannot be free from the limitations of the particular people and their culture which gave birth to these isms. Besides, many of these are already out of date. The principles of Marx have changed both with the changing times as well as with varying conditions, to the extent that parrot-like repetition of Marxism for solving the problems facing our country, would amount to a reactionary attitude rather than a scientific and pragmatic one. It is indeed surprising, that they who claim to reform the society by removing dead traditions, themselves fall prey to some outdated foreign traditions.

Learn, But Do Not Ape Others

Every country has its own peculiar historical, social and economic situation, and its leaders decide the remedies for the ills that beset the country from time to time, taking into consideration its background. It is illogical to believe that remedies which the leaders of one country decide to try for their problems are likely to be effective as such to all other peoples. A simple illustration will suffice. Even though the basic organic activity is the same in all human beings, the drugs which may be helpful in England may not prove equally helpful in Bharat. Diseases also depend upon climate, water, dietary habits and heredity. Even though the external symptoms may be apparently similar, the same drug does not necessarily cure all persons. Those who apply a single panacea to all diseases must be considered quacks rather than doctors. Therefore, Ayurveda states i.e. for the disease in each place, a remedy suitable to that place must be found. Therefore, it is neither possible nor wise to adopt foreign isms in our country in the original form in toto. It will not be helpful in achieving happiness and prosperity. On the other hand, it needs to be realised that not all the thoughts and principles that have sprung up elsewhere are necessarily local in space and time. The response of human beings in a particular place, time and social atmosphere may, and does, in many cases, have relation and use to other human beings elsewhere and at other times. Therefore, to ignore altogether the development in other societies, past or present, is certainly unwise. Whatever truths these developments contain must be taken note of and accepted. The rest must be scrupulously avoided. While absorbing the wisdom of other societies, it is only proper that we avoid their mistakes or perversities. Even their wisdom should be adapted to our particular circumstances. In brief, we must absorb the knowledge and gains of the entire humanity so far as eternal principles and truths are concerned. Of these, the ones that originated in our midst have to be clarified and adapted to changed times, and those that we take from other societies have to be adapted to our conditions.

Nationalism, Democracy and Socialism

Western political thought has accepted Nationalism, Democracy, and Socialism or Equality, as ideals. Besides, now and then, there have been attempts directed at world unity which took the shape of the League of Nations, and after the Second World War, the United Nations Organisation. For a variety of reasons these have not succeeded. However, these definitely were attempts in that direction. All these ideals have in practice proved to be incomplete and mutually opposing. Nationalism led to conflict between nations which led in turn to global conflict. Whereas if status quo is regarded as synonymous with world peace, the aspirations of many small nations to be independent would remain ever unfulfilled. World unity and nationalism conflict with each other. Some advocate suppression of nationalism for world unity, whereas others regard world unity as a utopian ideal and emphasise national interest to the utmost. Similar difficulty arises in reconciling socialism and democracy. Democracy grants individual liberty, but the same is used by the capitalist system for exploitation and monopolisation. Socialism was brought in to end exploitation, but it destroyed freedom and dignity of the individual. Mankind stands confused and is unable to decide what the correct path is for future progress. The West is not in a position to say with confidence that, "This alone and no other", is the right path. It is itself groping. Therefore, simply to follow the West would be an instance of the blind being led by the blind.

Claim of Bharatiya Culture

In this situation, our attention is claimed by the Bharatiya culture. Is it possible that our culture can point the direction to the world? From the national standpoint we shall have to consider our culture, because that is our very nature. Independence is intimately related to one's own culture. If culture does not form the basis of independence, then the political movement for independence would be reduced simply to a scramble by selfish and power-seeking persons. Independence can be meaningful only if it becomes an instrument for the expression of our culture. Such expression will not only contribute to our progress, but the effort required will also give us the experience of joy. Therefore, both from the national as well as human standpoint, it has become essential that we think of the principles of Bharatiya culture.

If with its help, we can reconcile the various ideals of Western political thought, then it will be an added advantage for us. These Western principles are a product of revolution in human thought and social conflict. They represent one or the other aspiration of mankind and it is not proper to ignore them.

Conflict – Sign of Cultural Regression

Unity in diversity and the expression of unity in various forms have remained the central thought of Bharatiya culture. If this truth is wholeheartedly accepted, then there will not exist any cause for conflict among various powers. Conflict is not a sign of culture or nature; rather it is a symptom of perversion. The law of the jungle – 'Survival of the Fittest' - which the West discovered in recent years was known to our philosophers. We have recognised desire, anger, etc, among the six lower tendencies of human nature, but we did not use them as the foundation or the basis of civilised life or culture. There are thieves and robbers in society. It is essential to save ourselves and society from these elements. We cannot consider them as our ideals or standards of human behaviour. 'Survival of the Fittest' is the law of the jungle. Civilisations have developed not on the basis of this law, but by consideration of how the operation of this law could be reduced to the minimum in human life. If we wish to progress, we have to keep this history of civilisation before our minds.[49]

Ironically, though it may sound for a man who lived abstemiously, Deendayal's end was perhaps precipitated by the sudden luxury of comfort which was bestowed upon him by members of his party. All through his life, he had only travelled in a third-class train compartment, until he became President in December 1967, when it was decreed that he should now travel only first class.

On 10 February 1968, Deendayal Upadhyaya was in Lucknow when he received news that he urgently needed to attend the party's Working Committee meeting in Patna. That same night, his party workers saw him off at the station as he got into the Sealdah-Pathankot Express. However, the train's schedule underwent a last-minute change and wasn't any longer bound for Patna. The first-class compartment that Deendayal was travelling in was detached from the Sealdah-Pathankot Express, and was instead fastened to the Delhi-Howrah Express at Mughalsarai, the big junction in UP which now bears his name. As scheduled, the train arrived in Patna the next morning, but Deendayal Upadhyaya did not alight from it. A big commotion had ensued at the Patna station even as party leaders began making frantic enquiries about the missing leader. Meanwhile, in Mughalsarai, a body was discovered next to the railway tracks, a short distance away from the platform. A huge crowd had surrounded the unclaimed body when suddenly one voice, belonging incidentally to a Jana Sangh worker, was heard, 'that is Deendayal Upadhyaya ji, the Jana Sangh President.'

He was murdered and the case remains unsolved till date. Many people believed the murder to be politically motivated. On 12 February 1968, Deendayal Upadhyaya was cremated in Delhi's Nigambodh Ghat.

In his condolence message, the RSS sarsanghchalak M.S. Golwalkar had likened Deendayal to Yudhishthir's character in the Mahabharata, a man 'who was devoid of any bitterness in word, action and thought.' The comparison was indeed apt because, much like the iconic warrior who was torn between righteousness and the horrors of war, Deendayal Upadhyaya was, for most part of his life, divided between his commitment to ideology and duty as the head of a political party. However, as one of the most illustrious RSS workers, he had fulfilled what was mandated upon him by his leadership, creating a robust space for the organisation in the history of Indian politics. Deendayal Upadhyaya's short octave may have reached early and macabre end, but with a flourish which remains unmatched in the annals of the RSS.

Bibliography

For Reference and further reading

1. Hindu Maha Sabha in Colonial North India 1915-1930, Constructing Nation and history, By Prabhu Bapu, 2nd Editiion
2. A Review of the History and Work of the Hindu Mahasabha and The Hindu Sanghathan movement, By Indra Prakash
3. Life and Time of Lokmanya Tilak, By N.C.Kelkar
4. The Complete works of Swami Vivekananda, Volume 3
5. Hindu Nationalism a reader, By Christophe Jaffrelot
6. The Hindu Nationalist Movement in India, By Christophe Jaffrelot
7. Hindu Nationalism, Origin, Ideologies and Modern myths, By Chetan Bhatt
8. Hindutva – Exploring the Idea of Hindu Nationalism, By Jyotirmaya Sharma, 1st Edition
9. Lala Lajpat Rai, Socio Political Ideology, By S.R Bakshi
10. Madan Mohan Malviya and Indian Freedom Movement, By Jagannath Prasad Mishra
11. The Great Indian Patriots, by P. Rajeshwar Rao, 2nd Volume
12. Hindutva, Origin, Evolution and Future, By Aravindan Neelakandan
13. Shraddhanand Swami, By M R Jambunathan
14. Hindu Sanghathan- Saviour of the Dying Race, By Swami Shraddhanand

15. Biography of Ganesh Damodar Savarkar, By Sunitha Deshpande, First Edition.
16. Savarkar-the true Story of the Father of Hindutva, By Vaibhav Purandare
17. Veer Savarkar Allegations and Reality, By Akshay Jog, 1st Edition
18. Hindutva – Who is a Hindu, By Vinayak Damodar Savarkar, Revised Edition
19. RSS Evolution from an Organization to a movement, By Ratan Sharda
20. RSS 360*, Demystifying Rastriya Swayamsevak Sangh, By Ratan Sharda
21. RSS A Vision in Action, By H.V. Seshadri
22. Partition-Days, The Fiery Saga of RSS, By Manik Chandra vajpayee
23. Understanding RSS, By Dr. Rakesh Sinha
24. The Brotherhood in Saffron, By Walter k Andersen and Shridhar Damle
25. Disaster Relief and the RSS, By Malini Chatterjee
26. The RSS, Icons of the Indian Right, By Nilanjan Mukhopadhay
27. The Saffron Surge, Untold Story of RSS leadership, By Arun Anand
28. Hindu Nationalism and Indian Politics, The Origin and development of the Bharatiya Jana Sangh, By Bruce Graham
29. Builders of Modern India, Dr. Keshav Baliram Hedgewar, by Rakesh Sinha
30. Encyclopedia of Eminent Thinkers, The political thought of M.S.Golwalkar, By Jai Narain Sharma
31. Portrait of a Martyr, A Biography of Dr.Shyama Prasad Mookherjee, By Balraj Madhok
32. Syama Prasad Mookherjee, Life and Times, By Tathagata Roy
33. Deendayal Upadhayaya, A Great Proponent of Hindutva ideology, By Rajesh Kr.Singh
34. Deendayal Upadhayaya, Life of an ideologue politician, By Shiv Shakti nath Bakshi.

Detailed Footnote

Evolution of Ideology and Akhil Bharat Hindu Mahasabha

1. https://www.hindusamaj.in/mission
2. https://en.wikipedia.org/wiki/Hindu_Nationalism
3. https://en.wikipedia.org/wiki/Raja_Ram_Mohan_Roy
4. https://en.wikipedia.org/wiki/Hindu_Nationalism
5. https://en.wikipedia.org/wiki/Ishwar_Chandra_Vidyasagar
6. Collected works of swami Vivekananda Vol 3 Pg 300 to 303
7. The Arya Samaj | Official Web Portal of Arya Samaj
8. Hindu nationlists of modern India by J.Kuruvachira, Pg 29-30

Bibliography

9. https://en.wikipedia.org/wiki/Arya_samaj
10. Hindu Nationalism – Origins,ideologies and Myths by Chetan Bhatt,Pg26-29
11. https://en.wikipedia.org/wiki/Anushilan_samiti
12. https://en.wikipedia.org/wiki/Surat_split
13. Hindu nationlists of modern India by J.Kuruvachira, Pg 67-96
14. Bipin Chandra Pal - Thoughts on Hinduism and Indian Nationalism - Cultural Samvaad| Indian Culture and Heritage
15. Hindu Mahasabha in Colonial North 1915-30 by Prabh bapu,Pg 105-106
16. https://en.wikipedia.org/wiki/Gandhi and rama rajya
17. The Hindutva Legacy of Netaji Subhas Chandra Bose. | Struggle for Hindu Existence
18. Hindutva And Cultural Nationalism: The Missing Chapter In Netaji's Life (swarajyamag.com)
19. Hindu Mahasabha in Colonial North 1915-30 by Prabh bapu,Pg 16-17
20. ibid ,Pg 19-20
21. www.abhm.org.in/about.aspx
22. A review of the History & work of the Hindu Mahasabha and the Hindu Sanghthan Movement Pg225-287
23. Hindu Mahasabha in Colonial North 1915-30 by Prabh bapu,Pg 50
24. Ibid Pg 52-53
25. Ibid Pg 82-83
26. Ibid Pg34-38
27. https://amritmahotsav.nic.in/unsung-heroes-detail.html
28. https://en.wikipedia.org/wiki/laxman_bhopatkar
29. https://en.wikipedia.org/wiki/Jagat_Narain_Lal
30. https://en.wikipedia.org/wiki/Jugal_kishore_birla
31. https://en.wikipedia.org/wiki/Narayan_Bhaskar_Khare
32. Savarkar's Hindu Mahasabha wrote a constitution that treated Hindus and Muslims as equals (theprint.in)
33. Maharashtran Brahmin Genocide - 8000 Killed • Hindu Genocide
34. The Great Indian Patriots, by P Rajeshwar Rao ,2nd Volume,Pg14-17
35. Hindu Nationalism – Origins,ideologies and Myths by Chetan Bhatt,Pg48-49
36. Ibid, Pg52-54
37. Ibid,Pg70-75

38. The Collected works of Lala Lajpat Rai, Volume 5, Provincial Hindu Conference
39. Hindu Nationalism a reader, by Christopher Jaffrelot, Pg 70-73
40. The Great Indian Patriots, by P Rajeshwar Rao, 2nd Volume, Pg10-13
41. https://en.wikipedia.org/wiki/Madan_Mohan_Malviya
42. Madan Mohan Malviya and Indian Freedom Movement by Jagannath Prasad Mishra, Pg 145 – 150
43. A review of the History & work of the Hindu Mahasabha and the Hindu Sanghthan Movement Pg168-169
44. Madan Mohan Malviya and Indian Freedom Movement by Jagannath Prasad Mishra, Pg 151 – 158
45. Hindu Nationalism a reader, by Christopher Jaffrelot, Pg 64-69
46. A review of the History & work of the Hindu Mahasabha and the Hindu Sanghthan Movement Pg168-169
47. The Great Indian Patriots, by P Rajeshwar Rao, 2nd Volume, Pg194-199
48. https://en.wikipedia.org/wiki/C. Vijayaraghavachariar
49. A review of the History & work of the Hindu Mahasabha and the Hindu Sanghthan Movement Pg118-122
50. Ibid Pg189-190
51. Dr Balakrishna Shivaram Moonje (amritmahotsav.nic.in)
52. A review of the History & work of the Hindu Mahasabha and the Hindu Sanghthan Movement Pg102-108
53. https://en.wikipedia.org/wiki/Round_table_conference(India)
54. A review of the History & work of the Hindu Mahasabha and the Hindu Sanghthan Movement Pg178-185
55. Rajah-Moonje Pact: The Forgotten Model For Social Justice And Integration Of Dalits (swarajyamag.com)
56. N C KELKAR (1872-1947) - One India One People Foundation
57. A review of the History & work of the Hindu Mahasabha and the Hindu Sanghthan Movement Pg109-128
58. Ibid 189-199
59. The Arya Samaj | Bhai Parmanand
60. Hindutva-Origin, Evolution and Future, By Aravindan Neelakandan, Pg 249-262
61. How 'seculars' falsely blame the Two Nation Theory on 'Hindu nationalists' (opindia.com)

Bibliography

62. https://en.wikipedia.org/wiki/Bhai_Mahavir
63. https://en.wikipedia.org/wiki/Swami_Shraddhanand
64. Swami Shraddhanand by M.R.Jambunathan,Pg100-164
65. Hindu Nationalism a reader , by Christopher Jaffrelot ,Pg 77-79
66. http://wikibio.in/ganesh-damodar-savarkar
67. Biography of Ganesh Damodar Savarkar by Sunitha Deshpande,Pg126-162
68. https://savarkar.org/en/index.html
69. The Rss Icons of the Indian Right by Nilanjan Mukhopadhyay,Pg 58-59
70. When BJP's Hindutva icon Savarkar met communist Vladimir Lenin in London - India Today
71. The Rss Icons of the Indian Right by Nilanjan Mukhopadhyay,Pg 62-66
72. Veer Savarkar Allegations and Reality , by Akshay Jog , Pg21-28
73. Savarkar-True story of the Father of Hindutva by Vaibhav Purandare,Pg150-158
74. Veer Savarkar Allegations and Reality , by Akshay Jog , Pg150-153
75. Right Word | Netaji, Savarkar and the making of INA: A glorious chapter of India's independence movement – Firstpost
76. Veer Savarkar Allegations and Reality , by Akshay Jog , Pg113-119
77. Ibid , Pg164-172
78. The Rss Icons of the Indian Right by Nilanjan Mukhopadhyay,Pg 86-88
79. Hindu Nationalism a reader , by Christopher Jaffrelot ,Pg 87-96
80. Hindu Rashtra Darshan, Pg4-8
81. Essential implications of Hindutva Pg 30-34

Rashtriya Swayamsevak Sangh

1. The Hindu Nationalist movement in India by Christophe Jafferelot,Pg72-73
2. Rss Evolution from an organization to a movement by Ratan Sharda,Pg 35
3. Hindu Nationalism and the Language of Politics in Late Colonial India by William Gould,Pg160-180
4. Vision and Mission - Rashtriya Swayamsevak Sangh (rss.org)
5. The Hindu Nationalist movement in India by Christophe Jafferelot, Pg40-41
6. RSSFACTS: How RSS drills sense of patriotism in swayamsevaks
7. The RSS Roadmaps 21st Century,By Sunil Ambekar,Pg40
8. The Hindu Nationalist movement in India by Christophe Jafferelot, Pg62-63

9. Rss's Tryst with Politics , By Pralay Kanungo,pg 72
10. Rss Evolution from an organization to a movement by Ratan Sharda, Pg 78-79
11. Understanding RSS by Dr.Rakesh Sinha, Pg 161
12. 12.Partition Days – The Fiery Saga of RSS by Manik Chandra Vajpayee, Pg331-338
13. Ibid Pg 14-15
14. RSS Vision in Action, by H.V.Seshadiri, Pg112-115
15. Rss's Tryst with Politics, By Pralay Kanungo,pg 141-148
16. Ibid pg150
17. Disaster Relief and RSS, Malini Bhatarcharjee
18. Dr.Keshav Balirm Hedgewar, Prabhat Prakshan,Pg 2.
19. The Saffron surge – Untold Story of RSS Leadership,By Arun Anand, Pg 12
20. Dr.Keshav Balirm Hedgewar, Prabhat Prakshan, Pg 4.
21. The Saffron surge – Untold Story of RSS Leadership,By Arun Anand, Pg 14
22. Dr.Hedgewar, Seer, Patriot and Nation Builder, P3
23. Ibid, Pg5
24. The Saffron surge – Untold Story of RSS Leadership,By Arun Anand,Pg 19
25. Dr.Hedgewar, Seer,Patriot and Nation Builder ,P5
26. The Saffron surge – Untold Story of RSS Leadership,By Arun Anand,Pg 20-30
27. Dr.Hedgewar, Seer,Patriot and Nation Builder ,P6-10
28. The Brotherhood in Saffron by Walter Andersen and Shridhar Damle,Pg69
29. Dr.Hedgewar, Seer,Patriot and Nation Builder ,P10-12
30. The Saffron surge – Untold Story of RSS Leadership,By Arun Anand,Pg 20-30
31. Dr.Hedgewar, Seer,Patriot and Nation Builder ,P10-12
32. Dr. Hedgewar The Epoch-Maker ,Pg 60
33. Ibid Pg 65-70
34. Dr.Hedgewar, Seer,Patriot and Nation Builder ,P15
35. Dr. Hedgewar The Epoch-Maker ,Pg 50
36. Rss Evolution from an organization to a movement by Ratan Sharda,Pg 40-41
37. Dr.Hedgewar, Seer,Patriot and Nation Builder ,P18
38. The Saffron surge – Untold Story of RSS Leadership,By Arun Anand,Pg 30-40
39. Dr.Hedgewar, Seer,Patriot and Nation Builder ,P20

Bibliography

40. Rss's Tryst with Politics ,By Pralay Kanungo,pg 159
41. The Saffron surge – Untold Story of RSS Leadership,By Arun Anand,Pg 42
42. Builders of Modern India, Dr. Keshav Baliram Hedgewar, by Rakesh Sinha,Pg23
43. Builders of Modern India, Dr. Keshav Baliram Hedgewar, by Rakesh Sinha,Pg41
44. Dr.Hedgewar, Seer,Patriot and Nation Builder ,Pg40
45. M.S. Golwalkar: His Life and Mission ,by Nagendra Singh Pg2-4
46. The Saffron surge – Untold Story of RSS Leadership,By Arun Anand,Pg 68
47. M.S. Golwalkar: His Life and Mission ,by Nagendra Singh Pg10-14
48. The Saffron surge – Untold Story of RSS Leadership,By Arun Anand,Pg 69-73
49. M.S. Golwalkar: His Life and Mission ,by Nagendra Singh Pg20-21
50. The Saffron surge – Untold Story of RSS Leadership,By Arun Anand,Pg 73-80
51. Reawakening to a Secular Hindu Nation: M. S. Golwalkar's Vision of a Dharmasapeksa Hindurastra , Shrinivas Tilak pg45
52. Rss's Tryst with Politics ,By Pralay Kanungo,pg 50
53. The Saffron surge – Untold Story of RSS Leadership,By Arun Anand,Pg 82
54. Rss's Tryst with Politics ,By Pralay Kanungo,pg 54
55. The Saffron surge – Untold Story of RSS Leadership,By Arun Anand,Pg 82-84
56. Rss Evolution from an organization to a movement by Ratan Sharda,Pg 78-79
57. The Saffron surge – Untold Story of RSS Leadership,By Arun Anand,Pg 82-84
58. M.S. Golwalkar: His Life and Mission ,by Nagendra Singh Pg60-68
59. The Saffron surge – Untold Story of RSS Leadership, By Arun Anand, Pg 84-89
60. 60.ibid 89-90
61. M.S. Golwalkar: His Life and Mission, by Nagendra Singh Pg 68-72
62. The Saffron surge – Untold Story of RSS Leadership,By Arun Anand,Pg 89-93
63. Rss Evolution from an organization to a movement by Ratan Sharda,Pg 80-82
64. The Saffron surge – Untold Story of RSS Leadership,By Arun Anand,Pg 94
65. The Brotherhood in Saffron by Walter Andersen and Shridhar Damle, Pg61-63
66. The Saffron surge – Untold Story of RSS Leadership, By Arun Anand,Pg 96-97
67. The Brotherhood in Saffron by Walter Andersen and Shridhar Damle,Pg129
68. The Saffron surge – Untold Story of RSS Leadership, By Arun Anand,Pg 99-100
69. Rss Evolution from an organization to a movement by Ratan Sharda, Pg 144
70. Biography - Madhav Sadashivrao Golwalkar(Golwalkar.in)

71. The Saffron surge – Untold Story of RSS Leadership, By Arun Anand, Pg 103
72. Rss Evolution from an organization to a movement by Ratan Sharda, Pg 145-147
73. The Saffron surge – Untold Story of RSS Leadership, By Arun Anand, Pg 104-107
74. Rss's Tryst with Politics, By Pralay Kanungo, pg 116-117.
75. The Saffron surge – Untold Story of RSS Leadership, By Arun Anand, Pg 108-111
76. Biography - Madhav Sadashivrao Golwalkar(Golwalkar.in)

Bharatiya Jana Sangh

1. The Hindu Nationalist movement in India by Christophe Jafferelot, Pg115-116
2. Hindu Nationalism and Indian Politics, The Origin and development of the Bharatiya Jana Sangh By Bruce Graham, Pg 30-40
3. The Hindu Nationalist movement in India by Christophe Jafferelot, Pg123-124
4. Hindu Nationalism and Indian Politics, The Origin and development of the Bharatiya Jana Sangh By Bruce Graham, Pg 40-60
5. Mauli Chandra Sharma - Wikipedia
6. Prem Nath Dogra - Wikipedia
7. Debaprasad Ghosh - Wikipedia
8. Pitamber Das - Wikipedia
9. Avasarala Rama Rao - Wikipedia
10. Raghu Vira - Wikipedia
11. Bachhraj Vyas - Wikipedia
12. Balraj Madhok - Wikipedia
13. The Hindu Nationalist movement in India by Christophe Jafferelot, Pg204-208
14. Hindu Nationalism and Indian Politics, The Origin and development of the Bharatiya Jana Sangh By Bruce Graham, Pg 147-155
15. The Brotherhood in Saffron by Walter Andersen and Shridhar Damle, Pg100-110
16. ibid 120-124
17. Indian National Congress (Organisation) - Wikipedia
18. Hindu Nationalism and Indian Politics, The Origin and development of the Bharatiya Jana Sangh By Bruce Graham, Pg 160
19. Indian National Congress (Organisation) - Wikipedia
20. Janata Morcha - Wikipedia
21. Janata Party - Wikipedia

Bibliography

22. Dr. Shyama Prasad Mookerjee
23. The RSS,Icons of the Indian Right,by Nilanjan Mukhopadhyay,Pg 170-179
24. Syama Prasad Mookerjee Life and Times,By Tathagata Roy,Pg81-88
25. The RSS,Icons of the Indian Right,by Nilanjan Mukhopadhyay,Pg 183-185
26. Syama Prasad Mookerjee Life and Times,By Tathagata Roy,Pg118-120
27. Ibid 122-124
28. The RSS,Icons of the Indian Right,by Nilanjan Mukhopadhyay,Pg 188-185
29. Portrait of a martyr-A Biography of Dr.Shyama Prasad Mukherjee, Prof.Bal Raj Madhok, Pg70-71
30. ibid 77-80
31. Syama Prasad Mookerjee Life and Times, By Tathagata Roy, Pg221-225
32. Portrait of a martyr-A Biography of Dr.Shyama Prasad Mukherjee, Prof.Bal Raj Madhok, Pg82-84
33. The RSS, Icons of the Indian Right, by Nilanjan Mukhopadhyay, Pg 192-200
34. Syama Prasad Mookerjee Life and Times, By Tathagata Roy, Pg298-300
35. ibid 308-309
36. Portrait of a martyr-A Biography of Dr.Shyama Prasad Mukherjee, Prof.Bal Raj Madhok, Pg92
37. The RSS,Icons of the Indian Right, by Nilanjan Mukhopadhyay, Pg 204-208
38. Syama Prasad Mookerjee Life and Times, By Tathagata Roy, Pg 372-383
39. Deendayal Upadhyaya - Wikipedia
40. The RSS, Icons of the Indian Right, by Nilanjan Mukhopadhyay, Pg 214
41. Deendayal Upadhyaya Life of an Ideologue Politician, Shiv Shakthi Nath Bakshi, Pg4-7
42. Ibid Pg7-8
43. The RSS,Icons of the Indian Right,by Nilanjan Mukhopadhyay,Pg 221-224
44. Deendayal Upadhyaya A Great Proponent of Hindutva Ideology,Rajesh Kr. Singh,Pg226-227
45. The RSS, Icons of the Indian Right, by Nilanjan Mukhopadhyay, Pg 218-219
46. Deendayal Upadhyaya A Great Proponent of Hindutva Ideology, Rajesh Kr. Singh, Pg116-168
47. Rss's Tryst with Politics, By Pralay Kanungo, pg 121
48. The RSS,Icons of the Indian Right,by Nilanjan Mukhopadhyay,Pg 240-244
49. Integral Humanism,by Deendayal Upadhyaya,Pg13-48